6/9 2

DATE DUE

DEMCO 38-296

American Political Leaders

AMERICAN *Political* LEADERS

From Colonial Times to the Present

Steven G. O'Brien

Editor
Paula McGuire

Consulting Editors
James M. McPherson
Gary Gerstle

ABC-CLIO

Santa Barbara, California
Denver, Colorado
Oxford, England

Library of Congress Cataloging-in-Publication Data

O'Brien, Steven.
    American political leaders : from colonial times to the present /
Steven G. O'Brien : editor, Paula McGuire : consulting editors,
James M. McPherson, Gary Gerstle.
        p.   cm.—(Biographies of American leaders)
    Includes bibliographical references.
        1. Politicians—United States—Biography—Dictionaries.   2. United
States—Biography—Dictionaries.   I. McGuire, Paula.
II. McPherson, James M.   III. Gerstle, Gary, 1954–   .   IV. Title.
V. Series.
E176.027   1991   973′.0992—dc20   91-30755
    [B]

ISBN 0-87436-570-8

98 97 96 95 94 93 92 91   10 9 8 7 6 5 4 3 2 1

BIOGRAPHIES OF AMERICAN LEADERS

Developed by Visual Education Corp., Princeton, N.J.

ABC-CLIO, Inc.
130 Cremona Drive, P.O. Box 1911
Santa Barbara, California 93116-1911

This book is printed on acid-free paper ∞.
Manufactured in the United States of America

Contents

Biographical Profiles, 1

List of American Political Leaders

Abzug, Bella Savitzky, 1
Acheson, Dean Gooderham, 2
Adams, Charles Francis, 3
Adams, John, 4
Adams, John Quincy, 6
Adams, Samuel, 8
Adams, Sherman, 10
Agnew, Spiro Theodore, 10
Albert, Carl Bert, 11
Aldrich, Nelson Wilmarth, 12
Anderson, John Bayard, 13
Arnold, Thurman Wesley, 13
Arthur, Chester Alan, 14
Atchison, David Rice, 16
Bacon, Robert, 16
Baker, James Addison, III, 17
Baker, Newton Diehl, 18
Ballinger, Richard Achilles, 19
Bankhead, William Brockman, 19
Banks, Nathaniel Prentiss, 20
Barbour, Philip Pendleton, 21
Barkley, Alben William, 22
Baruch, Bernard Mannes, 22
Bayard, Thomas Francis, 23
Belknap, William Worth, 24
Bell, John, 25
Benjamin, Judah Philip, 26
Bennett, William John, 27
Benson, Ezra Taft, 28
Benton, Thomas Hart, 29
Berger, Victor Louis, 30
Beveridge, Albert Jeremiah, 31
Biddle, Nicholas, 32
Birney, James Gillespie, 33
Black, Hugo LaFayette, 34
Black, Jeremiah Sullivan, 35
Blaine, James Gillespie, 36
Blair, Francis Preston, 37
Bland, Richard Parks, 38
Borah, William Edgar, 39
Bowles, Chester Bliss, 40
Boyd, Lynn, 41
Bradford, William, 42
Brandeis, Louis Dembitz, 43
Breckinridge, John Cabell, 44
Bristow, Benjamin Helm, 45

Brooke, Edward William, 46
Brooks, Preston Smith, 47
Browder, Earl Russell, 47
Bruce, Blanche Kelso, 48
Bryan, William Jennings, 49
Brzezinski, Zbigniew Kazimierz, 50
Buchanan, James, 52
Bundy, McGeorge, 54
Burger, Warren Earl, 54
Burr, Aaron, 56
Bush, George Herbert Walker, 58
Butler, Andrew Pickens, 60
Butler, Benjamin Franklin, 60
Byrnes, James Francis, 61
Byrns, Joseph Wellington, 62
Calhoun, John Caldwell, 63
Cameron, Simon, 65
Cannon, Joseph Gurney, 66
Cardozo, Benjamin Nathan, 66
Carlisle, John Griffin, 67
Carter, James (Jimmy) Earl, Jr., 68
Casey, William Joseph, 71
Cass, Lewis, 72
Chafin, Eugene Wilder, 73
Chase, Salmon Portland, 73
Chase, Samuel, 75
Cheves, Langdon, 76
Chisholm, Shirley Anita St. Hill, 77
Clark, James Beauchamp, 78
Clay, Henry, 78
Clayton, John Middleton, 80
Cleveland, Stephen Grover, 81
Clifford, Clark McAdams, 83
Clinton, DeWitt, 84
Clinton, George, 85
Cobb, Howell, 86
Colby, Bainbridge, 87
Colfax, Schuyler, 87
Conkling, Roscoe, 88
Coolidge, Calvin, 89
Cox, James Middleton, 91
Crawford, William Harris, 91
Creel, George, 92
Crisp, Charles Frederick, 93
Crittenden, John Jordan, 94
Curtis, Charles, 95

Editor's Preface

*A*merican Political Leaders: From Colonial Times to the Present is a biographical reference work containing over 400 profiles of American men and women who have been elected to or nominated for national office or appointed by the president, as well as some who earned special prominence in other positions. Intended for students and general readers as a quick guide to the outstanding leaders—past and present—in American government, it presents in concise form their lives with emphasis on their accomplishments as political figures.

The profiles include every president, every unsuccessful candidate for the presidency (including major third-party candidates), every vice president, every secretary of state, every chief justice of the Supreme Court, and every Speaker of the House. The remaining profiles include a number of diplomats, government agency directors, presidential advisers, associate justices, senators, and representatives. Several colonial and revolutionary figures have also been chosen, as have a few people who do not fit any of the categories (such as Jefferson Davis, president of the Confederate States of America; Richard Daley, chairman of the Cook County [Chicago] Democratic Central Committee; and Francis Preston Blair, newspaper editor and unofficial presidential adviser) and who were included because of their unusual influence on national affairs. Subjects were chosen from a survey of persons mentioned in the leading secondary and college textbooks and from an additional list of those whose accomplishments the consulting editors considered historically most important.

It should be carefully noted that, because the book has been specifically limited to *national political* leaders, it does not include leaders of social movements, such as civil rights, the women's movement, gay rights, or leaders in other categories, such as state and local governments, the military, education, or culture. However, the editors have sought to include women and minority leaders wherever possible.

The headnote of each profile states the subject's name, birth and death dates, and offices held, listed in the order of executive branch, judicial branch, and legislative branch. Based on authoritative sources, the profile texts aim to give brief, accurate information about a subject's life, built upon that person's accomplishments and significance and giving the important biographical and historical facts. Anecdotes and quotations are included when they serve to give further information about a subject or characterize him or her. The purpose of the condensed form of the profile is to give the student or general reader an easily accessible overview of the subject that is valuable for factual information or as a jumping-off place for further study. Each profile contains a bibliography for further reference, and the reader is urged to consult a library for additional materials.

To make good use of the space available, a simple cross-reference system is used. Within the profiles, the printing of subject names in SMALL CAPITALS indicates a cross-reference, of which there are two kinds. A name in small capitals alone indicates immediately to the reader that the person mentioned has a profile that will be found in its alphabetical position. A name in small capitals preceded by the word "see" indicates that the reader may turn to that profile for an explanation of a term or historical event just mentioned. Great care has been taken to describe significant events and legislative acts and to define important terms. Because the book is intended for American students and readers, some basic familiarity with people and events in American history is assumed. However, the editors have also aimed to connect people and events through the system of cross-references so as to give a comprehensive historical account.

At the back of the book, the reader can find a timeline that includes each person profiled in the book. This timeline places each person, by office and date, within the proper presidential administration.

Approximately one hundred profiles are accompanied by black-and-white portraits of the subjects.

The editor wishes to acknowledge the contributions of all the people who worked on this book. Steven G. O'Brien's clear (and often lively) expository style—the result of years of teaching and writing—was made to order for this reference project. The editor is extremely grateful for the author's tireless research and painstaking work. Special thanks are owed to the consulting editors Gary Gerstle and James M. McPherson who, in addition to giving advice about the planning and scope of the vol-

ume, read critically every profile. The time and care they gave to the project are much appreciated. The editor is indebted to her colleagues at Visual Education Corporation: Susan Tatiner, for coordinating the copyediting; Amy Lewis, for special editorial assistance; Suzanne Eckert and Jocelyn Flint, for fact checking; Richard Lidz and Dale Anderson, for their advice and encouragement; and Cindy Feldner, for her excellent preparation and proofreading of the manuscript. The editor is particularly grateful to Laura Daly for her careful copyediting and constructive editorial suggestions.

Paula McGuire

Consulting Editors' Preface

As consulting editors to *American Political Leaders: From Colonial Times to the Present,* our task has been twofold: first, to aid in the identification of those political leaders included in the book; second, to read each profile submitted by the author, Steven G. O'Brien, for general accuracy, balance (of the biographical and political), and historical perspective.

In performing this second task, we have been guided by a desire to add an interpretive dimension to this work, so that readers could turn to this book not only for essential biographical information but also for a sense of how historians have evaluated the contributions of particular leaders and of the reform programs, political movements, and events (such as wars) associated with their names. There are sharp limits on how much interpretation can be introduced to a reference work of this sort. For the shorter profiles of lesser known leaders, the emphasis is conventionally biographical. Nevertheless, we think that enough interpretation has been included to make this volume an uncommon book of reference. Readers can learn something about how historians now interpret the political legacy of Jacksonian democracy; Abraham Lincoln's role in winning the Civil War and

abolishing slavery; the political significance of the Socialist party of America when Eugene Debs was its presidential candidate; why Franklin Delano Roosevelt's New Deal is still regarded as such a watershed event in our history; and why historians view the presidencies of Herbert Hoover and Dwight D. Eisenhower more favorably than contemporaries did. These are but a few examples of the many interpretive assessments appearing in this book.

We have also encouraged the writer to be alert to the telling anecdote, quotation, or character trait that would offer readers some insight into the personality and motivation of particular leaders and, wherever possible, to incorporate such information into the profiles. A significant number of profiles contain, as a result, "human interest" material that serves both to enliven the text and to capture a bit of the spiritedness, forcefulness, idiosyncrasy, and humor that have been such intrinsic features of our nation's political life. We hope that this personal dimension, in combination with the interpretive one, will make this a rich and rewarding reference work.

James M. McPherson
Gary Gerstle

American Political Leaders

Abzug, Bella Savitzky

(July 14, 1920–   )
Representative

During her six years in Congress Bella Abzug assumed a national leadership role in the anti–Vietnam War (see LYNDON BAINES JOHNSON and RICHARD MILHOUS NIXON) movement, the women's rights campaign, and efforts to abolish the seniority system in the House of Representatives.

Abzug was the first Jewish woman ever elected to Congress. Born Bella Savitzky in the Bronx, New York, she earned her bachelor's degree from Hunter College in 1942, married Martin Abzug, and had two children. Five years later, she was awarded a law degree from Columbia University, was admitted to the bar, and began the practice of law in New York. During the 1950s and 1960s she earned considerable national attention for her civil rights work, mostly gratis, as a lawyer for the American Civil Liberties Union and for the Civil Rights Congress.

From 1961 to 1970, in her role as the national legislative representative of the Women Strike for Peace, Abzug led efforts to elect candidates opposed to the Vietnam War. In 1970, as the candidate of the Reform Democrats, she unseated the Democratic incumbent in the primary and won the first of three consecutive terms in Congress (1971–1977). In the House her efforts to abolish the seniority system resulted in some reforms, but not enough to satisfy her and other congressional insurgents.

As a first-term congresswoman, Abzug very much wanted to be a member of the House Armed Services Committee—one deemed too prestigious for such an inexperienced representative. Abzug rallied against the seniority system that only allows representatives to advance slowly to positions on choice committees (and also prevents certain representatives from going to the committee that lies within their area of expertise). Despite her outspoken appeals, she did not get Armed Services and was instead given Government Operations and Public Works committees. No specific reforms were instituted as a result of her protests, but for a while, attention was drawn to the seniority system and some freshman representatives (including SHIRLEY CHISHOLM) were given better committee assignments.

Abzug did not seek reelection in 1976. The following year she presided over the National Women's Conference in Houston, Texas, and in 1978 was appointed cochair of the President's National Advisory Council for Women. She was a candidate for the House of Representatives in 1986 but did not win the election.

BIBLIOGRAPHY

Abzug, Bella, *Bella! Ms. Abzug Goes to Washington*, 1972, and with Mim Kelber, *Gender Gap: Bella Abzug's Guide to Political Power for Women*, 1984.

Acheson, Dean Gooderham

(April 11, 1893–October 12, 1971)
Secretary of State

As secretary of state from 1949 to 1953, Dean Acheson helped create the North Atlantic Treaty Organization (NATO; see HARRY S TRUMAN), engineered the 1951 peace treaty with Japan, and implemented President Truman's policies in Korea.

Born in Middletown, Connecticut, Acheson attended Groton School and graduated from Yale University in 1915. He earned his law degree from Harvard Law School in 1918 after briefly serving in the navy during World War I. From 1919 to 1921 Acheson was Supreme Court Justice LOUIS D. BRANDEIS's private secretary. Except for a brief stint as President FRANKLIN D. ROOSEVELT's under secretary of the treasury in 1933, Acheson practiced corporate and international law from 1921 to 1941.

Appointed by Roosevelt as assistant secretary of state in 1941, Acheson helped secure congressional passage of the Lend-Lease Act (see FRANKLIN DELANO ROOSEVELT) and later of the Bretton Woods Monetary Agreement. The latter, made at an international conference in 1944, set up international banking funds and revaluated European currencies following World War II.

As under secretary of state from 1945 to 1947, Acheson played a vital role in the formulation of the Truman Doctrine (see HARRY S TRUMAN) in 1947, which pledged the United States to the worldwide containment of communism. He also worked closely with GEORGE MARSHALL in devising the Marshall Plan (see GEORGE CATLETT MARSHALL and HARRY S TRUMAN), a massive economic aid program designed to promote the recovery of the European economies and thus thwart the appeal of communism.

In 1949 President Truman selected Acheson as the new secretary of state. Acheson's two greatest accomplishments involved the creation of NATO, a military alliance of ten (eventually fourteen) European nations, Canada, and the United States designed to prevent the expansion of Soviet power in Europe, and the conclusion of a peace treaty with Japan in 1951. Although a staunch opponent of communism who believed that it was "economically fatal to a free society and to human rights and fundamental freedom," Acheson, like his mentor, George Marshall, became the target of Republican critics, who virulently and unfairly attacked him for "losing" China to the communists. His critics assailed him for encouraging the communist North Koreans to invade South Korea in 1950, thereby involving the United States in a costly and inconclusive four-year war. He also came under fire for his defense of Alger Hiss (see RICHARD MILHOUS NIXON), a State Department official accused of spying for the communists. Part of what made him politically vulnerable to these charges was the perception of many "mainstream" Americans that he belonged to an Eastern Establishment whose internationalism, elitism, and New Deal liberalism were out of step with basic American values.

After leaving office at the end of the Truman administration, Acheson returned to his law practice, wrote books on international diplomacy, and served as an unofficial policy adviser to presidents.

BIBLIOGRAPHY

Acheson, Dean Gooderham, *Power and Diplomacy,* 1958, and *Present at the Creation,* 1970; Acheson, Dean, *Morning and Noon,* 1965; Smith, Gaddis, *Dean Acheson,* 1972.

Adams, Charles Francis

(August 18, 1807–November 1, 1886)
Diplomat, Representative

Minister to Great Britain during the American Civil War, Charles Francis Adams played a superb diplomatic role in keeping the British, courted by the Confederacy and starved for cotton as a result of the Union's naval blockade of the South, from taking sides in the conflict.

Charles Francis Adams, son of JOHN QUINCY ADAMS and grandson of JOHN ADAMS, was born in Boston but raised abroad until the age of ten while his father fulfilled his diplomatic duties. Adams graduated from Harvard College in 1825 and, after studying law in DANIEL WEBSTER's office, was admitted to the bar four years later. His marriage, in 1829, to Abigail Brooks, the daughter of a multimillionaire, enabled him to pursue a career in journalism and politics.

From 1840 to 1845 Adams served in the Massachusetts legislature as a member of the Whig party. An abolitionist, he was the Free-Soil party's unsuccessful vice presidential nominee on the ticket with MARTIN VAN BUREN in 1848. Adams was elected to Congress as a Republican in 1858 and reelected in 1860.

In 1861 President ABRAHAM LINCOLN appointed Adams minister to Great Britain. His performance in this difficult post during the Civil War was exemplary. His early schooling in England came to be an asset. He not only understood the English, but his own reserved, logical, yet impassioned manner complemented theirs. The major goal of his diplomatic mission consisted of ensuring that Great Britain did not recognize the Confederacy or intervene diplomatically in the Civil War.

Adams's superb skills as a statesman served the interests of the United States brilliantly on at least two occasions. The first involved the *Trent* affair, when a U.S. warship stopped the British steamer *Trent* in 1861 and removed two Confederate commissioners bound for England. The seizure enraged the British, but war was averted when Adams helped arrange for the two men to be released.

The second occasion was slower to develop. Once in England, Adams protested the building of ships, such as the infamous Confederate raider *Alabama*, in British shipyards in violation of international neutrality laws. A crisis finally developed in 1863 when two ironclads, capable of breaking the Northern blockade of the South, were ready to sail for the United States. At the last moment the British reconsidered their position and gave orders to prevent the departure of the ships.

Ever aware of the need to avoid offending British public opinion, Adams retained a calm exterior in the moment of his greatest diplomatic triumph. He carefully expressed no emotion that might let enemies claim he was gloating over England's embarrassment, but in his diary he wrote: "I know not that even in the *Trent* case [had] I felt a greater relief." The ships never left England and, thanks to the British reluctance to condone slavery and the Union victory at Antietam, which marked a turning point in the North's military fortunes, England never intervened in the Civil War.

Adams resigned his diplomatic post in 1868 and returned to Boston. His last position as a public servant was in 1872 when he served as U.S. commissioner on the international tribunal that arbitrated the *Alabama* claims. This was the demand by American merchants for compensation for the damage done to Union ships during the Civil War by Confederate raiders built in Great Britain. Adams held that Britain should have to honor only direct war claims. Radicals pressed for indirect punitive damages, but Adams stood firm, claiming that the United States had to set an example to all nations in appealing to the highest principles of international law instead of behaving vindictively. His view prevailed.

Liberal reform elements in the Republican party, who were appalled at the rampant corruption in the administration of ULYSSES S. GRANT, considered but finally did not choose Adams as a candidate in 1872.

Adams spent the rest of his life working in various civic organizations, writing history books, and preparing his father's diary, *Memoirs of John Quincy Adams*, for publication. Earlier publications included two volumes of the letters of Abigail Adams (his grand-mother) and the biography and multivolume papers of John Adams (his grandfather).

BIBLIOGRAPHY

Adams, Charles Francis, Jr., *Charles Francis Adams*, 1980; DiPace, Aida, et al. (eds.), *The Diary of Charles Francis Adams*, 1964; Duberman, Martin, *Charles Francis Adams, 1807–1886*, 1961.

Adams, John

(October 19, 1735–July 4, 1826)
President, Diplomat, Revolutionary Leader

Brilliant and vain, industrious and argumentative, John Adams used his powers to help launch the movement for independence and, as president and diplomat, to launch the new nation. Adams's wife, Abigail, née Smith, whom he married in 1764, was a well-informed woman whose letters to her husband give us a lively and intelligent view of life in colonial times. John and Abigail were the first presidential family to inhabit the White House and the only presidential parents whose son, JOHN QUINCY ADAMS, became president. Their grandson, CHARLES FRANCIS ADAMS, also became a prominent statesman.

Born in Braintree (now Quincy), Massachusetts, Adams graduated from Harvard College in 1755, was admitted to the bar in 1758, and quickly established a successful Boston

Library of Congress

practice. Although by nature an upholder of the law and not a revolutionist, Adams opposed the Stamp Act of 1765, which required Americans to place stamps on all legal documents and newspapers, because the colonists had never given their consent to such taxation. The resolutions of protest against British rule he prepared for Braintree were adopted throughout Massachusetts.

In 1770, though he knew it was an unpopular cause, Adams was one of the lawyers who agreed to defend the British soldiers involved in the Boston Massacre, which, in part, had been instigated by his cousin, SAMUEL ADAMS. The soldiers, who had fired into a mob and killed five men, were acquitted of murder. His prestige untarnished, Adams was then elected to the Massachusetts General Court as a representative from Boston. In 1774 he was chosen to be one of the delegates from Massachusetts to the First Continental Congress. At the Second Continental Congress in 1775, Adams pressed for a complete break with England and was responsible for GEORGE WASHINGTON's appointment as commander in chief. The following year, it was Adams who seconded the motion of RICHARD HENRY LEE for a declaration of independence and was appointed to the committee to draft the document.

While in Congress (1775–1777), Adams served on many important committees. In 1778 he was sent to Europe to obtain a treaty of alliance with France, only to find when he arrived that this had already been accomplished by BENJAMIN FRANKLIN. Jealous of Franklin's popularity and unhappy with his own position, Adams returned to Massachusetts and immediately plunged into working on a new state constitution, becoming its principal author. In 1781 Congress asked him to go back to Europe to help negotiate peace and commercial treaties. As minister to Holland, Adams secured that country's recognition of the United States, as well as some badly needed loans for the new nation. Later Adams returned to France and, in concert with Benjamin Franklin and JOHN JAY, negotiated the Treaty of Paris (1783) with Great Britain to end the Revolution.

Adams remained in Europe as the American minister to Great Britain until 1788. Upon his return, he was elected the first vice president of the United States, to which post he was reelected in 1792 despite the opposition of ALEXANDER HAMILTON. Hamilton and Adams disliked each other; Hamilton felt that Adams did not believe strongly enough in the need for a powerful central government and in protecting the rights of the newly emerging wealthy business class, and Adams was sure that Hamilton wanted to establish aristocratic rule in the United States. In 1796 Adams overcame Hamilton's opposition to his candidacy to win a narrow victory for the presidency.

The Adams administration was dominated by the growth of the two-party system and the repercussions of the French Revolution. Adams assumed the office of the presidency during the emergence of two national political parties—the Federalists, nominally led by Hamilton; and the Democratic-Republicans (more often called Republicans), led by THOMAS JEFFERSON. Jefferson and his supporters felt that Adams, who actually considered himself above party affiliation, was a Federalist and a man who wanted to be king and subject the populace to his tyranny. To the Republicans, Adams did not believe strongly enough in the need to keep the central government weak in order to forestall threats to individual liberty, and a deep antagonism developed between Adams and Jefferson, his vice president.

President Adams followed Washington's advice of maintaining strict American neutrality in the war between England and France. His efforts were complicated by the fact that Hamilton and other Federalists were sympathetic to England, while Jefferson and his Republicans were sympathetic to France and the French Revolution. France, angry over the United States' refusal to help its cause and what it perceived to be U.S. support for Great Britain, began attacking American ships. As soon as he became president, Adams sent agents to France to resolve the disagreement, but the French government refused to meet with them. When secret agents of the French government demanded that the United States agree to loan France $10 million and pay a bribe of $250,000 before talks could begin, Adams relayed the insult to Congress. The incident became known as the XYZ affair after the initials Adams substituted in his report for the names of the French secret agents.

Adams's popularity soared as he strengthened the nation's defenses, though he himself was against war. He nominated Washington as commander in chief and supported a naval buildup, including the outfitting of the frigate *Constitution* ("Old Ironsides"). Between 1798 and 1800 an undeclared naval war raged between the United States and France. Full-scale war seemed inevitable, but by 1800 passions cooled. Napoleon had gained control in France and, preoccupied with other matters, wanted peace with the United States. Adams seized the opportunity to negotiate a peaceful resolution to the problem. Although a wise decision for the nation, it was a costly one politically: Adams's action infuriated Hamilton and his Federalist supporters, who had been pressing for war. But it was characteristic of Adams to choose his country over self-interest.

However, the outbreak of hostilities with the French in 1798 also had enabled the Federalists to push through Congress the repressive Alien and Sedition Acts (see THOMAS JEFFERSON). The acts were aimed against the many foreign-born (especially French and Irish) Republican critics of the government and made it more difficult for them to become American citizens. The acts also allowed the government to prosecute citizens who expressed opposition. Ten men, mostly newspaper editors, were convicted for their opinions. Although no one was deported, immigration was discouraged and some foreigners left the country. The laws were vigorously opposed by Jefferson and the Republicans, who felt the acts violated the First Amendment's guarantee of free speech.

Without the support of many of the Federalists and vilified by the Republicans for not vetoing the Alien and Sedition Acts, Adams was defeated for reelection by Thomas Jefferson in 1800. One of his final actions as president was to appoint Federalists (known as Midnight Judges) to newly created federal judgeships. The appointments were later voided (see JOHN MARSHALL). His appointment of John Marshall as chief justice of the Supreme Court, however, would endure for thirty-four years.

Adams retired to Braintree after leaving the White House in 1801. He spent the last twenty-five years of his life corresponding with friends, among them Jefferson, with whom he had a warm reconciliation, writing about contemporary affairs, and recording his experiences in politics. He died on July 4, 1826, exactly fifty years to the day from the signing of the Declaration of Independence. His last words are reported to have been "Thomas Jefferson still survives." He did not know that Jefferson had himself succumbed that very day.

BIBLIOGRAPHY

Adams, James Truslow, *The Adams Family,* 1974; Shepherd, Jack, *The Adams Chronicles,* 1975; Smith, Page, *John Adams,* 1962.

Adams, John Quincy

(July 11, 1767–February 23, 1848)
President, Secretary of State, Diplomat, Representative

As able and principled as he was, John Quincy Adams was an ineffectual president who was hampered by politics and his own forbidding personality. He is far better remembered for his earlier accomplishments as secretary of state and his postpresidential years in Congress.

Born in Braintree (now Quincy), Massachusetts, Adams was educated in Paris, Leiden, Amsterdam, Leipzig, and London while he was traveling with his father, JOHN ADAMS, then a foreign minister and later the second U.S. president. The younger Adams graduated from Harvard College in 1787 and was admitted to the Massachusetts bar in 1790. He established his practice in Boston, but after having served as his father's secretary when he was minister to France and as the secretary to the minister to Russia, it was politics, not the practice of law, that attracted his keen mind. In 1791 he published an anonymous series of articles in answer to THOMAS PAINE's *Rights of Man.* These articles were so well thought out that they were attributed to the senior Adams.

Library of Congress

President GEORGE WASHINGTON appointed the twenty-seven-year-old Adams minister to the Netherlands in 1794 and then minister to Prussia. After Adams's father became president, Washington squelched any misgivings about the propriety of the younger Adams serving in the foreign service with the comment, "Adams is the most valuable public character we have abroad . . . he will prove himself to be the ablest of all our diplomatic corps." Adams returned to Massachusetts in 1801 and was elected to the state senate in April 1802. However, he was referred to by his Federalist party colleagues as "too unmanageable" and was defeated in a close race for Congress that November. The following year he was elected by the state legislature to the U.S. Senate. He proved to be just as "unmanageable" there. Against party lines he supported the Louisiana Purchase; THOMAS JEFFERSON's handling of the impressment issue, especially during the *Chesapeake* incident; and finally the implementation of an embargo as an alternative to war (see THOMAS JEFFERSON). He so infuriated the Federalist party leadership in Massachusetts that they named his successor a full two years before the end of his term. Rather than stay in office in the face of such hostility, Adams resigned from his Senate seat

in 1808. He declined to run for office as a Republican.

Adams served Presidents Jefferson and JAMES MADISON as minister to Russia from 1809 to 1814 and chaired the commission that negotiated the Treaty of Ghent, which ended the War of 1812 (see JAMES MADISON). Extremely religious and by nature a loner, the intellectual Adams seldom mixed with his fellow delegates. Often, when HENRY CLAY and his friends would be retiring from their card games in the early hours of the morning, Adams would already be rising for his daily walks and Bible reading.

By the time he was selected in 1817 to be President JAMES MONROE's secretary of state, no candidate had ever been more superbly trained or qualified. During the Monroe administration Adams performed his duties magnificently. He defended ANDREW JACKSON's invasion of Florida; worked out the treaty by which Spain ceded Florida to the United States (see ANDREW JACKSON); reached a compromise agreement with England for the joint occupation of the Oregon Territory; maintained U.S. neutrality during the course of the wars for independence by Spain's Central and South American colonies; and assisted in the drafting of the Monroe Doctrine (see JAMES MONROE).

There were four Republican party candidates for the presidency in 1824: Henry Clay, WILLIAM CRAWFORD, Andrew Jackson, and John Quincy Adams. Jackson received the largest number of popular votes, but none received an electoral majority. It was left to the House of Representatives to decide the election. Since Clay's nationalistic beliefs were closer to those of Adams than to those of Jackson, Clay gave his crucial support to Adams, who won. When Adams appointed Clay secretary of state,

Jackson's supporters suggested loudly that Adams and Clay had struck a "corrupt" bargain to support each other for the presidency. They argued that Clay gave Adams the presidency now in return for his appointment to the State Department, a stepping-stone to the White House.

Adams attempted to ignore the Jackson charges, but their effect was to divide the Republicans and doom the programs Adams wished to have enacted. Adams had hoped to use the powers of the central government for internal improvements (see JOHN CALDWELL CALHOUN)—a cornerstone of Clay's American System (see HENRY CLAY), promoting the sciences and the arts and establishing a national university. His high-minded but ineffectual presidency was frustrated by a Congress torn by politics and sectional conflicts. It opposed his requests for funds for national improvements, thwarted his attempts to deal diplomatically with Latin America, and was strongly divided over the protectionist tariff of 1828. After a bitter and personally abusive campaign, Andrew Jackson won a decisive election for the presidency in 1828.

The second most important part of Adams's political career began after he left the White House in 1829. Adams expected to return to Massachusetts and retire in obscurity like his father. Instead, the people of the Plymouth district elected him to Congress. Although he had not entered his name as a candidate, Adams accepted the position and was reelected eight times, from 1831 to 1848. This was a remarkably productive period in his life. He became a spokesman for the antislavery movement and fought for the impartial application of the right of petition. During the rise of the antislavery movement in the 1830s, Congress had passed a series of gag rules in order to avoid hearing petitions from abolitionists. Adams was frequently the target of motions of censure initiated by Southern members infuriated by his antislavery speeches and attempts to overturn the gag rules. Because of his heroic efforts on behalf of the sanctity of the First Amendment in 1844, when the gag rules were finally repealed, he was nicknamed Old Man Eloquent. On February 21, 1848, he suffered a stroke while at his desk in the House. He died two days later in the Speaker's room without having regained consciousness.

That same year, John Quincy Adams's son, CHARLES FRANCIS ADAMS, as candidate for vice president, was beginning his own career as statesman.

BIBLIOGRAPHY

Bemis, Samuel F., *John Quincy Adams*, 1956; East, Robert, *John Quincy Adams*, 1962.

Adams, Samuel

(September 27, 1722–October 2, 1803)
Revolutionary Leader

Popular patriot and agitator Sam Adams is famous for organizing the Boston Tea Party and for helping to incite the Boston Massacre. Never as successful in politics as his cousin, JOHN ADAMS, Sam nevertheless earns an important place in American history as a fiery revolutionary leader and propagandist.

Born in Boston, Massachusetts, Adams graduated from Harvard College in 1740, where he also obtained his master's degree three years later. He tried studying law but gave it up; failed at running his own business; and, after inheriting his father's brewery business and property, did so poorly in managing it that he soon fell into debt and was reduced to relying on friends in order to provide for his family, a situation that he found himself in frequently throughout his life.

In 1747 Adams became influential in local politics and wrote newspaper articles on current affairs. In 1764 and 1765 he was chosen to draft the instructions from the Town of Boston to its representatives concerning the Stamp Act (see JOHN ADAMS).

Adams seized upon the Stamp Act as a means to sway popular opinion in Massachusetts. He never openly encouraged violence, but he was a leading influence in turning popular opinion against the conservatives. On September 27, 1765, he was elected to the lower house of the Massachusetts colonial legislature. As a member of the legislature, he worked to fill the house with radicals, fought against the Townshend Acts (revenue acts passed by Parliament to replace the repealed Stamp Act), and drafted letters to the assemblies of other colonies.

Adams formulated the basic premises for the break with England as early as 1765. When popular support for confronting the Crown died down in 1772 after the Townshend Acts were repealed, Adams kept the controversy alive with a steady stream of articles warning people against being lulled into accepting British tyranny. On November 2, 1772, the Boston town meeting, on Adams's motion, appointed a committee of correspondence ". . . to state the rights of the Colonists . . . and to communicate the same to the several towns and to the world." He drafted the committee's declaration of rights.

Adams organized the resistance to the Tea Act of 1773 (the Boston Tea Party) and the Coercive Acts of 1774. Upon learning that the other colonies were unwilling to adopt nonin-tercourse measures, Adams concluded that an intercolonial congress was an absolute necessity. He and four other delegates were chosen to represent Massachusetts at the First Continental Congress.

Before leaving for Philadelphia, Adams was active in organizing the convention that adopted the Suffolk Resolves on September 9, thereby placing Massachusetts in a state of virtual rebellion. At Philadelphia he used his influence to commit the Continental Congress to approval of the Suffolk Resolves.

Reelected to the Second Continental Congress, Adams returned to Philadelphia in 1775. He proposed a confederation of the colonies in favor of immediate independence and later signed the Declaration of Independence.

Once the break with Great Britain was achieved, Adams's political influence began to decline. He served in the Continental Congress until 1781 and then returned to Boston, where he was a delegate to the convention that drafted the Massachusetts constitution. Under the new Massachusetts government, he served as a senator and member of the council. He supported the adoption of the federal Constitution, with the provision that the Bill of Rights be added. He failed to win election to the U.S. Congress in 1788 but was elected lieutenant governor in 1789 and governor in 1794, the office from which he retired to private life in 1797.

BIBLIOGRAPHY

Cushing, H. A. (ed.), *Writings of Samuel Adams,* 1904–1908; Harlow, Ralph V., *Samuel Adams: Promoter of American Revolution,* 1923; Miller, John C., *Sam Adams: Pioneer in Propaganda,* 1936.

Adams, Sherman

(January 8, 1899–October 27, 1986)
Representative, Presidential Adviser

As White House chief of staff from 1953 until 1958, Sherman Adams established the model for the strong presidential chiefs of staff that were to follow.

Adams was born in East Dover, Vermont, and grew up in Providence, Rhode Island. He served in the Marine Corps during World War I, and, after graduating from Dartmouth College in 1920, settled in New Hampshire. Before entering politics he was an executive in the lumber industry.

In 1940 Adams was elected as a Republican to the New Hampshire House of Representatives. He was reelected in 1942 and served as speaker in 1943 and 1944. In 1944 he was elected to the U.S. House of Representatives. He served one term in the House (1945–1947) and two terms as governor of New Hampshire (1949–1953). As governor, he oversaw the reorganization and streamlining of the state government.

Adams was one of DWIGHT D. EISENHOWER's earliest political supporters. At the Republican national convention in 1952, he played a vital role in securing Eisenhower's nomination for president. He then managed Eisenhower's successful 1952 campaign for president.

In 1953 President Eisenhower appointed Adams as chief of staff. The efficiency with which Adams organized the president's day and the firmness with which he controlled who had access to the president earned him the nickname assistant president. Adams was forced to resign in 1958 when a House subcommittee investigation revealed that he had accepted expensive gifts, including a vicuña coat, from a textile manufacturer seeking federal assistance.

BIBLIOGRAPHY

Adams, Sherman, *Firsthand Report: The Story of the Eisenhower Administration*, 1961.

Agnew, Spiro Theodore

(November 9, 1918–   )
Vice President

Spiro T. Agnew received an unusually large amount of press coverage for his outspoken and controversial views while serving as RICHARD NIXON's vice president. In 1973, he became the first vice president to resign the office.

Born in Baltimore, Maryland, to Greek immigrant parents, Agnew served as an army officer in World War II. He earned his law degree from the University of Baltimore in 1947, established a successful law practice, and became active in Republican state politics during the 1950s.

In 1962 Republican Agnew was elected chief executive of overwhelmingly Democratic Baltimore County. Once again, in 1966, he managed to secure enough Democratic votes as a reform candidate to win election, this time to the governor's office. In 1968 Richard Nixon chose the relatively unknown Agnew to be his vice presidential running mate.

As vice president, Agnew was often in the news for his sarcastic speeches attacking critics of the Nixon administration. Among other things, he claimed that the media was biased against Nixon and that the administration could not hope to receive fair treatment because "a small and unelected elite, . . . an effete corps of impudent snobs . . . composed of nattering nabobs of negativism . . . and radical liberals" controlled the nation's most powerful newspapers, magazines, and television stations. His charges struck a responsive chord among conservative Republicans, and during the 1970 congressional elections Agnew became a much sought after speaker for Republican fund-raising dinners. Most people believed that Agnew was speaking for President Nixon.

After the Nixon-Agnew ticket was reelected by an overwhelming majority in 1972, charges against Agnew surfaced as part of a large, long-term federal government investigation. It was alleged that he had accepted bribes for awarding contracts while serving as Baltimore County chief executive and governor of Maryland. Agnew denied the charges, but when he was confronted with the evidence against him by federal prosecutors, he decided to accept a plea bargain offer rather than to go to trial for income tax evasion. In 1973 he pleaded nolo contendere (no contest) for tax evasion, resigned from office, paid a $10,000 fine, and was placed on probation for three years. (In 1981 a Maryland state court ordered Agnew to repay some $248,000 to the state for bribes he took while in office.)

Agnew retired from politics and established his own import consulting firm for a small group of clients.

BIBLIOGRAPHY

Agnew, Spiro, *Go Quietly . . . Or Else,* 1980; Coyne, John R., Jr., *Impudent Snobs: Agnew vs. the Intellectual Establishment,* 1972.

Albert, Carl Bert

(May 10, 1908–   )
Speaker of the House, Representative

Carl Bert Albert was born in McAlester, Oklahoma, the son of a farmer and coal miner. After graduating in 1931 from the University of Oklahoma at Norman with a B.A. degree in political science, he received a Rhodes scholarship to study law at St. Peter's Hall, Oxford University. Upon his return to the United States in 1934, he worked briefly as a lawyer in the Federal Housing Administration in Oklahoma City. After being admitted to the Oklahoma bar in 1935, he practiced law in Oklahoma City until he joined the legal department of the Ohio Oil Company in 1940. During World War II Albert served as an officer in the Army Air Force and the Judge Advocate General's Department.

In 1946 Albert won election to the U.S. House of Representatives from the congressional district that contained his hometown. As a moderate Democrat, he quickly earned a reputation as a hard worker and loyal party member. In general, he supported President HARRY TRUMAN's legislative goals and voted according to party lines during the Republican administration of DWIGHT D. EISENHOWER. In the 1960s he played a vital role in obtaining enactment of LYNDON JOHNSON's Great Society programs. He was also a staunch supporter of Johnson's handling of the Vietnam War (see LYNDON BAINES JOHNSON and RICHARD MILHOUS NIXON).

Albert was elected majority whip in 1955. He served in that office until he became majority leader in 1962, and served as majority leader until he was named Speaker of the House in 1971. He was a harsh critic of President RICHARD NIXON's efforts to curb inflation in the early 1970s, but he presided with impartiality over the House investigation during the Watergate scandal (see RICHARD

MILHOUS NIXON) that led to Nixon's resignation in 1974.

When the office of vice president was vacant in 1973 and 1974, first because SPIRO AGNEW resigned and then because GERALD FORD replaced Nixon as president, Albert was next in line to the presidency. He retired from the House in 1977, having established a reputation for relying on persuasion and compromise, rather than intimidation, in his use of political power.

BIBLIOGRAPHY

Brady, James, "Class," *Esquire,* August 1975; "Good Soldier," *Newsweek,* December 2, 1974; Sherrill, R., "Running from the Presidency," *New York Times Magazine,* December 9, 1973.

Aldrich, Nelson Wilmarth

(November 6, 1841–April 16, 1915)
Senator, Representative

The most powerful political figure in Rhode Island from 1881 to 1910, Nelson Aldrich launched his political career as a Providence city councillor in 1869. Already a wealthy businessman with millions invested in Rhode Island industry and trade, he rose rapidly in the political world, winning election to the state legislature in 1875, to the U.S. House of Representatives in 1879, and to the U.S. Senate in 1881.

Aldrich won national recognition in the 1880s and 1890s for his leadership in the Republican party on three issues: tariff, commerce, and monetary reform. In the 1897 and 1909 great tariff battles, Aldrich opposed efforts to lower tariffs in the interests of big business, fighting especially, with the aid of protectionist lobbies, against the reform efforts of WILLIAM HOWARD TAFT and ROBERT LA FOLLETTE.

Aldrich supported President THEODORE ROOSEVELT in his first term; but when Roosevelt began moving in a Progressive direction after 1904, Aldrich became a leader of the opposition. He and Roosevelt engaged in a fierce battle in 1906 over the Hepburn Rate Bill, which was designed to give the Interstate Commerce Commission the power to determine railway rates. Aldrich succeeded in modifying the bill so that the railroad companies could appeal any rate changes the commission made to the circuit courts "to enjoin, set aside, or suspend orders of the Commission."

Aldrich's interest in monetary issues first surfaced in his efforts to secure the passage of the Gold Standard Act of 1900. In the wake of the 1907 financial panic, banking reform became his passion. He even retired from the Senate in 1910 in order to promote a plan he had developed for reforming the U.S. banking system. The Aldrich Plan provided for a system of emergency currency based on the rediscounting of commercial paper and called for the creation of a national reserve association with fifteen regional branches. Although Aldrich's hopes of participating in putting the new banking system into practice vanished with the victory of the Democrats in the 1912 elections, he did live to see important elements of his plan incorporated in WOODROW WILSON's Federal Reserve Act of 1913. His last years were spent in political retirement.

BIBLIOGRAPHY

Stephenson, N. W., *Nelson W. Aldrich, a Leader in American Politics,* 1971.

Anderson, John Bayard

(February 15, 1922–)
Candidate for President, Representative

Born in Rockford, Illinois, John B. Anderson graduated from the University of Illinois and earned a degree in law before joining the army in 1943. Upon his discharge in 1945, Anderson moved to Boston and taught at Northeastern University. He acquired another law degree from Harvard University in 1949.

In 1952 Anderson joined the U.S. foreign service. He was stationed in West Berlin and served as adviser to the U.S. high commissioner for Germany until 1955.

Anderson began his political career in 1956 by winning the race for state's attorney of Winnebago County in Illinois. Four years later, he was elected as a Republican to the House of Representatives.

In Congress Anderson's traditional Republican views evolved into a blend of liberal approaches on social legislation and conservative interests in fiscal restraint. He supported civil rights and gun control legislation, backed the Equal Rights Amendment, and advocated eliminating duplication in defense programs. In 1968 Anderson assumed the chairmanship of the prestigious House Republican Conference.

After an unsuccessful effort to win the Republican nomination for president in 1980, Anderson decided to run anyway as an independent candidate. He selected a Democrat and a former governor of Wisconsin, Patrick J. Lucey, as his new National Unity party vice presidential running mate. During the campaign Anderson presented himself as an honest and forthright candidate willing to speak the truth about America's economic and international condition and what he would do about it. His most famous line was a barb at Republican presidential candidate RONALD REAGAN in which he declared that the only way Reagan could keep his campaign pledge of cutting taxes while raising defense spending and maintaining government social services was with mirrors. An eloquent speaker, he briefly became the darling of the media and of university youth before fading badly in the general election. Although he won 7 percent of the popular vote, he did not win any electoral votes.

BIBLIOGRAPHY

Bisnow, Mark, *Diary of a Dark Horse: The 1980 Anderson Presidential Campaign*, 1983; Brown, Clifford W., Jr., and Robert J. Walker, *A Campaign of Ideas: The 1980 Anderson/Lucey Platform*, 1984; Galubovskis, George M., *Crazy Dreaming— The Anderson Campaign, 1980*, 1981.

Arnold, Thurman Wesley

(June 2, 1891–November 7, 1969)
Assistant Attorney General

Thurman Arnold vigorously enforced the provisions of the Sherman Anti-Trust Act as assistant attorney general in charge of the federal government's Antitrust Division from 1939 to 1943.

Arnold was born in Laramie, Wyoming. He earned a B.A. from Princeton in 1911 and a law degree at Harvard Law School in 1914. After briefly practicing law in Chicago, he enlisted in the U.S. Army and spent three years fighting, first in Mexico and then in France during World War I.

After the war Arnold settled in Laramie. He was elected mayor and served a term in the state legislature before leaving in 1927 in order to become the dean of West Virginia University Law School. Three years later, he became a law professor at Yale University. While teaching at Yale, he worked as special counsel to the Agricultural Adjustment Administration (1933) and trial examiner for the Securities Exchange Commission (1935). In March 1939 he was appointed assistant attorney general in charge of antitrust cases.

Arnold disagreed with critics who argued that new antitrust laws were needed. He maintained that the problem, which he planned to remedy, was that the old ones were not being properly enforced. During his five years in office Arnold filed hundreds of antitrust suits, targeting firms in construction, the movies, dairy production, tobacco manufacturing, and many other industries.

Arnold's decision to indict unions (including the International Fur and Leather Workers' Union) and trade associations angered organized labor. His critics charged that he was succumbing to the same inclination to prevent unions from striking as his predecessors. Arnold replied that he was merely seeking balance in pursuing all those who engaged in the "restraint of trade."

Despite his reputation as a "trust buster," Arnold was actually little interested in breaking up large economic institutions. He preferred to regulate the marketing practices of large corporations rather than dismantle the corporations themselves. He was more of a "trust regulator" than a "trust buster."

The growing involvement of the United States in World War II made even this form of trust regulation unacceptable. Arnold was first prevented from investigating an industry in 1940 when the National Defense Commission forbade action against several oil companies on the grounds that antitrust litigation would "complicate and delay" the national preparedness program.

In 1943 Arnold was appointed associate justice of the U.S. Court of Appeals for the District of Columbia. He resigned two years later to go into private practice.

BIBLIOGRAPHY

Arnold, Thurman Wesley, *The Folklore of Capitalism*, 1937, *The Symbols of Government*, 1935, and *The Bottlenecks of Business*, 1940; *Christian Science Monitor Magazine*, May 11, 1940.

Arthur, Chester Alan

(October 5, 1830–November 18, 1886)
President, Vice President

C hester Alan Arthur, the Gentleman Boss, is remembered for the about-face he did against the spoils system when he succeeded to the presidency.

Born in Fairfield, Vermont, Arthur graduated from Union College in 1848. He was admitted to the New York state bar and developed a successful law practice before the Civil War. As a militia officer in the Union army from 1860 to 1863, Arthur carried out important administrative duties. He served in the posts of New York's engineer in chief, inspector general, and quartermaster general. An active Republican, his importance to the party was recognized by President ULYSSES S. GRANT in 1871 when he was appointed customs duty collector for the Port of New York. For seven years in that capacity, Arthur was responsible for the honest handling of the customs revenue collected by the federal government; although as a practical politician and open defender of the spoils system under the influence of ROSCOE CONKLING's New York Republican machine, he knew he presided over a post in which there were far more employees—hired for political reasons—than necessary. When President RUTHERFORD B. HAYES, also a Republican, was elected in 1876, his goal of reforming the federal civil service made the removal of Arthur and the reduction of the number of employees at the Port of New York a priority. After a bitter fight, Hayes succeeded in replacing Arthur in 1878, over the opposition of the New York Republican party. Arthur, in the eyes of his fellow Republicans, became a martyr to party loyalty.

At the divided Republican national convention in 1880 (see ROSCOE CONKLING), the Stalwarts backed Grant for a third term. Anti-Grant forces united to nominate JAMES A. GARFIELD, a known Half-Breed, and placated the Stalwarts by placing Arthur on the ticket as the vice presidential candidate. The ticket won the nomination and the election.

President Garfield was shot in 1881 by a man who claimed he had committed the murder in order to make Arthur president. With the Congress almost evenly split along party lines, Arthur assumed the presidency under the most difficult of circumstances and attempted to maintain a delicate political balance.

Library of Congress

As president, Arthur surprised everybody by working for civil service reform, but he kept many of Garfield's appointees even as he urged legislators to enact a civil service law. He succeeded in securing the passage of the Pendleton Act of 1883, which set up a bipartisan Civil Service Commission to oversee examinations that would determine, on a merit basis, whether or not a candidate was fit for federal appointment. (A first Civil Service Commission, authorized by Congress in 1871, had been short-lived.) A limited list of civil service jobs was also set up, and the law forbade political campaign contributions by federal officeholders. Contrary to his party's past position, Arthur also favored reducing tariff duties. Much to the dismay of the Stalwarts, Arthur thus refused to adopt a "to the victor belongs the spoils" attitude in the staffing of government offices. This attitude and his insistence upon nonpartisanship in his administration lost him key Stalwart supporters, and he was unable to gain the nomination in 1884.

The following year Arthur failed to receive a nomination from New York Republicans for a seat in the U.S. Senate. Exhausted by the strain of office, he died less than two years after leaving the White House.

BIBLIOGRAPHY

Howe, George F., *Chester A. Arthur*, 1934.

Atchison, David Rice

(August 11, 1807–January 26, 1886)
Senator

David Rice Atchison was born in Frogtown, Kentucky. After graduating from Transylvania University, he studied law in Lexington, was admitted to the bar there in 1830, and moved to Missouri.

Atchison was elected to the Missouri state legislature in 1834 and again in 1838. From 1841 until his appointment to the Senate in 1843, he served as a Platte County circuit court judge. Having completed the Senate term of the deceased L. F. Finn, Atchison won election to a full six-year term in 1849. In the Senate Atchison served as chairman of the Committee on Indian Affairs and worked to secure land grants to help Missouri's railroad companies to expand. He hoped to lay the foundation for a transcontinental railroad.

A proslavery Democrat, Atchison fought a fierce battle with the leader of the antislavery Missouri Democrats, THOMAS H. BENTON, for control of the Democratic party. The rivalry did not help either in Missouri politically; both failed to win election to the Senate in 1855. The loss of his Senate seat marked the end of Atchison's political career. His major accomplishment while in the Senate was in helping to secure the repeal of the Missouri Compromise (see HENRY CLAY) through support of the passage of the Kansas-Nebraska Act (see FRANKLIN PIERCE).

After his political defeat in 1855, Atchison became one of the leaders of the proslavery border terrorists who attacked antislavery settlements in "Bleeding Kansas" during 1855 and 1856 (see FRANKLIN PIERCE).

He supported the Confederacy in the Civil War while living in Texas. Atchison, Kansas, is named for him.

BIBLIOGRAPHY

Parrish, William E., *David Rice Atchison of Missouri*, 1961.

Bacon, Robert

(July 5, 1860–May 29, 1919)
Secretary of State, Diplomat

Born in Jamaica Plain, Massachusetts, and educated at Harvard College, Bacon gained prominence as a partner in J. P. Morgan & Co. in 1894. Three of the important enterprises he took part in while at Morgan included the relief of the federal government in the panic of 1895, the formation of the United States Steel Corporation in 1901, and the negotiations resulting in the creation of the Northern Securities Company in 1902. He resigned from the firm in 1903.

Bacon became an assistant secretary of state in 1905 and, in January 1909, replaced Secretary of State ELIHU ROOT, who entered the Senate, for the remaining weeks of President THEODORE ROOSEVELT's administration. President WILLIAM H. TAFT appointed him ambassador to France in December 1909, a post from which he resigned in January 1912.

After an unsuccessful 1916 run for the U.S. Senate, Bacon was commissioned a major in the quartermaster corps of the U.S. Army and sailed for France in 1917 with General John Pershing. He left Paris for home in March 1919 and died two months later as a result of the overexertion and strain he had endured as chief of the American Military Mission.

BIBLIOGRAPHY

Scott, James Brown, *Robert Bacon: Life and Letters*, 1923.

Baker, James Addison, III

(April 28, 1930–)
Secretary of State, Secretary of the Treasury, Presidential Adviser

Widely regarded as one of the premier Republican party national campaign strategists in the 1980s, James Baker's reputation for pragmatism and patience was confirmed by his success in a number of difficult positions within the administrations of RONALD REAGAN and GEORGE BUSH.

Baker was born in Houston, Texas, into a prominent family. After graduating from Princeton University in 1952, he spent two years in the Marine Corps. In 1957 he earned a law degree from the University of Texas at Austin and began practicing law in Houston.

In 1970 Baker helped to manage the campaign of Texas congressman George Bush, a longtime friend who was running for the U.S. Senate. As the state Republican party's finance chairman, Baker played an important role in the 1972 reelection campaign of President RICHARD NIXON. Three years later, President GERALD R. FORD appointed Baker under secretary of commerce, but Baker served in this position only a year before resigning to direct Ford's primary and then general election campaigns. Baker's growing reputation as a campaign tactician of uncommon ability was reinforced in 1980 when, as George Bush's national primary campaign manager, he almost managed to secure the Republican nomination for Bush against the heavily favored Ronald Reagan.

After the election of the Reagan–Bush ticket in November 1980, President Reagan appointed Baker White House chief of staff. As

U.S. Department of State

chief of staff, Baker displayed remarkable skill in managing ideological and personal conflict within the White House as well as between the executive and legislative branches of government. He played a major role in helping to secure the passage of the president's controversial "supply-side" tax and budget package in 1981.

In 1985 Baker was appointed secretary of the treasury. Although his so-called Baker plan (a strategy designed to help developing nations meet their debt payments and also stimulate their economies) failed, his surprise program to lower the value of the dollar did temporarily alleviate debt burden distress.

In 1988 Baker resigned his post to manage Vice President Bush's successful effort to obtain the Republican party nomination for president, then orchestrated the Bush defeat of the early favorite, Democrat MICHAEL DUKAKIS, in the general election. Following the election, Bush appointed Baker secretary of state. As secretary of state, Baker proposed a comprehensive Middle East peace plan and encouraged a careful and prudent American response to the collapse of Soviet rule in Eastern Europe, the reunification of Germany, and economic and political reforms in the Soviet Union.

BIBLIOGRAPHY

"The Bush Bunch?" *U.S. News and World Report,* August 15, 1988; "Bush's Team: Some Old, Some New," *Business Week,* November 21, 1988;

Christian Science Monitor, December 30, 1980; "The Eyes of Texas Are Upon Them," *Life,* 1989; *New York Times,* November 15, 1980, January 17, 1982; *New York Times Magazine,* April 18, 1981.

Baker, Newton Diehl

(December 3, 1871–December 25, 1937)
Secretary of War

While presiding over the massive build-up of American military forces during World War I, Secretary of War Newton Diehl Baker recruited a remarkable group of talented young administrators to public service and instituted the framework for the present civil service structure of the federal government.

Baker was born in Martinsburg, West Virginia. He graduated from Johns Hopkins University in 1892 and Washington and Lee Law School in Lexington, Virginia, in 1894. After briefly practicing law in Martinsburg, Baker served as secretary to the postmaster general in the cabinet of President GROVER CLEVELAND. In 1897 he moved to Cleveland, Ohio, to practice law and to be able to participate in the Progressive (see THEODORE ROOSEVELT) urban political movement there. Three years later, he became city solicitor in the reform administration of the Progressive Democrat Tom Johnson. In 1911 he was elected mayor of Cleveland and continued the reform efforts and sound city government goals of his mentor. He obtained a new home rule charter for the city, built a municipal electric power plant, organized a municipal orchestra, and improved the city hospital facilities.

An early supporter of WOODROW WILSON for president, Baker had played a pivotal role in securing the nomination for Wilson in 1912 at the Democratic national convention by delivering all nineteen of Ohio's delegate votes. When Baker's term as mayor ended in 1916, Wilson appointed him secretary of war. The scholarly, quiet Baker and President Wilson developed a close working relationship.

Once the United States was committed to war, Baker, despite his pacifist inclination, moved swiftly to institute and supervise the military draft. Under his administrative leadership the army grew from 95,000 to over 4 million men, and in less than two years 2 million American soldiers had served—in American units under American commanders, as requested by General John Pershing—in France. Although severely, and perhaps unfairly, criticized during a Senate investigation for the army's lack of preparedness in 1917, Baker's team of talented administrators managed the hugely expanded armed forces with efficiency and honesty.

After President Wilson was incapacitated by a series of strokes in 1919, Baker became his staunchest defender and carried on in his behalf during the fierce political debate about American participation in the League of Nations (see WOODROW WILSON). Baker resumed his law practice in Cleveland at the conclusion of the Wilson administration in 1921. He continued to support U.S. membership in the league and in 1928 was appointed to the Permanent Court of Arbitration at The Hague. Initially a supporter of President FRANKLIN D. ROOSEVELT's New Deal, Baker broke with the administration over the Tennessee Valley Authority. The debilitating effects of a heart attack in July 1937 effectively ended his political career.

BIBLIOGRAPHY

Baker, Newton D., *Why We Went to War,* 1936; Palmer, Frederick, *Newton D. Baker—America at War,* 2 vols., 1931; "Where Are the Pre-War Radicals?" *Survey,* February 1, 1926.

Ballinger, Richard Achilles

(July 9, 1858–June 6, 1922)
Secretary of the Interior

As secretary of the interior, Richard A. Ballinger became involved in one of the most controversial disputes of the early twentieth century: What was to be the federal government's role in regulating land use by private corporations?

Ballinger was born in Boonesboro (now Boone), Iowa. He graduated from Williams College in 1884, was admitted to the bar two years later, and moved to the Pacific Northwest just as Washington was about to become a state in 1890. In 1894 he served as superior judge in Jefferson County and from 1904 to 1906 as the mayor of Seattle. In 1907 he became commissioner of the General Land Office, and in 1909 he was appointed secretary of the interior by President WILLIAM HOWARD TAFT.

Ballinger's three years as secretary of the interior were filled with controversy. Shortly after he assumed office a subordinate, L. R. Glavis of the General Land Office, protested to President Taft that Ballinger had improperly halted an investigation into allegedly fraudulent coal land claims in Alaska. Taft authorized Ballinger to fire Glavis, and Glavis struck back with an article in *Collier's Weekly*.

Other conservationists became aroused, most notably GIFFORD PINCHOT, chief of the Bureau of Forestry and the most famous conservationist of the Progressive era (see THEODORE ROOSEVELT) and a dispute over conservation policies grew into a national controversy. Ballinger, a corporate lawyer, stood accused of abandoning the Progressives' newly formulated but intensely felt commitment to conservation. Others went further in saying he would have allowed the Alaskan land claims. A congressional investigation into Ballinger's handling of national resources eventually cleared him of any wrongdoing, but Ballinger realized he had become a liability to the Taft administration and resigned in March 1911.

In the 1912 election both Theodore Roosevelt and WOODROW WILSON capitalized on the incident as proof that President Taft did not support Progressive conservationist goals.

BIBLIOGRAPHY

Hays, Samuel P., *Conservation and the Gospel of Efficiency: The Progressive Conservation Movement, 1890–1920*, 2d ed., 1972.

Bankhead, William Brockman

(April 12, 1874–September 15, 1940)
Speaker of the House, Representative

William Brockman Bankhead was born into a prominent family (both his father and brother were U.S. senators) in Moscow, Alabama. After graduating from the University of Alabama in 1893, he earned his law degree from Georgetown University in 1895 and established a practice in Huntsville, Alabama. Bankhead entered politics in 1900 when he was elected to the state legislature.

Although he lost his first race for the U.S. Congress in 1914, Bankhead won election to the House of Representatives in 1916 and was reelected every two years thereafter until his death. While in Congress, Bankhead was a loyal Democrat. His longevity and staunch support of the party's legislation led to his election as chairman of the House Rules Committee in 1933, then Democratic majority leader in 1935, and finally Speaker of the House in 1936. As Speaker from 1936 until 1940, Bankhead played a vital role in securing the enactment of New Deal legislation, even though he had reservations about the dramatic increase in the size and power of the federal government.

In 1940 Bankhead gave the keynote address at the Democratic party's national convention. Conservative delegates, hoping to block the choice of liberal HENRY A. WALLACE as vice president, placed Bankhead's name in nomination. Bankhead obtained a surprising 329 delegate votes, but his popularity was not sufficient to prevent the convention from supporting President FRANKLIN D. ROOSEVELT'S choice of Wallace.

Bankhead died a few weeks later.

BIBLIOGRAPHY

Bankhead, W. B., "I'm Proud to Be a Politician," *True Story Magazine,* September 1940; *Current Biography,* 1940; *New York Times,* September 16, 1940; Owen, Thomas McA., *History of Alabama and the Dictionary of Alabama Biography,* 1921.

Banks, Nathaniel Prentiss

(January 30, 1816–September 1, 1894)
Speaker of the House, Representative

Library of Congress

Nathaniel Banks was known as the Bobbin Boy of Massachusetts because, after only a few years of formal schooling, he had to go to work in his father's cotton mill. Banks refused to let his humble origins impede his ambition. He was admitted to the state bar at the age of twenty-three; after briefly serving as an inspector in the Boston customshouse, he spent the next three years as the proprietor and editor of a weekly newspaper.

After seven unsuccessful tries, Banks was elected to the Massachusetts House of Representatives in 1849. He was elected speaker in 1851. The next year he was elected to the U.S. House of Representatives as a Democrat, but he alienated so many of his Democratic party supporters by voting against the Kansas-Nebraska Act (see FRANKLIN PIERCE) that he had to be reelected to Congress for a second term in 1854 as a member of the American or Know-Nothing party (see MILLARD FILLMORE). Elected Speaker of the House as an antislavery candidate in a bitterly contested struggle in 1856, Banks believed that the Speaker's office should be viewed as an executive rather than partisan political position. His decisions were prompt and impartial.

In 1856 Banks declined the North American party's nomination for president in order to lead the antislavery wing into the new Republican party. In 1857 he left Congress to run for governor of Massachusetts as a Republican. He served as an effective and progressive governor from 1858 to 1860.

Banks moved to Chicago in January 1861 to become president of the Illinois Central Railroad. As soon as the Civil War began, however, he joined the Union army as a major general in the militia. After being twice defeated by Stonewall Jackson, he assisted ULYSSES S. GRANT at Vicksburg by laying siege to and capturing Port Hudson. This was to be his only military success. Placed in charge of the poorly conceived Red River campaign in 1864 against his wishes, his army was badly defeated at Mansfield.

Banks returned to Boston and served in the U.S. House of Representatives from 1865 to 1873 as a Republican. In Congress he opposed reducing the supply of money in circulation, was a member of the Committee of Five to investigate the Crédit Mobilier charges (see SCHUYLER COLFAX), and supported the purchase of Alaska (see WILLIAM HENRY SEWARD). Because of his opposition to the reelection of Grant in 1872 and support for Democrat HORACE GREELEY, Banks was not reelected. He returned to Congress in 1875, first as a Democrat and then, two years later, as a Republican, serving until 1879. He served his last term from 1889 to 1891 as a Republican.

BIBLIOGRAPHY

Harrington, Fred H., *Fighting Politician: Major General N. P. Banks*, 1948.

Barbour, Philip Pendleton

(May 25, 1783–February 25, 1841)
Chief Justice of the Supreme Court, Speaker of the House, Representative

An early leader of the South's hostile reaction to the growth of federal power, Barbour was born in Barboursville, Virginia. He attended the College of William and Mary in 1801, studied law, and practiced in Virginia. He was elected to the Virginia House of Delegates in 1812 and served in the U.S. Congress from 1815 to 1825 and from 1827 to 1830. An advocate of states' rights and a strict constructionist, Barbour opposed in Congress the tariffs and internal improvements pushed by HENRY CLAY and JOHN C. CALHOUN, and the extension of federal jurisdiction by the Supreme Court under JOHN MARSHALL. He served as Speaker of the House from 1821 to 1823 and as president of the Virginia constitutional convention from 1829 to 1830.

Barbour opposed using nullification (see JOHN CALDWELL CALHOUN) as a method of defending states' rights, but he supported the right of a state to secede. As a strict constructionist, he did not believe that Congress had the authority to impose terms for the admission of Missouri as either a slave or a free state.

In 1830 Barbour accepted an appointment by President ANDREW JACKSON to be the U.S. district court judge for eastern Virginia and in 1836 an appointment to the Supreme Court, where he served until his death in 1841.

BIBLIOGRAPHY

The brief accounts of Barbour's life, such as the one found in Peters's *Supreme Court Reports,* XV, are based on W. W. Story's sketch in *Life and Letters of Joseph Story,* II, 1851.

Barkley, Alben William

(November 24, 1877–April 30, 1956)
Vice President, Senator, Representative

Alben Barkley capped off a long and distinguished political career in Congress by becoming one of the most popular vice presidents the nation has ever had. He was also the oldest vice president ever to serve.

Born in Graves County, Kentucky, Barkley graduated from nearby Marvin College and then studied law at Emory College in Georgia and the University of Virginia. He began practicing law in Kentucky in 1901 and became a judge in 1909.

Barkley was elected to Congress in 1912 and served in the House until he was elected to the Senate in 1926. Elected to four consecutive Senate terms, Barkley became majority leader in the Senate in 1937. His strong support for President FRANKLIN D. ROOSEVELT's New Deal and President HARRY S TRUMAN's Fair Deal legislation made him a strong vice presidential possibility for nearly twenty years before Truman asked him to be his running mate in 1948.

Truman had wanted WILLIAM O. DOUGLAS, associate justice of the Supreme Court, to be his running mate; but after Douglas refused to join the ticket, Truman had agreed on Barkley, even though he believed that at age seventy Barkley was too old. After Truman's surprising election victory over THOMAS E. DEWEY, Barkley became an unusually active vice president. Truman included Barkley in important meetings and discussed major issues with him.

When Barkley's grandson called him the Veep, the nickname stuck to Barkley and to the office. Although deemed too old to run for president in 1952 by Democratic party leaders, he was reelected to the Senate in 1954. He died suddenly two years later.

BIBLIOGRAPHY

Barkley, Alben W., *That Reminds Me,* 1954.

Baruch, Bernard Mannes

(August 19, 1870–June 20, 1965)
Government Agency Director, Presidential Adviser

In addition to his remarkable and unique role as adviser to American political leaders, Baruch was also chairman of the War Industries Board during World War I, a member of President WOODROW WILSON's staff at the Paris peace negotiations in 1919 (see WILSON), and U.S. representative to the United Nations Atomic Energy Commission in 1946.

Born in Camden, South Carolina, Baruch graduated from the College of the City of New York in 1889 and became a Wall Street bond salesman and stockbroker. He quickly decided to start investing in stocks himself and by the age of thirty was a millionaire.

Baruch left Wall Street in 1916 to advise President Wilson on national defense. In the summer of 1916 he served on the seven-member Advisory Commission to the Council for National Defense, and in 1918 became the chairman of the newly formed War Industries Board (WIB). Under his leadership, the WIB successfully managed the nation's economic mobilization and became a model for subsequent efforts at national planning.

In 1919 President Wilson asked him to serve as a staff member at the Paris peace conference. Baruch was dismayed by the British and French war reparations demands upon Germany. He was convinced of the soundness of Wilson's vision of the need for new forms of cooperative arrangements between nations as well as among traditionally hostile interest groups within the nation.

During the 1920s and 1930s Baruch championed the need for the United States to be prepared for the possibility of another world war. He was convinced that the only way to ensure maximum coordination between civilian businesses and military needs in the event of war was to create a more powerful version of the War Industries Board he headed during World War I. He was frequently consulted by government officials and supported President FRANKLIN D. ROOSEVELT's domestic and foreign policy initiatives. When the United States entered World War II, Roosevelt appointed Baruch to be a special adviser to the director of the Office of War Mobilization.

In 1946 President HARRY TRUMAN appointed Baruch U.S. representative to the United Nations Atomic Energy Commission. In June of that year Baruch presented what became known as the Baruch Plan. It promised that the production of atomic bombs by America would cease as soon as all nations agreed to give the World Atomic Authority of the United Nations full manufacturing control of all their nuclear weapons development facilities. The rejection of the plan by the Soviets was one of Baruch's greatest disappointments. After he resigned from the commission in 1947, his influence waned because he became increasingly out of step with the domestic and foreign policy views of the Truman administration.

BIBLIOGRAPHY

Baruch, Bernard, *Baruch: My Own Story*, 1957, and *Baruch: The Public Years*, 1960; Coit, Margaret L., *Mr. Baruch*, 1957; Schwarz, Jordan A., *The Speculator, Bernard M. Baruch in Washington, 1917–1965*, 1981.

Bayard, Thomas Francis

(October 29, 1828–September 28, 1898)
Secretary of State, Diplomat, Senator

Thomas Bayard was born into a family of distinguished public servants in Wilmington, Delaware. Instead of attending college, he embarked on a business career in a New York mercantile firm. When his older brother died, he returned to Wilmington, studied law with his father, and was admitted to the state bar in 1851. Bayard was appointed U.S. attorney for Delaware in 1853 but resigned the next year in order to resume his law practice.

Elected as a Democrat to succeed his father in the U.S. Senate in 1869, he served there until 1885. Although he received considerable support, he was unable to capture the presidential nomination in 1880 and 1884. In 1885 Bayard became President GROVER CLEVELAND's secretary of state. His tenure ended before he could resolve the major issues of the time: fishing rights with Canada in the North Atlantic; a dispute with Canada and Great Britain about jurisdiction over the Bering Sea and its seal herds; and a compromise among the United States, Great Britain, and Germany over conflicting interests in Samoa.

After Cleveland was elected for a second term in 1892, Bayard was appointed ambassador to Great Britain. In 1895 the Cleveland administration demanded to arbitrate the Venezuelan–British Guiana (now Guyana) boundary dispute with Great Britain, invoking the Monroe Doctrine (see JAMES MONROE) in a belligerent way. Bayard openly criticized Cleveland, causing the House of Representatives to pass a censure resolution against him in 1896. Bayard's health had begun to deteriorate while abroad; less than a year after his return in 1897, he died in Dedham, Massachusetts.

BIBLIOGRAPHY

Tansil, C. C., *Congressional Career of Thomas F. Bayard, 1869–1885*, 1946, and *Foreign Policy of Thomas F. Bayard, 1883–1897*, 1969.

Belknap, William Worth

(September 22, 1829–October 13, 1890)
Secretary of War

Born in Newburgh, New York, William Belknap attended the College of New Jersey (now Princeton University) and studied law at Georgetown University. He was admitted to the bar in 1851 and began his practice at Keokuk, Iowa. He served in the Iowa legislature as a Democrat in 1857 and 1858. At the outbreak of the Civil War, he received a commission as a major in the state militia. He served with distinction at Shiloh, was promoted to general, and received numerous commendations from William T. Sherman and ULYSSES S. GRANT for his leadership qualities in combat.

After the war ended in 1865, Belknap returned to Iowa and became a tax collector. President Grant chose him to be his secretary of war in 1869, a post that led to his disgrace. Accused of taking a bribe for making an appointment at a military installation, Belknap was impeached. A trial was held in the Senate, but Grant had already allowed Belknap to resign. Many senators felt that Belknap was no longer under Senate jurisdiction, and they failed to deliver enough votes for conviction. There was also the possibility that Belknap's wife had made the arrangements for taking the bribe without her husband's knowledge. In any event, Belknap's public career was over, and he spent his last years in Philadelphia and Washington, D.C., practicing law.

BIBLIOGRAPHY

No biography of Belknap exists. For records of his impeachment trial, see *Reports of Committees of the House of Representatives* and *Congressional Record*, vol. 4.

Bell, John

(February 15, 1797–September 10, 1869)
Secretary of War, Candidate for President, Senator, Representative

Born in Nashville, Tennessee, Bell graduated from nearby Cumberland College in 1814. Before he was twenty-one he had completed his legal studies, been admitted to the bar, served one term as a senator in the state legislature, and established his law practice at Franklin, Tennessee. In 1827 he won a seat in the U.S. House of Representatives. Bell considered himself a Jacksonian Democrat and supported ANDREW JACKSON's policies in Congress until the president began his war against the national bank (see NICHOLAS BIDDLE and ROGER BROOKE TANEY). Then, despite Jackson's threat to destroy him, Bell publicly broke with the president.

Library of Congress

Following MARTIN VAN BUREN's election, Bell left the Democratic party and became a Whig. For the next two decades, the Whig party, with Bell its acknowledged leader, dominated politics in Tennessee.

Bell served briefly as WILLIAM HENRY HARRISON's secretary of war in 1841. Six years later, he was elected to the U.S. Senate, where he served until 1859. In the growing controversy over slavery, Bell advocated moderation. He believed in the constitutionality of Congress prohibiting slavery in the territory acquired as a result of the Mexican War (see JAMES KNOX POLK), but he did not want to pursue the issue in any formal manner. He opposed parts of HENRY CLAY's compromise measures of 1850 that dealt with slavery and the territories, but after their adoption he supported them.

Bell parted with his Southern colleagues in 1854 when he opposed the Kansas-Nebraska Act (see FRANKLIN PIERCE), and in 1858 he refused to support the admission of Kansas under the proslavery Lecompton Constitution (see JAMES BUCHANAN and ROBERT J. WALKER). For this and his publicly stated opposition to forcing slavery upon new states, he was denounced in the South.

In 1860, with the Whig party dead, Bell and a number of other moderate former Whigs founded the Constitutional Union party in an effort to avoid civil war. Bell was nominated for the presidency and EDWARD EVERETT of Massachusetts for the vice presidency. Their ticket carried only three states: Tennessee, Kentucky, and Virginia.

Bell opposed secession, but he believed ABRAHAM LINCOLN was wrong in resorting to force to preserve the Union. When Union troops entered Tennessee, Bell, who advocated "resistance at any cost, and by arms," was forced to flee farther south. His career over, he retired to Georgia, returning only after the war to Tennessee. He died in 1869 in Bear Spring Furnace.

BIBLIOGRAPHY

Parks, Joseph H., *John Bell of Tennessee*, 1950.

Benjamin, Judah Philip

(August 6, 1811–May 6, 1884)
Senator

Dubbed the brains of the Confederacy by Northern journalists in recognition of his legal brilliance, former Louisiana senator Judah P. Benjamin served as JEFFERSON DAVIS's attorney general, secretary of war, and secretary of state.

Benjamin was born to Jewish parents on St. Thomas, then British West Indies. His family later moved to Charleston, South Carolina. Benjamin attended Yale, then went to New Orleans and supported himself by teaching while he studied law. He was admitted to the bar there in 1832 at age twenty-one and established a prosperous legal practice. A few years later, he acquired a national reputation for his discussion of the institution of slavery in America under international as well as domestic law in the case of the brig *Creole*.

Benjamin was soon wealthy enough to purchase a large sugar plantation. Entering politics, he was elected as a Whig to the Louisiana state legislature in 1842 and the U.S. Senate in 1852.

In the Senate Benjamin was a staunch defender of Southern policy. He also assisted in the creation of the Jackson Railroad Company (later the Illinois Central) and other commercial ventures. In 1856, after the collapse of the Whig party over the slavery issue, Benjamin joined the Democratic party. Two years later, he was reelected to the Senate, but he became increasingly convinced that the South could not hope to receive fair treatment in the Union. He was one of the first senators to support secession after the election of ABRAHAM LINCOLN, and as soon as Louisiana voted to secede in 1861, resigned from the Senate.

While in Congress, Benjamin had become a close friend as well as a political ally of Jefferson Davis. The new president of the Confederacy appointed Benjamin attorney general and, with the outbreak of fighting a few months later, secretary of war. Benjamin lost the considerable popularity he had acquired in the South during his reign as secretary of war. He was unjustly blamed for Southern military defeats and lack of military preparedness in the first year of the Civil War. The loss of Roanoke Island to Union forces in 1862 led to an effort to remove Benjamin from office that infuriated President Davis, who viewed the action as a challenge to his leadership. To spite his political opponents, he named Benjamin secretary of state. Davis's action did not enhance Benjamin's standing, but Benjamin ignored public hostility and diligently pursued the vain goal of securing foreign recognition of the Confederacy. In the waning, desperate days of the war, Benjamin publicly suggested enrolling slaves in the Confederate forces and emancipating them.

After the collapse of the Confederacy, Benjamin managed to escape to the West Indies and from there to Great Britain. He spent the remaining years of his life abroad.

BIBLIOGRAPHY

Evans, Eli, *Judah P. Benjamin, the Jewish Confederate*, 1988; Meade, Robert D., *Judah P. Benjamin*, 1943; Osterweis, R. G., *Judah P. Benjamin, Statesman of the Lost Cause*, 1943.

Bennett, William John

(July 31, 1943–   )
Secretary of Education

William J. Bennett rose to national prominence as the controversial chairman of the National Endowment for the Humanities. He continued to attract attention for his blunt outspokenness and conservative beliefs while secretary of education and later as director of the Office of National Drug Control Policy.

Bennett was born in Brooklyn, New York. After graduating from Williams College in 1965, he earned his doctorate in philosophy from the University of Texas in 1970, and a degree from Harvard Law School a year later.

Upon completing his studies at Harvard, Bennett became a professor and administrator at Boston University. In 1976 Bennett founded the National Humanities Center in North Carolina and served as its executive director and then as its president. During this period he wrote numerous articles explaining his conservative viewpoints on such contemporary issues as affirmative action, bilingual programs, and multiculturalism in the schools.

In 1981 President RONALD REAGAN appointed Bennett chairman of the National Endowment for the Humanities. Bennett eliminated funding for many programs launched by his liberal predecessor and brought the organization into line with his conservative view of its mission—to promote the study of the humanities, "not faddishly innovative programs." In "To Reclaim a Legacy: A Report on the Humanities in Higher Education" (1984), he argued that while the non-Western world must be taken into account in college curricula, "the core ... should be the civilization of the West."

President Reagan chose Bennett as secretary of education in January 1985. Though some critics thought that Bennett would lose visibility in this minor cabinet post (during his first term, Reagan had wanted to abolish it), he used it to enlarge his reputation as the leading conservative spokesperson on educational matters.

In 1989 President GEORGE BUSH chose Bennett to lead the war on drug abuse. Bennett was confident that victory could be achieved, but he conceded that the battle was going to be much more difficult than most people anticipated. Known as the drug czar, he resigned the post in 1990.

BIBLIOGRAPHY

Bencivenga, Jim, "Education Chief Takes 'Radical' Stand for Tough Standards," *Christian Science Monitor*, March 12, 1985, p. 3; Boyd, Gerald M., "President Names 3 for His Cabinet in Key Job Shifts," *New York Times*, January 11, 1985, p. 1.

Benson, Ezra Taft

(August 4, 1899–   )
Secretary of Agriculture

As a secretary of agriculture, the president of the Church of Jesus Christ of Latter-Day Saints (Mormons), and a leader of the farmers' cooperative movement, Ezra Benson has devoted his life to improving conditions for American farmers and to fulfilling his religious ideals.

Benson was born into a prominent Mormon family in Whitney, Idaho. He grew up on the family farm, graduated from Brigham Young University in 1926, and earned a master's degree in agricultural economics at Iowa State College in 1927. He also briefly pursued graduate studies in agriculture at the University of California in 1937.

After owning and operating his own farm from 1923 to 1929, Benson spent the next nine years as a county agricultural agent and farm marketing specialist for the University of Idaho's extension service. For many years he was also a leader of the farmers' cooperative movement.

Although not actively involved in the Republican party, Benson supported the nomination of ROBERT A. TAFT for president in 1952. He regarded the Democratic party's New Deal approach of subsidizing agricultural prices as patronizing paternalism: "The virus of subsidies," he warned, "permeates the economic body and eats it up once it gets its proboscis under the skin."

President-elect DWIGHT D. EISENHOWER chose Benson as secretary of agriculture in 1952. Two years later, Congress adopted Benson's program for reducing the federal govern-ment's role in agriculture. His system of flexible price supports for basic farm products allowed for at least some traditional free-market effects on agricultural supply and demand. Benson's flexible supports failed to stimulate farm prices, however, and a bitter reaction by farmers to his leadership began within two years. In 1956 the Republicans lost a number of congressional seats in the farm states. Enthusiasm for flexible supports dwindled in Congress, and a number of rigid agricultural price supports were reinstituted. Critics blamed Benson for the 1956 Republican election defeats, but he remained in office to become one of only two cabinet officials to serve the entire eight years of the Eisenhower administration. The federal government, moreover, would remain committed to some version of Benson's flexible price support program for the next twenty-five years.

In addition to his agricultural and political careers, Benson is a high official of the Mormon church. In 1985 he was elected its president.

BIBLIOGRAPHY

Dales, Douglas, "Eisenhower Names Adams as Top Aide; Benson in Cabinet," *New York Times,* November 25, 1952, p. 1; Jennings, Melvin K., "Incoming Agriculture Secretary Traces Career to Hoe," *Christian Science Monitor,* December 6, 1952, p. 15.

Benton, Thomas Hart

(March 14, 1782–April 10, 1858)
Senator, Representative

Thomas Hart Benton became one of the country's greatest backers of Manifest Destiny (see JAMES KNOX POLK) and the granting of free homesteads to farmers in the West. A farmer himself, Benton moved in 1801 from his birthplace in Hillsboro, North Carolina, to Tennessee to help his widowed mother run her estate. He was elected in 1809 to the North Carolina state senate, where he became involved in land ownership issues and the rights of slaves in capital trials. He was admitted to the state bar in 1811.

Library of Congress

After serving in the War of 1812 (see JAMES MADISON), Benton moved to St. Louis, Missouri, where he practiced law and became editor of the *St. Louis Enquirer*. He was elected to the U.S. Senate in 1820 from Missouri and was against restricting slavery in that state. By 1828, however, he had come to favor the gradual abolition of slavery. As a firm advocate of acquiring new territory and nationally improving road and river communications (see JOHN CALDWELL CALHOUN), Benton was beginning to see slavery as an impediment to the development of the West.

A follower of ANDREW JACKSON's democratic ideas, Benton was the Senate floor leader during Jackson's war on the national bank, an institution Benton thought bred inequalities (see NICHOLAS BIDDLE). Nicknamed Old Bullion, Benton backed gold coinage and paying for public lands in hard currency, and thus opposed the bank's power to issue notes. In 1831 he introduced a resolution opposing the scheduled rechartering of the national bank and endorsed removal of government deposits prior to the expiration of the charter. His support enabled Jackson's veto of the bank charter to hold, thus making the rechartering of the national bank an important issue in the 1832 presidential campaign.

Benton was initially opposed to the annexation of Texas (see JAMES KNOX POLK) because it was tied to slavery, but he backed the subsequent war with Mexico. While opposed to outright abolition, he backed the right of Congress to legislate on slavery in the territories. Always the moderate, he believed in the rights of states but not in nullification (see JOHN CALDWELL CALHOUN). Eventually, he began to see the intransigent defense of slavery by the Southern leadership as a grave threat to peace and the preservation of the United States.

His opposition to Southern demands during the debate on the Compromise of 1850 (see HENRY CLAY) cost him his support in Missouri, and he subsequently lost the Senate seat he had held for thirty years. Though he had championed essential Western interests, such as the pony express, the telegraph, and the building of a transcontinental railroad, his constituents could not tolerate his antislavery views. Undiscouraged, Benton won a seat in the House of Representatives, where he fought the repeal of the Missouri Compromise (see CLAY), only to lose his seat there as well.

He was defeated in a run for the Missouri governorship in 1856 and retired from political life to write *Thirty Years' View* (1856) and the *Abridgement of the Debates of Congress* (1857–1861). He died in Washington, D.C., in 1858.

BIBLIOGRAPHY

Chambers, William N., *Old Bullion Benton,* 1956; Roosevelt, Theodore, *Thomas H. Benton,* 1969; Smith, Elbert B., *Magnificent Missourian: Thomas Hart Benton,* 1958.

Berger, Victor Louis

(February 28, 1860–August 7, 1929)
Representative

Victor Louis Berger was the first socialist ever elected to the U.S. House of Representatives.

Born in Nieder-Rehbach, Austria, Berger grew up in Leutschau, Hungary. After attending universities in Vienna and Budapest, he emigrated to America. From 1878 until 1881 he lived in Bridgeport, Connecticut, working at a number of menial and semi-skilled jobs. In 1881 he moved to Milwaukee and became a German language teacher in the public school system there. He also became active in a number of local socialist organizations, trade unions, and reform movements. Berger believed in gradual reform and cooperation among socialist groups. He and EUGENE DEBS founded the Social Democratic party in 1899, which became the foundation of the Socialist party (formed in 1901). Berger became known as a right-wing socialist because of his commitment to gradual reform through the electoral process and his opposition to left-wing socialists who advocated revolutionary change.

Berger's political influence was enhanced by his role as a newspaper editor. He founded the *Wisconsin Vorwärts,* a Milwaukee German-language daily, in 1892 and served as its editor until 1898. From 1901 until 1911 he ran the weekly *Social Democratic Herald.* He then became the editor of the *Milwaukee Leader,* a position he held until his death. Berger helped to make Milwaukee a showcase of "municipal socialism," which featured municipal ownership of urban utilities and transportation systems.

In 1910 Berger became the first socialist ever elected to Congress when he was narrowly chosen to represent the city of Milwaukee and neighboring suburbs. During his two-year term in the House of Representatives, Berger championed the eight-hour day, protective child labor laws, federal farm aid, and old-age pensions. He also fought for international disarmament. He failed to win reelection in 1912 and 1914, but he was elected in 1918 on a strong antiwar platform. However, Berger was excluded from membership in November of 1919 on the grounds of giving aid and comfort to the enemy and being disloyal to the United States.

Like most American socialists, Berger opposed U.S. participation in World War I, a position also popular among his largely German immigrant constituents. The Espionage Act of 1917 and the Sedition Act of 1918 allowed the government to jail socialist leaders and other individuals simply for expressing their opposition to war. Berger was sentenced to twenty years for sedition before the Supreme Court overturned his conviction. In 1919 Berger was reelected to fill his vacant seat but was again refused admission. In 1922 the vindicated Berger won the first of three more successive terms in Congress. The socialist movement, however, never recovered its prewar appeal.

BIBLIOGRAPHY

Berger, Victor L., *Voice and Pen of Victor L. Berger*, 1929; Chafee, Zechariah, Jr., *Free Speech in the United States*, 1941; Salvatore, Nick, *Eugene V. Debs, Citizen and Socialist*, 1982.

Beveridge, Albert Jeremiah

(October 6, 1862–April 27, 1927)
Senator

Political leader and historian Albert Jeremiah Beveridge was born in Highland County, Ohio, and grew up on a small farm in Illinois. He graduated from Asbury College (now DePauw University) in Greencastle, Indiana, in 1885 and moved to Indianapolis, where he was admitted to the bar in 1887 and started a practice.

Beveridge established a substantial political reputation by traveling around the state speaking on behalf of Republican candidates. When a deadlock developed between two Republican candidates for the U.S. Senate in 1899, Beveridge was agreed upon as the compromise choice. He was reelected in 1905.

In the Senate Beveridge supported President THEODORE ROOSEVELT's buildup of the navy, regulation of trusts, and conservation programs. He also worked for legislation to control child labor and drafted a pioneering meat inspection law.

Because of his association with the Progressive wing of the Republican party and opposition to the Payne-Aldrich Tariff Act of 1909 (see WILLIAM HOWARD TAFT), angry elements within his own party worked with the Democratic party to successfully block Beveridge's reelection in 1911.

In 1912 Beveridge helped found the Progressive or Bull Moose party (see THEODORE ROOSEVELT). He delivered the keynote address at its first national convention, entitled "Pass Prosperity Around," and ran unsuccessfully as its candidate for governor of Indiana later that same year. He made two more unsuccessful tries for the Senate, first in 1914 as a Progressive and then in 1922 as the Republican candidate, before retiring from politics.

In addition to his political career, Beveridge was a prolific writer and accomplished historian. He wrote the four-volume Pulitzer Prize–winning biography *The Life of John Marshall* (1916–1919), in which he traced JOHN MARSHALL's role in developing the Supreme Court as a powerful branch of the federal government. Beveridge had begun work on an equally ambitious biography of ABRAHAM LINCOLN, but he did not complete writing all four volumes before his death. Volumes 1 and 2 of *Abraham Lincoln, 1809–1858* were published posthumously in 1928.

BIBLIOGRAPHY

Bowers, Claude, *Beveridge and the Progressive Era*, 1932.

Biddle, Nicholas

(January 8, 1786–February 27, 1844)
Diplomat, President of the Second Bank of the United States

Born in Philadelphia, Pennsylvania, Biddle entered the University of Pennsylvania at age ten, graduated at thirteen, and completed his advanced studies at the College of New Jersey (now Princeton University) in 1801. He traveled to France in 1804 as the U.S. minister's secretary and then to London in the same post, returning to Philadelphia in 1807. He was admitted to the bar in 1809. Interested in the law more as an academic endeavor than as an occupation, Biddle pursued the life of an intellectual, writing literary articles, participating in discussions at the elite Tuesday Club in Philadelphia, and preparing the official account of the Lewis and Clark Expedition from the explorers' notes and journals. He served one winter term, 1810 to 1811, in the Pennsylvania House of Representatives and was elected to the state senate in 1814.

The president was allowed to name five of the twenty-five directors of the Bank of the United States, and in 1819 President JAMES MONROE asked Biddle to become one of them. Biddle succeeded LANGDON CHEVES to become president of the bank in 1823. Under his leadership, the bank expanded and established public confidence by furnishing a stable currency and restraining state banks from engaging in unsound business ventures.

Although Biddle had made it an absolute rule that the bank should be neutral in politics, he, along with others who regarded the bank as a necessity, realized the threat posed by the election of ANDREW JACKSON in 1828. Jackson was bitterly opposed to the national bank. Biddle and most other prominent supporters of the bank mistakenly believed that only a lack of knowledge about currency, finance, and economics could be the basis for opposition to the institution. They embarked on a campaign to educate the public through the publication of articles. Biddle also wooed a number of influential politicians and editors to his cause, mainly by granting banking favors. He relied on HENRY CLAY and DANIEL WEBSTER for advice, and it was they who urged him to apply to Congress for a new charter in 1832, four years before the expiration of the bank's charter. President Jackson vetoed the bill and made his opposition to the rechartering of the bank a major issue of the presidential campaign of 1832. After Jackson's reelection, the Second Bank of the United States was doomed. In 1836 it became a state bank, and in 1841 it declared bankruptcy. Biddle resigned in 1839 and spent the last five years of his life writing and entertaining American and European intellectuals at his Delaware home.

BIBLIOGRAPHY

Govan, Thomas Paine, *Nicholas Biddle, Nationalist and Public Banker, 1786–1844*, 1959; McGrane, R. C. (ed.), *The Correspondence of Nicholas Biddle Dealing with National Affairs, 1807–1844*, 1966.

Birney, James Gillespie

(February 4, 1792–November 25, 1857)
Candidate for President

Despite his slave-owning background, James G. Birney progressed from a position of mild support to militant leadership in the antislavery movement. He thereby earned an uncommon place for himself in American history.

Born in Danville, Kentucky, Birney graduated from the College of New Jersey (now Princeton University) in 1810. Admitted to the bar in 1814, Birney established a law practice at Danville. In August 1816 he was elected to the lower house of the Kentucky state legislature.

In 1818 Birney moved to Madison County, Alabama. Although he owned slaves and was not a member of the Alabama constitutional convention, Birney was largely responsible for the inclusion in that state's constitution of certain provisions of the Kentucky constitution permitting the legislature to emancipate slaves and prohibiting the introduction of slaves into the state for sale. In 1819 he was elected a representative to the first General Assembly of Alabama, but his opposition to a resolution supporting the candidacy of ANDREW JACKSON for president was so unpopular he was not reelected.

A visit to New England and New York in 1829 convinced Birney that slavery was impeding the economic development of the South. In August 1832 he became an agent of the American Colonization Society, but by the mid-1830s he realized that sending American blacks back to Africa was unjust and became a strong supporter of the abolitionist cause. He freed his six slaves in 1834, and in 1839 he emancipated the twenty-one slaves he had inherited from his father.

Birney helped found the Kentucky Anti-Slavery Society in 1835. In 1836 he began publishing a weekly newspaper, *The Philanthropist*, which was met with great hostility. In it he not only attacked Democrats and Whigs for their attitudes toward slavery, but he also urged upon the abolitionists the need for political action. In 1837 he was elected executive secretary of the American Anti-Slavery Society and moved to New York. In 1840 his best-known work, *American Churches, Bulwarks of American Slavery*, was published in England.

Birney was selected to be the antislavery Liberty party's candidate for president in 1840. He polled an insignificant 7,069 votes. He was again nominated by the Liberty party in 1844, this time polling 62,300 popular votes. He retired from political life in 1845.

BIBLIOGRAPHY

Birney, William, *James G. Birney and His Times*, 1969; Fladeland, Betty L., *James Gillespie Birney: Slaveholder to Abolitionist*, 1969.

Black, Hugo LaFayette

(February 27, 1886–September 25, 1971)
Associate Justice of the Supreme Court, Senator

Library of Congress

A strong advocate of judicial activism during his thirty-four-year career as an associate justice of the Supreme Court, Hugo Black had a major influence on American judicial history.

Born in Clay County, Alabama, Black earned his law degree from the University of Alabama in 1906. From 1907 to 1927 he practiced law in Ashland and Birmingham. Active in the Democratic party, Black held a number of local political offices. From 1910 to 1911 he was police court judge, and from 1915 until he joined the army in 1917, prosecuting attorney of Jefferson County. During the 1920s, Black was briefly a member of the revived Ku Klux Klan (see ULYSSES SIMPSON GRANT), though he repudiated it later.

In 1926 Black was elected to the U.S. Senate; he was reelected in 1932. Black became a staunch supporter of FRANKLIN D. ROOSEVELT and of such important New Deal programs as the Tennessee Valley Authority. He won national attention with his investigation of merchant marine subsidies in 1933 and the lobbying practices used by the opponents of the Public Utilities Holding Company Act of 1935. President Roosevelt appointed Black to the Supreme Court in 1937.

Black's liberal views while serving on the Court from 1937 until one week before his death in 1971 surprised some of those who had criticized his appointment. People had as-sumed that, because of his Southern background and one-time membership in the Ku Klux Klan, Black would oppose using the Court to foster social change. Instead, just the opposite happened. Black became a critical member of the liberal majority of the Court under EARL WARREN that endorsed judicial activism on behalf of civil and human rights.

Black believed that decisions on constitutionality had to be made by the justices without regard to the legislature. "If, as I think," he wrote to a law professor, "the judiciary is vested with the supreme, constitutional power and responsibility to pass on the validity of legislation, then I think it cannot 'defer' to the legislative judgment 'without abdicating its own responsibility.'"

Throughout his Supreme Court career, Black held that the Fourteenth Amendment extended the protections contained in the Bill of Rights to all citizens at all times. This resulted in important civil rights decisions, especially those pertaining to the unconstitutionality of racial segregation. Black also believed that the rights to freedom of speech, freedom of assembly, and freedom of religion guaranteed by the First Amendment were absolute. Among the many specific views he supported were court-enforced legislative reapportionment, separation of church and state (Black wrote the majority opinion declaring prayer in public schools unconstitutional), and the strong enforcement of antitrust laws.

BIBLIOGRAPHY

Dilliard, Irving (ed.), *One Man's Stand for Freedom: Supreme Court Opinions of Hugo Black*, 1963; Frank, John P., *Mr. Justice Black*, 1949; Mendelson, Wallace, *Justices Black and Frankfurter*, 2d ed., 1966; Simon, James F., *The Antagonists: Hugo Black, Felix Frankfurter and Civil Liberties in Modern America*, 1989; Strickland, Stephen P. (ed.), *Hugo Black and the Supreme Court: A Symposium*, 1967; Williams, Charlotte, *Hugo L. Black*, 1950.

Black, Jeremiah Sullivan

(January 10, 1810–August 19, 1883)
Secretary of State, Attorney General

Born near Stony Creek, Pennsylvania, Black studied law privately and was admitted to the bar in 1830. In 1842 he was appointed judge of the Court of Common Pleas for the Sixteenth District. After nine years he was elected to the Pennsylvania Supreme Court and reelected in 1854. His principal contribution as a judge was his clear statement defining the meaning of corporation charters.

In 1857 President JAMES BUCHANAN appointed Black to be attorney general. Black considered his uncovering of widespread fraud in California land title claim settlements his greatest achievement. He was not successful in his attempts to enforce the fugitive slave law in the North (see MILLARD FILLMORE), nor in his support for the proslavery Lecompton Constitution in Kansas (see JAMES BUCHANAN), where his efforts ran afoul of fellow Democrat STEPHEN A. DOUGLAS.

When ABRAHAM LINCOLN's election made secession appear certain, Black was asked by President Buchanan for advice. Opposed to secession, he argued that although the president was not authorized by the Constitution to force a seceding state back into the Union, he must enforce the laws and protect federal property. Black urged that proper garrisons be placed in the federal forts in the South as a precautionary measure. When Buchanan refused to do this, Secretary of State LEWIS CASS resigned in protest. For the remainder of his presidency, Black served as secretary of state and gave lip service to the prosecution of the war.

The Senate refused to confirm Buchanan's appointment of Black to the Supreme Court in 1861. Republicans, Douglas Democrats, and Southerners were also against Black. Black retired to York, Pennsylvania, only to discover that a relative had improperly invested and lost his life savings. In December 1861 he was appointed U.S. Supreme Court reporter and prepared *Black's Reports*, volumes 1 and 2. His knowledge of the California land cases enabled him to quickly earn a new fortune through legal fees. In 1867 he became an adviser to President ANDREW JOHNSON and served briefly as one of his attorneys during his impeachment trial. He took up another unpopular cause by defending SAMUEL TILDEN's claims in the contested presidential election of 1876 (see RUTHERFORD BIRCHARD HAYES).

BIBLIOGRAPHY

Black, Jeremiah S., *Essays and Speeches*, 1885; Brigance, William N., *Jeremiah Sullivan Black, A Defender of the Constitution and the Ten Commandments*, 1971.

Blaine, James Gillespie

(January 31, 1830–January 27, 1893)
Secretary of State, Candidate for President, Speaker of the House, Senator, Representative

James G. Blaine was known as the Plumed Knight of the Republican party because of his ability to make any cause he supported seem like a noble crusade. He was born in West Brownsville, Pennsylvania, and educated at Washington College. From 1852 to 1854 he taught in the Pennsylvania Institute for the Blind in Philadelphia while he studied law. After purchasing the *Kennebec Journal* in 1854, he moved to Maine.

In 1856 Blaine was a delegate to the first national Republican convention, and by 1859 he was elected chairman of the Republican state committee. He continued to hold this post for the next twenty-two years. In 1858 he was elected to the state legislature and was chosen speaker of the Maine lower house.

Blaine began his national political career in 1860 and was elected to the U.S. House of Representatives in 1862. He was a strong supporter of the antislavery movement and of black civil rights. Although he did not serve in the Civil War, his "bloody shirt" speeches extolling the heroism of those who did endeared him to veterans. In 1869 he was elected Speaker of the House, serving until 1875. In 1876 he became a senator, holding that office until 1881.

During these years Blaine became a well-known national figure. He supported black suffrage, sound currency, and tariff reduction,

Library of Congress

positions that put him squarely in line with the moderates of his party and earned him considerable support in the West.

Blaine was the most likely candidate to secure the Republican party's nomination for president in 1876. However, accusations that he engaged in conflict of interest activities with respect to railroad stocks while Speaker in 1869 caused the convention to choose RUTHERFORD B. HAYES instead. Blaine tried unsuccessfully to be nom- inated again in 1880.

President JAMES GARFIELD selected Blaine to be secretary of state, but Blaine's term was cut short when Garfield was assassinated in his first year in office. However, with the publication of the first volume of his *Twenty Years in Congress* in 1884, Blaine's political fortunes rose. The influence of his supporters in the party grew steadily, and at the convention of 1884, Blaine was nominated for president on the first ballot.

Largely because of the taint of corruption still attached to him, Blaine was defeated by his Democratic opponent, GROVER CLEVELAND. Blaine also made a costly blunder when he did not quickly disavow a supporter's slander of Irish American Democrats at a political rally with the phrase "Rum, Romanism, and Rebellion." He declined to be a candidate for president in 1888 but helped BENJAMIN HARRISON secure the nomination.

Blaine was appointed secretary of state in 1889, and it was in this position that he had his greatest influence. Harrison and Blaine were pioneers in coordinating the strategic, diplomatic, and economic interests of the United States into a coherent foreign policy. Among the issues Blaine focused on were improving relations with the nations of Latin America, securing an interoceanic canal across the isthmus of Panama under the control of the United States, securing the annexation of the Hawaiian islands, and protecting seals in the Bering Sea. As secretary of state, Blaine presided over the first Pan-American Conference in 1889 and sought hemispheric solidarity based on "friendship, not force." He predicted that "just law and not the violence of the mob" would characterize inter-American relations. He also negotiated reciprocal trade treaties with Latin American nations.

Blaine resigned his cabinet post in 1892 in order to try one more time for the presidential nomination. He was soundly defeated by Harrison on the first ballot. His health failed rapidly after the election, and he died the next year, at the age of sixty-two.

BIBLIOGRAPHY

Muzzey, David S., *Twenty Years of Congress: From Lincoln to Garfield*, and *James G. Blaine*, 1934.

Blair, Francis Preston

(April 12, 1791–October 18, 1876)
Presidential Adviser

As the editor of the official Jacksonian newspaper, the *Washington Globe*, Francis Preston Blair exercised considerable political power during the administrations of both ANDREW JACKSON and MARTIN VAN BUREN.

Blair was born into a prominent family in Abingdon, Virginia, but spent most of his youth in Kentucky. After graduating from Transylvania University in 1811, he studied law and was admitted to the Kentucky bar six years later. Instead of practicing law, he embarked upon a political career. He became a writer and then editor of the *Argus of Western America*, a Kentucky newspaper known for its pro–Jacksonian Democratic party perspective.

After his articles in the *Argus* attacking the national bank (see NICHOLAS BIDDLE and ROGER BROOKE TANEY) attracted nationwide attention, Blair was asked in 1830 to found a pro–Jackson administration newspaper in Washington, D.C. With its motto "The World Is Governed Too Much," which summed up Blair's own philosophy of government, the *Globe* quickly became the nationally recognized voice of Jacksonian democracy. Blair's blatantly partisan articles unmercifully ridiculed supporters of the Bank of the United States, Southern proponents of nullification (see JOHN CALDWELL CALHOUN), and Whig political opponents. Blair soon wielded considerable political power as a close confidant of Andrew Jackson and an influential member of the president's unofficial Kitchen Cabinet.

In 1834 Blair, with his partner John C. Rives, also began publishing the *Congressional Globe* (now the *Congressional Record*), which contained a record of the debates and daily proceedings in Congress.

Jackson's designated successor, Martin Van Buren, continued to use the *Globe* as his official news organ. However, after winning election in 1844, JAMES K. POLK forced Blair to relinquish his interests in the *Globe* to Thomas Ritchie, a political supporter. Blair retired to his country estate, Silver Spring, near Washington, D.C., in 1845 and concentrated upon furthering the political careers of his sons, Montgomery and Francis P. Blair, Jr.

Blair's opposition to the spread of slavery into the West and conviction that the Democratic party had been taken over by "nullifiers" led him to abandon the party and to help found the Republican party. As a reward for his support in the 1860 presidential election, ABRAHAM LINCOLN appointed Blair's son Montgomery postmaster general. In 1865 Blair attempted to initiate a compromise settlement of the Civil War. His efforts culminated in the unsuccessful Hampton Roads peace conference, at which Confederate vice president Alexander Stephens could not negotiate recognition of an independent South with Lincoln and Secretary of State WILLIAM H. SEWARD.

After the war the Blairs supported President ANDREW JOHNSON's moderate policy of reconciliation toward the South. The result was their alienation from the Radical-dominated Republican party and decision to rejoin the Democratic party. The senior Blair's hope that one of his sons would become president was crushed in 1868 when Francis P. Blair, Jr., lost the race for vice president on the Democratic ticket.

The elegant Washington home Blair gave to his son Montgomery in 1853 was used as a temporary White House during the administration of President HARRY S TRUMAN and is now an official government guest house.

BIBLIOGRAPHY

Hendrick, B. J., *Lincoln's War Cabinet*, 1946; Schlesinger, A. M., Jr., *The Age of Jackson*, 1945; Smith, W. E., *The Francis Preston Blair Family in Politics*, 1933.

Bland, Richard Parks

(August 19, 1835–June 15, 1899)
Representative

Richard Bland was known as Silver Dick because of his lifelong fight in Congress on behalf of the minting of silver dollars. He was born near Hartford, Kentucky, and attended Hartford Academy. He spent ten years working in silver-mining camps throughout California, Colorado, and Nevada before opening a law office in Lebanon, Missouri, in 1869.

In 1872 Bland was elected as a Democrat to Congress, where, with the exception of 1895 to 1897, he was reelected every term until his death in 1899. In his second term in Congress he became chairman of the Committee on Mines and Mining and began his fight in support of "free silver" (see WILLIAM JENNINGS BRYAN). (Free silver referred to the minting of as many silver dollars as the supply of silver ore allowed. Farmers and miners hoped that the increase in the supply of money would reduce their debts and push up the value of their goods.) Bland was appointed to the congressional Silver Commission of 1876–1877;

he became a member of the Committee on Coinage, Weights, and Measures in 1879, and its chairman in 1883.

Bland became a national figure in 1878 with the passage, over RUTHERFORD HAYES's veto, of the Bland-Allison Act, which required the government to buy at least $2 million worth of silver bullion monthly, to be coined into silver dollars. Bland succeeded in defeating the repeal of the act in 1886, but he never managed to obtain a bill for the unlimited minting of silver dollars. The climax of his fight for free silver came in 1893 with his leadership of the unsuccessful opposition to the repeal of the Sherman Silver Purchase Act unless accompanied by the passage of a free-silver bill.

In his famous "Parting of the Ways" speech of August 11, 1893, Bland served notice that the western Democrats would put the free-silver issue above party loyalty. He was defeated in 1894 by only seventy votes because of the impact of a Populist party candidate, but he was immediately returned to Congress in 1896.

The power of the free-silver lobby at the 1896 Democratic convention made Bland one of the contenders for the nomination, but the convention chose William Jennings Bryan instead after his famous "Cross of Gold" speech. Bland declined the vice presidential nomination but campaigned hard for Bryan in the election. He served in Congress until his death in 1899.

BIBLIOGRAPHY

Byars, W. V., *An American Commoner*, 1900.

Borah, William Edgar

(June 29, 1865–January 19, 1940)
Senator

A Progressive Republican in the Senate who advocated the creation of a department of labor and the popular election of U.S. senators, William Borah is chiefly remembered for his fierce opposition to American membership in the League of Nations (see WOODROW WILSON).

William Edgar Borah was born near Fairfield in Jasper Township, Illinois, and attended the University of Kansas. Admitted to the bar in Kansas in 1887, he became a prominent attorney in Boise, Idaho.

First elected to the Senate in 1907, Borah served there until his death thirty-three years later. Shortly after winning election to the Senate, Borah attracted considerable national attention for his prosecution of William Haywood. Haywood, founder of the Industrial Workers of the World (IWW), was accused but acquitted of complicity in the murder of former Idaho governor Frank Steunenberg.

In the Senate, Republican party member Borah was dubbed "the Great Opposer" because of his frequent refusal to vote in support of Republican-sponsored legislation. He sponsored bills to create the Department of Labor, the Children's Bureau, and an eight-hour day on government contracts. He also favored the implementation of the federal income tax, the direct election of senators, and the enforcement of antitrust legislation. In 1912 he supported THEODORE ROOSEVELT's effort to capture the presidential nomination from President WILLIAM H. TAFT, but he did not join the Progressive (Bull Moose) party (see THEODORE ROOSEVELT).

In 1919 Borah toured the nation delivering speeches in opposition to WOODROW WILSON's proposal that the United States join the League of Nations. He felt that American politics would become contaminated by exposure to the machinations and corruptions of European politics. His fiery condemnation of the idea of U.S. membership in the league left no room for compromise. "If the Savior of mankind would revisit the earth and declare for a League of Nations," he declared, "I would be opposed to it."

When the Republicans regained control of the White House and Congress in the 1920s, Borah's power grew. From 1925 to 1933 he was chairman of the Senate Foreign Relations Committee. In this position he supported the recognition of the Soviet Union, favored collection of World War I debts, and opposed intervention in Latin American countries to protect U.S. investments.

An advocate of disarmament and the outlawing of war, he introduced the resolution in the Senate that led to the Washington Disarmament Conference of 1921–1922, which established the 5:5:3 ratio of naval tonnage for the United States, Britain, and Japan, and the five-year naval holiday adopted by the administration of HERBERT HOOVER in 1931. He also promoted the Kellogg-Briand Pact, or Pact of Paris, of 1928, which outlawed war as a tool of national policy, and the Neutrality Act of 1935, which outlawed shipments of arms to belligerent nations and forbade U.S. citizens from traveling on belligerent ships.

His political independence worked against him in 1936 when he vainly sought the Republican party presidential nomination. During his last years in the Senate, Borah criticized many New Deal programs (see FRANKLIN DELANO ROOSEVELT) on constitutional grounds and advocated strict neutrality when war broke out in Europe.

BIBLIOGRAPHY

Johnson, Claudius O., *Borah of Idaho,* 1936; McKenna, Marian C., *Borah,* 1961; Maddox, Robert J., *William E. Borah and American Foreign Policy,* 1970; Vinson, John Chalmers, *William E. Borah and the Outlawry of War,* 1957.

Bowles, Chester Bliss

(April 5, 1901–May 25, 1986)
Diplomat, Government Agency Director, Representative

During a long and distinguished career Chester Bowles was a successful businessman, U.S. government administrator, politician, and diplomat.

Bowles was born in Springfield, Massachusetts, graduated from Yale University in 1924, and founded the well-known New York advertising firm of Benton and Bowles in 1929.

During World War II he served as the Connecticut director of the Office of Price Administration and, in 1943, became the head of the Office of Price Administration in Washington, D.C. He was also a member of the War Production Board and the Petroleum Council for War.

From February to July 1946 Bowles served as President HARRY S TRUMAN's director of the Office of Economic Stabilization. After serving as the American delegate to the United Nations Educational, Scientific and Cultural Organization conference at Paris in 1946, he became a special consultant to the secretary general of the United Nations from 1947 to 1948.

Bowles was elected Democratic governor of Connecticut in 1948 (his second attempt) but suffered defeat in his reelection bid in 1950. He served as the American ambassador to India and Nepal from 1951 to 1953.

After winning one term as a member of the U.S. House of Representatives from Connecticut (1959–1961), Bowles became under secretary of state and special presidential representative for Asian, African, and Latin American affairs. He served another term as American ambassador to India from 1963 to 1968.

BIBLIOGRAPHY

Bowles, Chester, *Tomorrow without Fear*, 1946, *Ambassador's Report*, 1954, *The New Dimensions of Peace*, 1955, and *Africa's Challenge to America*, 1956; *Harper*, November 1952; *New York Times Magazine*, March 3, 1946.

Boyd, Lynn

(November 22, 1800–December 17, 1859)
Speaker of the House, Representative

Born in Nashville, Tennessee, Lynn Boyd grew up in Christian County, Kentucky, where he obtained little formal schooling and earned a living as a common laborer. He was elected to the state legislature in 1827, and reelected in 1828 and 1829. Although an unsuccessful candidate for the U.S. House of Representatives in 1833, he was elected in 1835. He served one term but failed to win reelection. Undaunted, Boyd returned to Congress in 1839 and served continuously there until 1855.

Boyd was a staunch supporter of the policies of President ANDREW JACKSON and played a prominent role in maneuvers leading up to the joint resolution of Congress for the annexation of Texas (see JAMES KNOX POLK). During the Mexican War (see POLK) he held the important chairmanship of the committee on military affairs and later became chairman of the committee on territories. He led the fight in the House for the Compromise of 1850 (see HENRY CLAY) to preserve the Union, and served as Speaker from 1851 to 1855.

Returning to Kentucky in 1855, Boyd decided to become a senator. As a step in securing a Senate seat, he sought the governorship in 1859. He had to settle for the lieutenant governor's position, an office he did not live long enough to fill.

BIBLIOGRAPHY

Thompson, G. W., *Biographical Sketch of Hon. Lynn Boyd*, 1852.

Bradford, William

(ca. March 29, 1590–May 9, 1657)
Colonial Leader

William Bradford was the most important person involved in the establishment of the first permanent English colony in New England. From 1621 until 1656, with the exception of five years (1633–1636, 1638, and 1644) when he was an assistant to the governor, Bradford served as governor of Plimoth Plantation, or Plymouth Colony.

Bradford was born in Austerfield, Yorkshire, England. At age sixteen he joined the Separatist congregation at Scrooby (religious reformers who had left or separated from the official Church of England). Three years later, to avoid persecution by the Crown, Bradford emigrated with the Scrooby Separatists to Holland. In Leiden he learned the trade of cloth making and studied theological literature.

At that time Holland was the only country in Europe that allowed religious freedom. The Separatists wanted their children to grow up English and not Dutch, however. By 1617 Bradford was among those lobbying for a move to the New World to establish a settlement uniquely their own. In 1620 Bradford joined 102 other Pilgrims aboard the ship *Mayflower*. Through its agents in London the group had received permission to settle in the Virginia colony. Instead, the Pilgrims, as they are now known, landed on the New England coast on December 21, 1620. They decided to settle there and named the colony after the town from which they had sailed. Since they were outside their permitted settlement area, they were technically without the rule of English law. To avoid disputes once ashore, Bradford and the other leaders drew up a document specifying the terms of self-government under which the colony would function.

Before disembarking, the colonists signed this document, the Mayflower Compact.

The Pilgrims were unprepared for the severity of New England winters. By the spring of 1621, more than half of them had died, including John Carver, the first governor of the colony. They were on the verge of abandoning Plimoth Plantation when Bradford was chosen to serve the first of his thirty years as governor. He was the ideal choice to lead the fledgling colony. Bradford immediately established a food-rationing system; implemented programs that led to successful fishing, trade, and agricultural industries; negotiated peaceful relations with the Narragansett Indians; paid off the English merchant investors who had financed the expedition; maintained the settlement's independence from the more powerful Massachusetts Bay Colony; and prevented rebellion against continued Separatist rule.

Although not as liberal as ROGER WILLIAMS, the founder of the colony of Rhode Island, Bradford was more tolerant of different religions than his Separatist peers. "It is too great an arrogancie for any man or church," he wrote, "to thinke that he or they have so sounded the word of God to the bottome."

About 1630 Bradford began writing his monumental *History of Plimoth Plantation*, a record of the establishment of the colony to be passed on to his descendants. Since it was not written for publication, he included personal feelings and intimate stories. The combination of his simple, direct prose and anecdotal narrative history created one of the most readable and important historical works by a seventeenth-century American.

Bradford was proud of his efforts to make Plimoth Plantation a commercial success, but by the time of his death he was deeply disappointed by the failure of the colony to create a model religious community. In 1655 he wrote with "grief and sorrow" of the growing secularism and the loss of "constant faithfulness" among the colonists.

BIBLIOGRAPHY

Briggs, Rose T., *Plymouth Rock: History and Significance*, 1968; Cummins, D. Duane, and William G. White, *Our Colonial History: Plymouth and Jamestown*, 1980; Davis, W. T. (ed.), *Bradford's History of Plymouth Plantation 1606–1646*, 1908; Willison, G. F., *Saints and Sinners*, 1945.

Brandeis, Louis Dembitz

(November 13, 1856–October 5, 1941)
Associate Justice of the Supreme Court

A long with his colleague OLIVER WENDELL HOLMES, Louis Brandeis became famous for his dissenting opinions in support of liberal causes while an associate justice of the Supreme Court.

Brandeis was born in Louisville, Kentucky, to Jewish parents who had immigrated to the United States in 1848 from Bohemia. After studying at the Annen-Realschule in Dresden, Germany, Brandeis graduated from Harvard Law School in 1877. Two years later, he established a successful law practice in Boston with Samuel Warren, Jr.

Library of Congress

From the beginning of his legal career, Brandeis insisted on breaking with tradition and introducing statistical and sociological information into his legal briefs. Committed to using the law as a tool to serve the public good, he once remarked, "A lawyer who has not studied economics and sociology is very apt to become a public enemy."

Passionately committed to social reform, by the turn of the century Brandeis had become well known as an articulate liberal advocate. Nicknamed the People's Attorney, he frequently donated his legal services on behalf of a great variety of worthy causes. Brandeis's idealism was grounded in a deep appreciation for the need to balance change with a respect for the underlying reasons for the structure of social institutions and working within the law.

From 1900 to 1907 Brandeis served as counsel for the people in proceedings involving the constitutionality of wages and maximum working hours laws in Oregon, Illinois, Ohio, and California. In 1910 he successfully argued before the Interstate Commerce Commission against railroad rate increases, and opposed the creation of a transportation monopoly in New England. Brandeis was also an arbiter in a strike of New York garment workers in 1910 and played a major role in securing the "Protocols of Peace" settlement, a highly touted model of industrial relations between management and labor.

In 1916 President WOODROW WILSON nominated Brandeis as an associate justice, the first person of Jewish background to serve on the Supreme Court. Brandeis's Jewish faith, combined with his liberal political activism, caused a bitter four-month battle before the Senate voted to confirm his appointment along strict party lines.

During his twenty-three years on the Supreme Court, Brandeis, a proponent of judicial activism, supported legislation created "to remold . . . economic practices and institutions to meet changing social and economic needs" (*New State Ice Co.* v. *Liebmann,* 1931) and opposed government actions that inhibited freedom of speech, assembly, the press, and religion. Although he wrote relatively few dissents (44 out of 528 decisions), his opinions were very significant because they frequently provided the basis upon which the law would be reinterpreted by a more liberal and activist Supreme Court.

A supporter of the need to establish a Jewish state in Palestine, Brandeis devoted his energy both before and after his retirement from the Court in 1939 to the Zionist movement.

BIBLIOGRAPHY

Mason, Alpheus T., *Brandeis,* 1956; Rabinowitz, Ezekiel, *Justice Louis D. Brandeis: Zionist Chapter of His Life,* 1968; Strum, Philippa, *Louis D. Brandeis: A Justice for the People,* 1984; Todd, Alden L., *Justice on Trial: Brandeis,* 1964, and *Brandeis: A Free Man's Life;* Vrofsky, Melvin, and David W. Levy (eds.), *Letters of Louis D. Brandeis, 1870–1907,* 1971.

Breckinridge, John Cabell

(January 15, 1821–May 17, 1875)
Vice President, Candidate for President, Senator

John Cabell Breckinridge shares the distinction with AARON BURR of being one of two vice presidents charged with treason. Born near Lexington, Kentucky, Breckinridge briefly attended the College of New Jersey (now Princeton University) in 1840 and Transylvania College from 1840 to 1841 to study law before establishing his own law practice in Lexington, Kentucky.

At first unenthusiastic about the Mexican War (see JAMES KNOX POLK), Breckinridge changed his mind in 1847 and led a regiment of Kentucky volunteers in Mexico. In 1849 he was elected to the state legislature as a proslavery Democrat. Two years later, he was elected to Congress as a Democrat from a former Whig district. Reelected for a second term, Breckinridge was tremendously popular and was chosen to be JAMES BUCHANAN's vice presidential running mate in 1856. He was so well liked in Kentucky that he was elected to the U.S. Senate a year before his term as vice president ended.

When the Democratic party broke apart in 1860 over the slavery question, Breckinridge attempted to remain out of the fray; but when the Southern faction of the party met in Baltimore and nominated him to be its candidate, he accepted. During the campaign he stated that he supported the Union, but he believed that the Constitution did not give Congress the authority to interfere in the territories concerning slavery. He received seventy-two electoral votes, all from the South.

After ABRAHAM LINCOLN's election, Breckinridge attempted to walk a neutral line. He believed states had the right to secede, but he felt secession was not necessary in 1861. He also believed that the federal government could not use force to coerce a state to remain in the Union once it had decided to secede. His fence straddling on the secession issue caused STEPHEN A. DOUGLAS to comment, "Breckinridge may not be for disunion, but all the disunionists are for Breckinridge."

As a member of the Senate in early 1861, Breckinridge refused to support Lincoln's call for troops. After Union troops drove all Confederate forces from Kentucky, Breckinridge fled south and joined the Confederate army. The federal government immediately indicted Breckinridge for treason since he had gone over to the rebel side from a state that had not seceded. Commissioned a brigadier general in the Confederate army, Breckinridge served with distinction at Shiloh, Vicksburg, Chickamauga, Cold Harbor, and many other battles before being selected in the closing days of the war by JEFFERSON DAVIS to be the Confederacy's secretary of war.

After Lee's surrender at Appomattox, Breckinridge, with an indictment out for his arrest on treason charges, was in grave danger. After more than two months of playing hide-and-seek with federal troops, he managed to escape to Cuba. Supported by English admirers and prosperous Southern expatri- ates, he lived in Europe until 1868 and then moved to Toronto, Canada. On Christmas 1868 President ANDREW JOHNSON issued a general amnesty proclamation, and Breckinridge's long years of exile ended. He returned to Kentucky in March 1869 and was greeted enthusiastically wherever he traveled. (It felt, one observer noted, as if Kentucky had waited until after the war to secede.) Breckinridge decided not to seek public office and spent his last years working to build railroads in the Midwest as vice president of the Elizabethtown, Lexington & Big Sandy Railroad.

It was not until January 1958 that a Kentucky circuit court judge dismissed the 1862 indictment for treason and conspiracy against Breckinridge and other Kentuckians who had fought for the Confederacy.

BIBLIOGRAPHY

Harrison, Lowell H., *John Breckinridge: Jeffersonian Republican*, 1969.

Bristow, Benjamin Helm

(June 20, 1832–June 22, 1896)
Secretary of the Treasury

Born in Elkton, Kentucky, Bristow graduated from Jefferson College in Pennsylvania in 1851 and was admitted to the bar in that state in 1853. He moved to Hopkinsville, Kentucky, in 1858. In 1861 he was commissioned a lieutenant colonel in the state militia. He was seriously wounded at Shiloh but returned to active duty. Bristow left the army in 1863 when, nominated as a candidate without his knowledge, he was elected to the state senate. He organized support in Kentucky for passage of the Thirteenth Amendment and worked for ABRAHAM LINCOLN's reelection.

Bristow resigned from the state senate in 1865 and moved to Louisville, where he was appointed an assistant U.S. attorney and then the U.S. attorney for the Kentucky district. He worked diligently to stop Ku Klux Klan violence against blacks in the years following the Civil War and to arrest illegal whiskey distillers. His skill and courage attracted national attention. When Congress created the post of solicitor general in 1870, President ULYSSES S. GRANT promptly appointed Bristow to the office.

Bristow left office in 1872 to become counsel of the Texas and Pacific railroads. However, he quickly realized he hated the work and returned to Kentucky to practice law. President Grant appointed him secretary of the treasury in 1874, at a time when the department had been rocked by scandal. Bristow moved quickly and successfully to reestablish the integrity of the office by instituting internal investigations and badly needed reforms.

Bristow's greatest accomplishment was in breaking up the notorious Whiskey Ring, a conspiracy of revenue officials (one of whom was a Grant appointee) and distillers to defraud the government of liquor taxes. He initiated over 250 civil and criminal suits that resulted in the recovery of more than $3 million in taxes, 176 indictments (including Grant's personal secretary), and 110 convictions.

After members of the Whiskey Ring succeeded in convincing the president that Bristow's real goal was to secure the Republican nomination, Grant forced Bristow to resign in 1876. Efforts to have him nominated by reform elements in the party at the Republican presidential convention failed.

Bristow moved to New York in 1878 and remained active in law until his death, arguing many cases before the Supreme Court. He was elected the second president of the American Bar Association in 1879.

BIBLIOGRAPHY

Willcox, David, "Memorial of Benjamin H. Bristow,"
   *Annual Reports, Association of the Bar of the City
   of New York,* 1897.

Brooke, Edward William

(October 26, 1919–   )

Senator

In 1966 Edward Brooke became the first popularly elected black U.S. senator in U.S. history.

Brooke was born in Washington, D.C. After graduating from Howard University in 1941, he served as an infantry officer in Italy in World War II. In 1948 and 1949 he earned a law degree and then a graduate law degree from Boston University.

After running unsuccessfully for the Massachusetts legislature as a Republican in 1950 and 1952, Brooke abandoned politics for eight years to concentrate on his legal practice. He then ran a close but losing race for secretary of state of Massachusetts in 1960 and afterward was appointed chairman of the Boston Finance Commission. Although head of this municipal government watchdog committee for little more than a year, Brooke skillfully used this position for political advantage by securing widespread news coverage of his uncovering of corruption by several city officials.

In 1962 Brooke was elected state attorney general. During his first two years in office he vigorously ferreted out incidents of political corruption that led to indictments of numerous government officials. The tremendous publicity he garnered for these muckraking efforts enabled him to win reelection in 1964 by the widest margin in the state's history for a Republican. His popularity brought him the Republican nomination for senator and then victory in the 1966 general election.

Brooke established a record as a moderate while in the Senate and easily won reelection in 1972. He failed to win a third term in 1978, however, after allegations by his daughter of financial misdealing in regard to his estate destroyed his image as a crusader for virtue in government. In 1979 the Senate Ethics Committee concluded that the former senator committed only minor violations of congressional conduct rules, which were insufficient to warrant punishment.

In 1984 Brooke was named chairman of the Boston Bank of Commerce.

BIBLIOGRAPHY

Cutler, John Henry, *Ed Brooke: Biography of a
   Senator,* 1972.

Brooks, Preston Smith

(August 6, 1819–January 27, 1857)
Representative

Had Preston Brooks not physically attacked Senator CHARLES SUMNER in public on the floor of the Senate, he may never have been remembered in U.S. history books. Born on his family's plantation in Edgefield, South Carolina, Brooks graduated from South Carolina College in 1839. He practiced law and served two terms in the South Carolina legislature before joining the army at the outbreak of the Mexican War (see JAMES KNOX POLK). He served as a captain in Mexico, where he developed a reputation as a severe disciplinarian for making his men strictly observe military etiquette.

He was first elected to Congress in 1852 and reelected in 1854. In May 1856, during a debate on the Kansas-Nebraska Act (see FRANKLIN PIERCE) Senator Charles Sumner of Massachusetts, a brilliant, outspoken abolitionist, delivered a speech in the Senate that he called "The Crime Against Kansas." In it he attacked the South and several of its proslavery senators with a long list of insults. One of the senators Sumner attacked was Brooks's uncle, Senator Charles Butler of South Carolina. Infuriated at this insult to his family's honor, Brooks, after unsuccessfully trying to catch Sumner outside of Congress for two days in order to demand an apology, spotted him working at his desk in the Senate. Brooks waited until the Senate adjourned, then without warning walked up to Sumner from behind and beat him savagely over the head with his cane until Sumner slumped to the floor unconscious.

The country's response to the attack was indicative of how much the slavery question had divided the nation along sectional and party lines at the time. A motion to have Brooks expelled from the House for his actions failed to secure enough votes to pass. Brooks resigned after explaining that his attack was an appropriate response to Sumner's speech, only to be unanimously reelected by the people of his congressional district.

Though seriously injured, Charles Sumner recovered enough from Brooks's attack to serve many more years in the Senate. Brooks later admitted that the attack had been a mistake since it had hurt the cause of the South.

BIBLIOGRAPHY

Bigelow, John, *Retrospection of an Active Life,*
1909–1913; Campbell, James E., "Sumner, Brooks,
Burlingame, or the Last of the Great Challenges," in
Ohio Archives and Historical Society Publications, XXXIV, 1925; Pierce, Edward L., *Memoir and Letters of Charles Sumner,* vol. 3, 1893.

Browder, Earl Russell

(May 20, 1891–June 27, 1973)
Candidate for President

Earl Browder led the American Communist party during the Great Depression and World War II, the period of its largest following.

Browder was born in Wichita, Kansas. Largely self-educated, he joined the Socialist party in 1907. During World War I Browder was imprisoned for sixteen months for refusing to register for the draft and for encouraging others to do likewise. Upon his release from prison, Browder immediately became active in the newly formed American

Communist party and especially its Trade Union Educational League. In 1930 Browder, at the Soviet Union's behest, joined the secretariat of the American Communist party. A few years later, he became the party's general secretary.

In 1935 the Communist International, or Comintern, decided to urge cooperation with Socialist and liberal political parties in capitalist nations to halt the spread of fascism. This, as well as the effects of the Great Depression, enabled Browder to establish links with American trade unions and the liberal intellectual community. The combination of the party's antifascism position on foreign policy, insistence on the need for unemployment insurance, support for the labor movement, and slogan "Communism Is Twentieth-Century Americanism" attracted considerable interest. The Communist party enrolled 80,000 to 100,000 new members during the late 1930s. This did not carry over into national electoral support, however, as Browder captured only 80,159 popular votes in the 1936 presidential campaign.

The American Communist party's support of the nonaggression pact between Germany and the Soviet Union in August 1939 and the subsequent invasion of Poland by Germany aroused the wrath of most Americans. In 1940 Browder was convicted of passport fraud (he had traveled under several assumed names while abroad in the 1920s) and in March 1941 began serving a four-year term in federal prison. After Germany invaded the Soviet Union in June 1941, the American Communist party began urging all-out American participation in the war against Germany. President FRANKLIN D. ROOSEVELT commuted Browder's sentence in May 1942 to the time he had already been imprisoned.

After World War II, Browder opposed Joseph Stalin's prohibition of any further Communist cooperation with Socialist and liberal capitalist parties. The result was first his removal from any leadership role in 1945, then his expulsion from the party in 1946 for harboring "right [-wing] deviationist" beliefs. Browder repudiated his involvement with the party ten years later: "The Communist party of the United States today is a contemptible sect with no roots in American life. I don't call myself a Communist anymore. . . ."

BIBLIOGRAPHY

Browder, Earl Russell, *Communism in the United States,* 1935, *What Is Communism?* 1936, *The People's Front,* 1938, *War or Peace with Russia,* 1947, and *Marx and America,* 1956; Isserman, Maurice, *Which Side Were You On?* 1982; Klehr, Harvey, *The Heyday of American Communism,* 1984.

Bruce, Blanche Kelso

(March 1, 1841–March 17, 1898)
Senator

Blanche Kelso Bruce was the second black person ever to serve in the U.S. Senate.

Born in Farmville, Virginia, Bruce grew up as a slave in Missouri. Tutored by his master's son, he moved to Ohio at the outbreak of the Civil War and attended Oberlin College for two years. In 1868 he moved to Mississippi, then under the rule of a Reconstruction government, and purchased enough land to acquire a substantial plantation.

As one of only a few educated and affluent blacks in Mississippi, he immediately assumed a leadership position in the community. After teaching for a brief period, he entered politics and held several state government positions, including sergeant at arms in the state senate in 1870, assessor of Bolivar County in 1871, and county sheriff from 1872 to 1875.

In 1874 Bruce was elected as a Republican to the U.S. Senate near the end of the rule of the Reconstruction government in Mississippi. During his one term in the Senate, Bruce fought to protect the voting rights of newly enfranchised blacks in the South, to deal fairly with Indians, and to improve flood control and navigation routes for the Mississippi River. He opposed the exclusion of Chinese immigrants to America (see BENJAMIN HARRISON) and the awarding of disability pensions to former Confederate soldiers.

Bruce had no hope of reelection in 1880 due to the demise of the Reconstruction government in Mississippi. President JAMES GARFIELD appointed him as register of the treasury in 1881, a position Bruce held for four years. In 1889 President Benjamin Harrison appointed him recorder of deeds in the District of Columbia, a position Bruce retained until President WILLIAM MCKINLEY reappointed him register of the treasury in 1895. He was still serving in this post at the time of his death.

BIBLIOGRAPHY

Journal of Negro History, 1922; Swain, Charles, *Blanche K. Bruce: Politician,* 1989.

Bryan, William Jennings

(March 19, 1860–July 26, 1925)
Secretary of State, Candidate for President, Representative

Called by his admirers the Great Commoner, William Jennings Bryan was a tireless defender of the poor against the rich and a prophet of reform and humanitarianism. Without a doubt he was the voice of the Democratic party at the turn of the century, and his style and dedication kept him at center stage for thirty-five years of turbulent American politics.

Born in Salem, Illinois, Bryan graduated from Illinois College in 1881. He studied at the Union College of Law in Chicago,

Library of Congress

early displaying outstanding debating ability. For the next few years he practiced law in Illinois and Nebraska. Running as a Democrat, he was elected to the House of Representatives from Nebraska in 1890 and was reelected in 1892. Defeated in his 1894 campaign for the U.S. Senate, he became the editor in chief of the *Omaha World Herald.*

During the 1880s and 1890s the issue of "free silver" was hotly debated. Those in favor wanted the federal government to be able to replace gold dollars with the free coinage of silver, an inflationary measure using cheaper and more available metal. They believed this would work to the advantage of debtors and farmers. Hoping for the nomination, Bryan went to the 1896 Democratic convention in Chicago as a leading advocate of free silver and as a loyal spokesman for the Midwest and Far West. In a fiery speech, he declared that "you shall not press down upon the brow of labor this crown of thorns, you shall not crucify mankind upon a cross of gold." Gaining the votes not only of the Democrats but also of the Populists (see JAMES BAIRD WEAVER), Bryan won the nomination.

Bryan campaigned energetically, staging one of the first national traveling campaigns, but nonetheless lost by ninety-five electoral votes to his Republican opponent, WILLIAM McKINLEY, who remained at home. In 1900 Bryan was defeated again by McKinley, this time by 137 electoral votes. In his third and final try for the presidency in 1908, he was defeated by WILLIAM HOWARD TAFT.

At the Democratic convention of 1912, Bryan was instrumental in securing the nomination of WOODROW WILSON. In return, even though Bryan had no experience in international affairs, Wilson named him secretary of state. Bryan performed ably, working to protect U.S. interests in the Panama Canal and negotiating treaties with some thirty nations for the investigation of disputes. As a pacifist, he disagreed with Wilson's strong stand against German aggression and resigned in 1915 when asked to send a stern note protesting the sinking of the *Lusitania*.

Though never elected president, the handsome, charismatic Bryan was revered by the masses for whom he was such an ardent spokesman. During the last years of his life Bryan remained a strong proponent of several causes, including Prohibition, a graduated income tax, woman suffrage, and world peace and disarmament. A fundamentalist crusader, he took a militant position against the theory of evolution. In the summer of 1925 he appeared as prosecutor in the famous Scopes trial and won his case against the teaching of evolution in schools, though he suffered heavy ridicule of his biblical beliefs in cross-examination from the defense attorney Clarence Darrow. Bryan died in his sleep a few days after the trial ended, but the fundamentalist-modernist argument over evolution has not been resolved to this day.

BIBLIOGRAPHY

Bryan, William Jennings, *Memoirs*, 1925; Coletta, Paolo E., *William Jennings Bryan*, 3 vols., 1964–1969; Curti, Merle, *Bryan and World Peace*, 1931; Glad, Paul W., *The Trumpet Soundeth: William Jennings Bryan, 1896–1912*, 1960; Koenig, Louis W., *Defender of the Faith: William Jennings Bryan, 1915–1925*, 1965.

Brzezinski, Zbigniew Kazimierz

(March 28, 1928–)
Presidential Adviser

Foreign policy specialist Zbigniew Brzezinski served as an adviser to Democratic presidents JOHN F. KENNEDY, LYNDON B. JOHNSON, and JIMMY CARTER.

As a consultant, as a member of the State Department, and as President Jimmy Carter's assistant to the president for national security affairs, Brzezinski urged the United States to adopt a foreign policy that emphasized human rights, firm opposition to all attempts by the Soviet Union to increase its influence in the third world, and improved relations with China.

Brzezinski was born in Warsaw, Poland. Because his father was a Polish diplomat, Zbigniew lived in France and Germany before the family settled in Montreal, Canada, in 1938. Brzezinski earned a B.A. in 1949 and an M.A. in 1950 in economics and political science from McGill University in Montreal. In 1953 he earned his doctorate from Harvard University and taught at Harvard until he was appointed a professor of public law and government at Columbia University in 1960. In 1961 he became the director of Columbia's newly formed Institute on Communist Affairs.

During the turbulent cold war era of the 1960s, Brzezinski became well known for his prediction that the changes brought about by the emergence of the postindustrial, highly technical culture in the United States, Europe, and Japan would ease tensions between capitalist and communist nations, but increase the gap between them and less-developed countries.

In addition to writing numerous articles on foreign policy issues, Brzezinski served as one of John F. Kennedy's preinaugural foreign policy advisers. He strongly supported American involvement in the war in Vietnam (see LYNDON BAINES JOHNSON and RICHARD MILHOUS NIXON) on the grounds that unless the United States managed to impose peace in Asia through the creation of a stable balance of power as it had in Europe, wars there would be endless. President Lyndon B. Johnson appointed Brzezinski to the Department of State's Policy Planning Council in 1966. Two years later, Brzezinski orchestrated the foreign policy positions of presidential candidate HUBERT H. HUMPHREY.

In 1976 President-elect Jimmy Carter appointed Brzezinski to serve as assistant to the president for national security affairs. In this post Brzezinski became locked in a battle with Secretary of State CYRUS VANCE to be the primary foreign policy adviser to the president. The two clashed severely over how to contain the Soviet Union. Brzezinski favored confronting Soviet foreign policy initiatives wherever they occurred, even if that prevented successful negotiations on a nuclear arms control agreement.

During the early phases of the revolution in Iran, Brzezinski supported informing the Shah and his military leaders that the United States would not oppose an effort by the Iranian military to maintain control. Secretary of State Vance disagreed. An ambiguous message was eventually transmitted to the Shah.

Shortly after the seizing of the American embassy and the subsequent holding of Americans in Iran as hostages by the newly installed revolutionary government, Brzezinski pressed for a rescue mission against the objections of Vance. After the rescue attempt authorized by the president ended in failure in the Iranian desert, Vance resigned in protest.

After completing his term of office in January 1981, Brzezinski resumed teaching, lecturing, consulting, and writing on foreign policy issues.

BIBLIOGRAPHY

Brzezinski, Zbigniew, *Power and Principle: Memoirs of the National Security Adviser, 1977–1981*, 1983, and *The Grand Failure: The Birth and Death of Communism in the Twentieth Century*, 1990.

Buchanan, James

(April 23, 1791–June 1, 1868)
President, Secretary of State, Diplomat, Senator, Representative

James Buchanan was the last U.S. president to believe at his inauguration that he could facilitate the compromise necessary between slave and antislavery factions to preserve the Union peacefully. "The great object of my administration," he wrote, "will be to arrest, if possible, the agitation of the slavery question at the North, and to destroy sectional parties." The religiously fatalistic, gentle, and diplomatic Buchanan failed completely to achieve his goal.

Library of Congress

The son of a storekeeper, Buchanan was born near Mercersburg, Pennsylvania. He graduated from Dickinson College in 1809, was admitted to the bar three years later, and quickly developed a lucrative Pennsylvania law practice.

Elected to the Pennsylvania legislature in 1814 as a Federalist, Buchanan was reelected in 1815, then elected to the U.S. Congress in 1820. He became a Democrat and supporter of ANDREW JACKSON in 1824. In June 1831 he retired from Congress to become the U.S. minister to Russia until 1833. Upon his return to the United States, he was elected to the Senate, where he served from 1834 to 1845.

Buchanan's good looks, charm, experience, northern constituency, and belief that it was the constitutional duty of the national government to protect slavery where it existed made him an attractive presidential possibility to Democratic party leaders. First suggested in 1844, he lost the nomination to JAMES POLK but still proceeded to work hard enough to secure Pennsylvania for the Democrats in the elec-

tion. As a reward, President Polk chose Buchanan to be secretary of state in 1845. The two men battled at cabinet meetings for the next four years. Polk wrote, "If I would yield up the government into his hands, and suffer him to be in effect President . . . I have no doubt he would be cheerful and satisfied."

While secretary of state, Buchanan negotiated a compromise settlement of the Oregon Territory dispute with Great Britain and participated in the drafting of the peace treaty with Mexico that ended the Mexican War (see JAMES KNOX POLK). Buchanan wanted to protect American interests from British encroachment in Central America and was largely responsible for President Polk's vigorous reaffirmation of the Monroe Doctrine in 1845. Although his efforts to secure the purchase of Cuba from Spain were unsuccessful, Buchanan remained committed to the annexation of the island for the rest of his life.

Although Buchanan had promised Polk upon becoming secretary of state that he would not seek the nomination for president in 1848, he quietly tried to obtain votes at the convention. LEWIS CASS was nominated instead. After retiring from office in 1849, Buchanan made another unsuccessful attempt to win the Democratic presidential nomination in 1852.

While serving as President FRANKLIN PIERCE's minister to Great Britain from 1853 to 1856, Buchanan participated in the writing of the controversial Ostend Manifesto, which advocated the U.S. acquisition of Cuba. The one great benefit to being out of the country at that time was that he played no part in the adoption of the divisive Kansas-Nebraska Act (see FRANKLIN PIERCE).

Buchanan returned to the United States in 1856 and was selected on the seventeenth ballot to be the Democratic party's presidential candidate. He won the general election by denouncing the abolitionists, promising not to allow any interference with the Compromise of 1850 (see HENRY CLAY and MILLARD FILLMORE), and supporting the principle of noninterference by Congress with slavery in the territories.

As president, Buchanan recommended, for military purposes, constructing a national railroad to the Pacific; he also advocated paying off the public debt and slightly increasing the size of the navy. He hoped that the slavery issue in the territories would be settled by the Dred Scott decision (see ROGER BROOKE TANEY) and urged Congress to admit Kansas as a slave state under the Lecompton Constitution (drawn up at a state convention without the participation of antislavery representatives). Buchanan was convinced that as soon as Kansas became a state the slavery issue would be peacefully resolved by its citizens, but when he submitted the fraudulent Lecompton Constitution to Congress in 1858, Senator STEPHEN A. DOUGLAS informed Buchanan that he would have to oppose it. The resulting break between the two men further split the Democratic party and weakened Buchanan's effectiveness as president. Another dangerous step had been taken along the road to civil war.

Buchanan made several major political blunders during his administration. His support for the tariff bill of 1857 infuriated his fellow Pennsylvanians and greatly aided the growth of the Republican party there. He did not protect the credit of the government after the financial panic of 1857, and he so mishandled the admission of Kansas that the Democratic party split along pro- and antislavery interest lines. He will be remembered most, however, for his refusal to take steps to prevent the South from seceding in the last months of his term. He did not reinforce the U.S. garrisons in the ports of the South in 1860 because he did not feel the Constitution gave the president the authority to do so.

Before his inauguration, Buchanan, who believed that one term was all any president ought to serve, had decided not to seek reelection. The Democrats split their votes between Stephen A. Douglas and JOHN C. BRECKINRIDGE, and Republican candidate ABRAHAM LINCOLN won with less than a popular vote majority. As it turned out, Lincoln would have won an electoral college majority even if the Democrats had united. Upon leaving office, Buchanan supported Lincoln's resort to arms after Fort Sumter had been fired upon. He spent the last years of his life at his home in Pennsylvania. Blamed by critics for the outbreak of the Civil War, Buchanan observed the situation before his death in 1868: "The world," he said, "had forgotten the circumstances. . . ."

BIBLIOGRAPHY

Curtis, George T., *The Life of James Buchanan*, 1883; Klein, Philip S., *President James Buchanan*, 1962; Moore, J. B. (ed.), *Works of James Buchanan*, 1908–1911.

Bundy, McGeorge

(March 30, 1919–   )
Presidential Adviser

McGeorge Bundy was one of the young, brash, and brilliant advisers who gave the administration of JOHN F. KENNEDY its reputation for intellectual prowess and ideological toughness. An architect of U.S. involvement in Vietnam (see LYNDON BAINES JOHNSON and RICHARD MILHOUS NIXON), he quickly became disillusioned by the failure of that intervention to produce a quick and decisive victory, an outcome that triggered his early retirement from politics.

Bundy was born in Boston. After graduating from Yale in 1940, he served as an intelligence officer in World War II, worked with the Council on Foreign Relations, and then taught at Harvard. He became dean of the faculty of arts and sciences at Harvard in 1953 and a professor of government in 1954.

In 1961 President Kennedy appointed Bundy special assistant for national security affairs. He became one of Kennedy's closest advisers and played an important role in the Cuban Missile Crisis and in the decision to intervene in South Vietnam. After President Kennedy's assassination, President Lyndon B. Johnson retained Bundy as a special assistant. Bundy participated in the decision to intervene in the Dominican Republic's civil war in 1965 and supported the escalation of the American military involvement in South Vietnam. However, as American casualties mounted, Bundy became less committed to the war, and in 1966 he resigned from the government to become the director of the Ford Foundation. During his thirteen-year tenure at the Ford Foundation he supervised influential reports on the future potential of educational television and satellite communications. After he retired from the Ford Foundation in 1979, Bundy became a history professor at New York University.

BIBLIOGRAPHY

Bundy, McGeorge, *The Strength of Government*, 1968, and with Henry L. Stimson, *On Active Service in Peace and War*, 1948; Halbertstam, David, *The Best and the Brightest*, 1972.

Burger, Warren Earl

(September 17, 1907–   )
Chief Justice of the Supreme Court

Although appointed to halt, even to roll back, the expansive approach taken by the liberal Warren Court (see EARL WARREN) toward issues of civil rights and civil liberties, Warren Burger in fact was not particularly successful in assembling majorities to overturn crucial Warren decisions or in articulating a new constitutional theory to guide Court rulings. His tenure as chief justice is recalled chiefly for his efforts to draw attention to the need for streamlining and modernizing the operations of the federal court system.

Warren Earl Burger was born in St. Paul, Minnesota. After taking extension courses at the University of Minnesota from 1925 to 1927, Burger entered the St. Paul College of Law (now Mitchell College of Law), where he attended night classes while earning his living as a life insurance salesperson. He was admitted to the bar in 1931 and began a successful practice in St. Paul while teaching law at Mitchell College.

In 1934 Burger helped organize the Minnesota Young Republicans. Four years later, he played an important role in Harold Stassen's successful campaign for governor. During the 1940s and early 1950s he became well known for his efforts to improve race relations in Minnesota.

Burger supported Harold Stassen's unsuccessful bid to win the Republican nomination in 1948 and 1952. At the 1952 convention, once it became clear Stassen could not win, Burger helped to secure DWIGHT D. EISENHOWER's nomination by pledging the Minnesota delegation to support him.

President Eisenhower appointed Burger assistant attorney general in charge of the civil litigation division of the Justice Department in 1953. Three years later, Eisenhower chose him to serve on the U.S. Court of Appeals for the District of Columbia. During his thirteen years on the court of appeals Burger became well known as a conservative judge, especially in cases involving criminal justice. His views often clashed with opinions handed down by the much more liberal Supreme Court. In 1969 he wrote: "This seeming anxiety of judges to protect every accused person from every consequence of his voluntary utterances is giving rise to myriad rules, subrules, variations, and exceptions, which even the most sophisticated lawyers and judges are taxed to follow. . . ."

Burger's "conservative" views were shared by Republican president RICHARD NIXON. When illness forced Chief Justice Earl Warren to retire in 1969, Nixon named Burger to take his place.

As a member of the Supreme Court, Burger proved to be a moderate, middle-of-the-road justice. The Burger Court initially upheld the use of busing to achieve school integration (only in the 1980s did the Court significantly reduce its application as a remedy for segregation) and ruled that the Constitution protected a woman's right to an abortion. Moreover, Burger concentrated on clarifying procedural issues and used his position to advocate the need for reforms that would modernize court administration, legal education, and correctional facilities.

In 1974 Burger joined with all his colleagues on the Supreme Court in ruling that President Nixon had to turn over the so-called White House tapes (recordings of conversations secretly made in the executive office by Nixon for reference use in his memoirs) to the Watergate (see RICHARD MILHOUS NIXON) special prosecutor. The evidence contained on the tapes proved decisive in forcing Nixon to resign.

Burger retired from the Supreme Court in September 1986. He was succeeded by fellow Republican WILLIAM REHNQUIST, who, aided by the addition of three justices appointed by RONALD REAGAN, quickly became a far more successful opponent of the Warren Court's jurisprudence than Burger had been.

BIBLIOGRAPHY

Alter, J., "A Chief in Transition," *Newsweek*, 107:21, June 30, 1986; "Empty Robe," *New Republic*, 194:4, July 14–21, 1986; *New York Post*, May 24, 1969; *New York Times*, May 22, 1969; Schwartz, Herbert, *The Burger Years: Rights and Wrongs in the Supreme Court, 1969–1986*, 1987; Thomas, E., "Reagan's Mr. Right," *Time*, 127:24, June 30, 1986; *Washington Post*, May 22, 1969.

Burr, Aaron

(February 6, 1756–September 14, 1836)
Vice President, Senator

A dynamic politician and adventurer, Aaron Burr is chiefly remembered as the man who killed ALEXANDER HAMILTON in a duel and who was almost executed for treason. Burr was born in Newark, New Jersey, into a family of wealth and intellectual accomplishment. His grandfather, Jonathan Edwards, was one of the leading New England theologians of the colonial period. His father, who died when Burr was only two, helped found the College of New Jersey (now Princeton University) and became its second president.

Library of Congress

Burr was brought up by a stern uncle and educated by a private tutor. Bright, but restless and hostile to authority, Burr managed to escape from his uncle's control by entering the College of New Jersey at age thirteen. He graduated three years later in 1772 and joined the American revolutionary army encamped around Boston in 1775. After serving on Benedict Arnold's staff, he briefly served on GEORGE WASHINGTON's staff before moving on to serve under General Israel Putnam. In July 1777, as a lieutenant colonel, Burr took over command of a regiment. He fought in the Battle of Monmouth and was angered by a rebuke from Washington he felt was unwarranted. Washington never forgave him for his decision to resign from the army on the grounds of illness in 1779.

Burr was admitted to the New York bar in 1782. His political career was complicated by the hostility of Alexander Hamilton. He and Hamilton had met during the Revolution and

had taken an instant dislike to one another. They were both remarkably intelligent and ambitious men who hoped to use a political power base in New York as a springboard to higher office. In addition to becoming rival lawyers, they soon became rival politicians.

Before the development of political parties, New York State was divided between Alexander Hamilton and GEORGE CLINTON factions. Burr became politically active in 1789, when Governor Clinton appointed him attorney general. In 1791 Burr managed to win a Senate seat by defeating Philip Schuyler, Hamilton's father-in-law. Defeated for reelection in 1797, he successfully ran for election to the state legislature. By 1800, Burr, through the establishment of a powerful New York City–based Republican political machine, controlled the state legislature. This meant he also controlled the choice of presidential electors. To ensure his support, the Republicans placed him on the ticket as candidate for vice president along with THOMAS JEFFERSON.

With the Federalists split in the election of 1800 between JOHN ADAMS and CHARLES PINCKNEY, Jefferson's victory seemed assured until the electoral votes were counted: Adams had sixty-five votes, Pinckney sixty-four, and Jefferson and Burr each seventy-three. (No distinction was then made on the ballots for president and vice president, an oversight corrected by the Twelfth Amendment.) With no clear winner, the Constitution provided that the choice between the two highest vote getters be made in the House of Representatives. The Federalists decided to thwart Jefferson by securing the choice of Burr instead. While the votes were counted again and again, Burr said nothing. Finally, after thirty-six ballots, Hamilton's influence helped secure the election of Jefferson for president and Burr for vice president.

Although Burr had never actually encouraged the Federalists, Jefferson never trusted him again. It quickly became apparent to Burr that he had no future with the Republicans. Burr began courting the Federalists. He ran for governor of New York in 1804, perhaps with the fantastic plan of uniting the state with a New England movement to secede; but once again, because of Hamilton's opposition his ambition was frustrated and he lost the election. Angered by a derogatory remark Hamilton made in a letter that was published, Burr challenged Hamilton to a duel. The two men faced each other on the morning of July 11, 1804, at Weehawken, New Jersey, and Hamilton was mortally wounded.

Surprised by the public outcry and the indictments for his arrest on murder charges issued by the states of New York and New Jersey, Burr fled to Philadelphia. While in Philadelphia, Burr hatched a scheme with JONATHAN DAYTON, another former senator, to create a vast empire in the West by conquering Mexico and encouraging the secession of the states west of the Appalachian Mountains. At the next session of Congress (1804–1805), Burr completed his term as vice president by presiding over the Senate and the impeach-ment trial of Supreme Court Justice SAMUEL CHASE as if nothing had happened.

After leaving office, Burr continued to work on launching his scheme. He attempted to secure British support and recruited new members to his conspiracy, one of whom, James Wilkinson, the governor of the Louisiana Territory, betrayed him to federal authorities just as he was about to begin implementing his plan in 1806. Burr was arrested and tried for treason in Washington in 1807.

Burr narrowly avoided conviction through the good fortune of having JOHN MARSHALL preside at his trial. Marshall's refusal to allow hearsay evidence and insistence upon at least two eyewitnesses to a treasonous act by Burr led to his acquittal; but Burr's political career and reputation were ruined.

To escape his creditors and to continue to recruit investors in new schemes, Burr traveled to Europe. He returned to New York in 1812, reestablished his law practice, and spent the last twenty-five years of his life in relative obscurity as a moderately successful lawyer.

BIBLIOGRAPHY

Abernethy, Thomas, *The Burr Conspiracy*, 1954; Cabell, James Alston, *Trial of Aaron Burr*, 1900; Carpenter, T., *The Trial of Aaron Burr;* Parmet, Herbert S., and Marie B. Hecht, *Aaron Burr*, 1967; Parton, James, *The Life and Times of Aaron Burr*, 1858; Schachner, Nathan, *Aaron Burr: A Biography*, 1937.

Bush, George Herbert Walker

(June 12, 1924–)
President, Vice President, Director of the Central Intelligence Agency, Diplomat, Representative

Before becoming president in 1989, George Bush's long career of public service included terms as a U.S. congressman, United Nations ambassador, Republican National Committee chairman during the Watergate (see RICHARD MILHOUS NIXON) era, envoy to China, director of the Central Intelligence Agency, and vice president.

Bush was born in Milton, Massachusetts, grew up in Greenwich, Connecticut, and attended Philips Academy, in Andover, Massachusetts. In 1942 he enlisted in the U.S. Naval Reserve. He was commissioned an ensign and became the youngest navy pilot in 1943. He entered Yale in 1945. After graduating with a B.A. three years later, he moved with his new wife to the oilfields of western Texas.

Bush learned the oil industry from firsthand experience and founded his own company with family money. He eventually merged his firm with others to form the Zapata Petroleum Corporation, but broke off on his own again in 1954 to develop the Zapata Offshore Company. He established the headquarters of his firm in Houston in 1958.

Like his father, a Republican senator from Connecticut from 1962 to 1972, Bush became active in politics. In 1964 he won the Texas Republican party nomination for senator, but his conservative, pro–BARRY GOLDWATER positions did not prove quite strong enough to defeat the Democratic incumbent. Two years

Library of Congress

later, Bush was elected to the first of two consecutive terms in the U.S. House of Representatives.

In Congress, Bush won an important appointment to the House Ways and Means Committee and supported a generally conservative approach to issues. He did, however, vote for enabling eighteen-year-olds to vote and for open housing legislation. His pro–civil rights vote riled many of his Texas constituents.

In 1970 Bush decided not to seek a third term in the House in order to make another try for the Senate. Although he ran a well-financed campaign, he was defeated by conservative Democrat Lloyd Bentsen. In appreciation for his effort, President Richard Nixon appointed Bush ambassador to the United Nations for two years, and in 1973 chairman of the Republican National Committee. Until the release of the Watergate tape that clearly implicated Nixon in a cover-up attempt, Bush loyally defended the president.

When Nixon's successor, GERALD FORD, allowed him to choose a new post, Bush decided to become the chief of the U.S. liaison office in the People's Republic of China. He served in this position from 1974 until December 1975, when he returned to the United States to become the director of the Central Intelligence Agency (CIA). The CIA had been beset by a series of embarrassing disclosures revealing its role in destabilizing third world governments through bribery, kidnapping, even support for assassinations. Although Bush headed it for only eight months, he had considerable success in restoring morale and implementing needed organizational reforms.

At the beginning of the 1980 race for the Republican presidential nomination, Bush unexpectedly pulled ahead of favorite RONALD REAGAN by winning the Iowa caucuses. A shocked Reagan altered his campaign strategy, recovered his momentum, and went on to defeat Bush for the nomination. Reagan then chose Bush as his running mate, and the ticket went on to a solid election victory against incumbent Democratic president JIMMY CARTER.

Reagan chose Bush to be his running mate again in 1984. During his eight years as vice president, Bush carefully cultivated conservative interests within the Republican party. By 1988 he had convinced most of his critics within the party that he really would support conservative Republican positions, and not the more liberal approach favored by the liberal wing of the party. He quickly knocked out his challengers for the presidential nomination in 1988, then went on to win a resounding upset victory against the Democratic candidate MICHAEL DUKAKIS. In the national election campaign, Bush promised to continue the Reagan administration's policies, especially the commitment to reduce government spending in order to balance the budget with no new taxes.

As president, Bush made curtailing drug abuse and lowering the budget deficit high priorities. It was his administration's "war on drugs" that led Bush to order an invasion of the Republic of Panama in 1989 in order to arrest its leader, Manuel Noriega. Noriega was accused of allowing his nation to be used as a drug-smuggling center. In the fall of 1990, faced with a growing budget deficit and a weakening economy, Bush publicly rescinded his no new taxes pledge. The move cost him the support of a substantial number of the Republican members of Congress, but a modest tax increase program was enacted that began to address the need to reduce the federal government's budget deficit.

In foreign policy, Bush encouraged the improvement of relations with the Soviet Union. The administration won praise for its speed in meeting the challenge of the unexpected collapse of communism in Eastern Europe in 1989 and 1990 and accepting the reunification of Germany. The first foreign policy crisis for the Bush administration occurred when Iraq invaded and annexed Kuwait in the Persian Gulf in August 1990. Bush immediately protested the invasion; ordered a huge buildup of American naval, air, and ground forces in the area (stationed primarily in Saudi Arabia); and successfully sought United Nations approval for an international trade embargo of Iraq to force it to withdraw from Kuwait. The two reasons he gave for the need to commit troops in the area were safeguarding oil supplies and protecting small nation-states from unprovoked aggression by more powerful neighbors. When economic sanctions did not lead to Iraq's withdrawal from Kuwait, Bush obtained support from the United Nations for the use of military force against Iraq.

BIBLIOGRAPHY

Bush, George, with Victor Gold, *Looking Forward: An Autobiography*, 1987; with Doug Wead, *Man of Integrity*, 1988; Green, Fitzhugh, *George Bush: An Intimate Portrait*, 1989; Plimpton, George, *The X Factor*, 1990; Ridley, Matt, *Warts and All: The Men Who Would Be Bush*, 1989.

Butler, Andrew Pickens

(November 18, 1796–May 25, 1857)
Senator

Born near Edgefield, South Carolina, Butler attended Wadell Academy. He graduated from South Carolina College in 1817 and two years later was admitted to the state bar. He established his law practice at Edgefield and was elected to the state legislature in 1824, where he became a strong supporter of JOHN C. CALHOUN and the right of a state to nullify a federal government law. In 1833 he was appointed circuit judge, and before the year was over he had moved up to become a court of appeals judge. He stepped down from the bench in 1846 to accept an appointment to the U.S. Senate. He was reelected in 1848 and 1854 without opposition.

In the Senate Butler was a strong supporter of his colleague and mentor, John C. Calhoun. He was appointed chairman of the Judiciary Committee, opposed the admission of California as a nonslave state, supported the fugitive slave law (see MILLARD FILLMORE), and fought for the Kansas-Nebraska Act (see FRANKLIN PIERCE). Butler's speech in support of the act prompted CHARLES SUMNER to deliver a sarcastic rebuttal. Three days later, Butler's nephew, Representative PRESTON S. BROOKS of South Carolina, attacked Sumner with a cane while he was seated at his desk in the Senate chamber. This played a crucial role in galvanizing Northern support for the new Republican party and in further polarizing the nation. Butler, who had been in poor health for some time, died the following year at his home.

BIBLIOGRAPHY

Brook, U. R., *South Carolina Bench and Bar*, 1908; "The Butlers of South Carolina," *South Carolina History and Genealogy Magazine*, October 1903; O'Neal, John B., *The Bench and the Bar of South Carolina*, 1859; Perry, B. F., *Reminiscences of Public Men*, 1883.

Butler, Benjamin Franklin

(November 5, 1818–January 11, 1893)
Candidate for President, Representative

Branded as "Beast Butler" by Southerners and hailed as an antislavery hero in the North, Benjamin Butler's long and controversial political career spanned more than thirty years, including the tumultuous years of the Civil War and Reconstruction.

After spending the first ten years of his life in Deerfield, New Hampshire, Butler moved, upon the death of his father, with his mother to Lowell, Massachusetts, in 1828. Mrs. Butler operated a "mill girl" or factory boarding house. Butler graduated from Waterbury (now Colby) College in 1838, was admitted to the bar at Lowell in 1840, and earned a fortune from his law practice and investments.

Butler was elected as a Democrat to the Massachusetts House of Representatives in 1853 and to the Massachusetts Senate in 1859. When the Democratic party divided into factions in 1860, Butler sided with the Southerners and voted for JOHN BRECKINRIDGE; but he did not support secession.

After helping to recruit a regiment in Massachusetts and playing a crucial role in preventing Maryland from seceding, Butler was appointed a major general of volunteers in

May 1861 by ABRAHAM LINCOLN. As a combat field commander Butler was a failure, but as an administrator of conquered Confederate territory he proved helpful to the Union cause. It was Butler who originated the idea that runaway slaves who came within Union lines ought to be treated as contraband of war. His most notorious assignment was as military governor of New Orleans for seven months in 1862. There he caused an international furor by seizing Confederate gold bullion that had been placed in the French consulate. He also earned the enmity of Southerners for his General Order No. 28, which declared that any woman showing disrespect for the Union flag or uniform should be treated as a "woman of the town, plying her trade." Infuriated residents claimed that "Beast Butler" was so corrupt that he "stole the spoons from the house he occupied."

In 1866 Butler was elected as a Radical Republican to Congress, where he was a strong proponent of the Reconstruction programs advocated by THADDEUS STEVENS. He was also one of the managers of the impeachment case against ANDREW JOHNSON. After two unsuccessful runs for governor of Massachusetts in 1871 and 1872, he was defeated for reelection to Congress in 1875. He returned to Congress in 1876 on a platform that supported the printing of paper money, without gold or silver backing, called greenbacks. Two more tries for the governor's office in 1878 and 1879 failed; but finally, in 1882, he succeeded in being elected. Defeated for reelection the next year, he concentrated on an unsuccessful bid for the Democratic nomination for president in 1884. He was nominated for president by two small political parties: the Anti-Monopoly party, which advocated an eight-hour day and national control of interstate commerce, and the National (Greenback) party (see JAMES BAIRD WEAVER). He received 175,370 popular votes but no electoral votes in the general election. He never ran for office again and died in his Washington, D.C., home nine years later.

BIBLIOGRAPHY

Butler, Benjamin F., *The Autobiography and Personal Reminiscences of Major-General Benjamin F. Butler,* 1892; Holzman, Robert S., *Stormy Ben Butler,* 1976; Trefousse, Hans L., *Ben Butler: The South Called Him Beast,* 1974; West, Richard S., Jr., *Lincoln's Scapegoat General: Benjamin F. Butler,* 1965.

Byrnes, James Francis

(May 2, 1879–April 9, 1972)
Secretary of State, Associate Justice of the Supreme Court, Senator, Representative

Born in Charleston, South Carolina, James F. Byrnes studied law while working as a court reporter. He was admitted to the bar in 1903 and, in addition to his legal work, owned and edited a newspaper in Aiken, South Carolina. From 1911 to 1925, Byrnes, a Democrat, served in the U.S. House of Representatives. His first bid to win a seat in the Senate in 1924 failed, but he succeeded in 1930 and won reelection in 1936.

In the Senate Byrnes became a budgetary expert. At first he backed President FRANKLIN D. ROOSEVELT's New Deal legislation, but after the 1936 elections he adopted a much more conservative attitude and grew increasingly disenchanted. He opposed increasing the amount of money devoted to direct relief programs and the Fair Labor Standards Act. In foreign policy matters, he continued to support the president and helped secure the repeal of the Neutrality Act of 1935 (see WILLIAM EDGAR BORAH) and passage of the Lend-Lease Act of 1941.

After supporting Roosevelt's reelection to a third term in 1940, Byrnes was appointed to the Supreme Court the following year as an associate justice. He served for only one year before resigning at President Roosevelt's request to become the director of economic stabilization, and then in 1943 director of the Office of War Mobilization. His broad authority to regulate the economy to produce war materiel without rampant inflation made him one of the most powerful men in Washington.

Byrnes's bid to win the nomination for vice president in 1944 failed due to Roosevelt's lack of support and opposition from northern liberals and labor leaders. In 1945 President HARRY S TRUMAN named him secretary of state. At first, Byrnes tried to improve relations with the Soviet Union, but his experiences in dealing with the Soviets in Europe and Iran convinced him of the need for the United States to negotiate from strength and to oppose communist expansion.

Byrnes, a states' rights Southern Democrat, fiercely opposed the growth of the power of the federal government. Truman and Byrnes were at odds with each other from the start, stemming partly from their competition for the 1944 vice presidency. The friction and distrust between them increased, and finally Byrnes resigned as secretary of state in 1947 and became one of Truman's harshest critics. As governor of South Carolina from 1951 to 1955, Byrnes opposed racial desegregation. In 1952, Byrnes supported Republican candidate DWIGHT D. EISENHOWER for president.

BIBLIOGRAPHY

Byrnes, James Francis, *Speaking Frankly,* 1947, and *All in One Lifetime,* 1958; Curry, George, *James F. Byrnes,* 1965.

Byrns, Joseph Wellington

(July 20, 1869–June 4, 1936)
Speaker of the House, Representative

Born on a farm near Cedar Hill, Tennessee, Byrns earned a law degree from Vanderbilt University in 1890. He was admitted to the bar the same year and established a practice in Nashville in 1891. Three years later, he began his political career in the Tennessee legislature. He was reelected in 1896 and 1898, and served as speaker during the 1899 session. Elected to the state senate in 1900, he suffered his first political setback two years later when he was defeated in a bid to be district attorney general of Davidson County.

In 1908 Byrns scored a surprising upset election victory by winning a seat in the U.S. House of Representatives against a popular Republican incumbent. During the campaign he had promised that if elected, he would obtain federal funding for the building of a dam and locks on the Cumberland River. He kept his word and remained in Congress for a total of twenty-eight years.

As a Democratic congressman, Byrns championed economy and frugality in government and favored lowering tariff rates. He was a strong supporter of WOODROW WILSON's programs and, as majority leader in the House in the 1930s, played an important role in securing passage of President FRANKLIN D. ROOSEVELT's New Deal legislation, even though much of it contradicted his own political beliefs. His commitment to party loyalty was rewarded in 1935 by his election as Speaker of the House, but he died suddenly after serving only a brief time.

BIBLIOGRAPHY

Galloway, J. M., "Joseph W. Byrns," manuscript in University of Tennessee Library; *Nashville Tennessean,* June 4 and 5, 1936; *Newsweek,* June 13, 1936; *New York Times,* June 4 and 7, 1936; *Time,* June 15, 1936; *Who's Who in America,* 1934–1935.

Calhoun, John Caldwell

(March 18, 1782–March 31, 1850)
Vice President, Secretary of State, Secretary of War, Senator, Representative

In a remarkable forty-year national political career, John C. Calhoun played a vital role in protecting Southern interests. As a political philosopher and statesman, he defended the institution of slavery as "a positive good" and the right of the South to nullify or refuse to obey laws passed by the national legislature viewed as harmful to its sectional interests.

John C. Calhoun was born in the South Carolina uplands near the Savannah River. He graduated

Library of Congress

from Yale College in 1804, was admitted to the bar in 1807, and established a law practice in Abbeville near his native home. In 1808 he was elected to the South Carolina legislature as a Republican. Two years later, he won a seat in the U.S. House of Representatives.

At the beginning of his congressional career, Calhoun was a militant nationalist. In Congress he joined the group of young men led by HENRY CLAY who were known as war hawks because of their desire to go to war with Great Britain, regardless of the consequences, to enable the United States to expand north and south, gaining Canada and Florida. Declaring that "our true system is to look to the country . . . to advance the general interest," Calhoun, in addition to supporting the War of 1812 (see JAMES MADISON), fought for implementation of Clay's American System (see HENRY CLAY), which consisted of federal funding for internal improvements, a national bank (see NICHOLAS BIDDLE and ROGER BROOKE TANEY), and protective tariffs.

At the end of his third term in Congress, Calhoun joined JAMES MONROE's cabinet as secretary of war. During the seven and a half years of his tenure, Calhoun worked to improve the strength of the army and navy.

In 1824 JOHN QUINCY ADAMS became president and Calhoun his reluctant vice president. Calhoun realized that the mood of the nation was in favor of ANDREW JACKSON, and as Senate president he showed his willingness to join the

Jackson camp by making no effort to curtail the fierceness of antiadministration speeches. Jackson rewarded Calhoun by selecting him to be his vice president in 1828.

Calhoun's hope of using the office of vice president as a stepping-stone for succeeding Jackson failed, however, in part owing to a peculiar social situation. Calhoun joined other members of Washington society in snubbing Secretary of War John Eaton's wife, Peggy, who, it was rumored, had lived with Eaton while she was still married to her first husband. Jackson despised such politically based slander; his own wife had undergone pain as a result of gossip about her divorce. Jackson became Peggy Eaton's champion. When MARTIN VAN BUREN also befriended Mrs. Eaton, Jackson was gratified and eventually settled on him as his successor.

Jackson's negative opinion of Calhoun was confirmed when he discovered that Calhoun had criticized his conduct during the Florida campaign of 1818 (see WILLIAM HARRIS CRAWFORD). The final break with Jackson occurred when Calhoun spoke out in support of nullification. Calhoun had come to believe that the high tariffs imposed in 1828 and the growing antislavery sentiment in the North posed dire threats to the South's economy. His *South Carolina Exposition,* published in 1828 at the request of the South Carolina legislature, argued that because the nation was composed of states that had originally been sovereign and independent, any state could refuse to obey (nullify) a federal law it believed unconstitutional. Therefore, if the tariff of 1828 was not reduced, South Carolina, along with any other states that wished to do so, could ignore the law.

When Congress declared protective tariffs essential to the economic well-being of the nation in 1832, the nullification crisis peaked. South Carolina proclaimed federal tariffs not "binding upon this State." After President Jackson issued a proclamation stating that nullification would not be tolerated, Calhoun, who by this time had placed defending the interests of the South ahead of party politics,

resigned the vice presidency. He was immediately appointed a senator from South Carolina and, amid threats of violence from both sides, led the fight to lower the tariff in the Senate. A compromise tariff avoided violence, but Calhoun's future role as the defender of the South had been cast.

From that point, in the Senate, as secretary of state under President JOHN TYLER, and in his writing, Calhoun attacked abolition and outlined his theory of "concurrent majorities." Rule by a numerical majority, he held, was "but Government of the strongest interests," which, "when not efficiently checked, is the most tyrannical and oppressive that can be devised. . . ." He argued that "Out of power interests" (such as the South) should be given the "right of self-protection"; each state, he believed, should have the right to agree with or veto any federal legislation.

Calhoun completed his term as secretary of state in 1845 and returned to the Senate, where, although his support for the annexation of Texas remained firm, he opposed going to war with Mexico (see JAMES KNOX POLK). The Wilmot Proviso (1846), which proposed prohibiting slavery in the area acquired from Mexico, caused Calhoun to claim that since all the states owned all the territories in common, any citizen could take whatever property he had in his state into a territory and enjoy the same protection for it that he enjoyed in his home state until the territory itself became a state. This line of reasoning rendered the Missouri Compromise (see HENRY CLAY) null and void.

Frustrated by the growing numerical superiority in the national legislature of the antislavery states, Calhoun called a conference of Southern senators in January 1849 to consider a scheme for uniting them against any effort by the North to abolish slavery. The meeting was unsuccessful. Most of the Southern senators decided not to accept Calhoun's dire warning of a looming crisis.

The effort to protect the interests of his beloved South in the framing of the Compromise of 1850 (see HENRY CLAY and MILLARD FILL-

MORE) drained Calhoun's remaining energy. Too weak to deliver his last formal speech on March 4, 1850, he expressed in writing one last time his view that although conflict had been avoided, he could not "see how two peoples so different and hostile can exist together in one common Union." He died less than a month later, bemoaning the fate of "the South, the poor South."

BIBLIOGRAPHY

Capers, Gerald M., *John C. Calhoun, Opportunist; A Reappraisal*, 1960; Coit, Margaret M. (ed.), *John C. Calhoun*, 1970; Niven, John, *John C. Calhoun and the Price of Union: A Biography*, 1988; Spain, August O., *Political Theory of John C. Calhoun*, 1968; Wiltse, Charles, *John C. Calhoun*, 3 vols., 1944–1951.

Cameron, Simon

(March 8, 1799–June 26, 1889)
Secretary of War, Diplomat, Senator

Born in Lancaster County, Pennsylvania, Cameron learned the printing business in Harrisburg. He moved to Washington, D.C., in 1822 to work in the printing house for the congressional debates. In 1824 he returned to Harrisburg, bought a local newspaper, and began to exercise considerable political influence as a staunch advocate of protective tariffs.

Eager for greater financial gain, Cameron left the newspaper business and acquired a fortune through various business interests in banking, insurance, and construction projects. He continued to be politically active and was involved in a scandal in 1838 when, as commissioner to settle certain claims of the Winnebago Indians, he had the claims adjusted through his own bank and to his benefit.

Cameron was elected to the Senate in 1845 as a Democrat but was defeated in two reelection attempts, the first in 1849 and the second in 1855, before returning to the Senate as a Republican in 1857. He remained a Republican for the rest of his life and devoted his energies and wealth to building up a strong party organization in Pennsylvania.

At the Republican convention in 1860, he bargained the votes of his Pennsylvania delegation to ABRAHAM LINCOLN for the promise of a cabinet post. Upon Lincoln's election, Cameron became secretary of war. Complaints against his favoritism and mismanagement became so overwhelming that Lincoln relieved him of his cabinet post by appointing him minister to Russia in 1862. Three months after his departure, the House censured his conduct in the handling of military contracts.

Upon his return from Russia, Cameron failed in his first Senate reelection attempt in 1863, but he succeeded in 1867 and again in 1873. He was so powerful in the Pennsylvania Republican party that he succeeded in having his son appointed secretary of war in ULYSSES S. GRANT's administration. When President RUTHERFORD B. HAYES refused to continue Cameron's son in that office, Cameron had the last laugh: he resigned from his Senate seat so that his son, who had assumed control of the Pennsylvania Republican party, could take his place. Cameron spent the last twelve years of his life in retirement on his farm in Donegal Springs.

BIBLIOGRAPHY

Bradley, Erwin S., *Simon Cameron, Lincoln's Secretary of War*, 1966.

Cannon, Joseph Gurney

(May 7, 1836–November 12, 1926)
Speaker of the House, Representative

As Speaker of the House from 1903 to 1911, Joseph Cannon was best known for an arbitrary and partisan style of rule called Cannonism. Born in Guilford County, North Carolina, Cannon was raised in Annapolis, Indiana. Trained as a lawyer, he first entered public life in 1861 as the attorney general for Illinois's twenty-seventh judicial district. He won his first congressional election as a Republican candidate from Illinois in 1872, a position he held virtually continuously until 1923.

Over the next thirty years, Cannon held many important committee posts in the House, was right-hand man to Speaker THOMAS B. REED from 1889 to 1891, and finally became Speaker himself in 1903. Cannon's name was never attached to any important legislation, but he was known for his staunch conservative outlook, especially in opposing President WILLIAM H. TAFT's attempt to lower tariffs. Dictatorial and coarse-spoken, "Uncle Joe," as he was called, recognized whom he wanted on the floor of the House and controlled the important Rules Committee absolutely. Associated with the Republican "Old Guard" (including Senator NELSON ALDRICH) and anathema to the progressive Republicans (see THEODORE ROOSEVELT) in Congress, Cannon eventually became the target of a drive to reform the House of Representatives in 1909. President Taft himself disliked Cannon and wanted his powers as Speaker curtailed, but Cannon's role in guiding the passage of legislation was so great—and his opposition to Taft's reform bill so firm—that Taft backed down from approving the progressive Republicans' revolt in Congress. As a result, a weak tariff bill finally was passed (see WILLIAM HOWARD TAFT), and it wasn't until the next year, in 1910, that the revolt against "Cannonism" was successful. Representative GEORGE NORRIS led a coalition of progressive Republicans and some Democrats in approving a resolution amending House rules on the formation of the crucial Rules Committee and thereby deprived Cannon of many of his powers.

Cannon lost his seat in the House in 1912 but bounced back in 1914. He remained in office for nearly another decade, but he never regained his status as congressional power-broker.

BIBLIOGRAPHY

Busbey, L. White, *Uncle Joe Cannon,* 1927; Gwinn, William R., *Uncle Joe Cannon,* 1957.

Cardozo, Benjamin Nathan

(May 24, 1870–July 9, 1938)
Associate Justice of the Supreme Court

Although an associate justice of the Supreme Court for only six years, Benjamin Nathan Cardozo left a legacy of reconciling the law's need to allow for evolutionary change in society while still providing stability.

Cardozo was born in New York City. He earned a B.A. degree (1889) and an M.A. degree (1890) from Columbia University. In 1891 Cardozo was admitted to the New York bar. He practiced law—primarily as an attorney for attorneys and as an expert in commercial law—before the New York Court of Appeals, the highest court in the state judicial system.

In 1913 Cardozo was elected as a reform candidate to the state supreme court. In 1917 he was elected—as the candidate of both the Democrat and Republican parties—to serve a fourteen-year term on the New York Court of Appeals. The logic Cardozo used while on the bench to adapt laws originally designed for an agrarian society to meet the needs of an industrialized culture was cited by lawyers throughout the English-speaking world.

President HERBERT HOOVER appointed Cardozo to succeed Associate Justice OLIVER WENDELL HOLMES on the Supreme Court in 1932, only the second Jewish judge ever chosen for the highest court. The six years Cardozo served as an associate justice before his death spanned a particularly tumultuous period in the Court's history. The Great Depression and the innovative regulatory and social welfare legislation spawned by the New Deal presented the Court with a difficult dilemma. Legal precedent did not provide the majority of the justices with sufficient justification to support the New Deal's approaches for coping with the national crisis. Cardozo joined Justices HARLAN STONE and LOUIS BRANDEIS in dissenting when the majority of the Court declared such programs as the National Regulatory Agency and the Agricultural Adjustment Act unconstitutional. Cardozo survived just long enough to see President FRANKLIN D. ROOSEVELT's "court-packing" plan defeated and for the majority of the Court to begin to reflect what had been his minority perspective.

BIBLIOGRAPHY

Elliott, Stephen P. (ed.), *A Reference Guide to the United States Supreme Court*, 1986; Hall, Margaret E. (ed.), *Selected Writings of Benjamin N. Cardozo*, 1947; Hellman, George S., *Benjamin N. Cardozo, American Judge*, 1940 (reprint 1969); Pollard, Joseph P., *Mister Justice Cardozo: A Liberal Mind in Action*, 1935 (reprint 1975).

Carlisle, John Griffin

(September 5, 1835–July 31, 1910)
Secretary of the Treasury, Speaker of the House, Senator, Representative

Born in Campbell (now Kenton) County, Kentucky, John Carlisle studied law in Covington, was admitted to the bar in 1858, and established a successful law practice.

Carlisle was elected to the Kentucky legislature in 1859 and reelected for a second term. He was a moderate on the slavery issue, opposing both secession and coercion of states back into the Union. When war broke out, he adopted a stance of neutrality. Before being elected lieutenant governor in 1871, he was elected to the state senate in 1865 and again in 1869.

In 1876 Carlisle was elected to the U.S. House of Representatives, where he soon became the leader of the Democrats. He was elected Speaker of the House in 1883, a post he also held for the next two Congresses. His knowledge of parliamentary procedure and the rules of the House, along with his impartial treatment of his colleagues, made him one of the greatest speakers. On May 26, 1890, he resigned his House seat to accept an appointment to the Senate.

President GROVER CLEVELAND chose Carlisle to be secretary of the treasury in 1893. As secretary, Carlisle became a strong supporter of the gold standard. After his effort to secure the Democratic nomination for president in 1896 failed (see WILLIAM JENNINGS BRYAN), Carlisle returned to Kentucky. There, because of his strong support for the gold standard, his prosilver neighbors almost mobbed his home. Carlisle, realizing the impossibility of ever having his gold standard views appreciated in Kentucky, retired from politics in 1897 and moved to New York, where he practiced law until his death.

BIBLIOGRAPHY

Barnes, James A., *John Carlisle: Financial Statesman*, 1931.

Carter, James (Jimmy) Earl, Jr.

(October 1, 1924–)
President

In 1976 former one-term governor of Georgia Jimmy Carter became the first president from the Deep South to win election without the benefit of incumbency since ZACHARY TAYLOR in 1848. During his term as president, Carter, an administrator with neither a liberal nor a conservative approach, proved unable to shake his image as a vacillator, unsure of how to cope with domestic economic turmoil and foreign policy crises.

Carter was born in Plains, Georgia, and grew up on the family farm in nearby Archery. He became, like his father, a pillar of the First Baptist Church of Plains. After attending Georgia Southwestern College for a year in 1941 and the Georgia Institute of Technology for another year, he received an appointment to the U.S. Naval Academy at Annapolis. He graduated in 1946, entered the navy in 1947, and a year later began his career as a submarine officer, first on conventional vessels and

Library of Congress

then as part of Hyman Rickover's nuclear submarine program.

Upon the death of his father in 1953, Carter resigned from the navy and returned to Plains to run the family farm and small general store. He began his involvement in politics by serving in a variety of local community political positions. Although he later chastised himself for not protesting more strongly the unfair treatment of blacks in Plains, he did refuse to join the local White Citizens' Council, and he was one of only two members of his church in 1965 to oppose a motion to exclude blacks from services.

In 1962 Carter ran in the Democratic primary for the state senate. He lost the primary election by a narrow margin because of illegal ballot box stuffing on the part of his opponent. Carter challenged the outcome and eventually succeeded in convincing the state Democratic Committee to place his name on the general election ballot. He won the general election and served in the state senate from 1963 to 1966.

In 1967, after losing his first try to win the Democratic party nomination for governor, Carter became a "born again" Christian. His second effort to win the governor's office in 1970 was successful.

As governor, he opened the Georgia government to women as well as blacks and established a number of innovations designed to improve efficiency and economy. He reorganized 300 state agencies into 22 superagencies and required each department to justify its total budget annually (zero-based budgeting). He instituted a sunshine law that required government meetings to be open to the public, pushed for legislation to protect the environment, and added large tracts of open land to the state park system. He also maintained a strong anticrime image by supporting capital punishment and harsh sentences for drug dealers.

The Georgia constitution prevented Carter from running for a second term. An effort to secure the vice presidential spot on the 1972 Democratic ticket with GEORGE MCGOVERN was unsuccessful, but Carter began campaigning for the 1976 Democratic presidential nomination as soon as he left the governor's office in January 1975.

Carter correctly sensed that the national electorate was eager for someone outside the Washington political establishment to vote for after the Vietnam War debacle (see LYNDON BAINES JOHNSON and RICHARD MILHOUS NIXON) and the Watergate scandal (see NIXON). He promised never to "tell a lie" and to return the government to the decency its citizens had every right to expect. By winning most of the thirty state primary elections, he was able to defeat his rivals for the nomination and to dispel doubts about his attraction to nonsouthern voters.

Carter chose WALTER MONDALE as his running mate and began the national campaign with a wide lead in the public opinion polls.

Victory seemed assured, but a surprisingly vigorous campaign by President GERALD FORD combined with what appeared to be Carter's vacillation on important issues resulted in a very close race: Carter won 297 electoral votes to Ford's 240.

After being sworn in as president on January 20, 1977, Carter walked from Capitol Hill with his family down Pennsylvania Avenue to the White House. The gesture of walking rather than riding in the presidential limousine demonstrated his desire to be perceived as a man of the people.

As a candidate for president, Carter had successfully turned his lack of national government experience into an asset; but as president, his outsider image and approach to dealing with Congress and the federal bureaucracy became a liability. The Democrats had an overwhelming majority in the House and Senate during his administration, but Carter seldom obtained much congressional support for his legislative proposals.

The domestic issues that dominated the nation during the Carter years concerned unemployment, inflation, and energy. When Carter assumed office, the unemployment rate was approximately 7 percent and the annual inflation rate was 6.8 percent. Carter had promised to reduce unemployment, cut the inflation rate, and balance the budget. He failed in all three areas. By 1980 unemployment was over 8 percent, inflation was about 12 percent, and the projected budget deficit was nearly $59 billion. Not all the fault lay with Carter, but nothing he did to improve the situation ever seemed to work. On one hand, he supported full employment and refused to recognize a connection between employment rates and inflation (reduced employment leads to less demand, which in turn results in lower prices). On the other hand, Carter appointed a conservative economist, PAUL VOLCKER, to head the Federal Reserve Board. Volcker advocated forcing an economic recession (increasing unemployment) by tightening the money supply (raising interest rates).

By 1980 Carter, the man who had promised to cut taxes while campaigning in 1976, was saying new taxes were necessary.

Carter had no better luck in dealing with a shortage of oil import supplies in 1979 caused by the overthrow of the Shah of Iran. The United States had been plagued by rising energy costs ever since the 1973 Arab oil embargo, but even though Carter had submitted a comprehensive energy bill to Congress designed to reduce U.S. dependence on foreign oil with the statement that "nothing less than the moral equivalent of war" was at stake, he was unable to rally support. In the fall of 1978 he settled for enactment of a much weaker piece of legislation than he knew was necessary. Thus, when prices began to skyrocket in the summer of 1979, there was little he could do except urge conservation and institute a gasoline rationing system through the newly created Department of Energy. The rationing system failed to avoid fuel shortages: tempers flared in long gasoline station lines, prices continued to soar, and Carter was blamed. Carter appeared on television and announced that he was submitting another comprehensive energy bill to Congress that instituted procedures for developing synthetic fuels and conservation incentives. This time most of his suggested measures were enacted, but it was too little, too late.

The basic tenets of Carter's foreign policy objectives—to pursue diplomatic solutions to world problems, initiate détente (see HENRY ALFRED KISSINGER) with the Soviet Union, plan strategic arms reduction, and strengthen relations with China—were goals consistent with the Ford and Nixon administrations. However, Carter's human rights policy of holding nations accountable for the treatment of their citizens made his foreign policy different. Critics charged that the fundamental flaw in Carter's approach was that the United States was able to exert pressure on allies—often destabilizing their governments and making them prone to revolution, as in Nicaragua—while it could do little or nothing to influence what happened in communist nations. Yet, histori-

ans may well credit Carter's insistence on human rights as providing critical support to dissidents in Eastern Europe and Russia, thus accelerating the collapse of communism.

The two foreign policy successes of the Carter administration, the negotiation and ratification by the Senate of a new Panama Canal treaty in 1978 and the facilitating of the negotiations that led to the signing of the Camp David Accords between Egypt and Israel in 1979 (the first peace treaty between Israel and one of its Arab neighbors), were overshadowed by events in Iran.

Perhaps no issue exemplified the image of a confused leader so much as the way Carter dealt with the ramifications of the overthrow of the Shah of Iran in 1979. During the convoluted course of Iran's revolution, fifty-two American citizens were seized at the American embassy and held hostage for 444 days. Carter pledged not to use military force that might endanger the lives of the hostages. Instead, he relied on world opinion and economic sanctions. In addition, after the Soviet Union invaded neighboring Afghanistan in order to prop up a puppet communist government, an outraged Carter ordered further economic sanctions, appealed to the United Nations for support, and sent a U.S. fleet to the area in an ineffectual display of force.

In 1980, in an effort to retain the Democratic presidential nomination in a close race with Senator EDWARD KENNEDY, Carter announced on the eve of several important primary races that the release of the hostages was on the verge of being secured. Finally, desperate after an agreement for their release was never reached, Carter ordered a military rescue attempt that failed and led to the death of eight servicemen and the resignation of Secretary of State CYRUS VANCE. As Hamilton Jordan, Carter's chief campaign strategist later noted: "The hostage crisis had come to symbolize the collective frustration of the American people. And in that sense, the President's chances for re-election probably died on the desert of Iran with eight brave soldiers. . . ."

The hostages were finally released on the day Republican RONALD REAGAN, Carter's successor, became president in exchange for U.S. concessions that included the unfreezing of Iranian assets in the United States and the procurement of medical supplies.

Carter retired to Plains, Georgia, with the lowest presidential popularity rating ever recorded. In Plains he wrote his memoirs, rebuilt the family business, and established the Carter library. He also began to rebuild his public esteem through goodwill work. He helped the homeless by rebuilding houses, and served as a roving peace ambassador who employed his negotiating skills to facilitate compromise settlements and democratic solutions to conflicts in Nicaragua and Ethiopia.

BIBLIOGRAPHY

Abernathy, M. Glenn, et al., *The Carter Years: The President and Policy Making*, 1984; Brzezinski, Zbigniew, *Power and Principle: Memoirs of the National Security Adviser, 1977–1981*, 1983; Carter, Jimmy, *Why Not the Best?* 1975; Hyatt, R., *The Carters of Plains*, 1977; Jordan, Hamilton, *Crisis: The Last Year of the Carter Presidency*, 1982; Lasky, Victor, *Jimmy Carter: The Man and The Myth*, 1979; Muravchik, Joshua, *The Uncertain Crusade*, 1986.

Casey, William Joseph

(March 13, 1913–May 6, 1987)
Director of the Central Intelligence Agency

William J. Casey was born in Elmhurst, Queens, New York. After graduating from Fordham University in 1934, he did graduate work at the Catholic University of America in Washington, D.C., and earned a law degree from St. John's University in 1937. He was admitted to the New York bar the following year. From 1941 to 1946, he served with Army Intelligence and the Office of Strategic Services in London, directing spy missions in German-held territory. After the war he was associated with U.S. aid programs in Europe.

Casey lectured in tax law at New York University from 1948 to 1962. He was also a partner in both Wall Street and Washington, D.C., law firms. In 1971, three years after working on RICHARD NIXON's successful campaign for the presidency, Casey was appointed chairman of the Securities and Exchange Commission and then undersecretary of state for economic affairs. From 1974 to 1975 he served as chairman of the Export-Import Bank, and in 1976 was a member of the Foreign Intelligence Advisory Board.

In 1981, after managing RONALD REAGAN's successful 1980 presidential campaign, Casey was appointed director of the Central Intelligence Agency (CIA) by President Reagan with a mandate to increase support for anticommunist military and political efforts in third world countries. Casey became the first director of the CIA to be treated as a full cabinet member.

Casey gave staff members wide latitude to circumvent a congressional prohibition on giving aid to anti-Marxist forces (Contras) fighting to overthrow the government in Nicaragua. He authorized the covert mining of Nicaraguan harbors and the use of "selective violence" against civilian officials. He was also allegedly deeply embroiled in what became known as the Iran-Contra scandal. This scandal involved the sale of American weapons to

Iran to secure the release of Americans held hostage by Middle Eastern terrorists. Profits from the arms sales were then used to provide military aid to the Nicaraguan rebels in violation of a congressional ban prohibiting U.S. military support for the Contras.

Exactly what Casey did or did not authorize is not known. He resigned as director in February 1987 during the investigation and could not be thoroughly questioned because of the debilitating effects of a brain tumor. He died three months later.

BIBLIOGRAPHY

Pace, Eric, "William Casey, Ex-C.I.A. Head, Is Dead at 74," *New York Times,* May 7, 1987; Persico, Joseph E., *Casey: From the OSS to the CIA,* 1990; Woodward, Bob, *Veil: The Secret Wars of the CIA, 1981–1987,* 1987.

Cass, Lewis

(October 9, 1782–June 17, 1866)
Secretary of State, Secretary of War, Candidate for President

Always a defender of the Union, Lewis Cass ended a distinguished career of service to his country by resigning his cabinet position in protest against a president who refused to take a stand against secession.

Born in Exeter, New Hampshire, Cass was educated at Phillips Exeter Academy. He studied law in Ohio and established a practice there. At age twenty-four he was elected to the Ohio legislature as a Jeffersonian Democrat. Cass served in the army in the War of 1812 (see JAMES MADISON), and from 1813 to 1831 was governor of the Michigan Territory. As governor, he negotiated important treaties with the Indians resulting in large U.S. land acquisitions.

Cass was appointed secretary of war in 1831 by President ANDREW JACKSON and minister to France in 1836. He supported Jackson in the South Carolina nullification crisis (see JOHN CALDWELL CALHOUN) and carried out his Indian removal program. This program, begun with THOMAS JEFFERSON, involved moving all eastern tribes west of the Mississippi. In the case of the Cherokees in Georgia, their removal in 1838 defied a Supreme Court ruling. Cass backed JAMES K. POLK in 1844 and the annexation of Texas. He was elected U.S. senator from Michigan, serving from 1845 to 1848 and from 1849 to 1857. He took an anti-British stand on the Oregon question (see JAMES KNOX POLK), pushed for the occupation of Mexico, and backed both the Compromise of 1850 (see HENRY CLAY) and the Kansas-Nebraska Act of 1854 (see FRANKLIN PIERCE).

Endorsing the position that the question of slavery in the territories should be left to the people who lived there, Cass ran for the presidency in 1848 as the Democratic candidate, but he lost the election to the Whig candidate, ZACHARY TAYLOR, when the Free-Soil party (see MARTIN VAN BUREN) split the Democrats. Cass lost his Senate seat in 1856 but was appointed secretary of state by JAMES BUCHANAN in 1857. He resigned in 1860 to protest Buchanan's refusal to take a strong stand against the Southern states that were threatening to secede from the Union. Cass retired to a private life of writing and lived to see the Union restored.

BIBLIOGRAPHY

Bemis, S. F. (ed.), "Lewis Cass" in *The American Secretaries of State and Their Diplomacy,* vol. 6, 1928; McGlaughlin, Andrew C., *Lewis Cass,* 1899; Woodford, Frank B., *Lewis Cass: Last Jeffersonian,* 1950.

Chafin, Eugene Wilder

(November 1, 1852–November 30, 1920)
Candidate for President

Eugene Wilder Chafin was born in East Troy, Wisconsin. After graduating from the University of Wisconsin in 1875, Chafin established a practice in Waukesha and became active in local politics, serving in a number of community elected offices that included justice of the peace and member of the school board. Always interested in the temperance movement, Chafin abandoned the Republican party in 1881 to run for Waukesha County district attorney as a member of the Prohibition party. This campaign was followed by unsuccessful campaigns for the U.S. House of Representatives in 1882, the state attorney general's office in 1886 and 1900, and the governor's office in 1898. Chafin moved to Chicago in 1901 and became superintendent of the Washingtonian Home for Inebriates. He also launched new campaigns for the U.S. House of Representatives in 1902 and the attorney general's office of Illinois in 1904.

By 1904 he had given up the practice of law to devote all his energy to campaigning for Prohibition. In 1908 and 1912, he was the Prohibition party's candidate for president. After the adoption of the Eighteenth Amendment in 1919, prohibiting the manufacture, sale, and transportation of intoxicating liquors in the United States, Chafin devoted his efforts to the world temperance movement. He traveled in 1919 to Australia and New Zealand to provide support to temperance organizations there.

BIBLIOGRAPHY

Dickie, Samuel, "The Prohibitionists and Their Cause," *Review of Reviews*, September 1908; *Who's Who in America*, 1912–1913.

Chase, Salmon Portland

(January 13, 1808–May 7, 1873)
Secretary of the Treasury, Chief Justice of the Supreme Court, Senator

Salmon Portland Chase was the founder of the national banking system and, as chief justice of the Supreme Court, managed to ensure that President ANDREW JOHNSON received a fair impeachment trial.

Born in Cornish, New Hampshire, Chase graduated from Dartmouth College in 1826 and briefly served as a headmaster of a boys' school in Washington, D.C., before being admitted to the bar in 1829. After settling in Cincinnati in 1830, Chase became deeply involved in antislavery activities. During the 1830s he gained such prominence as a defense attorney for runaway slaves that he was scornfully dubbed an "attorney general for runaway Negroes."

At first a Whig, Chase was active in the Liberty party (see JAMES GILLESPIE BIRNEY) in 1841 and helped organize the Free-Soil party (see MARTIN VAN BUREN) in 1848. Enlisting the support of both Free-Soilers and Democrats in Ohio, he won a six-year term in the Senate in 1849. While in the Senate, Chase continued to subordinate party interests to the central issue of slavery. He opposed extending slavery into the territories, attempted to block the Missouri Compromise of 1850 (see HENRY CLAY and MILLARD FILLMORE), and described the

Kansas-Nebraska Act (see FRANKLIN PIERCE) as a "criminal betrayal of precious rights" because the choice to accept or reject slavery should remain with the residents of the territories.

Chase helped establish the Republican party in Ohio in 1854. The following year he was elected the first Republican governor of Ohio. He was reelected in 1857. Chase was proposed for the presidential nomination in 1856 and 1860, but he failed to secure enough support due to the inability of the Ohio delegation to unite behind his candidacy. He was reelected to the Senate in 1860 but resigned to become ABRAHAM LINCOLN's secretary of the treasury in 1861.

Library of Congress

As secretary of the treasury during the Civil War, Chase developed the national banking system in 1863 and, despite reservations, finally supported the issuing of greenbacks (paper currency) to help finance the war. Chase's righteousness and uncompromising attitude frequently led him to challenge President Lincoln's policy decisions at cabinet meetings. Chase believed that Lincoln was much too lax in attending to administrative matters and that he was responsible for the slow prosecution of the war. His protest letters of resignation were routinely denied by Lincoln; but as the support by Lincoln's critics for nominating Chase as the next Republican presidential candidate in 1864 grew, the increasing tension between the two men finally led Lincoln to accept Chase's resignation in June 1864. Four months later, Lincoln appointed Chase chief justice of the Supreme Court. It was an appointment many felt Lincoln made in order to remove the potential rival candidate from active political life. If that was the case, Lincoln failed. While chief jus-

tice, Chase unsuccessfully campaigned for the presidency, at first as a candidate for the Republican party's nomination, then as a candidate for the Democratic party's nomination in 1868 on a platform of universal amnesty (for Confederate soldiers and political leaders) and universal suffrage (for blacks and whites).

As chief justice, Chase was required to preside over the impeachment hearings of President Andrew Johnson. He disapproved of the trial: "I do not believe . . . in the subversion of the executive and judicial departments by Congress, no matter how patriotic the motive may be." Although he was accused of being a partisan for the president (Chase had briefly served as an informal adviser to President Johnson after Lincoln's assassination), neutral observers agreed that he managed to ensure a fair trial by maintaining an impartial judicial role during the proceedings.

The major decisions authored by Chase while on the Supreme Court resulted from the Civil War and the Reconstruction period. In *Ex parte Milligan* (1866) he ruled that civilians could not be tried in military courts unless civil courts were inoperative or martial law had been declared. His opinion in *Mississippi* v. *Johnson* and *Georgia* v. *Stanton* upheld the power of the president and the cabinet to enforce the Reconstruction Acts, thus avoiding a political confrontation between the Supreme Court and the ruling Radical Republicans in Congress. In *Cummings* v. *Missouri* and *Ex parte Garland* (1867) secession was declared invalid, and attempts to keep former Confederates from holding public office were repudiated. In *Texas* v. *White* (1869) Chase reinforced the view that the Union had never been dissolved. In *Hepburn*

v. *Griswold* (1870) he held as unconstitutional the Legal Tender Act of 1862, which he had administered as secretary of the treasury. When the *Hepburn* decision was overturned the very next year, he wrote a dissenting opinion that reaffirmed his 1870 position. In the *Slaughterhouse Cases* (1873), in which the Fourteenth Amendment was first examined by the Court, Chase dissented from the extremely narrow interpretation of the amendment that the majority adopted.

Chase died in New York City while serving as chief justice.

BIBLIOGRAPHY

Belden, Thomas G., and Marva R. Belden, *So Fell the Angels*, 1956; Donald, David, *Inside Lincoln's Cabinet: The Civil War Diaries of Salmon P. Chase*, 1954; Hart, Albert B., *Salmon P. Chase*, 1899; Schuckers, J. W., *Life and Public Services of Salmon P. Chase*, 1874.

Chase, Samuel

(April 17, 1741–June 19, 1811)
Associate Justice of the Supreme Court, Revolutionary Leader

A prominent political leader during the American Revolution, Samuel Chase was the only Supreme Court justice ever impeached. His narrow escape from conviction established the precedent that Supreme Court justices would not be removed for purely political reasons.

Chase, the son of an Anglican minister, was born in Somerset County, Maryland. He studied law in Annapolis and was admitted to the bar there in 1761. Immediately attracted to politics, he served in the Maryland Assembly from 1764 to 1784. In 1765 he was a principal instigator of the opposition to the Stamp Act (see JOHN ADAMS and SAMUEL ADAMS) and became a member of the Maryland Committee of Correspondence. He was such a success as a patriot crusader in prompting Maryland to support independence that he was denounced by the loyalist mayor of Annapolis as a "busy, restless incendiary, a ringleader of mobs, a foul-mouthed and inflaming son of discord." From 1774 to 1778 he was a member of the First Continental Congress, and in 1776 he was appointed along with BENJAMIN FRANKLIN and Charles Carroll to the futile mission to persuade Canada to join the American Revolution.

Chase served for one year in the Second Continental Congress in 1784, and in 1788 moved to Baltimore and became chief justice of the criminal court. Three years later, amidst considerable controversy over his decision to remain on the criminal court, he was appointed chief judge of the general court of Maryland.

Although he led the opposition in Maryland to the ratification of the U.S. Constitution because of the lack of civil liberties guarantees, he eventually became a Federalist after the Bill of Rights was added. In 1796 President GEORGE WASHINGTON nominated him for the Supreme Court. A series of brilliant and influential decisions in which he defined a direct tax (*Hylton* v. *United States*, 1796), ex post facto laws (*Calder* v. *Bull*, 1798), and the supremacy of national treaties over state laws (*Ware* v. *Hylton*, 1796) demonstrated Chase's legal brilliance and made him the most outstanding justice to serve on the court prior to the appointment of Chief Justice JOHN MARSHALL in 1801.

Despite his record of outstanding accomplishment on the Supreme Court, Congress voted to impeach Chase in 1804. Chase's support of the Federalist-backed Alien and Sedition Acts (see JOHN ADAMS and THOMAS JEFFERSON) and his overly zealous handling of treason and sedition trials involving Jeffersonians caused him to anger the president and his backers in Congress. While spared by only a narrow margin, Chase was acquitted, with the result that his trial discouraged future attempts to impeach justices for purely political reasons. Chase remained on the Supreme Court for the rest of his life.

BIBLIOGRAPHY

Meyers, Gustave, *History of the Supreme Court*, 1919; Sanderson, John, *Biographies of the Signers of the Declaration of Independence*, 1917.

Cheves, Langdon

(September 17, 1776–June 26, 1857)
Speaker of the House, Representative, President of the Second Bank of the United States

Born in Bull Town Fort, South Carolina, Cheves briefly attended a private school at Charleston before studying law and being admitted to the bar in 1797. He began his political career as a member of the state legislature in 1802 and became attorney general in 1809. A year later, he was elected to the U.S. House of Representatives and served as Speaker from 1814 to 1815.

One of the most effective debaters in the House, Cheves played a prominent role in securing the passage of the U.S. declaration of war against Great Britain in 1812 (see JAMES MADISON). After the war ended in 1815, Cheves decided to retire from Congress. He refused the position of secretary of the treasury and returned to his law practice in Charleston. In 1816 he was elected a justice of the court of appeals of South Carolina, a position he left in 1819, when he was elected a director of the Second Bank of the United States (see NICHOLAS BIDDLE) and then chosen to be its president. Cheves restored the bank's disastrous financial condition to solvency through shrewd management. He resigned in 1822 when Nicholas Biddle took control.

Cheves practiced law in Philadelphia and then in Lancaster, Pennsylvania, until he returned to South Carolina in 1829. Though a strong believer in secession, Cheves opposed separate state action. The unpopularity of his views caused him to retire from public life. He acquired a fortune through the development of his plantation near Savannah, Georgia, during the last twenty years of his life.

BIBLIOGRAPHY

O'Neall, John B., *Biographical Sketches of the Bench and Bar of South Carolina*, 1975.

Chisholm, Shirley Anita St. Hill

(November 30, 1924–   )
Representative

Shirley Anita St. Hill was born in Brooklyn, New York. She graduated from Brooklyn College and received a master's degree in elementary education at Columbia University. After teaching in the New York public school system, she became a director of daycare centers and a recognized authority on early childhood education. She married Conrad Q. Chisholm in 1949 and became increasingly active in local political affairs.

In 1964 Shirley Chisholm made a successful bid to win election to the state legislature, where she served for four years. In 1968 she became the first black woman ever elected to the U.S. House of Representatives. Shortly after being sworn into office in January 1969 she observed: "I am an historical person at this point and I'm very much aware of it."

A native of the poor, predominantly black and Hispanic section of New York she represented, Chisholm had an unusually weak connection to the Democratic party organization in her area and a very strong bond with her constituents. She had promised that, if elected, she would not be a quiet freshman in Congress, and she kept her word. When she was appointed to the forestry and rural villages

Copyright Washington Post;
Reprinted by permission of the D.C. Public Library

subcommittee of the Agriculture Committee, she protested to the Democratic House leaders and the press: "Apparently," she commented, "all they know here in Washington about Brooklyn is that a tree grew there." Her point was that only nine blacks were serving in Congress at that time, and they could best serve the nation as members of committees relevant to inner city issues. Her committee assignment was changed, but to the Veterans Affairs Committee rather than to the one she wanted—Education and Labor. She served in Congress until she retired in 1982.

In 1972 she became the first black woman ever to run for a major political party's presidential nomination by making a symbolic bid to win the Democratic party's nomination. When her name was placed before the convention, she garnered 10 percent of the delegate votes.

BIBLIOGRAPHY

Brownmiller, Susan, "This Is Fighting Shirley Chisholm," *New York Times Magazine*, April 13, 1969; Chisholm, Shirley, *Unbought and Unbossed*, 1970, and *The Good Fight*, 1973; *Ebony*, February 1969.

Clark, James Beauchamp

(March 7, 1850–March 2, 1921)
Speaker of the House, Representative

James Beauchamp ("Champ") Clark was born near Lawrenceburg, Kentucky. He graduated from Bethany College in West Virginia in 1873 and settled in Bowling Green, Missouri. Admitted to the Missouri bar in 1875, he served as a Democrat in the Missouri legislature from 1889 to 1891 before winning election to the U.S. House of Representatives in 1892. Although defeated for reelection in 1894, he won on his third try in 1896 and was elected every two years thereafter until 1920.

A talented speaker and debater, Clark was elected leader of the Democrats in the House in 1907. His principal accomplishment in the House involved forging the alliance between disenchanted Republicans and Democrats that ended the reign of the domineering and extremely powerful JOSEPH G. CANNON as Speaker. Clark was elected Speaker himself in 1911 and served in that office until 1919.

Clark was a leading candidate for the Democratic nomination for president in 1912. However, after obtaining the most votes on the first ballot at the national convention, he was unable to secure enough to win and finally had to accept defeat when WILLIAM JENNINGS BRYAN decided to support WOODROW WILSON's candidacy.

As Speaker of the House, Clark loyally supported Wilson's New Freedom legislative goals, but he stubbornly opposed the establishment of the military draft even after the United States entered World War I. Largely because of the reforms he had helped to pass to curtail the power of Speaker, his ability to control events in the House was limited. When the Republicans regained control of the House in 1918, Clark again became the minority Democratic party leader. He was not reelected in 1920 and died before the end of his term in Washington, D.C.

BIBLIOGRAPHY

Clark, Champ, *My Quarter Century of American Politics*, 1920.

Clay, Henry

(April 12, 1777–June 29, 1852)
Secretary of State, Candidate for President, Speaker of the House, Senator, Representative

More than anything else, Henry Clay wanted to be president of the United States, an office he ran for unsuccessfully three times. Though he never became president, Clay was better loved and sometimes more powerful during his thirty years in Congress than some of the men who actually held that office.

Born in Hanover County, Virginia, in 1777, Clay was admitted to the bar in 1797. He moved to Lexington, Kentucky, the next year and established his own practice. Clay specialized in criminal law and soon had a substantial reputation because, according to local legend, he never lost a client to the hangman.

In 1803 Clay, a Jeffersonian Republican, was elected to the Kentucky legislature, where he served until 1806. He received his first taste of national politics when he was twice appointed to complete Senate terms, from 1806 to 1807 and from 1810 to 1811. Preferring to be more directly connected to his constituents, Clay decided in 1810 to leave the Senate and run for the House of Representatives. After winning election to Congress, he became Speaker of the House in 1811 and the leader of the group of young men known as war hawks because they favored war with England in order to gain new territory for the United States.

Following the War of 1812, President JAMES MADISON asked Clay to join the other American peace negotiators scheduled to begin bargaining with England. Clay agreed and helped bring the negotia-

Library of Congress

tions to a successful conclusion at the end of 1814. Upon his return home, Clay was reelected to Congress in 1815, and then again to the Speaker's office, a position he held until he decided to step down in 1820 after brilliantly handling the passage of the Missouri Compromise. This 1820 measure admitted Maine to the Union as a free state and Missouri as a slave state, and excluded slavery from the Louisiana Purchase north of 36°30'.

Clay desperately wanted to be appointed secretary of state by President JAMES MONROE in 1817. At that time, whoever held the office was considered the president's designated successor. When JOHN QUINCY ADAMS received the position instead, Clay vengefully refused to allow the swearing in ceremony to take place in the House.

A westerner, Clay was interested in developing his section of the country in particular, but he also wanted to strengthen American business in general. His American System, which consisted of building roads and canals for transportation, rechartering the Bank of the United States to provide credit, and raising the tariff for the protection of American in-

dustries, was based on a broad interpretation of the federal government's constitutional powers. The national bank (see NICHOLAS BIDDLE) was rechartered and a protective tariff was passed in 1816, but Clay's internal improvements program (see JOHN CALDWELL CALHOUN) was never passed as a whole because many legislators doubted that the national government had the right to appropriate money for roads, canals, and land development.

Clay's frustrated ambition to be president made him a perennial candidate. After finishing last in a four-man field in 1824, he threw his support as Speaker of the House to John Quincy Adams. He was subsequently appointed secretary of state in what ANDREW JACKSON's supporter's labeled a "corrupt bargain." The one major diplomatic initiative Clay attempted while secretary of state—the participation of the United States in a Pan-American conference—was stymied by political opposition in Congress.

Adams was defeated by Jackson in 1828, and Clay secured a seat in the Senate in 1831. The next year he ran for president as an anti-Jackson National Republican but was badly beaten. He sought the Whig party nomination in 1840, 1844, and 1848, managing to win it in 1844 only to be beaten in the general election by JAMES K. POLK. In 1849, after a year's retirement in Kentucky, he saw the clouds of disunion forming again and returned to the Senate, where he sponsored the most important legislation of his career, the Compromise of 1850 (see MILLARD FILLMORE).

The question of whether slavery would be allowed in the territory acquired as a result of the Mexican War (see JAMES KNOX POLK) threatened to tear the nation apart in 1850. The Northern demand to exclude slavery fueled rapidly building sentiment for secession in the South. The essence of the crisis to Clay was not the extension or restriction of slavery, but the preservation of the Union. Helping to craft and guide a bundle of bills that became known as the Compromise of 1850 through Congress was Clay's final political triumph. As a result of the compromise, California was admitted as a free state, a new strong fugitive slave law (see MILLARD FILLMORE) was enacted, the slave trade was abolished in the District of Columbia but slavery would still be protected there, and the settlers themselves would decide through the ballot box (popular sovereignty) whether slavery would be allowed in the New Mexico and Utah territories.

Clay died two years after enactment of the Compromise of 1850, unaware that his efforts to prevent the secession of the South had only delayed the "irrepressible conflict" for ten years.

BIBLIOGRAPHY

Eaton, Clement, *Henry Clay and the Art of American Politics*, 1962; Mayo, Bernard, *Henry Clay*, 1937; Poage, George R., *Henry Clay and the Whig Party*, 1965; Van Deusen, Glyndon G., *The Life of Henry Clay*, 1979.

Clayton, John Middleton

(July 24, 1796–November 9, 1856)
Secretary of State, Senator

Although John Middleton Clayton served over a quarter of a century in a variety of state and national government elective and appointive offices, he is remembered for negotiating the controversial Clayton-Bulwer Treaty of 1850.

Born in Dagsborough, Delaware, Clayton graduated from Yale College in 1815 and was admitted to the Delaware bar four years later. He established a practice in Dover and became noted for his cross-examination skill.

His political activities in the Whig party were rewarded in 1828 when he was chosen to serve in the Senate. His devotion to protecting the Union led him to support ANDREW JACKSON during the nullification controversy (see JOHN CALDWELL CALHOUN), but he opposed Jackson's hostility to the rechartering of the Bank of the United States (see NICHOLAS BIDDLE) and worked with HENRY CLAY for lower tariff rates. Although reelected to the Senate in 1834, he resigned two years later because of family obligations. From 1837 to 1839 he served as chief justice of Delaware, but he retired from politics to concentrate on developing his scientific farm near New Castle.

Reelected to the Senate in 1845, Clayton reluctantly supported the Mexican War (see JAMES KNOX POLK). In the presidential election of 1848 he gave his support to ZACHARY TAYLOR and was rewarded with the position of secretary of state, which he held until Taylor's death in 1850. As secretary of state, he negotiated the Clayton-Bulwer Treaty of 1850, which provided for joint control of any canal across Central America and, through compromise, managed to check British expansion in Central America while improving relations between the two nations.

Returning to the Senate in 1852, Clayton died in office. In addition to his political career, he won considerable fame for his work as a scientific agriculturist.

BIBLIOGRAPHY

Bemis, Samuel F., *American Secretaries of State and Their Diplomacy,* vol. 6, 1928.

Cleveland, Stephen Grover

(March 18, 1837–June 24, 1908)
President

Library of Congress

Grover Cleveland is remembered for being the only president who served two terms nonconsecutively. The fifth child of a Presbyterian clergyman, Cleveland was born at the parsonage in Caldwell, New Jersey. Four years later, the family moved to Fayetteville, New York, and then to Clinton in 1850, where Cleveland's father died in 1853. Cleveland worked in the New York Institution for the Blind, and through the financial help of an uncle he studied law. He was admitted to the bar in 1859 and in 1863 became an assistant district attorney of Erie County. The financial burden of needing to take care of his mother and sister prevented him—to his political disadvantage—from enlisting in the army during the Civil War. He paid a substitute to go in his place, a legitimate practice at the time. His willingness to stay at home enabled two brothers to serve.

A forty-four-year-old bachelor with a modest law practice, Cleveland was selected by the Democratic party in 1881 to be its reform candidate for mayor of Buffalo. He did such a thorough job of cleaning out corruption in Buffalo that the party chose him to be its reform candidate for governor in 1882. His refusal to accept the spoils system or to support legislation favored by the party leaders and Tammany Hall (see WILLIAM MARCY TWEED) earned him powerful enemies as well as the dismay of some of his supporters, but it endeared him to the voters.

When the scandal-tainted JAMES G. BLAINE was nominated by the Republicans in 1884, the Democrats saw in Cleveland a candidate who, because of his record for honesty, could win the general election by drawing dismayed Republican votes. During the campaign the Republicans attacked Cleveland for not serving in the Civil War and for fathering an illegitimate child. When Cleveland's supporters asked how they should respond to the charge that he had had a child out of wedlock, he replied, "Tell the truth." He had fathered an illegitimate child and, although he had refused to marry the woman, had faithfully contributed to the child's financial support. He was elected in a close race, and thus, at the age of forty-eight, became the first Democrat to be elected president after the Civil War. Cleveland was also the first president to be married in the White House, in 1886.

As the first Democratic president in twenty-four years, Cleveland attempted to chart a middle course concerning patronage appointments, but all his effort resulted in was enraging party regulars and disappointing civil service reformers. Cleveland accomplished little during his first two years in office. This was partly because he didn't believe the president should do much and partly because the Republicans retained control of the Senate.

In 1887 he signed the Interstate Commerce Act into law and risked considerable political popularity by resisting pension abuse. A generous Congress with a surplus in the treasury and the desire to win votes had made it extremely profitable to find an excuse to earn a military pension. Fraudulent claims were frequently being granted through the passage of private pension bills. In 1886 Cleveland started vetoing pension bills he felt were without merit, and in 1887 he vetoed a general pension bill that allowed any veteran who had served ninety days and was in need to receive financial benefits. Supporters of the bill branded Cleveland an enemy of old soldiers.

Later in the year Cleveland made a damaging political mistake. He decided to return Confederate battle flags that were in the possession of the War Department to their states of origin. The same act twenty years later would be applauded, but in 1887 it was still too soon for someone who had not fought in the war to make such a symbolic gesture of forgiveness to the South.

The most damaging political decision Cleveland made was to push for a reduction in tariff rates in order to eliminate the budget surpluses. He was convinced that surplus revenue invited extravagant government spending. He was determined to end "unnecessary taxation." The Republicans responded by advocating even higher rates in the name of protectionism. Their platform in the presidential campaign of 1888 stressed the need for a high tariff to protect "the general business, the labor, the farming interests of the country."

Cleveland won the popular vote but lost the election to BENJAMIN HARRISON by 233 electoral votes to 168. In the controversial Electoral College system provided by the Constitution for a presidential election, a state is apportioned as many electoral votes as it has senators and representatives in Congress. The winner of the popular vote in a state is awarded all of that state's electoral votes, and the winner of the majority of the electoral votes in the country becomes president. It can happen that by carrying a particular combination of states, a candidate will end up with enough electoral votes to win the election, even though an opposing candidate may have more popular votes. Thus it happened that Cleveland, who garnered 90,000 more popular votes than Harrison, nevertheless lost the election of 1888. (The popular vote winner also failed to win the elections of 1824 and 1876.)

Cleveland returned to New York in 1889 to resume the practice of law. The high-tariff policy led to growing discontent and defeat for the Republican party at the polls in 1890. Cleveland was renominated on the first ballot of the 1892 Democratic convention. He went on to defeat Benjamin Harrison by more than 370,000 popular votes and 277 electoral votes to 145.

Cleveland's second term was overwhelmed by the effects of a deep financial depression. One immediate problem stemmed from the flow of gold from the Treasury. Under the Sherman Silver Purchase Act of 1890, treasury notes issued to buy silver could be redeemed for gold. Since gold dollars were more valuable than silver dollars, people were turning in their silver treasury notes for gold dollars. By law the Treasury had to keep reissuing the notes even though they were being turned in for gold. Cleveland called a special session of Congress and managed, after both parties split on the issue, to have the act repealed.

The depression worsened, however, and Cleveland seemed powerless to help the common man. He opposed the cheap money provided by the silver purchase act and failed to bring tax relief. In 1894 he authorized the use of federal troops in Chicago, over the objections of the governor of Illinois, to restore order when violence occurred during the Pullman strike (see EUGENE VICTOR DEBS). In the congressional elections of 1894, the Republicans regained control of the House and Senate in a massive public display of anger and disappointment.

When the repeal of the Sherman Silver Purchase Act did not provide sufficient relief in time to protect the nation's gold supply, Cleveland asked John Pierpont Morgan for help. Morgan organized a group of bankers who sold $65 million in U.S. bonds in Europe. Morgan's success solved the nation's problem, but the fortune he earned only served as further evidence to millions of Americans that Cleveland had sold out to the wealthy.

Cleveland's foreign policy actions were just as unpopular as his domestic policies. He refused to support the annexation of Hawaii and, despite tremendous popular opinion to do so and the passage of resolutions by both the House and the Senate, to recognize the revolutionary government of Cuba.

Cleveland had lost any hope of renomination long before the Democratic convention in 1896 (see WILLIAM JENNINGS BRYAN), but the lengths to which his fellow Democrats went to denounce him and his support for the gold standard were exceptional. He retired to Princeton, New Jersey, where he wrote articles and gradually regained the grudging admiration of the public for his refusal to sacrifice his principles to popular opinion. In 1905 he undertook the difficult task of reorganizing the scandal-plagued Equitable Life Assurance Society. He was briefly mentioned as a possible candidate for nomination to a third term in 1904, but he never seriously considered running again before his death at age seventy-one in 1908.

BIBLIOGRAPHY

Merrill, Horace, *Bourbon Leader*, 1957; Nevins, Allan, *Grover Cleveland: A Study in Courage*, 1932; Tugwell, Rexford G., *Grover Cleveland*, 1968.

Clifford, Clark McAdams

(December 25, 1906–   )
Secretary of Defense

After more than two decades of service as a trusted adviser to three Democratic presidents, Clark Clifford concluded his public service career by serving as secretary of defense during the last year of the administration of President LYNDON B. JOHNSON.

Clifford was born in Fort Scott, Kansas, and grew up in St. Louis, Missouri. After earning his law degree from Washington University in St. Louis in 1928, Clifford was admitted to the Missouri bar and embarked upon a successful career specializing in corporation and labor law.

Commissioned a lieutenant in the U.S. Naval Reserve in 1944, Clifford served as assistant to President HARRY S TRUMAN's naval aide, James K. Vardaman. In January 1946 he succeeded Vardaman and undertook a number of special research projects for the president, one of which included working on the establishment of the National Intelligence Authority (the forerunner of the Central Intelligence Agency). At the end of his military service in June 1946, Clifford became special counsel to the president and quickly became one of Truman's most intimate advisers, especially in foreign affairs. He returned to private law practice in 1950.

In 1960 President-elect JOHN F. KENNEDY appointed Clifford to serve as his liaison during the transition of the control of the government from President DWIGHT EISENHOWER. In May 1961 Clifford joined Kennedy's Foreign Intelligence Advisory Board and oversaw the activities of the Central Intelligence Agency. After Kennedy's assassination, Clifford served President Lyndon Johnson in a number of capacities, culminating in his appointment as secretary of defense in 1968.

Because he had advised against the temporary halt to U.S. bombing raids on North Vietnam in 1966 (see LYNDON BAINES JOHNSON and RICHARD MILHOUS NIXON), Clifford was widely viewed as a "hawk" (advocate of a military solution). However, as secretary of defense, he is credited with convincing President Johnson to begin peace negotiations with North Vietnam. He also publicly advocated beginning a gradual process of American disengagement from the war. Clifford returned to his law practice in January 1969.

BIBLIOGRAPHY

National Observer, January 22, 1968, p. 2 and March 11, 1968, p. 1; *New York Times Magazine*, January 28, 1968, p. 21.

Clinton, DeWitt

(March 2, 1769–February 11, 1828)
Candidate for President, Senator

DeWitt Clinton was chiefly responsible for the building of the Erie Canal, which was completed in 1825. It was one of the most important developments of the era.

Clinton was born in Little Britain, New York, into an affluent, politically influential family. After graduating from Columbia College and being admitted to the bar, Clinton, with the help of the political influence of his uncle, GEORGE CLINTON, the former governor of New York, was elected to the state assembly in 1797. The following year he won a four-year term in the state senate.

After he was named in 1801 as one of the four state senators who sat on the governor's appointments council, Clinton managed to overcome the new governor's opposition and gain the right to make appointments himself. He used his power to replace as many Federalists as possible with fellow Republicans and is often blamed for establishing the spoils system in American politics. Clinton was appointed to the U.S. Senate in 1802 but left in 1803 to become mayor of New York City, a position he held until 1815, with the exception of two annual terms in 1807–1808 and 1810–1811. While mayor he was also a state senator (1806–1811) and lieutenant governor (1811–1813). During his administration he strongly supported public education and health facilities and took special interest in developing the shipping trade.

An antiwar faction of the Republicans who were opposed to JAMES MADISON's decision to go to war with Great Britain nominated Clinton for the presidency in 1812. The Federalists also gave Clinton their support. Since Clinton had accomplished this by promising each group that he would pursue its aims, Madison lost no time in pointing out his rival's remarkable duplicity. Clinton received 89 electoral votes to Madison's 128. Dismayed by his courting of Federalist votes, the Republican party did not renominate Clinton for lieutenant governor after the presidential election, and he was ousted from the mayor's office in 1815.

In 1816 the state legislature approved the canal system Clinton had long advocated, and work on the Erie Canal began. The following year Clinton was elected governor. After serving two terms as governor he shrewdly decided not to try for a third. He continued to hold the post of canal commissioner until his political opponents removed him from office in 1824. Seizing upon the public anger his ouster as canal commissioner aroused, Clinton managed to win another two terms as governor. Thus, appropriately enough, he presided over the opening of his beloved Erie and Champlain canals in 1825 before his sudden death in 1828.

BIBLIOGRAPHY

Bobbe, Dorothie, *DeWitt Clinton*, 1933; Remwick, James, *Life of DeWitt Clinton*, 1842.

Clinton, George

(July 26, 1739–April 20, 1812)
Vice President, Revolutionary Leader

Affectionately described as the father of his state because of his years of service as New York's governor, George Clinton was born in Little Britain, New York. After practicing law with little distinction, Clinton began his political career in 1768 by winning election to the New York Provincial Assembly. In the assembly he became the rival of Philip Schuyler to be the leader of the small but growing number of supporters of revolution.

In 1775 Clinton was elected a delegate to the Second Continental Congress, but he did not sign the Declaration of Independence because he left Congress to accept a commission as a brigadier general of the militia.

After a military career, which he summed up as dismal due to the loss of several important engagements, Clinton returned to New York politics. In July 1777 he became the new state's first governor. During his six successive terms, Clinton took advantage of the immense patronage of his office to build a powerful political organization.

Although a failure as military leader while in the army, Clinton was very successful as a wartime governor. He adroitly managed the state's precarious finances, achieved considerable success in dealing with the hostile Indians in western New York, and gained tremendous popularity by dealing harshly with the Loyalists in New York.

Believing that because of its geographical location and tremendous commercial power New York stood to lose much more than it would gain by joining a strong central government, Clinton opposed ratification of the Constitution. Writing under the name Cato, he published seven letters arguing against ratification. Nevertheless, ALEXANDER HAMILTON and other Federalists managed to secure New York's support in spite of Clinton's powerful opposition.

A narrow election victory in 1789 convinced Clinton of the need to attract new support. After securing the help of AARON BURR's New York City organization by appointing him to the Senate in 1791, Clinton still barely managed to win reelection in 1792 and decided not to seek office in 1795.

Clinton did not hold office again until the Republicans wrested control of the state from the Federalists in 1800. He was chosen to be THOMAS JEFFERSON's running mate in 1804 because of the importance of New York to the Republican national ticket's victory.

While vice president, Clinton began building support for a run for the presidency on his own. As the election of 1808 approached, he unsuccessfully attempted to form a coalition of the Federalist party with dissatisfied New York and Pennsylvania Democratic-Republicans. Although he was convinced that the election of fellow Republican JAMES MADISON would "make our situation still worse if possible," after his own presidential bid failed, Clinton accepted renomination to the vice presidency. Ironically, the Republican party leaders had only offered Clinton the position because they did not wish to lose support in New York and had expected him to decline.

Clinton often gave President Madison reason to regret the vice president he inherited from Jefferson. Clinton's last important political act occurred in 1811 when he broke a Senate tie by voting against the rechartering of the Bank of the United States (see NICHOLAS BIDDLE), thereby defeating one of Madison's most important legislative goals.

In April 1812, after a long period of poor health, Clinton became the first vice president to die in office.

BIBLIOGRAPHY

Spaulding, Ernest, *His Excellency George Clinton, Critic of the Constitution*, 1938; Hastings, Hugh, and J. A. Holden (eds.), *Public Papers of George Clinton*, 10 vols., 1899–1914.

Cobb, Howell

(September 7, 1815–October 9, 1868)
Secretary of the Treasury, Speaker of the House, Representative

Georgia political leader Howell Cobb fought to preserve the Union in the volatile pre–Civil War period, but he is remembered chiefly for his abrupt decision to support secession after the election of ABRAHAM LINCOLN.

Cobb was born into a wealthy family in Jefferson County, Georgia. He graduated from the University of Georgia in 1834 and was admitted to the bar in 1836. One year later, he became solicitor general of the western judicial circuit of Georgia, an area composed primarily of pro-Union, small farmers. In 1842 he won election to the U.S. House of Representatives from this same region.

In Congress Cobb supported the annexation of Texas (see JAMES KNOX POLK) and the Mexican War (see POLK). He was elected floor leader of the Democrats in 1848 and then, from 1849 to 1851, served as Speaker of the House.

Cobb played a major role in briefly uniting the wing of the Georgia Democratic party that he led, called the Union Democrats, and the Whig party in Georgia into the Constitutional Union party. This enabled him to secure Georgia's support for the passage of the Compromise of 1850 (see HENRY CLAY and MILLARD FILLMORE) and to be elected governor, a position he occupied from 1851 to 1853. Although unable to reunite the Georgia Democratic party in 1854, he was reelected to Congress in 1855. Two years later, President JAMES BUCHANAN appointed him secretary of the treasury.

Even though he had spent his political career supporting compromise efforts to preserve the Union, after Abraham Lincoln's election in 1860 Cobb resigned from the cabinet. Believing Republican victories meant the doom of the South within the Union, Cobb, like many other former Unionists, was jolted into advocating immediate secession for the South. He chaired the meeting in Montgomery, Alabama, in 1861 that organized the Confederacy. During the Civil War Cobb served in the Confederate army first as a brigadier general, later as a major general, but saw little combat.

BIBLIOGRAPHY

Hendrick, B. J., *Statesman of the Lost Cause*, 1939; Johnson, Zachary T., *Political Policies of Howell Cobb*, 1929; Montgomery, Horacek, *Howell Cobb's Confederate Career*, 1959.

Colby, Bainbridge

(December 22, 1869–April 11, 1950)
Secretary of State

Bainbridge Colby was born in St. Louis, Missouri. He graduated from Williams College in 1890. Two years later, after earning his law degree from New York Law School and being admitted to the state bar, he became a successful New York attorney. In 1901, as a Republican, he was elected to one term in the New York Assembly. Ten years later, Colby abandoned the Republican party, joined the Progressive party (see THEODORE ROOSEVELT), and supported Theodore Roosevelt's unsuccessful presidential reelection bid. In 1914 and 1916 Colby was an unsuccessful Progressive party candidate for the Senate. In the presidential campaign of 1916, he actively supported WOODROW WILSON's bid for reelection. During World War I Colby was commissioner of the U.S. Shipping Board and a member of the Emergency Fleet Corporation.

In March 1920 President Wilson appointed Colby secretary of state. Colby developed a close relationship with the partially paralyzed president and served as secretary of state until the end of the Wilson administration the following March. Although secretary of state for only a year, he improved relations with Latin America and capably handled issues relating to League of Nations (see WOODROW WILSON) mandates. (Following World War I, member nations of the league [the mandatories], under the supervision of the league, took over the governing of former German and Turkish colonies and territories [the mandates] until such time as they were considered able to govern themselves.) Colby also participated in the difficult task of developing an official U.S. policy toward the newly established Soviet Union and its Communist rulers.

At the end of his term in March 1921, Colby briefly established a law partnership with the still seriously ill Wilson. He then returned to New York City to practice law and write.

BIBLIOGRAPHY

Colby, Bainbridge, *Papers Relating to the Foreign Relations of the U.S., 1920, 1921,* 1935–1936, and *The Close of Woodrow Wilson's Administration and the Final Years,* 1930; Smith, Daniel M., "Bainbridge Colby and the Good Neighbor Policy, 1920–1921," *Mississippi Valley Historical Review,* June 1963, and *Aftermath of War: Bainbridge Colby and Wilsonian Diplomacy, 1920–1921,* 1970.

Colfax, Schuyler

(March 23, 1823–January 13, 1885)
Vice President, Speaker of the House, Representative

Born in New York City in 1823, Schuyler Colfax moved to Indiana in 1836 where he began his career as an auditor, clerk, and newspaper correspondent. In 1845 he bought an interest in a South Bend newspaper, became its editor, and turned it into the leading Whig newspaper in northern Indiana.

Colfax's direct involvement in political activities began in 1844, when he made campaign speeches for HENRY CLAY. Defeated as a Whig candidate for Congress in 1851, he joined the Republican party. After playing an important role in organizing the new party in Indiana, he won the first of seven consecutive terms in Congress in 1855 as a Republican.

Colfax was recommended by supporters for the cabinet-level position of postmaster general in 1861. ABRAHAM LINCOLN declined to make the appointment on the grounds that he "[is] a young man, is already in position, is running a brilliant career, and is sure of a bright future in any event."

His position as Speaker from 1863 to 1869 and his strong support for political rights of blacks in the South gave Colfax a considerable advantage over other vice presidential hopefuls at the Republican convention in 1868, and he duly served as vice president under President ULYSSES S. GRANT. Six months before the end of his term as vice president, Colfax was implicated in the Crédit Mobilier affair. The Crédit Mobilier construction company helped to build the Union Pacific Railroad. A few railroad stockholders awarded large fraudulent contracts to the construction company, taking for themselves the money, part of which came from government subsidies. To avoid congressional investigation, they bought off Colfax and other key politicians with stock in Crédit Mobilier, but the scandal came to light. Colfax was allowed to finish his term, as the investigators reasoned the wrongdoing had occurred before Colfax became vice president, but he was ruined politically and retired in 1873 in disrepute.

BIBLIOGRAPHY

Smith, Willard H., *Schuyler Colfax*, 1952.

Conkling, Roscoe

(October 30, 1829–April 18, 1888)
Senator, Representative

Roscoe Conkling was the undisputed leader of the Republican party in New York while ULYSSES S. GRANT was president. After Grant retired from office and Conkling lost the right to dispense all federal patronage positions in New York, his political power rapidly declined.

Born in Albany, New York, Conkling briefly attended the Mount Washington Collegiate Institute in New York City before being admitted to the bar in 1850. He was immediately appointed district attorney of Albany. Eight years later, he became mayor of Utica and then served in Congress from 1859 until 1867, with the exception of a term from 1863 to 1865.

In Congress Conkling became a member of the radical wing of the Republican party. The popularity of his support in New York for a thorough Reconstruction policy toward the South and the impeachment of President ANDREW JOHNSON enabled Conkling to gain control of the state's Republican party and win election to the U.S. Senate in 1867. He was reelected to the Senate in 1873 and 1879.

Conkling's national political ambitions brought him into increasing conflict with JAMES G. BLAINE, who also sought control of the national Republican party. While Ulysses S. Grant was president, Conkling's power base in New York was secure. However, after Grant retired from office in 1877, Conkling began a desperate, unsuccessful campaign to persuade newly elected president RUTHERFORD B. HAYES to continue to allow him to dispense all federal appointments in New York.

Furious at Hayes for supporting civil service reform (see CHESTER ALAN ARTHUR and RUTHERFORD BIRCHARD HAYES) and for launching an investigation of corruption at New York's customhouse, Conkling became the leader of the elements within the Republican party known as Stalwarts. (Blaine became the leader of the faction known as Half-breeds; see HAYES.) In addition to opposing civil service reform because of its debilitating effects on patronage, Stalwarts supported the nomination of Ulysses S. Grant for a third term as president in 1880 and wanted to continue providing federal protection of the voting rights of the newly enfranchised—largely pro-Republican—former slaves in the South.

When JAMES A. GARFIELD won the nomination and the presidency instead, and also refused to allow Conkling the patronage powers he sought, Conkling resigned from the Senate in 1881 in protest. He mistakenly assumed that his position would be vindicated with his reelection by the New York legislature. The legislature, however, chose someone else, and Conkling retired from politics.

BIBLIOGRAPHY

Chidsey, D. B., *The Gentleman from New York: A Life of Roscoe Conkling*, 1935; Conkling, A. R., *Life and Letters of Roscoe Conkling*, 1889; Jordan, David M., *Roscoe Conkling of New York*, 1971.

Coolidge, Calvin

(July 4, 1872–January 5, 1933)
President, Vice President

Following the scandalous and corrupt administration of WARREN HARDING, taciturn, frugal, and honest Calvin Coolidge seemed the perfect antidote when he succeeded to the presidency in 1923 after Harding's sudden death in office. His determination to foster old-time morality, big business, and isolationism at a time of material prosperity took the form of doing nothing, a talent that "suits the mood and certain needs of the country . . . suits all the businesses which want to be left alone . . . and suits all those who have become convinced that government in this country has become dangerously complicated and top-heavy," wrote the journalist Walter Lippman in 1926.

Three presidents—THOMAS JEFFERSON, JOHN ADAMS, and JAMES MONROE—died on July 4; but only one, Calvin Coolidge, was born on the

Library of Congress

Fourth of July. His father ran the general store in Plymouth Notch, Vermont. Coolidge spent his childhood there, attended the Black River Academy in nearby Ludlow, Vermont, and then graduated from Amherst College in western Massachusetts in 1895. After being admitted to the bar and marrying in 1905, he practiced law in nearby Northampton, Massachusetts.

Although he longed "to keep store like my father had done," the lure of politics proved irresistible. He began his political career in 1898 as an unsalaried member of the Northampton city council. In 1906 he was elected as a Republican to the Massachusetts House of Representatives and then elected to two terms as mayor of Northampton before winning a seat in the state senate in 1911. He was elected president of the senate in 1913.

Coolidge's conservative antigovernment brand of politics can be summed up in his observation: "It is more important to kill bad bills than to pass good ones." A shy, quiet man, Coolidge avoided the public limelight until he was elected lieutenant governor of Massachusetts in 1915. Then, his efforts to develop a statewide following were so successful that he was reelected in 1916 and 1917. He was elected governor in 1918. As governor, Coolidge broke into the national spotlight in 1919 when he refused to reinstate striking Boston police officers and uttered the oft-quoted statement, "There is no right to strike against the public safety by anybody, anywhere, any time."

After the Boston police strike, Coolidge thought his political career was over. Instead, an enthusiastic press boosted him to reelection and then into the 1920 presidential race as the Republican party's vice presidential nominee. When President Harding died in 1923, Coolidge became the nation's thirtieth president, sworn in—his hand on the family Bible—by his father, who was a notary public. He inherited the oil lease (Teapot Dome) scandals from Harding, but managed to avoid being tainted with corruption himself.

In the 1924 presidential campaign Coolidge said and did very little. Incapable of small talk, "Silent Cal" Coolidge was known for his brevity. Once, when asked why he said so little in public, he replied, "I never felt sorry about something I didn't say." The rural, small-town, back-to-old-fashioned-values Coolidge personified a longing among many Americans for a simpler life after a period of extravagance and waste. He won the election with an electoral vote of 379 to Democrat JOHN W. DAVIS's 139 and Progressive party candidate ROBERT M. LA FOLLETTE's 13.

Content to be an administrator and not a leader, Coolidge made few recommendations to Congress. The fact that those he did make were usually ignored did not bother Coolidge.

That was the way he thought it should be. "If the federal government should go out of existence," he said, "the common run of the people would not detect the difference for a considerable length of time." According to Coolidge, it was profitable businesses that made the whole nation happy and prosperous. "The man who builds a factory builds a temple there." Regulatory agencies, like the Federal Trade Commission and the Federal Reserve Board, were put in the charge of men who would help the businesses. Coolidge's laissez-faire attitude extended to the farmers, who were suffering from low prices. "Farmers have never made money. I don't believe we can do much about it," he explained, as he vetoed the McNary-Haugen Bill in 1927 and again in 1928, which would have authorized the government to buy and store crop surpluses.

Coolidge left the management of foreign policy mainly to his cabinet officials and followed a policy of noninvolvement with most international cooperative plans. He refused to consider refinancing European World War I loans and to reduce import tariffs on foreign goods. He did, however, support passage of the Kellogg-Briand Pact, an international peace plan outlawing war with no commitment to enforcement.

The nation was stunned when the popular president, never able to recover fully from the tragic death of his son, decided in 1928 not to seek reelection with the simple statement, "I do not choose to run." The country was prosperous, and people associated the good times with Coolidge. During the profligate Jazz Age of the 1920s, he championed the traditional values of diligence and thrift. He reduced taxes and managed to reduce the $20 billion national debt by a billion dollars a year, but he failed to control the speculation in business that would lead to the great stock market crash (see HERBERT HOOVER) only months after he left office.

The secret of his political success, Coolidge once explained, was in "avoiding the big problems." It was a phrase many critics would recall to sum up what was wrong with his administration after the United States had plunged into the Great Depression.

After leaving the White House, Coolidge retired to a modest house in Northampton to write until his death from a heart attack four years later. Half a century later, his antigovernment sentiments would make him the hero of another popular Republican president, RONALD REAGAN.

BIBLIOGRAPHY

Coolidge, Calvin, *The Autobiography of Calvin Coolidge,* 1989; Fuess, Claude M., *Calvin Coolidge: The Man From Vermont,* 1965; McCoy, Donald R., *Calvin Coolidge: The Quiet President,* 1988; White, William A., *A Puritan in Babylon: Calvin Coolidge,* 1939.

Cox, James Middleton

(March 31, 1870–July 15, 1957)
Candidate for President, Representative

James Middleton Cox was born in Jacksonburg, Ohio. Unable to afford college, he briefly taught school before becoming a reporter. As a young, self-educated reporter, Cox found so many things astounding that he was called Astounding Cox. A short, stocky, energetic man, Cox lived up to his nickname. He eventually became the editor and then the publisher of several Ohio newspapers worth millions of dollars.

In 1908 he was elected to the first of two terms in Congress as a Democrat, and in 1912 he won the Ohio governor's office. As governor, Cox championed the rights of labor and reform. He was defeated by conservative elements in 1914, then reelected in 1916 and 1918.

Nominated for president on the forty-fourth ballot at the 1920 Democratic convention, Cox chose young FRANKLIN D. ROOSEVELT, the assistant secretary of the navy, to be his running mate. During the campaign, one observer noted, Cox approached his audiences "a little like a frontier badman shooting up the meeting." Committed to Wilsonian progressivism and U.S. entry into the League of Nations (see WOODROW WILSON), Cox was overwhelmingly defeated by WARREN G. HARDING's conservative, "back to normalcy" campaign. Harding won 16,152,200 popular votes and 404 electoral votes to Cox's 9,147,353 popular votes and 127 electoral votes. Disillusioned after his crushing defeat, Cox retired from politics. In 1933 he served as an American delegate to the World Monetary and Economic Conference.

BIBLIOGRAPHY

Cox, James M., *Journey Through My Years,* 1946.

Crawford, William Harris

(February 24, 1772–September 15, 1834)
Secretary of the Treasury, Secretary of War, Diplomat, Candidate for President, Senator

It is possible that only a series of paralyzing strokes in 1823 kept William Crawford from becoming the sixth president of the United States. Born in Tye River, Virginia, the tall, handsome, amiable southerner served in the U.S. Senate from 1807 to 1813. Crawford made many influential friends in Washington, yet he basically remained the maverick conservative he had been when he started his political career in the Georgia legislature in 1803.

Although a strong supporter of states' rights, while in the Senate Crawford advocated a moderate protective tariff and the rechartering of the national bank (see NICHOLAS BIDDLE). President JAMES MADISON appointed him minister to France in 1813. When he resigned this post in 1815, Madison selected him to be secretary of war and then secretary of the treasury.

At this time Crawford was the choice of most Republicans for president over Madison's favorite, JAMES MONROE. Madison prevailed in winning the nomination for Monroe in 1816 with the argument that Monroe was the last of the great men of the American Revolution and deserved the nomination over a much younger Crawford, who could have his turn at a later date. Crawford served as Monroe's secretary of the treasury for eight years, working effectively for internal improvements. His ambition and influence were strong, and he knew the power of patronage: "Crawford's Act" of 1820 limited the tenure of minor federal appointees to four years.

In the free-for-all that developed to succeed Monroe, JOHN QUINCY ADAMS, HENRY CLAY, and ANDREW JACKSON all knew they had to beat Crawford, who had the support of MARTIN VAN BUREN, Madison, and THOMAS JEFFERSON (see JOHN QUINCY ADAMS). Every effort was made by the supporters of these candidates to discredit Crawford, but still, in 1823, he was the acknowledged front-runner. Then Crawford suffered a paralyzing stroke from which he never recovered. His nomination by a small congressional caucus was merely a gesture of respect and friendship. In the general election he won only forty-one electoral votes and ran a distant third in the race.

Crawford's last years were spent in forced inactivity. The judgeship his friends secured for him did not relieve his anger and bitterness over his fate. In 1830 he published a letter in which he said it was John C. Calhoun and not he who had proposed in 1818 that Andrew Jackson be disciplined for his actions in Florida (see JOHN CALDWELL CALHOUN; ANDREW JACKSON). The resulting rift between the two men was exactly what Crawford had sought to create. He was still living under the delusion that if the party split, he could win the nomination.

BIBLIOGRAPHY

Cobb, Joseph Beckham, *Leisure Labors; or, Miscellaneous, Historical, Literary, and Political,* 1858; Mooney, Chase C., *William H. Crawford,* 1974; Shipp, John Edgar Dawson, *Giant Days; or, The Life and Times of William H. Crawford,* 1909.

Creel, George

(December 1, 1876–October 3, 1953)
Government Agency Director

The journalist and Progressive (see THEODORE ROOSEVELT) political reform leader George Creel organized and directed the first federal government attempt in this century to project a positive image of America abroad and to manage the news at home.

Creel was born in Lafayette County, Missouri. Largely self-educated, he embarked upon a career as a journalist after leaving school in the ninth grade. In 1899 he cofounded the Progressive *Kansas City Independent* newspaper. In 1909 he moved to

Denver, briefly worked for the *Denver Post,* then founded the much more aggressive, muckraking *Rocky Mountain News.*

Creel vigorously supported President WOODROW WILSON's reelection in 1916, and the following year President Wilson appointed him chairman of the Committee on Public Information (CPI). As head of the CPI until 1919, Creel orchestrated an unprecedented effort on the part of the national government to provide literature and posters in support of the U.S. war effort. He combined his dynamic personality and flair for stirring up controversy with new advertising techniques to develop a massive propaganda campaign in support of Wilsonian Progressivism at home and abroad. His supporters credited CPI for lining up American public opinion behind the war effort, while his opponents blamed CPI for starting the national hysteria that culminated in the postwar "Red scare" (see ALEXANDER MITCHELL PALMER).

After leaving the government in 1920, Creel returned to journalism and settled in San Francisco. During the 1930s he made an unsuccessful bid to win the Democratic primary for governor of California (1934), served on the National Advisory Committee of the Works Progress Administration (WPA; see FRANKLIN DELANO ROOSEVELT), and wrote a biweekly commentary column for *Collier's* magazine.

During World War II Creel became convinced that the government was growing so large that it posed more of a threat to national well-being than did business special interests. By the time of his death he had come to believe that an international conspiracy had seized control of the American liberal (Progressive) community to foster the spread of communism.

BIBLIOGRAPHY

Creel, George, *Rebel At Large,* 1947, *Children in Bondage,* with B. B. Lindsey and Edwin Markham (1913), and three reports on his CPI performance published in 1920: *Complete Report of the Chairman of the Committee on Public Information, How We Advertised America,* and *The War, The World and Wilson;* Kennedy, David, *Over Here: The First World War and American Society,* 1980; Mock, James R., and Cedric Larson, *Words that Won the War: The Story of the Committee on Public Information, 1917–1919,* 1939.

Crisp, Charles Frederick

(January 29, 1845–October 23, 1896)
Speaker of the House, Representative

Born in Sheffield, England, while his actor parents were traveling there, Crisp grew up near Savannah, Georgia. Only sixteen when the Civil War began, he spent three years fighting in Virginia's Tenth Infantry, rising to the rank of lieutenant, before being captured and spending a year as a prisoner of war. After the war, Crisp studied law, was admitted to the Georgia bar, and established his law practice in Americus.

In 1872 he was appointed solicitor general of the Georgia southwest superior court circuit. Five years later he accepted an appointment as a judge in that circuit. Crisp resigned from the bench in 1882 to accept the Democratic nomination for Congress, which virtually guaranteed his election.

Crisp mastered the procedures of the political process so well that he became the Democratic leader in the House and then

Speaker in 1891, serving until 1895. In Congress Crisp played a major role in securing the passage of the Interstate Commerce Act of 1887. He was also a champion of the Sherman Silver Purchase Act of 1890, which provided for the limited coinage of silver. Crisp ran for the Senate on a free-silver platform in 1896 (see WILLIAM JENNINGS BRYAN) and, based on public sentiment in Georgia at that time, would have been elected had he not died suddenly.

BIBLIOGRAPHY

Knight, L. L., *Reminiscences of Famous Georgians*, 2 vols., 1907.

Crittenden, John Jordan

(September 10, 1787–July 26, 1863)
Attorney General, Senator, Representative

John J. Crittenden ended a long and distinguished public career by leading a valiant, futile effort to avoid the outbreak of fighting between the North and South through compromise after the election of ABRAHAM LINCOLN.

Crittenden was born in Woodford County, Kentucky. After graduating from the College of William and Mary in 1807, he returned home to establish a successful law practice.

In 1811 Crittenden was elected to his first term in the Kentucky legislature, where he served, except for two brief interruptions, for the next twenty-four years. From 1817 to 1819 he served in the U.S. Senate. During the War of 1812 (see JAMES MADISON) he saw action with the Kentucky militia at the Battle of the Thames.

A close friend and political ally of HENRY CLAY, Crittenden was elected as a member of the Whig party to the U.S. Senate in 1835. In 1840 President WILLIAM HENRY HARRISON appointed Crittenden attorney general. However, when Harrison died shortly after assuming office, Crittenden followed the example of most of the cabinet and submitted his resignation rather than serve under President JOHN TYLER.

Reelected to the Senate in 1842, Crittenden favored negotiation rather than war with Mexico (see JAMES KNOX POLK). He opposed the U.S. annexation of Texas, and advocated a two-year delay in the acquisition of Oregon (see POLK). He returned to Kentucky to serve as governor from 1848 to 1850, and from 1850 to 1853 was President MILLARD FILLMORE's attorney general.

Returning to the Senate in 1855, Crittenden concentrated his talents on averting war between the North and South. When the Southern states began to secede after the election of Abraham Lincoln in 1860, Crittenden attempted to calm their fears by offering a legislative proposal that became known as the Crittenden Compromise. It called for the guarantee of slavery in the South and the District of Columbia through a constitutional amendment and the reinstitution of the Missouri Compromise (see HENRY CLAY) line to divide free and slave states.

Crittenden's proposal failed to attract sufficient support prior to the Confederate attack on Fort Sumter, and the speed with which the outbreak of fighting between Union and Confederate troops escalated quickly rendered Crittenden's proposal moot. During the Civil

War Crittenden fought to keep Kentucky in the Union, but he supported its declaration of neutrality and opposed the state's occupation by Union troops. As a member of the House of Representatives from 1861 to 1863, Crittenden attempted to keep the hope of conciliation alive by opposing all measures that interfered with the institution of slavery, such as the Emancipation Proclamation (see ABRAHAM LINCOLN) and the enlistment of blacks in the Union army.

BIBLIOGRAPHY

Coleman, Ann M. B., *Life of John J. Crittenden*, 2 vols., 1871; Kirwan, Albert D., *John J. Crittenden*, 1962.

Curtis, Charles

(January 25, 1860–February 8, 1936)
Vice President, Senator, Representative

Indian" Curtis concluded a political career of thirty-five years in the U.S. Congress by serving as HERBERT HOOVER's vice president from 1929 to 1933.

Curtis was born in North Topeka, Kansas. His mother was part Kaw Indian (hence his nickname). Curtis attended mission and public schools before being admitted to the state bar in 1881. After serving as attorney for Shawnee County, Kansas, from 1884 to 1888, he was elected in 1892 to the U.S. House of Representatives. He served in the House until moving to the Senate in 1907. After losing his first Senate reelection effort in 1912, he succeeded in taking the Republican nomination away from Senator Joseph L. Bristow and winning election in the general election in 1914.

Curtis served in the Senate from 1914 until he assumed the office of vice president in 1929. Although a liberal newspaper editor described Curtis as the "apotheosis of mediocrity," his colleagues in the Senate were more charitable. They elected him majority leader in 1924. Senator WILLIAM BORAH said Curtis was "a great reconciler, a walking encyclopedia, and one of the best political poker players in America."

When his efforts to secure the Republican nomination for president failed in 1928, Curtis accepted the second spot on the ticket with Herbert Hoover. He served in the undemanding position without incident until 1933 and then retired from public office.

BIBLIOGRAPHY

Ewy, Marvin, *Charles Curtis of Kansas: Vice President of the United States, 1929–1933*, 1961.

Daley, Richard Joseph

(May 15, 1902–December 20, 1976)
Chairman of the Cook County (Chicago) Democratic Central Committee

Richard Daley was the head of Chicago's Democratic party machine and one of the most powerful Democrats in the country for more than two decades. During the height of his power in the 1960s, he became synonymous with Chicago's image: powerful, rough, restless, and prosperous.

Daley was born in the Chicago district of Bridgeport. After completing business courses at the De La Salle Institute in 1918, he worked as a clerk in the stockyards while attending De Paul University Law School at night. In 1933 he was admitted to the Illinois bar.

Daley had become a Democratic party precinct captain at the age of twenty-one. After working as a clerk and administrative assistant in the city treasurer's office, he formed a law firm with several colleagues in 1936, the same year he won election to the state legislature, where he served in both houses until 1946. From 1946 until he won election as the powerful chairman of the Cook County (Chicago) Democratic Central Committee in 1953, Daley held a variety of state and county positions. By never relinquishing his Central Committee chairmanship after he won election as mayor of Chicago in 1955, he managed to gain control of the party's nominations for state offices and the distribution of its patronage.

Since Daley controlled the Democratic party in Illinois, and Illinois was one of the large industrial states Democratic candidates for president had to win, his support was crucial to presidential aspirants. "Daley," Senator ROBERT F. KENNEDY succinctly explained, "means the whole ball game." Facts confirmed his judgment: In 1960 Daley played a crucial role in winning both the nomination and the election of JOHN F. KENNEDY. Many political scholars attribute Kennedy's narrow victory in Illinois to the ability of Daley's Cook County machine to produce the necessary votes.

Under his leadership in the early 1960s, Chicago became a showcase of urban management. Daley reduced graft, reformed the police and fire departments, and through urban renewal spurred a downtown building boom. However, he never managed to establish harmonious relations with the burgeoning black population of the city. In response to charges of racial insensitivity, he met with Martin Luther King, Jr., and other minority group leaders in 1967 and launched a program aimed at ending de facto housing discrimination. When rioting occurred on Chicago's West Side after the 1968 assassination of King, though, Daley issued his infamous "shoot to kill" order to police.

Daley's hope of savoring his powerful role at the 1968 Democratic national convention in Chicago turned to frustration when the already badly divided and disorganized Democrats attacked each other inside the convention hall, while the Chicago police and anti–Vietnam War protestors clashed outside. The nation watched the televised drama of the brawl in the streets (more than 700 protesters were treated for injuries); the image of Daley drawing his index finger across his throat in a signal to the podium to cut the sound system on Senator Abraham Ribicoff for criticizing the behavior of the Chicago police became forever fixed in viewers' minds. Vice President HUBERT HUMPHREY, Daley's candidate, won the 1968 presidential nomination; but the Democratic party was left in shambles and Daley was looked upon by many in the national party leadership as an embarrassingly old-fashioned, corrupt big-city boss.

From 1972 on, Daley suffered a number of defeats. Although he managed to regain firm control of the Democratic party in Illinois, the decline of his statewide and national political power was reflected in the election of a Republican governor in 1976 and his inability to deliver the electoral votes of Illinois to JIMMY CARTER.

BIBLIOGRAPHY

Rakove, Milton L., *Don't Make No Waves—Don't Back No Losers*, 1975; Royko, Mike, *Boss: Richard J. Daley of Chicago*, 1971.

Dallas, George Mifflin

(July 10, 1792–December 31, 1864)
Vice President, Diplomat, Senator

George Dallas was born in Philadelphia and graduated from the College of New Jersey (now Princeton University). He was appointed secretary to ALBERT GALLATIN on a peace mission to Russia in 1813. Upon his return to the United States in 1814, Dallas established a law practice in Philadelphia and became active in Republican state politics. Originally a follower of JOHN C. CALHOUN, he switched to ANDREW JACKSON after the election of 1824.

In 1831 Dallas was appointed to complete a Senate term; but after serving two years, Dallas decided not to seek a full term in the Senate and returned to Philadelphia. He became the attorney general of Pennsylvania until his party lost power in 1835. Between 1837 and 1839 Dallas spent two years as the U.S. minister to Russia.

Dallas became the Democratic nominee for vice president in 1844 after Silas Wright, a loyal MARTIN VAN BUREN supporter, refused to be JAMES K. POLK's running mate. A major reason for Dallas's selection was his championship of Texas annexation (see JAMES KNOX POLK). As vice president he supported Polk's policies, even when they were not compatible with his own views, as in 1846 when he cast the deciding vote in the Senate for lower tariffs.

After his term as vice president, Dallas retired from public life until FRANKLIN PIERCE appointed him minister to Great Britain in 1856. While in that post he negotiated a settlement between conflicting British and United States interests in Central America. The Civil War ended his political career. The moderate, conciliatory Dallas despised abolitionists and secessionists alike. He voted for the candidates of the Democratic party throughout the Civil War, the end of which he did not live to see.

BIBLIOGRAPHY

Dallas, Julia (ed.), *A Series of Letters from London Written During the Years 1856, '57, '58, '59, and '60*, 1896; Dallas, Susan (ed.), *Diary of George Mifflin Dallas while U.S. Minister to Russia, 1837–39, and to England, 1856–61*, 1892.

Daugherty, Harry Micajah

(January 26, 1860–October 12, 1941)
Attorney General

While attorney general during the administration of WARREN G. HARDING, Harry Daugherty abused the trust of the president and undermined the integrity of the Justice Department.

Daugherty was born in Washington Court House, Ohio. After earning his law degree from the University of Michigan in 1881, he established a law practice in Washington Court House and immediately became active in the Republican party. He served two terms in the Ohio state legislature from 1890 to 1894 but never succeeded in winning the Republican nomination for any state or federal office again. Nevertheless, Daugherty continued to play an active, if divisive, role in Ohio Republican party politics. In 1896 he worked on the national campaign of WILLIAM MCKINLEY and in 1908 and 1912 served as WILLIAM HOWARD TAFT's Ohio campaign chairman.

An early supporter of Warren G. Harding for president, Daugherty predicted the manner in which Harding would emerge from a deadlocked convention with the Republican nomination for president in 1920. Harding rewarded Daugherty for his support by appointing him attorney general in 1921. The appointment proved to be controversial, but Harding died before he ever realized just how inept and corrupt the man he had placed in charge of the Justice Department really was.

In 1922 Daugherty alienated organized labor when he issued a sweeping injunction against striking railroad shopmen. Little more than a year later, a Senate investigation revealed that Daugherty had used the Federal Bureau of Investigation to harass and discredit a senator who had denounced Daugherty's role in the Teapot Dome scandal (the fraudulent sale of federal government oil leases during the Harding administration; see WARREN GAMALIEL HARDING). Daugherty was accused, moreover, of abusing his supervisory role concerning property confiscated during World War I under the Alien Property Custodian's office and of receiving payments from Prohibition violators.

President CALVIN COOLIDGE asked for Daugherty's resignation as attorney general in 1924. Three years later, Daugherty was prosecuted for conspiracy to defraud the U.S. government, but the case was dismissed after two juries could not reach agreement on a verdict.

Daugherty spent much of his later life trying to prove his claims of innocence.

BIBLIOGRAPHY

Daugherty, Harry M., and Thomas Dixon, *The Inside Story of the Harding Tragedy,* 1932; Giglio, James N., *H. M. Daugherty and the Politics of Expediency,* 1978.

Davis, David

(March 9, 1815–June 26, 1886)
Associate Justice of the Supreme Court, Senator

As an associate justice of the Supreme Court, a U.S. senator, and the decisive vote caster on a special presidential election commission, David Davis remained at the center of American national politics for more than two decades.

Davis was born in Cecil County, Maryland. After graduating from Kenyon College in Gambier, Ohio, in 1832 and Yale Law School three years later, he settled in Bloomington, Illinois, and established a legal practice. In 1844 he won election as a Whig to the state legislature, and from 1848 to 1862, presided over the eighth judicial circuit in Illinois. While serving on the circuit bench, Davis established a close personal friendship with ABRAHAM LINCOLN.

At the Republican national convention in 1860, Davis managed the successful effort to secure the presidential nomination for Lincoln. Lincoln's trust in Davis was demonstrated when, in 1862, he appointed Davis to the U.S. Supreme Court. Four years later, in *Ex parte Milligan,* Davis wrote the majority opinion in one of the most important decisions in Supreme Court history. The decision, which denounced the arbitrary use of military power by declaring that martial law within areas not threatened by military action was unlawful, is famous for its clear protection of civil liberties in the United States.

Davis did not let his position on the Supreme Court interfere with his political ambitions. However, his allegiance to the Republican party after Lincoln's assassination was tenuous. In 1872 he accepted the nomination for president from the radical Labor Reform party, although he then changed his mind and declined it.

In 1877 Davis's lack of party allegiance led to his appointment as the neutral or independent fifth member (two Democrats and two Republicans) on the special commission established to decide the winner in the disputed 1876 presidential election (see RUTHERFORD BIRCHARD HAYES). He raised a storm of controversy when he resigned from the Supreme Court before the commission met to accept election to the U.S. Senate by the Democratic-dominated Illinois legislature. Ironically, although elected to the Senate by the Democrats, he earned their enmity by supporting the election of the Republican Rutherford B. Hayes for president. In his role as presiding officer of the Senate after Vice President CHESTER A. ARTHUR became president, Davis frequently cast the deciding vote in the evenly divided Senate in favor of the Republican position. He retired at the end of his single six-year term in the Senate in 1883 to Bloomington, Illinois.

BIBLIOGRAPHY

King, Willard L., *Lincoln's Manager: David Davis,* 1960.

Davis, Jefferson

(June 3, 1808–December 6, 1889)
Secretary of War, Senator, Representative, President of the Confederate States of America

Military hero and successful politician Jefferson Davis accepted the office of president of the Confederacy "as a man," said his wife, "might speak of a sentence of death." He would have preferred a military command and had little taste for political intrigue and infighting.

Born in Kentucky but raised in Wilkinson, Mississippi, Davis attended several private schools before securing an appointment to West Point in 1824. The six-foot-tall, strong-willed, and emotionally intense Davis thrived in the military. Upon graduation in 1828, Davis was stationed on the Northwestern frontier. He served in the Black Hawk War in the early 1830s. After marrying the daughter of his commander, ZACHARY TAYLOR, in 1835, he resigned his commission to develop Brierfield, a 1,000-acre plantation in Mississippi. His wife lived only three months after their marriage. Davis remarried in 1845.

Convinced that blacks were biologically inferior and that the Bible supported the institution of slavery, Davis sincerely believed that slavery benefited blacks as much as white slaveholders. The profits he made from his plantation and the good care he took of his slaves corroborated his beliefs.

Elected to Congress in 1845, Davis resigned to fight in the Mexican War (see JAMES KNOX POLK) and became a hero at Buena Vista. In 1847 he became U.S. senator from Mississippi. He supported President James K. Polk in his expansionist policies, and opposed the admission of California without slaves and the Wilmot Proviso (see JOHN CALDWELL CALHOUN). After the Compromise of 1850 (see HENRY CLAY and MILLARD FILLMORE) was adopted over his protest, Davis resigned his Senate seat to run an unsuccessful campaign for governor of Mississippi. In appreciation of his campaign help in 1852, FRANKLIN PIERCE appointed Davis secretary of war in 1853.

Library of Congress

While secretary of war, Davis increased the size of the army; improved military regulations, equipment, and salaries; and unsuccessfully attempted to replace seniority with merit as the basis for promotion. His greatest accomplishment lay in encouraging railroad construction through the authorization of survey parties to prepare detailed reports on possible railroad routes. Davis supported a southern route for the first transcontinental railroad and played an important role in the Gadsden Purchase (see FRANKLIN PIERCE). He also favored acquiring Cuba and Nicaragua.

Reelected to the Senate in 1857, Davis quickly became the chief spokesman for Southern legislators who saw no contradiction between their support of the Union and advocacy for the extension of slavery into the territories. Unlike STEPHEN DOUGLAS, Davis held the view that since the Constitution protected slavery and also protected private property, no federal legislation could be passed that inhibited the right of slave owners to take their slaves anywhere in the United States. Indeed, the Constitution made it the duty of the federal government to protect the property of slaveholders. Davis disagreed with John C. Calhoun's idea of nullification and argued instead that the United States was composed of sovereign states that, because they had voluntarily joined the Union, could also choose to leave it. By the 1850s Davis had come to regard the South as a country within a country and himself as its spokesman.

After the Democratic party split over the slavery issue in 1860, Davis supported the candidacy of JOHN C. BRECKINRIDGE. Realistic enough to know that secession would not be accomplished peacefully, Davis supported efforts to find some kind of compromise solution to the crisis posed by ABRAHAM LINCOLN's election. However, when Mississippi voted on January 5, 1861, to secede, he resigned from the Senate and went with his state.

As president of the Confederacy, Davis frequently tried to force his own military strategies for victory upon his generals. His insistence upon the need for a strong central government in order to win the war (he favored general conscription and suspending the writ of habeas corpus) convinced many in the South that he was unsympathetic to states' rights. Davis justified his actions with the reply, "We are fighting for independence, and that, or extermination, we will have." His obstinate refusal to negotiate for peace on any basis other than between "the two countries" caused Lincoln to remark that Davis "affords us no excuse to deceive ourselves."

After the war Davis was arrested. Although twice threatened with indictment for treason, he was released after serving two years in prison. He never asked for, nor was he ever granted, a pardon. At first unpopular in the South and blamed for defeat, Davis's harsh treatment by the North and unwavering devotion to the South gradually restored his popularity there. Hollow-cheeked, gaunt, and blind in one eye, Davis supported himself as a private businessman and author (*The Rise and Fall of the Confederate Government,* 1881) until his death at age eighty-one in 1889. He never wavered in his view that the South was a victim of Northern aggression, but shortly before his death he advised, "The past is dead; let it bury its dead, its hopes, and its aspirations; before you lies the future of expanding national glory before which all the world shall stand amazed."

BIBLIOGRAPHY

Ballard, Michael B., *Long Shadow: Jefferson Davis and the Final Days of the Confederacy,* 1986; Catton, William, and Bruce Catton, *Two Roads to Sumter,* 1971; Davis, Jefferson, *Papers of Jefferson Davis,* vols. 1–4, 1971–1985; Eaton, Clement, *Jefferson Davis,* 1979; Escott, Paul D., *After Secession: Jefferson Davis and the Failure of the Confederate Nationalism,* 1978; Patrick, Rembert W., *Jefferson Davis and His Cabinet,* 1944; Wiley, Bell, *Road to Appomattox,* 1968.

Davis, John William

(April 13, 1873–March 24, 1955)
Diplomat, Candidate for President, Representative

The presidential choice of the seventeen-day-long Democratic convention of 1924, John Davis was a man everyone agreed had exceptional ability; "the type," noted one political observer, that people call "a mighty fine man."

Born in Clarksburg, West Virginia, Davis graduated from Washington and Lee University in 1895, was admitted to the bar, and briefly taught at Washington and Lee University Law School before being elected to the West Virginia state legislature in 1899. Twelve years later he won a seat in the U.S. House of Representatives, where he helped to write the Clayton Antitrust Act. He resigned from the House in 1913 in order to become WOODROW WILSON's solicitor general and then Wilson's ambassador to Great Britain from 1918 to 1921. He advised Wilson at the Versailles peace conference and staunchly supported the League of Nations (see WOODROW WILSON).

One of several favorite sons at the 1924 Democratic convention, Davis was nominated on the 103d ballot as a compromise candidate in order to break the deadlock that had developed between AL SMITH and WILLIAM G. MCADOO. Running against Republican CALVIN COOLIDGE and Progressive ROBERT M. LA FOLLETTE, Davis was defeated in a landslide Republican victory.

Davis's politics were shaped as much by his membership in a prestigious Wall Street law firm (whose clients included John Pierpont Morgan) as by his West Virginia birth. He was opposed to the New Deal politics of FRANKLIN DELANO ROOSEVELT. Following his unsuccessful candidacy, he was thereafter ignored by the Democratic party. Davis devoted the rest of his life to his law practice, and before his death in 1955 he had argued more cases before the U.S. Supreme Court than any other attorney in history.

BIBLIOGRAPHY

Huntley, Theodore A., *The Life of John W. Davis,* 1924.

Dawes, Charles Gates

(August 27, 1865–April 23, 1951)
Vice President, Diplomat

As President CALVIN COOLIDGE's strong-willed, outspoken vice president, a Nobel Peace Prize recipient, and an international financier, Charles Gates "Hell and Maria" Dawes was one of the nation's most able statesmen.

Born in Marietta, Ohio, Dawes graduated from Marietta College in 1884 and Cincinnati Law School in 1886. He practiced law in Lincoln, Nebraska, from 1887 to 1894. Dawes then moved to Evanston, Illinois, where he became so active in banking that he relinquished his law practice and became a full-time business investor and financier. He moved to Chicago in 1895 and the next year managed Republican WILLIAM MCKINLEY's presidential campaign in Illinois. After McKinley's election, Dawes was appointed comptroller of the currency, but he resigned after little more than a year in office to make an unsuccessful bid for a Senate seat.

A brigadier general during World War I, Dawes was in charge of all matériel purchases for the U.S. forces in Europe. Called to testify about military spending before a congressional investigating committee after the war, Dawes became so enraged by the nature of the questions he was being asked that he exploded with a famous outburst: "Hell and Maria, we weren't trying to keep a set of books, we were trying to win the war!"

In 1921 Dawes became the nation's first director of the Bureau of the Budget. A year later he assumed the chairmanship of a special commission composed of American and European delegates meeting in Paris to resolve the complex problem of German war reparations. The results of the commission's efforts, known as the Dawes Plan and accepted by the Germans, won him the Nobel Peace Prize in 1925. The plan included a graduated schedule of reparation payments and a huge foreign loan for the Germans. In 1924 Dawes was nominated by the Republican party to be President Calvin Coolidge's vice president.

Completing his term as vice president, Dawes declined to seek reelection as HERBERT HOOVER's running mate in 1928. Instead, he accepted the position of ambassador to Great Britain in 1929, then chairman of the Reconstruction Finance Corporation (see HERBERT HOOVER) in 1932. He retired from government service five months later.

BIBLIOGRAPHY
Dawes, Charles G., *Journal,* 1950; Timmons, Bascom N., *Charles G. Dawes,* 1953.

Day, William Rufus

(April 17, 1849–July 9, 1923)
Secretary of State, Diplomat, Associate Justice of the Supreme Court

Diplomat and Associate Justice of the Supreme Court William Rufus Day was born in Ravenna, Ohio. He graduated from the University of Michigan in 1870 and was admitted to the Ohio bar two years later.

Day practiced law in Canton, Ohio, and served from 1886 to 1890 as judge of the county court of common pleas. In 1897 he became assistant to the secretary of state. When war was declared against Spain in April 1898 (see WILLIAM MCKINLEY, JR.), he reluctantly agreed to temporarily become secretary of state. Although only in that position for the first few months of the war, he was successful in persuading France and Germany to remain neutral. Day resigned as secretary of state to become chairman of the U.S. commission that arranged peace after the Spanish-American War. Opposed to U.S. acquisition of Spanish colonial possessions without compensation, Day insisted that the U.S. purchase the Philippines for $20 million from Spain rather than just claiming the islands by right of conquest.

In 1899 Day was appointed a federal circuit court of appeals judge. Four years later, President THEODORE ROOSEVELT nominated him to be an associate justice of the Supreme Court.

The most noted opinion the philosophically conservative Day delivered in his almost twenty years on the Supreme Court was in *Hammer* v. *Dagenhart* (1917), in which he held that a federal anti–child labor law was unconstitutional. He resigned from the Supreme Court in 1922 and, due to failing health, only briefly served on the Mixed Claims Commission authorized to settle American claims against Germany from World War I.

BIBLIOGRAPHY

McLean, Joseph Erigina, *William Rufus Day: Supreme Court Justice from Ohio*, 1946.

Dayton, Jonathan

(October 16, 1760–October 9, 1824)
Speaker of the House, Senator, Representative

Jonathan Dayton was born in Elizabeth-Town, New Jersey. After graduating from the College of New Jersey (now Princeton University) in 1776, he joined his father in the American army and served as a captain at the Battle of Yorktown. In 1786 he was elected to the New Jersey Assembly, and the next year, although only twenty-seven years old, was chosen to be a delegate to the Constitutional Convention when his father declined. At the convention Dayton vigorously participated in the debates that shaped the federal government. Although he had strong reservations, he signed the final draft of the Constitution.

Dayton declined to be a representative in the first Congress in 1789. Instead, he served two more years in the state assembly and then, in 1791, began the first of his four consecutive terms in the U.S. House of Representatives. He was elected Speaker during his last term in the House, and he served one term in the Senate from 1799 to 1805.

Dayton owned 250,000 acres between the Big and Little Miami rivers in Ohio, and was a strong force behind the building of the Miami Canal around the Ohio Falls. The city of Dayton, Ohio, was named after him.

A close friend of AARON BURR, Dayton was implicated in Burr's infamous and ill-fated attempt at empire building in the West. He was indicted for treason in 1807 as a result of his involvement with Burr, but the case against him was dropped by the federal prosecutor before coming to trial. Although his national political career was over, he served two more terms in the New Jersey Assembly in 1814 and 1815 before finally retiring from politics.

BIBLIOGRAPHY

Benton, T. H., *Abridgement of the Debates of Congress*, 1861; Farrand, Max (ed.), *The Records of the Federal Convention of 1787*, 3 vols., 1927; Hatfield, E. F., *History of Elizabeth, New Jersey*, 1868.

Debs, Eugene Victor

(November 5, 1855–October 20, 1926)
Candidate for President

As a leader of organized labor and a candidate for president of the Socialist party in five national elections, Eugene Debs passionately fought for radical social change in the United States. No other American socialist has ever achieved his fame or stature.

Debs was born in Terre Haute, Indiana, to immigrant parents from Alsace, France. Largely self-educated, he left school at age fifteen to work in the Terre Haute and Indianapolis Railway as a locomotive fireman. He immediately became active in the Brotherhood of Locomotive Firemen. In 1879 he was elected as a Democrat to a four-year term as city clerk. Five years later, he won election as a Democrat to the state legislature. After completing a term in the state legislature (1885–1887), Debs concentrated on his union-building activities.

Debs turned to socialism as a result of the severe depression of the 1890s and the use of government power, first to break a new union he had helped form, then to put him in jail. In 1893 Debs had organized the American Railway Union (ARU), the nation's first industrial union (a labor union open to all workers in an industry irrespective of their craft or skill). As president of the ARU, Debs successfully negotiated several labor disputes. Then the employees of the Pullman Company went out on strike against Debs's advice, and the results were completely different.

The ARU leadership felt bound to aid the Pullman workers and called a national strike

Library of Congress

that quickly tied up the nation's railroads. Violence occurred and President GROVER CLEVELAND sent troops to restore order (see CLEVELAND). The federal courts supported the railroad companies by applying the Sherman Antitrust Act (see BENJAMIN HARRISON) against organized labor. The act had been passed to control large corporations, but the court ruled that the ARU was, in effect, an illegal trust and issued an injunction to halt the strike. The use of an injunction against a union provided companies with a powerful new weapon. It made the strikers criminals if they refused to obey the court order to go back to work.

Debs, along with the other ARU leaders and the workers on strike, ignored the injunction. In July 1894 he and three other ARU leaders were arrested and later convicted of contempt of court. During the six months he spent in jail, Debs read socialist literature. After his release, he returned to a hero's welcome in Chicago and announced that he had become a socialist. Debs's socialist beliefs were uniquely American. He hoped to marry Jeffersonian republicanism and Marxism into an attractive idealistic social vision that would become a reality through the ballot box rather than violence. His vision had widespread support among immigrants, laborers, and disgruntled midwestern farmers. In 1900, as the presidential candidate of the Social Democratic party, the core of which consisted of what was left of the old ARU organization, Debs won 96,000 votes. In 1904, as the candidate of the new Socialist party (formed in 1901), he polled 402,000 votes.

Shortly after the 1904 election, Debs became the editor of the Midwest-based Socialist weekly *Appeal to Reason*, which reached a circulation of 700,000. The following year he helped to found the Industrial Workers of the World (IWW) but, due to what he perceived to be grave organizational problems, decided not to remain involved in the IWW. He did, however, defend its members when he felt they were unfairly attacked by the government for their radical political beliefs and union-building efforts.

Frustrated and angered by the inequities he saw around him, Debs lectured across the nation to large crowds about the evils of capitalism and the inability of trade unions to serve as agents for social change. He was a gifted public speaker and frequently drew large crowds to his political rallies. He drew 420,793 votes as the socialist candidate for president in 1908, and in the turbulent election of 1912, he garnered 901,062 votes, the largest popular vote percentage (6 percent) of his career. Historians differ on the significance of this showing, some treating it as relatively unimportant and others as the beginning of a mass radical party. What is clear is that issues dear to the socialists—the need to break the power of the trusts (industrial monopolies) and to aid working men and women—increasingly dominated public debate and spurred on the great reform movement known as Progressivism (see THEODORE ROOSEVELT).

The Socialist party refused to support the participation of the United States in World War I and suffered as a result. At first Debs maintained a low antiwar profile; but, in 1918, angered by the government's arrest of political radicals for sedition, he delivered a harsh speech in Canton, Ohio, attacking the administration of WOODROW WILSON for its unconstitutional use of the Espionage Act to imprison radicals. He himself was then indicted under the Espionage Act for sedition, tried, and sentenced to serve two concurrent ten-year terms in federal prison.

In the 1920 presidential election, while still an inmate at the Atlanta federal penitentiary, Debs won 901,255 votes. After President WARREN G. HARDING commuted his sentence in 1921, Debs was released, but his health was broken. He spent his last years editing the new socialist weekly *American Appeal* and writing a book about the need to improve prison conditions, *Walls and Bars*.

Debs summarized his views in this 1908 campaign speech:

> [There] will be no material change in the condition of the people until we have a new social system based upon the mutual economic interests of the whole people; until you and I and all of us collectively own those things that we collectively need and use. . . . As long as a relatively few men own . . . the sources and means of life—they will corrupt our politics, they will enslave the working class, they will impoverish and debase society, they will do all things that are needful to perpetuate their power as the economic masters and the political rulers of the people. . . .

Although he was the presidential candidate of the Socialist party, Debs was never its intellectual leader. His faith in socialism was passionate and unshakable, but he initiated few of the policies of the party. His complicated personality rendered him charismatic before a large crowd but ineffectual when it came to internal party politics.

BIBLIOGRAPHY

Debs, Eugene V., *Writings and Speeches*, 1948; Ginger, Ray, *The Bending Cross: A Biography of Eugene Victor Debs*, 1949; Karsner, Davis, *Debs: His Authorized Life and Letters*, 1919; Morgan, Wayne H., *Eugene V. Debs: Socialist for President*, 1962; Salvatore, Nick, *Eugene V. Debs: Citizen and Socialist*, 1982.

Denby, Edwin

(February 18, 1870–February 8, 1929)
Secretary of the Navy, Representative

Edwin Denby was born in Evansville, Indiana. After graduating from high school, he went abroad with his father, who was U.S. minister to China, and worked for ten years in the Chinese customs service. Denby earned his law degree from the University of Michigan in 1896 and, after a stint in the navy in 1898, practiced law in Detroit.

He was elected to the Michigan legislature in 1903, and two years later, as a Republican, to the first of his three successive terms in the U.S. House of Representatives. President WARREN G. HARDING's appointment of Denby as secretary of the navy in 1921 caught political observers as well as Denby by surprise.

Secretary Denby had virtually no influence upon U.S. naval organization or policy development while in office. He is remembered primarily for his indirect involvement in the notorious Teapot Dome scandal (see WARREN GAMALIEL HARDING).

To camouflage secret leasing of naval oil reserves at Teapot Dome, Wyoming, and Elk Hills, California, without competitive bidding, the conspirators, Edward L. Doheny, Harry F. Sinclair, and Secretary of the Interior ALBERT B. FALL decided that the secretary of the navy should also sign the lease documents.

When the conspiracy to defraud the government was discovered in 1924, the Senate, unable to reach Fall, who had retired from office, vented its fury upon Denby and requested President CALVIN COOLIDGE to dismiss him from the cabinet. Coolidge refused, and Denby defiantly dared the House to begin impeachment proceedings if it had any evidence of wrongdoing on his part. The pressure on Denby grew so great, however, that he resigned his office in March to save the administration "further embarrassment."

Denby retired from public life and returned to Detroit.

BIBLIOGRAPHY

"Edwin Denby Dies in His 59th Year," *New York Times*, February 9, 1929, p. 19.

De Priest, Oscar Stanton

(March 9, 1871–May 12, 1951)
Representative

Oscar Stanton De Priest was the first black from the North ever elected to serve in the U.S. House of Representatives.

De Priest was born in Florence, Alabama, to parents who were former slaves. He graduated from Salina (Kansas) Normal School in 1888 and later settled in Chicago, where he accumulated a fortune managing real estate on the city's South Side. A Republican in a predominantly Democratic local political environment, De Priest managed to hold a number of city offices because of his ability to deliver the black vote and to play factions of the Republican and Democratic parties against each other. In 1915 he became the first black elected to the city council. In 1923, in return for help he provided the successful Republican candidate for mayor, De Priest was appointed assistant Illinois commerce commissioner, a position that included patronage appointment powers.

In 1928 De Priest supported the white Republican candidate for Congress over a black candidate in the primary election. The white candidate died shortly after winning the nomination. De Priest took his place and went on to win the general election that fall for the House of Representatives.

In Congress De Priest filed a number of bills designed to protect the civil rights of black Americans. He also traveled extensively in the South at considerable personal peril to encourage blacks to organize politically. Although attacked by Southern newspapers for stirring up racial hostility by advocating social equality, De Priest refused to be intimidated.

Reelected in 1930, De Priest even managed to hold onto his seat in the 1932 Democratic landslide of FRANKLIN D. ROOSEVELT, despite his initial opposition to New Deal federal relief. Although his personal popularity remained high, he lost his bid to win a fourth term in Congress to a black Democratic party candidate in 1934. Still active in local politics, he was again elected alderman from Chicago's Third Ward from 1943 to 1947.

BIBLIOGRAPHY

Gosnell, Harold F., *Negro Politicians: The Rise of Negro Politics in Chicago*, 1935 (reprint 1967).

Dewey, Thomas Edmund

(March 24, 1902–March 16, 1971)
Candidate for President

Library of Congress

Elected governor of New York three times and nominated for president twice, Thomas Dewey is remembered chiefly for his unexpected presidential election loss to HARRY TRUMAN in 1948.

Born in Owosso, Michigan, Dewey graduated from the University of Michigan in 1923 and Columbia University Law School in 1925. Hard working and efficient, Dewey was named chief assistant U.S. attorney for the Southern District of New York before his twenty-ninth birthday.

In 1935 Herbert H. Lehman, the Democratic governor of New York, appointed the Republican Dewey to be a special prosecutor in charge of investigating organized crime. Dewey was so successful that two years later he was elected district attorney of New York County. Dewey earned national fame in this post after a series of spectacular prosecutions that culminated in the destruction of the infamous underworld organization Murder, Inc.

Although he lost his first race for governor in 1938, Dewey came so close to victory that he was recognized as one of the Republican party's most powerful figures in the state. Successful in his next bid to be elected governor in 1942, Dewey was reelected in 1946 and 1950, but his real focus between 1942 and 1948 was on becoming president.

Dewey won the Republican party's presidential nomination in 1944 but was defeated by Franklin D. Roosevelt. Nominated again in 1948, Dewey expected to coast to victory against the vulnerable Harry S Truman, whose party had split in disagreement over his policies. The southern conservatives in the Democratic party were backing "Dixiecrat" Strom Thurmond in opposition to Truman's stand on civil rights, and the left-wing faction had nominated Henry A. Wallace on a new Progressive party ticket with a view toward forming stronger domestic policies.

Because the polls gave him such a wide lead, Dewey became overconfident. He assumed the stance of the front-runner and issued bland campaign statements. Truman barnstormed the country, reminding the voters of their prosperity and blaming the "do nothing" Republican Eightieth Congress for the nation's ills. "Give 'em hell" Harry Truman's tactics succeeded brilliantly against the wooden Dewey, who always seemed just a bit too concerned with his perfectly groomed mustache and neatly parted hair. As one of his critics, Alice Roosevelt Longworth, quipped,

"How can you vote for a man who looks like the bridegroom on a wedding cake?" Truman managed to defeat Dewey in one of the greatest upset victories in modern politics.

Dewey was elected to his third and final term as governor of New York in 1950. During his three terms, Dewey provided an honest, efficient administration; oversaw the implementation of a huge highway construction program; obtained the passage of the first state law prohibiting racial or religious discrimination in employment; created a labor mediation board; and improved unemployment and disability benefits. He retired from political office in 1954.

BIBLIOGRAPHY

Beyer, Barry, *Thomas E. Dewey: A Study in Political Leadership,* 1978; Dewey, Thomas E., *The Case Against the Underworld,* 1940, *Journey to the Far Pacific,* 1952, *On the Two Party System,* 1966, and *Twenty Against the Underworld,* 1975; Smith, Richard Norton, *Thomas E. Dewey and His Times,* 1982.

Dickinson, John

(November 8, 1732–February 14, 1808)
Revolutionary Leader

Although he held a number of political positions in pre– and post–revolutionary war America, John Dickinson's most outstanding contribution to American independence was his *Letters from a Pennsylvania Farmer to the Inhabitants of the British Colonies* (1767) and *Essay on Constitutional Power of Great Britain over the American Colonies* (1774). His writings, which were widely read in both America and England, helped to define American grievances.

Born in Talbot County, Maryland, Dickinson studied law in Philadelphia and at the Middle Temple in London. In 1757 he began a very successful law practice in Philadelphia. Three years later he was elected to the Delaware Assembly and in 1762 to the Pennsylvania legislature, where he served until 1765 and again from 1770 to 1776.

While a member of the Continental Congress from 1774 to 1776, Dickinson wrote its *Address to the Inhabitants of Quebec* and *Petitions to the King.* He also may have written *Declaration of the Causes of Taking Up Arms.* In addition, he helped to write the Articles of Confederation.

Dickinson was strongly conservative in temperament. He did not sign the Declaration of Independence, because he considered it ill advised to take such a step without a foreign ally, and he still hoped to achieve a compromise solution with England. He did, however, fight with the Delaware militia during the Revolution. He later helped to write the U.S. Constitution and worked to obtain its adoption.

Before he retired from public service in 1787, Dickinson served as president of Delaware from 1781 to 1782 and governor of Pennsylvania from 1782 to 1785.

BIBLIOGRAPHY

Ford, Paul Leicester (ed.), *The Writings of John Dickinson*, vol. 1, *Political Writings 1764–1774*, 1895; Stille, C. J., *The Life and Times of John Dickinson*, 1891.

Dies, Martin, Jr.

(November 5, 1901–November 14, 1972)
Representative

As the first chairman of the House Un-American Activities Committee, Dies endeavored to discredit New Deal programs and organized labor unions by exposing alleged communist infiltration.

Born in Colorado, Texas, Dies grew up in Beaumont. He graduated from the University of Texas at Austin in 1919. After earning his law degree from National University in Washington, D.C. (now George Washington University), in 1920, Dies established a practice in Orange County, Texas.

Dies served as a Democratic U.S. Representative from 1931 to 1945 and from 1953 to 1959. He was chairman of the House Un-American Activities Committee from 1938 to 1945. His sensational investigations and claims, largely through the use of guilt by association, of communist infiltration in government and organized labor made him nationally known. Dies's attempt to win election to the Senate in 1941 failed, however. Because Dies did not seek reelection in 1944, he was not in a position to capitalize on the national preoccupation with "uncovering" communist infiltrators and liberals "soft" on communism that occurred due to the start of the cold war, the fall of mainland China to communism, and the repercussions of U.S. participation in the Korean War (see JOSEPH RAYMOND MCCARTHY).

Dies did win reelection to Congress in 1952, however, at the height of the McCarthy era. Ironically, he did not obtain a seat on the infamous committee he had once chaired during his three new terms in office from 1953 to 1959. A second bid to win election to the Senate in 1957 failed.

BIBLIOGRAPHY

Dies, Martin, *The Martin Dies Story*, 1963.

Dillingham, William Paul

(December 12, 1843–July 12, 1923)
Senator

During his four terms in the U.S. Senate from 1900 to 1923, William Paul Dillingham became the leading congressional authority on immigration. In 1921 he introduced legislation that served as the basis for the quota system established by the United States to control immigration.

Dillingham was born in Waterbury, Vermont. After attending Kimball Union Academy in Meriden, New Hampshire, he completed his legal training with his father, who was then governor of Vermont. From 1866 to 1888 he served the state in various legal and legislative capacities and in 1888 won a two-year term as governor.

In 1902, two years after winning election to the U.S. Senate to fill the vacancy caused by the death of Justin S. Morrill, Dillingham won the first of four full six-year terms. In the Senate Dillingham was assigned to the Committee on Immigration. From 1903 to 1911 he was the committee's chairman, and from 1907 to 1910 he also chaired the U.S. Immigration Commission, which conducted intensive studies of immigrants in the United States. In 1913 he introduced legislation to restrict immigration through a system of quotas. The effort to pass the bill was dropped during World War I, but in 1920 Dillingham reintroduced the measure. It was passed by Congress but vetoed by President WOODROW WILSON. On his third try in 1921, Dillingham's bill became law, thus ending the traditional open immigration policy of the United States. Each country (except those in Asia, the inhabitants of which were completely excluded) was allotted an annual 3 percent quota, based on the number of immigrants from that country resident in the United States in 1910; the ceiling on the total yearly immigration was set at 370,000.

The Dillingham quota system became the basis of the Immigration Act of 1924, which allotted each country an annual 2 percent quota based on the number of immigrants from that country resident in the United States in 1890. That act was meant to discriminate against the immigrants of southern and eastern Europe, whom Dillingham and others regarded as being of "inferior racial stock" and incapable of assimilating into American life. This act (with minor modifications) remained in effect until 1968, when it was replaced by a more equitable system created by the Immigration and Nationality Amendments of 1965 and the later immigration reform acts of 1986 and 1990.

BIBLIOGRAPHY

Congressional Record, 64 Congress, I Session, pp. 12,769–12,777; Senate Report No. 17, 67 Congress, I Session; *The Vermonter,* November 1900, November 1902, February 1924.

Dirksen, Everett McKinley

(January 4, 1896–September 7, 1969)
Senator, Representative

Everett Dirksen served as an effective minority leader of the Republicans in the Senate during the 1950s and 1960s. Born in Pekin, Illinois, Dirksen attended the University of Minnesota for three years before joining the army in 1917. In 1926 he was elected to local office in Pekin but lost a bid for a seat in the U.S. House of Representatives in 1930. In 1932 his second try to win election to Congress from Illinois was successful, and he won reelection every two years until failing eyesight caused him to decide to retire in 1948.

After ten months of rest and medication cured his vision difficulties, Dirksen made a remarkable political comeback. In 1950 he defeated the Democratic party incumbent for the U.S. Senate. A conservative philosophically but a pragmatist by nature, Dirksen was quickly chosen to be the leader of the Republican minority in the Senate. As minority leader, Dirksen worked closely with both Republican DWIGHT D. EISENHOWER and Democrats JOHN F. KENNEDY and LYNDON B. JOHNSON when it was politically advantageous to do so.

Dirksen's support for the 1963 Nuclear Test Ban Treaty was a major factor in obtaining its ratification by the Senate and the easing of cold war tensions. He also played a pivotal role in securing the passage of the Civil Rights Act of 1964 when he, a conservative Republican with close ties to southern segregationists, committed himself to black equality. His decision to vote for closure was crucial to ending the southerners' filibuster against the 1964 Civil Rights Act. Dirksen said at the time, in words taken from Victor Hugo: "Stronger than all the armies is an idea whose time has come." This stance made him a hero of sorts to liberals, even though on other welfare and civil rights issues (such as Medicare and Medicaid, and the open-housing provisions of the 1964 Civil Rights Act) he took customary conservative positions.

During the Vietnam War (see LYNDON BAINES JOHNSON and RICHARD MILHOUS NIXON), Dirksen was one of President Johnson's most important congressional supporters. Dirksen favored pursuing the conflict to military victory and did not agree with Johnson's decision to enter into peace negotiations with the North Vietnamese in 1968 "without prior conditions." He died in office in 1969.

As a senator, Dirksen became famous for his deep voice and languid style of speaking as well as for his ability to deliver remarkably disarming but effective comments. He once noted in a debate, "You know, you add a few hundred million dollars here and a few hundred million dollars there, and before you know it you're talking some serious money."

BIBLIOGRAPHY

McNeil, Neil, *Dirksen: Portrait of a Public Man,* 1971.

Dole, Elizabeth Hanford

(July 29, 1936–)
Secretary of Labor, Secretary of Transportation

First as a Democrat, then as an independent, and finally as a Republican, the politically astute and talented Elizabeth Hanford Dole has served in a wide variety of roles during the administrations of LYNDON JOHNSON, RICHARD NIXON, GERALD FORD, JIMMY CARTER, RONALD REAGAN, and GEORGE BUSH.

Born into an affluent family in Salisbury, North Carolina, Dole graduated from Duke University in 1958. After spending the summer at Oxford University in 1959, she returned to earn a master's degree in education at Harvard University in 1960 and a law degree there in 1965. Once she had her law degree, "Washington was like a magnet," she later recalled, and she decided to settle there.

In 1966 she became staff assistant to the assistant secretary for education in the Department of Health, Education, and Welfare. She specialized in the educational problems of the handicapped. In 1967 she organized the first National Conference on Education of the Deaf. In 1968 she became associate director of legislative affairs for President Johnson's Committee on Consumer Interests. Three years later, after the election of Richard Nixon, she became deputy director of the newly created White House Office of Consumer Affairs. It was in that position that she met Senator ROBERT DOLE, Republican of Kansas. They were married in 1975.

U.S. Department of Labor

In 1973 President Nixon appointed her to a seven-year term on the Federal Trade Commission (FTC). To avoid any possibility of conflict of interest, she took a leave from her FTC post in 1976 to participate in the election campaign of her husband, who had been chosen as Gerald Ford's vice presidential running mate. When her husband ran for president in the 1980 primary elections, Dole resigned from her FTC post to play an active role in his campaign.

President Reagan appointed Dole assistant to the president for public liaison in 1981 and in 1983 secretary of transportation. As secretary of transportation, she presided over the deregulation of the airline and trucking industries. Dole resigned from her cabinet position in 1987 to help her husband wage an unsuccessful bid to secure the Republican party's presidential nomination. The man who defeated her husband and went on to win the presidency in the general election, George Bush, chose her to be secretary of labor when he assumed office in January 1989. Dole resigned from this post in 1990 to head the American Red Cross.

BIBLIOGRAPHY

Dole, Robert, and Elizabeth Dole, with Richard Norton Smith, *The Doles: Unlimited Partners,* 1988.

Dole, Robert Joseph

(July 22, 1923–   )
Senator, Representative

Republican Senate majority leader from 1980 to 1986, candidate for vice president of the Republican party in 1976, and two-time unsuccessful candidate for the Republican party's nomination for president in 1980 and 1988, Senate minority leader Robert Dole continues to play a major role in national politics.

Born in Russell, Kansas, Dole was so severely wounded while a soldier in Italy during World War II that even after three years of intensive physical therapy, he was never able to regain the use of his right arm. His handicap did not hinder his drive to succeed. After his discharge from the army, Dole earned his bachelor's degree and then, in 1952, his law degree from Washburn University in Topeka. After serving in the Kansas state legislature and acting as a county attorney, Dole was elected to the U.S. House of Representatives in 1960. He remained there until he won election to the U.S. Senate in 1968.

In Congress Dole became a staunch advocate for agricultural interests. Although his voting record in Congress was basically conservative, he supported civil rights programs, the food stamp program, and legislation to aid the handicapped. A loyal Republican, Dole defended Republican president RICHARD NIXON against Democratic attacks on Nixon's conduct of the Vietnam War, Supreme Court nominees, and involvement in the Watergate burglary (see RICHARD MILHOUS NIXON). Dole was not involved in nor tainted by the collapse of the Nixon administration due to the Watergate scandal.

As chairman of the Senate Finance Committee, Dole played a pivotal role in securing passage of a major Republican-sponsored tax bill in 1982. He is admired for his professional accomplishments and his caustic wit in political debate. Dole is married to ELIZABETH HANFORD DOLE, who served as secretary of transportation in the Reagan administration and was chosen by President GEORGE BUSH to be secretary of labor.

BIBLIOGRAPHY

Dole, Robert, and Elizabeth Dole, with Richard Norton Smith, *The Doles: Unlimited Partners*, 1988; Edsall, Thomas B., "Dole's Transformations: Ideological Blur Characterizes Career," *Washington Post*, March 9, 1987, p. 1; Greenhouse, Linda, "Ford Picks Senator Dole as Running Mate; Says He Wants Debate, and Carter Agrees," *New York Times*, August 20, 1976, p. 1.

Donnelly, Ignatius

(November 3, 1831–January 1, 1901)
Representative

Brilliant and iconoclastic, Ignatius Donnelly was an important advocate of radical political reform in nineteenth-century America.

Born in Philadelphia, Donnelly studied law in Pennsylvania and moved to Nininger, Minnesota, in 1856. When his land speculation efforts failed during the panic of 1857, he became a farmer and entered politics. Two years later, at age twenty-eight, he was elected lieutenant governor of Minnesota. From 1863 until 1869, as a Republican, he served three terms in Congress.

After his assistance in securing land grants for railroad companies was challenged in Congress by ELIHU B. WASHBURNE, the Minnesota Republican party leadership refused to support Donnelly's renomination for office and his political career in Washington ended.

Donnelly was convinced that much more reform than was being suggested by either the Republican or Democratic parties had to be initiated to correct the ills industrialization was causing in America. First as a Liberal Republican, then as a Greenback Democrat (see JAMES BAIRD WEAVER) and editor of the weekly newspaper the *Anti-Monopolist* from 1874 to 1879, and finally as a leader of the Populist party (see WEAVER) and editor of its newspaper, the *Representative*, Donnelly fought for reform.

Although he never held national political office again after 1869, Donnelly was elected to five terms in the Minnesota state senate from 1874 to 1878 and ran for governor of Minnesota on the Populist ticket in 1892. In 1892 Donnelly wrote the Populist party's platform, the preamble of which became famous as the party's creed. He was also nominated by the Populist party for vice president of the United States in 1900.

In addition to his political achievements, Donnelly had a career as a best-selling author. One of his books, *The Great Cryptogram* (1888), was not a financial success, but it is the one he is still remembered for today. In it, Donnelly attempted to prove that Francis Bacon was the real author of the plays attributed to William Shakespeare.

BIBLIOGRAPHY

Ridge, Martin, *Ignatius Donnelly: Politician*, 1962.

Donovan, William Joseph

(January 1, 1883–February 8, 1959)
Diplomat, Government Agency Director

During World War II William Donovan organized and directed the Office of Strategic Services, the military precursor of the Central Intelligence Agency.

Donovan was born in Buffalo, New York. After earning his bachelor's degree in 1905 and law degree in 1907 from Columbia University, he established a successful practice in Buffalo. While serving as an officer in the U.S. Army during World War I, he was wounded three times and awarded the Congressional Medal of Honor for bravery. After the war he returned to Buffalo, resumed the practice of law, and became active in New York Republican politics.

In 1924 Donovan was appointed assistant attorney general in charge of criminal matters.

One year later he rose to assistant U.S. attorney general for the Antitrust Division, a post he held until he resigned in 1928 to work in the election campaign of HERBERT HOOVER for president.

Donovan was a strong advocate of the need to increase the military preparedness of the United States in the 1930s. Several highly publicized trips to Europe, after which he reported on the growing Axis military threat to government officials, convinced Donovan that war in Europe was inevitable and that the United States would have no recourse but to become involved.

The quality of the military intelligence data Donovan gathered in the 1930s convinced U.S.

government officials of his espionage expertise. At the beginning of World War II, Secretary of the Navy FRANK KNOX asked Donovan to assess England's military capabilities. His trip to Great Britain was followed by another secret one to southeastern Europe and the eastern Mediterranean.

In July 1941 President FRANKLIN D. ROOSEVELT asked Donovan to create a new U.S. intelligence service designed to analyze information, implement counterpropaganda techniques, and direct special secret operations (subversion, sabotage, and counterintelligence) overseas. The Office of Strategic Services (OSS) was the result, and from 1942 to 1945, Donovan, with the rank of major general, served as its director.

In 1944 Donovan recommended that the United States create a permanent peacetime intelligence agency modeled after the OSS. President HARRY S TRUMAN disagreed and dissolved the OSS in 1945 as part of the national war demobilization. Donovan returned to his law practice. However, the cold war soon convinced the president and the Congress that such an agency was needed to fight communism, and in 1947 legislation was drafted to create the Central Intelligence Agency (CIA).

Donovan, an early supporter of the presidential candidacy of DWIGHT D. EISENHOWER, hoped to be appointed to head the CIA. Instead, in 1953 President Eisenhower chose CIA Deputy Director ALLEN DULLES to be the agency's first civilian director. Eisenhower named Donovan ambassador to Thailand. He served in Thailand from 1953 to 1954.

BIBLIOGRAPHY

Ford, Corey, *Donovan of OSS,* 1970; Smith, R. Harris, *OSS: The Secret History of America's First Central Intelligence Agency,* 1972; Stevenson, William, *A Man Called Intrepid: The Secret War,* 1976.

Douglas, Stephen Arnold

(April 23, 1813–June 3, 1861)
Candidate for President, Senator, Representative

The tragedy of Stephen A. Douglas's political career was that the harder he worked to find a middle-of-the-road position on slavery that would hold the Democratic party together, the more he inflamed the passions of both the supporters of slavery and the abolitionists.

Born in Brandon, Vermont, and raised in New England, Douglas received only a minimum of formal education. After attending the Canandaigua Academy in New York and beginning the study of law, Douglas abruptly decided to join the wave of immigrants flooding into the Mississippi valley.

After being admitted to the Illinois bar in 1834, Douglas established a law practice at Jacksonville, but politics was his true passion. Within a year he was elected state's attorney for the first judicial district; and only six years later, "Judge Douglas," as he was called for the rest of his life, was appointed to serve on the bench of the Illinois Supreme Court.

Following a brief stint in the state legislature in 1836, Douglas ran for Congress the next year as a Democrat and turned what was supposed to be a hopeless race into a narrow loss. He assumed the leadership of the Democratic party's statewide campaign efforts in 1840, served as the Illinois secretary of state, and then made an unsuccessful try for the U.S. Senate in 1842 while holding onto his state supreme court seat.

In 1843, after the Democratic party–dominated legislature had redrawn election districts to its advantage, Douglas won a close election to the House. He quickly earned a reputation as a popular, persuasive nationalist. He was reelected to Congress and in 1847 elected by the Illinois legislature to the Senate.

Library of Congress

At the beginning of the 1850s Douglas was at the peak of his personal and political life. The speculative real estate investments he had made after moving to Chicago earned Douglas a fortune. Short, muscular, and flamboyant, to his contemporaries Douglas seemed like a "steam engine in britches" as he urged that all of Oregon be taken (see JAMES KNOX POLK), supported the Mexican War (see JAMES KNOX POLK), and helped guide the Compromise of 1850 (see HENRY CLAY and MILLARD FILLMORE) through Congress. After almost winning the presidential nomination at the Democratic national convention in 1852, he was easily reelected to the Senate.

After 1852 Douglas's life seemed to lose the magic momentum it had had earlier. His wife died, and Douglas entered the most turbulent period in his career. Apparently blind to the growing popular hostility to politicians who attempted to maintain a middle-of-the-road position concerning slavery, Douglas continued to argue that the issue of whether or not a territory allowed slavery ought to be left to the settlers living there. This "popular sovereignty" proposal was the basis of his concessionary Kansas-Nebraska bill of 1854 (see FRANKLIN PIERCE). Since Douglas wanted the Nebraska territory organized (thus clearing the way for a transcontinental railroad that would benefit Northern speculators, of which he was one),

Douglas wooed Southern support for the bill by including an amendment that repealed the antislavery clause of the Missouri Compromise (see HENRY CLAY). The bill became law, but its passage enraged Northerners, increased divisiveness between the parties, and triggered the murder and mayhem that occurred over the next two years in "Bleeding Kansas."

Having thus alienated Northerners with the Kansas-Nebraska Act, Douglas proceeded to stick to his guns on popular sovereignty and anger the South with his position on the territory of Kansas's fraudulent Lecompton Constitution (see JAMES BUCHANAN and ROBERT JOHN WALKER). When in 1857, on the heels of the Dred Scott decision (see ROGER BROOKE TANEY), President James Buchanan supported the proslavery Lecompton Constitution, Douglas, knowing that most of the Kansas voters were against slavery in the territory, broke with his party and led the fight for congressional rejection of the constitution.

Prior to the congressional elections of 1858, Republican candidate ABRAHAM LINCOLN challenged Douglas to seven debates in their home state of Illinois, debates that would galvanize the nation with the candidates' clear presentations of opposing positions on slavery. "If each state will agree to mind its own business," argued Douglas at Quincy, "this republic can exist forever divided into free and slave States." Lincoln replied by thanking Douglas for making it clear that "his policy in regard to . . . slavery contemplates that it shall last forever."

Douglas argued in the debate at Freeport (an argument that subsequently became known as the Freeport Doctrine) that, despite the Dred Scott decision, a territory could legally exclude slavery. The Dred Scott decision had ruled that slaves were property and that the Fifth Amendment prohibited Congress from taking property without due process of law. Slavery, Douglas said, could not exist a day without "local police regulations," and all a territory need do was fail to enact such regulations. This, in effect, would keep the slaveholders out of the territory.

The Democrats managed to retain control of the Illinois legislature, and Douglas was returned for another term to the Senate in 1858. In 1860 he was nominated for president as the candidate of the Northern and Western wings of the Democratic party. His hopes of leading a united party were shattered as the rift between Democrats over slavery became solidified: the Southern wing split away and nominated JOHN C. BRECKINRIDGE on a separate slate. Legend has it that the cause of Douglas's failure to keep the support of Southern Democrats for his candidacy in 1860 was the Freeport Doctrine. In truth, his argument at Freeport was not new and had been stated earlier many times. It was important to him at Freeport to hold on to his Illinois constituency, as he knew he had already lost Southern voters because of his opposition to the Lecompton Constitution.

By the middle of the summer of 1860, Douglas knew he could not win, but he toured the nation to speak out for the preservation of the Union. After the election he gave President Lincoln his complete support. Before he died in 1861, he pleaded for everyone to "rally 'round the flag."

BIBLIOGRAPHY

Capers, Gerald M., *Stephen A. Douglas: Defender of the Union*, 1959; Johannsen, Robert W., *Stephen A. Douglas*, 1973; Milton, George F., *The Eve of Conflict: Stephen A. Douglas and the Needless War*, 1963.

Douglas, William Orville

(October 16, 1898–January 19, 1980)
Associate Justice of the Supreme Court

During his record thirty-six years on the Supreme Court, William O. Douglas was a consistent champion of individual civil liberties. In hundreds of opinions, frequently delivered in dissent, Douglas consistently voted for a broad exercise of the Supreme Court's powers to limit government power when it threatened to infringe on individual liberties.

Douglas was born in Maine, Minnesota. His father was an impoverished Presbyterian minister. Shortly after his birth, the family moved to California and later Yakima, Washington. There, in 1905, William was stricken with poliomyelitis. He recovered and, in order to build up his stamina, became an avid hiker.

Douglas graduated from Whitman College in 1920 and earned his law degree from Columbia University Law School in 1925. He joined a Wall Street law firm, but quickly became disenchanted and decided to become a law professor. After briefly teaching at Columbia, he settled at Yale in 1928 and became an expert on financial law.

President FRANKLIN D. ROOSEVELT appointed Douglas to the Securities and Exchange Commission (SEC), a New Deal agency created to regulate Wall Street business practices, in

1936. Nine months later, Douglas became the SEC chairman. In 1939 President Roosevelt appointed him to the Supreme Court, where he served until ill health forced him to resign in 1975.

During his long, controversial tenure on the Court, Douglas vigorously argued that the Bill of Rights was applicable to the states through the due process clause of the Fourteenth Amendment. After the 1961 decision in *Mapps* v. *Ohio*, when a majority of the Court agreed that the Fourth Amendment prohibition of unreasonable searches and seizures did apply to the states, Douglas's perspective on this issue was usually upheld. However, he still frequently spoke in the minority when it came to interpreting just how much individual liberty the Constitution protected.

In advocating what he termed "full and free discussion even of ideas we hate," Douglas read the First Amendment as a virtually absolute curb on governmental interference with speech of all kinds, with the press, with peaceable assembly, and with association: "The First Amendment makes confidence in the common sense of our people and in the maturity of their judgment the great postulate of our democracy.... When ideas compete in the market, full and free discussion exposes the false and they gain few adherents."

Douglas was also outspoken in seeking to protect people from unreasonable search and seizure, from erosions of their privilege against self-incrimination, from intrusions into their privacy, and from what he saw as lapses in due process: "It is no answer that a man is doubtlessly guilty. The Bill of Rights was designed to protect every accused against practices of the police which history showed were oppressive."

Douglas was extremely sensitive to the historical role of the Court in protecting the rights of "political, religious, and racial minorities," and advocated using whatever judicial tools were available or could be created through a broad interpretation of the Constitution by the Court to promote equality. He was a "judicial activist," in the sense of believing that the Court could be used to promote social change; as such, he helped to define the character of the Court under EARL WARREN.

In addition to his work on the Supreme Court, Douglas was an avid world traveler, wilderness hiker, prolific writer, naturalist, and conservationist.

BIBLIOGRAPHY

Douglas, William O., *An Almanac of Liberty*, 1954, *Democracy's Manifesto*, 1962, *A Wilderness Bill of Rights*, 1965, *Points of Rebellion*, 1970, and *Go East Young Man*, 1974.

Dukakis, Michael Stanley

(November 3, 1933–   )
Candidate for President

Michael Stanley Dukakis was born of Greek-American parents in Brookline, Massachusetts, where he has resided ever since. He graduated from Swarthmore College in 1955 and, following military service in the U.S. Army in Korea from 1955 to 1957, Harvard University Law School in 1960.

As a member of the Massachusetts House of Representatives from 1963 to 1971, Dukakis was the first legislator in America to introduce a no-fault automobile insurance bill. From 1971 to 1973 Dukakis was the moderator of public television's "The Advocates." In 1974 he was elected governor of Massachusetts.

When he was sworn into office as governor in January 1975, the state faced a budget deficit of over half a billion dollars. When he left office four years later, after losing the Democratic party's nomination for reelection in the primary to a conservative rival, the state had a budget surplus of $200 million.

Dukakis entered Massachusetts politics determined to rid it of corruption and patronage. He represented a new breed of liberal, one who was socially conscious—about minority and women's rights, and the environment—but fiscally prudent. He took pride in his honesty and analytic abilities, and disdained the process of political compromise and negotiation. This disdain came across as arrogance and was a major cause of his upset reelection defeat in the Democratic gubernatorial primary in 1978.

Between leaving office in 1979 and winning election to a second term as governor in 1982, Dukakis taught at Harvard University's Kennedy School of Government. He returned to politics a "changed" politician, willing to cultivate allies and make political appointments. He had the good fortune of winning election just as Massachusetts was entering an economic boom based on high-technology growth and President RONALD REAGAN's increased defense spending. After Dukakis was reelected to a third term as governor in 1986, the so-called Massachusetts miracle, allegedly the work of a Democrat in the age of Reagan, made him attractive to large constituencies of northern and western liberals, as well as to significant groups of progressive businesspeople, and catapulted him to the position of Democratic presidential nominee in 1988.

In the campaign, however, many of his old liabilities—his arrogance, stiffness, technocratic mind-set, and inability to arouse enthusiasm among working-class voters—resurfaced, and he went down to a resounding defeat at the hands of GEORGE BUSH.

During his last two years in office, Dukakis's popularity plummeted in Massachusetts as the state experienced a recession and accompanying tax revenue shortfall that necessitated new taxes.

BIBLIOGRAPHY

Dukakis, Kitty, *Now You Know,* 1990; Gaines, Richard, and Michael Segal, *Dukakis: The Man Who Would Be President,* 1987; Kenney, Charles, *Dukakis: An American Odyssey,* 1988.

Dulles, Allen Welsh

(April 7, 1893–January 30, 1969)
Director of the Central Intelligence Agency, Diplomat

Allen Dulles played a major role in the creation and organization of the Central Intelligence Agency (CIA) and served as the CIA's first civilian director from 1953 until 1961.

Dulles was born in Watertown, New York, earned his bachelor's degree in 1914 and master's degree in 1916 at Princeton University, then joined the foreign service. During World War I he was stationed at Bern, Switzerland, and placed in charge of intelligence activities that involved establishing connections with enemy agents in the Balkans and Austria-Hungary. In 1918, while serving as a member of the

American Commission to Negotiate the Peace, he helped to draw the new national boundaries in Eastern Europe.

Dulles returned to the United States in 1920, attended law courses at George Washington University, and, after obtaining his law degree in 1926, left the State Department to join a prestigious Wall Street law firm.

During the 1930s Dulles called on the United States to recognize the threat of Adolf Hitler. When the United States entered World War II, Dulles joined the new Office of Strategic Services (OSS), an agency under the jurisdiction of the Joint Chiefs of Staff, headed by his friend WILLIAM DONOVAN. He was placed in charge of the OSS's New York City office and in 1942 was again assigned to establish an enemy intelligence gathering center at Bern, Switzerland. In 1945 Dulles negotiated the surrender of the German forces in northern Italy. Critics questioned his exclusion of the Soviets from the negotiations, but his clandestine effort solidified his national reputation as America's greatest covert operations expert.

When President HARRY S TRUMAN disbanded the OSS after World War II, Dulles returned to his Wall Street law practice. In 1947 he helped to draft the legislation that created the Central Intelligence Agency. He returned to full-time government service in 1950 when President Truman asked him to help organize the agency he envisioned. From 1950 to 1953 Dulles was the deputy director of the CIA, and in 1953 President DWIGHT D. EISENHOWER appointed Dulles to be the CIA's first civilian director. (His brother, JOHN FOSTER DULLES, also served in the Eisenhower administration as under secretary and then secretary of state.)

In the 1950s, during the height of the cold war, the CIA under Dulles's leadership exercised tremendous power. Dulles believed that the United States had to fight communism "fire with fire." He orchestrated the overthrow of governments in Iran in 1953 and Guatemala in 1954, and authorized high reconnaissance flights by U-2 aircraft over the Soviet Union. However, the agency also suffered major failures, as in its unsuccessful effort in 1958 to install a pro-American government in Indonesia, and the shooting down of a U-2 by the Soviet Union (which prompted the cancellation of the 1960 American/Soviet summit). Dulles was forced to resign as director of the CIA in 1961 by President JOHN F. KENNEDY after the CIA-orchestrated invasion of Cuba at the Bay of Pigs ended in a humiliating fiasco.

BIBLIOGRAPHY

Dulles, Allen, *The Craft of Intelligence*, 1963, and *Secret Surrender*, 1966; Mosley, Leonard, *Dulles: A Biography of Eleanor, Allen, and John Foster Dulles and Their Family Network*, 1978; *New York Times*, January 31, 1969; Ranelagh, John, *The Agency: The Rise and Decline of the CIA*, 1986; Smith, Bradley, *The Shadow Warriors: OSS and the Origins of the CIA*, 1983, and with Elena Agarossi, *Operation Sunrise: The Secret Surrender*, 1979; Smith, R. Harris, *OSS: The Secret History of America's First Central Intelligence Agency*, 1972.

Dulles, John Foster

(February 25, 1888–May 24, 1959)
Secretary of State, Diplomat, Senator

Over the course of a fifty-two-year career, John Foster Dulles fulfilled a wide variety of important international diplomatic roles. As secretary of state in the Eisenhower administration, Dulles became famous for his strong anticommunist views and insistence that the United States help small countries to withstand aggression.

Born in Washington, D.C., Dulles had planned to become a minister; but after his grandfather took him, at age nineteen, to the Second Hague Peace Conference in 1907 (which attempted to establish codes for warfare and steps for disarmament) to serve as secretary to the Chinese delegation, Dulles decided on a diplomatic career. He graduated from Princeton in 1908, attended the Sorbonne in Paris, and obtained his law degree from George Washington University in 1911. That same year he was admitted to the bar and began working for a New York City law firm.

During World War I Dulles was counsel to the War Trade Board and was one of President WOODROW WILSON's advisers at the Versailles treaty negotiations. After his work at Versailles, he returned to private law practice in New York City and became a leading international lawyer.

Dulles served as a delegate to the United Nations from 1946 to 1948 and in 1950. In 1951, with the rank of ambassador, he helped negotiate the Japanese peace treaty, which formally ended World War II. He was also a special adviser to the secretary of state at the

Library of Congress

Councils of Foreign Ministers in London in 1945, Moscow in 1947, and Paris in 1949. Governor THOMAS E. DEWEY of New York appointed Dulles to complete a U.S. Senate term in July 1949, but he lost the general election for the seat that fall.

Appointed secretary of state in 1953 by President DWIGHT D. EISENHOWER, Dulles was given unprecedented authority in shaping American foreign policy. "I think he is the wisest, most dedicated man that I know," said the president. Critics questioned the wisdom of Dulles's belief that communism was a monolithic moral evil that had to be contained through "massive retaliation." Dulles threatened such retaliation against the Soviet Union and China if they attacked any country. It was necessary, he warned, to go to "the brink of war." He believed that his strategy of "brinkmanship" had succeeded in ending the Korean War, settling the Indochina War (between the French and the Vietnamese communists), and ensuring the independence of the Nationalist Chinese forces on the island of Formosa (Taiwan). The inability of the United States to aid the people of Hungary in their 1956 revolt against Soviet domination, however, revealed the limitations of a strategy so dependent on brinkmanship.

During his six-year tenure as secretary of state, Dulles argued against compromising with the Soviet Union and China, and he played an important role in keeping China from attacking two islands in the Formosa

Strait (Quemoy and Matsu). But Dulles also understood the need to undertake actions that would reduce the appeal of communism to the third world. He opposed the 1956 Anglo-French-Israeli invasion of Egypt on these grounds; he also urged Eisenhower to protect the rights of black schoolchildren in Little Rock, Arkansas, in 1957 to bolster the image of America among the emerging African nations.

Dulles was instrumental in the promulgation of the Eisenhower Doctrine (see DWIGHT DAVID EISENHOWER), the establishment of the Southeast Asia Treaty Organization (SEATO),

and the Baghdad Pact, later called the Central Treaty Organization (CENTO). Critics dubbed his efforts to encircle the Soviet Union and Communist China by treaty alliances "Pactomania."

Dulles was forced to resign from office in April 1959 due to illness. He died the next month from cancer.

BIBLIOGRAPHY

Beal, John R., *John Foster Dulles*, 1957; Gerson, Louis L., *John Foster Dulles*, 1968.

Durkin, Martin Patrick

(March 18, 1894–November 13, 1955)
Secretary of Labor

The son of an Irish immigrant, Martin Durkin was born in Chicago. At age seventeen he left school to become a steamfitter's apprentice. After serving in the army during World War I, Durkin began his career in 1921 as the business manager of the largest local chapter of the national plumbers and pipefitters union. Six years later, he was elected vice president of the Chicago Building Trades Council.

In 1933 Durkin was appointed by the Democratic governor of Illinois as the state director of labor. During his eight years in office he oversaw the establishment of minimum wage guidelines, unemployment compensation programs, maximum working hours for women and children, safe working condition requirements, and labor dispute mediation and conciliation services. He lost this position in 1941 as a result of his denial of unemployment benefits to striking members of the United Mine Workers (UMW). The Congress of Industrial Organizations (CIO), the labor federation to

which the UMW belonged, felt unfairly treated by Durkin, whose union loyalties lay with the American Federation of Labor (AFL), the CIO's archrival.

Durkin returned to his union career and in 1943 was elected national president of the plumbers and pipefitters union, to which he still belonged.

In addition to his union responsibilities, Durkin served during World War II on the National War Labor Board. In 1951, during the Korean War, he served on the National Security Resources Board.

Republican President-elect DWIGHT D. EISENHOWER chose Democrat Durkin as his secretary of labor in 1952. Durkin's membership in the conservative AFL made him acceptable to Eisenhower, but he was a controversial appointment for others. Conservative Republicans attacked the selection of a Democratic union official, and union leaders bemoaned the willingness of a leader of organized labor to serve in the cabinet of an antilabor Republican administration. Durkin resigned after serving just eight months in office when his suggestions for modifications to the Taft–Hartley Act (see HARRY S TRUMAN) were rejected by the Eisenhower administration.

BIBLIOGRAPHY

Frier, David A., *Conflict of Interest in the Eisenhower Administration*, 1969; Goulden, Joseph C., *Meany*, 1972.

Ehrlichman, John Daniel

(March 20, 1925–   )
Presidential Adviser

John Ehrlichman, President RICHARD NIXON's domestic affairs adviser from 1969 to 1973, was imprisoned for his participation in the Watergate scandal (see RICHARD MILHOUS NIXON).

Ehrlichman was born in Tacoma, Washington. After serving as an aircraft bomber navigator in Europe during World War II, he earned a bachelor's degree at the University of California at Los Angeles in 1948 and obtained a law degree from Stanford University three years later. He settled in Seattle, established a successful law practice, and in 1967 became an instructor in law at the University of Washington.

At the encouragement of his friend H. R. HALDEMAN, Ehrlichman gradually became more involved with supporting Nixon's ambitions for the presidency. In 1962 he worked on Nixon's campaign for governor of California, and in 1968 managed Nixon's national campaign schedule. His loyalty, industriousness, and willingness to follow orders without question led to his appointment by President-elect Nixon in 1968 as presidential counsel. In 1969 he was promoted to presidential assistant for domestic affairs.

Ehrlichman was forced to resign from the White House staff in April 1973 after two Nixon administration officials had implicated him in the Watergate scandal. He was convicted on January 1, 1975, of conspiracy, obstruction of justice, and two counts of perjury. After serving eighteen months in federal prison at Safford, Arizona, he settled in Santa Fe, New Mexico, and became a writer. He also did volunteer legal counseling for local Indian and Chicano community groups.

BIBLIOGRAPHY

Ehrlichman, John, *The Company*, 1976, and *The Whole Truth*, 1979; *Esquire*, July 1976; *Newsweek*, December 23, 1974; *Washington Post Magazine*, April 29 and May 8, 1979.

Eisenhower, Dwight David

(October 14, 1890–March 28, 1969)
President

For almost twenty years Dwight David Eisenhower, as supreme commander of the Allied forces in Europe during World War II, commander of North Atlantic Treaty Alliance (NATO; see HARRY S TRUMAN) forces from 1950 to 1952, and president of the United States from 1953 to 1961, played a major role in the events that shaped the modern world.

One of six sons, Eisenhower was born in Denison, Texas, but grew up in Abilene, Kansas. After graduating from West

Courtesy Dwight D. Eisenhower Library

Point in 1915, he commanded a tank training school during World War I in Pennsylvania. In 1933 he became Army Chief of Staff General Douglas MacArthur's administrative assistant. Eisenhower accompanied MacArthur to the Philippines in 1935 and assisted in building up the commonwealth's defenses until 1940. Lieutenant Colonel Eisenhower attracted considerable public attention in 1941 when the troops he commanded in huge war game maneuvers in Louisiana defeated their opponents through the careful coordination of infantry, tank, and airplane forces.

Promoted to brigadier general, Eisenhower returned to Washington after the attack by the Japanese on Pearl Harbor to be the assistant chief of staff to GEORGE C. MARSHALL. In this position he helped draft the U.S. military's World War II global strategy, outlined a plan for a cross–English Channel invasion of France, and designed the European theater of operations command that he was appointed to lead in June 1942.

As supreme commander of the Allied Expeditionary Forces in World War II, Eisenhower directed the invasions of North Africa, Italy, France, and Germany. He was not a colorful figure like General George Patton or Field Marshal Bernard Montgomery. However, his style of firm, calm leadership proved to be ideally suited for welding the disparate forces of the Allies into an efficient military machine capable of accomplishing the largest amphibious invasion in history at Normandy in 1944 and then crushing Nazi Germany. "He has the power of drawing the hearts of men towards him as a magnet attracts the bit of metal. He merely has to smile at you, and you trust him at once," said General Montgomery in an attempt to explain Eisenhower's leadership charisma.

After Germany's defeat, Eisenhower oversaw the demobilization of American troops before leaving the service to become president of Columbia University in 1948. In 1950 President Harry S Truman appointed Eisenhower supreme commander of NATO, a position he held until his decision to seek the Republican nomination for president in 1952. The immensely popular Eisenhower, nicknamed Ike by reporters, was viewed by the American public as the architect of a peaceful world order and the personification of traditional American goodness.

Efforts to embroil Eisenhower in the controversy raging around McCarthyism (see JOSEPH RAYMOND McCARTHY) failed, and he made a brilliant campaign promise to go to Korea and end the fighting there. Eisenhower, with the young, conservative RICHARD M. NIXON as his running mate, obtained 442 electoral votes to his Democratic challenger ADLAI E. STEVENSON's 89, winning by a plurality of more than 6 million votes.

Eisenhower's administration is remembered chiefly for its lack of legislative initiatives and calm style of consensus management during a period of national prosperity. Eisenhower believed that most problems would be better solved at the local government level than through programs designed and managed, like those of the New Deal, from Washington. He had campaigned on the promise of cutting back on government—on the size of the budget, on taxes, and on regulation of the nation's business. Once in office, however, Eisenhower, always a practical man, recognized how popular the New Deal programs were and instead of ending them actually expanded some, such as Social Security benefits. His efforts to eliminate the budget deficit and to end price supports for farm products failed.

In *Brown* v. *Board of Education* (1954; see EARL WARREN) the Supreme Court ordered that integration of the public schools must go forward "with all deliberate speed." Eisenhower did not believe that a president should publicly approve or disapprove of Supreme Court decisions. Southerners, he said, should be given a chance to adjust to the great social changes integration would entail. The process would have to go ahead slowly. "We have got to have reason and sense and education, and a lot of other developments that go hand and hand in the process—if this process is going to have any real acceptance in the United States." But mob violence occurred in Little Rock, Arkansas, in 1957 when black children attempted to attend school, and the illegal opposition of the governor of the state to integrating the public schools drove the president to take action. Eisenhower sent more than a thousand paratroopers to Little Rock and federalized 10,000 Arkansas National Guardsmen.

He also supported the establishment of the Civil Rights Commission. Neither of these actions, however, meant that Eisenhower was making civil rights a priority of his administration. In general, Eisenhower left the issue of civil rights up to the Supreme Court and local authorities.

Eisenhower suffered a heart attack in September 1955 but returned to his duties within two months' time. He ran for reelection in 1956, once again against Adlai Stevenson, and won a landslide electoral vote of 457 to 73.

In foreign policy the Eisenhower years stand out as a period of relative peace. One month after his election in 1952, Eisenhower traveled to Korea and halted the fighting through an uneasy truce with North Korea. For much of his eight-year administration, he avoided stark confrontations with the Soviet Union; he even hoped to improve U.S.–Soviet relations to the point where the two superpowers might contemplate weapons' reductions.

Nevertheless, Eisenhower could not escape the realities of the cold war. He relied upon the threatened use of American nuclear weapons to deter Soviet and Communist Chinese aggression (see JOHN FOSTER DULLES). He involved the United States in the affairs of Asian, Middle Eastern, and Latin American nations in the pursuit of U.S. cold war objectives.

In 1954 he committed the United States to the Southeast Asia Treaty Organization to protect Southeast Asian nations from communist attack. This commitment helped to draw the United States ever deeper into the war between the communists and noncommunists in Vietnam.

In 1956 Eisenhower opposed the invasion of Egypt by Britain, France, and Israel for fear of driving Arab states into the Soviet camp. (This invasion was a response to the Egyptian president Gamal Abdal Nasser's nationalization of the Suez Canal.) In 1957, having just promulgated the Eisenhower Doctrine, which pledged U.S. aid to any Middle Eastern country threatened by international communism, Eisenhower sent 5,000 marines to Lebanon to suppress an internal revolt against the U.S.–supported government. Also in 1957, when the Soviet Union shocked America by launching Sputnik, the first artificial satellite into space, a reluctant Eisenhower authorized America's entry into the "space race."

Finally, on the island republic of Cuba, located only 90 miles from Key West, Florida, a corrupt pro-American dictatorship was overthrown by Fidel Castro in 1959. Initial American approval of Castro turned to hostility as he began turning Cuba into a communist dictatorship. Eisenhower broke diplomatic relations with Cuba just before leaving office in January 1961.

For those and other reasons, Eisenhower's efforts to improve relations between the United States and the Soviet Union were unsuccessful. A hoped-for Paris summit in 1960 was canceled when an American U-2 spy plane was shot down over the Soviet Union and Eisenhower refused to apologize for the incident. The inability to achieve any weapons reductions agreements was Eisenhower's greatest disappointment. He feared the danger posed by "the acquisition of unwarranted influence, whether sought or unsought, by the military-industrial complex" in American life.

Popular and beloved by Americans after leaving the White House, Eisenhower retired to his farm in Gettysburg, Pennsylvania, in 1961. Following another serious heart attack in 1965, he concentrated until his death four years later on writing his memoirs, playing golf, hunting, fishing, and painting.

The image of Eisenhower as an uninvolved, figurehead president has recently been reconsidered. Revisionist historians have come to view Eisenhower as a quietly activist and extraordinarily shrewd president who projected an air of simplicity, naiveté, and simplemindedness in order to pursue his objectives more effectively behind the scenes. This argument may appear strongest in Eisenhower's restrained use of military adventurism abroad—less than in either Harry Truman's or JOHN F. KENNEDY's presidencies—and in his determination to curb the power of the military and of the military-industrial complex in American politics.

BIBLIOGRAPHY

Ambrose, Stephen E., *The Supreme Commander: The War Years of General Dwight D. Eisenhower*, 1970, *Eisenhower, Soldier, General of the Army, President-Elect, 1890–1952*, vol. 1, 1983, and *Eisenhower, The President, 1953–1961*, vol. 2, 1984; Divine, Robert A., *Eisenhower and the Cold War*, 1981; Eisenhower, David, *Eisenhower at War: 1943 to 1945*, 1986; Ferrell, Robert H. (ed.), *The Eisenhower Diaries*, 1981; Greenstein, Fred I., *The Hidden Hand Presidency*, 1982; Sixsmith, E. K., *Eisenhower as Military Commander*, 1983; Wills, Garry, *The Kennedy Imprisonment*, 1982.

Ellsworth, Oliver

(April 29, 1745–November 26, 1807)
Chief Justice of the Supreme Court, Senator

O liver Ellsworth was notable chiefly for drafting the Judiciary Act of 1789, the basis for organizing the federal judiciary in the United States.

A native of Windsor, Connecticut, Ellsworth attended Yale and the College of New Jersey (now Princeton University). He was admitted to the bar in 1771. Active in local politics, Ellsworth was appointed state's attorney for Hartford County and then elected to the Continental Congress. In 1780 he became a member of the governor's council of Connecticut, and in 1784 he was named to the state superior court.

Little is known of Ellsworth's activities as a member of the Continental Congress. His importance as a national political figure began in 1787, when he became a delegate to the Constitutional Convention. There he played a major part in developing the Connecticut Compromise (see ROGER SHERMAN), which established the bicameral legislature (Senate and House of Representatives) that provided balanced representation between states and population. Each state sent two senators to Congress, but the number of representatives it elected was determined by population.

Ellsworth was elected one of Connecticut's first two U.S. senators and served from 1789 to 1796. During his term he drafted the Judiciary Act of 1789, which provided for the Supreme Court (one chief justice and five associates), thirteen district courts, and three circuit courts, and established the attorney general's office. He also drafted the first set of Senate rules, presented from the conference committee the final form of amendments to the Constitution that became known as the Bill of Rights, drafted the bill for North Carolina's admission to statehood, and drew up the first bill regulating the consular service. JOHN ADAMS remarked of Ellsworth's Senate work that he was the "firmest pillar of his (GEORGE WASHINGTON's) whole administration."

In 1796 Ellsworth was appointed chief justice of the Supreme Court and held that position until 1800.

Ellsworth's special talent was as an advocate, rather than as a learned jurist; his success in the Continental Congress, the Constitutional Convention, and the Senate was due more to his skill as a lawyer than as a judge. His judicial decisions were more a product of common sense than knowledge of law and legal precedent.

At the request of President John Adams, Ellsworth assisted in negotiations with the French in 1799, although he was unhappy with the position. The treaty of 1800 (see JOHN ADAMS) that resulted was not very auspicious for the United States, but it did help avoid war. Ellsworth became ill in Europe. He resigned from the Supreme Court in 1800 and avoided any further involvement in politics.

BIBLIOGRAPHY

Brown, William G., *The Life of Oliver Ellsworth*, 1970.

Ervin, Samuel James, Jr.

(September 27, 1896–April 23, 1985)
Senator, Representative

Although he always described himself as "just an ol' country lawyer," Senator Sam Ervin played a vital and sophisticated role in guiding the Senate's hearings on the Watergate break-in and cover-up that eventually led to the resignation of President RICHARD NIXON.

Ervin's prominence at the end of a twenty-year career in the Senate obscured a complex record that could combine traditional southern opposition to civil rights with the scrupulous defense of the constitutional separation of church and state. Born in Morganton, North Carolina, Ervin attended the University of North Carolina. After serving in France during World War I, he attended Harvard Law School. He was elected to the state legislature in 1923, where he served three terms over a ten-year period. In 1925 he voted against a bill that would have banned the teaching of evolution in the public schools with the comment, "Only one good thing can come of this. The monkeys in the jungle will be pleased to know that the North Carolina legislature has absolved them from any responsibility for humanity. . . ."

Ervin became a county judge in 1935, a superior court judge in 1937, and a member of the U.S. House of Representatives in 1946 and 1947 before being named to the North Carolina Supreme Court in 1948. In 1954 he was appointed to fill a Senate vacancy. Well-liked for his down-home style and frequent Bible quotations, Ervin was reelected to the Senate until he decided to retire in 1974.

As a member of the Senate Judiciary Committee, Ervin quickly established a reputation as a constitutional law expert with a conservative outlook. He opposed the civil rights legislation of the 1960s and consistently voted against social welfare legislation such as Medicare, the Model Cities program, and Head Start. However, he was a sponsor of the 1964 Criminal Justice Act, which provided for free legal counsel for indigent defendants in federal court. He also led the Senate fight against a proposed constitutional amendment in 1966 to permit prayer in the public schools. "The government," he said, "must keep its hands off religion if our people are to enjoy religious freedom."

Because of his colorful use of language and persistent quest for the truth, Ervin gained national recognition during the televised Watergate hearings (see RICHARD MILHOUS NIXON) in 1973 when he headed the Senate Select Committee on Presidential Campaign Activities. Assigned to investigate the events that surrounded the 1972 burglary at the Democratic party's national headquarters, by 1974 the committee had evidence that incriminated many of the Nixon administration's highest officials and forced the resignation of President Nixon. Ervin's dogged pursuit of justice during these investigations, in combination with his evident decency and sense of humor, made him a hero to millions of Americans. He spent the last decade of his life practicing law in Morganton and writing about his career.

BIBLIOGRAPHY

Clancy, Paul R., *Just A Country Lawyer*, 1974; Dabney, Dick, *A Good Man*, 1976; Ervin, Sam J., Jr., *The Whole Truth: The Watergate Conspiracy*, 1981.

Evarts, William Maxwell

(February 6, 1818–February 28, 1901)
Secretary of State, Attorney General, Diplomat, Senator

William Maxwell Evarts managed to combine a brilliant legal career with a successful political one. In addition to arguing cases before the Supreme Court, Evarts was President ANDREW JOHNSON's defense attorney during the impeachment proceedings, represented the Republican party before the committee established by Congress to settle the disputed Hayes–Tilden presidential election (see RUTHERFORD BIRCHARD HAYES), and was named U.S. counsel before the *Alabama* claims (see CHARLES FRANCIS ADAMS) tribunal at Geneva, Switzerland.

Born in Boston, Evarts graduated from Yale College in 1837. After studying at Harvard Law School, he was admitted to the New York bar in 1841. From 1849 to 1853 he was assistant U.S. attorney for the southern district of New York. After playing an important part in the creation of the Republican party, he served as chairman of the New York delegation to the Republican convention of 1860.

During the Civil War Evarts made two trips to London as a representative of the U.S. government to persuade the British to stop providing aid to the Confederacy. After the war he backed the effort to have JEFFERSON DAVIS tried for treason and argued a number of cases before the Supreme Court.

Evarts served as attorney general from July 1868 to March 1869, the last eight months of President Johnson's administration. Two years later, he represented U.S. claimants seeking war damages from Great Britain for its assistance in helping the Confederacy to procure raider warships like the *Alabama*.

From 1877 to 1881 he served as President Rutherford B. Hayes's secretary of state. As secretary of state, he supported the construction of a U.S.–built, owned, and operated canal across Central America. The Panama Canal was opened in 1914.

In 1885 Evarts was elected to the Senate. Deteriorating eyesight forced him to retire at the end of his term in 1891.

BIBLIOGRAPHY

Barrow, Charles L., *William M. Evarts,* 1941; Dyer, Brainerd, *The Public Career of William M. Evarts,* 1933; Evarts, Sherman (ed.), *Arguments and Speeches of William M. Evarts,* 3 vols., 1919.

Everett, Edward

(April 11, 1794–January 15, 1865)
Secretary of State, Diplomat, Senator, Representative

Restless and brilliant, Edward Everett was a Unitarian minister, college professor, and successful politician before he discovered his true avocation and became the most famous public speaker of his time.

Everett was born in Dorchester, Massachusetts, into an affluent and prominent family. He graduated from Harvard College in 1811 and earned his master's degree in theology there three years later. From 1814 to 1815 Everett was a Unitarian minister in Boston. In 1815 he accepted an appointment as a professor of Greek at Harvard, studied in Europe, and was awarded his doctorate in philosophy from the University of Göt-

Library of Congress

tingen in 1817. While teaching at Harvard from 1819 to 1825, Everett edited the influential *North American Review.*

As a member of the U.S. House of Representatives from 1825 to 1835, Everett sided with his New England colleagues and opposed President ANDREW JACKSON's policy against the Second Bank of the United States (see NICHOLAS BIDDLE and ROGER TANEY). Although he personally detested slavery, Everett refused to attack the institution. He was sure that the issue was so volatile that a civil war was possible.

Everett left Congress in 1835 to begin the first of four consecutive one-year terms as governor of

Massachusetts. As governor, he improved public education and encouraged railroad expansion.

In 1841 Everett was appointed minister to Great Britain. He served in England for four years and then became president of Harvard College for the next three.

After DANIEL WEBSTER's death in 1852, Everett served as secretary of state for the last four months of President MILLARD FILLMORE's term. In this brief period he helped to write the note Commodore Matthew Perry carried with him to Japan on the journey that ended Japanese isolation from the West.

Elected to the Senate while secretary of state, Everett served only fifteen months of his term before resigning in 1854 rather than denounce the Kansas-Nebraska Act (see FRANKLIN PIERCE), as his constituents and political party colleagues demanded. He believed that the act offered the only hope of avoiding conflict between the North and the South.

After leaving the Senate, Everett concentrated upon using his considerable powers as a public speaker to raise money for worthy causes. He continued to denounce abolitionist extremists and even campaigned across the nation for compromise in 1860 as the vice presidential nominee of the Constitutional Union party. Once the Civil War began, Everett drew immense crowds as he traveled throughout the North speaking on behalf of the Union cause. His most famous speech, now virtually completely forgotten, was the two-hour soliloquy he delivered at Gettysburg just before President ABRAHAM LINCOLN delivered his much shorter, but far more enduring, Gettysburg Address.

BIBLIOGRAPHY

Frothingham, Paul R., *Edward Everett, Orator and Statesman*, 1925.

Fairbanks, Charles Warren

(May 11, 1852–June 4, 1918)
Vice President, Senator

Born in a one-room farmhouse in Unionville, Ohio, Charles W. Fairbanks attended Ohio Wesleyan University. After being admitted to the bar in 1874, Fairbanks moved to Indianapolis, Indiana, and earned a considerable fortune as a successful attorney for railroad companies.

Long active in Indiana Republican party politics, Fairbanks first attracted national attention as the keynote speaker at the Republican convention in 1896. The following year he was elected to the U.S. Senate, serving from 1897 to 1905. While in the Senate, Fairbanks played an important role in securing the passage of WILLIAM MCKINLEY's programs.

Although his conservative, pro–big business political views were very different from President THEODORE ROOSEVELT's, Fairbanks was selected to be Roosevelt's running mate in 1904 to balance the Republican ticket and to secure the votes of Indiana. Fairbanks hoped to use the national exposure provided by the 1904 campaign and the position of vice president as a stepping-stone to the presidency. He visited thirty-three states and traveled 25,000 miles during the campaign. After the election was won, however, President Roosevelt ignored Fairbanks in public and mocked him in private.

Passed over for the presidential nomination in 1908, Fairbanks did manage to exact some revenge. In 1912, as the chairman of the Republican convention, he supported WILLIAM HOWARD TAFT against Roosevelt. Fairbanks died two years after his effort to be nominated for president in 1916 failed.

BIBLIOGRAPHY

Harris, Addison C., "Charles Warren Fairbanks," *North American Review*, May 1908.

Fall, Albert Bacon

(November 26, 1861–November 30, 1944)
Secretary of the Interior, Senator

Born in Frankfort, Kentucky, Albert B. Fall moved to Clarksville, Texas, in 1881. Six years later, after exploring the area on a mining expedition, he purchased a ranch and established a law practice in Las Cruces, New Mexico. His clients were primarily large development, mining, and lumber corporations.

From 1890 to 1897 and again from 1902 to 1904, as a Democrat, Fall served in the New Mexico territorial legislature. From 1893 to 1895 he was an associate justice of the New Mexico Supreme Court. Twice, in 1897 and in 1907, he served briefly as territorial attorney general.

In 1908 Fall abandoned the Democratic party and became a Republican. When New Mexico became a state in 1912, he became one of its first U.S. senators. He served in the Senate until President WARREN G. HARDING appointed him secretary of the interior in 1921.

Three months after taking office, Fall convinced President Harding and Secretary of the Navy EDWIN DENBY to transfer control of naval oil lands to him. He then accepted a $404,000 bribe for granting exclusive drilling rights to the Teapot Dome Naval Oil Reserve in Wyoming. In March 1923 Fall resigned his cabinet post because his proposal to transfer the Forest Service from the Agriculture to the Interior Department was blocked by conservationists. That October, hearings were begun in the Senate that uncovered Fall's, and eventually other Harding administration officials', larcenous behavior. The investigation of the Teapot Dome scandal (see WARREN GAMALIEL HARDING), as the incident came to be called, was used to great effect by the Democrats in the 1924 and 1928 elections.

When called to testify, Fall denied ever receiving a bribe. However, after the men who had provided the bribe confessed, Fall was convicted of lying under oath and conspiracy to defraud the government, and sentenced to one year in prison. Fall served his time in jail in 1931, at age sixty-nine, and thus became the first cabinet officer ever convicted and imprisoned for a serious crime committed while in office.

BIBLIOGRAPHY

Bates, J. Leonard, *The Origins of the Teapot Dome: Progressives, Parties and Petroleum, 1909–1921*, 1963; Stratton, David H., "New Mexico Machiavellian? The Story of Albert B. Fall," *Montana: The Magazine of Western History*, October 1957, and "The Memoirs of Albert B. Fall," *Southwestern Studies*, March 15, 1966.

Farley, James Aloysius

(May 30, 1888–June 9, 1976)
Postmaster General

A prosperous businessman born in Grassy Point, New York, James Farley managed the key political campaigns that brought FRANKLIN D. ROOSEVELT national attention. He played an important role in helping Roosevelt to win election as governor of New York in 1928 and 1930, in securing the Democratic party's presidential nomination for Roosevelt in 1932, and, as national party chairman, in managing Roosevelt's 1932 and 1936 election and reelection campaigns. In appreciation of his political talent and efforts, President Roosevelt appointed Farley postmaster general in 1933.

Although Farley and Roosevelt were political allies, they were never close friends. Farley did not support many of Roosevelt's New Deal programs and felt that the men who composed the president's brain trust, or inner circle of advisers, did not deserve the power they wielded because they were not loyal Democrats.

Farley's relationship with Roosevelt ended when he opposed Roosevelt's decision to seek a third term in 1940. After his own effort to secure the Democratic presidential nomination failed, Farley resigned from the cabinet, became an executive at the Coca-Cola Company, and never participated in national politics again.

BIBLIOGRAPHY

Farley, James A., *Behind the Ballots*, 1938, and *Jim Farley's Story*, 1948.

Ferraro, Geraldine Anne

(August 26, 1935–)
Representative

Geraldine Ferraro was the first woman and the first Italian American ever nominated for vice president by a major political party. The Democratic party lost the presidential race in 1984, but Ferraro's strong performance under intense media scrutiny and political pressure challenged gender and ethnic stereotypes.

Ferraro was born in Newburgh, New York, to Italian immigrant parents. The death of her father when she was eight years old meant economic hardship for Ferraro and her mother and younger sister. With the help of a scholarship, Ferraro was able to attend Marymount Manhattan College. She became a public school teacher after graduation in 1956 and worked on her law degree at nights at Ford-

ham University Law School. In 1960 she earned her law degree and married John A. Zaccaro. Ferraro kept her maiden name in honor of her mother. She was admitted to the bar in 1961.

Ferraro practiced law part-time for ten years, primarily in her husband's growing real estate business, so that she would have time to take care of their three children. When the youngest entered school in 1974, she became an assistant district attorney in Queens. Four years later she successfully ran for the U.S. House of Representatives.

In Congress Ferraro accomplished the difficult task of reconciling her personal beliefs with those of her predominantly blue-collar, Catholic constituents. As a Roman Catholic, she was opposed to abortion; but as a feminist, she was committed to the right of women to be free to choose whether or not to have an abortion without government interference. Offsetting her position on this question was her opposition to busing to desegregate schools and support for tax credits for private (parochial) schools. She easily won reelection in 1980 and 1982 while building a reputation as a solid supporter of the women's movement.

Democratic party presidential nominee WALTER F. MONDALE picked Ferraro to be his running mate in 1984. Besides her regional and ethnic appeal for the ticket, it was hoped Ferraro would attract female voters. The campaign had no sooner begun than the intense scrutiny by the media of her personal life began to take its toll. The complex intertwining of Ferraro's husband's business with her political

campaign funds made headlines after an investigation disclosed that he had been involved in two legally questionable real estate transactions. These investigations sharply limited her ability to attract voters to the Democratic party ticket and to make a dent in President RONALD REAGAN's enormous popularity.

Since her vice presidential election defeat, Ferraro has returned to private law practice and has written a book about her campaign experience.

BIBLIOGRAPHY

Doerner, William R., "A Credible Candidacy and Then Some," *Time,* November 19, 1984; Ferraro, Geraldine, with Linda Bird Franche, *My Story,* 1985; Rosenblat, Roger, "Mondale: This Is an Exciting Choice!" *Time,* July 23, 1984.

Fillmore, Millard

(January 7, 1800–March 8, 1874)
President, Vice President, Representative

Millard Fillmore became the thirteenth president of the United States upon the death of ZACHARY TAYLOR in 1850. Unable to obtain effective control of the Whig party or to unite it behind his conciliatory attitude toward the South's "peculiar institution" of slavery, he was not nominated for president in 1852. An unsuccessful bid to make a political comeback in 1856 as the American or Know-Nothing party's presidential candidate ended his political career.

The second of nine children, Millard Fillmore was born in Locke (now Summerhill), New York. Although from a poor family, Fillmore's ambition, exceptional intelligence, and good looks caught the attention of a local judge, who helped him to study law. He was admitted to the bar in 1823, and five years later was elected to the state legislature. In 1830 Fillmore moved to Buffalo and became a

member of the Whig party. After serving three terms in the state legislature, where he helped to develop the public school system, he was elected to Congress in 1832. He served in the House from 1833 to 1835 and from 1837 to 1843.

As chairman of the Ways and Means Committee from 1840 to 1842, Fillmore played a major role in the drafting and passage of the protective tariff of 1842. In 1844 he failed to secure the Whig vice presidential nomination and lost the race for governor of New York. Three years later, his political fortunes turned, and he was elected comptroller of New York in 1847. In 1848 he was elected vice president on the Whig ticket with President Taylor.

Fillmore believed that the election of the Whigs meant that the slavery issue would be resolved through compromise. He wrote to a friend, "I regard this election as putting an end to all ideas of disunion. It raises up a national party, occupying a middle ground, and leaves the fanatics and disunionists, North and South, without hope of destroying the fair fabric of our Constitution."

Zachary Taylor's sudden death on July 9, 1850, made Fillmore president. His quick replacement of Taylor's cabinet with his own political allies—DANIEL WEBSTER as secretary of state, JOHN J. CRITTENDEN as attorney general, and Nathan Kelsey Hall as postmaster general—clearly identified him with the

Library of Congress

moderate wing of the Whig party that favored compromise in coping with sectional issues and the extension of slavery.

As president, Fillmore faced an almost impossible task. The Compromise of 1850 (see HENRY CLAY), sections of which Taylor had opposed, could now become law. The support Fillmore and his cabinet gave to the compromise helped to ensure the passage of the various bills: California was admitted as a free state; New Mexico and Utah were organized as territories with the question of slavery left open to the decision of the voters; a strict fugitive slave law was passed that required all runaway slaves to be sent back to their owners; and the slave trade was abolished in Washington, D.C.

The new fugitive slave law imposed penalties for sheltering runaway slaves and denied slaves a trial by jury or even the right to summon witnesses on their behalf. It provided machinery for federal enforcement through creation of a new office of commissioners with plenary powers to decide fugitive slave cases. Fillmore knew the enforcement of the law would be extremely difficult and that attempting to uphold it after the sensational success

of Harriet Beecher Stowe's *Uncle Tom's Cabin* would alienate him from the growing antislavery sentiment of the North. Nevertheless, in the name of conciliation, he attempted to force the North to abide by its provisions.

The hopes of Fillmore and other moderates that the slavery issue would disappear from the national political scene were completely frustrated by the growing abolitionist sentiment in the North. Certain states enacted personal liberty laws to block the operation of the fugitive slave law. According to these laws, fugitives were presumed free until proven to be runaway slaves. In addition, local officials were forbidden to help in the capture or return of runaway slaves, in violation of the provisions of the federal fugitive slave law. The controversy further split the Whig party. The efforts by both Daniel Webster and Fillmore to appeal to the moderates in the party at the national convention in 1852 enabled the popular military hero and antislavery candidate WINFIELD SCOTT to win the party's presidential nomination.

Fillmore tried again to return to the White House four years later. In 1856 he was nominated as the presidential candidate of the American party. Its members were known as the Know-Nothings because they would reply, "I don't know," when asked about the party's secret activities. The American party was formed to combat the rising influence of what its members deemed "foreign" groups, primarily Catholics. Fillmore ran a poor third behind Democrat JAMES BUCHANAN and Republican JOHN FRÉMONT, carrying only one state.

With his political career effectively finished, Fillmore returned to Buffalo and became the first chancellor of the University of Buffalo. In

1861 he entertained President and Mrs. ABRA-
HAM LINCOLN on their way to the White House,
but he soon became a bitter critic of the Lincoln administration's handling of the South's
secession. In 1864 he backed the presidential
candidacy of GEORGE McCLELLAN; and, after
Lincoln's murder, he supported ANDREW
JOHNSON's Reconstruction policies.

BIBLIOGRAPHY

Grayson, Benson Lee, *The Unknown President: The
Administration of President Millard Fillmore*,
1981; Griffis, W. E., *Millard Fillmore*, 1915;
Raybeck, Robert J., *Millard Fillmore*, 1959;
Severance, F. H. (ed.), *Millard Fillmore Papers*,
1907.

Fish, Hamilton

(August 3, 1808–September 6, 1893)
Secretary of State, Senator, Representative

President ULYSSES S. GRANT's selection of
Hamilton Fish as secretary of state was
his most astute cabinet appointment.
Fish respected Grant and fulfilled the duties
of his office with distinction while deploring
the corruption that swirled around the Grant
administration.

Born in New York City, Fish graduated from
Columbia College in 1827 and was admitted to
the bar in 1830. Fish began his political career
as a member of the Whig party. He was
elected to the U.S. House of Representatives
in 1842, where he served until 1845. He was
elected lieutenant governor of New York in
1847, served as governor of New York from
1848 to 1850, and a year later began a six-year
term as U.S. senator.

In the Senate Fish opposed the Kansas-Nebraska Act (see FRANKLIN PIERCE) and, after the
Whig party dissolved, became a Republican in
1856. During the Civil War he avoided politics
and served in minor government posts. Surprised when offered the position of secretary
of state in 1869 by President Grant, Fish at
first declined the post but was quickly convinced by friends to change his mind. He
served as secretary of state for the full eight
years of the Grant administration.

With the help of CHARLES FRANCIS ADAMS,
Fish managed the settlement of claims against
England, which had supplied warships, including the *Alabama*, to the Confederacy. The negotiations were complicated by the harsh
reparation demands made by the Radical Republicans in Congress. Fish shrewdly waited
until the political climate had calmed and
then, in 1871, negotiated the moderate Treaty
of Washington. The treaty led to an equitable
settlement that improved relations between
the two nations and opened the way for an
agreement on Canadian fishing rights and
boundaries (see CHARLES FRANCIS ADAMS).

In 1873 Spain captured the *Virginus*, a
steamer that was being used by Cuban revo-
lutionaries although it flew the American flag.
Many of the crew, including some Americans,
were executed. Fish averted a serious incident
by proving that the ship was registered illegally and settling death claims. He then successfully demanded that Spain end the Cuban
revolt.

After leaving office, Fish returned to New
York City and became an elder statesman in
the conservative wing of the Republican party.

BIBLIOGRAPHY

Nevins, Allan, *Hamilton Fish: The Inner History of the
Grant Administration*, 1957.

Foley, Thomas Stephen

(March 6, 1929–)
Speaker of the House, Representative

Highly regarded by members of both parties, Thomas Foley has been an effective congressional leader for more than twenty-five years.

Born in Spokane, Washington, Foley earned his B.A. degree from the University of Washington in Seattle in 1951, as well as his law degree in 1957. In 1958 Foley became deputy prosecutor of Spokane County and two years later was named assistant state attorney general. He also served as a special counsel on the Senate Interior and Insular Affairs Committee from 1961 to 1964.

In 1964 Foley won an upset election to the U.S. House of Representatives as a Democrat by unseating a Republican incumbent with twenty-two years in office. Foley has been re-elected every two years ever since.

In Congress Foley has established a generally liberal voting record. He supported President LYNDON JOHNSON's Great Society programs, but he gradually came to oppose the administration's support for U.S. involvement in Vietnam (see LYNDON BAINES JOHNSON and RICHARD MILHOUS NIXON). Although a Roman Catholic, Foley has supported a woman's right to decide whether or not to have an abortion without state interference, and has been opposed to prayer in public schools, capital punishment, and a constitutional amendment requiring a balanced federal budget.

In 1980 Foley became the Democratic majority whip in the House. In this position he supported enactment of President RONALD REAGAN's 1982 tax bill designed to reduce the federal deficit, and helped to obtain passage of the Gramm–Rudman–Hollings deficit reduction bill in 1985. This act established mandatory automatic spending cuts as a means of achieving a balanced budget.

Foley became the Democratic majority leader in the House in 1987, and two years later, after Speaker JIM WRIGHT was forced to resign over alleged financial improprieties, Foley became Speaker of the House. As Speaker, he has shepherded bills through Congress that increased the minimum wage and established minimum clean air standards.

BIBLIOGRAPHY

New Yorker, 65:48+, April 10, 1989; *New York Times*, D, p. 20, August 18, 1982; *Time*, 133:36, June 5, 1989.

Ford, Gerald Rudolph, Jr.

(July 14, 1913–)
President, Vice President, Representative

Gerald R. Ford, Jr., was successor to the only U.S. president ever to resign. A moderate Republican who had been a popular congressional leader, Ford helped to heal the country's wounds after the Watergate scandal (see RICHARD MILHOUS NIXON), but he left no innovative program for the future.

Ford grew up in Grand Rapids, Michigan, the adopted son of a paint salesman. A superb football player, he graduated from the University of Michigan in 1935 and earned his law degree at Yale. He was admitted to the Michigan bar in 1941. Ford had barely started his practice when the Japanese attack on Pearl

Harbor (see FRANKLIN DELANO ROOSEVELT) occurred, and he joined the navy. During the war he served as a gunnery officer and assistant navigator on a light aircraft carrier that was involved in virtually every major battle in the South Pacific. After his discharge from the navy in 1946, Ford returned to Grand Rapids and joined a large law firm.

In 1948 Ford managed to beat the incumbent and win Michigan's fifth congressional district seat. In Congress he was appointed to the Public Works Committee, and in 1951 moved to the powerful House Appropriations Committee, where, ten years later, he earned considerable influence as the ranking minority member of the Defense Appropriations Subcommittee.

Ford supported HARRY TRUMAN's foreign policy, endorsing the Marshall Plan (see GEORGE CATLETT MARSHALL and HARRY S TRUMAN), Truman's Point Four program for aid to underdeveloped countries, and increases in the defense budget. He opposed Truman's domestic policy, however, especially such prolabor initiatives as repeal of the Taft–Hartley Act (see TRUMAN) and a minimum wage hike. He also voted to override Truman's veto of the McCarran–Walter immigration bill, which removed the ban against Asians, included screening measures to keep out subversives, and allowed the attorney general to deport immigrants who had communist affiliations. Later, Ford regretted that he did not speak out against the communist witch-hunt instigated by Senator JOSEPH MCCARTHY in the early 1950s.

Ford was an early supporter of DWIGHT D. EISENHOWER for the 1952 Republican presidential nomination. A friend of Vice President

Courtesy Gerald R. Ford Library

Richard Nixon from the time of their service in the House of Representatives together, Ford fought to help him remain as the vice presidential candidate on the Republican national ticket in 1956 and supported his nomination for president in 1960. In 1963 Ford was named chairman of the House Republican Conference.

After President JOHN KENNEDY's assassination in November 1963, President LYNDON B. JOHNSON appointed Ford as one of the two Republican congressmen to serve on the Warren Commission, which investigated the murder. Ford, with the help of a commission assistant, published *Portrait of the Assassin* in 1965 to explain why he fully endorsed the Warren Commission's conclusion that Lee Harvey Oswald had acted alone.

During the 1960s Ford was criticized by black leaders for voting to weaken civil rights legislation. He opposed the establishment of Medicare and denounced the Johnson administration's War on Poverty as "a lot of washed-up old programs." In 1965 he was elected House minority leader. As minority leader, Ford frequently criticized the conduct of the Vietnam War (see LYNDON BAINES JOHNSON and RICHARD MILHOUS NIXON) by demanding that the president unleash American military might to win the war or withdraw.

After the election of Richard Nixon as president in 1969, Ford was among the administration's strongest supporters. He argued for Nixon's "peace with honor" Vietnam policy, the cutting back of social welfare programs, détente with the Soviet Union (see HENRY ALFRED KISSINGER and RICHARD MILHOUS NIXON), the recognition of China, and the imposition of wage and price controls.

When two conservative Nixon Supreme Court nominees were rejected by the Senate, Ford headed a movement to impeach Justice WILLIAM O. DOUGLAS, the Court's most liberal member, citing Douglas's paid activities on behalf of the Parvin Foundation, a charitable organization with alleged ties to organized crime. When critics pressed that Douglas's actions did not warrant impeachment, Ford replied: "An impeachable offense is whatever the majority of the House of Representatives considers it to be at a given moment of history; conviction results from whatever offenses two-thirds of the Senate considers to be sufficiently serious to require removal of the accused from office."

Following Vice President SPIRO AGNEW's resignation in 1973, President Nixon selected Ford to be the first vice president appointed according to the provisions of the Twenty-fifth Amendment to the Constitution.

Vice President Ford defended Nixon throughout the long Watergate scandal ordeal. Upon Nixon's resignation in August 1974, Ford assumed the presidency. He selected NELSON ROCKEFELLER to be his vice president and kept Nixon's cabinet members. In September President Ford granted "a full, free and absolute pardon" to Nixon on the grounds that he had suffered enough and that his lengthy trial would only serve to arouse "ugly passions."

Facing a depressed economy at home, Ford acted to curb inflation and lower the deficit. In foreign affairs, he oversaw the withdrawal of U.S. forces from a defeated South Vietnam and worked with both Israel and Egypt to bring about a truce. Ford narrowly survived two assassination attempts. He lost his bid to be elected president in 1976 when he was defeated by Democrat JIMMY CARTER. Since leaving the White House and retiring to Rancho Mirage, California, Ford has concentrated on business activities.

BIBLIOGRAPHY

Ford, Gerald, *A Time to Heal,* 1979; Hersey, John, *The President,* 1975; Reeves, Richard, *A Ford, Not a Lincoln,* 1975.

Forrestal, James Vincent

(February 15, 1892–May 22, 1949)
Secretary of Defense, Secretary of the Navy

While under secretary of the navy during World War II, James Forrestal became known as the man who "bought the fleet that won the war." The nation's first secretary of defense, he helped shape American foreign policy during the early years of the cold war.

James Vincent Forrestal was born in Matteawan (now Beacon), New York. He attended Dartmouth College (1911–1912) and Princeton University (1912–1915), but left Princeton six weeks before graduation after failing an English course. Forrestal began a career as a Wall Street investment banker at the firm of William A. Read and Company (later Dillon, Read and Company) and, with the exception of naval aviator service during the First World War, stayed at Read, rising to partner in 1923, vice president in 1926, and president in 1937.

In June 1940 President FRANKLIN D. ROOSEVELT summoned Forrestal to Washington, D.C., to serve as a special administrative assistant. Two months later, Roosevelt appointed Forrestal under secretary of the navy. Upon the death of FRANK KNOX in 1944, Forrestal was named secretary of the navy.

As under secretary and secretary of the navy during World War II, Forrestal oversaw the procurement of necessary war supplies and the deployment of troops. He also managed, amid considerable controversy, to maintain civilian control of the navy in the face of strong opposition for operational control by Admiral Ernest J. King. After the war Forrestal opposed the unification of the U.S. armed forces, but he agreed to become the first secretary of defense in 1947.

Although he failed to persuade President HARRY S TRUMAN to take a hard-line position, Forrestal nevertheless influenced the design and implementation of the American position toward the Soviet Union that emerged after World War II. It was Forrestal who convinced GEORGE KENNAN to publish his "Mr. X" article in the July 1947 issue of *Foreign Affairs*, which publicly explained the need for an American foreign policy of containment toward the Soviet Union.

During his tenure as secretary of defense, Forrestal became involved in an escalating series of disputes with Truman: Forrestal fought for a "balanced forces" approach to national defense, while the budget-conscious Truman administration chose to emphasize reliance upon strategic bombers; Forrestal opposed the partition of Palestine (which led to the creation of Israel), but Truman supported it;

Forrestal supported military rather than civilian control over nuclear weapons, while Truman authorized civilian control through the Atomic Energy Commission; Forrestal worked to strengthen the power of the National Security Council, even though Truman felt that the council posed a potential threat to presidential authority. Finally, in March 1949, Truman requested, and received, Forrestal's resignation.

The distraught Forrestal suffered a nervous breakdown shortly after leaving office. After a suicide attempt in April, he was admitted to Bethesda Naval Hospital for intensive psychiatric treatment. He plunged to his death from an unguarded sixteenth-story hospital window a month later.

BIBLIOGRAPHY

Borklund, Carl W., *Men of the Pentagon: From Forrestal to McNamara*, 1966; Caraley, Demetrios, *The Politics of Military Unification*, 1966; Connery, Robert H., *The Navy and Industrial Mobilization in World War II*, 1952; Hammond, Paul Y., *Organizing for Defense: The American Military Establishment in the Twentieth Century*, 1961; Millis, Walter (ed.), *The Forrestal Diaries: A Study of Personality, Politics, and Policy*, 1936.

Forsyth, John

(October 22, 1780–October 21, 1841)
Secretary of State, Diplomat, Senator, Representative

John Forsyth was born in Fredericksburg, Virginia. He graduated from the College of New Jersey (now Princeton University) in 1799, was admitted to the bar three years later, and established a law practice in Augusta, Georgia. Forsyth's political career began in 1808 with his appointment as attorney general of Georgia. In 1812 he was elected to the U.S. House of Representatives and six years later to the Senate, but he quickly resigned his Senate seat to become minister to Spain in 1819. During his four-year term in Spain, Forsyth secured the ratification by the Spanish government of the treaty by which Spain transferred ownership of Florida to the United States (see ANDREW JACKSON).

In 1822, while he was still in Spain, Forsyth was reelected to Congress. He served in the House of Representatives from 1823 until he was elected governor of Georgia in 1827. Two years later, he returned to the Senate and played an important role in the forced removal of all Indian tribes west of the Mississippi River, known as the Trail of Tears (see ANDREW JACKSON). Forsyth's strong support of President Jackson in the nullification controversy (see JOHN CALDWELL CALHOUN) severely undermined his political support in Georgia, where public opinion favored Calhoun's position.

Forsyth resigned from the Senate in 1834 to become secretary of state, a post he held in the administrations of Andrew Jackson and MARTIN VAN BUREN. While secretary of state, Forsyth was chiefly concerned with securing payment by France, according to a previously agreed upon installment schedule, for claims made by Americans for damages during the Napoleonic wars. Other issues he dealt with concerned the question of the annexation of Texas (see JAMES KNOX POLK), which he opposed, and the dispute over the Maine boundary with Canada (see MARTIN VAN BUREN).

BIBLIOGRAPHY

Duckett, Alvin L., *John Forsyth*, 1962.

Foster, John Watson

(March 2, 1836–November 15, 1917)
Secretary of State, Diplomat

Diplomat John W. Foster was born in Pike County, Indiana. He graduated from Indiana University in 1855, studied at Harvard Law School, and was admitted to the Indiana bar in 1857. In addition to establishing his law practice at Evansville, Indiana, Foster also earned a master's degree from Indiana University in 1858.

After serving with the Union army in the Civil War, he edited the *Evansville Daily Journal* from 1865 to 1869, then served as Evansville's postmaster from 1869 to 1873. In 1872 Foster became chairman of the Indiana Republican party. One year later, he was appointed minister to Mexico, where he served until becoming minister to Russia in 1880 and, from 1883 to 1885, minister to Spain.

In 1892 President BENJAMIN HARRISON appointed Foster secretary of state. Before he left office the next year, Foster negotiated a treaty of annexation with Hawaii (later rescinded by President GROVER CLEVELAND), and represented the United States during the arbitration of the Bering Sea dispute with Great Britain over sealing rights.

After 1893 Foster became an international lawyer. He represented China in the peace negotiations that ended the Sino-Japanese War of 1894–1895, and the United States in the settlement of the Alaska boundary dispute with Great Britain in 1903.

BIBLIOGRAPHY

Foster, J. W., *A Century of American Diplomacy, 1776–1876*, 1900, *The Practice of American Diplomacy*, 1906, and *Diplomatic Memoirs*, 2 vols., 1909.

Frankfurter, Felix

(November 15, 1882–February 22, 1965)
Associate Justice of the Supreme Court

A renowned liberal legal activist before becoming a Supreme Court justice, Frankfurter became known over the course of his twenty-three-year career as a leading proponent of the need for the Court to exercise judicial restraint.

Born in Vienna, Austria, Frankfurter immigrated with his parents to the United States in 1894 at age twelve. He quickly learned English, graduated third in his class from the City College of New York in 1902, and went on to complete his education at Harvard Law School in 1906.

Frankfurter was assistant U.S. attorney in New York from 1906 to 1910. He then became legal officer in the Bureau of Insular Affairs from 1911 to 1914 before becoming a professor at Harvard Law School, a position he retained from 1914 to 1939 while serving in a number of intermittent government positions. During World War I he was Secretary of War NEWTON D. BAKER's legal adviser on industrial problems, secretary and then counsel to the President's Mediation Commission, and in 1918 chairman of the War Labor Policies Board. These positions led to his involvement in a number of controversial labor disputes, such as the forced removal of more than 1,000 striking Bisbee, Arizona, copper miners in 1917, which he opposed, much to the consternation of the conservative business community.

In 1919 Frankfurter served as President Wilson's legal adviser at the Paris Peace Conference (see WOODROW WILSON) and then returned to his teaching post at Harvard. Active in liberal political circles, Frankfurter helped found the American Civil Liberties Union and the magazine *New Republic.* His efforts to secure a new trial for the doomed anarchists Nicola Sacco and Bartolomeo Vanzetti gained him a national liberal political reputation after the publication in 1927 of an article by him in the *Atlantic Monthly* on their behalf. Many of his Harvard law students became important figures in FRANKLIN D. ROOSEVELT's administration in the 1930s.

When President Roosevelt appointed Frankfurter as an associate justice of the Supreme Court in 1939, most people assumed, in light of his previous commitment to liberal causes, that Frankfurter would continue along the same liberal path. Yet Frankfurter, who had strongly supported New Deal social reform legislation, gradually came to be perceived as the leader of the conservative block on the Court. Ironically, this development was not due to Frankfurter's inconsistency, but to the changing definition of what constituted liberal judicial behavior.

Frankfurter believed, like Justice OLIVER WENDELL HOLMES, that judges should exercise great restraint before overruling, or nullifying, a law. This was a liberal viewpoint early in the twentieth century because the major opposition to innovative social legislation was often centered in the judicial branch. Frankfurter and other liberals argued that it was not the judicial branch of the government but the elected legislature that should have the primary say. "Indeed," Frankfurter once wrote to Associate Justice JOHN HARLAN, "must not the Court put on the sackcloth and ashes of deferring humility" in deciding whether the legislative judgment should be overturned?

Yet, by 1940 a new political climate had emerged in the liberal community that advocated judicial intervention in support of civil liberties over the opposition of the legislature. Frankfurter, however, could never bring himself to believe that the short-term gain for human rights won by overruling the legislative branch would outweigh the long-term danger of undermining the democratic process and the separation of powers in the American federalist system. It was essential, Frankfurter continued to argue throughout his career on the Supreme Court, that judges remember that the legislative function did not belong to them. The Constitution had wisely given the people, through their elected representatives, and not a handful of judges, the power to learn by failure.

Following his judicial restraint beliefs often compelled Frankfurter to contradict his personal feelings. For example, in 1940 Frankfurter wrote the Court's opinion upholding a law requiring schoolchildren to salute the flag even though he personally opposed the requirement. He did so, he explained, because the Court should "not exercise our judicial power unduly, and as though we ourselves were legislators." When the Court overruled the decision three years later, Frankfurter delivered an impassioned dissent.

The result of Frankfurter's refusal to alter his conviction that it was a judge's duty to decide cases and not to create a new world through judicial intervention was that by the end of his career on the Supreme Court in 1962, Frankfurter was generally perceived by the liberal community as an obstacle rather than an asset to badly needed social reform on behalf of human rights.

BIBLIOGRAPHY

Frankfurter, Felix, *The Public and Its Government*, 1930, and *Felix Frankfurter Reminisces: Recorded in Talks with Harlan B. Phillips*, 1960; Kurland, Philip B. (ed.), *Of Law and Life: Papers and Addresses of Felix Frankfurter, 1956–1963*, 1965; Mendelson, Wallace, *Justices Black and Frankfurter*, 2d ed., 1966; Simon, James F., *The Antagonists: Hugo Black, Felix Frankfurter and Civil Liberties in Modern America*, 1989; Thomas, Helen S., *Felix Frankfurter*, 1960.

Franklin, Benjamin

(January 17, 1706–April 17, 1790)
Revolutionary Leader

Benjamin Franklin achieved worldwide renown as a writer, scientist, statesman, and diplomat. Besides writing *Poor Richard's Almanack*, developing the unified field theory of electricity, and negotiating crucial French aid during the American Revolution, he invented numerous practical labor-saving devices, served as a colonial representative in England prior to the revolution, signed the Declaration of Independence, and helped to draft the Constitution.

Franklin was born in Boston into a religiously pious, but humble, Puritan family. Self-educated, he began to work full-time at the age of ten, but he did not let lack of time or schooling impede his intellectual development. While still a teenager, he had already acquired enough sophistication to comprehend Isaac Newton's theories of physics and John Locke's philosophical perspective about the nature of man and its relationship to government.

After five years of working as an apprentice for his autocratic brother in order to learn the trade of printer, Franklin left his service and at age seventeen sailed to England. He earned a living there as a printer and savored the world of young writers. He returned to the Colonies in 1725 and settled in Philadelphia, where he became the owner of the *Pennsylvania Gazette*. Through hard work and frugality he soon managed to obtain most of the public printing business of Pennsylvania. In 1732 he published the first edition of his perennial best-seller—*Poor Richard's Almanack*. The work consisted of popular sayings and homilies given a deft turn of phraseology that have since become an integral part of American culture: "Early to bed and early to rise, makes a man healthy, wealthy, and wise."

And, "If you would not be forgotten, as soon as you are dead and rotten, either write things worthy reading, or do things worth the writing."

As his personal wealth increased, Franklin developed his civic and scientific interests. He organized a debating club (1727), which led to the founding of a circulating library in 1731, the first in America; the American Philosophical Society (1743); and an academy (1751) that evolved into the University of Pennsylvania. He also studied foreign languages and began his scientific experiments

Library of Congress

(such as the famous kite-flying incident) that led to his hypothesis of a unified theory of electricity. Always interested in practical applications of science from his research, Franklin deduced the benefit of lightning rods to protect homes from natural electrical catastrophe. The Franklin stove and bifocal glasses are two of the best known of his over 200 inventions. In recognition of his wide-ranging scientific research, but especially for his work in electricity, Franklin was elected to England's Royal Society in 1756 and to the French Academy of Sciences in 1772.

Franklin could have retired to enjoy the life of a wealthy businessman and scientist in the 1750s; instead, he decided to enter politics. In 1751 he was elected to the Pennsylvania colonial legislature and began a phenomenally successful and broad career of thirty-nine years of public service.

From 1753 to 1774, as deputy postmaster general, Franklin developed an efficient and financially self-supporting postal system. In 1754, as a delegate to the Albany Congress, he proposed a plan to unite the Colonies in the war against the French and Indians that won

the endorsement of the congress but was rejected by the Crown as too democratic. Still a loyal Englishman, Franklin helped fund and direct Pennsylvania's contribution to winning the French and Indian War (1754–1763), even leading a military expedition into the Lehigh Valley.

In 1757 Franklin journeyed to England as the agent of the Pennsylvania Assembly. During the five years it took him to accomplish his mission of winning Crown support for ending the proprietary rights of the Penn family, he reveled in the attention lavished upon him for his scientific accomplishments and traveled in Europe. He returned to Philadelphia in 1762 and spent the next two years traveling from southern Virginia to Massachusetts.

Largely because of his opposition to the abuse of Indians, Franklin failed to win reelection to the state legislature in 1764. However, he was again appointed the Pennsylvania Assembly's agent to London. While in England, he also became the agent for Georgia (1768), New Jersey (1769), and Massachusetts (1770). Although he was at first firmly committed to the colonies' remaining under British rule, Franklin warned Parliament that measures such as the Stamp Act (see JOHN ADAMS and SAMUEL ADAMS) and the Townshend Acts would sour the dispositions of the people and if enforced could eventually precipitate civil strife. As his warnings went unheeded, Franklin became increasingly frustrated by British indifference to American grievances and began to contemplate the need to create an independent nation.

In 1774 letters written by Governor THOMAS HUTCHINSON of Massachusetts to government officials and friends in London were surreptitiously obtained by Franklin and passed on to patriots in Boston. Their publication, which Franklin had warned against, by SAMUEL ADAMS and JOHN HANCOCK was such a serious breach of etiquette that Franklin's effectiveness as a colonial representative was severely undermined. Forced to leave England under the threat of imprisonment, Franklin arrived in the United States in April 1775 just as armed conflict broke out between the colonists and British troops at Lexington and Concord, Massachusetts. He was elected to the Second Continental Congress in time to participate in the drafting and signing of the Declaration of Independence, but his stay in America was to be brief. In October 1776 he accepted an appointment as one of the three commissioners to France assigned to obtain French aid and recognition.

Franklin shrewdly capitalized on his reputation as a "republican" philosopher and scientist. Much to the chagrin of the other American commissioners, he savored the notoriety of being a celebrity among the French aristocracy. He played upon the cliché of "frontiersman" by not wearing a wig and by dressing in a plain brown suit. John Adams was infuriated by Franklin's pursuit of popularity and "indolence." What he failed to appreciate at the time was how brilliantly Franklin managed to insinuate himself with powerful figures for the good of the American cause. Where others failed (Adams was expelled from the French court), Franklin obtained war loans, military equipment, naval and troop support, recognition of the American republic after the victory of the Battle of Saratoga in 1777, and finally a declaration of war by France against England. Fortunately, the Continental Congress realized his value and retained him in France throughout the war for independence. After the massive British defeat at Yorktown in 1781 by American and French forces, Franklin served on the negotiating committee that obtained the recognition of the independence of the United States by England in 1783.

Franklin returned to the United States in 1785. Despite being almost eighty years old, he accepted election as president of the executive council of Pennsylvania. Two years later, although too weak to stand in debates, he participated in the Constitutional Convention. He helped to calm tempers through the judicious use of humor and wise advice about the need to compromise. Even though he admitted that, like most of the delegates, he had reservations about the final document, in a concluding speech he requested that they join him in urging its ratification by acknowledging the need to doubt their own infallibility.

BIBLIOGRAPHY

Clark, Ronald W., *Benjamin Franklin: A Biography*, 1983; Crane, Verner W., *Benjamin Franklin and a Rising People*, 1954; Ketcham, Ralph L., *Benjamin Franklin*, 1965; Labaree, Leonard W., et al. (eds.), *Autobiography of Benjamin Franklin*, 1964, and *The Papers of Benjamin Franklin*, 13 vols., 1959–1970; Smyth, Albert H., *The Writings of Benjamin Franklin*, 10 vols., 1905–1907 (reprint 1969); Van Doren, Carl, *Benjamin Franklin*, 1938.

Frelinghuysen, Frederick Theodore

(August 4, 1817–May 20, 1885)
Secretary of State, Senator

Frederick T. Frelinghuysen was born in Millstone, New Jersey. After graduating from Rutgers College in 1836, he was admitted to the bar in 1839 and established a practice at Newark. Ten years later, he became city attorney of Newark and was later elected to the city council. From 1861 until 1866 Frelinghuysen, a Republican, served as attorney general of New Jersey. In 1866 he accepted a three-year appointment to complete a term in the U.S. Senate and, after a brief return to the practice of law, won election to a full six-year term from 1871 to 1877.

While in the Senate, Frelinghuysen supported Radical Republican Reconstruction policies and joined the Stalwart faction (see ROSCOE CONKLING) of his party. He fought for the impeachment of President ANDREW JOHNSON and served on the 1876 election commission (see RUTHERFORD BIRCHARD HAYES) that decided in favor of Republican presidential candidate Hayes.

President CHESTER A. ARTHUR appointed Frelinghuysen secretary of state on December 19, 1881. During his term in office, which lasted until the end of the Arthur administration on March 4, 1885, Frelinghuysen urged reciprocity agreements with Latin American countries; secured a treaty with Nicaragua that granted the United States the right to build a canal there (later rescinded by President GROVER CLEVELAND); negotiated for a naval base at Pearl Harbor, Hawaii; initiated diplomatic relations with Korea; supported efforts to protect U.S. commercial interests in Europe; and authorized U.S. participation in the Berlin Conference of 1884, which resolved the administration of the African Congo and mediated a border dispute between Mexico and Guatemala.

BIBLIOGRAPHY

Bemis, S. F. (ed.), *The American Secretaries of State*, 1928; Hageman, John Frelinghuysen, *Life, Character and Services of F. T. Frelinghuysen*, 1886; Swan, H. Kels (comp.), *Raritan's Revolutionary Rebel: Frederick Frelinghuysen, Fatherless Protégé of Dirck Middagh*, 1967.

Frémont, John Charles

(January 21, 1813–July 13, 1890)
Candidate for President, Senator

The explorer and soldier John C. Frémont, known as the Pathfinder of the West, was chosen as the first presidential candidate of the new Republican party in 1856.

The handsome, bright, and daring Frémont displayed a remarkable talent early in life for attracting the attention and support of powerful sponsors. Born in Savannah, Georgia, Frémont grew up in Charleston, South Carolina. After the death of his father in 1818, an attorney sponsored his early education and secured his admission to Charleston College. Frémont attended college from 1829 until 1831 and then joined the navy. His real career began when he resigned from the navy in 1835 and became a surveyor. Commissioned a second lieutenant in the U.S. Topographical Corps in 1838, he became famous after writing a lively account of a journey he made with the frontiersman Kit Carson as his guide in 1842 to chart the best route to Oregon.

His marriage the year before, in 1841, to Jessie Benton, the daughter of Senator THOMAS HART BENTON of Missouri, played a major part in his success. Senator Benton worked hard for his son-in-law's advancement and fired him with enthusiasm about the exploration of the West. Jessie helped her husband write his reports and memoirs. She also supported the family in the 1870s and 1880s by contributing short stories to periodicals.

In 1843 Frémont was given the choice assignment of surveying Oregon. He remained out of touch while he spent the next year exploring virtually the entire Northwest, including northern California. His return to St. Louis in August 1844 created a sensation, and his account of his adventure, which included detailed maps and scientific observations, became an important travel guide to the West.

In 1845 Frémont, on another exploratory journey in northern California, received word from President JAMES K. POLK that war with Mexico was imminent (see JAMES KNOX POLK). He journeyed to Sonoma and encouraged American settlers there to revolt against Mexican rule on June 14, 1846. He then took command of the Bear Flag Republic, the nickname of the newly independent Republic of California (its flag featured a grizzly bear). American troops arrived in California in July, and Commodore Robert F. Stockton proclaimed California to be a part of the United States and named himself as governor.

A conflict in instructions from Washington over the formation of a civil government brought trouble. Frémont was appointed governor by Stockton and refused to accept orders from General Stephen W. Kearny, who also had orders from Washington. This led to Frémont's arrest and court-martial. The trial, held in the glare of intense publicity in Washington, D.C., resulted in Frémont's conviction for disobedience and mutiny. He was subsequently sentenced to dismissal from the army, but President Polk canceled his punishment.

Nevertheless, Frémont indignantly resigned from his commission.

After his resignation, Frémont led an unsuccessful privately funded expedition to prove that the Sangre de Cristo and San Juan mountains were passable for railroad traffic in the winter. Gold was discovered during this expedition on land that had been purchased for Frémont by supporters in the Sierra foothills of California. Frémont used his newfound wealth to invest in San Francisco real estate and to develop his huge ranch at Mariposa.

Although now famous and wealthy, Frémont's restless nature kept him on the move. In December 1850 he was elected one of California's first U.S. senators. His term lasted only a few months. He traveled to Europe two years later, and led one more winter expedition to find a southern railroad route to the Pacific in 1853.

In 1856 Frémont was nominated as the new Republican party's first antislavery presidential candidate. Party officials hoped that his fame might overcome the lack of national organization of the Republicans. "Free soil, free speech, and Frémont" was their slogan in the campaign, recalling the Free Soil party slogan in the 1848 campaign (see MARTIN VAN BUREN). Among those distinguished citizens who supported him were Ralph Waldo Emerson, William Cullen Bryant, and Henry Wadsworth Longfellow. Support by the intellectuals and Northern abolitionists was insufficient, however, to counteract fears of Southern secession, and Frémont lost to the Democratic candidate JAMES BUCHANAN 174 electoral votes to 114. Frémont returned to California to develop his mining interests, but the gold had run out and he lost his entire Mariposa estate in a vain effort to finance the discovery of more.

Soon after the Civil War broke out, Frémont was chosen to head the Department of the West, but his decision to free the slaves of Confederate owners under his jurisdiction without the approval of President ABRAHAM LINCOLN prompted Lincoln to relieve him of his command. It was feared that Frémont's action might cause the secession of several of the slaveholding border states that had remained in the Union. This was not the only reason Lincoln removed him, however. Frémont's defects as an administrator and a military commander, along with corruption in war contracts, played a major role.

Transferred to western Virginia, Frémont soon resigned from the army. He was nominated for the presidency by a group of Radical Republicans in 1864, but he withdrew from the race four months later.

This was Frémont's last major role in national affairs. Although he served as governor of the Arizona Territory from 1878 to 1883, his remaining years were spent in private pursuits. Frémont lost the remainder of his fortune in the 1870s through bad railroad investments. Congress voted him a pension just before his death in 1890.

BIBLIOGRAPHY

Brandon, William, *The Men and the Mountain*, 1955; Ferol, Egan, *Frémont: Explorer for a Restless Nation*, 1985; Jackson, Donald, and Mary L. Spence (eds.), *The Expeditions of John Charles Frémont*, 3 vols., 1970–1984; Nevins, Allan, *Frémont: Pathmarker of the West*, 1939.

Fulbright, James William

(April 9, 1905–)
Senator, Representative

In a long and successful career as a U.S. senator from Arkansas, Fulbright became famous for his intellectual criticism of the destructive "arrogance of power" course the United States pursued in South Vietnam (see LYNDON BAINES JOHNSON and RICHARD MILHOUS NIXON) and for sponsoring legislation that established a student foreign exchange program.

Fulbright graduated from the University of Arkansas in 1925, spent a year at Oxford as a Rhodes scholar in 1928, and earned a law degree from George Washington University in 1934. After working as an attorney in the U.S. Department of Justice, Antitrust Division, from 1934 to 1935, Fulbright taught law at George Washington University before being chosen president of the University of Arkansas, a position he held from 1939 to 1941.

In 1942 Fulbright was elected to the U.S. House of Representatives as a Democrat. During his first year in Congress he gained national attention as the author of a resolution that supported U.S. participation in the development of what was to become the United Nations. He left the House two years later to make a successful run for the Senate in 1944. He was reelected to the Senate without interruption for the next thirty years.

Building on the positive experience he had had as a Rhodes scholar, Fulbright sponsored legislation in 1946 that established scholarships for American and foreign exchange students. The Fulbright Scholarship program (expanded in 1961 by the Fulbright-Hayes Act), provides U.S. government financial awards for graduate study, research, teaching, or professional training in other countries for U.S. recipients, and in the United States for foreign recipients.

From 1955 to 1959 Fulbright was chairman of the Committee on Banking and Currency and from 1959 until 1974 chairman of the Senate Committee on Foreign Relations. It was in this position that his views on foreign policy eventually brought him into open conflict with President Lyndon Johnson. Fulbright wrote that "the most striking characteristic of a great nation is . . . the wisdom and restraint . . .

with which power is exercised." He was convinced that "excessive moralism" in U.S. foreign policy had blinded the nation's leaders to the new political realities of the world in the 1960s.

Fulbright believed that the United States had, in Southeast Asia, revealed an "arrogance of power." He also felt that the nation tended, as in the case of the Dominican Republic invasion in 1965, to make "exaggerated estimates of communist influence." These views made Fulbright a leader of those who opposed the administration's policy in South Vietnam. After the huge American military buildup did not lead to victory, Fulbright argued that the cost of a military victory there would far exceed "the requirements of our interest or of our honor." He urged the United States to seek a "negotiated settlement involving major

concessions by both sides," and a war-weary public began to hear the message.

Although remarkably sophisticated and prophetic on matters of foreign policy, as a senator from the Deep South, Fulbright favored going slowly on integration and opposed all federal civil rights legislation.

In a surprise election upset, Fulbright lost the Democratic nomination for senator in the 1974 Arkansas primary and retired to lecture and write.

BIBLIOGRAPHY

Coffin, Tristram, *Senator Fulbright,* 1966; Johnson, Haynes B., and Bernard M. Gwertzman, *Fulbright: The Dissenter,* 1968; Meyer, Karl E. (ed.), *Fulbright of Arkansas,* 1962.

Fuller, Melville Weston

(February 11, 1833–July 4, 1910)
Chief Justice of the Supreme Court

Although his lack of national prominence surprised the nation when President GROVER CLEVELAND nominated him to be chief justice of the Supreme Court, Melville Weston Fuller proved to be an exceptionally capable and popular chief justice.

Born in Augusta, Maine, Fuller graduated from Bowdoin College in 1853 and briefly studied at Harvard Law School. After being admitted to the Maine bar in 1855, Fuller moved to Chicago and became a prominent attorney. In addition to handling cases ranging from ecclesiastical disputes to municipal contracts, he became active in the Democratic party. In 1862 he was a delegate to the Illinois constitutional convention, in 1863 and 1864 he served in the Illinois legislature, and he was a delegate to all the Democratic national conventions between 1864 and 1884 except 1868.

His successful efforts in Illinois to defeat Maine Republican JAMES G. BLAINE's campaign for president in 1884 were so appreciated by Grover Cleveland that he nominated Fuller to be chief justice of the Supreme Court. However, Fuller's reputation as a fervid states' rights Democrat who had been highly critical of the conduct of the Civil War and the lack of any national political standing were factors that worked against him. The result was that his appointment was not confirmed by the Senate until 1888.

Although Fuller believed in a strict constructionist (see THOMAS JEFFERSON) interpretation of the Constitution (Congress derived its powers from specific language in the Constitution and not from broad interpretations of implied powers or an underlying national sovereignty), he had no difficulty in establishing a warm and friendly relationship with those on the Court who disagreed with him, such as OLIVER WENDELL HOLMES. His colleagues appreciated his sense of humor while presiding over cases, impartiality in assigning cases, and efforts to encourage consensus on difficult issues through compromise.

Fuller's talent proved to be primarily administrative while serving as chief justice. Although he wrote more than 850 opinions, few are still cited today. Perhaps his most important opinion was rendered in 1895. It involved two cases known as *Pollock* v. *Farmers' Loan and Trust Company,* in which the Court held the Income Tax Act of 1893 unconstitutional.

He also vigorously dissented in the series of cases after the Spanish-American War (see WILLIAM MCKINLEY, JR.) that determined the status of the new American colonial acquisitions.

While chief justice, Fuller served as a commissioner to help settle the British-Venezuelan boundary dispute in 1899 and was a member from 1900 to 1910 of the Permanent Court of Arbitration at The Hague.

BIBLIOGRAPHY

King, Willard L., *Melville Weston Fuller,* 1950.

Gadsden, James

(May 15, 1788–December 26, 1858)
Diplomat

As a railroad promoter and minister to Mexico, James Gadsden never managed to achieve his dream of purchasing northern Mexico; but he did succeed in obtaining enough land for his planned southern railroad route along the Gila River, which was built after his death.

Gadsden was born into a prominent Charleston, South Carolina, family. He graduated from Yale in 1806 and served as an army officer in the War of 1812 (see JAMES MADISON) and in the war against the Seminole Indians in Florida (see ANDREW JACKSON).

In 1823 President JAMES MONROE appointed Gadsden commissioner in charge of moving all Seminole Indians onto a reservation in southern Florida. After losing several attempts to win election to Congress from Florida, Gadsden moved back to Charleston in 1839 and became president of the South Carolina Railroad Company a few years later.

Gadsden's dream was to create a single great railroad network in the South. Such a network, he believed, could enable the South to compete with the North in attracting the trade of the West after a line was constructed across the southern U.S. frontier to the Pacific Ocean.

Gadsden never managed to convince enough railroad companies in the South to merge with his line to create a single link from the Atlantic to the Mississippi River. His obsession finally drove the stockholders of the South Carolina Railroad Company to vote him out of the presidency in 1850. Gadsden seems to have viewed his dismissal as merely a temporary setback and continued his efforts to promote the construction of a southern transcontinental railroad route. By 1853 he was convinced that land needed to be purchased from Mexico to enable construction of a railroad from Texas to California along the Gila River. He secured an appointment from President FRANKLIN PIERCE to be the U.S. minister to Mexico.

Gadsden became convinced that the Mexican leader Santa Anna was so desperate for money that he would sell northern Mexico to the United States. The federal government authorized Gadsden to purchase the area for up to $50 million, but all he was ever able to obtain was a relatively small portion of territory (45,535 square miles) known as the Gadsden Purchase (see FRANKLIN PIERCE)

along the Gila River for $10 million in 1854.

BIBLIOGRAPHY

Garber, Paul Neff, *The Gadsden Treaty*, 1923.

Gallatin, Albert

(January 29, 1761–August 12, 1849)
Secretary of the Treasury, Diplomat, Senator, Representative

Albert Gallatin was an outstanding secretary of the treasury, superb diplomat, and successful Jeffersonian political leader. Born in Switzerland and educated at the Geneva Academy, Gallatin decided at the age of nineteen to reject his family fortune and make his own way in newly independent America.

Arriving in Massachusetts in 1780, Gallatin earned a living teaching French at Harvard College and selling goods to Maine farmers. He used the few thousand francs he had brought with him to invest in land in western Pennsylvania. He was not a success as a farmer or as a speculator, but his residence in frontier Pennsylvania proved to be the perfect place for him to launch a political career.

After establishing himself in local politics as a strong supporter of states' rights, anti-Federalist Gallatin was elected to the state legislature in 1790 and then to the U.S. Senate in 1793. However, his demands that Secretary of the Treasury ALEXANDER HAMILTON issue a detailed report of all the financial activities of the new government from 1789 until January 1, 1794, drew an angry letter from Hamilton about "unexpected, desultory, and distressing calls for lengthy and complicated statements." In retaliation, Gallatin was forced by the Federalists to give up his seat in February on the grounds that he had not been a citizen for the full nine years required by the Constitution.

Gallatin returned home in 1794 to find western Pennsylvania in political uproar over the Whiskey Rebellion (see ALEXANDER HAMILTON and GEORGE WASHINGTON). Gallatin, who was sympathetic to the farmers' protest over the excise tax placed on distilled liquor, at first joined the protest meetings. However, he quickly realized "his only political sin" in supporting armed resistance and successfully used his political skills to guide the anger of his neighbors into peaceful resistance.

The result was that Gallatin returned to Washington less than a year after losing his place in the Senate to start the first of three consecutive terms in Congress, from 1795 to 1801. Quickly recognized as an authority on financial affairs, he helped to create the Ways and Means Committee and continued to urge financial reforms. As the leader of the Republicans in the House during the THOMAS JEFFERSON/AARON BURR controversy after the election of 1800, Gallatin led the successful effort to elect Jefferson.

President Jefferson chose Gallatin to be secretary of the treasury when he assumed office in 1801. During Jefferson's first term, Gallatin, who favored reducing taxes and curtailing government expenditures, was quite successful at accomplishing both. But the prewar embargo imposed by Jefferson and the War of 1812 (see JAMES MADISON) ruined Gallatin's attempts to bring about lasting financial stability and brought Senate opposition to his policies. Gallatin continued in office during the administration of James Madison, but he requested service abroad in 1813. President Madison named him to the delegation that formulated the Treaty of Ghent ending the War of 1812. Gallatin also negotiated commercial treaties and became minister to France from 1816 to 1823. Returning to America after ten years of diplomatic service abroad in 1823, Gallatin planned to become a gentleman farmer, but in 1826 he was appointed minister to Great Britain for one year. After securing new vitally important commercial treaties, he resigned.

Although officially retired, Gallatin remained active politically, publishing articles attacking the banking and tariff policies of AN-DREW JACKSON and the expansionist goals of JAMES K. POLK. From 1831 until 1839 he served as president of the newly established National Bank of New York. Gallatin was also the first president of the University of the City of New York and the founder of the American Ethnological Society. In the last years of his life he conducted valuable studies of American Indian tribes.

BIBLIOGRAPHY

Adams, Henry, *Life of Albert Gallatin*, 1879; Balinsky, Alexander, *Albert Gallatin: Fiscal Theories and Policies*, 1958; Walters, Raymond, Jr., *Albert Gallatin: Jeffersonian Financier and Diplomat*, 1969.

Garfield, James Abram

(November 19, 1831–September 19, 1881)
President, Representative

Renowned for his evangelical debating style, James Garfield capped a career of almost two decades of service in the House of Representatives by winning election as president of the United States in 1880, only to be assassinated by a deranged office seeker a few months after assuming office.

Born in Cuyahoga County, Ohio, Garfield worked his way through the Western Reserve Eclectic Institute (later Hiram College) for a term in 1850. He taught school until 1854, when he had saved enough money to

Library of Congress

complete his education at Williams College in Massachusetts. Two years later, he returned to Hiram College and became its president. He also became an accomplished lay minister and evangelical preacher.

Garfield was elected to the Ohio senate in 1859. Commissioned a colonel in the Ohio volunteers at the start of the Civil War, he quickly learned basic military discipline and combat techniques by studying military manuals. He won a Union victory at the battle of Middle Creek in 1862, for which he was promoted to brigadier general. In September

1862, even though he made it clear he would not leave the army to serve in Congress, he was elected to the House of Representatives.

Early in 1863, Garfield became General W. S. Rosecrans's chief of staff. In this capacity Garfield, alone among Rosecrans's officers, recommended that Rosecrans attack the Confederate forces under General Bragg in Tennessee. Rosecrans's assault was repulsed by Bragg at Chickamauga. Rosecrans was discredited, while Garfield, who had behaved bravely during the battle, emerged a hero.

In December 1863, Major General Garfield resigned from the army to take his seat in the House of Representatives, where he was assigned to the important Appropriations and Ways and Means committees. An advocate of implementing a stern Reconstruction program, Garfield was disappointed by ABRAHAM LINCOLN'S moderate approach but still supported his fellow Republican's reelection campaign in 1864.

When House Republican leader THADDEUS STEVENS retired in 1868, JAMES G. BLAINE and Garfield took his place and, although very different in temperament from one another, became an effective Republican leadership team. In 1876 Blaine moved on to the Senate. Garfield would have joined him there, except that newly elected Republican president RUTHERFORD B. HAYES asked him to remain in the House, where he could provide badly needed legislative leadership. At the end of Hayes's presidency in 1880, Garfield finally secured election to the Senate by the Ohio legislature. He was scheduled to begin his first term in the Senate in 1881, but in the interim he was elected president.

The Republican party split into two factions in 1880. The Stalwarts, led by Senator ROSCOE CONKLING of New York, favored the nomination of former president ULYSSES S. GRANT for a third term. The Half-Breeds, led by Blaine, favored Blaine's nomination. Garfield backed the compromise candidacy of JOHN SHERMAN. Grant's supporters were unable to secure enough votes at the convention to guarantee his nomination. After Blaine's and Sherman's efforts to win the nomination also

failed, Garfield became a candidate himself. On the thirty-sixth ballot, after Sherman withdrew and encouraged his supporters to back Garfield, he won the nomination. CHESTER A. ARTHUR was chosen to be Garfield's running mate in order to pacify the Stalwarts.

The Democrats might have been able to defeat Garfield if they had concentrated on his involvement in the Crédit Mobilier scandal (see SCHUYLER COLFAX). During the Grant administration Garfield had received a $329 dividend check for stock in Crédit Mobilier of America. Although he had never purchased any stock in the company, he had accepted the dividend check. The Democrats were effectively ridiculing his excuse that he thought it was a campaign contribution and identifying Garfield with corruption through use of the derisive slogan "three twenty-nine" ($329). However, the publication of a letter in a Democratic newspaper ostensibly signed by Garfield and advocating support of unrestricted immigration of Chinese backfired. The letter was exposed as a forgery, and Garfield won the election by a close popular but comfortable electoral vote, 214 to 155.

The split in the Republican party continued after Garfield assumed office. His effort to balance the distribution of patronage positions plagued him, and a scandal involving fraud in the postal department forced him to launch an investigation that revealed long-term and widespread Republican abuse of the department for kickbacks and no-show patronage positions. To Garfield's credit, he did not try to impede the investigation, which played a significant role in pressuring Congress to implement civil service reform.

On July 2, 1881, Garfield was shot twice at the Washington, D.C., train station by a man who had been unable to secure a diplomatic appointment. After firing at Garfield he yelled, "I am a Stalwart and now Arthur is President!" One bullet only grazed Garfield's arm, but the other lodged in his back. His doctors, unable to locate the bullet in his back, kept the wound open so they could probe for the bullet before it caused an infection. Ironically, his body had formed a protective cyst around the bullet, and he would have completely healed in a few weeks if he had been left alone. Instead, Garfield died eleven weeks later from infection.

BIBLIOGRAPHY

Brown, Harry J., and Frederick D. Williams (eds.), *Diary of James A. Garfield,* 2 vols., 1967; Caldwell, Robert G., *James A. Garfield, Party Chieftain,* 1931; Doenecke, Justus D., *The Presidencies of James A. Garfield and Chester A. Arthur,* 1981; Garfield, James A., *A Diary,* 1848–1874; Hoyt, Edwin P., *James A. Garfield,* 1964; McElroy, Richard L., *James A. Garfield—His Life and Times,* 1986; Peskin, Allan, *Garfield,* 1978; Smith, Theodore C., *Life and Letters of James Abram Garfield,* 2 vols., 1925.

Garner, John Nance

(November 22, 1868–November 7, 1967)
Vice President, Speaker of the House, Representative

"Cactus Jack" Garner had served in the House of Representatives for thirty years before becoming FRANKLIN D. ROOSEVELT's vice president in 1933. Having earned the opposition of organized labor, Garner was once described by union leader John L. Lewis as "a labor-baiting, poker-playing, whiskey-drinking, evil old man."

Born near Detroit, Texas, Garner studied law in Clarksville and established his practice in Uvalde, Texas, in 1890. After acquiring ownership of a local newspaper, Garner quickly established a political power base. He won appointment and then reelection as judge of Uvalde County in 1893, and served two terms in the Texas House of Representatives. In 1902 he began his national political career by winning election to the U.S. House of Representatives, where he served without interruption until 1933.

Elected Speaker in 1931, Garner earned a reputation as a superb politician who could be counted upon to deftly maneuver legislation through the Congress.

The knowledge that the presidency was within their grasp due to the debacle of the Great Depression calmed the passions of the various factions within the Democratic party in 1932. Although in many respects Franklin D. Roosevelt seemed the ideal candidate, he did not win the nomination until Garner withdrew from the race after the third ballot and instructed his Texas and California delegates to vote for Roosevelt in the interests of party unity. To help ensure Democratic victory, Garner then agreed to be Roosevelt's running mate.

At first, Garner supported Roosevelt's political goals, but he was never comfortable with Roosevelt's "too liberal" New Deal programs (see FRANKLIN DELANO ROOSEVELT), and grew increasingly alarmed at Roosevelt's advocacy of greater executive authority. He finally broke with Roosevelt over the latter's plan to "pack" the Supreme Court. A futile effort to defeat Roosevelt's bid for a third term and to secure the presidential nomination for himself failed in 1940.

Embittered, Garner retired from politics and returned to his home in Uvalde, Texas. Although he kept his vow to never return to Washington, Garner never tired of recommending to visiting reporters on his birthday that the office of vice president be abolished: "The Vice President is just a waiting boy, waiting just in case something happens to the President." The office of vice president is "not worth a pitcher full of warm spit."

BIBLIOGRAPHY

Timmons, Bascom N., *Garner of Texas,* 1948.

Gerry, Elbridge

(July 17, 1744–November 23, 1814)
Vice President, Diplomat, Representative

Born in Marblehead, Massachusetts, in 1744 to a wealthy shipping family, Elbridge Gerry graduated from Harvard College in 1762. While working in his father's shipping business, he became a follower of SAMUEL ADAMS. Because of his strong anti-British views, he was elected to the Massachusetts colonial legislature in 1772. Four years later, he was elected a representative to the Continental Congress. In addition to signing the Declaration of Independence, Gerry served on the important treasury board. Angry at what he felt were infringements upon states' rights by the Continental Congress, Gerry resigned in 1780 but returned again in 1783 and served until 1785.

In 1786 Gerry was elected to the Massachusetts state legislature and a year later was chosen as a delegate to the Constitutional Convention. Although he actively participated in the debates that created the Constitution, Gerry refused to sign or support its ratification because he felt it contained too many ambiguities that could prove dangerous to republicanism. However, once the Constitution was adopted, he supported ALEXANDER HAMILTON's Federalist financial policies as a member of the House of Representatives from 1789 to 1793.

President JOHN ADAMS chose Gerry, as a representative of the anti-Federalists whom he trusted, to join JOHN MARSHALL and CHARLES PINCKNEY on a peace commission to France in 1797. In Paris, the French diplomat Talleyrand managed to take advantage of Gerry's pro-French feelings to divide the American mission. Much to the distress of Pinckney and Marshall, Gerry refused to join them when they returned to the United States after rejecting Talleyrand's infamous bribery request that became known as the XYZ affair (see JOHN ADAMS). When Gerry returned home by command of President Adams, he was snubbed by the Federalists and embraced by the Republicans.

In 1810, while Massachusetts was still a Federalist stronghold, Gerry, running as a Republican, managed to win the governorship. To help his party, he supported a bill in 1812 that redistricted the state in such a way that more Republican state senators than Federalists could be elected. This was accomplished by putting all strong Federalist voting areas into a few districts and connecting disparate Republican voting areas into numerous new election districts no matter how irregularly shaped they might have to be. This technique of rearranging the boundaries of voting districts to favor the party in power became known as gerrymandering.

Gerry was in his sixties when he was nominated as Republican presidential candidate JAMES MADISON's vice president in 1812. Gerry was considered valuable to the ticket because he was a Republican from a Federalist state. He died in office in Washington, D.C., two years after being elected.

BIBLIOGRAPHY

Austin, James T., *Life of Elbridge Gerry,* 1970; Morison, Samuel E., "Elbridge Gerry, Gentleman-Democrat," in *By Land and By Sea; Essays and Addresses,* 1953.

Giddings, Joshua Reed

(October 6, 1795–May 27, 1864)
Representative

Joshua Reed Giddings was born in Athens, Pennsylvania, and grew up on a small farm in Ohio. He had very little formal education, but with the help of tutors he studied law and was admitted to the Ohio bar in 1821. He immediately established a successful law practice in Jefferson, Ohio, and became active in local politics.

Giddings served one term in the Ohio legislature in 1826, and in 1838 he was elected as a Whig to the U.S. House of Representatives to represent the Western Reserve. In Congress Giddings voted against the Mexican War and the annexation of Texas (see JAMES KNOX POLK), and fiercely opposed the spread of slavery into the territories.

Reacting to an incident in which the U.S. Navy seized the mutinous slave ship *Creole*, Giddings introduced measures that protested the coastal slave trade. This was in violation of the House's self-imposed gag rules (see JOHN QUINCY ADAMS) prohibiting the raising of the slavery issue in Congress. Giddings was censured for his antislavery position by his colleagues in the House and resigned in protest. He was vindicated, however, when he was promptly reelected by his constituents despite the opposition of his own Whig party leaders.

A staunch abolitionist, Giddings supported the Free-Soil party (see MARTIN VAN BUREN) in 1848 and helped to found the Republican party in 1854. Due to illness, Giddings was not renominated in 1858, and his career in Congress came to an end in 1859. In 1861 President ABRAHAM LINCOLN appointed him consul general to Canada. He held this post until his death.

BIBLIOGRAPHY

Julian, George W., *Joshua Reed Giddings*, 1892.

Gillett, Frederick Huntington

(October 16, 1851–July 31, 1935)
Speaker of the House, Senator, Representative

Frederick Gillett was born in Westfield, Massachusetts. He graduated from Amherst College in 1874 and completed his studies at Harvard Law School in 1877. After being admitted to the state bar in 1877 and establishing a practice in Springfield, he became assistant attorney general of Massachusetts from 1879 to 1882. In 1890 he was elected, as a Republican, to the Massachusetts House of Representatives; two years later, he began the first of sixteen consecutive terms in the U.S. House of Representatives.

As a member of the House Appropriations Committee, Gillett played an important part in the establishment of the Bureau of the Budget in 1921. After serving as Speaker of the House from 1919 to 1925, Gillett served one term in the U.S. Senate (1925 to 1931) before retiring from public service.

BIBLIOGRAPHY

Amherst Graduate Quarterly, August–September, 1935; *New York Times*, July 31 and August 1, 1935; *Worcester Telegram and Springfield Union*, August 1, 1935.

Goldberg, Arthur Joseph

(August 8, 1908–January 19, 1990)
Secretary of Labor, Diplomat, Associate Justice of the Supreme Court

Arthur Goldberg's rise to national prominence was inextricably linked to the dramatic growth of organized labor from the 1930s to the 1960s.

The youngest of eight children in a poor Russian Jewish immigrant family, Goldberg worked his way through a Chicago junior college and then Northwestern University. He received his bachelor's degree in 1929 and his doctorate in law the next year. Specializing in union law, Goldberg opened his own practice in 1933 and represented many of the nation's largest unions in litigation. During World War II he served in the Office of Strategic Services.

In 1948 Goldberg became general counsel of both the Congress of Industrial Organizations (CIO) and the United Steelworkers union. In 1955 he played a significant part in the merger of the American Federation of Labor (AFL) and the CIO. The merged AFL-CIO had a membership estimated at 15 million. As a result of his work for labor union legislation, Goldberg met Senator JOHN F. KENNEDY.

When Kennedy became president in 1960, he appointed Goldberg secretary of labor. As secretary of labor, Goldberg fought for increased federal aid to the unemployed and mediated a number of major labor disputes. President Kennedy nominated him as an associate justice of the Supreme Court in 1962. Goldberg remained on the Court only a few years because President LYNDON B. JOHNSON implored him to become ambassador to the United Nations in 1965. Frustrated by his inability to influence President Johnson's Vietnam War policies (see LYNDON BAINES JOHNSON and RICHARD MILHOUS NIXON), Goldberg resigned his position in 1968.

After losing a race for governor of New York in 1970, Goldberg returned to the private practice of law. He also assisted with international arbitration cases and served as a U.S. ambassador at large in 1977 and 1978. Goldberg died in January 1990.

BIBLIOGRAPHY

Moynihan, Daniel P. (ed.), *Public Papers of Arthur J. Goldberg,* 1966.

Goldwater, Barry Morris

(January 1, 1909–)
Candidate for President, Senator

Leader of the conservative political forces in the Republican party in the 1960s, Barry Goldwater won the party's nomination for president in 1964 but lost in the general election to LYNDON JOHNSON. His campaign slogan, "In your heart you know he's right," caused one political commentator to sum up the voters' overwhelming rejection of Goldwater for president with the comment "too far right."

Born in Phoenix, Arizona, Goldwater graduated in 1928 from Staunton Military Academy in Virginia. After attending the University of Arizona for one year, he dropped out upon the death of his father to work in the family's Phoenix department store. A member of the

National Guard, he was assigned to the air force in 1941 and served as a pilot during World War II. He remained in the Air Force Reserve after the war and became a major general in 1962.

Named to the Phoenix City Council in 1949, Goldwater won election as a Republican to the U.S. Senate in 1952. In the Senate his consistent stern conservatism and militant anticommunism eventually made him the hero of the American right. He frequently refused to support measures sponsored by moderate Republicans and opposed any increase in federal government powers and programs except when it came to laws regulating unions or expanding the military. He was reelected in 1958 and, after RICHARD NIXON's defeat by JOHN KENNEDY in 1960, decided to make a run for the presidency himself.

Goldwater's conservative supporters gradually gained control of a majority of Republican party state organizations and succeeded in securing his nomination for president in 1964 over moderate Republicans NELSON ROCKEFELLER and William Scranton. Goldwater stated in his acceptance speech at the convention that "extremism in the defense of liberty is no vice" and "moderation in the pursuit of justice no virtue." Such views, combined with his opposition to civil rights legislation and willingness to use nuclear weapons to stop the spread of communism, convinced many Americans that Goldwater was a right-wing extremist. In the general election Goldwater won only 52 electoral votes to Johnson's 486.

Goldwater's decisive defeat seemed to spell the end of the Republican right's mobilization; Goldwater himself retired to private life. But the conservative Republican wing continued its resurgence, its leadership now in the hands of RONALD REAGAN, who had given such a stirring and convincing speech in support of Goldwater at the 1964 Republican convention. The continued rise of the New Right prompted Goldwater's return to public service in 1968 when he was elected to the Senate. Reelected in 1974 and 1980, he gradually emerged as an elder statesman in the Republican party. By the time he retired to his Phoenix home in 1987, he was perceived as a moderating rather than a radicalizing force in the party.

BIBLIOGRAPHY

Goldwater, Barry M., *The Conscience of a Conservative*, 1960, and *Why Not Victory*, 1962; Parsons, Robert P., *Mr. Conservative: Barry Goldwater*, 1962.

Grant, Ulysses Simpson

(April 27, 1822–July 23, 1885)
President

Born in Pleasant Point, Ohio, Grant attended public school in nearby Georgetown until his father secured an appointment for him to West Point in 1839. Upon graduation in 1843, he was assigned to the infantry. He served two years in Missouri and Louisiana before joining General ZACHARY TAYLOR's army in Texas.

Although he felt that the Mexican War (see JAMES KNOX POLK) was unjustly provoked by the United States, he fought valiantly, first with General Taylor's army, then with General WINFIELD SCOTT's troops on the long march from Veracruz to Mexico City.

In 1852 Grant was transferred to the West Coast. He was stationed first at isolated Fort

Vancouver, and then, after being promoted to captain, at even more remote Humboldt Bay. Lonely, miserable, and unable to obey his commanding officer's warning not to drink to excess, Grant was forced to submit his resignation from the army in 1854.

Grant returned to Illinois and failed at a number of occupations: farmer, real estate agent, candidate for county engineer, and clerk in a customhouse. The Civil War rescued Grant from the oblivion of spending his

Library of Congress

life as a clerk in his father's general store. He secured an appointment as a colonel in the state militia, and then, in August 1861, was promoted to brigadier general. He became a national hero in February 1862, after he led his troops into Tennessee and captured Fort Donelson on the Cumberland River, along with its garrison of approximately 14,000 men.

After almost being defeated at Shiloh, Grant devised and implemented a brilliant campaign to split the Confederacy in half along the Mississippi River. He moved 30,000 men south of Vicksburg, ferried them across the Mississippi River without supplies, and then, by separately defeating two Confederate armies before they could unite, finally forced the garrison in Vicksburg to surrender on July 4, 1863, after a six-week siege. After Grant snatched victory from defeat by rescuing a large army at Chattanooga, President ABRAHAM LINCOLN chose him to command all the armies of the United States.

As general in chief of the Union forces, Grant provided the leadership necessary to coordinate the superior military and industrial resources of the North against the South. While his numerically superior forces wore down General Robert E. Lee's army, Grant dis-

patched other generals to attack elsewhere in the South to ensure that Lee could not receive any reinforcements or supplies. Although criticized for the ruthlessness and destructiveness of his tactics, both in terms of human life and in civilian property, the success of his "total war" approach was proven when Lee was forced to surrender at Appomattox Courthouse on April 9, 1865.

After Lincoln's assassination, an unpopular President ANDREW JOHNSON became locked in a furious battle with the ruling majority of Radical Republicans in Congress, who disagreed with Johnson's Reconstruction plan. Grant attempted to avoid entanglement in Johnson's political problems, but this proved impossible. He moved away from Johnson's policy and toward that of congressional Republicans in 1866, before Congress enacted Negro suffrage. The reason was the increasing intransigence and violence of Southern whites, not only against blacks and Republicans, but against any Northerners in the South, including the army, of which Grant was general in chief.

The Radicals gained effective control of the party and swept the elections of 1866. They were able to override Johnson's vetoes (see ANDREW JOHNSON) and make laws curtailing executive powers, including the Tenure of Office Act (1867). This prohibited Johnson from firing a cabinet officer without the consent of Congress. When Johnson fired Secretary of War EDWIN STANTON, Grant agreed to act as secretary until a replacement was appointed. However, when the Senate refused to accept the dismissal of Stanton, Grant refused to continue in the office. President Johnson's public accusation that Grant had betrayed him infuriated Grant and drove him into the arms of the Radical Republicans.

While the battle between President Johnson and Congress raged, Grant savored the gifts bestowed upon him by a grateful nation. He was given the rank of lieutenant general and named general in chief. In Philadelphia a group of businessmen gave him a magnificent fully furnished house. Merchants in New York gave him $100,000. Wealthy businessmen in Washington, refusing to be outdone, gave him another home and $75,000.

Grant's nomination for president by the Republican party in 1868 seemed almost inevitable. During the campaign he made no speeches and took no positions on any major issues. Still, due to his military glory, he defeated his Democratic opponent, New York Governor HORATIO SEYMOUR, 214 electoral votes to 80. His popular majority was only 30,000 in a total of 5.7 million.

Grant believed his job as president consisted of implementing the programs Congress created, not of suggesting programs or using the position of the presidency to galvanize public opinion in order to lead Congress. Still, with the exception of a disastrous effort to secure the annexation of Santo Domingo and the attempt by the financial speculators Jay Gould and Jim Fisk to corner the gold market in 1869, Grant's first term was relatively successful.

The economy was prosperous, immigrants were flowing into the United States, and the West was being settled. On matters of Reconstruction, Grant supported the efforts of the Radical Republicans to enfranchise blacks and spoke out for the need to control secret societies known as the Ku Klux Klan in the South. These openly terroristic groups tried to frighten and even physically keep blacks from voting. In 1871 Grant decided to enforce vigorously the Ku Klux Klan Act of that year. The Justice Department made a major effort in this area, successfully breaking up the Klan by 1872. Terrorist groups subsequently rose again in the South but under different names. Confused about what course of action to fol-

low, Grant decided to continue to implement the reforms, but only to use the remnants of troops stationed in the South as an absolute last resort.

Fortunately, in the foreign policy arena, Grant generally followed the advice of his secretary of state, HAMILTON FISH. Fish managed to convince Grant to curb his desire to recognize the rebel government in Cuba; but he failed to prevent Grant's politically disastrous drive to annex the Dominican Republic. In a treaty with Great Britain in 1871, the *Alabama* claims—demands by American merchants that Great Britain pay for the damages caused by Confederate gunboats built there during the Civil War (see CHARLES FRANCIS ADAMS)—were settled through the use of an international arbitration court at Geneva, Switzerland.

Shortly after Grant was reelected in 1872 (see HORACE GREELEY), the nation sank into a deep depression and corruption scandals began to plague the administration. The secretary of the treasury and the secretary of the interior were forced to resign, and Secretary of War WILLIAM W. BELKNAP was impeached. Belknap avoided conviction only because Grant allowed him to resign. By the end of the Grant administration, congressional investigating committees had indicted the collector of internal revenue and over 230 other government employees and distillers for involvement in a whiskey tax kickback scheme. Even Grant's personal secretary, Orville E. Babcock, was indicted (see also SCHUYLER COLFAX). Although there was never any evidence that Grant received any illegal money, as the economy continued to remain mired in stagnation and the scandals mounted, Grant's popularity declined.

After leaving the White House in 1877, Grant embarked on a trip to Europe. Elated by the warm greeting he received by leaders and crowds abroad as a great Civil War leader, Grant decided to spend two years traveling around the world with his family. When his bid for a third term in 1880 failed, he became a partner in a Wall Street investment firm.

Grant's last years were sad ones. He was forced to declare bankruptcy and to sell his war souvenirs to raise money because of the actions of a crooked business partner, Fred Ward. Financially devastated, Grant struggled, often in excruciating pain from cancer of the throat, to write his *Personal Memoirs* in order to pay off creditors and provide for his wife. He died a week after finishing the manuscript, unaware that he had written a great military history. His work, published by Mark Twain, became a phenomenal financial success.

BIBLIOGRAPHY

Catton, Bruce, *Grant Takes Command,* 1969, and *Grant Moves South,* 1960; Grant, Ulysses S., *Personal Memoirs,* 2 vols., 1982; McFeely, William S., *Grant: A Biography,* 1982; Smith, Gene, *Lee and Grant,* 1988.

Greeley, Horace

(February 3, 1811–November 29, 1872)
Candidate for President, Representative

Horace Greeley was more a social reformer than a politician when he ran for president as a Democrat in 1872. Born in Amherst, New Hampshire, Greeley's irregular formal education ended at fourteen when he was apprenticed to the editor of the local newspaper. At twenty Greeley moved to New York in search of typesetting work; he found employment in printshops and wrote for Whig newspapers. In 1840 Greeley, an active member of the Whig party, accepted the editorship of the party's weekly newspaper, *Log Cabin.* Immediately successful in the political partisan arena, Greeley shrewdly realized his true calling and, with borrowed money, founded and became the editor of the widely read *New York Tribune* in 1841.

In the first issue of the *Tribune,* Greeley pledged that his paper would stand "removed alike from servile partisanship on the one hand and from gagged, mincing neutrality on the other." He succeeded in both objectives, shaping public opinion through the high moral tone of his editorials. Espousing Fourierism (the belief that people should live in small communities in which everything is shared equally), homestead legislation, labor unions, and women's rights (though not suffrage), Greeley used the platform provided by his newspaper to attack all forms of social and economic tyranny. He supported the antislavery cause and the free-soil movement (see MARTIN VAN BUREN); and while he advocated preservation of the Union, he was willing to see it dissolved rather than allow the extension of slavery. He advocated "determined resistance" to the execution of the Kansas-Nebraska Act (see FRANKLIN PIERCE) and assisted those who sought to arm the Kansas Free-Soilers. Some of his phrases, such as "Go West, young man," appealed to millions and earned him lasting fame.

While his newspaper flourished, Greeley's political career languished. Although he was selected to complete the remainder of a fellow Whig's term in the U.S. House of Representatives in 1848, he was not reelected to the post. He also failed in a bid for the Senate in 1863, and was an unsuccessful candidate for the House in 1866 and 1870.

One of the early members of the new Republican party, Greeley decided on the eve of the voting at the Republican convention in 1860 to support ABRAHAM LINCOLN. Greeley was bitterly disappointed when he failed to secure WILLIAM SEWARD's seat in the Senate. During the Civil War he criticized Lincoln for not immediately emancipating the slaves, adopting a conciliatory attitude toward the border states, and refusing to negotiate with delegates from the Confederacy for peace. Greeley's vacillation on the question of pursuing the war to victory and in backing Lincoln's reelection, publicly expressed in his newspaper, seriously undermined his credibility for political leadership.

A strong supporter of the Radical Republican Reconstruction program and an advocate of the impeachment of President ANDREW JOHNSON, Greeley at first applauded ULYSSES S. GRANT's election, but he soon denounced the new administration as corrupt and illiberal toward the South. When the Liberal Republicans split from the regular party in 1872, Greeley became their candidate. In a desperate effort to block the reelection of Grant, the Democratic party also nominated Greeley for president.

Urging a conciliatory attitude toward the South, Greeley failed to carry a single Northern state. His opponents' personal hostility and attacks upon his character in the campaign hurt him deeply. Crushed by the magnitude of his defeat (he carried only six border and Southern states), the death of his wife, and the inability to resume his role as editor of the *Tribune*, Greeley collapsed physically and mentally. He died insane only a few weeks after the election.

BIBLIOGRAPHY

Greeley, Horace, *Recollections of a Busy Life*, 1868; Hale, William H., *Horace Greeley*, 1950; Isely, J. A., *Horace Greeley and the Republican Party, 1853–1861*, 1947; Lunde, Erik S., *Horace Greeley*, 1981; Van Deusen, Glyndon, *Horace Greeley: Nineteenth-Century Crusader*, 1953.

Gresham, Walter Quintin

(March 17, 1832–May 28, 1895)
Secretary of State, Secretary of the Treasury, Postmaster General

Born in Harrison County, Indiana, Walter Quintin Gresham attended Indiana University for one year in 1852 before leaving to study law. After being admitted to the bar in 1854, he helped organize the Indiana Republican party and was active in the campaign to elect JOHN FRÉMONT president in 1856. In addition to working for ABRAHAM LINCOLN's election in 1860, he won a seat in the Indiana legislature.

During the Civil War, Gresham served in the Union army under ULYSSES S. GRANT and William Sherman. After a wound at Atlanta ended his military service, he returned to Indiana and established a successful law practice. Defeated in two tries for a seat in the House of Representatives in 1866 and 1868, he accepted an appointment by President Grant in 1869 to be a federal district judge in Indiana. Although mentioned as a possible Senate candidate for his loyal party work, Gresham never ran for public office again.

In 1883 President CHESTER ARTHUR appointed him postmaster general. In recognition of his reform efforts in that office, Arthur appointed Gresham secretary of the treasury the following year, but he served only a month before becoming a U.S. circuit judge in 1884.

Gresham tried but failed to win the Republican nomination for president in 1888. The nomination went instead to his Indiana political rival, BENJAMIN HARRISON. Gresham was opposed to the high protective tariff policy of the Republican party, and the passage of the protective McKinley tariff of 1890 was the final blow that caused Gresham to leave the party. After declining the Populist party nomination for president in 1892, he supported the presidential candidacy of Democrat GROVER CLEVELAND. President Cleveland recognized the importance of Gresham's help by appointing him secretary of state in 1893, but Gresham achieved little of lasting importance before dying in office nearly two years later.

BIBLIOGRAPHY

Gresham, Matilda, *The Life of W. Q. Gresham*, 1919.

Grow, Galusha Aaron

(August 31, 1822–March 31, 1907)
Speaker of the House, Representative

Born in Ashford (now Eastford), Connecticut, Galusha Aaron Grow graduated from Amherst College in 1844 and was admitted to the bar in Susquehanna County, Pennsylvania, in 1847. He established a practice in Towanda and in 1850, as a compromise candidate agreed upon to avoid a Democratic party split, was elected to the House of Representatives to take the place of his law partner, DAVID WILMOT. In 1854 he joined the newly created Republican party and was reelected every two years to Congress until 1862.

In Congress Grow led the drive for a homestead law to distribute western lands to settlers at minimal cost. While serving as Speaker of the House from 1861 to 1863, he took advantage of the absence of Southern opposition legislators to secure passage of the Homestead Act.

Gerrymandered out of office (see ELBRIDGE GERRY) by the Democratic Pennsylvania legislature in the election of 1862, Grow returned to his law practice in Pennsylvania and developed successful financial interests in the oil, coal, and lumber industries. From 1871 to 1875 he was president of the International and Great Northern Railroad of Texas.

Grow remained active in Pennsylvania politics, but his efforts to return to Congress were stymied until he finally managed to win reelection in 1894. Still primarily concerned with legislation affecting education and western lands, he served in the House until 1903 and then retired to Glenwood, Pennsylvania.

BIBLIOGRAPHY

DuBois, James T., and G. S. Mathews, *Galusha A. Grow*, 1917.

Haig, Alexander Meigs, Jr.

(December 2, 1924–)
Secretary of State, Presidential Adviser

Alexander Meigs Haig, Jr., was born in Philadelphia. He graduated from the U.S. Military Academy at West Point in 1947 and served briefly as an aide to General Douglas MacArthur in Japan before earning his master's degree from Georgetown University in 1961.

After two years as a staff officer at the Pentagon in Washington, D.C., Haig became a special assistant to Secretary of Defense ROBERT MCNAMARA in 1964.

In 1966, Haig volunteered for a year of combat duty in South Vietnam as an infantry unit battalion commander. Upon his return to the United States in 1967, he was assigned to West Point as deputy commandant. Two years later, he returned to duty in Washington, D.C., but in the White House instead of the Pentagon. Moving rapidly up the bureaucratic ladder, Haig was first appointed military assistant to HENRY KISSINGER, then assistant to the president for national security affairs, and in 1971 deputy assistant to the president for national security affairs.

Shortly after President RICHARD M. NIXON chose Haig to serve at the Vietnam peace talks in Paris, he was promoted to major general. In 1973 Nixon made him army vice chief of staff with the rank of four-star general. During the traumatic last year of the Nixon administration, Haig became chief of the White House staff.

After President Nixon's resignation following the Watergate scandal in 1974 (see RICHARD MILHOUS NIXON), President GERALD FORD appointed Haig supreme allied commander of the North Atlantic Treaty Organization (NATO) forces in Europe. Five years later, Haig resigned from that post and from the army. After a brief period as a business executive, Haig was appointed secretary of state in December 1980 by President RONALD REAGAN and confirmed by the Senate a month later. However, only a little more than a year later, frustrated at his lack of ability to influence administration foreign policy, Haig resigned and resumed his business activities. His efforts to win the Republican nomination for president in 1988 were a dismal failure.

BIBLIOGRAPHY

Duggan, Ervin S., "The Little Engine of Alexander Haig," *Washington Magazine*, November 1981; Morris, Roger, *Haig: The General's Progress*, 1982; Thimmesch, Nick, "Chief of Staff," *Washington Post*, November 25, 1973; Ungar, Sanford J., "Alexander Haig: Pragmatist at State," *Atlantic Monthly*, March 1981.

Haldeman, Harry Robbins

(October 27, 1926–)
Presidential Adviser

H. R. Haldeman presided over the most notorious White House staff of the twentieth century.

Harry Robbins Haldeman was born in Los Angeles, California, into a wealthy and conservative family known for its staunch anticommunism. After graduating from the University of California at Los Angeles in 1948, Haldeman became an advertising executive for the J. Walter Thompson Company.

Haldeman's volunteer staff work in RICHARD NIXON's 1956 vice presidential reelection campaign and in the 1958 Republican congressional campaign won him enough recognition to be chosen chief advance man for Nixon's campaign for president in 1960. Haldeman discouraged Nixon from running for governor of California in 1962 but agreed to manage the unsuccessful effort. When Nixon decided to run for president in 1968, Haldeman devised a careful campaign strategy that employed advertising techniques to merchandise and package a "new" Nixon. To avoid his candidate's tendency to blurt out sarcastic and caustic remarks when exhausted, Haldeman kept Nixon's campaign appearances to a minimum and took maximum advantage of television's power to project the image of Nixon as a calm, experienced world leader who would "bring the nation together again." The same strategy was followed in Nixon's successful 1972 reelection campaign.

President Nixon appointed Haldeman as his chief of staff in 1969. Haldeman quickly developed a reputation as the "Iron Chancellor" because of his successful efforts to determine who did and did not have access to the president. When federal prosecutors began to investigate the June 17, 1972, burglary of the Democratic National Committee's headquarters in the Watergate complex in 1973 and discovered a connection to the White House, Haldeman and his colleague JOHN EHRLICHMAN resigned on April 30, 1973, to protect the president. They sought to take full responsibility for the affair, but the discovery of tape recordings (made by the president for his personal use) containing conversations with Nixon of their plans to cover up White House involvement in the break-in eventually forced Nixon to resign from the presidency in August 1974.

Haldeman was convicted of perjury, conspiracy, and obstruction of justice in federal court. From June 1977 to December 1978, he was imprisoned in the federal minimum security facility at Lompoc, California. After his release in December 1978, Haldeman reflected upon his role in the Watergate scandal and concluded: "I put on too much pressure, and in the process laid the groundwork for the mental attitude that 'the job must be done,' which badly served the cause when Watergate struck. By then, our whole crew was so strongly indoctrinated in the principle that there were to be results, not alibis, that they simply once again swung into action—doing what they felt was expected of them."

BIBLIOGRAPHY

Ambrose, Stephen E., *Nixon*, 1987; Cook, Fred J., *The Crimes of Watergate*, 1981; DiMona, Joseph, and H. R. Haldeman, *The Ends of Power*, 1978; Kutler, Stanley I., *The Wars of Watergate: The Last Crisis of Richard Nixon*, 1990; Woodward, Bob, and Carl Bernstein, *The Final Days*, 1976.

Hale, John Parker

(March 31, 1806–November 19, 1873)
Diplomat, Candidate for President, Senator, Representative

Born in Rochester, New York, Hale graduated from Bowdoin College in Brunswick, Maine, in 1827. He practiced law in New Hampshire and became noted for his persuasive skill with juries. After serving as U.S. district attorney from 1834 to 1841, he was elected to Congress from New Hampshire as a Democrat.

During his term in the House of Representatives from 1843 to 1845, Hale defended the right of citizens to petition Congress about abolishing slavery and opposed the annexation of Texas (see JAMES KNOX POLK) as a slave state. His refusal to vote for the annexation of Texas caused his expulsion from the Democratic party in 1846. His election to the Senate that year as an independent by the New Hampshire legislature made him the first senator elected on the basis of his abolitionist views.

During his first term in the Senate from 1847 to 1853, Hale led efforts to reform U.S. Navy regulations that resulted in the end of flogging and of distribution of grog. He resigned from the Senate in 1852 to accept the nomination for president by the Free-Soil party (see MARTIN VAN BUREN). Two years later, he was returned to the Senate, where he served until he was defeated for reelection in 1864 under a barrage of corruption accusations pertaining to his actions as naval committee chairman. In 1865 he became minister to Spain, where he served until he was recalled in 1869, once again under a cloud of corruption accusations.

BIBLIOGRAPHY

Ela, J. H., "Honorable John P. Hale," *Granite Monthly,* July 1880; Julian, G. W., "A Presidential Candidate of 1852," *Century,* October 1896; Sewell, Richard H., *John P. Hale,* 1965.

Hamilton, Alexander

(January 11, 1755 or 1757?–July 12, 1804)
Secretary of the Treasury

Alexander Hamilton dedicated his life to establishing a strong national government in America. Widely admired as a political philosopher, statesman, and public servant, Hamilton was also condemned by some for his distrust of the masses and preference for rule by an established aristocracy.

Born of a common-law marriage on the island of Nevis in the West Indies, Hamilton grew up on the nearby island of St. Croix. Virtually abandoned by his aristocratic but financially destitute father after the death of his mother when he was eleven, Hamilton obtained work

Library of Congress

in the office of a trading firm in Christiansted, St. Croix. The exceptionally bright, religious, and industrious Hamilton made such an impression upon the ruling class of the island that a scholarship fund was established to send him to New York to acquire a proper education.

The teenage Hamilton arrived in New York City in 1772, his impoverished life as an illegitimate child left behind forever. At King's College (now Columbia University), he was caught up in the revolutionary fervor sweeping the American colonies. After giving rousing speeches and writing impassioned articles against British rule, he joined a local militia regiment. In March 1776 he was commissioned captain of a New York artillery company. After fighting bravely in the battles around New York City, at White Plains, and at Princeton, Hamilton was promoted to lieutenant colonel and selected to serve on GEORGE WASHINGTON's staff.

Impressed by his performance and loyalty, Washington began to rely more and more on Hamilton's advice and assistance. During the course of the war Hamilton became Washington's most trusted personal aide. It was while serving as an officer under Washington that Hamilton began to develop his theories of democratic rule. After being admitted to the bar in 1783 and serving as a delegate to the Continental Congress, Hamilton began to campaign for a convention to enlarge the powers of the federal government in order to establish a system of federal taxation and a national bank. He attended the Constitutional Convention of 1787 as a delegate from New York.

At the Constitutional Convention Hamilton argued that, in order to survive, the nation would have to be what it was not under the Articles of Confederation—firmly united. He believed that only a strong national government could keep the separatist tendencies of the states in check, defend the country against foreign attack, and maintain a sound economy. He also favored government support of American commerce and the encouragement of an educated, well-to-do ruling class, whose interests would be closely tied to the interests of the nation. Many of his ideas, drawn from the British political system, clashed with the strong republican feelings of those (particularly THOMAS JEFFERSON) who favored a less strong central and urban government and the maintenance of power in the hands of ordinary farmer-citizens. His plan for a national government did not attract support, and at the end of the convention he admitted, according to JAMES MADISON, that "no man's ideas were more remote from the Constitution than his own were known to be."

Nevertheless, Hamilton served as a member of the Committee of Style that produced the finished document; pleaded for its unanimous approval by the delegates; wrote, with the help of Madison and JOHN JAY, arguments in favor of ratification in *The Federalist Papers;* and masterminded a campaign that secured the ratification of the Constitution in New York.

In the battle to secure the ratification of the Constitution, Hamilton persuasively argued in a series of masterful political essays that the new Constitution, imperfect though it might be, offered a viable alternative to the "anarchy and convulsion" that would otherwise surely engulf the new nation under the Articles of Confederation. His *Federalist* pieces also articulated many of the Constitution's general principles so well that they became classics of American political theory.

Appointed secretary of the treasury by Washington in 1789, Hamilton continued to endeavor to strengthen the powers of the federal government and became the central figure in the Federalist party as it developed. Once again Washington came to rely heavily on Hamilton's advice. As secretary of the treasury, Hamilton successfully insisted that the United States assume full responsibility for its war debts and for those of the states. This served to unite the wealthy creditor class behind the new central government and to stabilize the economy. He also wanted to establish a national bank as a safe repository of government funds, to issue loans and currency, and to keep an eye on government bonds. A federal excise tax on whiskey, however, was objected to by farmers in western Pennsylvania in 1794. Hamilton persuaded Washington to make a show of military force against the so-called Whiskey Rebellion and thereby confirmed the right of the federal government to tax.

By the time Hamilton completed his term as secretary of the treasury in 1795, he had laid the groundwork for the rapid expansion of the nation's economy. However, his bold Federalist policies and proud personality had aroused tremendous opposition; his inability to compromise his strong political beliefs resulted in the creation of a new political party, the Republicans, under the leadership of Thomas Jefferson.

Out of office after the election of JOHN ADAMS to the presidency, Hamilton hoped to revive his declining political fortunes by achieving military glory in a war with France that threatened in 1798. He secured the appointment as inspector general of the army from John Adams, but the peaceful resolution of the crisis in 1800 doomed his prospects.

His support for CHARLES COTESWORTH PINCKNEY over John Adams split the Federalist party in the 1800 election and enabled the Republican ticket of Jefferson and AARON BURR to win. The election was thrown into the House of Representatives for resolution, however, because the ballots for president and vice president were not so labeled, and Burr and Jefferson were tied. Hamilton encouraged Federalist legislators to vote for Jefferson for president as the lesser evil. Four years later, when Hamilton helped defeat Burr's election as governor of New York with the comment that Burr was "a man of irregular and insatia-

ble ambition . . . who ought not to be trusted with the reins of government," Burr challenged Hamilton to a duel.

Too proud to refuse, Hamilton decided to confront Burr at Weehawken, New Jersey, on the morning of July 11, 1804, but—because he was opposed to the practice—determined not to fire. Burr shot Hamilton, fatally wounding him, and the man Thomas Jefferson had once described in frustration as "a colossus" died the next day in New York City.

BIBLIOGRAPHY

Cooke, Jacob E. (ed.), *Alexander Hamilton*, 1967, and *Alexander Hamilton*, 1982; Flexner, James T., *The Young Hamilton*, 1978; Hendrickson, Robert A., *The Rise and Fall of Alexander Hamilton*, 1985; McDonald, Forrest, *Alexander Hamilton*, 1982; Miller, John Chester, *Alexander Hamilton: Portrait in Paradox*, 1959; Morris, Richard B., *Witnesses at the Creation: Hamilton, Madison, Jay and the Constitution*, 1964; Stourzh, Gerald, *Alexander Hamilton and the Idea of the Republican Government*, 1970.

Hamlin, Hannibal

(August 27, 1809–July 4, 1891)
Vice President, Diplomat, Senator, Representative

One of ABRAHAM LINCOLN's earliest supporters in New England, Hannibal Hamlin served as vice president during the nation's grimmest period. Born in Paris Hill, Maine, Hamlin attended Hebron Academy before being admitted to the bar in 1833. Active in Democratic politics, Hamlin served in the state legislature from 1836 to 1841, during most of which time he was speaker. Elected to the U.S. House of Representatives in 1842, Hamlin developed a strong antislavery reputation. This led to his selection in 1848 by the antislavery wing of the Democratic party in

Maine to complete a Senate term. He won election to a full term in 1851.

Dissatisfied with the Democratic party's position on slavery, Hamlin joined the Republican party in July 1856. His election as governor of Maine that year marked the emergence of the Republican party as the dominant political force in New England; however, he resigned as governor after a few weeks and returned to the Senate. Hamlin's strong antislavery views and New England origins made him a logical choice for the Republican vice presidential nomination with Lincoln in 1860, and he served as vice president throughout Lincoln's first term. In need of a southern vice presidential running mate in 1864, Lincoln chose ANDREW JOHNSON instead of Hamlin.

Hamlin was again elected to the Senate in 1868, where he remained until his retirement in 1881. While in the Senate, he firmly supported Radical Republican Reconstruction programs. At the Republican national convention in 1880, he played an important role in preventing former president ULYSSES S. GRANT's

nomination for a third term. His final post was minister to Spain, from 1881 to 1882, and he died in Maine in 1891.

BIBLIOGRAPHY

Hamlin, Charles E., *The Life and Times of Hannibal Hamlin*, 1899; Hunt, H. Draper, *Hannibal Hamlin: Lincoln's First Vice President*, 1969.

Hammond, James Henry

(November 15, 1807–November 13, 1864)
Senator, Representative

Both as a journalist and as an elected representative to Congress, James Henry Hammond was an early and consistent supporter of the South's right to secede from the Union to preserve the institution of slavery.

Born in Newberry County, South Carolina, Hammond graduated from South Carolina College (now the University of South Carolina) in 1825. He was admitted to the bar in 1828 and established a lucrative practice in Columbia.

Immediately active in local politics, Hammond established a newspaper, the *Southern Times*, in 1830 to support opposition to protective tariff legislation and the right of states to nullify federal legislation. When the nullification crisis (see JOHN CALDWELL CALHOUN) seemed on the verge of precipitating a civil war in 1832, Hammond raised a regiment and eagerly prepared to lead it in battle. He opposed HENRY CLAY's compromise (for a gradual lowering of taxes) that averted conflict in 1833 and advocated continued preparedness for war, but he did not believe any secession attempt should be made unless at least five Southern states agreed to work together.

By the time he was elected to the U.S. House of Representatives in 1834, Hammond had acquired by marriage a large cotton plantation and hundreds of slaves. Hammond regarded slavery as the cornerstone of the Southern way

of life. While in Congress he advocated the death penalty for abolitionists as well as the right of Southern states to secede to prevent emancipation. Because of illness Hammond did not seek reelection to the House in 1836, but he recovered and won election to a two-year term as governor of South Carolina in 1842.

In March 1858, after winning election to the Senate the year before, Hammond made his famous "Cotton Is King" speech. It was delivered in reply to Senator WILLIAM H. SEWARD's comment that, due to its reliance upon slavery, the economically backward South was doomed to eventually be ruled by the industrial North. Hammond claimed that the factory workers in the North lived lives of even worse degradation than the South's slaves and defiantly warned, "You dare not make war on cotton—No power on earth dares make war upon it. Cotton is king."

Hammond resigned from the Senate upon the election of ABRAHAM LINCOLN in 1860. Although a fierce critic of JEFFERSON DAVIS and the Confederate congress, he staunchly supported the war effort until his death.

BIBLIOGRAPHY

Merritt, Elizabeth, *James Henry Hammond*, 1923.

Hampton, Wade

(March 28, 1818–April 11, 1902)
Senator

Perhaps no other man lived a life as close to the stereotypical image of the Southern aristocrat before and after the Civil War than Wade Hampton.

Born in Charleston, South Carolina, into a prominent family, Hampton learned to be an excellent horseman and hunter before he graduated from South Carolina College in 1836. Then, in addition to improving the family plantations in Mississippi, Hampton served in the state legislature from 1852 until his resignation in 1861.

Hampton did not feel that secession was necessary or practical in 1860. He believed the institution of slavery to be uneconomical and did not see the election of ABRAHAM LINCOLN as sufficient grounds to dissolve the Union. Nevertheless, he was sure that states had a constitutional right to secede. As soon as South Carolina voted to do so, he pledged the resources of his plantations to the cause of defending the Confederacy and organized a regiment known as the Hampton Legion.

As General James E. B. ("Jeb") Stuart's second in command, Hampton fought heroically throughout the Civil War despite several serious wounds. After the defeat of the Confederacy, Hampton tried to establish a working relationship with the new and overwhelmingly Republican black voters while running unsuccessfully for governor of South Carolina as a Democrat in 1865 and 1868. For the next decade, while the Radical Republican Reconstruction government ruled South Carolina, Hampton assumed a low political profile and concentrated upon rebuilding his Mississippi plantations.

In 1876, at the end of Reconstruction, Hampton returned to the political arena in South Carolina once again as the Democratic party candidate for governor. This time, however, largely through the widespread use of intimidation against black voters, Hampton was elected along with a Democratic-dominated state legislature.

Fortunately, the violence between the races many feared would erupt after the last federal troops were withdrawn from South Carolina did not occur. This was due largely to the efforts of Hampton, who sought to curtail the mob actions of embittered whites as well as to chart a moderate, if patronizing, attitude toward blacks. Two years later, Hampton was reelected governor and, in 1878, elected to the U.S. Senate, where he served two successive six-year terms. After failing to win reelection to the Senate in 1890, Hampton retired from politics. From 1893 until 1899, he was the commissioner of Pacific Railways.

BIBLIOGRAPHY

Jarell, Hampton M., *Wade Hampton and the Negro: The Road Not Taken*, 1949.

Hancock, John

(January 23, 1737–October 8, 1793)
Revolutionary Leader

The patriot leader John Hancock signed his name to the Declaration of Independence with such exceptional size and clarity that today his name is used informally to mean a person's signature.

Hancock was born in Braintree, Massachusetts. He was adopted while still a young boy by a wealthy uncle upon the death of his father. After graduating from Harvard College in 1754, he went to work in his uncle's firm, Thomas Hancock & Company, the leading mercantile firm in Boston. John inherited the company in 1764, at age twenty-seven.

Library of Congress

Because of the flamboyant Hancock's blatant contempt for the efforts of the British Crown to regulate and tax colonial trade, customs agents attempted to arrest him for smuggling. In 1768 Hancock's ship *Liberty* was seized and confiscated in Boston after some wine was smuggled ashore from its cargo hold by other merchants. A riot broke out when Hancock's vessel was towed out to a British warship for impoundment, and Hancock was charged with smuggling. Since he owned the ship, Hancock was technically responsible for what happened to its cargo, even though he was not the one who attempted to bring it ashore illegally. He hired JOHN ADAMS to handle his defense and was eager to stand trial, but Crown officials decided, in the face of the strong popular support for Hancock in Boston, that it was wiser to drop the case before trial. The long-term impact of the incident was significant: Hancock, one of the wealthiest men in New England, became a staunch supporter of the need for radical revolution. He never recovered his ship, but he was hailed as a martyr and in 1769 won election to the Massachusetts General Court.

The wealthy Hancock and the firebrand SAMUEL ADAMS quickly became revolutionary allies. In 1770, after the Boston Massacre, Hancock became head of the Boston patriot committee. Three years later, he played a leading role in publishing private letters illegally obtained in England written by loyalist governor THOMAS HUTCHINSON that contained unflattering references to the people of Massachusetts. Adams and Hancock's efforts to incite armed resistance to the British authorities in Massachusetts after the implementation of the Coercive Acts in 1774 led General Thomas Gage to issue a warrant for their arrest in April 1775. Paul Revere's famous warning enabled them to escape capture on the day that the battles of Lexington and Concord began the American Revolution.

Hancock served as president of the Massachusetts provincial congress from 1774 until he was elected in May 1775 to the Second Continental Congress. Two weeks after his arrival in Philadelphia, the convivial and popular Hancock was elected the first president of the Continental Congress. He served as president until 1777 and as a delegate to Congress until 1780. Hancock felt slighted when he was not named commander in chief of the Continental Army, but time proved that GEORGE WASHING-

TON was a much better choice. Hancock performed poorly in his only military leadership position. In 1778 he commanded a Massachusetts contingent of 5,000 men in a mismanaged and bungled attack upon British forces in Rhode Island.

In 1780 Hancock, who had carefully maintained his local political power base while serving in Congress, was elected governor of Massachusetts. He held office until 1785, when dire financial conditions in the state due to an economic depression and an attack of the gout led to his resignation. He was reelected governor in 1787 and remained in office until his death six years later.

In addition to serving as governor, Hancock presided over the Massachusetts convention called to ratify the U.S. Constitution in 1788. His support proved helpful in securing the state's adoption of the Constitution.

BIBLIOGRAPHY

Allan, Herbert S., *John Hancock*, 1948; Sears, Lorenzo, *John Hancock, the Picturesque Patriot*, 1912.

Hancock, Winfield Scott

(February 14, 1824–February 9, 1886)
Candidate for President

Named for the hero of the War of 1812 (see JAMES MADISON), General WINFIELD SCOTT, Hancock entered West Point at age sixteen. Graduating in 1844, he served in the Mexican War (see JAMES KNOX POLK), and performed duty in Florida, Kansas, and Utah. As a major general in the Civil War, Hancock commanded divisions in the battles of Fredericksburg and Chancellorsville and, as commander of the Second Corps, played a particularly important role at Gettysburg, where he won fame for selecting the field of battle, repulsing repeated attacks by Lee, and being severely wounded during General Pickett's assault. In 1864 his Second Corps became General ULYSSES S. GRANT's shock troops in the long and bloody campaign from the Wilderness to Petersburg.

A career officer, Hancock remained in the army after the Civil War. During this period he led an expedition against hostile Indians while in command of the Central Military Department in 1867. The same year he was placed in command of the Department of Louisiana and Texas. Hancock was one of the conservative generals ANDREW JOHNSON appointed to try to frustrate Republican policies in the South, and Hancock's wise and restrained leadership angered the radicals in Congress. He was relieved of duty for giving civil tribunals jurisdiction over all crimes and offenses not involving forcible resistance to federal authority. He went on to command the Department of Dakota (1870–1872), the Division of the Atlantic (1872–1876), and finally, the Department of the East with headquarters at Governor's Island, New York.

Because of his war record, Hancock was first mentioned for the Democratic nomination for president in 1868, but it wasn't until twelve years later that he was actually nominated. The presidential campaign of 1880, devoid of major policy issues, focused on the character of the candidates. Unable to find anything in Hancock's past on which to attack him, besides an offhand remark that "the tariff question is a local issue," the Republicans resorted to smearing him as someone who did "nothing but eat, drink, and enjoy himself sensually."

After losing to JAMES A. GARFIELD by a narrow margin of popular votes (214 electoral votes to 155), Hancock resumed his military duties as commander of the Division of the Atlantic and of the Department of the East. He died on Governor's Island, New York, six years later.

BIBLIOGRAPHY

Denison, Charles W., *Hancock "the Superb,"* 1880; Junkin, D. X., and F. H. Norton, *The Life of Winfield Scott Hancock,* 1880; Walker, Francis A., *General Hancock,* 1987.

Hanna, Marcus Alonzo

(September 24, 1837–February 15, 1904)
Senator

A wealthy businessman and political leader, Mark Hanna is credited with introducing preconvention campaign techniques to the American political system through his successful efforts on behalf of Republican president WILLIAM MCKINLEY.

Born in New Lisbon, Ohio, Hanna moved with his family to Cleveland in 1852. After a brief stint in college, Hanna left to begin a remarkably successful career in business. Through M. A. Hanna and Company, with its interests in shipbuilding, coal, and iron, he accumulated a substantial fortune. From this base he invested in the *Cleveland Herald* and the Cleveland Opera House, and in control of Cleveland's streetcar system.

Hanna saw political power as a means to promote business. Prosperous companies provided jobs, and jobs increased the wealth of the nation. An unusual capitalist, Hanna was not opposed to the right of labor to organize. A strong supporter of the need to implement protective tariffs and to keep to the gold standard (that is, to use gold to back currency), Hanna lobbied for Republican senator JOHN SHERMAN for president in 1888. He was unable to muster sufficient support for Sherman's nomination at the Republican national convention. However, at the convention Hanna met Representative William McKinley and decided that the Ohio congressman had the right qualities and beliefs to be president.

With the help of Hanna's financial backing and organizational management skills, McKinley was elected governor of Ohio in 1891 and reelected in 1893. Hanna decided to begin working to secure McKinley's nomination for president by recruiting delegates long before the 1896 Republican convention. As a result, McKinley won the nomination in 1896 on the first ballot, and Hanna became chairman of the Republican National Committee and managed McKinley's "front porch" campaign (see WILLIAM MCKINLEY, JR.). The election occurred in the midst of a severe economic depression. Advertising McKinley as the "advance agent of prosperity," Hanna raised several million dollars that helped to ensure McKinley's election against Democratic candidate WILLIAM JENNINGS BRYAN.

Elected to the Senate in 1897, Hanna was reelected in 1903. He was President McKinley's most intimate adviser but did not, as critics charged, control McKinley.

Following McKinley's assassination in 1901, Hanna served as one of President THEODORE ROOSEVELT's advisers. As time went by, he became increasingly unhappy with Roosevelt. He might have challenged Roosevelt for the Republican nomination in 1904 had he not died unexpectedly.

BIBLIOGRAPHY

Beer, Thomas, *Hanna,* 1929; Croly, Herbert D., *Marcus Alonzo Hanna,* 1912.

Harding, Warren Gamaliel

(November 2, 1865–August 2, 1923)
President, Senator

In 1920 Republican presidential candidate Warren Harding promised "less government in business and more business in government" to help bring prosperity back into American lives. But prosperity was no substitute for leadership, as his incompetent, scandal-ridden administration would soon prove.

The oldest of eight children, Warren Gamaliel Harding was born on a farm in Blooming Grove, Ohio. He attended Ohio Central College from 1879 to 1882 and briefly taught school before becoming a newspaper editor and publisher.

Library of Congress

After losing an 1892 race for county auditor, Harding was elected to the state senate in 1898. "It was not long," wrote a reporter, "before Harding was the most popular man in the legislature. He had the inestimable gift of never forgetting a man's name. He was a regular he-man . . . a great poker-player, and not at all averse to putting a foot on the brass rail." Harding was an ideal conciliator for the faction-ridden Ohio Republican party.

In 1902 he was elected lieutenant governor with the help of HARRY M. DAUGHERTY, head of the Ohio Republican machine. He twice tried unsuccessfully to be elected governor, in 1910 and 1912, before being elected to the U.S. Senate in 1914. A traditional Republican, Senator Harding voted along conservative lines. In Washington, as in Ohio, his charm and good looks served him well. Known as someone who preferred the golf course to the office, the ball park to the Senate chamber, and a poker game to almost anything, Harding quickly became Washington's most popular senator.

The Republican party chose Harding as its candidate for president in 1920 because of his genial personality, good looks, and noncontroversial Senate record and because of a conviction by the party's bosses that he could be controlled. Harding conducted a "front porch" campaign. He promised to keep America out of the League of Nations (see WOODROW WILSON) and to return the country to "normalcy," or the way it used to be before the traumas of World War I, postwar inflation, labor unrest, and recession. It was precisely the right theme for the time. He defeated his Democratic rival, JAMES M. COX, by 7 million popular votes.

After becoming president, Harding admitted to his friend Daugherty, "I knew that this job would be too much for me." He was right. Although most of his appointments consisted of friends, including Daugherty as attorney general, and people he felt he owed jobs to for supporting his campaign, he did make some outstanding appointments to his cabinet: CHARLES EVANS HUGHES, secretary of state; ANDREW MELLON, secretary of the treasury; and HERBERT HOOVER, secretary of commerce. When Mellon's budget-reform program was passed in June 1921, Harding appointed the able CHARLES G. DAWES director of the Budget Bureau. He also named former president WILLIAM HOWARD TAFT chief justice of the Supreme Court.

The most successful foreign policy accomplishment of the Harding administration was the naval disarmament conference chaired by Secretary of State Hughes in Washington, D.C., in November 1921. Great Britain, France, Italy, Japan, and the United States agreed to a ten-year moratorium on the construction of capital ships. Harding, poorly informed about international affairs, had left the organization of the conference to Secretary Hughes.

Baffled and overwhelmed by the responsibilities of his office, Harding was dependent upon the honesty and competence of his appointed officials. Unfortunately, many of his closest friends and supporters disappointed him. When rumors began to spread in 1923 of rampant corruption in his administration, Harding began to realize the extent to which he had been betrayed. He admitted as he left Washington for a cross-country trip in 1923, "I am not worried about my enemies. It is my friends that are keeping me awake nights." He suffered a stroke and died that summer in San Francisco. His death elevated Vice President CALVIN COOLIDGE to the presidency and saved Harding from having to confront the disgrace his friends brought upon his administration.

Congress began a public investigation of the corruption rumors in 1924. The widespread abuse of the public trust by Harding's cronies shocked the nation. The most notorious abuse was by Secretary of the Interior ALBERT B. FALL. He had leased two government oil deposits—the Teapot Dome reserve in Wyoming and the Elk Hills fields in California—to private interests from which he had received at least $125,000 in personal "loans." Fall was eventually convicted of bribery and sent to prison. Attorney General Daugherty was acquitted of conspiracy charges in another matter and resigned at the request of President Coolidge. It would be Coolidge's task to restore trust in the presidency.

BIBLIOGRAPHY

Downes, Randolph C., *Rise of Warren Gamaliel Harding, 1865–1920*, 1970; Murray, Robert K., *Harding Era*, 1969; Russel, Francis, *Shadow of Blooming Grove*, 1968; Sinclair, Andrew, *Available Man*, 1965.

Harlan, John Marshall

(June 1, 1833–October 14, 1911)
Associate Justice of the Supreme Court

John Marshall Harlan earned the title of liberal dissenter for his passionate arguments on behalf of civil liberties while serving as an associate justice of the Supreme Court for almost thirty-four years.

Harlan was born into a prominent family in Boyle County, Kentucky. He graduated from Centre College in Danville, Kentucky, in 1850, studied law at Transylvania University in Lexington, and was admitted to the bar in 1853. A slave owner with considerable sympathy for the Southern perspective, Harlan began his political career as a Whig, briefly joined the American or Know-Nothing party (see MILLARD FILLMORE), then became a leader of the Kentucky Union party. In 1858 he was elected to a one-year term as judge of the court of Franklin County, but the following year he lost a bid for Congress.

At the outbreak of the Civil War, Harlan raised a regiment of Kentucky volunteers. He served as a colonel in the Union militia until the death of his father led to his resignation and return home in 1863. He was promptly elected state attorney general on the Union party ticket. The following year Harlan worked to prevent the reelection of President ABRAHAM LINCOLN and the adoption of the Thirteenth Amendment, which ended slavery.

Harlan resigned as state attorney general in 1867 to resume his private law practice. After the collapse of the Union party, he joined the Republican party. In 1871 and 1875, as the leader of the conservative wing of the Kentucky Republican party, he made two unsuccessful attempts to win election as governor. Appalled at the violence employed to prevent blacks from exercising their civil rights in Kentucky, Harlan reevaluated his beliefs about the proper role of the federal government and became an advocate for the need to provide adequate government protection.

In 1877, in return for Harlan's vital support as the leader of the Kentucky delegation at the Republican national convention, President RUTHERFORD B. HAYES appointed him to the Supreme Court. For the next three decades, Harlan earned the reputation of being the Supreme Court's most outstanding, and for a great deal of the time only, liberal dissenter.

Philosophically, Harlan was a strict constructionist (see THOMAS JEFFERSON and MELVILLE WESTON FULLER). He believed that the Constitution should be construed as closely as possible to match the intent of the framers within the dictates of common sense. For example, in what he felt was his most important dissenting opinion, he disagreed that Congress had no power under the Fourteenth Amendment to protect blacks from discrimination practiced by individuals because it was the need for just such protection that had prompted the authors to frame the amendment. He also vainly argued in 1883 in support of upholding the constitutionality of the Civil Rights Act of 1875 and opposed the legitimization of the separate-but-equal racial segregation policy of the South in *Plessy* v. *Ferguson* (1896).

In addition, Harlan supported the constitutionality of the graduated income tax in *Pollock* v. *Farmers' Loan and Trust Co.* (1895) on the basis of the right of the national government to raise revenue through taxation, and refused to concur in the weakening of the power of the Sherman Anti-Trust Act (see BENJAMIN HARRISON) in *Standard Oil Co.* v. *U.S.* and *U.S.* v. *American Tobacco Co.* on the grounds that the Court had no right to read the word "unreasonable" into the act (see EDWARD DOUGLASS WHITE). Many of Harlan's important dissents were eventually supported when the composition of the majority of the Court changed.

In 1892 President Benjamin Harrison appointed Harlan as the American representative on the tribunal that met in Paris to settle the Bering Sea controversy with Great Britain. From 1899 to 1910 he lectured on constitutional law at Columbian (now George Washington) University.

BIBLIOGRAPHY

Abraham, Henry J., "John M. Harlan," *Virginia Law Review*, 41, 1955, p. 871; Clark, F. B., *Constitutional Doctrines of Justice Harlan*, 1915; Westin, Alan F., "John Marshall Harlan and Constitutional Rights of Negroes," *Yale Law Journal*, 66, 1957, p. 637.

Harris, Patricia Roberts

(May 31, 1924–March 23, 1985)
Secretary of Health, Education, and Welfare; Secretary of Housing and Urban Development; Diplomat

Patricia Harris was the first black woman to serve as a U.S. ambassador and the first to hold a presidential cabinet position.

The daughter of a Pullman car waiter, Patricia Roberts Harris was born in Mattoon, Illinois. She received her bachelor's degree from Howard University in 1945 and earned her law degree from George Washington University in 1960.

Harris was an early and consistent advocate of black civil rights. In 1943 she participated in her first sit-in in Washington, D.C., to desegregate a cafeteria.

In 1964 she served on the Commission on the Status of Puerto Rico. One year later, President LYNDON B. JOHNSON appointed her the ambassador to Luxembourg and an alternate delegate to the United Nations. She served in these posts for two years and then became the dean of Howard University Law School.

President-elect JIMMY CARTER appointed Harris secretary of Housing and Urban Development in November 1976 and in 1979 secretary of Health, Education, and Welfare (HEW, renamed the Department of Health and Human Services).

As an administrator, Harris was well known for her demanding, no-nonsense personal style and for her skills in protecting her department both from other federal bureaucracies and from grass-roots groups seeking to turn HEW to their own advantage.

After leaving the White House in January 1981, Harris became a professor at the George Washington University National Law Center.

BIBLIOGRAPHY

Boyd, Gerald M., "Patricia R. Harris, Carter Aide, Dies," *New York Times*, March 24, 1985, p. 36; *Current Biography*, 1965.

Harrison, Benjamin

(August 20, 1833–March 13, 1901)
President, Senator

Little Ben" Harrison (he was 5 feet, 6 inches tall) became twenty-third president of the United States, one of the few presidents elected without a plurality of popular votes (see GROVER CLEVELAND). Grandson of President WILLIAM HENRY HARRISON, Benjamin Harrison was born near Cincinnati, Ohio, and attended Farmer's College before graduating from Miami University in 1852. He was admitted to the state bar in 1854. A firm antislavery advocate and loyal Republican, he was elected city attorney in 1857, served as secretary to the Republican state central committee in 1858, and was elected reporter of the Indiana Supreme Court in 1860 and 1864.

At the outbreak of the Civil War, Harrison raised a regiment of Indiana infantry. In 1864 he led his troops in the attack on Atlanta and won praise from General Joseph Hooker before returning briefly to Indiana to help in the reelection campaign of ABRAHAM LINCOLN. After the war he became a successful corporate lawyer. Although unable to secure the Republican nomination for governor of Ohio in 1872, he did win it in 1876, only to be defeated.

After commanding the state militia during the national railroad strike in 1877 and playing a prominent role in assuring the nomination of JAMES A. GARFIELD in 1880, Harrison was elected to the U.S. Senate in 1881. He was mentioned as a possible vice presidential candidate in 1884, but Harrison made it clear he would not accept the nomination.

While in the Senate from 1881 to 1887, Harrison developed a reputation as a moderate, independent, and progressive legislator. As chairman of the Committee on Territories he guided through the Senate the bill that granted civil government to Alaska and fought to protect the rights of Indians and homesteaders from the railroads. He also supported passage of the Interstate Commerce Act, labor legislation, a moderate protective tariff bill in 1883, pension legislation for Civil War veterans, and civil service reform (see CHESTER ALAN ARTHUR and RUTHERFORD BIRCHARD HAYES). He opposed, at considerable political cost, the Chinese Exclusion Act of 1882, which prohibited the immigration of Chinese to the United States. He was defeated for reelection in 1886 by a margin of one vote, but this did not end his political career. In 1888 he was nominated as the Republican presidential candidate.

The decision of President GROVER CLEVELAND in 1887 to advocate reducing tariffs—the customs duties placed on imported goods—was the major issue of the campaign. Harrison, who took the Republican stand of supporting the need for high protective tariffs, won the presidency in a "front porch" campaign conducted without traveling. He defeated Cleveland in the electoral college by 233 votes to 168, even though he lost in the popular vote by 100,000 votes.

Library of Congress

Although Harrison tried to establish cordial relations with Congress, his effort to adopt a moderate position concerning civil service reform and his cold personality alienated Republican Party leaders. Republican senator Shelby Cullom of Illinois said, "I suppose he treated me about as well in the patronage as he did any other Senator, but whenever he did anything for me it was done so ungraciously that the concession tended to anger rather than please."

Harrison worked diligently to overcome the administrative problems associated with the opening of the Oklahoma Territory to settlement in 1889, and he strongly supported the Pan-American Congress conducted by his secretary of state, JAMES G. BLAINE. A firm believer in the destiny of the United States to be a world power, Harrison took great pride in the new navy of steel ships constructed during his administration. He pushed U.S. claims in Samoa, and submitted a treaty to Congress for the annexation of Hawaii.

Although he played only a minor role in their passage, significant laws were enacted in his administration. These include the Sherman Anti-Trust Act, which prohibited the "restraint of free trade" by businesses; the McKinley Tariff Act, which placed high import tax rates on numerous goods; the Sherman Silver Purchase Act, which doubled the amount of silver purchased by the government and the paper money issued based upon it; and the Dependent Pension Act, which provided benefits for any veterans who had served more than ninety days in the army during the Civil War. The increase in taxes and prices that resulted from this legislation led to the Democrats' regaining control of Congress in the elections of 1890 and set the stage for Harrison's reelection defeat.

Harrison was renominated in 1892, but he lacked strong support inside his own party. His efforts to curtail patronage combined with the labor strife resulting from the Homestead strike (at the Carnegie Steel Company in Homestead, Pennsylvania), the rise in prices caused by the implementation of the McKinley tariff, and the birth of the Populist party (see JAMES BAIRD WEAVER) doomed his campaign. A renominated Cleveland defeated Harrison 277 electoral votes to 145, with a victory margin of more than 370,000 popular votes.

Harrison returned home to Indianapolis and led a busy and productive life. His first wife having died in 1892, Harrison married again in 1896, and the couple had a child (Harrison's third) the next year. Harrison had a vigorous law practice, including cases that took him before the Supreme Court. He also successfully defended Venezuelan claims against England in the final arbitration of an international boundary dispute in 1899 (see THOMAS FRANCIS BAYARD).

BIBLIOGRAPHY

Sievers, Harry J. (ed.), *Benjamin Harrison,* 1969; Volewiler, Albert T. (ed.), *The Correspondence between Benjamin Harrison and James G. Blaine, 1882–1893,* 1940.

Harrison, William Henry

(February 9, 1773–April 4, 1841)
President, Senator, Representative

Indian fighter and War of 1812 (see JAMES MADISON) military hero, William Henry Harrison was born into a distinguished Virginia family in Charles County, Virginia. After attending Hampden-Sidney College, Harrison joined the army. As aide-de-camp to General Anthony Wayne, he fought in the Indian wars in the Northwest Territory. He resigned from the army in 1798 and was appointed secretary of the Northwest Territory. He was elected its first delegate to Congress in 1799.

On May 12, 1800, President JOHN ADAMS appointed Harrison governor of the Indiana Territory. One of his main tasks was to make treaties with the Indians that gained white settlers the right to occupy millions of acres of Indian land. Harrison deplored the unfair treatment the Indians received from whites, but he realized the tide of white immigrants spelled their doom. When the Shawnee leader Tecumseh attempted to stop the white advance by uniting the tribes of the region, Harrison led the militia assault upon Tecumseh's village at Tippecanoe Creek in 1811, thereby earning the nickname Tippecanoe. Unable to crush Tecumseh at that time, Harrison requested military assistance from President JAMES MADISON. His pleas for more troops were ignored until the outbreak of the War of 1812 the next year. Then, after Detroit had been captured by the British and Harrison had taken charge of efforts to halt the British advance, he was made overall military commander of the Northwest.

After recapturing Detroit in 1813, Harrison pursued the retreating British forces into Canada. At the Battle of the Thames, the British troops and the Canadian militia, along with their Indian allies, were so soundly defeated that they never posed a threat to the security of the Northwest Territories again. (Tecumseh was killed in the battle.) The victory at the Battle of the Thames made Harrison a national hero.

After resigning his commission in the army for a second time, Harrison was elected as a Whig to the House of Representatives in 1816 as a follower of HENRY CLAY. In 1819 he was elected to the Ohio state senate. His ambivalence about slavery prevented his reelection and undermined his unsuccessful 1821 bid for election to the U.S. Senate. However, another try for the Senate in 1825 was successful, and he served there until his appointment three years later as ambassador to Colombia.

National Portrait Gallery, Smithsonian Institution

Newly elected President ANDREW JACKSON recalled Harrison in 1829 to replace him with a Democrat.

After his return to the United States, Harrison entered private life, where he suffered a number of business and family losses but managed to provide for his family from his North Bend, Ohio, farm and the income derived from his appointment in 1834 as county recorder. Harrison was mentioned as a Whig presidential candidate in 1836; but instead of selecting a single candidate, the Whig party split and nominated three sectional candidates: DANIEL WEBSTER of Massachusetts, Senator HUGH L. WHITE of Tennessee, and Harrison from Ohio. Democrat MARTIN VAN BUREN won easily against the fragmented Whigs, but in the states north of the Ohio River Harrison obtained almost as many votes as Van Buren. Encouraged, Harrison and his supporters immediately began working to win the Whig nomination in 1840.

At its first national nominating convention in 1840, held in Harrisburg, Pennsylvania, the party chose Harrison because he was a military hero and, unlike rival candidate Henry Clay, did not have a political record that indicated how he felt about controversial issues. Not having any strong issues for their platform, the Whigs realized that as a party representing largely upper-income and business voters, who stood in opposition to Andrew Jackson's egalitarian democracy, they needed a candidate who would appeal to a wider electorate. To complement Harrison's popularity in the Northwest, the party chose as his running mate JOHN TYLER of Virginia.

When a Democratic newspaper reported that Harrison only wanted to retire eventually with a pension to a log cabin and an abundance of hard cider, the Whigs seized upon the comment as proof that Harrison was a man of the people. Model log cabins and kegs of hard cider became Whig campaign symbols, along with the slogan using Harrison's nickname, "Tippecanoe and Tyler too!" Harrison carried all but seven states, won 53 percent of the popular vote, and swept the electoral vote 234 to incumbent Van Buren's 60.

The sixty-eight-year-old Harrison caught a cold after his inauguration that developed into pneumonia, and he died after serving only one month in office.

BIBLIOGRAPHY

Cleaves, Freeman, *Old Tippecanoe: William Henry Harrison*, 1939; Goebel, D. B., *William Henry Harrison*; Green, J. A., *William Henry Harrison*, 1941.

Hay, John Milton

(October 8, 1838–July 1, 1905)
Secretary of State, Diplomat

Poet, novelist, and historian as well as secretary of state under Presidents WILLIAM MCKINLEY and THEODORE ROOSEVELT, John Milton Hay achieved success as both a writer and a diplomat.

Born in Salem, Indiana, Hay graduated from Brown University in 1858. One week after he was admitted to the Illinois bar in 1861, Hay was asked to serve as one of newly elected president ABRAHAM LINCOLN's assistant private secretaries. Shortly before Lincoln's assassination in 1865, Hay accepted a position in the diplomatic corps in Paris. During the next four years he traveled extensively in Europe, serving two years in Paris and one each in Vienna and Madrid.

While abroad Hay decided to become a writer. Upon his return to the United States in 1870, he succeeded in having several very well received pieces published in major literary magazines. He also secured a position as an editorial writer for the *New York Tribune.* Marriage in 1874 to Clara Louise Stone, the daughter of a millionaire, provided Hay with financial and social stature to match his literary success. Hay's most important work is the ten-volume *Abraham Lincoln: A History* (1890), which he wrote with John George Nicolay.

From November 1878 to March 1881, Hay served as assistant secretary of state. His role as one of McKinley's advisers during the campaign of 1896 led to his appointment as ambassador to Great Britain in 1897. A year and a half later, McKinley appointed Hay secretary of state.

McKinley and Hay were in agreement on the way to deal with the important international issues facing the United States. As a result, McKinley had complete confidence in Hay and often let him lead the development of what became administration foreign policies.

Hay's most important foreign policy achievement concerned American involvement in China. In 1900 Hay made the position of the United States in China clear with the announcement of U.S. support for the Open Door policy. Hay stated that it was the goal of the United States in China to ensure equality of commercial exploitation opportunity. The pronouncement did not actually prevent the partition of China—the United States was not powerful enough in 1900 to do that—but Americans believed that it did, because China was not, like Africa, carved up into separate colonial possessions. The apparent success of the Open Door policy enhanced the prestige of Hay and the McKinley administration. When resentment in China over foreign domination exploded in the Boxer Rebellion, Hay successfully encouraged McKinley to demonstrate American interest in the region by dispatching American troops to China to assist in its suppression. The Boxers were a secret group of Chinese who resented the strong influence of foreigners in China. In 1899 they made violent attacks on foreigners and, in 1900, besieged foreign embassies in Peking (now called Beijing).

After the assassination of McKinley in 1901, Hay accepted President Theodore Roosevelt's request that he remain in office, but under Roosevelt, Hay never had the wide discretion he enjoyed with McKinley. Nevertheless, before his death in 1905, Hay engineered a number of important diplomatic achievements. For example, the Alaska panhandle boundary dispute with Canada was resolved (1903), and the Hay-Pauncefote Treaty with Great Britain (1901) and treaties with Colombia and Panama (1903) were signed, clearing the way for the construction of the Panama Canal. During the Boer Rebellion in South Africa, despite substantial American popular sympathy for the Boers, Hay enforced a policy of strict American neutrality. Hay died in office at the beginning of President Roosevelt's second term.

■■■
BIBLIOGRAPHY

Brown University Library, *Life and Works of John Hay, 1838–1905,* 1961; DeConde, Alexander, *The American Secretary of State: An Interpretation,* 1962; Hay, John, *Complete Poetical Works of John Hay,* 1916, and *Letters of John Hay and Extracts from His Diary,* 3 vols., 1908; Thayer, William R., *John Hay,* 2 vols., 1916; Thurman, Kelly, *John Hay as a Man of Letters,* 1974.

Hayes, Rutherford Birchard

(October 4, 1822–January 17, 1893)
President, Representative

The controversial way in which Rutherford B. Hayes was elected has tended to overshadow his presidency. However, the integrity and conciliatory manner displayed by Hayes as president restored much of the dignity to the office that had been undermined by the impeachment trial of President ANDREW JOHNSON and the corruption associated with President ULYSSES S. GRANT's administration.

During his four years in office, Reconstruction was formally concluded through the removal of the last federal troops from South Carolina and Louisiana, and significant progress was made in implementing civil service reform (see CHESTER ALAN ARTHUR).

Hayes was born in Delaware, Ohio. After graduating from Kenyon College in 1842 and Harvard Law School in 1845, he became a moderately successful attorney in Cincinnati. Hayes helped to found the Ohio Republican party in 1856 and began his political career by winning election as city solicitor.

Commissioned a major in the Ohio militia during the Civil War, Hayes was wounded three times in battle and rose to the rank of major

Library of Congress

general. Despite his protestations that he would not leave active duty until the war was over, he resigned from the service after he was elected to the U.S. House of Representatives in 1864.

While in Congress from 1865 to 1867, Hayes unenthusiastically supported Radical Republican Reconstruction policies. His one personal accomplishment was in helping to establish the Library of Congress. He successfully introduced a bill to have the Smithsonian Institution's collection of books transferred there and obtained sufficient funding for the library to begin acquiring additional major book collections.

Hayes was reelected to Congress in 1866, but he resigned the next year to make a successful run for the office of governor of Ohio. In his first term as governor, despite the fact that the legislature was controlled by the Democratic party, Hayes managed to implement prison and poor-relief organization reform. Reelected in 1869 and aided by a newly installed Republican party majority in the state legislature, Hayes played a leading role in the establishment of Ohio State University;

secured the state ratification of the Fifteenth Amendment to the Constitution, which attempted to ensure the right of newly enfranchised blacks to vote; and improved the state's mental hospitals and public school system.

Bowing to tradition in Ohio, Hayes did not seek election to a third consecutive term as governor in 1871. However, four years later, he accepted the Republican nomination for governor once again. His reelection by a wide margin as a supporter of the gold standard made him a national figure. He was a logical compromise "dark horse" choice for the Republican nomination for president in 1876 by the forces opposed to JAMES G. BLAINE.

Upon winning the Republican party endorsement, Hayes promised that, if elected, he would serve only one term in office. In the general election Hayes received 4,036,572 popular votes to Democratic candidate SAMUEL J. TILDEN's 4,284,020. According to the tally the day after the election, Hayes had won 165 electoral votes to Tilden's 184. Due to election irregularities, the electoral votes of Louisiana, South Carolina, Florida, and Oregon (a total of 20) were disputed. Since a majority of 185 votes was required to win the election, and Tilden had 184, one short, Hayes needed all the disputed votes to claim victory. The Constitution provided no remedy for such a situation, so Congress resolved the matter by creating an ostensibly bipartisan commission to determine the winner. The fifteen-member commission voted 8 to 7 along strict party lines to give the disputed votes to Hayes, and Congress, avoiding a filibuster by Democrats and exacting certain pledges from the Republicans, finally ratified the commission's vote

just two days before the inauguration in March 1877.

The manner in which he was elected and his narrow margin of victory encouraged Hayes to choose a bipartisan cabinet and a moderate, conciliatory approach to issues while president. Many federal jobs were awarded by Hayes to Democrats in order to placate them and, unsuccessfully, to win support for the Republican party in the South.

His efforts while president to secure civil service reform and strong government support for the gold standard met with some success. In 1877 he issued an executive order prohibiting federal civil servants from taking active part in politics. After locking horns with the Stalwarts (see ROSCOE CONKLING), the wing of the Republican party that favored awarding government positions for patronage purposes, Hayes finally emerged victorious.

Hayes kept his word and did not seek reelection in 1880. After leaving office, he retired from politics and devoted the rest of his life to working for prison reform and improved public education.

BIBLIOGRAPHY

Barnard, Harry, *Rutherford B. Hayes and His America,* 1954 (reprint 1967); Bishop, Arthur (ed.), *Rutherford B. Hayes, 1822–1893,* 1969; Davidson, Kenneth E., *The Presidency of Rutherford B. Hayes,* 1972; Howells, William D., *Sketch of the Life and Character of Rutherford B. Hayes,* 1876; Williams, T. Harry (ed.), *Hayes: The Diary of a President, 1875–1881,* 1964.

Hayne, Robert Young

(November 10, 1791–September 24, 1839)
Senator

Robert Young Hayne was the leading Southern spokesman in the Senate during the 1830s for the right of states to nullify federal laws they deemed unconstitutional (see JOHN CALDWELL CALHOUN).

Hayne was born in Colleton district, South Carolina. He was admitted to the bar in 1812 and established a successful practice. Two years later, as a member of the Democratic-Republican party, Hayne was elected to the state legislature. He became speaker of the house in 1818 and attorney general of the state in 1819 for two years. He was elected to the U.S. Senate in 1822 and reelected to the Senate without opposition for a second term in 1828.

In the Senate Hayne focused on defeating efforts to implement high protective tariffs, which he deemed unwise and unconstitutional. In January 1830, in a series of famous debates that lasted two weeks, Hayne faced off against DANIEL WEBSTER. Webster supported the need for protective tariff legislation and argued for a broad interpretation of the Constitution (see THOMAS JEFFERSON and MELVILLE WESTON FULLER). Hayne argued that a broad interpretation opened the door to domination of the states by the federal government and, in the long run, the end of democracy.

Hayne resigned from the Senate in 1832 to become the governor of South Carolina. As governor, he supported HENRY CLAY's compromise approach to dealing with the tariff issue and played a leading role in calming hostility toward the federal government in South Carolina. After leaving the governor's office in 1834, Hayne was mayor of Charleston for one year and then devoted his energy to railroad development projects, which he vainly hoped would unite the West and South.

BIBLIOGRAPHY

Jervy, Theodore D., *Robert Y. Hayne and His Times*, 1909.

Hays, William Harrison

(November 5, 1879–March 7, 1954)
Postmaster General

Although an important Republican party political leader, Will Hays is recalled primarily for his role as president from 1922 to 1945 of the Motion Picture Producers and Distributors of America. As "czar" of the motion picture industry, he administered the moral guidelines—popularly known as the Hays Code—that restricted the content of American films. The code was promulgated in 1934 by agreement of the leaders of the motion picture industry in order to avoid government censorship of films.

William Harrison Hays was born in Sullivan, Indiana. He earned his law degree from Wabash College in 1900, joined his father's law practice, and immediately embarked upon a political career in the Indiana Republican party. After establishing a reputation for integrity and industriousness by holding a number of state party positions between 1904 and 1916, he was chosen chairman of the Republican National Committee in 1918. Two years later, he managed WARREN G. HARDING's successful campaign for the presidency. Harding rewarded Hays by appointing him postmaster general in 1921. During his year as postmaster general, Hays won widespread praise for his honesty, diligence, and efficient management skills.

Hays resigned as postmaster general to accept the more lucrative and potentially much more influential position of president of the Motion Picture Producers and Distributors of America. When he became the moral guardian of the film industry in 1922, seven states had passed movie censorship laws and many others were contemplating such action. By appointing the upright, pious Presbyterian elder Hays to guarantee the wholesomeness of the film industry, the Hollywood producers accomplished their goal of ending the trend to regulate films through state and federal government legislation. Instead, with the aid of Hays's close behind-the-scenes supervision, the industry imposed censorship on itself. This was a censorship, Hays shrewdly advertised to the general public, that was much more effective than legislation because it conformed to his high moral standards.

Hays resigned from his film industry position in September 1945. Times had changed, but Hays had not changed since his appointment twenty-three years before. Disputes with producers eager to provide the public with movies more sophisticated than Hays could countenance finally forced him to relinquish control. He spent the rest of his life practicing law and writing his memoirs.

BIBLIOGRAPHY

Hays, Will H., *Memoirs*, 1945; Moley, Raymond, *The Hays Office*, 1945.

Helms, Jesse A.

(October 18, 1921–   )
Senator

The first Republican in this century to represent North Carolina in the Senate, Jesse Helms is perhaps the staunchest member of that legislative body's conservative coalition.

Helms was born in Monroe, North Carolina. After studying at Wingate (North Carolina) Junior College and Wake Forest College, he worked as city editor of the *Raleigh Times* in 1941 and 1942. During World War II he served in the U.S. Navy.

Helms went to Washington, D.C., as administrative assistant to Senator Willis Smith in 1951; two years later, he briefly served in the same role to Senator Alton Lennon before returning to North Carolina. From 1953 to 1960 he was the executive director of the North Carolina Bankers Association, and until 1972 he served as executive vice president of the Capital Broadcasting Company.

At Capital Broadcasting Helms wrote and broadcast daily editorials designed to combat what he called the "consistent bias in national television network news programs." He attacked the national news media for its alleged bias in favor of black civil rights protestors, excessive academic freedom, a weak national defense and softness on communism, and toleration of waste in government spending.

Helms gradually became more involved in conservative political activities and in 1970 changed his party allegiance to Republican. In 1972 he won an upset victory against a heavily favored Democratic opponent to become the first Republican from North Carolina to win a seat in the Senate since the Reconstruction era. The only other elected office he had held was as a Raleigh city council member from 1957 to 1961.

In the Senate Helms quickly established a reputation as a militant conservative eager to be in the forefront of national debates on school busing, abortion, school prayer, law enforcement, defense spending, and federal funding of "lewd and obscene" artistic endeavors. Helms's approach to many issues is based on his belief that the fundamental cause of all contemporary ills in America is a loss of traditional values due to a decline in religious faith.

Helms supported the unsuccessful effort of RONALD REAGAN to win the Republican nomination for president in 1976. After winning reelection to the Senate by a wide margin in 1978, he played a vital role, even shaping the Republican party platform, in Reagan's successful bid for the presidency in 1980. Helms won reelection again in 1984 and 1990. He received massive financial support from direct mail appeals through national conservative political organizations.

BIBLIOGRAPHY

Washington Post, November 9, 1972, p. 22; *New York Sunday News,* August 15, 1976, p. 27.

Henderson, David Bremner

(March 14, 1840–February 25, 1906)
Speaker of the House, Representative

David Bremner Henderson was born in Old Deer, Scotland. His parents immigrated to Illinois in 1846 and lived there for several years before purchasing a farm in Iowa.

After briefly attending Upper Iowa University, Henderson volunteered to join the Union army. He was wounded twice during the Civil War. His second wound was so severe that he never fully recovered from the partial amputation of his leg.

After the Civil War, Henderson established a legal practice in Dubuque, Iowa, and became active in local Republican party politics. In 1882 he was elected to the House of Representatives, where he served for ten consecutive terms. In the House he voted along Republican party lines for protectionist tariff legislation and the gold standard, and strongly supported pension benefits for veterans. He served as Speaker from 1899 to 1902, when he retired from public service. He briefly practiced law in New York City in 1903 and then retired to his home in Iowa.

BIBLIOGRAPHY

Annals of Iowa, April 1906; Gue, B. F., *History of Iowa,* vol. 4, 1903; Smith, William H., *Speakers of the House of Representatives of the U.S.,* 1928; *Who's Who in America,* 1906–1907.

Henderson, Leon

(May 26, 1895–October 19, 1986)
Government Agency Director

Often described as a brilliant yet truculent economist, Leon Henderson was a leading advocate within the administration of FRANKLIN D. ROOSEVELT for direct federal government relief and the need to break up business monopolies.

Henderson was born in Millville, New Jersey. After graduating from Swarthmore College in 1920, he taught at the Wharton School of the University of Pennsylvania and at Carnegie Tech. Henderson left college teaching in 1923 to work in the Pennsylvania state government and, in 1925, for the Russell Sage Foundation.

In 1934 Henderson was appointed by President Franklin D. Roosevelt to head the New Deal's National Recovery Administration (NRA), division of research and planning. When it was declared unconstitutional by the Supreme Court, Henderson became the economic adviser to the Democratic National Campaign Committee. In this influential position he was soon recognized as the foremost advocate of the consumer purchasing-power theory to end the depression. (Sometimes called pump priming, this approach advocated increasing the purchasing power of the low-paid masses of workers so that their demand for goods would spur production and thus create jobs.)

After serving in 1938 as the executive secretary and "guiding genius" of the newly created Temporary National Economic Committee (designed to monitor the business practices of large corporations and to identify any antitrust violations), Henderson was appointed by Roosevelt to the Securities and Exchange Commission. Although the appointment aroused the wrath of businesspeople, who viewed Henderson as their ideological foe, Henderson served in this delicate post until he was appointed administrator of the Office of Price Administration and director of civilian supply for the Office of Production Management in 1941.

For two years Henderson worked to hold down prices while ensuring full economic production during World War II. In 1943 he resigned in bitterness, angry at the government for not giving state planners like himself enough power to regulate the economy and control business.

BIBLIOGRAPHY

Ennis, Thomas W., "Leon Henderson, a Leading New Deal Economist," *New York Times*, October 21, 1986, D31; McCormick, R., "Where the Thinking Starts," *Collier's*, 103:13, January 7, 1939; "Up Again Henderson," *Time*, 33:18, May 1, 1939.

Hendricks, Thomas Andrews

(September 7, 1819–November 25, 1885)
Vice President, Senator, Representative

Born in Muskingum County, Ohio, Thomas A. Hendricks was raised in Indiana and graduated from Hanover College in 1841. He was admitted to the bar in 1844. In 1848 Hendricks entered the Indiana state legislature as a Democrat and later served as a delegate to the state constitutional convention. In 1851 he was elected to Congress, and in 1855 President FRANKLIN PIERCE appointed him to be commissioner of the General Land Office.

After losing the Indiana governor's race in 1860, Hendricks was elected to the Senate in 1863 by a Democratic legislature that had come into power because of a voter backlash against the Republicans' antislavery, total-war policies. In the Senate Hendricks attacked the Republicans for instituting the military draft and for imposing heavy taxes to win the Civil War. He also opposed freeing the slaves. He believed emancipation was a state matter and that blacks were indeed inferior. After the war he opposed adopting the Fourteenth and Fifteenth Amendments, and supported President ANDREW JOHNSON's Reconstruction views.

Hendricks was a contender for the Democratic party's presidential nomination in 1868 but lost to HORATIO SEYMOUR. In 1872 he was elected governor of Indiana. As a Democratic governor of a Northern state after the Civil War, he held considerable political prominence. Four years later, he was the Democratic candidate for vice president on the unsuccessful SAMUEL J. TILDEN ticket. When GROVER CLEVELAND was nominated for the presidency in 1884, Hendricks was chosen for the second spot to pacify the Democratic party bosses and to strengthen the ticket in the Midwest, where his well-known support for the resumption of the printing of the paper money issued in the Civil War known as greenbacks was popular (see SAMUEL PORTLAND CHASE). He died suddenly of a heart problem nine months after assuming the office of vice president.

BIBLIOGRAPHY

Holcombe, John W., and Hubert M. Skinner, *The Life and Public Services of Thomas A. Hendricks,* 1886.

Henry, Patrick

(May 29, 1736–June 6, 1799)
Revolutionary Leader

G ive me liberty or give me death" and "If this be treason, make the most of it" are two of the most famous phrases attributed to Patrick Henry, one of America's greatest public speakers and early patriots.

Patrick Henry was born in Hanover County, Virginia. Largely self-taught, he was admitted to the Virginia bar in 1760 and within a few years had become a very successful attorney. Henry established his reputation as a spokesman for colonial rights in 1763 by the logic he used to persuade a jury to award only one penny in damages in the so-called Parson's Case.

Five years earlier, the Virginia legislature had sought to circumvent the British law that required the use of colonial tax revenue to pay the salaries of the ministers (parsons) of the state-supported Anglican church. The legislature was found guilty of evading the law in a suit brought by the parsons. Henry's task was to settle the amount of the reward owed to the parsons. He succeeded brilliantly in holding down the amount by arguing that it was inappropriate for the king to seek damages because, as the ruler of all his subjects, the king ought to have the well-being of his subjects as his first administrative priority. It was an extremely popular position to take, and Henry was elected to Virginia's House of Burgesses soon after the minuscule damages award to the parsons was announced by the jury.

Henry joined the Virginia House of Burgesses in 1765 just as the Stamp Act (see JOHN ADAMS and SAMUEL ADAMS) was beginning to arouse the fury of the colonists. He became an exceptionally eloquent advocate of the position that only colonial legislatures could require colonists to pay taxes. It was during a decisive speech on this issue that he associated King George III of England with Caesar and Charles I. When he was interrupted by cries of treason, he replied, "If this be treason, make the most of it."

Henry was a delegate to the First Continental Congress in 1774. Frustrated by his inability to win support for a united colonial stand, he returned to Virginia and lobbied intensively to begin preparations for war. When those fearful of war opposed his support for organizing a militia, he replied: "What is it that the gentlemen wish? What would they have? Is life so dear or peace so sweet as to be purchased at the price of chains and slavery? . . . I know not what course others may take, but as for me, give me liberty or give me death!"

Henry's hopes for a military career in the American Revolution were frustrated when he was not chosen to lead Virginia's troops. He became governor under a new Virginia constitution on June 29, 1776, instead. Reelected twice, he served as governor until 1779. Because he believed that foreign support needed to be acquired and the colonies united under a central government before independence from Great Britain could be achieved, he opposed the Declaration of Independence in 1776.

Library of Congress

After the Revolution, Henry served another term as governor from 1784 to 1786 and led the fight for the adoption of the Virginia Religious Freedom Act of 1785. At the special Virginia constitutional convention held in 1788, Henry opposed ratification. He believed the Constitution granted too much power to the central government at the expense of individual liberty and states' rights. After the Constitution's adoption, he helped lead the fight to have the Bill of Rights added. Over the next decade Henry's political outlook gradually evolved until he had become one of the new federal government's supporters in Virginia. President GEORGE WASHINGTON offered Henry the positions of secretary of state and chief justice, but he declined both. In 1798, at Washington's request, Henry ran for the state legislature. He was elected but died before the legislature convened.

BIBLIOGRAPHY

Axelrad, Jacob, *Voice of Freedom,* 1947 (reprint 1975); Henry, William W., *Patrick Henry: Life, Correspondence and Speeches,* 3 vols., 1891; Mayer, Henry, *A Son of Thunder,* 1986; Meade, Robert D., *Patrick Henry,* 2 vols., 1957–1969; Tyler, Moses Coit, *Patrick Henry,* 1898; Wirt, William, *Sketches of the Life and Character of Patrick Henry,* 1836 (reprint 1972).

Herter, Christian Archibald

(March 28, 1895–December 30, 1966)
Secretary of State, Representative

Christian A. Herter could be considered the model for the Eastern Establishment progressive, or "liberal," Republican. Born in Paris, France, of American parents, Herter graduated from Harvard in 1915 and joined the U.S. foreign service. For the next two years he was an attaché in the American embassies in Germany and Belgium. Upon America's entry into World War I, he joined the State Department and worked in Washington, D.C. At the Paris Peace Conference in 1919, he served as secretary to the American Commission to Negotiate Peace.

Herter resigned from the State Department in 1920 to become the assistant to HERBERT HOOVER, the director general of the American Relief Administration. The two men developed a close friendship as well as a harmonious working relationship. The next year, when Hoover was appointed secretary of commerce, Herter became his special assistant.

In 1924 Herter left government service and became a magazine publisher. Six years later, he won the first of five consecutive elections to the Massachusetts legislature as a moderate, reform-oriented Republican. He was elected speaker of the Massachusetts House in 1939 and 1941, and in 1942 won election to the U.S. House of Representatives. While serving in Congress from 1943 until 1953, Herter strongly supported the creation of the United Nations and the implementation of the Marshall Plan (see GEORGE CATLETT MARSHALL and HARRY S TRUMAN).

After helping to secure the Republican nomination for president for DWIGHT D. EISENHOWER in 1952, Herter was elected governor of Massachusetts. His most notable accomplishments as a two-term governor included the creation of a public housing program, the reorganization of the state tax collection agency, and an increase in benefits for the elderly and needy.

In 1957 Herter became under secretary of state. When illness forced Secretary of State JOHN FOSTER DULLES to resign in 1959, President Eisenhower chose Herter to succeed him. Herter's brief tenure as secretary of state from April 1959 to January 1961 was a personal disappointment. His hopes for obtaining an international arms control agreement and of ending the cold war confrontation between the United States and the Soviet Union were not realized. Nevertheless, Herter is still considered to have accomplished a great deal in a short period as secretary of state. His efforts to avoid confrontation and to resolve disputes with the Soviet Union through negotiation served as a necessary transition period from the hard-line, confrontational anticommunism that had typified American foreign policy in the 1950s during the Republican Eisenhower administration to the more flexible response approach of Democratic president JOHN F. KENNEDY.

From 1962 until 1966, during both Kennedy's and LYNDON BAINES JOHNSON's administrations, Herter served as a special representative for trade negotiations in Geneva.

BIBLIOGRAPHY

Ambrose, Stephen E., *Eisenhower: The President,* 1983; Beschloss, Michael R., *Mayday: Eisenhower, Khrushchev, and the U-2 Affair,* 1986; Kenworthy, E. W., "Quarterback of State's Team," *New York Times Magazine,* March 29, 1959; Noble, B. Bernard, "Christian A. Herter," in Robert H. Ferrell (ed.), *The American Secretaries of State and Their Diplomacy,* 1970; "Yankee Internationalist," *Time,* January 13, 1967.

Hoar, George Frisbie

(August 29, 1826–September 30, 1904)
Diplomat, Senator, Representative

Although a staunch Republican, as a senator George Hoar became a leader among those in Congress who opposed President WILLIAM McKINLEY's decision to make the United States an imperialist power after the Spanish-American War of 1898.

George Frisbie Hoar was born in Concord, Massachusetts. After graduating from Harvard College in 1846 and Harvard Law School three years later, he practiced law in Worcester, Massachusetts.

Strongly in favor of the Radical Republican Reconstruction program after the Civil War, he was elected as a Republican to the House of Representatives in 1868. As a member of the House from 1869 to 1877, Hoar fought for civil service reform, regulation of railroads, protection of the civil rights of newly freed slaves, and aid to public education. He also helped to uncover the corruption of fellow Republican President ULYSSES S. GRANT's administration.

Hoar was elected to the Senate in 1877 and served there until his death twenty-seven years later. In the Senate he led the doomed fight to prevent the acquisition of overseas colonies by the United States after the Spanish-American War and coauthored the 1890 Sherman Anti-Trust Act (see BENJAMIN HARRISON). As chairman of the Judiciary Committee, he wrote and helped obtain passage of the Presidential Succession Act of 1886. (This act detailed which cabinet officers would become president in the event the other designated government officials mentioned in the Constitution were also incapacitated.)

BIBLIOGRAPHY

Hoar, George Frisbie, *Autobiography of Seventy Years*, 2 vols., 1903; Welch, Richard E., Jr., *George F. Hoar and the Half-Breed Republicans*, 1971.

Hobart, Garret Augustus

(June 3, 1844–November 21, 1899)
Vice President

Born in Long Branch, New Jersey, Garret Augustus Hobart graduated from Rutgers College in 1863 and was admitted to the bar three years later. After quickly establishing a successful law practice, Hobart was elected to the state legislature in 1872 and 1873 and served as speaker in 1874. Hobart was then elected to the state senate in 1876 and 1879 and chosen that body's president in 1881. He experienced his first political setback in 1884 when he was defeated in a try

for the U.S. Senate. Although remaining active in Republican party politics, for the next decade he concentrated on his business and legal interests. By 1895 he was one of the wealthiest men in New Jersey and also one of the most powerful men in the New Jersey Republican party.

Hobart was nominated for vice president with WILLIAM McKINLEY in 1896 largely because the Republicans wanted someone on the ticket who would carry the traditionally Democratic state of New Jersey. Hobart's firm belief in the gold standard—"An honest dollar, worth 100 cents everywhere, cannot be coined out of 53 cents of silver, plus a legislative fiat"—also made him a very attractive running mate for McKinley.

As vice president, Hobart presided over the Senate with such diligence and administrative skill that Senator Henry Cabot Lodge of Massachusetts remarked, "He has restored the Vice Presidency to its proper position." A close friend and confidant to President McKinley, Hobart cast the deciding vote in the Senate against granting the Philippines independence. He died of a heart ailment in office in 1899.

BIBLIOGRAPHY

Magie, David, *Life of Garret Augustus Hobart, Twenty-fourth Vice-President of the U.S.,* 1910.

Hobby, Oveta Culp

(January 19, 1905–)
Secretary of Health, Education, and Welfare

Oveta Culp Hobby was the first director of the Women's Army Corps and the first secretary of the Department of Health, Education, and Welfare.

Born in Killeen, Texas, Oveta Culp Hobby attended Mary Hardin-Baylor College in Belton, Texas, and the University of Texas Law School. After an unsuccessful try to win election to the Texas legislature in 1929, she became the assistant to the city attorney of Houston. In 1931 she married William Pettus Hobby, former governor of Texas and publisher of the *Houston Post.* She held a number of positions at the *Post* before becoming the paper's executive vice president in 1938 and finally its managing editor.

During World War II Hobby was appointed to head the newly formed women's division of the War Department's Bureau of Public Relations (a $1-a-year position). She was also named director of the Women's Auxiliary Army Corps in 1942. Hobby created an organization that eventually numbered over 100,000 women and set the model later copied by the navy and air force women's services.

Hobby returned to her duties at the *Houston Post* after the war, becoming coeditor and publisher of the Houston Post Company in 1952.

Although active in the Democratic party prior to 1948, in that election year she announced her support for Republican presidential candidate THOMAS E. DEWEY. In 1952 she worked to organize voting drives in Texas for DWIGHT D. EISENHOWER.

In recognition of her support, Hobby was appointed administrator of the Federal Security Agency by President-elect Eisenhower in November 1952. In March 1953 the agency became the Department of Health, Education, and Welfare by act of Congress, and Hobby officially became its head in April of that year. Two years later, she resigned to return to the *Houston Post.*

BIBLIOGRAPHY

Anderson, John, and Valerie Wright, "The Texas 100—The 100 Richest People in Texas," *Texas Monthly,* 1989; *Business Week,* December 6, 1952; *New York Herald Tribune,* May 5, 1941; *U.S. News and World Report,* December 26, 1952.

Holmes, Oliver Wendell

(March 8, 1841–March 6, 1935)
Associate Justice of the Supreme Court

Oliver Wendell Holmes and JOHN MARSHALL are considered the two greatest justices in Supreme Court history. Holmes's more than 2,000 opinions and famous dissents in favor of individual liberties are still frequently quoted by attorneys today. His major legal work, *The Common Law*, published in 1881, is considered a classic of legal philosophy and is still in print; the Memorial Day address he gave at Harvard in 1895 is ranked for oratorical brilliance with ABRAHAM LINCOLN's Gettysburg Address.

Born in Boston, Massachusetts, into a wealthy and socially prominent family, Holmes graduated from Harvard College in 1861 and joined the Union army. He was discharged in 1864 after being wounded three times. His experiences in the war shaped his personal philosophy of life. He summed up his conclusion for the necessity of war in an 1895 Memorial Day address: "War, when you are at it, is horrible and dull. It is only when time has passed that you see that its message was divine. I hope it may be long before we are called again to sit at that master's feet. But some teacher of the kind we all need. In this smug, over-safe corner of the world we need it, that we may realize that our comfortable routine is no eternal necessity of things, but merely a little space of calm in the midst of the tempestuous untamed streaming of the world. . . ."

Holmes returned to Boston in 1864 a war hero and graduated from Harvard Law School

Library of Congress

two years later. The handsome, charming, and brilliant Holmes began practicing law in Boston. He became the editor of the *American Law Review* from 1870 to 1873 and lectured on constitutional law and jurisprudence at Harvard.

After publishing a new edition of Kent's *Commentaries* in 1873, he completed work on his masterpiece, *The Common Law*, in 1881, in which he summed up sociological jurisprudence with the observation: "The life of the law has not been logic; it has been experience."

In 1882, after completing one year as a full professor at Harvard Law School, Holmes was appointed to the Massachusetts Supreme Judicial Court. In 1899 he became chief justice, and three years later, at age sixty, was appointed by THEODORE ROOSEVELT to the U.S. Supreme Court, where he served as an associate justice until he retired in 1932 at age ninety.

On the bench Holmes earned the nickname the Great Dissenter because of the high judicial importance and legal and literary quality of the 173 dissents that he wrote. "My keenest interest is excited, not by what are called great questions and great cases, but by little decisions which the common run of selectors would pass by because they did not deal with the Constitution or a telephone company, yet which have in them the germ of some wider theory, and therefore of some profound interstitial change in the very tissue of the law." The constitutional doctrines he explained in his dissents were frequently cited decades later by a new majority on the bench that upheld his views.

Holmes fiercely defended the right of every American to freedom of speech. In one of his most famous dissents, delivered in the case of *Abrams* v. *United States* in 1919, he wrote: "In this case sentences of twenty years' imprisonment have been imposed for the publishing of two [procommunist] leaflets that I believe the defendants had as much right to publish as the Government has to publish the Constitution. . . . I think that we should be eternally vigilant against attempts to check the expression of opinions that we loathe and believe to be fraught with death, unless they so imminently threaten immediate interference with the lawful and pressing purposes of the law that an immediate check is required to save the country."

He reaffirmed his position in another dissent in 1925 in *Gitlow* v. *New York*. Gitlow had been convicted for publishing a leaflet advocating the overthrow of the government. "The publication," wrote Holmes, "presented no clear and present danger of substantive evils that the state had a right to prevent. . . . If in the long run, beliefs expressed in proletarian dictatorship are destined to be accepted by the dominant forces of the community, the only meaning of free speech is that they should be given their chance and have their way."

Holmes served on the Supreme Court at a time when the majority of the justices believed that states could not pass laws regulating the economy because such statutes would violate the Fourteenth Amendment by depriving businesses of their property without due process of the law. In 1905, when the majority of the Court in *Lochner* v. *New York* concluded that the sixty-hour work week law in New York for bakers was unconstitutional, Holmes disagreed. He believed in the right of the government to interfere with the freedom of contract and argued that the Court, with its logic, was guilty of perverting the traditional American meaning of the word "liberty." Holmes was a major contributor to the rise of legal realism: the philosophy that the nation's laws must constantly be tested against common social notions of justice, and if the two stand in opposition, it is the laws that would have to change.

Today, Holmes's "clear and present danger" guideline concerning free speech limits and belief that the government should have wide authority to regulate commerce are the accepted constitutional approaches.

Not all of Holmes's opinions were so visionary or humanitarian. A social Darwinist, he believed that all human affairs were subject to the rule of the survival of the fittest. In 1927, in an opinion concerning a case involving a statute in Virginia that authorized the sterilization of the mentally retarded, he wrote: "We have seen more than once that the public welfare may call upon the best citizens for their lives. It would be strange if it could not call upon those who already sap the strength of the state for these lesser sacrifices. . . . The principle that sustains compulsory vaccination is broad enough to cover cutting the fallopian tubes. . . . Three generations of imbeciles are enough."

Holmes had no traditional religious faith, but he did have a mystical belief in a divine order to the universe and the need to accept the power of fate.

BIBLIOGRAPHY

Bent, Silas, *Justice Oliver Wendell Holmes*, 1932; Burton, David H., *Oliver Wendell Holmes, Jr.*, 1980; Kellogg, Frederic R., *The Formative Essays of Justice Holmes*, 1984; Pohlman, H. L., *Justice Oliver Wendell Holmes and Utilitarian Jurisprudence*, 1984.

Hoover, Herbert Clark

(August 10, 1874–October 20, 1964)
President, Secretary of Commerce, Diplomat

Library of Congress

Brilliantly successful as an engineer and humanitarian, Herbert Hoover failed as a president to lead the nation effectively during the Great Depression because, in the words of the historian Arthur Schlesinger, Jr., he was "a man of high ideals whose intelligence froze into inflexibility and whose dedication was smitten by self-righteousness."

Born in West Branch, Iowa, to devout Quaker parents, Hoover was orphaned at age nine. He worked his way through Stanford University, graduating in 1895 with a degree in engineering. By 1914 he was a well-known international engineer. He had discovered major gold and coal deposits in Australia and China, and had accumulated a substantial fortune. He wrote: "To feel great works grow under one's feet and to have more men constantly getting good jobs is to be the master of contentment."

During World War I Hoover, living in London, headed the Commission for Relief in Belgium, which managed to save millions of people from starvation. When the United States entered the war, President WOODROW WILSON asked Hoover to return to the United States to serve as director of the Food Administration. While at the bureau, Hoover introduced the concept of standardized sizes for packages in order to prevent waste; to "Hooverize" meant to save food. At the end of the war, Hoover returned to Europe, first to head the Inter-Allied Food Council and then to become the director of the American Relief Administration. He also served as an adviser to President Wilson at the Versailles peace conference. His relief work significantly eased the threat of famine in Austria and Germany in 1919.

Upon his return to the United States in September 1919, Hoover conducted an unofficial and unsuccessful campaign for the Republican nomination for president. When WARREN G. HARDING was nominated instead and elected in 1920, Hoover accepted an appointment as secretary of commerce.

At the Commerce Department the frugal and energetic Hoover worked to reduce waste and eliminate bureaucratic inefficiencies. He counseled moderation in dealing with the new communist government in the Soviet Union and secured the shipment of food to that country with no political strings attached. Hoover believed in a doctrine of "associationalism," by which he meant the voluntary association of bankers with bankers, farmers with farmers, manufacturers with manufacturers, and so on. Such economic associations, he was convinced, would spur economic growth, encourage a wholesome spirit of cooperation and commonwealth in economic activity, and preclude the need for direct government interference in economic affairs. These views, along with his international relief work and his good performance as commerce secretary, made him an attractive choice for president in 1928.

With peace and prosperity on his side, Hoover felt confident that he would defeat anti-Prohibition and Catholic Democratic candidate ALFRED E. SMITH. During the campaign the stock market soared, and that August Hoover said in a speech, "We are nearer to the final triumph over poverty than ever before in the history of any land. The poorhouse is vanishing from among us. We have not yet reached the goal, but we shall soon with the help of God be in sight of the day when poverty will be banished from this nation." "The Great Engineer and Humanitarian" won 444 electoral votes to Smith's 87.

In October 1929, less than a year after Hoover took office, the stock market crashed and killed Hoover's dream of presiding over a period of increasing prosperity. At first, through a tax cut and in meetings with business leaders, Hoover tried to encourage expansion of public and private construction— "the greatest tool which our economic system affords for the establishment of stability"—in order to deal with what he viewed as a temporary economic collapse. He was convinced that the cause of the depression lay not in domestic affairs but in the structure of international finance. With what appeared to be a ruthless disregard for human suffering, Hoover remarked, "The sole function of government is to bring about a condition of affairs favorable to the beneficial development of private enterprise." When he vetoed a proposal to have the government build a huge electrical project in the Tennessee Valley at Muscle Shoals, he said, "I am firmly opposed to the Government entering into any business the major purpose of which is competition with our citizens." Relief activities belonged, he believed, to state and local governments. To tamper with that principle would "have struck at the roots of self-government." From the perspective of those in need of immediate relief, it appeared as though Hoover were helping the rich instead of the poor. Hoover's name became associated with the misery of the Great Depression: Shantytowns of the homeless and unemployed were called Hoovervilles, while the newspapers used to keep people warm were known as Hoover blankets.

As the economic depression deepened, however, the dynamic Hoover, who was genuinely interested in resolving economic tensions, actually started many of the innovative programs the New Deal later received credit for. In 1932, for example, he supported the creation of the Reconstruction Finance Corporation (RFC), through which the government lent money directly to companies and banks. This shifted the financial power from private institutions to the federal government.

Still, as the election of 1932 approached, Hoover appeared to cling to his worn-out, "meanspirited" convictions. He authorized the Reconstruction Finance Corporation to grant money to state governments for direct relief programs, but it was too late. The RFC had $500 million available for local relief but had spent only $37 million before the end of his term in office.

Renominated in 1932 by the Republican party, Hoover, appalled at the dangers the election of FRANKLIN DELANO ROOSEVELT portended, vigorously campaigned across the nation against "changes and so-called new deals which would destroy the very foundations of the American system." The American people rejected his arguments and elected Roosevelt, 472 electoral votes to 59.

A gloomy and depressed Hoover retired to Palo Alto, California, in 1933 to work at the Hoover Institute for War, Revolution, and Peace at Stanford University. After World War II Hoover returned to Europe at President HARRY TRUMAN's request to help organize food relief programs. In 1947, again at the request of President Truman, and in 1953 at the request of President DWIGHT EISENHOWER, Hoover headed commissions that studied ways to improve the efficiency of the executive branch of the federal government.

Hoover lived an active and vital life until his death at age ninety. By the time of his death the image of Hoover as inflexible and out of touch with the feelings of the people had been modified by a growing appreciation of his more dynamic and innovative efforts to cope with the overwhelming economic problems of the Great Depression. Even New Dealer REXFORD TUGWELL conceded: "We didn't admit it at the time, . . . but practically the whole New Deal was extrapolated from programs Hoover started." A combination of Hoover's deeply held principles and a crisis of unprecedented magnitude made it impossible for Hoover to carry his reform impulses far enough.

BIBLIOGRAPHY

Brandes, Joseph, *Herbert Hoover and Economic Diplomacy: Department of Commerce Policy 1921–1928*, 1962; Burner, David, *Herbert Hoover: A Public Life*, 1979; Hoover, Herbert, *Memoirs, 3 vols., 1951–1952*; Huthmacher, J. Joseph, and Warren Susman (eds.), *Herbert Hoover and the Crisis of American Capitalism*, 1973; Lyons, Eugene, *Herbert Hoover*, 1964; Wilson, Joan Hoff, *Herbert Hoover: Forgotten Progressive*, 1975; Wolfe, Harold, *Herbert Hoover: Public Servant and Leader of the Loyal Opposition*, 1956.

Hoover, John Edgar

(January 1, 1895–May 2, 1972)
Director of the Federal Bureau of Investigation

In 1924, at the age of twenty-nine, J. Edgar Hoover became the third director of the Federal Bureau of Investigation (FBI). By the time he died in office forty-eight years later, he had created a powerful federal government crime-fighting agency.

Hoover was appointed director of the FBI as a result of the Teapot Dome scandal (see WARREN GAMALIEL HARDING), in which several government officials in the Harding administration were implicated in the secret sale of federal oil lands. President CALVIN COOLIDGE, Harding's successor, hoping to keep his own administration free of the scandal's taint, appointed the distinguished jurist HARLAN STONE as his attorney general; Stone named J. Edgar Hoover as the FBI director.

Hoover, who was born in Washington, D.C., had earned a B.A. degree in 1916 and a master's degree in law in 1917 from George Washington University. After being admitted to the bar, he began his long career at the FBI (established in 1908 as an arm of the Justice Department). In 1919 he was appointed special assistant to Attorney General A. MITCHELL PALMER in charge of the drive against political radicals that accompanied the "Red scare" of the postwar years. The mass arrests of radicals in 1919, known as the Palmer raids after Attorney General Palmer, were actually directed by Hoover.

Upon assuming control of the FBI, Hoover established nonpolitical recruiting and training methods, consolidated and expanded the central fingerprint bureau, created the voluntary Crime Reporting Program (1930) so that the FBI could compile and publish annual crime statistics, and created the FBI laboratory (1932).

Anticommunism was the force that brought Hoover to power, and it was the force that defined both his career and the shape of the FBI from the 1920s to the late 1960s. In 1939 President FRANKLIN D. ROOSEVELT greatly increased the power of the FBI when he assigned it the task of protecting internal U.S. security and ferreting out enemy spies. The organizing principle behind Hoover's task was vigilance against all who would threaten lawful governmental authority—in particular, "Communists, subversives and pseudoliberals." Such a broad definition of the "enemy" gave the FBI under Hoover's ironfisted control tremendous investigative latitude.

Hoover decided early on never to collaborate with other government agencies in the collection or dissemination of information. His agents gathered all the information he requested, then he alone decided who would have access to it. He stood ready to answer a president's request for the most personal information about anybody, but the FBI's files remained closed to everyone—even presidents. They were an important source of his power.

Shrewdly aware of the value of publicity, he carefully avoided committing the limited resources of the FBI to the immense tasks of enforcing the drug laws and defeating organized crime. It took the vigor of both President JOHN F. KENNEDY and his brother, Attorney General ROBERT KENNEDY, to force Hoover to assign his agents to fight organized crime, and the determination of President LYNDON B. JOHNSON to push the FBI into enforcing civil rights laws.

By the time Hoover launched the Cointelpro, or counterintelligence program, against black radicals and the so-called New Left radical student movement in the late 1960s, his power and public esteem had begun to deteriorate. When records stolen from the FBI offices in Media, Pennsylvania, concerning the agency's domestic security operations—which included illicit wiretapping and false character-destroying efforts—were published in March 1971, the nation was stunned. Hoover immediately shut down all Cointelpro operations, but his reputation never recovered.

Richard Gid Powers, Hoover's biographer, summed up Hoover's career in this way:

> Hoover was at the very midst of the combat over the most important issues of the first three-quarters of the 20th century—Communism and racial justice. . . . From the beginning there were conflicting strains in Hoover of idealism but also of an almost savage sense of self-preservation. I don't think he will be understood as a sheer ogre. But the final assessment of him will be less than favorable. As time goes on he will be seen as a complex and significant figure who tested the outer limits of permissible political behavior.

Today, the FBI fulfills a wide range of necessary federal law enforcement tasks, the foundations for which—from the training academy at Quantico, Virginia, to the Uniform Crime Report statistics and sophisticated crime laboratory—were laid by J. Edgar Hoover.

BIBLIOGRAPHY

Hoover, J. Edgar, *Persons in Hiding*, 1938, *Masters of Deceit: The Story of Communism in America and How to Fight It*, 1958, *A Study of Communism*, 1962, and *J. Edgar Hoover on Communism*, 1969; Powers, Richard Gid, *G-Men: Hoover's FBI in American Popular Culture*, 1983, and *Secrecy and Power: The Life of J. Edgar Hoover*, 1987.

Hopkins, Harry Lloyd

(August 17, 1890–January 29, 1946)
Secretary of Commerce, Diplomat

Harry Hopkins was the principal architect of immediate relief programs during the New Deal and a major foreign policy adviser to President FRANKLIN D. ROOSEVELT during World War II.

Hopkins was born in Sioux City, Iowa, and grew up in nearby Grinnell. After graduating from Grinnell College in 1912, he moved to New York City and joined the staff of the Association for Improving the Condition of the

Poor. He became director of the Southern division of the American Red Cross in New Orleans in 1917 and in 1924 became director of the New York Tuberculosis Association.

After the stock market crash in 1929 (see HERBERT CLARK HOOVER), Hopkins became the administrator of the Red Cross's work relief program. Governor Franklin D. Roosevelt of New York used the Red Cross program, which stressed the need to provide jobs instead of just money, as the model for the state Temporary Emergency Relief Administration he established in 1931 and appointed Hopkins as its executive director. The New York relief program became the model for the Federal Emergency Relief Administration (FERA), created by Roosevelt when he became president in 1933. Roosevelt appointed Hopkins as head of FERA. Hopkins specialized in establishing immediate relief programs for the unemployed. He convinced Roosevelt to create the Civil Works Administration in 1933, and in 1935 he became head of the Works Progress Administration. He also played an important role in the development of the Social Security system. By the time he was appointed secretary of commerce in 1938, he had dispensed approximately $10 billion in employment relief.

Hopkins's integrity and commitment to social work were widely admired, but his blunt and abrupt manner often alienated colleagues; in addition, his passion for gambling and bridge provided ammunition for his critics. In 1940, after undergoing stomach cancer surgery, Hopkins resigned as secretary of commerce. He had planned to return to social work in New York, but President Roosevelt recalled him to Washington, D.C., to serve as his closest aide. Throughout World War II, Hopkins traveled around the world and met with political and military leaders on the president's behalf. In 1941 he took on the administration of the lend-lease program (see FRANKLIN DELANO ROOSEVELT), and it was largely upon his recommendation that lend-lease aid was extended to the Soviet Union.

After helping to ensure the smooth transition of the presidency to HARRY S TRUMAN upon the death of Roosevelt in April 1945, Hopkins, desperately ill and near death himself, became chairman of the Women's Cloak and Suit Industry in New York in July of that year.

BIBLIOGRAPHY

Adams, Henry H., *Harry Hopkins: A Biography*, 1977; Hopkins, Harry, *Spending to Save*, 1936; McJimsey, George, *Harry Hopkins: Ally of the Poor and Defender of Democracy*, 1987; Meriam, Lewis, *Relief and Social Security*, 1946; Searle, Charles F., *Minister of Relief: Harry L. Hopkins and the Depression*, 1963; Sherwood, Robert, *Roosevelt and Hopkins, An Intimate History*, 1948.

House, Edward Mandell

(July 26, 1858–March 28, 1938)
Diplomat

Through his genius for sympathetic understanding of different viewpoints and close relationship with President WOODROW WILSON during World War I, "Colonel" Edward Mandell House played a vital role in shaping American foreign policy during a critical period in world history.

House was born in Houston, Texas, into a prominent family and attended Cornell University. In 1890, ten years after the death of his father, House acquired enough wealth by selling his father's cotton plantations to be able to live off the interest for the rest of his life. This financial independence gave him the opportunity to indulge his passion for politics, and he moved to Austin, Texas, to be near the legislature.

House began his political career by managing Texas governor James S. Hogg's successful reelection campaign in 1892. Hogg placed him on his staff with the title of colonel, and "Colonel" House, as he was henceforth known, quickly became an important influence within the Texas Democratic party.

With the Democratic victory in Congress in 1910, House decided to enter the national political arena. He used his influence to secure the support of Texas for Wilson at the 1912 Democratic national convention, and helped to convince WILLIAM JENNINGS BRYAN to throw his support behind the Wilson nomination.

Preferring to play the role of confidant and unofficial adviser, House declined Wilson's offer of a cabinet appointment. Temperamentally and intellectually compatible, House and Wilson quickly developed a close working relationship. The president came to rely on House's wisdom and discretion in working with legislators and political interest groups, and House soon developed a reputation of being the president's "silent partner." Because Wilson did not trust the wisdom of Secretary of State William Jennings Bryan, he gradually came to rely on House to act as his spokesperson and emissary in foreign affairs.

Although he agreed with Wilson's position of U.S. neutrality at the start of World War I, House was strongly biased in favor of Great Britain. He was convinced that the United States and Great Britain ought to work together to preserve world peace, and most of his efforts were designed to accomplish this Anglo-American alliance. House was one of the most adamant supporters of the need for a strong American response to German submarine attacks in 1915 and 1916.

From 1914 to 1917 Wilson used House as his personal diplomatic agent. House met with British, French, and German political leaders, but he was never able to bring the belligerents together so that the United States could negotiate what Wilson hoped would be a "peace without victory."

After the United States entered the war in 1917, House served as Wilson's most important and trusted adviser in dealings with the Allies. He helped to write Wilson's Fourteen Points and served on the American delegation to the peace conference in Paris. The trust between the two men did not survive the peace conference, however. Wilson never forgave House for his support of the harsh treatment of Germany, even though he himself came to appreciate the need to accept reparations if the League of Nations (see WOODROW WILSON) was going to be created. House further angered Wilson by urging the president to compromise with his congressional opponents to secure the Senate's ratification of the Treaty of Versailles (see WOODROW WILSON). Wilson suffered a series of debilitating strokes in October 1919, and the two men never spoke to each other again.

During the long period of Republican domination of the White House from 1920 to 1932, House continued to meet with European intellectual and political leaders. In 1932 he supported the candidacy of Governor FRANKLIN D. ROOSEVELT of New York for president. Although Roosevelt met with the senior statesman of the Democratic party at the White House on occasion, House never joined the president's inner circle of advisers.

BIBLIOGRAPHY

George, Alexander L., and Juliette L. George, *Woodrow Wilson and Colonel House: A Personality Study,* 1956; Seymour, Charles, *The Intimate Papers of Colonel House,* 4 vols., 1926–1928; Smith, Arthur D. Howden, *The Real Colonel House,* 1918, and *Mr. House of Texas,* 1940; Viereck, George S., *The Strangest Friendship in History,* 1932.

Houston, Samuel

(March 2, 1793–July 26, 1863)
Senator, Representative

The first elected president of the "Lone Star" Republic of Texas, Sam Houston was born near Lexington, Virginia. After his father's death in 1807, he moved with his family to Maryville, Tennessee. One of ten children living on a frontier farm, Houston attended school only occasionally. At age sixteen he decided to try living with the Cherokee Indians. Four years later, he joined the army and served under General ANDREW JACKSON in the War of 1812 (see JAMES MADISON). In 1817, through the influence of Jackson, he became an Indian agent for the army. His duties involved the removal of all the Cherokee from Tennessee and their resettlement in present-day Arkansas.

Houston left the army to study law. He was elected to the House of Representatives as a Democrat in 1823, reelected in 1825, and made a successful run for governor of Tennessee in 1827. He was reelected in 1829, but he resigned soon after his term began when his wife deserted him. Heartbroken, he left Tennessee to live among the Cherokee in Texas.

Houston was among the settlers who petitioned the Mexican government to make Texas a self-governing state in 1833. When the war for independence with Mexico began in 1835, he was chosen to head the Texas rebel army. He commanded the troops that defeated the Mexican army at San Jacinto in 1836, which forced General Santa Anna to order the withdrawal of Mexican troops from Texas. With the victory, he was elected the first president of the Republic of Texas and served from 1836 to 1838.

Houston served as a member of the Texas congress from 1838 to 1841. Reelected president of Texas from 1841 to 1844, Houston successfully financed a $7 million debt, calmed Indian unrest, and warded off new Mexican army attacks.

After Texas was annexed by the United States in 1845 (see JAMES KNOX POLK), Houston was elected to the Senate for the next fourteen years. Houston often voted against measures, such as the repeal of the Missouri Compromise (see HENRY CLAY and MILLARD FILLMORE) by the Kansas-Nebraska Act of 1854 (see FRANKLIN PIERCE), that his fellow southern legislators supported. "I make no distinction between northern rights and southern rights ... I am for the Union ... it shall be preserved!" he explained. Because of his pro-Union stance and support for the principles of the Know-Nothing party (see MILLARD FILLMORE) in 1856, the Texas legislature did not reelect him to the Senate in 1859. Undaunted, Houston launched a successful campaign for governor. While in office he tried to discourage the secession of Texas from the Union. He was forced to resign as governor in 1861 for refusing to take the oath of allegiance to the Confederacy and retired from public life. He died two years later in Huntsville, Texas.

BIBLIOGRAPHY

Crane, W. C., *Life and Select Literary Remains of Sam Houston of Texas*, 2 vols., 1884; James, Marquis, *The Raven: A Biography of Sam Houston*, 1988.

Hughes, Charles Evans

(April 11, 1862–August 27, 1948)
Secretary of State, Candidate for President, Chief Justice of the Supreme Court,
Associate Justice of the Supreme Court

Charles Evans Hughes is remembered mainly for his superb performance as chief justice of the Supreme Court during the turbulent 1930s.

Born in Glens Falls, New York, Hughes was a graduate of Brown University and of Columbia University Law School. Practicing law in New York City, he distinguished himself as a prosecuting counsel for the New York legislature in a number of cases involving abuses by New York public utilities and life insurance compa-

Library of Congress

nies. Hughes's success in that role and the fame it brought him led to his nomination by the Republican party and election as governor of New York in 1906. His liberal and independent behavior led to frequent clashes with the leadership of his own party, but he was nevertheless reelected in 1908. During his administration, public service commissions were established and many progressive reforms were carried out.

Fortunately for Hughes, President WILLIAM H. TAFT's appointment of him as an associate justice of the Supreme Court in 1910 removed him from the political conflict that split the Progressives from the regular Republicans in 1912. Within a few years of serving on the Supreme Court, Hughes had established a national reputation as one of the Court's most distinguished justices. The Republicans needed someone in 1916 who could reunite the liberal and conservative wings of the party. Hughes was the logical choice. The only

problem was that Hughes did not want to run for office and refused to be a candidate. Undaunted, the party nominated him for president in 1916. This was a ploy to entice the Progressives back, and it worked, with Hughes receiving the support of the Progressive party after THEODORE ROOSEVELT refused the nomination.

Hughes, who believed that no citizen should decline the honor of such a nomination, resigned from the Supreme Court in order to run. However, even with Theodore Roosevelt's reluctant endorsement (Roosevelt called the bewhiskered Hughes the "bearded lady"), Hughes was narrowly defeated by WOODROW WILSON 277 electoral votes to 254. A bitter Republican-Progressive fight in California and the fear that a Republican administration would take the United States into World War I cost him victory.

Hughes resumed the private practice of law until the election of President WARREN G. HARDING. From 1921 to 1925 he served as secretary of state under Harding and CALVIN COOLIDGE. Among his accomplishments were the making of a separate peace treaty with Germany following World War I (the Senate had rejected the Treaty of Versailles—see WOODROW WILSON) and the negotiation at the 1922 Washington conference of the first successful agreement limiting naval armaments. He also helped develop plans to ease Germany's reparation burden and worked to improve relations between the United States and nations of Latin America. After his resignation as secretary of state in 1925, he became a member of the Permanent Court of Arbitration in 1926, and in 1930 was appointed a judge on the Permanent Court of International Justice.

Later in 1930, President HERBERT HOOVER selected Hughes to be the chief justice of the Supreme Court. During the controversial years of the New Deal under FRANKLIN D. ROOSEVELT, Hughes wavered between siding with those justices who were for the Roosevelt reforms to promote economic recovery and curtail private power interests and those who were against them. More often than not, Hughes voted to uphold the Roosevelt legislation. However, the Court infuriated President Roosevelt by declaring the National Recovery Administration and the Agricultural Adjustment Administration—two critical components of Roosevelt's New Deal—unconstitutional. In retaliation, Roosevelt asked Congress for the authority to expand the Court with up to six new justice positions, from the present nine to fifteen, if there were sitting members over age seventy

who refused to retire. The president's effort to "pack" the Court with new appointments who supported his policies resulted in a historic debate in Congress. In the end, after Hughes, who was over seventy, stated that more justices would not increase the efficiency of the Court, Congress refused to pass the necessary legislation. After the crisis had passed, Hughes led the Court, until his retirement in 1941, in upholding the constitutionality of such major New Deal reforms as the National Labor Relations Act and the Social Security Act.

BIBLIOGRAPHY

Glad, Betty, *Charles Evans Hughes and the Illusions of Innocence*, 1966; Hendel, Samuel, *Charles Evans Hughes and the Supreme Court*, 1951; Perkins, Dexter, *Charles Evans Hughes and American Democratic Statesmanship*, 1956; Pusey, Merlo J., *Charles Evans Hughes*, 2 vols., 1951; Wesser, Robert F., *Charles Evans Hughes: Politics and Reform in New York, 1905–1910*, 1967.

Hull, Cordell

(October 2, 1871–July 23, 1955)
Secretary of State, Senator, Representative

Although he had little experience in international diplomacy before he became FRANKLIN D. ROOSEVELT's secretary of state in 1933, Cordell Hull served almost twelve years in office during one of the most critical periods in the history of American foreign policy before illness forced him to resign in November 1944.

Born near Byrdstown, Tennessee, Hull attended National Normal University at Lebanon, Ohio, from 1888 to 1889. After studying law for five months at Cumberland Law School in Leb-

anon, Tennessee, he obtained his law degree in 1891.

Hull immediately entered politics as a Democrat and was elected a state legislator when only twenty-one years old. After briefly serving in the army in the Spanish-American War (see WILLIAM McKINLEY, JR.), Hull returned to Tennessee and in 1903 was appointed a state circuit judge. In 1906 he was elected to the U.S. House of Representatives and served there from 1907 until 1931, with the exception of one two-year term from 1921 to 1923. Elected to the Senate in 1930, he resigned in 1933 to become President Franklin Roosevelt's secretary of state.

In Congress Hull had supported President WOODROW WILSON's desire for U.S. participation in the League of Nations (see WILSON), but he correctly believed that Wilson's tactics to sway the Senate were incorrect. Hull was a member of the Democratic national committee from 1914 to 1928 and its chairman from 1921 to 1924. Prior to the Democratic convention of 1932, he helped to break AL SMITH's hold on the party and worked for Roosevelt's nomination. After winning election, Roosevelt chose the popular Hull as his secretary of state to quiet criticism that his cabinet appointments were biased toward northern liberals.

Almost from the moment he assumed office Hull endured Roosevelt's undercutting and bypassing of him in major foreign policy decisions. He briefly considered resigning during his first year in office, but after meeting with the president he changed his mind. Despite his domination by Roosevelt, prior to the outbreak of World War II Hull managed to exert considerable influence upon American foreign policy. His efforts to improve relations with Latin America by developing and then securing the passage of a program of tariff reciprocity played a major part in the creation of what became known as the Roosevelt Good Neighbor policy. However, after 1939 his influence waned as President Roosevelt stopped concentrating on domestic affairs and began personally conducting foreign policy.

Although he was awarded the Nobel Peace Prize in 1945, some of Hull's actions during his long tenure as secretary of state have been severely criticized. Most notably, his decision to adopt an increasingly inflexible hard line when negotiating with Japanese diplomats in 1941 has been attacked. Some historians argue that if Hull had been more patient and flexible, perhaps war with Japan might have been averted or at least postponed. Hull, his critics charge, should have worked harder to temper Roosevelt's efforts to prevent Japanese expansion in China and Southeast Asia, areas outside America's traditional sphere of national security interest.

Hull's major foreign policy success during World War II concerned American relations with the Soviet Union. Prior to the German invasion in 1941, Hull executed a policy of refraining from any actions that might have pushed the Soviet premier Joseph Stalin closer to Adolf Hitler. His decision to attend the Conference of Foreign Ministers in Moscow in 1943 greatly facilitated the wartime working relationship between the United States and the Soviet Union.

Influenced by Woodrow Wilson's vision after World War I, Hull was convinced that future wars could be avoided only through a combination of collective security and international economic cooperation. In honor of his tireless efforts to secure bipartisan support for the creation of the United Nations in Congress, Roosevelt called Hull the "father of the United Nations."

BIBLIOGRAPHY

Hinton, H. B., *Cordell Hull*, 1942; Hull, Cordell, *Memoirs*, 2 vols., 1942; Pratt, Julius W., *Cordell Hull, 1933–1944*, 1964.

Humphrey, Hubert Horatio

(May 27, 1911–January 13, 1978)
Vice President, Candidate for President, Senator

As a U.S. senator, vice president of the United States, and unsuccessful Democratic party candidate for president, Hubert Humphrey established a reputation as a leader in the civil rights struggle and war on poverty.

Born in Wallace, South Dakota, Humphrey earned a pharmacy degree from Denver College in 1933. After helping his father for several years in the family drugstore in Doland, Humphrey enrolled in the University of Minnesota, majored in political science, and graduated in 1939. In 1940 he earned his master's degree at Louisiana State University.

Library of Congress

After working in the Works Progress Administration (see FRANKLIN D. ROOSEVELT) and as a teacher at Louisiana State University and the University of Minnesota, Humphrey narrowly lost the election for mayor of Minneapolis in 1943. He helped to unite the Democratic and Farmer-Labor parties in Minnesota, and his second bid for mayor in 1945 was successful. He also cofounded with Arthur Schlesinger, Jr., Americans for Democratic Action, an anti-Communist, liberal political organization.

At the Democratic national convention in 1948, Humphrey succeeded in winning the endorsement of President HARRY TRUMAN's civil rights proposals. Elected to the U.S. Senate later that year, Humphrey established a close relationship with LYNDON JOHNSON, another new senator who had also been a teacher. A successful political career for both men hinged on a willingness to engage in hard bargaining and compromise. Later, when Johnson became Senate majority leader, he explained their successful working relationship: "[Senator Humphrey] is not like other liberals. He wants to get the job done." Humphrey's habit of always looking on the bright side and talking long after his audience had begun to lose interest earned the comment from Johnson: "He is the greatest coordinator of mind and tongue in the world, being able to prepare a speech in the time it takes to draw a deep breath."

Humphrey was reelected to the Senate in 1954. After an unsuccessful bid for the vice presidential nomination in 1956, he decided to run for president in 1960. Although favored at the start of the campaign to defeat JOHN F. KENNEDY, the Kennedy combination of youth, good looks, money, organization, and charm proved too much. After losing the West Virginia primary, Humphrey was forced to withdraw, though he continued his political career by winning reelection in the Senate.

In 1961 Humphrey became assistant majority leader in the Senate and helped secure approval of the nuclear test ban treaty in 1963. After President Kennedy's assassination, Humphrey strongly supported President Johnson's civil rights and War on Poverty programs.

In 1964 President Johnson selected Humphrey to be his running mate. An unusually active vice president, Humphrey chaired several important presidential commissions, traveled widely as a goodwill ambassador, and, much to the dismay of his liberal colleagues in the Senate, staunchly defended Johnson's conduct of the war in Vietnam (see LYNDON BAINES JOHNSON and RICHARD MILHOUS NIXON).

After President Johnson decided not to seek reelection, Humphrey, with the support of the regular party leaders and organized labor, entered the race for the nomination in competition with antiwar candidates EUGENE MCCARTHY and ROBERT KENNEDY. Robert Kennedy's assassination and McCarthy's inability to broaden his base of support enabled Humphrey to win the party's nomination for president in 1968. The convention was marked by fighting that raged in the Chicago streets outside the convention hall between protesters and Mayor RICHARD DALEY's police.

During the campaign Humphrey pulled away from his unequivocal support of Johnson's conduct of the war in Vietnam and almost succeeded in reuniting his badly fractured Democratic party. He lost to Republican candidate RICHARD NIXON by only 1 percent of the popular vote in a three-way race that included GEORGE WALLACE.

Humphrey was reelected to the U.S. Senate in 1970 and made another unsuccessful attempt to win the nomination for president in 1972. During his long political career Humphrey never wavered from his staunch support of organized labor. His most ambitious labor proposal, the Humphrey-Hawkins Full Employment Bill, was never passed by Congress.

In 1976, even though he underwent surgery for cancer, he was reelected to the Senate. He died two years later.

BIBLIOGRAPHY

Engelmayer, Sheldon D., and Robert J. Wagman, *Hubert Humphrey: The Man and His Dream, 1911–1978,* 1978; Solberg, Carl, *Hubert Humphrey: A Biography,* 1984.

Hunter, Robert Mercer Taliaferro

(April 21, 1809–July 18, 1887)
Speaker of the House, Senator, Representative

Politically conservative and renowned for his advocacy of states' rights, Robert M. T. Hunter changed political parties and his government allegiance during the course of his long political career.

Hunter was born on the family plantation in Essex County, Virginia. After graduating from the University of Virginia in 1828 and after studying law, he was admitted to the bar in 1830. Elected to the Virginia General Assembly in 1834, Hunter served there until he began his career in the U.S. House of Representatives in 1837 as a member of the Whig party. During his second term in the House, from 1839 to 1841, Hunter was elected Speaker.

A devout follower of JOHN C. CALHOUN, Hunter relinquished the speakership and, like Calhoun, became a states' rights Democrat in 1840. Gerrymandered (see ELBRIDGE GERRY) out of his House seat in 1843, Hunter worked unsuccessfully to help elect Calhoun president in 1844. He then won reelection to the House for one term before being chosen by the Virginia legislature to serve in the Senate in 1847.

Frustrated by Calhoun's failure to win the presidency in 1848 and the increasing hostility of the North toward the expansion of slavery, Hunter was convinced by 1850 that long-term cooperation between the North and South would prove impossible. Hunter resigned from the U.S. Senate a week after ABRAHAM LINCOLN became president to join the newly created Confederate government. From 1861 to 1862 he served as the secretary of state of the Confederacy and then, until 1865, as a senator in the Confederate legislature.

Imprisoned for several months following the defeat of the Confederacy and financially ruined, Hunter nevertheless played a major role in helping to establish the local conservative political party that saved Virginia from many of the hardships other former Confederate states experienced during Reconstruction. From 1874 to 1880 Hunter was treasurer of Virginia and, at the time of his death, tax collector for the port of Tappahannock.

BIBLIOGRAPHY

Ambler, C. H. (ed.), *Correspondence of Robert M. T. Hunter, 1826–1876,* 1918; Simms, H. H., *Robert M. T. Hunter: A Study in Sectionalism and Secession,* 1935.

Hutchinson, Thomas

(September 9, 1711–June 3, 1780)
Colonial Leader

Thomas Hutchinson was the colonial governor of Massachusetts at the outbreak of the American Revolution. Between 1765 and 1774 he came to symbolize those loyal to Britain in Massachusetts.

A descendant of the New England religious leader Anne Hutchinson, Thomas Hutchinson was born in Boston into a prominent family. After graduating from Harvard College in 1727 and receiving his master's degree in 1730, he began what became a lifelong study of the history of New England. Hutchinson began his political career in 1737 when he was elected a selectman of Boston and a member of the General Court (House of Representatives) of Massachusetts. (He served as speaker from 1746 to 1749.)

Hutchinson failed to win reelection in 1749. Embraced by the upper classes of Massachusetts and rejected by the masses for his advocacy of "hard money," Hutchinson aligned himself politically with the conservatives and was immediately chosen to be a member of the Governor's Council. While remaining a council member until 1766, Hutchinson was appointed a delegate to the Albany Congress in 1754, lieutenant governor in 1758, chief justice in 1760, acting governor in 1769, and royal governor in 1771.

Though he considered the Stamp Act (see JOHN ADAMS and SAMUEL ADAMS) unwise, after it was announced he favored strict enforcement. The unpopularity of his position caused a patriot mob to sack his mansion in 1765. The incident led to a further hardening of his distrust of the "common masses" and confirmed his belief in the need to enforce parliamentary law. The result was that he became ever more deeply involved in an escalating series of confrontations with patriot leaders Sam Adams and JAMES OTIS, which they shrewdly used to their advantage in turning the people of Massachusetts against Hutchinson and British colonial rule.

Hutchinson's support for punishing the colony to stifle political opposition to Parliament was unequivocally confirmed when letters he had written to British friends were obtained by BENJAMIN FRANKLIN in England and published in the Boston press. The incident served to further estrange him from the people of Massachusetts and clouded his political judgment. In 1773 he refused to let tea-laden ships clear Boston harbor until they had unloaded their cargo. It was his last executive decree and his greatest mistake. Angry colonists disguised as Indians boarded the ships and threw the tea into Boston harbor. The incident became known as the Boston Tea Party.

Efforts by Hutchinson to stymie revolutionary activity had actually encouraged it. In 1774 he was replaced as colonial governor by General Thomas Gage. The situation deteriorated so rapidly in Massachusetts later that year that Hutchinson decided to move temporarily to England. He was forced by the American Revolution to spend the rest of his life away from his beloved New England. Before his death he wrote the third volume of *The History of the Colony of Massachusetts Bay.* It was published by his grandson in 1828.

BIBLIOGRAPHY

Freiberg, Malcolm, "Thomas Hutchinson: First Fifty Years," *William and Mary Quarterly,* 3 ser., 15, 1958, 35; Hosmer, James K., *The Life of Thomas Hutchinson,* 1896; Hutchins, P. O. (ed.), *Diary and Letters of Thomas Hutchinson,* 2 vols., 1883–1886.

Ickes, Harold Le Claire

(March 15, 1874–February 3, 1952)
Secretary of the Interior

Harold Ickes was one of the ablest, most outspoken, and longest-serving members of FRANKLIN D. ROOSEVELT's New Deal administration. As secretary of the interior, he directed some of the New Deal's greatest successes through skillful management of natural resources and a vast program of public works.

Ickes was born in Frankstown Township, Pennsylvania. He earned his B.A. degree (1897) and his law degree (1907) from the University of Chicago. Originally a Republican, he joined the Progressive party (see THEODORE ROOSEVELT) in 1912 to help Theodore Roosevelt's presidential campaign and was the Illinois Progressive party's leader for three years. Thereafter, he returned to the Republican party and in 1924 served as Illinois campaign manager of HIRAM JOHNSON's second unsuccessful try for the nomination.

In 1932 Ickes led an effort to encourage Republicans to support Franklin D. Roosevelt, the Democratic presidential candidate. To the surprise of Roosevelt's aides, the new president appointed Ickes secretary of the interior. Ickes immediately embarked upon an intense drive to ensure the integrity of the department, which had been plagued by the Teapot Dome scandal (see WARREN GAMALIEL HARDING). He personally reviewed virtually every contract for which the department was responsible.

Some of the controversy that surrounded Ickes was unavoidable. As secretary of the interior, he was responsible for overseeing the utilization of federal lands, waterpower, and oil. Because his department provided public power at low cost, private utility companies charged unfair competition and oil producers eagerly joined in attacks on him because they were angered by his close supervision of their access to oil tracts. The criticism never undermined Roosevelt's confidence in Ickes.

In addition to his work at the Department of the Interior, Ickes served as head of the Public Works Administration from 1933 to 1939. During his tenure he allocated over $6 billion in construction funds with such care that no significant graft was ever uncovered while America obtained hundreds of schools, public buildings, libraries, sewer systems, hospitals, roads, bridges, dams, airports, military bases, and ships.

Ickes' zeal in rooting out corruption from his agencies (which sometimes prompted him to put his personnel under illegal surveillance) made him a controversial figure. His penchant for outlandish descriptions of political rivals (General Hugh Johnson had "mental saddle sores" and HUEY LONG "halitosis of the intellect") made him good newspaper copy, but his irascible personality often negated his positive publicity gains because of his frequent quarrels with journalists.

During World War II, as the petroleum and solid fuels coordinator, Ickes oversaw the rationing of coal and petroleum resources. After the death of President Roosevelt in 1945, Ickes was retained in his post by HARRY S TRUMAN, but the two men never established a close working relationship. In 1946 President Truman accepted Ickes's resignation.

BIBLIOGRAPHY

Ickes, Harold L., *The New Democracy*, 1924, *The Autobiography of a Curmudgeon*, 1943, and *Secret Diary*, 3 vols., 1953–1954; Watkins, T. H., *Righteous Pilgrim: The Life and Times of Harold L. Ickes, 1874–1952*, 1990.

Jackson, Andrew

(March 15, 1767–June 8, 1845)
President, Senator, Representative

Andrew Jackson, rough-hewn military hero of the Battle of New Orleans and bold national leader, left a political legacy known as Jacksonian Democracy that encompassed a new political party and a new interpretation of the role of the president.

Jackson was born in the Waxhaw, a wooded frontier region in South Carolina. His father, an immigrant from northern Ireland, died two weeks before his birth. Jackson received only a rudimentary education before he became a mounted courier at age thirteen for the patriot cause in the American Revolution. Although he was severely wounded by a saber blow while a prisoner of war after he refused to polish a British officer's boots, Jackson survived the war. His mother and two brothers did not.

In 1787, after studying law at Salisbury, North Carolina, Jackson was admitted to the bar. The next year he moved to the western district of North Carolina (now Tennessee) and became a public prosecutor. He settled in Nashville and had just begun to accumulate a substantial sum of wealth when the panic of 1795 deprived him of much of his fortune.

Jackson married Rachel Donelson Robards in 1791. Two years later, the couple learned that her first husband, contrary to what they had been led to believe, had just obtained a divorce. They immediately remarried in January 1794, but ugly rumors that Jackson had stolen another man's wife and lived with her out of wedlock haunted the couple for the rest of Rachel's life. Jackson fought several duels in the course of defending his wife's reputation.

When Tennessee became a state in June 1796, Jackson was elected to the House of Representatives. The next year, when his political mentor, William Blount, was expelled from the Senate, Jackson resigned from the House. To vindicate his party, he then won election to the U.S. Senate. He served only briefly in the Senate, however, before financial difficulties forced him to resign in 1798. His difficult personal financial situation was relieved when he was appointed a judge of the superior court of Tennessee. For the next six years Jackson was a popular frontier judge who told jurors to "do what is right between these parties. That is what the law always means."

With the outbreak of the War of 1812 (see JAMES MADISON), Jackson sought a commission in the regular army. He had to settle for the rank of major general of volunteers in charge of two expeditions to crush a Creek Indian uprising in Mississippi. It was during these campaigns, which culminated in the end of Indian resistance at the Battle of Horseshoe Bend in 1814, that he earned the nickname Old Hickory for his iron will in the face of adversity. Promoted to major general in the regular army, Jackson won national fame for his brilliant defense of New Orleans in January 1815. The battle was fought shortly before news reached America that a peace treaty had been agreed to in Europe. Jackson's overwhelming success (over 2,000 British casualties to 71 American casualties) contributed to the upsurge in American nationalism that followed the war.

In 1818 President JAMES MONROE dispatched Jackson to suppress attacks by Creek and Seminole Indians on settlers along the Florida frontier. Instead of just halting the raids, Jackson pursued the Indians to their villages in Florida, captured Pensacola, deposed the Spanish governor, and hanged two British citizens blamed for encouraging the Indian attacks. Amidst the outrage of Great Britain, President Monroe and Secretary of War JOHN C. CALHOUN denied authorizing Jackson's behavior and contemplated punishing him, but Secretary of State JOHN QUINCY ADAMS prevailed upon the president to seize the opportunity to pressure Spain into selling Florida. After all, argued Adams, negotiations would be greatly simplified by the fact that the United States

Library of Congress

already controlled the area. Jackson was not reprimanded, and, as Adams had predicted, Spain agreed to relinquish control of Florida to the United States the following year. Once again, Jackson's individual initiative made him a national hero.

President Monroe appointed Jackson governor of Florida in 1821, but the post held little appeal. He resigned after only four months in office and returned to Tennessee, where he was elected to the Senate in 1822. Pressure for Jackson to run for president in 1824 as the representative of the common man who epitomized the dreams of the expansionist West gradually mounted.

The election of 1824 was a four-way split in which all the candidates represented various wings of the Democratic-Republican party: John Quincy Adams's power base was in New England; WILLIAM H. CRAWFORD's support was primarily in the South; HENRY CLAY and Andrew Jackson shared the West, with Jackson clearly perceived as the true democrat. Although Jackson won the highest number of popular and electoral votes, no candidate won enough electoral votes to become president. The election had to be decided in the House of Representatives. The winner was settled when fourth-place Clay agreed to support second-place Adams. Jackson accepted the outcome with grace until Adams appointed Clay secretary of state. Then Jackson and his followers attacked Adams and Clay for their "corrupt bargain." It was, they claimed, clearly a case of two representatives of old vested interests combining to cheat the rightful victor and true representative of the people out of becoming president. For the next four years, while his backers worked to defeat Adams's legislative goals, Jackson began building support for the next presidential contest. In 1828 Jackson, at the head of the new Democratic party and with John C. Calhoun as his vice presidential running mate, won a landslide victory.

The inauguration of Jackson—and the beginning of the movement that became known as Jacksonian Democracy—marked the emergence of a new, much broader electorate on the American political scene due to the elimination of property and other qualifications for white men to vote. Jackson embraced these new "common man" voters as his own and moved to place them in governmental offices. The disorderly and disheveled rabble that attended Jackson's inauguration celebration appalled many in the upper middle class. Although Jackson did not replace any more government officeholders than Thomas Jefferson had during his first year in office, he was attacked for the quality of the replacements and accused of establishing the spoils system in the federal government. In policy matters, President Jackson relied upon several of his close friends. This so-called influential Kitchen Cabinet included William Lewis, Duff Green, Isaac Hill, and Andrew Jackson Donelson.

Jackson's first term in office was dominated by three issues: the firm manner in which the president opposed the states' rights doctrine of nullification (see John Caldwell Calhoun); the rival ambitions of Secretary of State Martin Van Buren and Vice President John C. Calhoun to be Jackson's successor; and the decision by Jackson to oppose the rechartering of the Bank of the United States.

At the start of Jackson's administration, John C. Calhoun seemed the most logical candidate to become his successor. Calhoun had a national reputation and a strong power base in the South. Martin Van Buren, the bachelor political organizer who had delivered New York's electoral votes in 1828, had no such national stature. However, over the course of Jackson's first term, Jackson and Calhoun became locked in a fierce political confrontation over the proper role of the federal government in fostering national economic development and states' rights. A personal animosity between the two men quickly developed soon after Jackson assumed office, first over an incident involving treatment of a cabinet member's wife accused of adultery, and second from Jackson's discovery of Calhoun's behavior during the Florida controversy.

Calhoun refused to make any effort to encourage his wife to treat Peggy Eaton (see John Caldwell Calhoun), Secretary of War John Eaton's wife, with respect. Jackson, sensitive to the harm caused because of the unfair labeling of his own wife, felt a personal need (which fellow widower Martin Van Buren supported) to defend Mrs. Eaton's honor. Nettled by Calhoun's attitude about Peggy Eaton, Jackson then discovered government documents describing how Calhoun had advocated that Jackson be reprimanded for his actions in Florida in 1818.

These matters, however, paled in comparison to the drama that unfolded over states' rights. Calhoun led efforts to oppose the tariff bills in 1828 and 1832 that protected the industrial Northeast at the expense of the South. As the spokesman of the South, Calhoun promulgated the doctrine of nullification—the belief that a state could refuse to obey a federal law—to justify South Carolina's refusal to honor the tariffs. At first, Calhoun hoped Jackson's support could be enlisted; but Jackson's toast at a dinner party in Washington in 1830—"Our Union, it must be preserved"—boldly and succinctly stated his opposition to nullification. Jackson's toast captured the mood of the nation and prompted a surge of nationalism.

In 1833, after a furious Jackson had threatened to use military force to ensure South Carolina's compliance with the tariff of 1832, a military confrontation was barely avoided by the enactment of a new compromise tariff. The matter, however, was only temporarily resolved. It convinced Calhoun and his loyal followers that their interests in the Union were endangered. They resolved to become even more adamant in refusing to compromise when they sensed Southern interests threatened. In the end, it would take the Civil War to resolve the issue.

Jackson's position concerning states' rights was not based on a philosophical foundation that he felt obligated to consistently enforce regardless of political consequences. When the Supreme Court ruled in 1832 that Georgia had to honor its treaties with the Cherokee Indians, Jackson did not hesitate to support Georgia's right to deal with the Cherokee without federal interference: "[Chief Justice] JOHN MARSHALL has made his decision, now let him enforce it." Jackson's position was a shrewd political ploy that successfully discouraged Georgia from supporting South Carolina's militant nullification stand. Jackson hoped that the Cherokee would quietly give up their tribal lands and become assimilated. They did not, and finally, in 1838, 15,000 Cherokee were forced by the U.S. Army to resettle west of the Mississippi in a long winter journey (the Trail of Tears) that caused great suffering.

Because he believed the federal government should play a carefully limited role in fostering national development, Jackson opposed federal funding for internal improvements (see JOHN CALDWELL CALHOUN). During his first term this belief, combined with his distrust of aristocrats and speculators, convinced him that the federal government charter granting the private Bank of the United States (see NICHOLAS BIDDLE and ROGER BROOKE TANEY) the right to handle all government funds should not be renewed in 1836. When Nicholas Biddle, president of the bank, supported by Henry Clay and DANIEL WEBSTER, persuaded Congress to pass a rechartering bill in advance in 1832, Jackson promptly vetoed it, and the veto stood.

After winning a massive reelection victory, with Martin Van Buren as his vice presidential running mate, Jackson kept his word. In 1833, with the help of treasury secretary ROGER B. TANEY, he began to remove government deposits from the national bank, placing them in small regional banks (pet banks). Biddle con-

tinued the war over the bank by keeping interest high and causing money to be scarce, hoping that by making borrowing more difficult, business would be hurt and the bank would be rechartered. But when unemployment occurred and businessmen applied to Jackson for relief, he said, "Go to Biddle." Biddle was finally forced to back down and grant credit on reasonable terms. Jackson had won, and the bank passed out of existence in 1836. However, economic troubles lay ahead for his successor.

In the foreign policy arena the Jackson administration managed to obtain the reopening of Britain's Caribbean colonies to U.S. trade. The United States also formally recognized the independence of Texas (see JAMES KNOX POLK). Jackson did not advocate the admission of Texas as a state in 1836 because he realized it would tear the Democratic party apart by disrupting the delicate balance that existed between the slave and free states.

Martin Van Buren, Jackson's designated successor, won an easy election victory over his Whig rival. Pleased with the outcome of the 1836 election, Jackson retired to The Hermitage, his Tennessee plantation.

Two political parties had been formally organized during the period—the Democrats and the opposing Whigs—and it was the Jackson presidency, built on strong leadership and the belief in limiting the power of the federal government, as well as opposing privilege in favor of the common man, that would help define not only the Democratic party, but an era.

BIBLIOGRAPHY

Bugg, James L., Jr., and Peter C. Steward, *Jacksonian Democracy: Myth or Reality?* 2d edition, 1986; Davis, Burke, *Old Hickory: A Life of Andrew Jackson,* 1977; Remini, Robert, *Andrew Jackson and the Course of American Empire, 1767–1821,* 1977, *Andrew Jackson and the Course of American Freedom, 1822–1832,* 1981, and *Andrew Jackson and the Course of American Democracy,*

1833–1845, 1984; Rogin, Michael P., *Fathers and Children: Andrew Jackson and the Subjugation of the American Indian*, 1975; Sellers, Charles G. (ed.), *Andrew Jackson: A Profile*, 1971; Syrett, H. C., *Andrew Jackson: His Contribution to the American Tradition*, 1953.

Jackson, Henry Martin

(May 31, 1912–September 1, 1983)
Senator, Representative

Four decades of public service in Congress, with membership on a number of key Senate committees and a shrewd appreciation for the need to address the concerns of the blue-collar "silent majority," enabled Henry "Scoop" Jackson to become a powerful leader of the Democratic party in the 1970s.

Jackson was born in Everett, Washington. He completed his undergraduate studies and earned a law degree from the University of Washington in Seattle in 1935; he was admitted to the bar later that year. In 1940 he won election to the U.S. House of Representatives. He served in the House, with the brief exception of a few months in the army in 1943–1944, until winning election to the U.S. Senate in 1952.

During his twelve years in the House and thirty years in the Senate, Jackson earned a reputation as a liberal on domestic affairs and a conservative on issues of foreign policy and national defense. He was a staunch supporter of organized labor, civil rights, military preparedness, U.S. involvement in Vietnam (see LYNDON BAINES JOHNSON and RICHARD MILHOUS NIXON), the survival of Israel, and freedom from persecution of Jews living in the Soviet Union.

In his first term in the Senate, Jackson was assigned to Senator JOSEPH MCCARTHY's permanent investigations subcommittee of the Committee on Government Operations. Appalled at the methods of investigation employed by McCarthy against alleged communists, Jackson helped to orchestrate the effort in the Senate that led to the vote to censure McCarthy in 1954.

In recognition of his superb handling of McCarthy, Jackson was appointed to a coveted position on the Senate Armed Services Committee. He quickly became a leading spokesman of the Democratic party on defense policy. In the late 1950s he was a strong proponent of the existence of a "missile gap" between the United States and the Soviet Union. A political ally of JOHN F. KENNEDY, Jackson was deeply disappointed when Kennedy chose LYNDON B. JOHNSON instead of him to be the 1960 vice presidential candidate.

As chairman of the Interior Committee (later the Committee on Energy and Natural Resources), Jackson was one of the key architects of the National Environmental Quality Act of 1969, which required federal agencies to submit environmental impact statements. He angered environmentalists, however, when he supported construction of the supersonic transport plane and the Alaska oil pipeline. To Jackson, the issue was one of balance: "It's fine for the people who have made it to say we won't have any more economic growth. . . . [But what] about the six million at the poverty level? We have an obligation to them."

Although Jackson failed to win the Democratic party nomination for president in 1972 and 1976 as a representative of the conservative wing of the party, his popularity in his home state never waned. He died a year after winning reelection to a sixth consecutive term in the Senate.

BIBLIOGRAPHY

Ognibene, Peter J., *Scoop: The Life and Politics of Henry M. Jackson*, 1975; Prochnau, William W., and Richard W. Larsen, *A Certain Democrat: Senator Henry M. Jackson*, 1972.

Jay, John

(December 12, 1745–May 17, 1829)
Diplomat, Chief Justice of the Supreme Court

As the first chief justice of the U.S. Supreme Court, delegate to both Continental Congresses, diplomat, and Federalist governor of New York, John Jay helped to shape the government of the United States.

Born to one of New York's most influential families, the self-confident Jay, like ALEXANDER HAMILTON, was marked from the beginning as a person of uncommon intellectual ability. He graduated from King's College (now Columbia University) in 1764 and was admitted to the New York bar four years later. In 1773, as secretary of the Royal Mixed Commission, Jay observed the settlement of a boundary dispute between New Jersey and New York through arbitration. The success of the arbitration technique evidently made a lasting impression upon him. Twenty-one years later he recommended arbitration as a way of resolving differences between the United States and Great Britain.

Jay's active involvement in the Continental Congress ended his private law practice and drew him into full-time public service. Afraid of unleashing the prejudices of the masses, Jay opposed independence, but once the decision was made, he loyally supported the Revolution. After helping to draft New York's new constitution and serving for a few months as the state of New York's first chief justice, Jay was elected president of the Continental Congress on December 10, 1778.

Jay served as minister to Spain from 1780 to 1782, then joined in the peace talks in Paris.

His insistence that the American commissioners be regarded as representatives of the United States, not of the "Colonies," delayed the negotiations and may have cost the United States possession of Canada, which the British might have been willing to cede in exchange for an early end to the war. Jay also shared responsibility with JOHN ADAMS for suing for peace without consultation with France. After the treaty ending the war (the Treaty of Paris) was signed in September 1783, Jay returned to New York.

Jay had planned to resume his private law practice upon his return. Instead, the Continental Congress, in his absence abroad, had elected him secretary of foreign affairs. The position obliged him to begin negotiations with Great Britain and Spain concerning trade agreements, relations with Indians on the frontier, and navigation rights on the Mississippi River. He remained in this post until the new government was organized and THOMAS JEFFERSON assumed the duties of secretary of state in 1790.

Like JAMES MADISON and Hamilton, Jay was convinced that the Articles of Confederation did not provide a strong enough central government. He wrote five *Federalist* papers in support of the new Constitution and vigorously campaigned for its ratification in New York.

President GEORGE WASHINGTON named Jay chief justice of the Supreme Court as soon as the new federal government was organized. *Chisholm* v. *Georgia* (1793), which affirmed the right of a citizen of one state to sue another sovereign state, was the most important case decided in Jay's brief tenure as chief justice; it did not stand long. The Eleventh Amendment, which effectively reversed the decision, was quickly adopted. While chief justice, Jay continued to serve as an adviser to Washington and even wrote the first draft of Washington's famous Proclamation of Neutrality of 1793.

Washington asked Jay to return to England in 1794 to cope with the threat of a new war by obtaining a treaty with Great Britain that recognized U.S. neutrality rights. Jay's success in dealing with the British representative, Lord Grenville, was limited. The treaty he returned with (known as Jay's Treaty) bought time and helped avoid a war, but it did not contain British acceptance of American neutrality rights or halt the impressment of American seamen.

Although vilified in the press for selling out the interests of the United States for the sake of helping Great Britain against France, Jay and the Federalist-dominated Senate realized that Jay had obtained all that America could hope for. The furor that surrounded the Senate ratification of the treaty effectively eliminated any chance Jay might have had of being elected president.

Jay resigned as chief justice in 1795 to become governor of New York. He served two terms.

In 1800, anticipating that the Republicans were going to win the next election, Jay decided not to seek reelection to a third term as governor. After declining an offer to again be chief justice because he believed "the Supreme Court lacked the energy, weight, and dignity which are essential to its affording due support to the national Government," he left office and public life for good in 1801. He died at his home twenty-eight years later.

BIBLIOGRAPHY

Jay, John, *Diary, during Peace Negotiations of 1782,* Monaghan, Frank (ed.), 1934; Jay, John, *Correspondence and Public Papers,* Johnston, H. P. (ed.), 4 vols., 1890–1893; Monaghan, Frank, *John Jay,* 1935; Morris, Richard B., *John Jay, the Nation, and the Court,* 1967.

Jefferson, Thomas

(April 13, 1743–July 4, 1826)
President, Vice President, Secretary of State, Diplomat, Revolutionary Leader

Thomas Jefferson wrote the lines inscribed on his tombstone: "Here was buried Thomas Jefferson, author of the Declaration of Independence and the Virginia Statute of Religious Freedom, and the father of the University of Virginia." It is a modest epitaph for a man who founded a major political party and served as minister to France, governor of Virginia, secretary of state, vice president, and president of the United States. He was also an accomplished writer, lawyer, farmer, naturalist, architect, musician, linguist, philosopher, scientist, geographer, surveyor, botanist, ethnologist, and paleontologist.

Jefferson was born into a prominent family at Shadwell in Albemarle County, Virginia. He graduated from the College of William and Mary in 1762 and was admitted to the bar in 1767 after an exceptionally thorough preparation in legal theory. Until the outbreak of the American Revolution, Jefferson lived the life of a wealthy Virginia aristocrat. He practiced law, married, began the construction of his mansion at Monticello, and served as magistrate, county lieutenant, and member of the House of Burgesses from 1769 to 1775.

There was no doubt in Jefferson's mind about the right of the colonists to refuse to obey the decrees of the British Parliament. In *A Summary View of the Rights of British America,* a pamphlet prepared for the Virginia convention in 1774, he argued that under English law the legal precedents of emigration and natural rights meant that the colonies owed allegiance to the king but did not have to obey Parliament in matters of taxation or trade.

A tall, lanky, and shy man, Jefferson impressed his colleagues through the quality of the written committee reports he prepared rather than by his speeches. As a member of the Second Continental Congress, Jefferson, along with BENJAMIN FRANKLIN, JOHN ADAMS, ROGER SHERMAN, and ROBERT R. LIVINGSTON, was asked to draw up a declaration of independence. The completed document was composed from ideas suggested by the committee members and the congress. Jefferson actually wrote the text, contributing the impassioned and stirring prose that inspired Americans in 1776. The vision of a world in which all people are treated equally regardless of their birth, class, or status and in which governments exist to improve the quality of life of their citizens, not to control them, still serves as a model for oppressed people today.

Jefferson resigned from the congress in September 1776 to serve in the Virginia House of Delegates and to be closer to his family. He concentrated his energies for the next several years in trying to institutionalize his ideas of political and religious freedom in Virginia. He believed that a social revolution as well as a

Library of Congress

war with Great Britain for independence needed to occur. His goal was to create a society in which a natural aristocracy based on talent and merit rather than wealth and birth could lead. Although he was disappointed by the results of his efforts in Virginia, he did manage to have all the feudal aspects of land ownership in Virginia abolished. He also led the successful effort to end government support for the Anglican church.

His most famous single bills were for Establishing Religious Freedom, introduced in 1779 but not adopted until 1786, which provided for the separation of church and state; and a Bill for the More General Diffusion of Knowledge to create a public education system, which was never adopted as he envisioned.

Jefferson was elected governor in 1779 and was in office when Virginia was devastated by the invasion of the British. He was blamed for the lack of Virginia's ability to defend itself, even though the restrictions on the powers of the office had given him little authority to act. After his term ended in 1781, a legislative inquiry cleared him of all charges of dereliction of duty, but Jefferson was so humiliated that he decided to retire from public life. He might have remained secluded at Monticello, but the death of his wife in September 1782 drove him to seek escape from his grief through work.

He returned to the Continental Congress in 1783 and served there until he was appointed a special commissioner to France in 1784 and then minister to France in 1785. A notable accomplishment in Congress was securing adoption of the decimal system of coinage. His *Report of Government for the Western Territory,* in which he advocated prohibiting slavery in all western territories, became the foundation for the Northwest Ordinance of 1787.

Jefferson remained in Paris as Benjamin Franklin's successor until 1789. While in Paris his *Notes on the State of Virginia* (1785), a highly respected natural history that established his reputation in Europe as a scientist, was published. It was from Paris that Jefferson reviewed the newly written Constitution and added his support to the need for amendments (the Bill of Rights) to ensure adequate protection of individual liberties. Before his return to the United States, Jefferson witnessed the early stages of the French Revolution. He could not hide his enthusiasm for the principles heralded in the revolt or his support for the moderate factions led by men such as the Marquis de Lafayette.

Shortly after his return to the United States in 1789, President GEORGE WASHINGTON asked him to become secretary of state. Jefferson reluctantly agreed and served in that post until the end of Washington's first term in 1793. It was during this period that the bitter rivalry began between Jefferson and Secretary of the Treasury ALEXANDER HAMILTON, which led to the formation of two major political parties in America.

Jefferson's fears about the dangers of a strong central government, his desire to protect small farmers—the people he believed constituted the foundation of a republic—and his wish to forge a close political bond with France were not shared by Hamilton. Hamilton advocated interpreting the Constitution broadly, or loosely, using the doctrine of "implied powers," so that the new central government could establish a strong nation with an expanding industrial base and increased trade with Great Britain. Each man sought to persuade George Washington of the correctness of his perspectives. Washington attempted to follow a middle path, but Jefferson, a strict constructionist who believed in a narrow interpretation of the Constitution, decided that the president had adopted Hamilton's perspective after he supported the establishment of a national bank (see ALEXANDER HAMILTON)

and the broad interpretation of the Constitution. Jefferson became the leader of those opposed to the Federalists and Alexander Hamilton's programs; he helped to found an opposition press and what became known as the Democratic-Republican party.

Finally convinced that he could not persuade Washington to adopt his perspective or stop Hamilton while serving in the cabinet, Jefferson decided to retire to Monticello in 1793. For the next three years his supporters and other opponents of Hamilton and the Federalist party worked to secure Jefferson's election to the presidency. In 1796, although Jefferson did no campaigning, he received only three fewer electoral votes than John Adams and therefore was elected vice president.

Relations between Jefferson and Adams were cordial at first, but Adams's decision to support most of Hamilton's programs and the Alien and Sedition Acts (see JOHN ADAMS) earned Jefferson's enmity. Jefferson opposed the Alien and Sedition Acts on the grounds that they stifled free speech and political opposition. He even went so far as to claim in his so-called Kentucky Resolutions (as JAMES MADISON did in the Virginia Resolutions) that states could declare the acts null and void. At this time Jefferson also used his experience of presiding over the Senate to compose *A Manual of Parliamentary Practice* (1801).

The tumult caused by the Alien and Sedition Acts, the growing international crisis precipitated by the French Revolution, and the domestic conflict arising from Hamilton's national economic development program culminated in Jefferson's election to the presidency in 1800. His taking office, however, was delayed several weeks as the result of a controversy caused by a flaw in the Constitution. AARON BURR, the vice presidential candidate, had received as many electoral votes as Jefferson because at that time there was no distinction made on the ballots between candidates for president and vice president. The man with the most votes became president, and the second-place finisher became vice president. In the event of a tie, the election was automatically thrown into the House of Representatives. Burr briefly capitalized on the confusion in the House to try to usurp Jefferson's election and win the office himself, but Hamilton's advice to Federalists to vote for Jefferson as the lesser of two evils helped settle the matter (see AARON BURR). The Twelfth Amendment remedied this defect in the Constitution by changing the procedure for the election of president and vice president.

During his first term in office Jefferson reduced the national debt, cut taxes, and sought unsuccessfully to reduce the power of the Federalist-dominated judiciary. Although he believed in a strict constructionist (see MELVILLE WESTON FULLER) interpretation of the Constitution in theory, in practice he was more flexible. When a unique opportunity was provided by Napoleon to purchase the Louisiana Territory, Jefferson committed the United States to the purchase although the Constitution did not specifically authorize the government to acquire foreign territory. The only foreign conflict he faced at this time was in ordering the small American navy to blockade Tripoli to suppress the raids of Barbary pirates on American shipping. Although the military effects of the action were mixed, the action was extremely popular, and the securing of a favorable treaty in 1805 with Tripoli seemed to justify his resort to force. His efforts to have western Florida included in the Louisiana Purchase failed, but overall his first term was remarkably successful and he was easily reelected in 1804.

Jefferson's second term was dominated by efforts to protect American neutral trade rights as warring England and France both established naval blockades. The British impressment of seamen was a constant grievance, and when a British ship fired upon and boarded a U.S. naval frigate, the *Chesapeake*, in 1807, the American public might have backed a declaration of war. Jefferson had never wanted to resort to war and, opposed to constructing a large navy, had decided to rely on economic pressure tactics. First the Nonimportation Act of 1806 was tried, then the Embargo Act of 1807. Unfortunately, these acts required Americans not to attempt to trade with their principal clients, England and France, and brought economic havoc to merchants as well as to shippers. New England, the maritime center of America, was especially hurt. In addition, enforcement of the embargo required infringements upon the very individual rights that Jefferson heralded as inviolate. The result was that by the time he left office in 1809, even though the Embargo Act had been repealed, he was the target of considerable public hostility.

The furor was not sufficient to prevent the election of Jefferson's chosen successor, James Madison, however. Jefferson retired to Monticello secure in the knowledge that his policies would be continued.

Retirement to Monticello in 1809 did not mean inactivity. Before his death he achieved one more major goal, the establishment of the University of Virginia. He was also active as the president of the American Philosophical Society (1797–1815).

Jefferson died on the fiftieth anniversary of the Declaration of Independence, shortly after noon and just a few hours before John Adams.

BIBLIOGRAPHY

Boorstin, Daniel J., *The Lost World of Thomas Jefferson*, 1948; Commager, Henry Steele, *Jefferson, Nationalism, and the Enlightenment*, 1975; Honeywell, Roy J., *The Educational Work of Thomas Jefferson*, 1931; Lehmann, Karl, *Thomas Jefferson: American Humanist*, 1947; Malone, Dumas, vol. 1, *Jefferson and His Time*, 1948; vol. 2, *Jefferson the Virginian*, 1948; vol. 3, *Jefferson and the Ordeal of Liberty*, 1962; vol. 4, *Jefferson the President: First Term, 1801–1805*, 1970; vol. 5, *Jefferson the President: Second Term, 1805–1809*, 1974; vol. 6, *The Sage of Monticello*, 1981; Martin, Edwin T., *Thomas Jefferson: Scientist*, 1952; Matthews, Richard K., *The Radical Politics of Thomas Jefferson: A Revisionist View*, 1984; Peterson, Merrill D., *The Jefferson Image in the American Mind*, 1960, and *Thomas Jefferson and the New Nation: A Biography*, 1970.

Johnson, Andrew

(December 29, 1808–July 31, 1875)
President, Vice President, Senator, Representative

Library of Congress

Andrew Johnson was the only U.S. president to endure the agony of an impeachment trial. He escaped conviction for high crimes and misdemeanors by one vote in 1868.

Johnson was born in Raleigh, North Carolina, and spent his childhood in grinding poverty. Apprenticed to a tailor, he learned the trade, and ran away, settling in Greeneville, Tennessee, where he married in 1827. Denied formal schooling, Johnson, with the help of his wife, educated himself. He developed a flare for public debate through contacts he made at Greeneville College and Tusculum Academy.

After being elected alderman and mayor of Greeneville, Johnson was elected to the state legislature in 1835, defeated in 1837, and reelected in 1839. In 1841 he was elected to the state senate; two years later, he won election to the U.S. House of Representatives as a Democrat. He served in the House until 1853, when he was elected to two terms as governor of Tennessee. He became a U.S. senator in 1857.

In both the state legislature and Congress Johnson identified with the common citizens and attacked anyone—which over the course of his career meant virtually everyone—who spoke against their interests. At the same time, Johnson was a staunch defender of states' rights and slavery (he owned a few slaves himself), although there were few slaves in the section of eastern Tennessee that he represented. Johnson quarreled with his fellow Democrats and became identified with the "radical" idea of basing political representation on the number of white persons in the area instead of counting slaves as three-fifths (as provided for in the Constitution at that time). He also was in favor of electing U.S. senators by popular vote, electing federal judges, and abolishing the electoral college. Johnson backed the passage of a homestead law that would grant small parcels of government-owned land in the West to settlers for free or at a nominal price, thus supporting the interests of the small laborer against the large plantation owner.

When the Democratic party met at Charleston in April 1860, Johnson's name was placed in nomination for the presidency by the Tennessee delegation, but any hope he had of being selected for the vice presidency vanished when the party broke into sectional factions. He supported Southerner JOHN C. BRECKINRIDGE in the general election. However, when the senators from seceding states withdrew from Congress in 1860, Johnson declared himself for the Union and remained in Washington, D.C. It was Johnson who wrote the resolution that explained the purpose of the North's resort to arms as solely to preserve the supremacy of the Constitution and the Union.

In March 1862, after the western half of Tennessee fell to Union forces, Johnson was appointed military governor of Tennessee by President ABRAHAM LINCOLN with instructions to reestablish the authority of the federal government in the state. As military governor, Johnson had the difficult task of balancing the needs of the army with the political interests of a hostile population, as well as trying to rally Unionists in the state around a moderate Reconstruction policy. After the Union forces had driven all Confederate troops from eastern Tennessee in 1863, Johnson managed to reestablish civil government and secure, by state constitutional convention and popular vote, the abolition of slavery. Johnson viewed his experience in Tennessee as a successful example of the approach that would be necessary for the North to follow in reconstructing the Union after the Civil War. His success in Tennessee also made Johnson the logical choice for Lincoln's vice presidential running mate in 1864.

When Johnson became president after Lincoln's assassination, he promised to continue Lincoln's policies and retain his cabinet. Congress was not in session when Johnson became president in April 1865 and was not scheduled to return until December. The Republicans wanted Johnson to call Congress into special session so that they could make the rules for the treatment of the conquered South. Johnson refused and decided to use the time to resolve the matter on his own.

Lincoln had favored leniency toward the South. He believed that since states could not legally secede, the Confederate states should be treated as if they had never left the Union. Therefore, as soon as one-tenth of the voting population in a state took an oath of allegiance to the Constitution and agreed to abolish slavery, they should be allowed to establish a new state government. The Radical Republicans in Congress disagreed. They argued in the Wade-Davis bill, passed in July 1864 but vetoed by President Lincoln, that since the Southern states had seceded, they would have to apply for readmission to the Union under new terms established by Congress. Among these terms was the requirement that 50 percent of the enrolled white male citizens take an oath of allegiance to the Constitution before a convention could be called to reestablish the state government. In order to be a delegate to the convention or vote for a dele-

gate, a person would have to take an "ironclad oath," swearing that he had never voluntarily fought against the United States or given aid to the rebels. Once the new state government was accepted by Congress, it could, if it wished, proceed to reenfranchise ex-Confederates.

Lincoln died before having to confront the Radical Republicans on the issue. Johnson proceeded to implement his own plan with the hope of presenting Congress with the fait accompli of a readmitted South when it convened in December. He almost succeeded, but his decision to let the Southern states determine their own courses of action proved his downfall.

Johnson suggested that Southern conventions—gathered under his interpretation of Lincoln's plan—ought to refuse to pay their war debts, nullify their ordinances of secession, and adopt the Thirteenth Amendment freeing the slaves. These conditions were the least the North might have accepted, but Johnson failed to make them requirements. The result was that South Carolina repealed rather than nullified its ordinance of secession. This implied that states had a right to secede. Mississippi refused to adopt the Thirteenth Amendment abolishing slavery, and both South Carolina and Mississippi refused to repudiate their war debts (although they were compelled to do so later). Further, many of the new Southern state legislatures adopted laws, called Black Codes, that severely restricted the civil rights of free blacks. They also proceeded to allow former high-ranking Confederate government officials to accept political office.

By the time Congress reconvened, the stage was set for a fierce battle between it and the president. Johnson refused to back down or seek compromise. Radical Republicans, led by THADDEUS STEVENS, refused to recognize the Southern representatives and passed various Reconstruction measures to protect the rights of the newly freed blacks. In February 1866 Congress passed a bill to extend and strengthen the Freedmen's Bureau. The bureau had been established for one year in 1865 to assist and protect freed slaves and settle them on abandoned lands in the South. Now Congress wanted to try in military courts anyone who attempted to deprive freedmen of their civil rights. Johnson, believing that the bill was unconstitutional, vetoed it. The attempt to override the veto failed. Congress then passed the Civil Rights Act, which granted citizenship to blacks. Johnson again vetoed this measure, but the bill was passed over his veto. This victory by the Radical Republicans allowed them to garner sufficient support for the passage of a new Freedmen's Bureau bill in July 1866.

The Tenure of Office Act of 1867, passed by Congress over Johnson's veto, set the stage for a final confrontation by prohibiting the president from dismissing his own cabinet members or other federal officeholders without the consent of the Senate. In August 1867 Johnson suspended Secretary of War EDWARD M. STANTON, pending Senate approval. When the Senate refused to approve his action, Johnson fired Stanton anyway in February 1868. The moment Radical Republicans had been hoping for had arrived. Impeachment proceedings for high crimes and misdemeanors began in the House. Johnson was tried by the Senate in March 1868. The trial lasted until the end of May, when the motion to impeach him failed by one vote short of the required two-thirds majority, 35 to 19.

While he retained office, Johnson's power was reduced. None of his vetoes were upheld during his last year in office. One of his last acts as president was to grant amnesty "without limitation to all who had participated in the rebellion."

Johnson returned to Tennessee in 1868. He sought election to the Senate in 1869 and the House of Representatives in 1872, and was elected to the Senate in 1875. He served in one special session of Congress before his sudden death while visiting his daughter near Carter Station, Tennessee.

BIBLIOGRAPHY

Lomask, Milton, *Andrew Johnson: President on Trial*, 1960; McKitrick, Eric L., *Andrew Johnson and Reconstruction*, 1988; Trefousse, Hans L., *Andrew Johnson: A Biography*, 1989.

Johnson, Hiram Warren

(September 2, 1866–August 6, 1945)
Senator

First as a reform-oriented California governor and then as a vehemently isolationist U.S. senator, Hiram Warren Johnson defied political party labels and successfully pursued his own independent political vision.

Johnson was born in Sacramento, California. He attended the University of California at Berkeley for two years, then studied law in his father's law office. Admitted to the California bar in 1888, he became a partner in his father's practice. In 1902 Johnson and his brother established their own practice in San Francisco.

Johnson's efforts to foster political reform in California attracted national attention in 1908. After the prosecutor was shot during the sensational trial of the corrupt political leader Abe Ruef, Johnson, who had helped prepare the case as an assistant district attorney, continued the trial and obtained the conviction of Ruef and several of his associates.

With the support of Progressive Republicans (see THEODORE ROOSEVELT), Johnson was elected governor of California in 1910 and instituted a wide range of progressive social, economic, and political reforms. In 1912 Johnson joined other disenchanted Republicans in establishing the Progressive or Bull Moose party. He was chosen by the new party to be Theodore Roosevelt's vice presidential running mate, but the ticket lost to Democratic candidate WOODROW WILSON in the general election.

In 1916, midway through his second term as governor, Johnson won election to the U.S. Senate, where he served until his death nearly thirty years later. Although he reluctantly supported President Wilson's declaration of war, he opposed ratification of the Treaty of Versailles (see WOODROW WILSON) and U.S. participation in the League of Nations (see WILSON).

In the Senate Johnson fought for progressive legislative reforms and opposed U.S. involvement in European affairs. Frequently at odds with his own Republican party during the 1920s and the Great Depression, Johnson backed FRANKLIN D. ROOSEVELT for president in 1932.

At first Johnson embraced Roosevelt's New Deal legislative program, but he quickly lost enthusiasm for it and did not support Roosevelt's reelection in 1936. He had grown to distrust such a concentration of power, and, in opposition to Roosevelt, advocated a U.S. foreign policy of isolationism.

After the Japanese attack on Pearl Harbor (see FRANKLIN DELANO ROOSEVELT), Johnson supported the U.S. war effort, but he never changed his viewpoint about the need to avoid all foreign entanglements. In 1945, shortly before his death, Johnson voted against U.S. adoption of the United Nations' charter.

BIBLIOGRAPHY

Olin, Spencer C., Jr., *California's Prodigal Sons: Hiram Johnson and the Progressives, 1911–1917*, 1968.

Johnson, Lyndon Baines

(August 27, 1908–January 22, 1973)
President, Vice President, Senator, Representative

Lyndon Johnson, one of the most controversial presidents of modern times, fought more for black equality than any president since ABRAHAM LINCOLN. He also led the United States into one of the worst foreign policy disasters in the nation's history.

Raised in Johnson City, Texas, Lyndon Johnson was born into a financially poor family with a rich political heritage—Johnson's father and grandfather (for whom Johnson City was named) had served in the Texas legislature. Johnson graduated from Southwest Texas State Teachers College in 1930 and briefly taught school before embarking on his political career by helping Richard M. Kleberg win a seat in the U.S. House of Representatives. Johnson accompanied Kleberg to Washington, D.C., where he served as his secretary for four years. In 1935 Johnson returned to Texas as state director of the National Youth Administration, a New Deal post in which he helped young people secure part-time employment so that they could attend college. In 1937 Johnson, campaigning as a fervent supporter of fellow Democrat FRANKLIN DELANO ROOSEVELT, was elected to the U.S. House of Representatives. Four years later, Johnson made an unsuccessful run for the U.S. Senate.

After the Japanese attack on Pearl Harbor in December 1941, Johnson joined the navy but served for only six months when President Roosevelt ordered all congressmen on active duty to return to Washington. During the war Johnson chaired a subcommittee of the Naval Affairs Committee, which was charged with investigating procurement procedures in order to eliminate waste. After the war Johnson adopted a more conservative political demeanor. Believing that unions had become too powerful, he voted for the Taft-Hartley Act of 1947 (see HARRY S TRUMAN). In 1948 Johnson won his second bid for a Senate seat by eighty-seven contested votes in the Democratic primary. Despite court challenges, "Landslide Lyndon" held on to his narrow victory and easily won the general election in 1948.

A willingness to do favors and work with Republicans enabled Johnson, by nature a pragmatist and master at persuasion, to advance rapidly in the Senate. Columnist Mary McGrory described the Johnson treatment as consisting of "an incredibly potent mixture of persuasion, badgering, flattery, threats, reminders of past favors and future advantages." In 1953 Johnson became minority leader in the Senate. In 1954, when he was reelected along with enough other Democrats for his party to regain control of the Senate, Johnson became majority leader. After recovering from a heart attack in 1955, he continued his policy

Franke Wolfe/Courtesy Lyndon B. Johnson Library

of working with President DWIGHT D. EISENHOWER in formulating bipartisan policies.

Johnson's ability to search for the common ground upon which a compromise could be reached enabled him to become one of the most powerful men in Washington. His decision in 1957 to personally direct the first civil rights bill through the Senate and in 1960 to guide the passage of the second led political commentator James Reston to observe: "Johnson has, on the race problem, been the most effective mediator [in Congress] between the North and South."

His hopes of winning the Democratic nomination for president in 1960 were crushed by JOHN F. KENNEDY. Johnson had based his nomination strategy on the hope that no clear winner would emerge from the primaries. After Kennedy defeated his opponents in the primaries, Johnson made an unsuccessful effort to discredit Kennedy as too young and inexperienced for the presidency. After Kennedy won the nomination on the first ballot, he offered the vice presidential position to Johnson. It was assumed the proud Johnson would decline the offer, but instead he accepted and campaigned vigorously for the ticket in the South.

Although Johnson participated in cabinet meetings and chaired several important committees as vice president, he was clearly unhappy in the office. He felt restricted by the limited powers of the vice president, and he hated the president's and his brother ROBERT KENNEDY's personal style. They, in turn, despised him. Then, on November 22, 1963, Kennedy was assassinated in Dallas, Texas, and Johnson assumed the office of president.

Adroitly capitalizing on the somber mood of the nation, Johnson swiftly achieved enactment of civil rights legislation and a tax cut program—legislation Kennedy had sought before his death—as a living memorial to the murdered president. His success with the Congress and promise that the United States would not become involved in another land war in Asia, this time in Vietnam, enabled him to easily win the nomination of his party for president in 1964 and then to go on to overwhelm Republican candidate BARRY GOLDWATER. The election also secured a large Democratic majority in both houses of Congress.

Claiming that the election was a mandate to create his vision of a "Great Society," Johnson began working to secure passage of a number of important programs and bills in 1965. These included Medicare, a system of health insurance for the elderly under the Social Security program, and the Voting Rights Act of 1965, which outlawed illiteracy tests that had been used to prevent blacks from voting. He established two new federal agencies, the Departments of Housing and Urban Development and Transportation, and increased federal aid to public education. As part of Johnson's War on Poverty program, Congress increased unemployment benefits, expanded the food-stamp program, created new youth employment opportunities, and provided legal services to the poor (Legal Services) and special preschool classes to underprivileged children (Head Start). These programs amounted to the most ambitious attempt at liberal reform since the New Deal (see FRANKLIN DELANO ROOSEVELT).

Johnson's success in domestic affairs was not matched in the foreign policy arena. By 1966 Johnson had committed almost half a million American troops to the defense of South Vietnam, and American planes were bombing North Vietnam. In 1965, fearful of communist involvement, Johnson ordered more than 20,000 American troops to suppress a revolution in the Dominican Republic. In contrast, Johnson's restrained behavior during the 1967 Arab-Israeli conflict helped avoid an international crisis.

As victory in Vietnam seemed to slip further away and casualties mounted, Johnson's popularity weakened along with his political power. His policies gave rise to a massive antiwar movement that involved hundreds of thousands, if not millions, of Americans, many of them college undergraduates. This movement accused Johnson and his administration of hiding the true financial and human costs of the war and of using the war to increase American power rather than to guarantee the rights of the Vietnamese. After the surprising primary election success of Senator EUGENE McCARTHY in 1968 and the entry into the race of Senator Robert Kennedy, a demoralized Johnson stunned the nation with his announcement on television that he would not seek another term as president.

Johnson retired to his ranch near Johnson City, Texas, to write his memoirs and died four years after leaving office.

BIBLIOGRAPHY

Bornet, Vaughn D., *The Presidency of Lyndon B. Johnson*, 1983; Caro, Robert A., *The Years of Lyndon Johnson: The Path to Power*, vol. 1, 1982, and *Lyndon B. Johnson: Means of Ascent*, vol. 2, 1990; Dugger, Ronnie, *The Politician: The Life and Times of Lyndon Johnson*, 1982; Johnson, Lyndon B., *The Vantage Point: Perspectives of the Presidency*, 1963–1969; Kearns, Doris, *Lyndon Johnson and the American Dream*, 1976; Miller, Merle, *Lyndon: An Oral Biography*, 1980; Redford, Emmette, and Richard T. McCulley, *White House Operations*, 1986; Schandler, Herbert, *The Unmaking of the President: Lyndon Johnson and Vietnam*, 1977; White, Theodore H., *The Making of the President*, 1964.

Johnson, Richard Mentor

(October 17, 1781–November 19, 1850)
Vice President, Senator, Representative

War hero, Kentucky state legislator, member of both houses of the national legislature, and vice president under MARTIN VAN BUREN, Richard Mentor Johnson was born in the frontier settlement of Beargrass (now Louisville), Kentucky. Johnson was admitted to the Kentucky bar in 1802 and established a successful practice before being elected to the state legislature in 1804. Two years later he began his thirty-year national political career by winning a seat in the U.S. House of Representatives as a Democrat.

In the War of 1812 Johnson commanded a regiment of mounted Kentucky riflemen. He was severely wounded leading a charge at the Battle of the Thames, during which he reputedly killed the Shawnee chief Tecumseh. Returning to Congress as a military hero, he supported military pensions, internal improvements, and protective tariffs, but he opposed the second Bank of the United States. He was also strongly in favor of government-sponsored education and played an active role in establishing George Washington University and other institutions.

Johnson resigned his seat in the House in 1819 in order to return to Kentucky, but the Kentucky legislature quickly elected him to the U.S. Senate. Defeated for reelection in 1829, he was promptly returned to the House of Representatives, where he remained until 1837.

A close friendship developed between Johnson and President ANDREW JACKSON. The two men shared common frontier and military backgrounds; moreover, while serving on the committee on military affairs during the 1818 controversy over General Jackson's actions in Florida, Johnson had been the only member of the committee to vote in support of Jackson. Johnson favored all of the Jackson administration's policies and was rewarded in 1836 when Jackson handpicked him as the vice presidential candidate on the successful Democratic ticket with Martin Van Buren. Because he did not secure a majority of votes in the Electoral College, Johnson became the first vice president to be elected by the Senate.

Johnson, a bachelor, was not renominated in 1840. His increasingly eccentric behavior and indiscreet relationships had made him a political liability. Undaunted by his party's rejection, Johnson ran an unsuccessful campaign for vice president anyway, touring the nation to the chant of "Rumpsey, dumpsey, Colonel Johnson shot Tecumseh," and displaying his battle scars. He returned to Kentucky in 1841 and served one more term in the state legislature before his death.

BIBLIOGRAPHY

Meyer, Leland W., *Life and Times of Colonel Richard M. Johnson of Kentucky*, 1966.

Jones, John Winston

(November 22, 1791–January 29, 1848)
Speaker of the House, Representative

Born in Amelia County, Virginia, John Winston Jones graduated from the College of William and Mary in 1810, was admitted to the bar in 1813, and, after establishing his own practice in Chesterfield County, settled at Bellwood, near Petersburg.

In 1818 he was appointed prosecuting attorney for the fifth Virginia judicial circuit, a position he held for seventeen years. In 1829 he was chosen to lead the county's delegation to the state constitutional convention and, in 1834, as a Democrat, was elected to the U.S. House of Representatives.

Jones was reelected to Congress for four successive terms. He served as chairman of the House Ways and Means Committee from 1841 to 1843 and was then elected Speaker. During his term as Speaker from 1843 to 1845, Jones established one important precedent. When his 1842 reelection to Congress was contested, he had the Speaker pro tempore decide which congressmen would serve on the investigating committee. This procedure became the standard practice for choosing committee members when the Speaker might have a personal interest in the outcome of a committee's deliberations.

Jones decided not to seek reelection in 1844 and returned to the practice of law in Chesterfield, but retirement from public service did not follow. Instead, he was unanimously elected to represent Chesterfield in the state legislature, where, from 1846 to 1847, he served as speaker of the House of Delegates.

BIBLIOGRAPHY

Journal of the House of Delegates, 1847–1848; Smith, W. H., *Speakers of the House of Representatives of the U.S.,* 1928.

Jordan, Barbara Charline

(February 21, 1936–   )
Representative

In 1972 Barbara Jordan became the first black woman ever elected to Congress from the Deep South.

Jordan was born in Houston, Texas. She graduated from Texas Southern University in 1956 and earned a law degree at Boston University in 1959. While engaged in private legal practice in Houston, Jordan worked as an administrative assistant to a county judge and became increasingly active in Democratic party politics.

After two unsuccessful efforts to win a seat in the Texas House of Representatives in 1962 and 1964, Jordan won election in 1966 to the state senate. She was the first black woman ever elected to that legislative body. Her political skills proved so strong that no opponent campaigned against her in 1968.

Jordan announced her decision to run for Congress in September 1971. In the May 1972 Democratic primary she defeated three male rivals in the four-candidate race by winning over 80 percent of the vote. She easily defeated her Republican opponent in the November general election, and began her first of three terms in the U.S. House of Representatives in January 1973.

In 1974, as a member of the House Judiciary Committee during the televised Watergate scandal hearings (see RICHARD MILHOUS NIXON), the eloquent and methodical Jordan attracted nationwide attention for her support of articles of impeachment against President Nixon. Two years later, her keynote address to the Democratic national convention won a tremendous ovation from the delegates. Although her political career seemed on the right track for obtaining a seat in the Senate or a cabinet-level appointment, Jordan decided to retire from politics in 1976 and accepted a teaching position at the School of Public Affairs at the University of Texas in Austin.

BIBLIOGRAPHY

Christian Science Monitor, March 18, 1974; *The Ebony Success Library,* vol. 2, 1973; *Washington Post,* October 22, 1972.

Kassebaum, Nancy Landon

(July 29, 1932–   )
Senator

Nancy Landon was born in Topeka, Kansas, the daughter of ALFRED M. LANDON, the Republican presidential candidate defeated by FRANKLIN D. ROOSEVELT in 1936. She earned a bachelor's degree from the University of Kansas in 1954 and two years later obtained a master's degree at the University of Michigan. In 1956 she married Philip Kassebaum. Over the next two decades she served as vice president of Kassebaum Communications (a family-owned concern that operates radio stations KFH and KBRA) and fulfilled a variety of local civic positions.

From 1975 to 1976 Kassebaum worked in the Washington office of Senator James B. Pearson. When Pearson decided not to seek reelection in 1978, Kassebaum announced her candidacy and, capitalizing on her father's fame, won both the Republican primary and the general election (Her campaign slogan was "A Fresh Face, A Trusted Kansas Name"). She was reelected in 1984 and 1990.

In the Senate, Kassebaum has generally voted along conservative Republican party lines. She has advocated reducing government spending instead of raising taxes, but not at the expense of the defense budget. Her record on feminist issues is mixed. She has opposed efforts to extend the time limit for obtaining ratification of the Equal Rights Amendment, but she has supported the federal funding of abortion on a limited basis. In 1980 she obtained a seat on the prestigious Senate Foreign Relations Committee and became a strong advocate of the need for strategic arms reductions.

BIBLIOGRAPHY

Christian Science Monitor, January 9, 1979; *Ladies Home Journal,* January 1970 and April 1979; *Washington Post,* November 30, 1978; *Working Woman,* October 1979.

Kefauver, Carey Estes

(July 26, 1903–August 10, 1963)
Senator, Representative

Estes Kefauver was born near Madison-ville, Tennessee. After graduating from the University of Tennessee in 1924 and Yale Law School in 1927, he became a successful banking and corporate lawyer in Chattanooga.

Active in local government reform efforts and an enthusiastic New Dealer, Kefauver won a special election to the U.S. House of Representatives in 1939. After five terms in the House, he was elected to the Senate in 1948 and reelected in 1954 and 1960.

In Congress Kefauver was one of the few Southerners to support labor unions and the protection of civil rights and civil liberties. He established a national political reputation as chairman of the Senate Crime Investigation Committee when the committee's sensational hearings exploring connections between underworld figures and political leaders were televised in 1950 and 1951.

Kefauver lost two tries to secure the Democratic party's presidential nomination in 1952 and 1956 to ADLAI STEVENSON, but he did manage to defeat Senator JOHN F. KENNEDY to win the vice presidential nomination in 1956.

However, the Stevenson–Kefauver ticket was buried in the landslide reelection of popular Republican president DWIGHT D. EISENHOWER.

As chairman of the Senate Antitrust and Monopoly Subcommittee during its investigations of monopolistic activities of organized professional sports and alleged price fixing by the drug, automobile, and steel industries, Kefauver again attracted national attention. He also helped achieve the ratification of the Twenty-fourth Amendment to the Constitution, which abolished the poll tax, and the passage of the Kefauver–Harris Drug Safety Act of 1962.

BIBLIOGRAPHY

Fontenay, Charles L., *Estes Kefauver: A Biography,* 1980; Gorman, Joseph Bruce, *Kefauver: A Political Biography,* 1971; Kefauver, Estes, *Crime in America,* 1951; Kefauver, Estes, and Jack Levine, *A Twentieth-Century Congress,* 1947; Kefauver, Estes, and Irene Till, *In a Few Hands: Monopoly Power in America,* 1965.

Keifer, Joseph Warren

(January 30, 1836–April 22, 1932)
Speaker of the House, Representative

Joseph W. Keifer was born in Bethel Township, Ohio. In 1858, after attending Antioch College for less than a year and working for two years in a Springfield law office, he was admitted to the Ohio bar. Keifer practiced law for the rest of his life in Springfield.

After serving with distinction as a volunteer in the Civil War, Keifer became active in local Republican party politics. He served in the Ohio Senate in 1868 and 1869, and won election in 1876 to the first of four consecutive terms in the U.S. House of Representatives. Keifer joined the Stalwart faction (see ROSCOE CONKLING) of the Republican party and in 1881 was elected Speaker. During his two-year term as Speaker, the House adopted a cloture rule, the parliamentary procedure by which debate is closed and the measure under discussion is brought up for an immediate vote. The goal of the cloture rule was to restrict the filibuster. However, Keifer's efforts to implement the new rule were not successful because he lacked the political skill to secure the required number of votes to invoke it. Building coalitions of legislators around issues and particular bills by negotiating compromises so that a consensus could emerge was a skill Keifer never mastered. Instead, by the end of his term as Speaker, he had even lost the support of members of his own party due to his narrow partisan committee appointments.

Keifer failed to win the Republican nomination for a fifth term in 1884, but he returned to the national political scene in 1904 by winning the first of three more consecutive terms (1905–1911) in the House.

BIBLIOGRAPHY

Fuller, H. B., *The Speakers of the House*, 1909; Keifer, Joseph Warren, *Four Years of War: A Political History of Slavery in the United States with a Narrative of the Campaigns and Battles of the Civil War in Which the Author Took Part: 1861–1865*, 1900.

Kellogg, Frank Billings

(December 22, 1856–December 21, 1937)
Secretary of State, Diplomat, Senator

Frank Billings Kellogg was born in Potsdam, New York, but moved to Olmsted County, Minnesota, when he was nine. In Minnesota he worked on his father's farm until he was ready to study law. Admitted to the bar in 1877, he was elected a year later as the attorney for Rochester, and in 1881 as state attorney general. In 1887 he joined a St. Paul law firm that represented large railroad and mining corporations. The success he achieved brought him wealth and power within the Republican party. Appointed special counsel to the U.S. attorney general in 1904, Kellogg played a major role in the government's successful prosecution of the Standard Oil and General Paper Compa-

Library of Congress

nies for violation of the antitrust laws (see EDWARD DOUGLASS WHITE).

Kellogg won election to the U.S. Senate in 1916 but failed to win reelection in 1922. After serving as ambassador to Great Britain from 1923 to 1925, President CALVIN COOLIDGE appointed him secretary of state. During his term as secretary of state, Kellogg improved relations with Mexico and helped negotiate a settlement to the Tacna-Arica dispute between Chile and Peru. His most important achievement was an international agreement to end war, known as the Kellogg-Briand Pact, which was signed in Paris in 1928.

In honor of his efforts to resolve international conflicts through diplomacy, Kellogg was awarded the Nobel Peace Prize in 1929, the same year he resigned from office. Before he retired from public life in 1935, Kellogg served as a judge on the Permanent Court of International Justice for five years.

BIBLIOGRAPHY

Bryn-Jones, David, *Frank B. Kellogg,* 1937; Ellis, L. Ethan, *Frank B. Kellogg and American Foreign Relations, 1925–1929,* 1961; Ferrel, Robert H., *Kellogg and Stimson,* 1961.

Kemp, Jack French

(July 13, 1935–)
Secretary of Housing and Urban Development, Representative

Jack Kemp was a star professional football quarterback before he embarked upon a political career as a conservative Republican congressman.

Kemp was born in Los Angeles. He graduated from Occidental College in 1957, served a year in the army, and from 1958 to 1969 played professional football as a quarterback for several teams, in particular, the Buffalo Bills. In 1965 he was named the American Football League's player of the year and was elected president of the league's players association.

In 1970 Kemp won election to Congress from New York's thirty-ninth congressional district. He developed great support among Buffalo's blue-collar Democrats, an early sign of the disintegration of the Democratic party's once solid working-class electoral base. He was reelected every two years thereafter until he decided not to seek reelection in 1988 in order to run for the Republican presidential nomination.

During the 1970s, anger at taxes was one of the strongest political sentiments in the United States. Kemp, who described himself as a "neo-conservative," was able to achieve national prominence at the time for his efforts in Congress to implement a large federal tax reduction for individuals and businesses. Kemp had embraced the "supply-side" thesis of economist Arthur B. Laffer, which held that the federal government's tax rates had reached the point of diminishing returns. Therefore, it was argued, cutting taxes would actually result in more revenue by increasing prosperity and the willingness of people to pay their fair share.

Kemp, along with his cosponsor, Senator William V. Roth of Delaware, introduced a bill in 1978 calling for a 33 percent reduction in taxes for individuals and a more moderate percentage drop for corporations. The Kemp–Roth bill languished in Congress until it was embraced by Republican presidential candidate RONALD REAGAN in 1980. Kemp's tax-cutting stand, conservative voting record, and youthful appearance made him a strong contender for the 1980 vice presidential Republican nomination, but Ronald Reagan chose GEORGE BUSH instead. Eight years later, Kemp was defeated by George Bush for the Republican presidential nomination.

In November 1988, President-elect Bush appointed Kemp secretary of the Department of Housing and Urban Development (HUD). As secretary of HUD, Kemp worked to transfer the ownership of government-subsidized housing to individual tenants.

BIBLIOGRAPHY

Kemp, Jack, *An American Renaissance: A Strategy for the 1980s,* 1979.

Kendall, Amos

(August 16, 1789–November 12, 1869)
Postmaster General

Amos Kendall was the most influential member of President ANDREW JACKSON's unofficial Kitchen Cabinet.

Kendall was born in Dunstable, Massachusetts, and graduated from Dartmouth College in 1811. He moved to Kentucky in 1814 and played an important role in helping Andrew Jackson to carry Kentucky in the presidential election of 1828. Jackson appointed him postmaster general in 1834, the post he also held in the administration of MARTIN VAN BUREN, Jackson's designated successor.

As an administrator, Kendall was noted for his honesty, organizational skills, and management expertise. But it was in his unofficial role as one of Jackson's closest advisers and perhaps the most influential member of the so-called Kitchen Cabinet for which Kendall is recalled. Kendall frequently wrote Jackson's state papers, letters, and speeches. He was the principal author of Jackson's message in 1832 announcing his decision to veto the recharter-

ing of the Bank of the United States (see NICHOLAS BIDDLE and ROGER BROOKE TANEY).

Back in private life, in 1845 he became the business manager and legal representative of F. B. Morse, the inventor of the telegraph. By 1859 the invention of the telegraph had made both Morse and Kendall wealthy.

The threat of the secession of the South caused Kendall to become politically active again. Although a Democrat with reservations about ABRAHAM LINCOLN's handling of the Civil War, Kendall opposed secession and vigorously supported the North.

After the war Kendall devoted his attention to religion and philanthropy.

BIBLIOGRAPHY

Stickney, William (ed.), *Autobiography of Amos Kendall*, 1872.

Kennan, George Frost

(February 16, 1904–   )
Diplomat

In a famous memorandum cabled from Moscow and published anonymously in *Foreign Affairs* in July 1947, George F. Kennan defined the central goal of U.S. foreign policy during the cold war—containment of the Soviet Union in its postwar sphere of influence. Kennan's recommendation provided the rationale for the Truman Doctrine (see HARRY S TRUMAN), the Marshall Plan (see GEORGE CATLETT MARSHALL and TRUMAN), and the North Atlantic Treaty Organization (see TRUMAN).

Kennan's advice was misconstrued to justify a massive buildup of U.S. military forces, a situation Kennan deplored as wasteful and counterproductive. He perceived the Soviet threat to be more political than military, and he thought that the economic well-being of the West, more than its military might, would deflate the Soviet challenge. Kennan would spend much of the rest of his life (after he was identified as the author of the famous memo) cautioning policymakers on the dangers of militarizing the conflict with the Soviets and relying upon nuclear weapons for security.

Kennan was born in Milwaukee. He graduated from Princeton University in 1925 and entered the U.S. foreign service the next year. As a vice consul, he was assigned first to Geneva and then Hamburg in 1927, Berlin in 1928, and Estonia and Lithuania in 1929. From 1929 until 1931 Kennan studied Russian language, culture, and history at the Berlin Seminar for Oriental Languages and the University of Berlin through a special program designed to provide the State Department with experts on the Soviet Union. During the 1930s, Kennan completed tours of duty in Moscow, Vienna, and Prague.

When the United States and Germany declared war in December 1941, Kennan was interned by the Nazis at Bad Nauheim. After being repatriated in June 1942, he served in neutral Portugal until late 1943, when he became counselor of the American delegation to the European Advisory Commission. From May 1944 to April 1946 he was minister-counselor in Moscow. Upon his return to the United States in 1946, he became a lecturer on foreign policy issues at the National War College in Washington, D.C., for a year, then director of the policy-planning staff of the State Department responsible for long-range planning of U.S. action in foreign affairs. It was at this time that his article, signed by Mr. "X," was published in the journal *Foreign Affairs,* advocating the containment of the Soviet Union's expansionist efforts.

From 1949 until his appointment as ambassador to the Soviet Union in 1952, Kennan was one of Secretary of State DEAN ACHESON's principal advisers. He served less than a year in Moscow as ambassador before the Soviet government demanded his replacement because he had spoken out against the treatment of diplomats in the Soviet Union. Kennan left the foreign service in 1953 to accept a faculty appointment at the Institute for Advanced Study at Princeton.

In 1957, in a series of lectures heard over the British Broadcasting Corporation, Kennan attacked what he viewed as a perversion of his containment policy toward the Soviet Union into a dangerous military confrontational situation that exposed the world to nuclear devastation. He advocated a policy of coexistence with the Soviet Union based upon a realistic assessment of the respective power and interests of that country and the United States. This lecture series, *Russia, the Atom and the West* (1958), like many others he delivered, was later published as a book. Kennan was also awarded the Pulitzer Prize in history in 1957 for *Russia Leaves the War* (1956). In these and other works, he argued for "realism" in foreign affairs and against the misguided "idealism" and moralism that, he felt, marred the foreign policy of WOODROW WILSON and like-minded presidents.

During the next two decades, through numerous speeches, lectures, and publications, Kennan offered a number of controversial foreign policy suggestions that eventually came to be shared by many Americans. They included the mutual withdrawal of American and Soviet troops from Europe, the reunification of Germany as a neutral nation, the avoidance of involvement in Vietnam (see LYNDON BAINES JOHNSON and RICHARD MILHOUS NIXON), the abolishment of nuclear weapons, and the protection of the environment from the ravages of industrialization.

BIBLIOGRAPHY

Gaddis, John Lewis, *Strategies of Containment: A Critical Appraisal of Postwar American National Security Policy,* 1982; Gellman, Barton D., *Contending with Kennan: Toward a Philosophy of American Power,* 1984; Kennan, George F., *Memoirs, 1925–1950,* 1967–1972, and *Sketches from a Life,* 1989; Mayers, David, *George Kennan and the Dilemmas of U.S. Foreign Policy,* 1989; Stephanson, Anders, *Kennan and the Art of Foreign Policy,* 1989.

Kennedy, Edward Moore

(February 22, 1932–   )
Senator

As a U.S. senator and leader of the liberal wing of the Democratic party, Edward (Ted) Moore Kennedy, the brother of assassinated President JOHN KENNEDY and Senator ROBERT KENNEDY, has played an important role in national politics since their deaths.

The youngest of the nine Kennedy children, Edward was born in Boston, Massachusetts. Although suspended from Harvard College in 1951 for cheating, he returned and graduated from Harvard in 1956 after completing a two-year stint in the U.S. Army as a private. Three years later, he earned his law degree at the University of Virginia.

In 1958 Ted managed his brother John Kennedy's reelection campaign to the U.S. Senate, and two years later oversaw Kennedy's presidential campaign in the West. Ted began his career in the Senate in 1962 by winning the special election to complete the term of his brother. Two years later, at age thirty-two, he won election to a full term in the Senate.

In the Senate Kennedy established a reputation for supporting liberal social reform legislation. He was the front-runner for the 1972 Democratic presidential nomination after the election of Republican president RICHARD NIXON in 1968, but he was forced to withdraw his name for consideration after he accepted responsibility for the tragic death of Mary Jo Kopechne in July 1969.

Kopechne, a passenger in a car Kennedy was driving, drowned when Kennedy lost control of the car. The vehicle plunged off a bridge on Chappaquiddick Island near Martha's Vineyard, Massachusetts, into eight feet of water. Kennedy escaped unhurt, but he was unable to answer questions about why it took him until the next day to seek help and to report the accident to the police. Although he pleaded guilty to leaving the scene of an accident, Kennedy was not held responsible for Kopechne's death. He was reelected to the Senate the following year. Nevertheless, unanswered questions about the cause of the tragedy seriously undermined Kennedy's desirability as a national candidate. In addition, Kennedy lost his bid to be reelected majority whip in the Senate.

Despite this and other personal crises, Kennedy won reelection to the Senate in 1976 and became chairman of the powerful Judiciary Committee in 1979. During this time, he became disenchanted with the domestic and foreign policies of fellow Democrat President JIMMY CARTER. A split developed within the Democratic party between those, like Kennedy, who wanted to maintain the party's commitment to an activist social welfare spending program and those, like Jimmy Carter, who wanted to curtail government power in the interest of fiscal prudence, lower spending, and laissez-faire economics. Kennedy launched an effort in 1979 to prevent Carter's renomination for another term by winning the presidential nomination for himself. Kennedy waged a vigorous campaign and almost succeeded in accomplishing his goal. Ironically, by weakening Carter, Kennedy helped elect the conservative Republican candidate, RONALD REAGAN.

During the Republican administrations of Presidents Ronald Reagan and GEORGE BUSH, Kennedy, who won reelection to the Senate in 1982 and in 1988, was an important critic and spokesman for the interests of the liberal elements within the Democratic party. While he has been associated with little successful legislation over the years, he has supported such measures as national health insurance, full employment, affirmative action, gun control, détente with the Soviet Union (see HENRY

ALFRED KISSINGER), and opposition to the Contras in Latin America.

Public doubts about Ted Kennedy's ability and character have haunted him throughout his career, but few of those doubts have affected Massachusetts voters, who have made him electorally unbeatable for thirty years.

BIBLIOGRAPHY

Honan, William H., *Ted Kennedy: Portrait of a Survivor,* 1972; Lerner, Max, *Ted and the Kennedy Legend: A Study in Character and Destiny,* 1980; Levin, Murray B., *Edward Kennedy: The Myth of Leadership,* 1980.

Kennedy, John Fitzgerald

(May 29, 1917–November 22, 1963)
President, Senator, Representative

The administration of John F. Kennedy, famous for its youth and style, ushered in a period of hope, vigor, and commitment for the country that would be cruelly cut short by Kennedy's assassination and more critically evaluated with the passage of time. John F. Kennedy, the youngest man ever elected president, was born in Brookline, Massachusetts, into a large, Irish Catholic family. His father, JOSEPH P. KENNEDY, stressed self-improvement and public service in a spirit of competition and victory. Due to a variety of illnesses, Kennedy spent much of his childhood sick in bed surrounded by books. After illness forced him to drop out of the London School of Economics and Princeton University, he graduated from Harvard College in 1940. His senior essay, *While England Slept,* briefly became a best-selling book.

Kennedy tried to enlist in the army in 1941, but he was rejected because of a back injury

Courtesy John F. Kennedy Library

he had sustained while playing football at Harvard. As a result of his father's influence, he managed to enlist in the navy. In 1943, after the PT boat he was commanding was sunk by a Japanese destroyer, he heroically saved the life of one of his crew members. In the process, however, he aggravated his back ailment and contracted—and almost died from—malaria. Painful complications from his war injuries plagued him for the rest of his life.

In 1946 Kennedy was elected as a Massachusetts Democrat to his first of three terms in the U.S. House of Representatives. In 1952, as a result of diligent campaigning and his father's money, Kennedy defeated the incumbent, HENRY CABOT LODGE, JR., for a seat in the Senate. The next year he married the Washington socialite Jacqueline Lee Bouvier and, while recuperating from back surgery, wrote *Profiles in Courage,* a book of political sketches that won the Pulitzer Prize.

After an unsuccessful attempt to become ADLAI STEVENSON's vice presidential running mate in 1956, Kennedy's political career was buoyed by an exceptionally wide victory margin in his reelection to the Senate in 1958. Kennedy decided to seek the Democratic party nomination for president in 1960. After defeating HUBERT HUMPHREY in the primaries, and LYNDON JOHNSON and Stevenson at the convention, Kennedy was nominated to run against RICHARD NIXON. During the campaign Kennedy faced the challenges of his young age (he was forty-three) and his Roman Catholic religion by openly confronting the concerns of voters in speeches and during four televised debates. He was narrowly elected by a margin of only 118,550 popular votes out of 68.3 million votes cast.

Kennedy brought a refreshing vigor, intelligence, and style to the presidency. In his inaugural speech, he inspired Americans to public service with the famous line "Ask not what your country can do for you, ask what you can do for your country." As president, he projected an image of a leader directly involved in formulating national and international policy.

Kennedy's rhetoric did not always match his actions. He promised a new American attitude toward Latin America based on trust and partnership through the Alliance for Progress, a program of U.S. aid calling for development and democracy. His efforts, however, were undermined by the disastrous U.S.-sponsored invasion of Cuba in the Bay of Pigs in 1961 to bring about the downfall of Fidel Castro. He opposed the use of American combat troops in Southeast Asia, yet he gradually increased the U.S. presence there until by the end of 1963 there were 16,732 military advisers in South Vietnam.

Relations with the Soviet Union were complicated by Kennedy's decision to increase defense spending for both conventional weapons and intercontinental ballistic missile development. Soviet leader Nikita Khrushchev misunderstood Kennedy's failure to ensure the success of the Bay of Pigs invasion as weakness and precipitated confrontations in Berlin and Cuba.

Khrushchev had been threatening to sign a separate peace treaty with East Germany, and when he ordered East Germany to build a wall in 1961 to cut off contact between East and West Berlin, Kennedy responded by calling up military reserve units and increasing defense spending. Khrushchev did not sign a treaty, and the crisis cooled. In 1962 American intelligence discovered sites in Cuba being prepared for the installation of Soviet intermediate-range ballistic missiles. Kennedy informed Khrushchev that the United States would not allow the missile sites to become operational and announced a naval arms blockade of Cuba. For thirteen days the world waited for Khrushchev's reaction as Soviet ships loaded with missiles steamed toward the island. Finally, the Soviet ships began to turn around; and on October 27, Kennedy and Khrushchev reached an acceptable compromise. The U.S. promised not to support any further invasions of Cuba and to remove some intermediate-range missiles in Turkey, and the Soviet Union agreed to dismantle the missile sites.

The Cuban Missile Crisis, once regarded as Kennedy's "finest hour," has led to sharp criticism by historians in recent years of Kennedy's willingness to risk war. Both Khrushchev and Kennedy seemed to have been humbled by the crisis. This led in 1963 to the first thaw in the cold war, when Great Britain and the Soviet Union joined the United States in banning nuclear tests in the atmosphere, in outer space, and underwater. But Kennedy's foreign policy idealism is perhaps best remembered for his creation of the Peace Corps and his decision to commit the United States to a race with the Soviet Union to put a man on the moon by 1970.

Domestic politics were dominated by the economy and the civil rights movement. Kennedy endorsed the use of tax cuts and increases in government spending to stimulate the economy. By 1964 the unemployment rate had dropped from 8.1 percent to 5.2 percent. Because Congress was dominated by a coalition of conservative southern Democrats and Republicans, Kennedy's initial civil rights focus was on executive rather than legislative action. His principal ally was his brother Attorney General ROBERT KENNEDY. Beginning in 1962, with the desegregation of the University of Mississippi, their efforts included an executive order ending discrimination in federally funded housing, the establishment of the President's Committee on Equal Employment Opportunity, the extension of the right to vote for blacks, the appointment of an unprecedented number of blacks to public office, and the filing of proposals for more complete civil rights legislation. It should be noted, however, that contemporary historians now view Kennedy's civil rights efforts as halfhearted and vacillating.

On November 22, 1963, while riding in a motorcade in Dallas, Texas, Kennedy was shot and killed by Lee Harvey Oswald. The magnitude of the tragedy and the speed with which the Warren Commission (headed by EARL WARREN) was forced to work in determining the cause of Kennedy's death have led people ever since to doubt the commission's conclusion that Oswald acted alone.

BIBLIOGRAPHY

Branch, Taylor, *Parting of the Waters: America in the King Years, 1954–63,* 1988; Schlesinger, Arthur, Jr., *A Thousand Days: John F. Kennedy in the White House,* 1965; Sorensen, Theodore C., *Kennedy,* 1965; Wills, Garry, *The Kennedy Imprisonment: A Meditation on Power,* 1982.

Kennedy, Joseph

(September 6, 1888–November 18, 1969)
Diplomat

The founder of the Kennedy political dynasty was the son of a Boston tavern owner and political ward boss. Joseph Kennedy graduated from Harvard in 1912. A stockbroker at thirty, he made a fortune as a master of the stock pool, the then-legal device in which a few traders conspired to inflate a stock's price, selling out just before other speculators caught on. He also made money as a movie producer in the 1920s and has been accused of profiting handsomely from illegal liquor trade during Prohibition. The bootlegging charges have never been proven, and it is more likely that he made his first millions through shrewd investments and skillful playing (and manipulation) of the thinly regulated stock market. Kennedy's intimate knowledge of the market and his political connections won him the chairmanship of the newly established Securities and Exchange Commission under FRANKLIN D. ROOSEVELT in 1934.

Kennedy's only other significant political involvement was as ambassador to Great Britain from 1937 to 1940. He argued against the United States becoming involved in World War II, on the grounds that such involvement would not save Great Britain from the Nazis. At odds with Roosevelt concerning aid to England, Kennedy resigned as ambassador in November 1940.

During the late 1930s and 1940s Kennedy invested in real estate. In 1945 he made the purchase that became the foundation of the massive Kennedy fortune: for $12.5 million he bought the Merchandise Mart in Chicago, a huge wholesale emporium that had cost over

$30 million to build. Within a few years, the annual gross rents exceeded the purchase price, and by 1957 *Fortune* magazine estimated Kennedy to be worth between $200 million and $400 million.

Although Kennedy established a few small charitable trusts, most notably for the retarded (his daughter Rosemary was retarded), he put most of his money into trusts for his family and used millions to finance the political careers of his sons. JOHN F. KENNEDY became the first Irish Catholic ever elected president, and his two other sons, ROBERT KENNEDY and EDWARD KENNEDY, were elected to the Senate.

BIBLIOGRAPHY

Beschloss, Michael R., *Kennedy and Roosevelt: The Uneasy Alliance,* 1980; Goodwin, Doris Kearns, *The Kennedys and the Fitzgeralds,* 1987; Koskoff, David E., *Joseph P. Kennedy: A Life and Times,* 1974; Wills, Garry, *The Kennedy Imprisonment: A Meditation on Power,* 1982.

Kennedy, Robert Francis

(November 20, 1925–June 6, 1968)
Attorney General, Senator

Library of Congress

Robert (Bobby) Kennedy served as campaign adviser and attorney general for his brother JOHN KENNEDY. After President Kennedy's assassination, Robert was elected to the U.S. Senate from New York. As a liberal Democrat strongly committed to civil rights and aiding the poor, he assumed an important place in national politics. Viewed as his brother's political heir, Kennedy decided to run for president in March 1968 after Senator EUGENE MCCARTHY's upset primary election victory in New Hampshire. After winning the important California primary on June 4, 1968, Bobby Kennedy was assassinated by Sirhan B. Sirhan, a young Jordanian Arab outraged by Kennedy's pro-Israeli sentiments.

Born in Brookline, Massachusetts, into a large, politically powerful Irish Catholic family, Kennedy attended Harvard College until 1944, when he entered the navy. He later graduated from Harvard in 1948 and earned his law degree from the University of Virginia Law School in 1951.

From 1951 to 1952 Kennedy helped prosecute income tax cases as an attorney in the U.S. Department of Justice. After managing his brother John's successful election to the Senate in 1952, Kennedy became an attorney for Republican JOSEPH MCCARTHY's Permanent Senate Subcommittee on Investigations. He resigned in 1953, along with the other Democratic members of the committee, in protest against its excesses. He rejoined the committee in 1954 as counsel for the Democratic minority.

In 1957 Kennedy became chief counsel of the Senate Select Committee on Improper Activities in the Labor or Management Field. In this capacity he began a long fight with Teamsters Union boss James Hoffa. Kennedy resigned from the committee in 1960 to manage his brother's successful presidential campaign. The decision of John F. Kennedy to name his brother as his attorney general aroused great criticism. Even thirty-six-year-old Robert thought the appointment ill-advised, but he gave in. "I saw nothing wrong," quipped John Kennedy, "with giving him [Robert] a little experience [as Attorney General] before he goes out to practice law." Criticism died down when Bobby Kennedy proved to be an able head of the Justice Department and an obviously crucial adviser to his brother, notably during the Cuban Missile Crisis (see JOHN FITZGERALD KENNEDY).

After President Kennedy's assassination in November 1963, Kennedy continued to serve in LYNDON B. JOHNSON's cabinet until 1964, when he left to run a successful campaign in New York for the U.S. Senate. At first a supporter and then an outspoken critic of the Johnson administration's handling of the war in Vietnam, Kennedy announced that he would be a candidate for president in March 1968 after Senator Eugene McCarthy's upset primary election victory in New Hampshire showed that Lyndon Johnson was vulnerable. Although Kennedy quickly eclipsed Eugene McCarthy as the principal alternative to Vice President HUBERT H. HUMPHREY for the Democratic party's presidential nomination, he still had not managed to win the support of party regulars when he was assassinated.

Bobby Kennedy, far more than his brother, wanted to improve the circumstances of the nation's poor, especially after the ghetto riots of the mid-1960s. His campaign in 1968 inspired great hope and emotion, making his assassination all the more shattering. He was buried near his brother in Arlington National Cemetery.

BIBLIOGRAPHY

Halberstam, David, *The Unfinished Odyssey of Robert Kennedy*, 1969; Navasky, Victor, *Kennedy Justice*, 1977; Schlesinger, Arthur M., Jr., *Robert Kennedy and His Times*, 1969; Sorensen, Theodore C., *The Kennedy Legacy*, 1969; Wofford, Harris, *Of Kennedys and Kings: Making Sense of the Sixties*, 1980.

Kerr, Michael Crawford

(March 15, 1827–August 19, 1876)
Speaker of the House, Representative

Michael C. Kerr was born in Titusville, Pennsylvania. After graduating from the University of Louisville in Kentucky in 1851, he was admitted to the Kentucky bar and in 1852 established a practice in New Albany, Indiana. Two years later, Kerr was elected the city attorney of New Albany. In 1856, after serving a year as the prosecuting attorney of Floyd County, he won election as a Democrat to the state legislature, where he served until 1860.

During the Civil War Kerr held the lucrative position of reporter to the Indiana Supreme Court. In 1864 he won the first of four consecutive terms in the U.S. House of Representatives. During the Reconstruction era Kerr supported the Democratic party position and advocated conciliatory treatment of the South. He was defeated for reelection in 1872 as a result of the redistricting of the state, but was elected to a fifth term in the House in 1874.

On December 6, 1875, Kerr was named Speaker of the House. Although he became increasingly incapacitated due to illness almost immediately after his election, Kerr continued to serve as Speaker until his death.

BIBLIOGRAPHY

Smith, William Henry, *Speakers of the House of Representatives of the United States,* 1928.

King, Rufus

(March 24, 1755–April 29, 1827)
Diplomat, Candidate for President, Senator

A great orator and diplomat, Rufus King was the last Federalist candidate for president.

Born in Scarboro, Maine, King graduated from Harvard College in 1777. Admitted to the bar in 1780, he served in the Massachusetts provincial legislature from 1783 to 1784 and as a delegate to the Continental Congress from 1784 to 1787.

Although at first opposed to the rewriting of the Articles of Confederation, after his arrival as a delegate to the Constitutional Convention he became a very eloquent and persuasive spokesman for a strong central government. After helping to secure the ratification of the Constitution by Massachusetts, King moved to New York City.

Shortly after his arrival in New York, King was elected to the state legislature, and then as one of New York's first U.S. senators from 1789 to 1796. As a Federalist leader, he played an important role in securing the passage of ALEXANDER HAMILTON's financial programs. From 1796 to 1803 he was minister to Great Britain.

After being defeated as the Federalist vice presidential candidate with CHARLES PINCKNEY in 1804, he retired to his Long Island home. Four years later, he tried for the same office only to lose again. Vigorously opposed to the War of 1812 (see JAMES MADISON), King returned to the Senate in 1813 to lead the opposition. However, once it became clear that the United States had been forced into a defensive position, he became a strong supporter of the need to prosecute the war to an honorable conclusion.

In 1816 he became the last candidate the dying Federalist party would ever nominate for president. Remaining in the Senate after his loss to JAMES MONROE, King turned his eloquence against the institution of slavery. He opposed the Missouri Compromise of 1820 (see HENRY CLAY) because it failed to offer any kind of long-range solution to the slavery question. He proposed a plan instead to pay for the emancipation of all slaves from the sale of public lands and their resettlement outside of the United States.

In 1825 President Adams again appointed him minister to England, but he soon became ill and had to return home, where he died.

BIBLIOGRAPHY

Ernst, Robert, *Rufus King: American Federalist,* 1968; King, Charles R., *Life and Correspondence of Rufus King,* 1894.

King, William Rufus de Vane

(April 7, 1786–April 18, 1853)
Vice President, Diplomat, Senator, Representative

Born in Sampson County, North Carolina, William R. King graduated from the University of North Carolina in 1803 and was admitted to the bar in 1806. He was elected to two terms in the North Carolina state legislature and served in the U.S. House of Representatives from 1811 to 1816. King resigned from the House in order to serve as William Pinckney's secretary of the U.S. legation in Naples and St. Petersburg.

In 1818 King returned from abroad to live in Alabama, where he was elected as one of the state's first U.S. senators the following year. A loyal follower of ANDREW JACKSON, King served as president pro tempore for five years.

King had been in the Senate nearly twenty-five years when, in 1844, President JOHN TYLER appointed him minister to France, where he worked successfully to prevent French interference in the U.S. annexation of Texas (see JAMES KNOX POLK). Returning to the Senate in 1848, he supported the Compromise of 1850 (see HENRY CLAY and MILLARD FILLMORE) and worked for the ratification of the Clayton-Bulwer Treaty (see JOHN MIDDLETON CLAYTON).

Elected vice president as FRANKLIN PIERCE'S running mate in 1852, King was allowed by a special act of Congress to take his oath of office in March 1853 in Havana, Cuba, where he had gone in a futile effort to cure his tuberculosis. He died in Alabama the following month, from which time the country was without a vice president until 1857.

BIBLIOGRAPHY

"William Rufus de Vane King," *History of Alabama and Dictionary of Alabama Biography,* vol. 3, 1921; Young, Donald, *American Roulette, The History and Dilemma of the Vice Presidency,* 1924.

Kirkpatrick, Jeane Duane Jordan

(November 19, 1926–   )
Diplomat

Jeane Duane Jordan (Kirkpatrick) was born in Duncan, Oklahoma. After graduating from Barnard College in 1948, she obtained her master's degree in political science from Columbia University in 1950. Five years later, she married Evron Kirkpatrick, a fellow professor and the future director of the American Political Science Association. Kirkpatrick earned her Ph.D. in 1968 at Columbia University.

While a professor at Georgetown University from 1967 to 1981, Kirkpatrick became active in Democratic party politics. In 1972 she formed the Coalition for a Democratic Majority to counteract what she deemed to be the dangerous "soft on communism" influence of Senator GEORGE MCGOVERN and his supporters within the Democratic party.

During President JIMMY CARTER's administration, Kirkpatrick, describing herself as a "neoconservative," attracted national attention for her harsh criticism of her fellow Democrat's foreign policy stand on human rights. Kirkpatrick claimed that Carter attacked human rights violations in right-wing military dictatorships that supported U.S. foreign policy objectives but overlooked them in communist dictatorships. She was one of the first foreign policy experts to introduce the distinction between authoritarian (noncommunist) and totalitarian (communist) regimes, arguing the former could be reformed but the latter could not. This distinction became Republican President RONALD REAGAN's justification for aiding noncommunist dictatorships.

President Reagan appointed Kirkpatrick U.S. ambassador to the United Nations in 1980. She served in that post from 1981 to 1985. Shortly after her return to academic life, Kirkpatrick joined the Republican party.

BIBLIOGRAPHY

Kirkpatrick, Jean, "Projecting and Protecting U.S. Interests in the U.N.," *Vital Speeches*, February 1, 1988, "Advice and Consent in Foggy Bottom," *U.S. News and World Report*, February 8, 1988, and "Beyond the Cold War," *Foreign Affairs*, Winter 1990; Green, Philip, "A Sort of Memoir," *Nation*, August 29, 1987.

Kissinger, Henry Alfred

(May 27, 1923–)
Secretary of State

D r. Henry Kissinger was the principal architect of U.S. foreign policy during the administrations of Republican Presidents RICHARD NIXON and GERALD FORD. For his efforts to negotiate a settlement of the Vietnam War (see LYNDON BAINES JOHNSON and RICHARD MILHOUS NIXON), he was awarded the Nobel Peace Prize in 1973.

Kissinger was born in Fürth, Germany, and immigrated with his parents to New York in 1938 to escape Nazi persecution. After serving in the U.S. Army and becoming a naturalized citizen during World War II, Kissinger obtained his B.A. in 1950, M.A. in 1952, and Ph.D. in 1954 from Harvard University.

While at Harvard, Kissinger cultivated political ties to the Council on Foreign Relations and to NELSON ROCKEFELLER. These connections brought him funds to write books that attracted wide attention. The first, *Nuclear Weapons and Foreign Policy* (1957), attracted wide attention and made him a recognized authority on international relations and nuclear weapons. The second, *The Necessity of Choice* (1961), argued that the United States should have a number of different options for responding to the Soviet threat in addition to the brinkmanship and massive retaliation approach employed during the administration of DWIGHT D. EISENHOWER.

While teaching at Harvard from 1957 to 1969, Kissinger was a consultant on foreign policy matters for both presidents JOHN F. KENNEDY and Lyndon B. Johnson. Kissinger's "flexible response" doctrine became the core of Kennedy's defense policy in 1961. In several more books on foreign policy issues, Kissinger outlined an approach that rested on his admiration for nineteenth-century balance-of-power schemes in which a handful of world powers, carefully balanced against each other, preserved world peace. Preserving such a balance in the modern world, and preserving peace, were more important to Kissinger than human rights or any kind of redistribution of power from the larger to the smaller nations.

In 1969 Republican President Richard Nixon appointed Kissinger assistant to the president for national security affairs and executive secretary of the National Security

Council. Kissinger's remarkable skills at political infighting and his sheer intellect combined to enable him to outwit far more experienced public servants. His most important task was to find a way to win a "peace with honor" (Nixon's campaign promise) in Vietnam. He played a vital role in forming the policies that led to the end of the draft, Vietnamization (withdrawal of American combat troops from South Vietnam), and escalation of the war in Southeast Asia (carrying the war to Cambodia in order to attack communist supply bases). He also conducted secret meetings with representatives of North Vietnam that culminated in a cease-fire agreement.

In large part because of him, the National Security adviser position came to rival secretary of state for importance and influence. This development also enlarged the area of government hidden from public oversight and, in combination with Kissinger's penchant for secrecy, raised troubling questions about accountability and the possibility of Democratic control of foreign policy. Kissinger also played a major role in the successful opening of diplomatic relations between China and the United States in 1971 and in the implementation of the policy of coexistence with the Soviet Union known as détente.

At the beginning of his second term in 1973, President Nixon appointed Kissinger secretary of state. He was the first foreign-born person to ever hold the office. That year Kissinger and North Vietnamese negotiator Le Duc Tho were jointly awarded the Nobel Peace Prize in recognition of their negotiation efforts that ended direct American military involvement in Vietnam. When President Nixon was forced to resign because of the Watergate scandal (see RICHARD MILHOUS NIXON), President Gerald Ford retained Kissinger as secretary of state.

Between 1973 and 1975 Kissinger's diplomatic efforts were focused on ending hostilities between Israel and neighboring Arab countries. To confront the immediate crisis precipitated by the outbreak of war in October 1973, Kissinger successfully employed numerous personal visits—nicknamed shuttle diplomacy—to all the major national leaders involved. He suffered his first major public failure when he was unable to secure a permanent settlement agreement between Israel and Egypt.

In addition, accusations by foreign policy critics—most notably, fellow cabinet member Secretary of Defense James Schlesinger—that Kissinger's policy of détente enabled the Soviet Union to pull ahead of the United States militarily gradually undermined public confidence and the president's support. In 1976, in a move to distance himself from Kissinger in his campaign for the presidency, President Ford dismissed him as his assistant for national security affairs.

After leaving office in 1977, Kissinger briefly served as a foreign policy commentator for NBC television and as a consultant for the Chase Manhattan Bank. During the 1980s he completed two books about his foreign policy experiences, resumed teaching, and was appointed by President RONALD REAGAN to lead a commission assigned to reevaluate American foreign policy options toward Latin America.

BIBLIOGRAPHY

Hersh, Seymour M., *The Price of Power: Kissinger in the Nixon White House,* 1983; Kissinger, Henry A., *White House Years,* 1979, and *Years of Upheaval,* 1982; Shawcross, William, *Sideshow: Kissinger, Nixon, and the Destruction of Cambodia,* 1979.

Knox, Henry

(July 25, 1750–October 25, 1806)
Secretary of War

The country's first secretary of war, Henry Knox had fought in the major battles of the Revolution and had become GEORGE WASHINGTON's trusted adviser and friend. Washington said, "There is no one whom I have loved more sincerely" than General Knox.

Seventh of his shipmaster father's ten sons, Knox was born in Boston. In 1762 he found work in a bookstore and opened his own successful shop in Boston in 1771. Abandoning his bookstore for full-time military service during the Revolution, he rose rapidly in rank. In 1775 he became Washington's artillery commander. The following year he was a brigadier general.

Knox commanded the expedition that hauled cannon over the mountains from Fort Ticonderoga to Dorchester Heights, forcing the British to abandon Boston. He fought in the subsequent disastrous battles in New York and then in the surprise attack on Trenton. Washington learned to count on his dependable support. He was with Washington at Brandywine, Valley Forge, Germantown, Mon-

Library of Congress

mouth, and Yorktown. A major general by 1781, his careful positioning of the American cannon at Yorktown, in Washington's opinion, "supplied the deficit of our means." It was Knox who suggested that a military academy for the army should be founded at West Point.

After resigning from the disbanded army in January 1784, he accepted election by the Continental Congress as secretary of war in 1785. Washington retained him in office when the new federal government was implemented. Knox's one major disappointment as secretary of war was Congress's rejection of his plan for a strong regular army and navy. He left national public office in 1794 and retired to his estate in Maine.

BIBLIOGRAPHY

Brooks, Noah, *Henry Knox, A Soldier of the Revolution,* 1900; Callahan, North, *Henry Knox: Washington's General,* 1958; Drake, Francis S., *Life and Correspondence of Henry Knox,* 1873.

Knox, Philander Chase

(May 6, 1853–October 12, 1921)
Secretary of State, Attorney General, Senator

Philander Chase Knox was best known as the secretary of state who pursued the policy known as dollar diplomacy. Born at Brownsville, Pennsylvania, Knox graduated from Mount Union College in Ohio in 1872 and was admitted to the bar in 1875 at Pittsburgh. He served as assistant district attorney for western Pennsylvania for a short time before forming a successful corporate law firm.

President WILLIAM MCKINLEY chose him to be his attorney general in 1899, but Knox declined because of his involvement at that time in the formation of the Carnegie Steel Company. When the position was reoffered in 1901, Knox accepted. While attorney general, he initiated a successful suit under the Sherman Anti-Trust Act (see BENJAMIN HARRISON) to prevent John Pierpont Morgan's plan to merge the Great Northern, the Northern Pacific, and the Chicago, Burlington and Quincy railroads into one corporation.

In 1903 Knox wrote the draft of the bill that resulted in the creation of the Department of Commerce and Labor. He also worked on the legislation that gave the Interstate Commerce Commission effective control of railroad rates.

In 1904, after the death of one of Pennsylvania's U.S. senators, Knox was appointed to complete his term and subsequently won election to a full term. In the Senate he quickly established a reputation as an expert on rail-road rate legislation, served on the Judiciary Committee, and was briefly chairman of the Committee on Rules before resigning to become secretary of state under President WILLIAM H. TAFT in 1909.

As secretary of state, Knox reformed the selection process of foreign service officers and pursued a policy—which his critics soon dubbed "dollar diplomacy"—of aggressively promoting private American investment overseas in underdeveloped regions as part of national policy. Disputes with Canada over North Atlantic fishing rights and Russia over the Bering Sea were also settled, but a reciprocity treaty with Canada and efforts to establish a general arbitration treaty process at The Hague with France and Great Britain failed.

At the end of the Taft administration in 1913, Knox returned to his private law practice. He was reelected to the Senate from Pennsylvania in 1916, where he played a major role in defeating the ratification of the Treaty of Versailles and participation of the United States in the League of Nations (see WOODROW WILSON).

BIBLIOGRAPHY

"Philander Chase Knox," *The American Secretaries of State and Their Diplomacy*, vol. 9, 1928.

Knox, William Franklin

(January 1, 1874–April 28, 1944)
Secretary of the Navy

The son of a grocery store owner, William Franklin (Frank) Knox was born in Boston, Massachusetts, but spent most of his youth in Michigan. He attended Alma College in Michigan but left school to join THEODORE ROOSEVELT's Rough Riders in the

Spanish-American War (see WILLIAM MCKINLEY, JR.). Later, in 1912, Knox was awarded his B.A. degree.

After the war, Knox returned to Michigan and became a journalist. He was Roosevelt's Midwest preconvention campaign manager in 1911 and supported his independent (Bull Moose; see THEODORE ROOSEVELT) effort to win the White House in 1912.

When the United States entered World War I, Knox, then forty-three years old, enlisted in the army. After the war he returned to journalism, first in Michigan, then in New Hampshire, and finally in Boston as a manager in the Hearst publishing organization. He moved to Chicago in 1931, after he bought a controlling interest in the *Chicago Daily News.*

A leading opponent of President FRANKLIN D. ROOSEVELT's New Deal programs, Knox was chosen to be Republican presidential nominee ALFRED LANDON's running mate in 1936. Four years after their ticket's overwhelming defeat, President Roosevelt, interested in forming a bipartisan cabinet, asked Knox to serve as secretary of the navy. In that position he oversaw the construction of the largest and most powerful two-ocean navy in history. He died in office in Washington, D.C.

BIBLIOGRAPHY

Alexender, Jack, "Secretary Knox," *Life,* March 10, 1941; Lobdell, George H., Jr., *A Biography of Frank Knox,* Ph.D. dissertation, University of Illinois, 1936; *New York Times,* "Knox Dies in Home of Heart Attack," April 29, 1944; "Who Is Frank Knox?" *Fortune,* November 1935.

Knudsen, William Signius

(March 25, 1879–April 27, 1948)
Government Agency Director

William Signius Knudsen was a major figure in the American automobile industry and a vital contributor to the successful conversion of the U.S. economy into a massive "arsenal of democracy" during World War II.

Knudsen was born in Copenhagen, Denmark. He immigrated to the United States in 1900 and in 1911 joined the Ford Motor Company. In 1914 he became a citizen.

During World War I Knudsen supervised the Ford production of military equipment. Dismissed from Ford during a company reorganization in 1921, Knudsen joined the General Motors Corporation as vice president in charge of production at the Chevrolet division. Under his leadership Chevrolet sales surpassed the Model T Ford as the best-selling car in the low-priced range. In 1933 Knudsen became executive vice president of General Motors, and four years later, president of the corporation. His intervention in the sit-down strike at General Motors plants in 1937 helped resolve the dispute and paved the way for the recognition of the United Automobile Workers union by the automobile industry.

From 1940 to 1945 Knudsen worked at getting American industry to produce what the Allies needed during World War II. He served on the National Defense Advisory Commission, directed the Office of Production Management, advised the under secretary of war, and directed the Air Technical Service. Until he retired from the army in May 1945 to return to General Motors, Knudsen was responsible for purchasing, distributing, and maintaining all aircraft and equipment used by the Army Air Force. He was the only civilian in American history to be commissioned a lieutenant general in the army.

After serving on the board of directors at General Motors for a year, Knudsen became the chairman of the board of directors of the Hupp Corporation. This was the position he held at the time of his death.

BIBLIOGRAPHY

Beasley, Norman, *Knudsen: A Biography,* 1947; Borth, Christy, *Masters of Mass Production,* 1945; Gray, L. C., "Defense Commissioner Knudsen," *Current History,* August 1940, p. 12; *New Yorker,* March 8, 15, and 22, 1941.

La Follette, Robert Marion

(June 14, 1855–June 18, 1925)
Candidate for President, Senator, Representative

Over the course of a twenty-five-year political career, "Fighting Bob" La Follette never let the lure of wealth or political power deter him from his successful efforts to champion progressive reforms in Wisconsin and Washington. Although his passionate commitment to reform earned him the wrath of his opponents during his lifetime, admiration for his courage and appreciation for his accomplishments have greatly enhanced his reputation since his death. He was voted one of the most outstanding senators of all time by the Senate in 1957.

Robert Marion La Follette was born in Primrose, Wisconsin, graduated from the University of Wisconsin in 1879, and established a law practice in Madison. He was elected district attorney of Dane County in 1880, was reelected in 1882, and two years later won election to the first of three successive (1885–1891) terms in Congress.

Library of Congress

After his reelection defeat in 1890, La Follette resumed his law practice. In 1891 a bitter dispute between him and Wisconsin senator and Republican party leader Philetus Sawyer caused a split in the Wisconsin Republican party between conservative Sawyer and progressive La Follette supporters that lasted for decades.

Stymied by the refusal of the Wisconsin Republican party leadership to support his nomination for governor in 1896 and 1898, La Follette went directly to the people and established a power base among farmers, small businessmen, professionals, and intellectuals that was independent of party affiliation. Through this support and by joining forces with other reformers in the Republican party in 1900, La Follette won the party's nomination for governor by acclamation and then triumphed in the general election.

Because the state legislature was still controlled by his opponents, La Follette again took his message directly to the people and, in addition to his own reelection in 1902, managed to secure the election of a reform-oriented majority in the new legislature.

La Follette was able to introduce and secure the passage of legislation that made Wisconsin the first state to adopt the direct primary. This provides a way for the voters to choose the party's candidates and is the most widely used method (as opposed to the caucus or convention) for nominating candidates in the United States today. He also introduced legislation to tax railroads on the basis of the true value of their property. In addition, under his administration a commission was established to regulate railroad rates, corporation taxes were increased, a civil service law was adopted, and state funding for education was increased.

La Follette was elected to the Senate in 1905 but delayed taking his seat until 1906, when he finished his third term as governor. In the Senate, La Follette continued his efforts to initiate progressive reforms designed to curb what he believed was the dangerous and excessive power of entrenched political leaders, wealthy businessmen, and corporations. He supported the need to regulate railroads and other industries and opposed high tariffs. He was a strong supporter of labor's right to organize and of the government's obligation to regulate working conditions.

La Follette's views on foreign policy hurt him politically. His refusal to support President WOODROW WILSON's hostility toward Germany, which he suspected was motivated by the desire of American bankers and businessmen to protect their loans and earn war profits, was at first popular with his isolationist, largely German and Scandinavian constituency. However, his decision to vote against going to war and his continued criticism of the U.S. war effort in 1917 and 1918 made him so unpopular that an effort to expel him from the Senate for disloyalty was barely avoided.

After the war, La Follette remained true to his convictions and opposed the Treaty of Versailles and U.S. membership in the League of Nations (see WOODROW WILSON). Ironically, by the time he was up for reelection in 1922, public disillusionment with American participation in the war had set in, and he was returned to office by an overwhelming majority.

Disappointed by the lack of commitment of either of the major political parties to significant reform, La Follette concluded that a third party needed to be created. In 1924 he accepted the nomination of the Progressive party (see THEODORE ROOSEVELT) for president. He waged an exceptionally vigorous campaign and managed to win over 5 million popular votes or 17 percent of all the votes cast. The strain of the campaign he conducted, however, proved fatal.

BIBLIOGRAPHY

La Follette, Belle C., and Fola La Follette, *Robert M. La Follette,* 2 vols., 1953; La Follette, Robert M., *La Follette's Autobiography,* 1960; Maxwell, Robert S., *La Follette and the Rise of Progressives in Wisconsin,* 1956; Stirn, E. W., *Annotated Bibliography of Robert M. La Follette,* 1937; Thelen, David P., *Robert M. La Follette and the Insurgent Spirit,* 1986; Young, D. (ed.), *Adventure in Politics,* 1970.

La Guardia, Fiorello Henry

(December 11, 1882–September 20, 1947)
Representative

While campaigning for reelection to Congress in 1922, Fiorello La Guardia said, "I stand for the Republicanism of ABRAHAM LINCOLN, and let me tell you that the average Republican leader east of the Mississip' doesn't know anything more about Abraham Lincoln than Henry Ford knows about the Talmud." The fact that he frequently made such comments helps to explain why La Guardia was viewed as such a political maverick. Nevertheless, for over three decades, first as a congressman and then as mayor of New York City, the dynamic "Little Flower" (the English translation of his name) played a unique and important role in American politics.

Fiorello Henry La Guardia was born in New York City. From 1885 to 1898, while his Italian-born father served as army bandmaster, La Guardia lived on U.S. Army posts in the West. His mother, originally from Trieste, Austria, was Jewish. After his father's death, La Guardia accompanied his mother to Trieste in 1898 and was employed by the American consular service in Hungary, Trieste, and Fiume from age nineteen to twenty-three.

He returned to New York City in 1906 and earned his law degree by attending New York University at night while working in the daytime for the immigration service. The multilingual and cosmopolitan La Guardia was admitted to the bar in 1910. Committed to improving life for the downtrodden in society, La Guardia almost immediately became active in politics.

Since the Irish American–dominated Democratic party seemed too corrupt and hostile toward Italians, La Guardia decided to join the Republican party. His first campaign to win a seat in the U.S. House of Representatives as a Republican failed in 1914; but his second attempt, running as an anti–Tammany Hall (see WILLIAM MARCY TWEED) reform candidate, in 1916 was successful, and he became the only Republican elected from the Lower East Side of New York. He served in the House (with the exception of his service in the army in 1917 and 1918 and his term as president of the New York City Board of Aldermen from 1920 to 1921) until 1932.

While in the House, La Guardia fought for numerous prolabor laws and sponsored the Norris–La Guardia anti-injunction bill, which limited the ability of employers to break up strikes by securing court-ordered injunctions against picketing and other forms of protest. He also denounced Prohibition, anti-immigration bills, and tax legislation of his own party on the grounds that the tax policy favored the rich.

Frustrated by what he viewed as the stupidity of the Republican party on the major issues and the unacceptability of the Democratic party, La Guardia decided to support the Progressive party's (see THEODORE ROOSEVELT) presidential candidate, ROBERT M. LA FOLLETTE, in 1924. He also successfully ran for reelection as a Progressive party candidate himself. As a liberal in the predominantly conservative Republican party, La Guardia summed up his political destiny in Congress in 1927 with the observation: "I am doomed to live in a hopeless minority for most of my legislative days."

In 1933 La Guardia won the first of three terms as mayor of New York. He relished the power and duties of the job, and thrived as the chief administrator of the city. He did not let the fact that the city's board of aldermen was composed of Democrats opposed to his ideas hinder his efforts to cope with the Great Depression. He overwhelmed their opposition through direct appeals to the people of New York over the radio and to the state legislature. A close ally of FRANKLIN D. ROOSEVELT, he and his city benefited greatly from the New Deal's largess.

During his three terms as mayor, La Guardia reduced political corruption, modernized and beautified New York City, brought about the adoption of a new city charter in 1938, introduced ambitious building and slum clearance projects, and improved health and sanitary conditions. La Guardia implemented such a vast program of reform during his first two terms in office that his name became associated with good government and the improvement of the quality of urban living throughout the nation. He seemed to be everywhere, doing everything. Once, during a newspaper strike in New York City, he even read the comics over the radio so New Yorkers would not miss out on the adventures of their favorite characters. His cosmopolitanism (he was not only part Italian and part Jewish, but a practicing Episcopalian) enabled him to reach out to a broad range of New Yorkers. La Guardia remains, to this day, the most beloved New York City mayor.

World War II broke out during La Guardia's third term. He was deeply disappointed when he could not secure a general's commission in the army or an important cabinet-level appointment. Instead, President Franklin D. Roosevelt chose him to be the director of Civil Defense, a post he could hold without relinquishing his mayoral duties.

La Guardia declined to run for a fourth term as mayor in 1945, and after serving a year as director of the United Nations Relief and Rehabilitation Administration, retired from public service just a few months before his death.

BIBLIOGRAPHY

Carter, John F., *La Guardia*, 1937; Garrett, Charles, *The La Guardia Years*, 1961; Mann, Arthur, *La Guardia*, 2 vols., 1959–1965; Moses, Robert, *La Guardia: A Salute and a Memoir*, 1957; Zinn, Howard, *La Guardia in Congress*, 1959.

Landon, Alfred Mossman

(September 9, 1887–October 12, 1987)
Candidate for President

Two-term governor of Kansas Alfred Landon won the Republican nomination for president in 1936, but in the general election he won the electoral votes of only Maine and Vermont against President FRANKLIN DELANO ROOSEVELT.

Landon was born in Pennsylvania, moved to Kansas with his parents at seventeen, and earned a law degree from the University of Kansas in 1908. After four years in banking, he established his own independent oil exploration and production company. During World War I he served in the chemical warfare division of the army.

A liberal Republican, Landon supported THEODORE ROOSEVELT's Bull Moose candidacy in 1912, and in 1922 he became the private secretary to the governor of Kansas. In 1928 he became the state party's central committee chairman. During his two terms as governor, from 1933 to 1937, supporters nicknamed him the "Kansas Coolidge" because of his record of reducing taxes and practicing strict fiscal government austerity.

Largely because he was the only Republican who had managed to win reelection in 1934 in the face of the Democratic party landslide, he was judged the strongest candidate available by the Republicans to run against President Franklin Roosevelt two years later. Nevertheless, Roosevelt's popularity overwhelmed Landon's criticism of New Deal programs.

Landon never ran for public office again, but he stayed active in Republican party politics while managing his oil company and three radio stations. He once quipped to a reporter: "I'm an oil man who never made his million, a lawyer who never had a case, and a politician who only carried Maine and Vermont."

BIBLIOGRAPHY

McCoy, Donald R., *Landon of Kansas,* 1966.

Lansing, Robert

(October 17, 1864–October 30, 1928)
Secretary of State, Diplomat

As secretary of state from 1915 to 1920, Robert Lansing attempted to play an important role in balancing what he perceived to be President WOODROW WILSON's visionary idealism with pragmatic political concerns.

Born in Watertown, New York, Lansing graduated from Amherst College in 1886 and was admitted to the New York bar three years later. Through his marriage in 1890 to Eleanor Foster, the daughter of Secretary of State JOHN W. FOSTER, Lansing acquired contacts that launched him on his career as a diplomat and international lawyer.

Lansing frequently served as counsel for the United States before international tribunals from 1892 until Woodrow Wilson appointed him counselor of the state department in 1914. At this time WILLIAM JENNINGS BRYAN was secretary of state, but Lansing actually wrote most of the official diplomatic dispatches that bore Bryan's signature. When Bryan resigned in 1915 in protest over the U.S. response to the sinking of the *Lusitania,* President Wilson appointed Lansing to succeed him.

Although President Wilson dealt with most major foreign policy issues on his own and relied much more on "Colonel" Edward M. House than Lansing for delicate international negotiations, Lansing nevertheless played an important role in setting the stage for U.S. involvement in World War I on the side of the Allies.

When Congress failed to pass legislation in 1917 authorizing the arming of U.S. merchant ships, Lansing convinced President Wilson that he already possessed the authority. And, after several American ships had been torpedoed, it was Lansing who argued most persuasively for a declaration of war on the grounds that Germany had broken its pledge not to engage in unrestricted submarine warfare.

Lansing viewed Wilson's pledge of "peace without victory" and commitment of the United States to support the creation of a world government as unrealistic, but this did not disrupt their working relationship until after the World War I Allied victory. At the peace conference in Paris, Wilson simply ignored Lansing's misgivings. Although chastened, Lansing did not resign. Wilson asked for his resignation in 1920, shortly after Lansing publicly expressed his personal apprehensions about the extent of the proposed U.S. commitment to the League of Nations (see WOODROW WILSON). (Officially, Lansing was dismissed for exceeding his authority by holding cabinet meetings while Wilson was incapacitated.)

After leaving government service, Lansing resumed his international law practice, continued editing the *American Journal of International Law*, and wrote extensively on foreign policy issues.

BIBLIOGRAPHY

Beers, Burton F., *Vain Endeavor: Robert Lansing's Attempts to End American-Japanese Rivalry*, 1962; Lansing, Robert, *The Peace Negotiations: A Personal Narrative*, 1921, and *War Memoirs*, 1935; Smith, Daniel M., *Robert Lansing and American Neutrality*, 1958.

Lee, Richard Henry

(January 31, 1732–June 19, 1794)
Senator, Revolutionary Leader

On June 7, 1776, Richard Henry Lee introduced the resolution in the Continental Congress that initiated the writing of the Declaration of Independence. Although he was away participating in the Virginia constitutional convention when Congress actually adopted the document on July 2, he signed it upon his return.

Born in Westmoreland County, Virginia, into a prominent family, Lee was educated in Europe. In 1758 he was elected to the Virginia House of Burgesses and spoke out in favor of halting the slave trade. He and PATRICK HENRY led colonial opposition to the Stamp Act of 1765 (see JOHN ADAMS and SAMUEL ADAMS), and organized a boycott of British goods in Virginia until the Stamp Act was repealed. Two years later, Lee was equally incensed by the Townshend Acts, which replaced the repealed Stamp Act, and again led boycott protest efforts. In 1773 he organized an intercolonial committees of correspondence network so that opposition leaders in the various colonies could coordinate their efforts.

At the first Continental Congress, Lee once again advocated the implementation of a boycott as a protest measure against England and served on the congressional committee that chose GEORGE WASHINGTON to command the nascent Continental army.

Lee served in Congress until 1779, when, because of age and ill health, he decided to resign. Along with Samuel Adams he led the opposition to the strong French role in American peacemaking efforts. Although he did not participate in the writing of the Articles of Confederation, he played an important role in the establishment of the Confederation government.

After the Revolution, Lee returned to Congress and was elected its president for the 1784–1785 session. Several years later, Lee and Patrick Henry led the fight against ratification of the new federal Constitution in Virginia on the grounds that it would destroy states' rights and threatened individual liberties. Deeply suspicious of centralizing power, Lee once observed: "The first maxim of a man who loves liberty should be never to grant to Rulers an atom of [unnecessary] power. . . ."

After the Constitution was adopted, however, Lee accepted election to the U.S. Senate and played an important role in securing the adoption of the first ten amendments (the Bill of Rights). Illness forced him to resign from the Senate in 1792.

BIBLIOGRAPHY

Ballagh, J. C. (ed.), *The Letters of Richard Henry Lee*, 2 vols., 1911–1914; Hendrick, B. J., *The Lees of Virginia: Biography of a Family*, 1935.

Lemke, William Frederick

(August 13, 1878–May 30, 1950)
Candidate for President, Representative

Born in Albany, Minnesota, William Lemke graduated from the University of North Dakota in 1902. After earning his law degree at Yale University in 1905, Lemke established a practice in Fargo, North Dakota, and became chairman of the Republican state committee in 1916. He was elected state attorney general in 1920 but was defeated for the U.S. Senate in 1926 as a candidate for the Farmer-Labor party. Elected to the House of Representatives as a Republican in 1932, Lemke worked particularly to improve credit and housing conditions for farmers during the Depression.

In 1936, angered by FRANKLIN D. ROOSEVELT's opposition to farm refinance legislation he favored, Lemke decided to accept the presidential nomination of the recently formed Union party. It was composed of the followers of the Reverend Charles Coughlin and his National Union for Social Justice, Dr. Francis Townsend, Gerald L. K. Smith, and the recently assassinated senator HUEY LONG, and was vehemently anti–New Deal (see FRANKLIN DELANO ROOSEVELT). Lemke won nearly a million popular votes but no electoral votes.

Defeated in a bid for a Senate seat in 1940, Lemke returned to the House in 1943 and served there until his death seven years later.

BIBLIOGRAPHY

Blackorby, Edward, *Prairie Rebel: The Public Life of William Lemke*, 1963.

Lilienthal, David Eli

(July 8, 1899–January 15, 1981)
Government Agency Director

More than any other individual, David Lilienthal made the Tennessee Valley Authority (TVA), the huge New Deal power and flood-control project established in 1933, into a widely acclaimed example of a government-funded and government-managed economic enterprise. Lilienthal would later bring this same commitment to the public regulation and control of the nation's resources to his chairmanship of the Atomic Energy Commission.

Lilienthal was born in Morton, Illinois, the son of Czechoslovakian immigrants. After graduating from DePauw University in 1920 and Harvard Law School in 1923, he practiced law in Chicago. In 1926, as a special attorney for the city of Chicago in a telephone rate–setting case, he forced a telephone utility to rebate $20 million to subscribers. The case earned him a statewide reputation as a specialist in utility law and as an opponent of privately held utilities.

In 1931 Governor Philip La Follette of Wisconsin appointed Lilienthal to the state public service commission. While on the commission, he enforced rate reductions on telephone companies and other utilities. Two years later, President FRANKLIN D. ROOSEVELT appointed Lilienthal one of the triumvirate to head the TVA.

During the 1930s, the TVA constructed dams and reservoirs, improved river navigation, instituted flood control, and provided cheap electric power for the region around the Tennessee River and its tributaries, covering 40,000 square miles and seven states. Though attacked for its constitutionality and investigated by Congress, the TVA thrived, and Lilienthal was given considerable credit for its success. In 1941 he became the chairman of the entire TVA.

Lilienthal left the chairmanship of the TVA in 1945 to work with the State Department on plans for atomic energy control. In 1946 President HARRY TRUMAN appointed Lilienthal as the first chairman of the Atomic Energy Commission. As chairman, Lilienthal led the program to develop nuclear energy for peaceful industrial and medical uses. His opposition to the development of the hydrogen bomb and his continued commitment to government planning made him an increasingly unpopular figure, especially once the cold war between the United States and the Soviet Union intensified in 1949. Lilienthal resigned from the Atomic Energy Commission in 1950 to become a private economic regional resource development consultant. From 1953 until 1971, as chairman of the Development and Research Corporation, Lilienthal continued to help launch development projects in Latin America and Asia.

BIBLIOGRAPHY

Lilienthal, David, *TVA—Democracy on the March*, 1944, *This I Do Believe*, 1949, *Big Business, A New Era*, 1953, *The Multinational Corporation*, 1960, *Change, Hope and the Bomb*, 1963, *Journals*, 1964–1976, and *Atomic Energy, A New Start*, 1980.

Lincoln, Abraham

(February 12, 1809–April 15, 1865)
President, Representative

Among all the presidents, Abraham Lincoln is perhaps the most loved. A photograph of Lincoln taken toward the end of the Civil War shows a gaunt, exhausted leader whose anguish moves every American. His words, always simple and eloquent, exhorting preservation of the Union, then asking forgiveness and peace for all who fought and suffered in the war, are equally familiar and moving. For most people, Lincoln personifies the American spirit of freedom and equality. Without his leadership and humanity, the country would certainly have taken a different course in history.

Lincoln grew up on frontier farms in Kentucky and Indiana. From an early age, despite his father's discouragement, he was obsessed with obtaining an education. The goal had to be innate, for, as he observed later, Indiana offered "absolutely nothing to excite ambition for education." Lincoln always attributed his love of books to his mother. "I owe everything I am to her," he said. She died when he was nine, but his stepmother encouraged him to continue his studying.

The year after the family moved to Illinois in 1830, Lincoln decided to live on his own. A job as a store clerk in New Salem gave him access to books and plenty of time to read. During the Black Hawk War, a conflict between the Sac and Fox Indians and the United States in 1832, Lincoln served a short stint in the militia but did not see combat. When he returned to New Salem, he ran unsuccessfully for the state assembly in a predominantly Democratic district as an anti-Jackson Whig. After his defeat, he purchased a general store with a partner. Their venture failed because of the partner's alcoholism. Although it took Lincoln fifteen years, he paid off all their debts in full, earning the nickname "Honest Abe."

In 1834 Lincoln won the first of his four two-year terms to the Illinois state assembly. As a state legislator, he generally supported internal improvements and the development of the nation's resources, and was soon the leader of the Whig minority. In addition to his work in the assembly, Lincoln began to study law. After moving to the new state capital in Springfield, he was admitted to the bar in 1836. In 1842 Lincoln married Mary Todd, and in 1846 he was elected to the U.S. House of Representatives. In his single term in the House, Lincoln opposed the Mexican War (see JAMES KNOX POLK) and the extension of slavery into the territories, and supported the right of voters in the District of Columbia to be able to abolish slavery.

In 1848 Lincoln vigorously campaigned across New England for ZACHARY TAYLOR. He was so disappointed when he did not obtain an expected appointment as commissioner of the general land office that he withdrew from politics and concentrated on his law practice for five years.

Lincoln returned to the political arena when reaction to the Kansas-Nebraska Act (see FRANKLIN PIERCE) helped forge the new Republican party. In 1856 he campaigned throughout Illinois, delivering speeches in favor of antislavery Republican presidential candidate JOHN C. FRÉMONT. In 1858 the Illinois Republican party nominated him to run for the Senate against Democrat STEPHEN A. DOUGLAS.

In his acceptance speech, Lincoln succinctly summed up his view of the situation the nation was in due to slavery: "A house divided against itself cannot stand. I believe

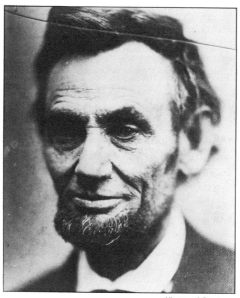
Library of Congress

this government cannot endure, permanently half slave and half free." Slavery, he warned, was a threat to free labor, and there was no way to reconcile it with a free society. By preventing its expansion, its ultimate extinction could be gradually obtained.

From town to town during the 1858 campaign, in a series of debates, Lincoln and Douglas appeared on the same stage. What they said was reported across the nation because Douglas was widely regarded as the front-runner for the Democratic party's presidential nomination in 1860. In his speeches, Lincoln repeated that slavery was morally wrong and attacked his opponent's "declared indifference" to it.

I hate it because of the monstrous injustice of slavery itself. I hate it because it deprives our republican example of its just influence in the world—enables the enemies of free institutions, with plausibility, to taunt us as hypocrites—causes the real friends of freedom to doubt our sincerity, and especially because it forces so many really good men amongst ourselves into an open war with the very fundamental principles of civil liberty—criticizing the Declaration of Independence, and insisting that there is no right principle of action but self-interest.

The Republicans won 4,000 more popular votes than the Douglas Democrats (125,000 to 121,000); but the Democrats still managed to win more seats in the state legislature, and Douglas was returned to the Senate. Friends consoled the disappointed Lincoln with the advice that, although he had lost the Senate race, he was now a strong candidate for the Republican nomination for president. Lincoln replied, "I . . . admit that I am ambitious, and would like to be President . . . but there is no such good luck in store for me. . . ." A prominent figure after the debates, Lincoln toured the nation giving speeches to increasingly enthusiastic crowds prior to the 1860 Republican convention. At the convention he was nominated on the third ballot over front-runner WILLIAM H. SEWARD.

The Republican platform in 1860 called for noninterference in the slave states, the exclusion of slavery from the territories, a homestead act to give free land to settlers, government support for the construction of a transcontinental railroad, and protective tariffs. Against a divided Democratic party, Lincoln was able to win election by securing the electoral votes of every nonslave state (180), even though he won only 40 percent of the popular vote.

Warned of an assassination plot, Lincoln had to enter Washington by secret train to assume office. He promised not to interfere with slavery in the South. However, the month before he took the oath of office, seven Southern states met at Montgomery, Alabama, to proclaim the Confederate States of America. One month after he assumed the presidency, Fort Sumter was fired upon. The Civil War, which would claim the lives of at least 620,000 Americans, had begun.

Lincoln moved swiftly to deal with the rebellion. At first he left the conduct of the war up to his generals; but following the dismal performance of the Union army in 1861, Lincoln began studying military tactics. After GEORGE B. MCCLELLAN's lack of success, Lincoln even tried to direct military operations himself. In 1864 he finally found a general he had faith in, ULYSSES S. GRANT. By executive decree Lincoln increased the size of the army and navy, suspended the writ of habeas corpus where necessary, placed treason suspects in military custody, and forbade the use of the mails for treasonable correspondence.

By mid-1862 Lincoln had decided that the war aims of the North had to include ending slavery. He felt, however, that he couldn't say so publicly as long as the South appeared to be doing well. Thus, as late as August, he still spoke of preserving the Union as the only goal.

Then, on September 22, 1862, after interpreting the bloody Battle of Antietam as a victory, Lincoln issued his preliminary Emancipation Proclamation. (He signed the final version on January 1, 1863.) He described the proclamation as "an act of justice as well as a fit and necessary war measure. . . . " Emancipation as a war goal of the North also made it extremely difficult for the British government to side with the South.

As the war dragged on and the casualties mounted, Lincoln's popularity fell to an all-time low. He despaired of being reelected but was renominated in 1864 for a second term by the Republicans. When the Democrats in turn nominated George B. McClellan on a platform of stopping the war and negotiating a settlement, Lincoln admitted to his cabinet: "It seems exceedingly probable that this Administration will not be reelected." But when a string of Union victories, especially General William T. Sherman's capture of Atlanta, indicated that the end of the war was in sight, Lincoln was elected for a second term. At his inauguration he recalled the sacrifice made to preserve the Union and looked forward to the need for reconciliation:

> Fondly we do hope—fervently we do pray—that this mighty scourge of war may speedily pass away. . . . With malice toward none, with charity for all, with firmness in the right as God gives us to see the right, let us finish the work we are in, to bind up the nation's wounds, to care for him who shall have borne the battle, and for his widow and for his orphans, to do all which may achieve and cherish a just, and lasting peace. . . .

The Confederate general Robert E. Lee surrendered at Appomattox Courthouse on April 9, 1865, effectively ending the war. Two days later, Lincoln addressed a crowd at the White House on reconstruction. He took a bold stand concerning a politically volatile issue. If the Confederate states had left the Union, as Northern radical politicians claimed, then they had abrogated their constitutional rights and could be treated as foreign territories. But if secession was impossible, the view favored by Lincoln and other moderates, then the citizens of the Confederate states who had re-mained loyal, as well as those who would promise to be loyal again, could reestablish state governments that supported civil liber-ties for blacks and elect representatives and senators to Congress. "Finding themselves safely at home," argued Lincoln, "it would be utterly immaterial whether they had ever been abroad." Lincoln cited the procedures followed in Louisiana and Arkansas, where 10 percent of the 1860 voting population was considered a sufficient number to set up state governments capable of petitioning for read-mission to Congress, as a model for how the course of Reconstruction might proceed.

The agony of the war, the death of his young son from typhoid in 1862, and the subsequent emotional breakdown of his wife caused Lincoln to age dramatically in of-fice. However, he had acquired tremendous wisdom about the underlying principles of American political institutions. His eloquent speeches expressed the vision he had of the long-term prospects for the nation. In his Get-tysburg Address, he began with the immortal lines, "Four score and seven years ago our forefathers brought forth on this continent a new nation, conceived in liberty and dedicated to the proposition that all men are created equal . . ." and concluded with the promise "that government of the people, by the people, for the people, shall not perish from the earth."

On the evening of April 14, 1865, Lincoln was fatally shot by the actor and Confederate sympathizer John Wilkes Booth as he watched a play at Ford's Theater in Washington, D.C. Lincoln's tragic death became a symbol of the human toll the Civil War cost the nation.

BIBLIOGRAPHY

Basler, Roy P. (ed.), *Abraham Lincoln: Collected Works*, 9 vols., 1963; Fehrenbacker, Don E. (ed.), *Abraham Lincoln: Speeches and Writings, Vol. 1, 1832–1858*, 1989, and *Abraham Lincoln: Speeches and Writings, Vol. 2, 1859–1865*, 1989; Luthin, Reinhard H., *The Real Abraham Lincoln*, 1960; Oates, Stephen, *With Malice Toward None*, 1977; Quarles, Benjamin, *Lincoln and the Negro*, 1962; Randall, James E., and Richard Current, *Lincoln the President*, 4 vols., 1945–1955; Thomas, Benjamin, *Abraham Lincoln*, 1952.

Livingston, Edward

(May 28, 1764–May 23, 1836)
Secretary of State, Diplomat, Senator, Representative

Born in Columbia County, New York, Ed-ward Livingston, brother of ROBERT R. LIVINGSTON, graduated from the College of New Jersey (now Princeton University) in 1781, was admitted to the bar in 1785, and established a practice in New York City.

Elected to three terms in Congress from 1795 to 1801 as a Jeffersonian Republican, Livingston consistently voted against Federal-ist measures, such as Jay's Treaty (see JOHN JAY) and the Alien and Sedition Acts (see JOHN ADAMS and THOMAS JEFFERSON). While serving in Congress, Livingston established a close per-sonal friendship with ANDREW JACKSON and from that time on was at Jackson's side at every critical phase of his career.

After serving simultaneously as U.S. attor-ney for the District of New York and mayor of New York City from 1800 to 1803, Livingston moved to New Orleans. During the War of

1812 (see JAMES MADISON), he played a crucial role in organizing the city's defenses by recruiting the aid of the pirates Jean and Pierre Laffite. During the Battle of New Orleans in 1815, he became General Jackson's aide-de-camp, confidant, and secretary. (He wrote most of the formal war dispatches.)

In 1822 Livingston was again elected to Congress. He served three terms, was defeated for reelection in 1828, but was then elected by the legislature to the U.S. Senate. He also campaigned for Jackson in 1828, to whom he had suggested the presidency as early as 1815. Jackson appointed Livingston secretary of state in 1831.

While Livingston took a moderate stance on the issue of the Second Bank of the United States (see NICHOLAS BIDDLE and ROGER BROOKE TANEY), he agreed fully with Jackson's opposition to nullification (see ANDREW JACKSON). Indeed, he wrote Jackson's firm, antinullification proclamation of 1832 from presidential notes (see JOHN CALDWELL CALHOUN).

Appointed minister to France from 1833 to 1835, Livingston initiated attempts to make France pay American claims dating from the Napoleonic Wars. Britain finally mediated the controversy, but not before Jackson's threats had brought the two nations to the brink of war.

BIBLIOGRAPHY

Hatcher, William B., *Edward Livingston*, 1940.

Livingston, Robert R.

(November 27, 1746–February 26, 1813)
Diplomat

Robert R. Livingston's role in the negotiation of the Louisiana Purchase in 1803 (see THOMAS JEFFERSON) capped a remarkable career of public service.

Born in New York City into one of the most prominent families in that area, Livingston was educated at King's College (now Columbia University) and admitted to the bar in 1770. As a delegate to the Continental Congress from 1775 to 1776, Livingston helped draft the Declaration of Independence but was absent when the document was signed. In two more terms as a member of the Continental Congress from 1779 to 1781 and from 1784 to 1785, Livingston served on a wide range of committees. Elected by Congress as the nation's first secretary of foreign affairs in 1781, he oversaw the signing of the Treaty of Paris before resigning in 1783.

Active in New York political affairs, Livingston, with JOHN JAY and Gouverneur Morris, helped write the state constitution. From 1777 to 1801 he was New York state chancellor; as such, he administered the presidential oath to GEORGE WASHINGTON in 1789. It was an appropriate duty for a man who had played a prominent part in obtaining New York's ratification of the U.S. Constitution.

When he did not receive what he felt was his just share of patronage positions, Livingston split with the Federalists in 1791 and joined the new Democratic-Republican party. After failing to win election as New York governor in 1798, Livingston was appointed by THOMAS JEFFERSON as minister to France in 1801. When Napoleon offered to sell all of Louisiana to the United States, Livingston, along with JAMES MONROE, boldly exceeded his authority and accepted.

After returning to the United States in 1804, Livingston helped finance Robert Fulton's development of the Hudson River steamship *Clermont*. Although clouded by almost continuous legal challenges, Livingston continued to exercise the monopoly on steam navigation he had obtained from the state of New York in 1798 for supporting Fulton until his death in 1813.

BIBLIOGRAPHY

Dangerfield, George, *Chancellor Robert R. Livingston, 1746–1813*, 1960.

Lodge, Henry Cabot, Jr.

(July 5, 1902–February 27, 1985)
Diplomat, Senator

Born into a prominent Massachusetts family and a member of the powerful Eastern establishment, Henry Cabot Lodge, Jr., was originally an isolationist who, in the years following World War II, became a proponent of American internationalism and a determined opponent of Soviet expansion. Television made him a national figure during the 1950s when he was ambassador to the United Nations, and he ran as vice presidential candidate on the unsuccessful Republican ticket of 1960.

After graduating from Harvard College in 1924, Lodge (he dropped the "Jr." in the 1950s) spent the next seven years working as a reporter on the *Boston Evening Herald* and the *New York Herald Tribune*. First elected to public office in 1932, Lodge served in the lower house of the Massachusetts legislature from 1933 to 1936. Then, based partly on his reputation for integrity and partly on his revered family name, he was elected to the U.S. Senate. He was reelected in 1942, but resigned in order to serve on active duty in the army in North Africa, the Mediterranean, and Europe.

After his discharge from the army in 1945, Lodge was again elected to the Senate from Massachusetts in 1946; but he failed to win reelection in 1952 against JOHN F. KENNEDY. In the Senate he was most proud of his role in securing passage of the Lodge-Brown Act. This legislation led to the formation of the Hoover Commission, with HERBERT HOOVER as chairman, which studied the operation of the executive branch of the government from 1947 to 1949 and from 1953 to 1955. The reforms initiated saved a total of about $10 billion.

President DWIGHT D. EISENHOWER appointed Lodge ambassador to the United Nations (UN) in 1953, where he served until 1960. Lodge worked for a cease-fire and the dispatch of a UN emergency force to the Middle East during the Suez Canal crisis of 1956. He defended U.S. intervention in Lebanon in 1958 and the Eisenhower administration's inept response when the Soviet Union shot down an American U-2 spy plane flying over its territory in 1960. Following Lodge's unsuccessful candidacy for vice president in 1960, President Kennedy named him ambassador to South Vietnam in 1963, where civil war was raging. Lodge recommended that the United States abandon its support of the corrupt regime of President Ngo Dinh Diem. Diem and his brother were later shot in a coup by the South Vietnamese military, aided, allegedly, by the Americans. From 1965 to 1967 Lodge was charged with overseeing U.S. efforts to stabilize the South Vietnamese government, as the American involvement in the war deepened.

Lodge filled the post of ambassador to West Germany from 1968 to 1969, when he was selected to head the American delegation to

Paris that began the negotiations to end the Vietnam War (see LYNDON BAINES JOHNSON and RICHARD MILHOUS NIXON). Lodge left the deadlocked negotiations ten months later. He was selected by President Richard Nixon to serve as special envoy to the Vatican in 1970, and he worked intermittently for the next seven years with Vatican officials to halt international drug trafficking and to implement humanitarian relief projects.

BIBLIOGRAPHY

Hatch, Alden, *The Lodges of Massachusetts*, 1973; Lodge, Henry Cabot, *As It Was*, 1976.

London, Meyer

(December 29, 1871–June 6, 1926)
Representative

Meyer London was one of the few individuals ever elected to Congress on a Socialist party ticket. Elected in the latter part of the heyday of American socialism, London served a largely immigrant, Jewish, and working-class district on New York's East Side.

London was born in the Russian-Polish province of Suwalki, immigrated to New York City in 1891, began to study law, and was admitted to the bar in 1898. London quickly established himself as a lawyer and spokesman for the garment unions on New York's East Side. He supported a powerful garment workers' union strike in 1910 and a twelve-week fur workers' union strike in 1912. A spokesman for the unions, a supporter of unrestricted immigration, and a loyal member of the Socialist party, London was nominated for Congress by the New York Socialist party in 1910 and in 1912. He was unsuccessful in both races but captured over 30 percent of the vote each time. In 1914, with the support of the garment unions, he was elected to the first of two consecutive terms in the U.S. House of Representatives.

London, who lived his whole life on the East Side, cared deeply about the issues that affected immigrants and the working class.

While in the House, he introduced legislation prohibiting child labor, as well as bills that would ensure a minimum wage, unemployment insurance, and old-age pensions. London became a controversial figure as domestic conflicts escalated over the entry of the United States into World War I. He opposed U.S. involvement, conscription, and wartime sedition laws, believing that the United States should serve only as a mediator in European affairs. His moderate antiwar position angered both his political allies and his constituents, many of whom wanted him to take a stronger stand on one side or the other. He lost the election of 1918; however, two years later, he reclaimed his congressional seat.

The split in the Socialist party, the gerrymandering (see ELBRIDGE GERRY) of his district, and the unity of Democrats and Republicans behind a rival candidate prevented him from winning reelection in 1922. He retired from politics and focused his energies on his law practice. In 1926 he was fatally injured in an automobile accident.

BIBLIOGRAPHY

Howe, Irving, *World of Our Fathers*, 1976.

Long, Huey Pierce

(August 30, 1893–September 10, 1935)
Senator

Huey (the Kingfish) Long rose from poverty to national prominence by ruthlessly building a powerful political organization in Louisiana and by shrewdly appealing to the populist sentiments of that state's poor. Critics described his tactics as fascistic, but no one denied his growing popularity prior to his assassination. He was the man FRANKLIN D. ROOSEVELT feared the most in 1935 as he plotted his reelection. One fellow politician observed: "If he's a lunatic, he's the smartest lunatic I ever saw."

Library of Congress

Long was born in Winnfield, Louisiana. After a dispute with his high school principal in his senior year, Long dropped out of school. He spent the next four years earning a living as a traveling salesman, then studied law at Tulane University for a year before being admitted to the bar in 1915.

Although he established a successful practice in Shreveport, Long had already decided that his true calling was politics. In 1918 he was elected to the state railroad commission and three years later to the public service commission. His populist-inspired attacks against the Standard Oil Company (see EDWARD DOUGLASS WHITE) and other large corporations while serving in these posts won him a large statewide following.

An unsuccessful campaign as a Democrat for governor in 1924 was followed by a second victorious try in 1928. Long's platform stressed massive highway construction, free textbooks for all public school children, and new and improved public hospitals, all to be paid for by increased corporate taxes. His efforts to fulfill campaign promises incurred the wrath of powerful conservative interests and led to impeachment proceedings. Long escaped impeachment for the misuse of public funds, but the experience convinced him of the need to create a political power base strong enough to ensure that no one would ever challenge his authority again. Numerous new state agencies were created to provide patronage positions for Long supporters; his opponents were methodically eliminated from the legislature through a combination of overwhelming organization pressure, voting fraud, bribery, and intimidation.

In 1930, although only halfway through his term as governor, Long won election to the U.S. Senate. The next year he resigned from the governor's office to begin his term in the Senate, but he did not relinquish control of the state government and continued to run Louisiana from Washington, D.C.

Long supported the election of Franklin D. Roosevelt in 1932, but in the Senate he quickly became convinced that Roosevelt's New Deal legislation did not go far enough in redistributing the nation's wealth and thus would not solve the problems of the Great Depression. In the Senate, on speaking tours, over the radio (which he, along with Roosevelt and the Reverend Charles Coughlin, used to remarkable effect in establishing a national following), and in his book *Every Man a King*,

Long savagely attacked Roosevelt and advocated his own "Share the Wealth" program. In a January 1935 radio address, Long described his plan, which attracted millions of supporters: "The great wealth and abundance of this great land belongs to all of us . . . we propose laws [that use estate and income taxes to ensure that no family owns more than $5 million in property or earns more than $1 million in income.] By limiting the size of the fortunes and incomes of the big men, we will throw into the government treasury the money and property from which we will care for the millions of people who have nothing; and with this money we will provide a home and the comforts of home, with such common conveniences as radio and automobile, for every family in America, free of debt."

In addition, every family in America would be guaranteed a minimum yearly income, free education for every child through college, "a thirty-hour work week, maybe less, and eleven months per year, maybe less . . . , a pension to all persons over sixty years of age, [and] a debt moratorium on all debts which people owe that they cannot pay." In attacking those who had too much wealth and in aligning himself with the average citizen, Long showed himself to be an heir of the Populist movement of the 1890s (see JAMES BAIRD WEAVER). A measure of Long's influence can be seen in the degree to which Franklin D. Roosevelt began attacking big business and defending ordinary Americans.

As his national following grew, Long completed his efforts to gain total political control in Louisiana. His efforts to eliminate all organized opposition down to the local government level alarmed critics. He seemed on the way to becoming a virtual dictator in Louisiana, but this did not seem to inhibit Long in the state or hurt him nationally with the millions who were enthralled with his democratic rhetoric.

Long made it clear that he hoped to run for the presidency at the head of the Democratic party in 1936 or 1940, but that if he could not secure the nomination he would run as an independent. He never had the chance. He was assassinated in September 1935 by the son-in-law of a political opponent he was attempting to destroy.

Huey Long's death did not end the Long family's influence in Louisiana. His wife was appointed to complete his Senate term in 1936; one of his brothers served three terms as Louisiana's governor; another was elected to the U.S. House of Representatives; and his son, Russell Long, first elected to the U.S. Senate in 1948, became a powerful political figure as chairman of the Senate Finance Committee.

BIBLIOGRAPHY

Brinkley, Alan, *Voices of Protest: Huey Long, Father Coughlin, and the Great Depression,* 1982; Graham, Hugh D. (ed.), *Huey Long,* 1970; Long, Huey P., *My First Days in the White House,* 1935; Sindler, Allan P., *Huey Long's Louisiana: State Politics, 1920–1952,* 1956; Williams, T. Harry, *Huey Long,* 1969.

Long, John Davis

(October 27, 1838–August 28, 1915)
Secretary of the Navy, Representative

John Davis Long was born in Buckfield, Maine. After graduating from Harvard College in 1857, he completed his formal education at Harvard Law School and was admitted to the bar in 1861. Two years later he established a successful practice in Boston and joined the Republican party. Within a decade, Long had become a leading political figure in Massachusetts. After serving in the Massachusetts House of Representatives from 1875 to 1878, he was elected lieutenant governor in 1879, and in 1880, 1881, and 1882 governor. From 1883 to 1889, he served in the U.S. House of Representatives.

In 1897, shortly before the Spanish-American War, President WILLIAM MCKINLEY appoin-ted Long secretary of the navy. He performed ably in this post during the war and earned considerable praise for the U.S. Navy's superb performance in the conflict. After briefly holding his post under President THEODORE ROOSEVELT, Long returned to the private practice of law in 1902.

BIBLIOGRAPHY

Long, John Davis, *The New American Navy*, 2 vols., 1903; Mayo, L. S. (ed.), *America of Yesterday, as Reflected in the Journal of John Davis Long*, 1923.

Longworth, Nicholas

(November 5, 1869–April 9, 1931)
Speaker of the House, Representative

Nicholas Longworth was born in Cincinnati, Ohio, into a wealthy and influential family. He graduated from Harvard College in 1891 and, three years later, from the Law School of Cincinnati College. After establishing his own law practice in Cincinnati, Longworth became active in the Republican party. He began his political career in 1898 by winning election to the Cincinnati board of education. With the help of local Republican party leader George Cox, Longworth was elected to the Ohio House of Representatives in 1898 and then to the state senate in 1900.

In 1902 he was elected to his first term in the U.S. House of Representatives and was re-elected every two years thereafter until the 1912 election. The decision of THEODORE ROOSEVELT to run for president again in 1912 against fellow Republican WILLIAM HOWARD TAFT placed Longworth in a particularly difficult position on a personal as well as a political level. He was married to Theodore Roosevelt's daughter, Alice Lee, but had promised Taft he would support his candidacy before Roosevelt had decided to run. In a remarkable feat of political dexterity, Longworth managed to keep his word to Taft and to avoid offending his father-in-law. Still, the Republican party split caused by Roosevelt's candidacy enabled the Democrats to capture control of Congress and cost Longworth his seat in the House. Two years later, he won reelection and was never defeated for reelection again. In 1923 he became floor leader of the Republican majority in the House and from 1925 until his death in 1931 served as Speaker.

BIBLIOGRAPHY

Chambrun, Clara Longworth, *Nicholas Longworth,* 1933; Longworth, Alice Roosevelt, *Crowded Hours,* 1933.

Luce, Clare Boothe

(April 10, 1903–October 9, 1987)
Diplomat, Representative

The successful politician, journalist, and playwright Clare Boothe Luce was born in New York. She began her career as a writer at *Vanity Fair* in 1929, became its managing editor in 1933, and resigned in 1934 out of frustration over her inability to include more coverage of politics in the magazine.

In 1935 she married Henry R. Luce, one of the nation's most influential publishers, whose magazines included *Time, Life,* and *Fortune.* Clare Luce could have basked in her husband's wealth, but instead she obtained fame on her own. She wrote several hit Broadway plays, served as a war correspondent during World War II, completed two terms (1943–1947) in the House of Representatives from Connecticut, and was the ambassador to Italy from 1953 to 1957.

President DWIGHT D. EISENHOWER nominated her as the ambassador to Brazil in 1959. Sen-

Library of Congress

ator WAYNE MORSE, who thought her conservative views made her an inappropriate diplomat to an increasingly discontented Latin America, brought attention to some earlier psychiatric care she had once had and caused her, as people began to question her suitability, to decline the nomination. The episode was made famous by her spirited and witty riposte that Wayne Morse had once been kicked in the head by a horse.

A committed conservative, Luce seconded the nomination of BARRY GOLDWATER at the 1964 Republican convention. After her husband died in 1967, she lived in Honolulu, Hawaii, until returning to Washington, D.C., in 1983. Her last position was as a member of the Foreign Intelligence Advisory Board.

BIBLIOGRAPHY

Shadegg, Stephen, *Clare Boothe Luce,* 1971.

McAdoo, William Gibbs

(October 31, 1863–February 1, 1941)
Secretary of the Treasury, Senator

Progressive Democratic politician William McAdoo is recalled for his superb management of the Treasury Department during the administration of Woodrow Wilson and effective use of the media to encourage the purchase of World War I bonds by the general public.

McAdoo was born near Marietta, Georgia. He attended the University of Tennessee from 1879 to 1882 and became a lawyer in 1885. When his Chattanooga, Tennessee, law practice failed, he moved to New York City in 1892 and made a fortune building four tunnels under the Hudson River to connect Manhattan and New Jersey.

As a Progressive (see Woodrow Wilson and Theodore Roosevelt) active in the Democratic party, he was an early supporter of Wilson's political career. McAdoo backed Wilson's successful run for governor of New Jersey in 1910 and managed his campaign for the presidency in 1912.

President Wilson appointed McAdoo secretary of the treasury in 1913, and McAdoo's ideas were important in establishing a centralized banking system through the Federal Reserve Act (1913). In 1914 he married Wilson's daughter, Eleanor. During World War I, McAdoo displayed superb organizational skills and a remarkable flair for arousing public enthusiasm for supporting the war effort. In addition to serving as secretary of the treasury, he was chairman of the Federal Reserve Board, the Federal Farm Loan Board, and the War Finance Corporation, as well as director of the railroads after their management was taken over by the government in 1917. The four Liberty Loan drives he organized to stimulate the purchase by the general public of government war bonds in 1917 and 1918 collected more than $18 billion for the Allied war effort.

McAdoo resigned from his cabinet post in 1919 and returned to the private practice of law in New York City. He was often mentioned as a possible nominee for president, but he never won the nomination. He came close in 1924, but his identification with William Jennings Bryan, Prohibition, and other culturally conservative positions aroused the opposition of the party's urban and immigrant constituencies. The 1924 Democratic convention dragged on for 103 ballots before rejecting McAdoo and Al Smith (who represented the party's urban wing) in favor of a compromise candidate, John W. Davis.

McAdoo had moved to California in 1922, and he continued to remain politically active there. He supported Franklin D. Roosevelt for president in 1932 and won election to the U.S. Senate himself that fall. In the Senate he supported the New Deal, but he lost his bid to win reelection in 1938 and retired from politics.

Bibliography

Burner, David, *The Politics of Provincialism,* 1967; McAdoo, William G., *Challenge—Liquor and Lawlessness Versus Constitutional Government,* 1928, and *Crowded Years,* 1938.

McCarthy, Eugene Joseph

(March 29, 1916–   )
Candidate for President, Senator, Representative

Eugene McCarthy's opposition to the Vietnam War (see LYNDON BAINES JOHNSON and RICHARD MILHOUS NIXON) and his electoral challenge to President Johnson in 1968 electrified the nation's college youth and brought thousands into active involvement in Democratic party affairs.

Born in Watkins, Minnesota, McCarthy graduated from St. John's University in Collegeville, Minnesota, and received his master's degree from the University of Minnesota in 1939. After teaching public high school from 1935 to 1940, McCarthy became a professor of economics and education at St. John's University until 1944, when he became a civilian technical assistant to the Military Intelligence Division of the War Department. From 1946 to 1948 he was a sociology professor at the College of St. Thomas in St. Paul, Minnesota.

In 1948 McCarthy was elected to the U.S. House of Representatives on the Democratic-Farmer-Labor ticket, and he served there for ten years. He was elected to the Senate in 1958 and reelected in 1964. While there, he established an independent, liberal voting record.

McCarthy opposed President Lyndon Johnson on several issues, most notably U.S. involvement in Vietnam, and ran against him in 1968 for the Democratic presidential nomination. McCarthy declared: "My decision to challenge the President's position [on Vietnam] has been strengthened by recent announcements by the Administration of plans for continued escalation and intensification of the war in Vietnam and, on the other hand, by the absence of any positive indications or suggestions for a compromise or negotiated political settlement. I am concerned that the Administration seems to have placed no limits on the price that it will pay for military victory."

The Tet offensive in January 1968 added to the public's loss of confidence in the administration and contributed to a growing desire to protest the course of the war. In March, McCarthy won a stunning 42.4 percent of the votes in the New Hampshire primary. His upset defeat of incumbent Johnson caused Senator ROBERT F. KENNEDY to enter the race for the nomination and led to President Johnson's surprise announcement on March 31, 1968, that he would not seek reelection.

After Senator Kennedy's assassination, Democratic party regulars supported Vice President HUBERT HUMPHREY, who won the nomination but lost the general election to Richard Nixon. McCarthy then decided not to seek reelection to the Senate in 1970. Never entirely comfortable with the adulation showered upon him in 1968, he failed to turn that outpouring of support into an ongoing political movement. When he campaigned again for president as an independent in 1976, he received only about 1 percent of the popular vote.

BIBLIOGRAPHY

McCarthy, Eugene, *The Limits of Power*, 1967, and *The Ultimate Tyranny: The Majority Over the Majority*, 1980.

McCarthy, Joseph Raymond

(November 14, 1908–May 2, 1957)
Senator

Although an undistinguished legislator, Joseph McCarthy was responsible for an indelible chapter of Senate history. Because of his unsubstantiated but politically popular charges that the government was infiltrated with communist agents, McCarthy earned the dubious distinction of having his name become synonymous with character assassination and guilt by association for political gain.

Library of Congress

Born in Grand Chute, Wisconsin, McCarthy graduated from Marquette University Law School in 1935. After winning election as a judge by lying about his opponent's qualifications and age, McCarthy performed so poorly on the bench that he was reprimanded by the Wisconsin Supreme Court.

At the outbreak of World War II McCarthy resigned from the bench to join the U.S. Marine Corps. He was assigned as an airplane tailgunner and adopted the nickname Tailgunner Joe, even though he never saw combat.

Upon his discharge, McCarthy decided to run as a Republican for the U.S. Senate against the Democratic incumbent, Robert M. La Follette, Jr. La Follette underestimated Tailgunner Joe McCarthy's vote-getting appeal and, in a major political upset, was defeated by McCarthy. McCarthy had managed to win a seat in the Senate, but once there he could not manage to establish any kind of political reputation that would guarantee him reelection.

Then, in 1950, McCarthy began to exploit the anticommunism hysteria already gripping the nation. Before McCarthy picked up the theme, President HARRY S TRUMAN had used the issue of communism to whip up support for his containment policies in 1947 and to institute loyalty oaths for federal employees. The House Un-American Activities Committee was already in existence and was hot on the trail of communists in Hollywood. Representative RICHARD NIXON of California had used communism to get elected in 1946 and was working with Wittaker Chambers to convict Alger Hiss as a spy (see RICHARD MILHOUS NIXON and DEAN GOODERHAM ACHESON). In 1949 China had fallen to the communists and the Soviet Union had exploded an atomic bomb. So, in many ways, McCarthy was as much a product of the postwar inquisition as he was its creator.

In a speech delivered on February 9, 1950, McCarthy brandished a piece of paper on which he claimed he had a list supplied by the Federal Bureau of Investigation (FBI) of 205 names of U.S. State Department employees who were known to be "card-carrying communists." It was a false claim, but his dramatic demeanor and the fact that he was a senator lent credibility to the charges. The massive public response to his charges surprised even McCarthy. Although he could not produce any evidence and kept changing the number of names he had when pressed by reporters, his power and influence grew.

McCarthy managed to stay ahead of his critics by making new charges instead of admitting that he had fabricated old ones and silencing those who attacked him in the

Senate by threatening them with defeat at the polls. McCarthy claimed that Owen Lattimore, a Johns Hopkins professor and diplomat for the State Department, was "the top Russian espionage agent" in the department. When Senator Millard Tydings of Maryland produced an FBI report that proved Lattimore had never been involved with communism or communist agents, McCarthy attacked Tydings's loyalty. McCarthy had a fake photograph made showing Tydings talking with the American Communist party leader Earl Browder. McCarthy's claim that Tydings had come to Lattimore's defense to divert attention from his own communist activities stuck and contributed to Tydings's electoral defeat in 1950.

Although McCarthy himself never unearthed a single communist spy, he became so powerful that even DWIGHT D. EISENHOWER, in his 1952 presidential campaign, did not dare to criticize him. Eisenhower even refused to challenge McCarthy's calumnious charge that GEORGE C. MARSHALL was the kind of man who "would sell his grandmother for any advantage," and therefore had become part of a communist "conspiracy so immense and an infamy so black as to dwarf any previous such venture in the history of man." Senator William Benton of Connecticut, who filed a motion to censure McCarthy for slandering Marshall, was defeated for reelection.

The Republican party capitalized on the hysteria McCarthy had generated in order to put Democratic candidates on the defensive in congressional races. Since no Democrat could afford to be labeled "soft on communism," many endeavored to earn reputations for being even more dedicated than McCarthy in defeating the supposed internal and external communist menace.

Finally, in 1954, after the Korean War had ended and the threat of World War III no longer appeared imminent, the mood of the nation began to shift. On April 22, 1954, after several years of enduring McCarthy's false charges about subversion in the military forces, the U.S. Army, represented by Attorney Joseph N. Welch, went on the offensive and attacked McCarthy with a charge of corruption. The army's charge was based on the fact that McCarthy and his counsel, Roy Cohn, had demanded special treatment for former associate Private G. David Schine. Cohn had threatened that if he (Cohn) was not satisfied, he would use his political influence as McCarthy's aide to "wreck the army."

In over a month of televised hearings, Attorney Welch proceeded to show via live televised congressional hearings how McCarthy had doctored photographs and created other false documents to provide evidence for his unsubstantiated earlier charges. McCarthy's erratic behavior and the constant traps Welch laid to catch him lying made it obvious to the television audience which side was telling the truth.

After the televised hearings and McCarthy's public humiliation, a majority of senators finally felt sufficiently secure enough to vote to censure him on December 2, 1954. He died a broken man three years later.

"McCarthyism" and "McCarthy tactics" are terms that have come to symbolize demagoguery in American politics. As a result of McCarthy's unsubstantiated charges and abuse of the privileges of his office, the careers and reputations of countless innocent victims were ruined.

BIBLIOGRAPHY

Adams, John G., *Without Precedent: The Story of the Death of McCarthyism,* 1985; Bristol, James E., *McCarthyism,* 1983; Crosby, Donald F., *God, Church, and Flag, Senator Joseph R. McCarthy and the Catholic Church,* 1978; Ewald, William B., Jr., *McCarthyism and Consensus,* 1986; Griffith, Robert D., *The Politics of Fear: Joseph R. McCarthy and the Senate,* 1970; Oshinsky, David, *A Conspiracy So Immense: The World of Joe McCarthy,* 1983; Rogin, Michael P., *The Intellectuals and McCarthy: The Radical Specter,* 1967; Rovere, Richard H., *Senator Joe McCarthy,* 1959.

McClellan, George Brinton

(December 3, 1826–October 29, 1885)
Candidate for President

George B. McClellan, West Point graduate and Mexican War veteran, seemed the logical choice to lead the Union forces in 1861, but his egotism and overcautiousness cost the Union the chance to end the Civil War quickly and finally forced Lincoln to relieve him of command in 1862. Thereafter McClellan identified with the political opposition to Abraham Lincoln and in 1864 ran unsuccessfully for president as a Democrat.

Born in Philadelphia, McClellan graduated from West Point in 1846. As a second lieutenant in the Engineer Corps, McClellan fought under General Winfield Scott in the Mexican War (see James Knox Polk and Winfield Scott). From 1848 to 1851, he served as an instructor at West Point and in 1855, after being promoted to captain, was assigned to visit Europe in order to study new military techniques. While in Europe, McClellan observed the siege of Sevastopol during the Crimean War. As a result of his trip, McClellan successfully proposed the adoption by the U.S. cavalry of a new type of saddle, which came to be known as the McClellan saddle.

In 1857 McClellan resigned his commission in order to become the chief engineer of the Illinois Central Railroad. The next year he was made vice president in charge of operations, and in 1860 he became president of the Ohio & Mississippi Railroad.

When the Civil War broke out, McClellan was commissioned a major general of the Ohio volunteers and then quickly appointed a major general in the regular army in command of the Department of the Ohio. Troops under his command drove Confederate forces from western Virginia. After the Union forces were routed at the first battle of Manassas (Bull Run), President Lincoln asked McClellan to assume command of the Washington theater of military operations. McClellan succeeded in whipping the disparate and demoralized troops he found there into soldiers quickly and efficiently enough to be appointed general in chief of all Union armies. Then, at the pinnacle of his military career, McClellan succumbed to indecisiveness. A perfectionist, he constantly overestimated the size and skill of his Confederate adversaries and underestimated the capability of his own men. As a result, he lost invaluable time obtaining more troops instead of obeying Lincoln's orders to go on the offensive.

A conspicuous example of this was the peninsula campaign in the spring of 1862, in which McClellan marched his army within earshot of the bells of Richmond, then failed to launch an attack on the city.

His downfall came, ironically, after a crucial victory at Antietam, when he halted Robert E. Lee's invasion of Maryland. Although Lee was forced to retreat, McClellan, much to the fury of Lincoln, did not pursue and destroy Lee's army before it could escape. On October 13 an exasperated Lincoln asked McClellan: "Are you not overcautious when you assume that you cannot do what the enemy is constantly doing?" A month later Lincoln relieved McClellan of command. McClellan never led an army in the field again.

McClellan was against issuing the Emancipation Proclamation (see Abraham Lincoln) after Antietam and sided with the Democrats, who opposed Lincoln's war aims of preservation of the Union *and* emancipation.

In 1864 the Democrats nominated McClellan for the presidency, depicting him as a scapegoat for administration political and military ineptness. Running on a platform advocating the pursuit of a negotiated peace, McClellan's chances seemed good until a series of Union military victories reestablished the voters' faith in Lincoln's leadership. Many Northern voters also distrusted the Democratic party as too pro-Southern. After Lincoln's reelection McClellan faded from public view, although he emerged to serve as governor of New Jersey from 1878 to 1881.

BIBLIOGRAPHY

Eckenrode, Hamilton J., and Bryan Conrad, *George B. McClellan*, 1941; Hassler, Warren W., Jr., *General George B. McClellan*, 1957; McClellan, George B., *McClellan's Own Story*, 1887; Myers, W. S., *A Study in Personality: General George Brinton McClellan*, 1934.

McCloy, John Jay

(March 31, 1895–)
Assistant Secretary of War, Diplomat

In one of his many important diplomatic posts during his years of public service, John J. McCloy earned the title "Architect of West Germany" for his work in helping to transform a war-torn occupied area into a prosperous, independent, democratic nation.

McCloy was born in Philadelphia. He graduated from Amherst College in 1916 and attended Harvard Law School until he enlisted in the army in May 1917. McCloy served as a captain in the U.S. forces in France and Germany for two years, then returned to the United States and completed his law studies at Harvard in 1921. From 1921 until he became Secretary of War HENRY L. STIMSON's expert consultant on counterespionage in October 1940, McCloy practiced corporate law in New York City.

In April 1941 McCloy was appointed assistant secretary of war by President FRANKLIN D. ROOSEVELT. He remained in this post throughout World War II. His duties included helping to secure passage of the Lend-Lease Act (see FRANKLIN DELANO ROOSEVELT); supporting the intelligence unit that broke the Japanese war codes; supervising the evacuation of Japanese Americans from the West Coast to internment camps in the country's interior; successfully lobbying for the creation of Japanese American army units; visiting the operational war theaters; participating in the Casablanca, Cairo, and Potsdam Conferences; and formulating the plans for the Nuremberg war crimes trials after World War II.

McCloy resigned as assistant secretary of war in November 1945 and returned to private law practice in New York. He remained involved in government affairs, however, serving in 1946 and 1947 as a member of the State Department's committee on atomic energy. From 1947 to 1949, as president of the International Bank for Reconstruction and Development, he succeeded in establishing the credibility of the institution in the eyes of the American investment community.

From 1949 to 1952 McCloy played an important role in the creation of democratic West Germany (the German Federal Republic). He served as the first U.S. high commissioner for Germany, chief Economic Cooperation Administration representative, and U.S. military governor of the American zone of occupied West Germany.

In 1953 McCloy became chairman of the board of the Chase Manhattan Bank. At the same time, he chaired the Council on Foreign Relations. In January 1961 President JOHN F. KENNEDY appointed McCloy as his chief adviser on disarmament. He resigned nine months later after first the Soviet Union, then the United States, resumed aboveground nuclear weapons testing. In 1963 and 1964, he served on the Warren Commission, which investigated the assassination of President Kennedy.

In addition to his law practice work in New York during the 1960s and 1970s, McCloy frequently served as a special consultant in foreign policy and national security matters to Presidents LYNDON JOHNSON, RICHARD NIXON, GERALD FORD, and JIMMY CARTER.

BIBLIOGRAPHY

Brinkley, Alan, "Minister Without Portfolio," *Harpers*, February 1983, p. 30; McCloy, John Jay, *The Challenge to American Foreign Policy*, 1953; "A Taste for Diplomacy," *New York Times*, January 3, 1961.

McCormack, John William

(December 21, 1891–November 22, 1980)
Speaker of the House, Representative

John William McCormack was born in South Boston, Massachusetts, into an impoverished Irish family. Forced to leave school at age thirteen to work full time, the largely self-taught McCormack studied law while working in a law office and was admitted to the bar in 1913. After serving in the army as a sergeant major during World War I, McCormack, who had always been active in local Democratic party politics, served in the Massachusetts legislature from 1920 to 1926. In 1928 he won the first of many elections to the U.S. House of Representatives.

As a freshman congressman, McCormack's love of poker and undeviating loyalty won the appreciation of JOHN NANCE GARNER, then Democratic minority leader. When Garner became Speaker of the House in 1931, he appointed McCormack to a coveted seat on the powerful House Ways and Means Committee. In this important position after only one term in the House, McCormack was able to play an important role in securing enactment of President FRANKLIN D. ROOSEVELT's New Deal legislation. A virulent foe of communism, McCormack sponsored several anticommunist measures during the 1930s, and in 1934 he was appointed the first chairman of the House Un-American Activities Committee. In 1941 he played a key role in securing passage of the unpopular legislation to extend draft enlistments just three months before the Japanese attack on Pearl Harbor (see FRANKLIN DELANO ROOSEVELT).

During his four decades in the House McCormack developed a reputation as a diligent legislator perhaps best categorized as a moderate liberal. He taught himself to be an expert on tax matters and served as majority floor leader from 1940 to 1961, except for the two brief periods the Republicans controlled the House (1947–1949 and 1953–1955), when he was minority whip.

Nicknamed the Archbishop by foes because of his strong identification with the Roman Catholic church in 1962, McCormack became the first Irish Catholic to be elected Speaker of the House. A consistent defender of minority rights, McCormack once replied to a hostile racist comment by Representative John Rankin of Mississippi: "A man's racial origin means nothing to me, a person's name means nothing to me. A person's religion I respect. But what does mean everything to me is a person's mind. And when I meet a person with a bigoted mind, I am meeting a person I do not like, a person I have nothing but contempt for." As Speaker, McCormack continued his careful negotiating of compromise positions between conservatives and liberals in the Democratic party that he had become well known for as majority leader. His help played a vital role in securing the passage of the Civil Rights Act of 1964 and other Great Society programs of LYNDON JOHNSON. McCormack retained the position of Speaker until his retirement from Congress in 1971.

BIBLIOGRAPHY

Current Biography, 1962; *New York Post Magazine*, February 18, 1962; *New York Times*, January 11, 1962; *Time*, January 19, 1962.

McGovern, George Stanley

(July 19, 1922–)
Candidate for President, Senator, Representative

George McGovern became one of Congress's most outspoken critics of the Vietnam War (see LYNDON BAINES JOHNSON and RICHARD MILHOUS NIXON) and the most prominent leader of the liberal wing of the Democratic party after Senator ROBERT F. KENNEDY's assassination in 1968. He secured the Democratic party's nomination for president in 1972 only to be overwhelmingly defeated by President Richard Nixon in the general election.

Born in Avon, South Dakota, McGovern grew up in Mitchell, where his father was a Methodist minister. Enrolled at Dakota Wesleyan University on a scholarship in 1940, McGovern left in 1943 to join the Army Air Force, serving as a B-24 bomber pilot in Europe during World War II.

After the war he was at first interested in becoming a minister, but he decided to study history and earned his Ph.D. at Northwestern University in 1953. McGovern began his political career in 1953 when he became executive secretary of the South Dakota Democratic party. In 1956 he was elected to the U.S. House of Representatives but lost a bid for the Senate in 1960. In 1961 President JOHN F. KENNEDY appointed him director of the Food for Peace Program, a post in harmony with his deep religious idealism. His second try to be elected to the Senate in 1962 was successful, and he served there until 1981.

In the Senate, although he had voted for the Tonkin Gulf Resolution in 1964, McGovern soon became one of the most outspoken critics of Lyndon Johnson's handling of the war in Vietnam. After an unsuccessful run for the Democratic party's presidential nomination in 1968, he supported, much to the chagrin of his antiwar colleagues, the candidacy of his mentor, Vice President HUBERT HUMPHREY.

Policies McGovern supported as chairman of the Democratic party's reform commission in 1969 greatly increased the importance of primaries in the selection of the party's presidential nominee. McGovern won the Democratic party's nomination in 1972, but his campaign in the general election was a disaster for several reasons.

The split that had occurred in 1968 in the Democratic party along class and ideological lines—doves and hawks, cultural liberals and cultural conservatives, middle class and working class—had not mended by 1972. McGovern was a representative of liberals and middle-class Democrats. His nomination prompted a wholesale flight of conservatives and working-class Democrats to the Republican party and Richard Nixon.

Given the deeply divided state of the Democrats, it is unlikely that a more conservative candidate would have been able to secure many more votes than McGovern, but his tactical blunders also contributed significantly to his wide margin of defeat. When it was discovered that the man he had chosen to be his vice presidential running mate, Senator Thomas F. Eagleton of Missouri, had received electric shock therapy for depression some years before, McGovern said he still supported him on the ticket "1,000 percent." However, as public concern mounted over Eagleton's dependability, McGovern replaced Eagleton with R. Sargent Shriver, Jr. This decision won McGovern many critics. When he backed off on a plan to establish a guaranteed annual income for every American family after Republicans successfully attacked it as a giveaway to those who would not work, some of his supporters saw this as another expedient decision. Because of his antiwar sentiment in the 1970s, McGovern was also perceived as soft on maintaining America's military defenses. In the general election results, President Nixon won every state except Massachusetts and the District of Columbia.

McGovern was reelected to the Senate in 1974, but he lost his seat in 1980 to a Republican. He made another doomed, largely symbolic effort to win the Democratic party's presidential nomination in 1984, after which he retired from politics.

BIBLIOGRAPHY

Anson, Robert S., *McGovern: A Biography,* 1977; Hart, Gary Warren, *McGovern—Right from the Start: A Chronicle of the McGovern Campaign,* 1973; McGovern, George, *A Time of War—A Time of Peace,* 1968, and *An American Journey,* 1974.

McKinley, William, Jr.

(January 29, 1843–September 14, 1901)
President, Representative

William McKinley was president when the United States became a world power at the turn of the century. During his administration the country defeated Spain in the Spanish-American War, annexed the Hawaiian islands, and acquired overseas colonial possessions.

Born in Niles, Ohio, McKinley attended Allegheny College for one term before illness forced him to withdraw. Unable to afford to return, he taught school and clerked in a post office until volunteering for the Ohio militia at the outbreak of the Civil War. During the war McKinley rose to the rank of major and

Library of Congress

established a permanent friendship with his commanding officer, RUTHERFORD B. HAYES. Upon his discharge in 1865, McKinley studied law for less than one term at Albany Law School and in 1867 established his own successful practice in Canton, Ohio. A Republican, the popular and confident McKinley immediately became active in local politics and won election as a prosecuting attorney in Stark County.

A tragic result of McKinley's quick climb to political and social success was his wife's deteriorating mental health over the course of their marriage. Apparently due to the death of their two children, she suffered increasingly frequent epileptic fits and prolonged periods of depression. McKinley, who remained a loyal and devoted husband, found solace in his deep religious faith.

The popular and convivial McKinley was elected to the U.S. House of Representatives in 1876. As congressman from Ohio, he supported civil service reform, efforts to ensure that newly enfranchised black males could exercise their right to vote, and the need for high tariffs. At the 1888 Republican national convention McKinley made an important friendship. Multimillionaire MARCUS HANNA, eager to use his fortune and organizing skills to elect a Republican president, was so impressed by McKinley's economic views and political skill that he vowed to use all his influence to help McKinley achieve the presidency.

In 1890 the Democratic Ohio legislature gerrymandered (see ELBRIDGE GERRY) McKinley's congressional district so that he failed to win reelection. However, before the end of his term, Congress passed the protectionist McKinley Tariff Act. The controversial tariff made McKinley a well-known national figure. The next year, with the support of Hanna's money and organizational skills, McKinley was elected governor of Ohio by a wide margin.

As governor, McKinley earned a reputation as someone who would look after the interests of the average voter as well as those of the business community. Although he called out the National Guard to crush a violent strike by coal miners in 1894, he also won legislation that established a board to arbitrate labor disputes and succeeded in reforming the Ohio tax code so that proportionately more money was collected from corporations than from small property owners.

McKinley's reelection as governor and Hanna's skill in securing delegate support before the Republican convention met combined to win McKinley the Republican nomination for president in 1896 on the first ballot. The most controversial issue in the election concerned the party's position on the use of gold and/or silver to back the nation's currency. The na-

tion was divided between those who believed in the unlimited coinage of silver and those who supported the exclusive use of gold. McKinley and the Republican party argued that the "existing gold standard must be maintained." The Democrats, with WILLIAM JENNINGS BRYAN as their nominee, supported the coinage of silver.

The well-financed and superbly organized McKinley campaign was orchestrated by Hanna. McKinley shrewdly conducted a restrained "front porch" campaign. Funds were provided for voters to visit him in Canton, Ohio, and the railroad companies issued free passes. Bryan, introducing a new style of campaign, stumped every section of the nation systematically. He spoke to millions of voters and apparently antagonized many, for McKinley won the election with 271 electoral votes to Bryan's 176.

McKinley's first priority in office was to secure the passage of a new high protective tariff, which he accomplished in 1897. However, the issue that dominated his first term was the war with Spain that began in 1898. Aroused by the brutal efforts of the Spanish to crush a rebellion in Cuba and the growing imperialist sentiment to acquire colonies, McKinley attempted to seek a diplomatic solution. Events, however, such as the publication of an insulting letter about McKinley by the Spanish ambassador, the explosion of the battleship *Maine* in Cuba, the inability of Spain to reach a settlement with the Cuban rebels, and the efforts of the Hearst newspaper chain to provoke a war, pushed a reluctant McKinley to request a declaration of war against Spain.

The badly prepared Spanish forces were defeated in only a few months of fighting by the modern U.S. Navy and the ill-equipped but still superior U.S. Army. Spain accepted the terms for peace: independence for Cuba, and the transfer of Puerto Rico and the island of Guam to the United States. The fate of the conquered Philippine islands was to be decided at the peace conference. During the war McKinley had also accomplished the annexation of the Hawaiian islands through a joint resolution of Congress.

The question over what to do with the conquered Philippines was the most controversial territorial acquisition decision McKinley had to make. He later said that he "walked the floor of the White House night after night until midnight, and I am not ashamed to tell you . . . I went down on my knees and prayed to Almighty God for light and guidance more than one night. And one night it came to me . . . that there was nothing left for us to do but to take them all, and to educate the Filipinos, and uplift them and civilize and Christianize them. . . . " McKinley overlooked the fact that the islands were already Christian and had a revolutionary government that had supported the U.S. invasion under the promise that the Philippines would obtain their independence. Spain surrendered the islands for $20 million.

The annexation of the Philippines stirred a frenzy of debate in Congress. The Treaty of Paris with Spain passed by only one more vote than needed in the Senate. The Filipinos did not accept American domination without resistance, and a fierce and costly guerrilla war began between Filipino independence fighters and U.S. forces that lasted three years.

Another foreign policy issue of great importance during McKinley's first term concerned the American reaction to the scramble of European powers to carve up China into colonial spheres of influence. In 1900 Secretary of State JOHN HAY made the position of the United States in China clear with the announcement of U.S. support for an Open Door policy, a policy actually originating with the British. Hay stated that it was the goal of the United States in China to ensure equality of commercial exploitation opportunity among all nations and guarantee existing Chinese rights and treaties.

The final accomplishment of the McKinley administration concerned the debate over whether gold or both gold and silver should be used to back the nation's currency. In 1900, with the passage of the Gold Standard Act by Congress, McKinley delivered on his campaign pledge to support gold exclusively.

Although tired, McKinley accepted nomination for a second term. His new vice presidential running mate was THEODORE ROOSEVELT. Once again, McKinley easily defeated Democratic candidate William Jennings Bryan. However, only six months into his second term, on September 6, 1901, McKinley was shot by an anarchist. He died eight days later.

BIBLIOGRAPHY

Glad, Paul W., *McKinley, Bryan, and the People*, 1964; Gould, Lewis L., *The Presidency of William McKinley*, 1980; Leech, Margaret, *In the Days of McKinley*, 1959; Morgan, H. Wayne, *William McKinley*, 1963; Olcot, C. S., *Life of William McKinley*, 2 vols., 1916.

McLane, Louis

(May 28, 1786–October 7, 1857)
Secretary of State, Secretary of the Treasury, Diplomat, Senator, Representative

Louis McLane was born in Smyrna, Delaware. He entered the navy at age twelve and served as a midshipman until 1801, when he briefly attended Newark College (now the University of Delaware) and began the study of law. After being admitted to the bar in 1807, he established a practice in Smyrna. McLane's political career began in 1817 when he was elected as a Democratic-Republican to the U.S. House of Representatives. He served in the House until he became a senator in 1827. In Congress he generally supported the party line, except for his refusal to condone attacks upon the Bank of the United States (see NICHOLAS BIDDLE and ROGER BROOKE TANEY).

In 1829 President ANDREW JACKSON repaid McLane for his help in the election of 1828 by naming him minister to England. What McLane really wanted was to be named to the Supreme Court. Three years later, he was recalled and appointed secretary of the treasury, a position he was forced to resign from because of his well-known support for the bank after Jackson vetoed the bill to recharter it in 1832. Even though McLane opposed Jackson's bank policy, he and the president remained friends. Jackson named him secretary of state in 1833, but McLane resigned from this post a year later after he realized he had virtually no chance of being nominated by Jackson for the Supreme Court.

After leaving the cabinet, McLane became president of the Morris Canal and Banking Company of New York from 1834 to 1837 and then president of the Baltimore & Ohio Railroad from 1837 to 1847. Again appointed minister to England in June 1845, McLane negotiated the compromise between the United States and Great Britain over the Oregon boundary line (see JAMES KNOX POLK) before returning to the United States in August 1846. He declined an appointment as minister to Mexico in 1848, served as a member of the convention that reformed the constitution of Maryland in 1850, and then retired.

BIBLIOGRAPHY

Bemis, S. F., *The American Secretaries of State and Their Departments*, 1928.

McNamara, Robert Strange

(June 9, 1916–   )
Secretary of Defense

Robert McNamara served as secretary of defense for seven years under Presidents JOHN F. KENNEDY and LYNDON B. JOHNSON. He brought the Defense Department under strict civilian control and successfully introduced management techniques he had developed during World War II for the air force and as controller at Ford Motor Company. These accomplishments were overshadowed, however, by his failure to achieve neither a victory nor a quick withdrawal from the war in Vietnam.

Born in San Francisco, McNamara graduated with honors from the University of California at Berkeley in 1937. Two years later, he earned his MBA at Harvard University's Graduate School of Business Administration. During World War II, while teaching a statistical systems course at Harvard, McNamara perfected a method of organizing the huge flow of men, equipment, and money necessary to conduct the war.

In 1949, McNamara accepted a position as controller at Ford Motor Company. He was promoted to vice president and had just become president of the company when President Kennedy nominated him to be secretary of defense in 1960.

McNamara strongly supported the diversification of American military forces (flexible response) and weapons systems in order to give presidents alternatives to massive retaliation and brinkmanship in times of crisis (see JOHN FOSTER DULLES). His no-nonsense statistical style and hardheaded management techniques quickly endeared him to Kennedy.

After Kennedy's assassination, President Johnson came to rely upon McNamara's advice in conducting the war in Vietnam (see LYNDON BAINES JOHNSON and RICHARD MILHOUS NIXON), which critics dubbed "McNamara's War." Johnson once remarked, "I thank God every night for Bob McNamara."

At first convinced that gradual military escalation by the United States could win the war in Vietnam, by 1967 McNamara had changed his mind and had come to conclude that the cost of military victory was too high, both in human lives and economically. Attacked by both military men for not supporting a rapid escalation of the war and antiwar critics for the continuance of fighting in Vietnam, McNamara decided to resign from his office to assume the position of president of the International Bank for Reconstruction and Development (World Bank) in 1968.

As president of the World Bank, McNamara obtained the admission of China to the bank's membership in 1980 and strongly supported increased aid to help the poor in underdeveloped nations. He retired from the bank in 1981 and since that time has written and spoken extensively on the threat of nuclear war.

BIBLIOGRAPHY

McNamara, Robert S., *The Essence of Security: Reflections in Office*, 1968, and *One Hundred Countries, Two Billion People*, 1973.

Macon, Nathaniel

(December 17, 1758–June 29, 1837)
Speaker of the House, Senator, Representative

Nathaniel Macon was born at Macon Manor, Edgecombe (now Warren) County, North Carolina. He studied at the College of New Jersey (now Princeton) from 1774 to 1776, served briefly in the New Jersey militia, then studied law for three years. From 1780 to 1782 he served in the Continental Army. He left the army after being elected to the first of three consecutive terms as a North Carolina state senator.

A devout defender of states' rights, Macon opposed the ratification of the Constitution on the grounds that it gave too much power to the central government. Nevertheless, he became an important figure in the new national government, where he served in the U.S. House of Representatives from 1791 to 1815 (as Speaker from 1801 to 1807) and in the Senate from 1815 to 1828 (as president pro tempore from 1826 to 1828).

As a friend and political ally of THOMAS JEFFERSON, Macon fought the programs of Secretary of the Treasury ALEXANDER HAMILTON and the policies of the Federalist party. He supported Jefferson's purchase of Louisiana and the War of 1812 (see JAMES MADISON) but opposed federal funding for internal improvements, protective tariffs, and the Missouri Compromise (see HENRY CLAY).

Macon retired from national government service in 1828, but in 1835 he agreed to serve as president of the North Carolina state constitutional convention.

BIBLIOGRAPHY

Dodd, W. E., *Nathaniel Macon*, 1903.

Madison, James

(March 16, 1751–June 28, 1836)
President, Secretary of State, Representative

James Madison earned the title "Father of the Constitution" for his critical role in the drafting of the U.S. Constitution. In addition to his remarkable contributions at the Constitutional Convention, Madison, over the course of a life dedicated to public service, was elected to four terms in the House of Representatives, completed eight years as secretary of state, and served two terms as president.

James Madison was born into a prominent family in Port Conway, Virginia. After graduating from the College of New Jersey (now Princeton University) in 1771, he remained for six additional months to pursue graduate study in law and theology with the goal of becoming either a minister or lawyer. He concluded, however, that neither profession was satisfactory and returned to his plantation in Orange County, Virginia, still in search of a career.

Like other members of the Virginia planter class, including THOMAS JEFFERSON and GEORGE WASHINGTON, Madison supported efforts to oppose British colonial policy. In 1775 he was made chairman of the Orange County Revolutionary Committee of Safety and one year later was elected to the convention that declared Virginia independent. He also helped to draft the new state constitution and managed to insert a strong religious freedom clause in that text. In 1780 he became the youngest person elected to the Continental Congress. During his almost four years as a member of the congress he became a well-known advocate of the need for a strong

Library of Congress

central government, as well as a highly respected debater.

While serving in the Virginia Assembly from 1784 to 1786, Madison played a major role in bringing about the series of meetings that led to the convening of the Constitutional Convention. Among the fifty-five delegates who met in Philadelphia in 1787 to correct flaws in the Articles of Confederation, Madison was recognized as the best-prepared scholar of political history. He also quickly became recognized as the leading advocate of a new government plan that contained a much stronger central government than could be crafted under the Articles of Confederation.

The physically frail Madison was an unlikely candidate for political greatness. A slight speech impediment and a tendency to talk very softly made public speaking a particular challenge. Nevertheless, through a combination of intense intellectual efforts and a deep appreciation for the need to check the evil as well as to count on the good of human nature, Madison managed to play the central role in the work at the convention.

Although the deliberations of the delegates were conducted in private, Madison took detailed notes of the proceedings and recomposed every day's events in his journal. It is from this document that historians have been able to obtain invaluable insight into how the structure of the central government of the United States was created.

After the Constitution was completed, Madison, along with ALEXANDER HAMILTON and

JOHN JAY, wrote the *Federalist Papers*. These essays brilliantly explained the goals and theory behind the organization of the new national government. Madison also led the successful ratification effort—part of which involved besting antiratification leader PATRICK HENRY in debate—in Virginia. Finally, as a member of the House of Representatives from 1789 to 1797, he helped to implement the new government by sponsoring the first ten amendments (the Bill of Rights), introducing revenue bills, and ensuring that the president alone was responsible for the conduct of the executive branch.

Although he had led the effort to establish a new federal government, Madison was appalled by Secretary of the Treasury Alexander Hamilton's vision of using it to facilitate the transformation of America from an agricultural to an industrial economy. Convinced that Hamilton's national financial program threatened the rights of the states and undermined the prosperity of small farmers—the people he believed history showed were absolutely essential to a successful republican government—Madison joined Thomas Jefferson in founding the opposition Democratic-Republican party. Their vision was to carefully adhere to the limits placed on the power of the federal government in the Constitution (see THOMAS JEFFERSON and MELVILLE WESTON FULLER).

In foreign policy, Madison favored developing close relations with the revolutionary government of France and avoiding entanglement with the "old world" government of Great Britain. Hamilton advocated restoring commercial relations with England and avoiding entanglement in the turmoil of the revolution in France. Bitterly disappointed by the ratification of Jay's Treaty (see JOHN JAY), which he viewed as a betrayal of the republican principles of the Revolution, Madison retired from Congress in 1797 to his plantation. He did not, however, retire from public life. The following year he drafted the Virginia Resolves, which protested the Alien and Sedition Acts (see JOHN ADAMS and THOMAS JEFFERSON). In this doc-

ument and a report defending it in 1800, Madison delivered a powerful defense of freedom of the press and voided the acts as unconstitutional on the grounds that, since the Constitution was based on a compact among states, the federal government had acted contrary to the compact. The states, according to the Virginia document, had the right and duty to "interpose for arresting the progress of evil."

After playing a major role in securing the election of Thomas Jefferson as president, Madison was appointed secretary of state. As secretary of state in the Jefferson administration from 1801 to 1809, Madison guided the successful negotiations for the purchase of the Louisiana Territory (see THOMAS JEFFERSON), demanded that Spain recognize U.S. ownership of the coastal territory between New Orleans and Florida, and supported the need for the United States to deal forcefully with the North African Barbary pirates (see THOMAS JEFFERSON). His area of greatest frustration concerned the inability of the United States to force Great Britain to recognize American neutral trade rights. Unable to cajole Britain to stop seizing (impressing) alleged deserters serving on American ships, Madison resorted to advocating the unsuccessful Embargo Act of 1807. When it had become clear by the end of Jefferson's second term that the embargo had failed, Madison accepted its repeal.

After overcoming a bid by JAMES MONROE to win the Democratic-Republican nomination for president, Madison easily won the general election for president in 1808. He made poor choices for cabinet positions in a vain attempt to maintain party unity without Jefferson's leadership. This, combined with his belief that the president should not play a strong role in shaping national policy, severely weakened his authority and reinvigorated Federalist party opposition in Congress. Finally, in 1812, having been unable to force Great Britain to stop impressing American sailors and facing a difficult reelection campaign, Madison decided to support a declaration of war.

Madison won reelection, but his hopes that the War of 1812 would be a short conflict leading to the annexation of Canada were crushed as the badly prepared American army failed in its efforts to invade Canada. The end of the Napoleonic wars in Europe led to a massive increase in British military power in America, culminating in the burning of Washington, D.C., in 1814. The performance of the American forces began to improve, but the war had wreaked such economic devastation on the economy of maritime New England that secession was openly discussed at the so-called Hartford Convention. The convention was made up of Federalist delegates from the New England states who met in secret at Hartford, Connecticut, in December 1814 to air their opposition to the war. The report of the meeting declared the right of nullification (much as the Kentucky and Virginia Resolutions had done; see THOMAS JEFFERSON), but the news of ANDREW JACKSON's victory at New Orleans discredited the proceedings and brought accusations of sedition against the delegates.

Although the peace treaty signed in December 1814 merely restored the nation to the territorial position it had occupied in 1812 and failed to resolve the issue of American maritime rights, the end of the Napoleonic wars and the successful defense of American independence led to a surge of American nationalism that Madison basked in during his last two years in office. Having matured in office, Madison overcame his initial opposition to the federal government's playing a strong role in economic development and in 1815 advocated the rechartering of the national bank (see NICHOLAS BIDDLE and ROGER BROOKE TANEY), a protectionist tariff, federal funding for internal improvements, the creation of a national university, and the maintenance of a professional navy and army.

After retiring to his Virginia plantation in 1817, Madison supported Thomas Jefferson's efforts to found the University of Virginia, served as a foreign policy adviser to President JAMES MONROE, and participated in the Virginia constitutional convention of 1829.

BIBLIOGRAPHY

Brugger, Robert J., et al. (eds.), *Papers of James Madison*, vol. 1, 1986; Ketcham, Ralph, *James Madison, A Biography*, 1971; Meyers, Marvin (ed.), *The Mind of the Founder: Sources of the Political Thought of James Madison*, 1981; Moore, Virginia, *The Madisons: A Biography*, 1979; Rutland, Robert A., et al. (eds.), *Papers of James Madison*, 1979–1985; Stagg, J. C., *Mr. Madison's War: Politics, Diplomacy, and Warfare in the Early American Republic, 1783–1830*, 1983.

Mangum, Willie Person

(May 10, 1792–September 7, 1861)
Candidate for President, Senator, Representative

Willie Person Mangum was born in Orange (now Durham) County, North Carolina. He graduated from the University of North Carolina in 1815, was admitted to the state bar two years later, and established a successful practice in Durham.

After serving in the North Carolina House of Commons in 1818 and 1819, Mangum served briefly as a superior court judge in 1820 and then, two years later, won election to the U.S. House of Representatives. Mangum supported WILLIAM H. CRAWFORD's unsuccessful presidential campaign in 1824 and won reelection, but he resigned from the House before the end of his term in 1826.

Mangum briefly returned to the bench to fill a vacancy as judge, but the appointment was not confirmed. He lost his first bid to win election to the U.S. Senate in 1828 but succeeded in 1830. In the Senate he championed states' rights and opposed protective tariffs. He entered the Senate as a Jacksonian Democrat, but he soon broke with ANDREW JACKSON over the president's handling of the rechartering of the Second Bank of the United States (see NICHOLAS BIDDLE and ROGER BROOKE TANEY) and the nullification controversy (see JOHN CALDWELL CALHOUN). While serving in the House, Mangum had opposed the national bank, but in the Senate he believed Jackson's attack on the bank and decision to make its continuing existence an issue in the 1832 election was a mistake. He voted against Jackson's rechartering bill and, although personally opposed to nullification, voted against Jackson's Force Bill in 1833. Mangum felt so strongly about these issues that he decided to resign from the Senate in 1835 rather than obey a directive from the North Carolina legislature to support Jackson's policies.

Mangum joined the Whig party after leaving the Senate, and in 1837, as an independent candidate, received the electoral votes of South Carolina for president. At the Whig national convention in 1839 he was offered, but declined, the nomination for vice president. The next year, as a Whig party candidate, he was reelected to the U.S. Senate.

From May 31, 1842, to March 4, 1845, Mangum was president pro tempore of the Senate and was thus acting vice president of the United States under JOHN TYLER. (Tyler had succeeded to the presidency following the death of WILLIAM HENRY HARRISON.) Defeated for reelection in 1852, Mangum retired from public service.

BIBLIOGRAPHY

Shanks, Henry T. (ed.), *Papers of Willie P. Mangum*, 5 vols., 1950–1956.

Marcy, William Learned

(December 12, 1786–July 4, 1857)
Secretary of State, Secretary of War, Senator

Although he had a long and distinguished political career, William Learned Marcy is most often recalled as the man who first used the phrase "To the victor belong the spoils" to describe the patronage methods employed by politicians.

William Marcy was born in Sturbridge (now Southbridge), Massachusetts. He graduated from Brown University in 1808, moved to Troy, New York, and was admitted to the bar there in 1811. Although he saw little action during the War of 1812 (see JAMES MADISON), he achieved the rank of adjutant general of the state militia. By 1819 Marcy, a staunch Jeffersonian Democratic-Republican, had begun what became a long and mutually beneficial friendship with MARTIN VAN BUREN. Together they and a number of other Van Buren supporters founded the powerful state Democratic political organization known as the Albany Regency.

In 1823 Marcy was appointed state comptroller of New York and moved to Albany. Six years later, Governor Van Buren appointed Marcy associate justice of the state supreme court. Marcy reluctantly resigned from the bench in 1831 after being elected to the U.S. Senate. He served only one year in the Senate before resigning to become governor of New York in 1833, but it was during this period that he uttered his famous statement in reply to an attack by Senator JOHN C. CALHOUN of South Carolina against Van Buren and the patronage practices of the Albany Regency.

During his three terms as governor of New York from 1833 to 1838, Marcy organized the first geological survey of the state. (The highest mountain in the Adirondacks is named in his honor.) He also refused to return a man accused of being an escaped slave to Alabama even though he disapproved of the activities of abolitionists as a threat to the Union, and he settled a boundary dispute with New Jersey.

From 1840 to 1842 Marcy served on the Mexican Claims Commission for President Van Buren. From 1845 to 1849 he served as secretary of war in JAMES K. POLK's administration. As secretary of war during the Mexican War (see JAMES KNOX POLK), Marcy earned a reputation as a capable administrator.

By 1848 Marcy had drifted away from supporting his mentor, Martin Van Buren, and had aspirations to accede to the presidency himself, but he failed to obtain the Democratic party's nomination in 1852. FRANKLIN PIERCE was nominated instead, and after winning election he appointed Marcy secretary of state. The next four years were the peak of Marcy's political career. Accomplishments during his term in office from 1853 to 1857 included the ratification of the Gadsden Purchase Treaty (see FRANKLIN PIERCE), along with a reciprocity trade agreement concerning Canada with Great Britain, and a treaty with Denmark opening its colonial possessions to U.S. consuls. Marcy also dispatched Townsend Harris as first U.S. minister to Japan in 1855 to build upon Commodore Matthew Perry's 1853 visit. The Harris mission led to a treaty that eventually opened trade and established formal diplomatic relations between Japan and the United States.

One glaring error of Marcy's term as secretary of state concerned his authorization of the preparation of a secret report, known as the Ostend Manifesto (see FRANKLIN PIERCE), for presentation to the State Department. The manifesto advocated the annexation of Cuba by the United States; when it was leaked to the press, a furor erupted in Spain and war was barely averted.

Marcy died only a few months after retiring from office.

BIBLIOGRAPHY

Spencer, Ivor D., *Victor and Spoils: William L. Marcy,* 1959.

Marshall, George Catlett

(December 31, 1880–October 16, 1959)
Secretary of State, Secretary of Defense

On September 1, 1939, the day World War II officially began in Europe, George C. Marshall became chief of staff of the U.S. Army. For the next twelve years, first as chief of staff and then as secretary of state, Marshall played a vital role in the military and political events that shaped the modern world. In 1953, shortly after his retirement, in recognition of his efforts to end and to avert war around the world, Marshall became the only professional soldier ever awarded the Nobel Peace Prize.

Born in Uniontown, Pennsylvania, Marshall began his army career in 1902, after graduating from the Virginia Military Institute. He served in the Philippines from 1902 to 1903 and then again from 1913 to 1916. In 1917 he went to France, where, as chief of operations for the First Infantry, he helped to plan the first U.S. campaigns in the war. Then, transferred to general headquarters, he was instrumental in plotting the successful strategy of the Saint-Mihiel and Meuse-Argonne offensives as First Army chief of operations.

With the exception of the period 1924 to 1927, when he was executive officer of an infantry regiment in China, Marshall served from 1919 to 1938 in a variety of capacities at various military bases around the United States.

The quiet, austere Marshall managed to make a favorable impression in both the peace and wartime army. One of his commanders described him as "the greatest military genius since Stonewall Jackson." Impressed by reports of Marshall's administrative skills and extraordinary ability to recognize talent, President FRANKLIN D. ROOSEVELT selected Marshall over thirty-four senior officers to be army chief of staff. Marshall occupied the position from 1939 to 1945.

Marshall saw his task during World War II as building a 200,000-man standing army into a force of millions that would be able to fight quickly a large-scale war against superbly trained and equipped, battle-hardened enemy forces. It was, he believed, up to the president to tend to the politics, to make the proper case with Congress and the American people in the face of mounting military manpower needs and materiel costs. But Roosevelt saw things differently. He wanted Marshall to push his ideas in Congress. This was not what Marshall had trained for or expected, but he felt it was the duty of subordinates to fulfill the president's wishes. He learned to lobby in Congress and to hold news conferences. Working with candor and respect, President Roosevelt and Marshall succeeded admirably as a team, but in the process the distinction between political leader and military leader became blurred.

Marshall was the principal military strategist for all Allied operations in Europe and the Pacific during World War II. When the time came to plan the cross-Channel invasion of the Continent, President Roosevelt asked Marshall who should command the Allied forces. Marshall was too modest to name himself and was disappointed when Roosevelt said, "Well, then, you'll stay in Washington. I feel I could not sleep at night with you out of the country." Marshall then suggested General DWIGHT D. EISENHOWER over 366 senior officers, and Roosevelt agreed to the appointment. In recognition of Marshall's efforts in training, planning, and supplying the Allies, Winston Churchill called him "the true organizer of victory."

After the war President HARRY S TRUMAN asked Marshall to undertake what turned out to be the hopeless task of trying to arrange some kind of negotiated peace between the Nationalist and Communist forces in China. As Truman's secretary of state from 1947 to 1949, Marshall, who believed the Soviets were bent on controlling Europe, helped the president to formulate his containment policy (see HARRY S TRUMAN). Convinced that economic instability aided Soviet Communist expansion, Marshall outlined, in a speech delivered at Harvard University in June 1947, a plan by which the United States would help to ensure Europe's economic recovery. The plan, he said, was not directed against a country or an idea, but "against hunger, poverty, desperation, and chaos. Its purpose should be the revival of a working economy in the world. . . . " He proposed that during the next several years the United States ought to help Europe with substantial grants and loans in order to prevent "economic, social, and political deterioration of very grave character."

The Soviet Union was invited to take part, but it refused on the grounds that the economic aid was really a sham for making Europe dependent upon the United States. Eastern European nations under Soviet control were also prevented from participating. The Soviet refusal to participate and the overthrow of the Czechoslovakian government by communists helped secure passage of the Marshall Plan through Congress.

Signed into law in April 1948, $5.3 billion in aid was provided to Europe the following year. Of the $12 billion spent in Marshall aid, more than half went to Great Britain, France, and West Germany. By 1950 these nations had increased their gross national products by over 25 percent. Their prosperity not only helped contain communism, but as they became more prosperous, they bought more American goods. This helped to fuel the postwar American economic prosperity. American policymakers would often refer to the success of the Marshall Plan to support aid programs for Asia, Latin America, and Africa.

Marshall resigned as secretary of state due to ill health in 1949, but President Truman asked him to return as secretary of defense at the outbreak of the Korean War in 1950. As secretary of defense from 1950 to 1951, Marshall rebuilt the armed forces, devised a plan for universal military training, helped create the North Atlantic Treaty Organization (NATO; see HARRY S TRUMAN), and successfully worked to keep the Korean War contained to the Korean peninsula.

In 1951 Senator JOSEPH MCCARTHY of Wisconsin assailed Marshall as a communist traitor who would "sell his grandmother for any advantage." Marshall, of course, had no connection to, or sympathy for, communism. McCarthy's attack on him demonstrated the hysterical and defamatory character of the senator's anticommunist crusade (see JOSEPH RAYMOND MCCARTHY). During the 1952 presidential campaign, Dwight D. Eisenhower refused, for political reasons, to condemn McCarthy's assault upon his former mentor.

The following year Marshall was awarded the Nobel Peace Prize.

───

BIBLIOGRAPHY

Bland, Larry (ed.), *The Papers of George Catlett Marshall*, 1981; Marshall, George C., *Memoirs of My Services in the World War*, 1945; Mosley, Leonard, *Marshall: Man for Our Times*, 1982; Parrish, Thomas, *Roosevelt and Marshall: Partners in Politics and War*, 1989; Pogue, Forrest C., *George C. Marshall*, 3 vols., 1963–1966, 1973.

Marshall, John

(September 24, 1755–July 6, 1835)
Secretary of State, Diplomat, Chief Justice of the Supreme Court, Representative

The chief justice who made the Supreme Court the final arbiter on the acceptability of laws had "one original . . . almost supernatural faculty," said a contemporary, WILLIAM WIRT: he could grasp an argument in a law court by "a single glance of his mind." This amazing capacity for concentration and insight was obvious to others even in Marshall's youth. After only a month of formal study and a few years of practice, he became one of Virginia's leading lawyers. And, although he never held a judicial post before his appoint-

ment to the Supreme Court, he became perhaps the nation's greatest chief justice.

The eldest child in a family of fifteen children, John Marshall was born to well-connected and, for the frontier, well-educated parents near Germantown, Virginia. Marshall served as an officer in the American Revolution from 1775 to 1781, first in the militia and then in the Continental Army. While awaiting his formal discharge from the army, Marshall was admitted to the Virginia bar in 1780. He quickly became a prominent Federalist political figure as well as a successful attorney in Richmond. He was elected to several terms in the state assembly (1782 and 1787) and executive council (1782–1784), and helped secure the ratification of the Constitution in Virginia (1788). Although he turned down several important political posts offered by Presidents GEORGE WASHINGTON and JOHN ADAMS because he preferred the practice of law, he did accept, primarily for personal business reasons, a diplomatic assignment to France by

Library of Congress

President Adams in 1797. Ironically, it was this mission that first brought him national fame as part of the infamous XYZ affair (see JOHN ADAMS).

After his return, Marshall declined an appointment to the Supreme Court. Instead, he was elected to Congress in 1799. President Adams nominated him as secretary of war in 1800, but Marshall declined. However, shortly afterward he agreed to become the secretary of state; and in the following year Adams selected him to become chief justice. The first official act Marshall performed in his remarkable thirty-four years in office was to administer the presidential oath to his cousin and political rival, THOMAS JEFFERSON.

Firmly committed to the need to create a strong and effective national government, Marshall's historic effect on the Court began with the first opinion he delivered in 1801. Until *Talbot* v. *Seeman*, each justice delivered his own separate opinion. Marshall substituted a single majority opinion and kept Court debate behind closed doors. Indeed, his influence was so strong that in the 1,106 decisions handed down, most of which he wrote, he disagreed with the majority opinion only nine times.

Out of the Jefferson-Marshall political antagonism came one of the Supreme Court's most momentous decisions. Shortly after assuming office, the Republican administration of Jefferson refused to deliver some last-minute appointments (known as Midnight Judges) by Federalist president John Adams. One of the men, William Marbury, denied his commission as justice of the peace, petitioned the Supreme Court to force Jefferson to have Secretary of State JAMES MADISON deliver the appointment as the Court was empowered to do by the Judiciary Act of 1789. Marshall sympathized with Marbury, but he realized the Court could not force Jefferson to do anything. So, instead of ordering Jefferson to do what Marbury asked, he used *Marbury* v. *Madison* (1803) to establish that the Supreme Court was the final arbiter on the constitutionality of laws. In his precedent-setting opinion, Marshall scathingly criticized Jefferson for not giving Marbury the commission he was legally entitled to, but then declared that the Court could not help Marbury because the section of the Judiciary Act of 1789 that had empowered the Court to issue such an order was unconstitutional.

Marshall's reputation as the author of a large body of constitutional doctrine is founded on the opinions rendered in such cases as *Fletcher* v. *Peck* (1810), the first Court decision holding a state law invalid under the federal constitution, which declared that the states, as well as private individuals, had an "obligation of contracts"; *U.S.* v. *Peters* (1809), *Cohens* v. *Virginia* (1821), and *Gibbons* v. *Ogden* (1824), which unified the federal court system and established its supremacy over state courts in federal matters; *McCulloch* v. *Maryland* (1819), which assigned powers to Congress that were implied rather than stated in the Constitution; and *Dartmouth College* v. *Woodward* (1819), which held contracts with states inviolable.

Marshall's support for the preeminence of the federal courts caused him to be savagely attacked by the advocates of states' rights. Nevertheless, he never let popular sentiment control his actions. In 1807, in the role of circuit justice, he presided over the trial of AARON BURR for treason and used the occasion to protect the rights of all Americans by narrowly defining the crime of treason. He ruled that hearsay evidence and mere membership in a conspiratorial group were insufficient grounds for conviction.

Marshall combined his belief in the need for a strong central government with a deep appreciation for the rights of individuals and the sanctity of private property. Fortunately for the nation, none of the efforts by his political adversaries to weaken the power of the Supreme Court or to force him to resign succeeded.

BIBLIOGRAPHY

Beveridge, Albert J., *Life of John Marshall*, 4 vols., 1916–1919; Corwin, Edward S., *John Marshall and the Constitution*, 1921; Faulkner, Robert K., *The Jurisprudence of John Marshall*, 1968.

Marshall, Thomas Riley

(March 14, 1854–June 1, 1925)
Vice President

"Democrats, like poets, are born, not made," said Thomas R. Marshall. A loyal member of the Democratic party, Marshall, a lawyer, was politically influential but held no public office until 1908 when, at the age of fifty-four, he was elected governor of his home state of Indiana.

During his four years in office, Marshall opposed rigid Prohibition laws and pushed forward an important program of social and labor legislation. Presented as a favorite son candidate at the Democratic convention of 1912, he was given the second spot on the ticket after the presidential nomination went to WOODROW WILSON.

As vice president, Marshall brought wit and humor to the routine task of presiding over the Senate. Once, during a particularly boring debate, he made a remark that became famous: "You know, what this country needs is a really good five-cent cigar."

He was nominated and reelected in 1916, the first vice president to succeed himself in half a century. Marshall's role as vice president was complicated after 1918 by President Wilson's long illness. While the president lay incapacitated, some members of the government felt that Marshall should assume Wilson's office; but since the Constitution was not specific on the matter, and because Marshall was unwilling to appear to be a usurper, he did nothing.

Marshall retired to his home in Indiana in 1921. In 1925 he published his *Recollections*, a humorous account of his life, in the hope, he declared, "that the tired Business Man, the Unsuccessful Golfer and the Lonely Husband whose wife is out reforming the world may find therein a half-hour's surcease from sorrow."

BIBLIOGRAPHY

Marshall, Thomas R., *Recollections*, 1925.

Marshall, Thurgood

(July 2, 1908–   )
Associate Justice of the Supreme Court

Thurgood Marshall, the first black American ever appointed to the U.S. Supreme Court, built a remarkable legal career on the premise that all forms of racial segregation were unconstitutional.

Born in Baltimore, Maryland, Marshall attended segregated public schools and graduated from Lincoln University in 1930 and Howard University Law School in 1933. He established a private practice and immediately volunteered his services to the National Association for the Advancement of Colored People (NAACP) to fight for civil rights cases. In his capacity as special counsel to the NAACP's legal defense fund, Marshall was a leader in the organization's attack on state segregation laws, especially in the field of education.

Marshall argued thirty-two cases before the U.S. Supreme Court and won all but three of them. He also helped write the briefs for eleven other cases. His efforts helped to obtain most of the major Supreme Court decisions that provided for orderly civil rights change in America during the 1950s and 1960s. Cases he argued secured voting rights for all qualified persons regardless of race, obtained the admission of minority students to state law schools, abolished segregation on interstate buses, and ended state-supported housing agreements that allowed segregation. His most dramatic success occurred in 1954, in *Brown* v. *Board of Education of Topeka, Kansas* (see EARL WARREN). This landmark case, which gave impetus to the civil rights movement, overturned the "separate but equal" doctrine that the Supreme Court had upheld in 1896 in *Plessy* v. *Ferguson.*

In 1961 Marshall was appointed to the U.S. Court of Appeals, second circuit, by President JOHN F. KENNEDY. He was named solicitor general four years later, and served in that post until 1967, when President LYNDON B. JOHNSON chose Marshall to become the first black justice of the Supreme Court.

As a Supreme Court justice, Marshall consistently voted to end economic, political, and social injustices experienced by minorities. During the more conservative years of RONALD REAGAN's presidency, Marshall continued to represent the minority, liberal faction on the Court. He strongly advocated a major role for the federal government in ensuring that the goal of obtaining meaningful equality for all Americans is not left up to state and local governments. Marshall retired in 1991.

BIBLIOGRAPHY

Kluger, Richard, *Simple Justice: The History of Brown v. Board of Education and Black America's Struggle for Equality,* 1975.

Martin, Joseph William, Jr.

(November 3, 1884–March 6, 1968)
Speaker of the House, Representative

During his forty-two years in the House of Representatives, Joseph W. Martin became one of the most influential legislators of his generation and the only Republican Speaker of the House in the last sixty years.

Martin was born in North Attleboro, Massachusetts. Instead of going to college on a football scholarship, he worked on several local and regional newspapers. In 1911 Martin was elected to the Massachusetts legislature, serving until 1917. In 1924 he won the first of twenty-one successful election campaigns for the U.S. House of Representatives.

Although a Republican, Martin supported some of FRANKLIN D. ROOSEVELT's New Deal programs. In 1936 he managed ALFRED M. LANDON's unsuccessful presidential campaign and then served as the chairman of the Republican Congressional Campaign Committee until 1938. The following year he was elected House Republican leader. By forging coalitions with conservative Democrats and picking his fights carefully, Martin proved to be an extremely effective opposition minority party leader. He also managed WENDELL WILLKIE's unsuccessful presidential campaign in 1940.

Martin was elected Speaker when the Republicans gained control of the House in 1946. In reaction to Roosevelt's four terms in office, Martin led the campaign to pass the Twenty-second Amendment, which limits presidents to two terms. He played a vital role in enacting the Taft–Hartley Act (see HARRY S TRUMAN) over President Harry S Truman's veto and in securing an override of Truman's veto of a tax cut. He dropped his opposition to the Democrats, however, in order to secure bipartisan support for the Marshall Plan (see GEORGE CATLETT MARSHALL and HARRY S TRUMAN).

In 1948 control of both houses of Congress was regained by the Democrats, and Martin resumed his old position as minority leader. He became a strong critic of the Truman policy of limited warfare in Korea, and in April 1951 made public a letter from General Douglas MacArthur, supreme commander in Korea, in which MacArthur stated his approval of Martin's criticisms. An infuriated Truman fired MacArthur, who had been ordered not to seek political support for his views, for insubordination.

After the Republicans retook control of both houses of Congress in the 1952 elections, Martin was again chosen Speaker. Overshadowed by the popular DWIGHT D. EISENHOWER, Martin fulfilled the role of loyal lieutenant. The Democrats recaptured Congress in 1954, and Martin once again served as minority leader until 1958. He retired to Hollywood, Florida, in 1967.

BIBLIOGRAPHY

Donovan, Robert J., *Conflict and Crisis: The Presidency of Harry Truman, 1945–1948*, 1977; Martin, William Joseph, Jr., *My First Fifty Years in Politics*, 1960; Neal, Steve, *Dark Horse: A Biography of Wendell Willkie*, 1984; Reichard, Gary W., *The Reaffirmation of Republicanism*, 1975.

Mason, George

(1725–October 7, 1792)
Revolutionary Leader

George Mason played an important role in securing Virginia's participation in the American Revolution, wrote the influential Virginia Declaration of Rights, served as a member of the Constitutional Convention, and framed the Declaration of Rights, which became the basis for the first ten amendments to the Constitution.

Mason was born into a prominent family in Fairfax County, Virginia. Educated by tutors, he acquired a deep knowledge of the law but never became a practicing attorney. He inherited a substantial estate and, while developing his plantation as a young man, built the magnificent Gunston Hall residence. He also began a lifelong service in local government.

While he opposed the Stamp Act in 1765 (see JOHN ADAMS and SAMUEL ADAMS), the Townsend Acts in 1767, and the closing of Boston Harbor in 1774 in retaliation for the Boston Tea Party, Mason did not play a major role in revolutionary politics until he replaced GEORGE WASHINGTON (who had become commander in chief of the Continental Army) in the Virginia House of Burgesses in 1775. The following year he wrote the Virginia Declaration of Rights and most of Virginia's new state constitution. The Declaration of Rights became a model for the other colonies and influenced the writing of the Declaration of Independence, the first ten amendments (Bill of Rights) to the U.S. Constitution, and the French Declaration of the Rights of Man.

During the American Revolution Mason took a particular interest in the affairs of the Northwest Territory. He had been actively involved in the development of the West as a member of the Ohio Company since 1752 and had an almost father–son relationship with George Rogers Clark, who would explore the region. He helped to secure the Great Lakes rather than the Ohio River as the northwestern boundary of the United States in the

Library of Congress

Treaty of Paris in 1783 and outlined the plan by which Virginia, and eventually the other states, relinquished control of their western lands to the United States.

By 1787 Mason was convinced of the need for a stronger central government than the one provided for in the Articles of Confederation and played a central role in the debates at the Constitutional Convention. However, at the end of the convention he still could not bring himself to sign the document (and fought against ratification in the Virginia Convention in 1788) because of the lack of a Bill of Rights and what he viewed to be the immoral and economically mistaken compromise between New England and the South that traded a tariff policy for the continuation of the slave trade and slavery. Mason consistently opposed slavery throughout his public career as "diabolical in itself and disgraceful to mankind." The eventual inclusion of the first ten amendments to the Constitution and the major conflict over slavery would prove his judgments on these issues to have been correct.

BIBLIOGRAPHY

Miller, Helen Hill, *George Mason: Gentleman Revolutionary,* 1975; Rowland, Kate M., *The Life of George Mason,* 2 vols., 1892 (reprint 1964); Rutland, Robert A., *George Mason, Reluctant Statesman,* 1961.

Mason, James Murray

(November 3, 1798–April 28, 1871)
Senator, Representative

James M. Mason was born in Georgetown, Washington, D.C., into a prominent family. After graduating from the University of Pennsylvania in 1818, he studied law at the College of William and Mary and established a practice in Winchester, Virginia, in 1820.

Mason served in the Virginia legislature from 1826 to 1831, with the exception of the 1827–1828 session, and one term in the U.S. House of Representatives from 1837 to 1839. In 1847 he was elected to complete the remainder of a term in the Senate. Two years later, he was elected to a full six-year term and reelected in 1855.

In the Senate Mason was a staunch ally of JOHN C. CALHOUN, another adamant defender of Southern rights. Like Calhoun, Mason believed that the industrial North was determined to destroy the agricultural South by abolishing the institution of slavery. In 1850 he was the principal drafter of the fugitive slave law (see MILLARD FILLMORE) and a defender of the right of the South to secede if the North refused to provide it with adequate protection for its way of life.

After ABRAHAM LINCOLN's election in 1860, Mason was one of the first border state political leaders to advocate immediate secession. JEFFERSON DAVIS appointed Mason the Confederate commissioner to England in 1861. His task was to secure British recognition of the Confederacy in order to obtain desperately needed financial loans and military assistance. Mason almost managed to precipitate a break in diplomatic relations between the United States and England before he ever arrived in London. Along with fellow Confederate diplomat JOHN SLIDELL, he was seized by a Union warship from the British mail packet *Trent* on the high seas and held at Fort Warren in Boston (see CHARLES FRANCIS ADAMS and JOHN SLIDELL). This breach of diplomatic etiquette strained relations between the United States and England, but Lincoln avoided a confrontation by releasing Mason and Slidell from captivity in January 1862. Mason completed his journey to England, but although he did succeed in raising some funds and military assistance, he never managed to accomplish his mission of securing British recognition.

After the war, Mason spent three years in Canada. He returned to Virginia in 1868 after President ANDREW JOHNSON's amnesty proclamation made it safe for ex-Confederates to return to the United States.

BIBLIOGRAPHY

Mason, Virginia, *Public Life and Diplomatic Correspondence of James M. Mason*, 1903.

Maverick, Fontaine Maury

(October 23, 1895–June 7, 1954)
Representative

The grandson of a Texas cattle baron and a proponent of radical change during the Great Depression, Maury Maverick never sacrificed his iconoclastic views and independence for political expediency. While administering the Smaller War Plants Corporation during World War II, he made a permanent contribution to American language by originating the term "gobbledygook" to describe the tendency of bureaucrats to use jargon instead of "plain English."

Maverick was born in San Antonio, Texas, into a prominent family. (The term "maverick" was originally used in reference to his grandfather's unbranded cattle that roamed southern Texas. "Maverick" evolved to mean "nonconformist.") He left the University of Texas before graduation, studied law on his own, and was admitted to the Texas bar in 1916 and the California bar in 1917. During World War I, Maverick served as a U.S. Army infantry officer in France. He never fully recovered from his combat injuries.

In addition to running his own construction and lumber businesses during the 1920s and early 1930s, Maverick served as tax collector of Bexar County. In 1932 he attempted to create a model communal-living community—Diga Colony—composed largely of destitute former army veterans and their families. Although it attracted national attention, the experiment failed, and Maverick abandoned it the following year.

In 1934 Maverick won a fiercely contested race for the U.S. House of Representatives as a Democrat. He became the leader of a bloc of independent legislators (nicknamed "Mavericks") that refused to follow the directions of party leaders. His pugnacious personality and brazen disregard for conventional political behavior and wisdom made him extremely popular with the press and, briefly, a national celebrity.

Maverick strongly supported New Deal economic legislation, especially the Tennessee Valley Authority, public works projects, and antitrust efforts. Before 1940, though, Maverick distanced himself from President FRANKLIN D. ROOSEVELT's foreign policy, which he feared would lead the country into another war. Instead, he helped to secure passage of neutrality legislation (see WILLIAM EDGAR BORAH).

Maverick was a dedicated defender of civil liberties. In 1935 and 1936 he helped to organize efforts to defeat legislation aimed at punishing radicals. Although he won reelection in 1936, his strong support in 1937 for an antilynching law and opposition to a bill requiring teachers in the District of Columbia to swear that they were not communists led to his electoral defeat in 1938.

In 1939 Maverick became the mayor of San Antonio. In 1940 he renounced his former support for American isolationism and joined with ADLAI STEVENSON and other prominent Americans to form the Committee to Defend America by Aiding the Allies. From 1942 until 1946 he served as chairman of the Smaller War Plants Corporation.

BIBLIOGRAPHY

Henderson, Richard B., *Maury Maverick: A Political Biography,* 1970.

Mellon, Andrew William

(March 24, 1855–August 26, 1937)
Secretary of the Treasury, Diplomat

The wealthy industrialist and financier Andrew Mellon was secretary of the treasury during the Republican administrations of WARREN G. HARDING, CALVIN COOLIDGE, and HERBERT C. HOOVER.

Mellon was born in Pittsburgh, Pennsylvania, into a prominent family. He entered the Western University of Pennsylvania (now the University of Pittsburgh) in 1868 but left several months before graduation in 1872 to found a successful lumber and construction business in nearby Mansfield, Pennsylvania. Two years later, Mellon joined the family bank, T. Mellon & Sons, and in 1882 took over the ownership.

Mellon's awesome success over the next thirty-five years in building a financial-industrial empire from this base hinged upon his genius for recognizing the growth potential of new industries and fully appreciating the profitable role a bank could play in supplying them with necessary financial support. Among the major companies his bank (after 1902, the Mellon National Bank) helped found were the Aluminum Company of America (Alcoa), the Gulf Oil Corporation, and the Union Steel Company, which later merged into United States Steel.

By 1910, Mellon had become an important financial supporter of conservative Republican candidates in Pennsylvania. In 1921 President Warren G. Harding selected Mellon to be secretary of the treasury. The appointment was a surprise because, although he was one of the wealthiest men in the world, the quiet, single Mellon was virtually unknown to the general public. Mellon proved so competent at dealing with the broad range of complicated issues confronting the nation in the 1920s that he was retained in this position in the succeeding Coolidge and Hoover administrations. He reduced individual and corporate tax rates and substantially cut the federal budget. He also significantly lowered the national debt, from $24 billion to $16 billion. His policies were hailed by many Americans during the prosperous 1920s but drew criticism as the country sank into a deep depression in the early 1930s. Similarly, his apparent success in arranging repayment schedules for the World War I loans the United States had made to European nations drew fire in the early 1930s, as one country after another, caught under a crushing burden of debt, defaulted.

Mellon had become a political liability to Hoover by 1931. In February 1932 he resigned to become ambassador to Great Britain, and in 1933 he returned to private life. Mellon later gave his extensive and valuable art collection to the federal government, along with funds to build the National Gallery of Art in Washington, D.C.

BIBLIOGRAPHY

Denton, Frank, *The Mellons of Pittsburgh*, 1948; Love, Philip H., *Mellon, Andrew W.*, 1929; O'Connor, Harvey, *Mellon's Millions*, 1933.

Mitchell, John Newton

(September 15, 1913–November 9, 1988)
Attorney General

John Mitchell was the first U.S. attorney general to ever be convicted of illegal activities and imprisoned. As the president's national campaign manager and confidant, he played a central role in the Watergate scandal (see RICHARD MILHOUS NIXON).

Mitchell was born in Detroit, Michigan, and grew up on Long Island in New York. He earned his law degree from Fordham University and was admitted to the New York bar in 1938. Except for three years' service in the navy, from 1938 until 1960 Mitchell practiced law in New York City.

Richard Nixon met John Mitchell when his law firm merged with Mitchell's in 1967. The two men became friends, and in 1968, with considerable trepidation, Mitchell agreed to become Nixon's presidential campaign manager.

During his successful 1968 campaign, Nixon turned over the details of the day-to-day operations to the superbly organized Mitchell. After he became president in January 1969, Nixon appointed Mitchell attorney general. Mitchell remained in office from 1969 until he resigned in 1972 to manage President Nixon's successful reelection campaign. As attorney general, Mitchell believed that the government's need for "law and order" justified restrictions on civil liberties. He advocated the use of wiretaps in national security cases without obtaining a court order and the right of police to employ the preventive detention of criminal suspects. He brought conspiracy charges against critics of the Vietnam War (see LYNDON BAINES JOHNSON and RICHARD MILHOUS NIXON), and demonstrated a reluctance to involve the Justice Department in civil rights issues. "The Department of Justice is a law enforcement agency," he told reporters. "It is not the place to carry on a program aimed at curing the ills of society."

In 1975 Mitchell was found guilty of conspiracy, obstruction of justice, and perjury and sentenced to two and a half to eight years in prison for his role in the Watergate break-in and cover-up. Tape recordings made by President Nixon and the testimony of others involved confirmed that Mitchell had participated in meetings to plan the break-in of the Democratic party's national headquarters in the Watergate complex. In addition, he had met, on at least three occasions, with the president in an effort to cover up White House involvement after the burglars were discovered and arrested.

BIBLIOGRAPHY

Grover, Stephen, "New Attorney General Poses Question Marks on Antitrust Rights," *Wall Street Journal*, January 17, 1969; Kutler, Stanley I., *The Wars of Watergate: The Last Crisis of Richard Nixon*, 1990; Morris, Roger, *Richard Milhous Nixon: The Rise of an American Politician*, 1990; "Nixon's Cabinet: 12 Men Who Will Lead Departments and Help Shape Policy," *New York Times*, December 12, 1968.

Mondale, Walter Frederick

(January 5, 1928–)
Vice President, Candidate for President, Senator

Walter Frederick Mondale, the son of a Methodist minister, was born in Ceylon, Minnesota. After graduating from the University of Minnesota in 1951, he served in the army. In 1956 Mondale earned a law degree from the University of Minnesota and established a practice in Minneapolis.

While attending college, Mondale worked to help elect candidates for the Minnesota Democratic-Farmer-Labor party. He continued these activities as an attorney and in 1960, after managing the successful reelection campaign of Governor Orville Freeman, was chosen to complete a term in the vacant office

of state attorney general. Mondale then won election to two full terms in that office in 1960 and 1962. In 1964, when Senator HUBERT HUMPHREY became vice president, Mondale was appointed to complete his term, and once again won election to two full Senate terms on his own in 1966 and 1972.

In Congress, Mondale established a solid record as a liberal Democrat. He supported busing to integrate public schools, the establishment of minimum wages and working conditions for migrant farmers, reform of the Indian reservation education system, and legislation designed to prohibit racial discrimination in housing. At first a strong supporter of U.S. involvement in the Vietnam War (see LYNDON BAINES JOHNSON and RICHARD MILHOUS NIXON), Mondale changed his mind after the 1968 Tet offensive.

JIMMY CARTER, the Democratic nominee for president in 1976, chose Mondale to be his vice presidential running mate. The two men established a close relationship during President Carter's administration. After the ticket's reelection defeat in 1980 by RONALD REAGAN, Mondale returned to Minnesota and prepared for a presidential run of his own in 1984. Following a difficult battle for the Democratic party's presidential nomination in the primaries, Mondale won the nomination and boldly chose a woman (the first), GERALDINE FERRARO, to be his running mate.

The Mondale–Ferraro ticket could not overcome the popularity of Ronald Reagan and his pledge of no tax increase. Instead of also pledging to avoid new taxes, Mondale stated that if desirable programs were not going to be harmed, taxes would have to be increased. Mondale claimed that he dared to tell Americans this because it was the responsibility of a leader to be honest: "Taxes will go up. Let's tell the truth. It must be done. Mr. Reagan will raise taxes, and so will I. He won't tell you. I just did."

Americans were in no mood to listen to such words from a "tax and spend" Democrat. Mondale carried only his home state of Minnesota and the District of Columbia in the general election. After this defeat, he retired from politics and returned to practicing law in Minnesota.

BIBLIOGRAPHY

Lewis, Finlay, *Mondale: Portrait of an American Politician,* 1980.

Monroe, James

(April 28, 1758–July 4, 1831)
President, Secretary of State, Secretary of War, Diplomat, Senator

James Monroe, the last of the eighteenth-century revolutionary patriots to lead the nation, served as president during the period known as the Era of Good Feelings, a time of exceptional national political consensus that briefly overshadowed some growing national problems.

Monroe was born in Westmoreland County, Virginia. He enrolled at the College of William and Mary in 1774 but left two years later before graduating to fight in the Ameri-

Library of Congress

can Revolution. He joined the Virginia militia and then served under GEORGE WASHINGTON in the Continental Army, incurring a severe wound at the Battle of Trenton. In late 1779 Monroe left active military service and studied law from 1780 to 1783 under THOMAS JEFFERSON. Jefferson became Monroe's mentor, and the friendship that developed between the two men provided the foundation of Monroe's public service.

Monroe began his political career in 1782 by winning election to a term in the Virginia legislature. The next year he was elected to the Confederation Congress, where he quickly became identified as a champion of states' rights and advocate for the development of the frontier. In 1788 Monroe supported PATRICK HENRY's efforts to prevent ratification of the Constitution by Virginia on the grounds that the new central government threatened to undermine the power of the states. After an unsuccessful effort to win election to the House of Representatives in 1788, he was elected two years later by the Virginia legislature to the U.S. Senate. During his four years in the Senate Monroe, acting as Thomas Jefferson's lieutenant in concert with JAMES MADISON and sometimes AARON BURR, proved to be an extremely effective opposition leader to ALEXANDER HAMILTON's Federalist policies.

In 1794 President George Washington appointed Monroe minister to France in the hope that his pro-French sentiments would calm hostilities between the United States and the revolutionary French government. While in France, Monroe managed to secure the release of the imprisoned American patriot THOMAS PAINE, but he failed to find support for Jay's Treaty (see JOHN JAY), and Washington recalled him.

Although Monroe's diplomatic mission to France was not successful, his political career flourished on his return to the United States because of the successful efforts of Jefferson and Madison to make it appear that his recall was based on partisan political grounds. Monroe became one of the leaders of the new Democratic-Republican party and from 1799 to 1802 served another term as governor of Virginia.

Just over two years after winning election as president in 1800, Thomas Jefferson dispatched Monroe to France as a special envoy. He remained in Europe until 1807. During this period of his diplomatic career, Monroe assisted ROBERT R. LIVINGSTON in negotiating the Louisiana Purchase (see THOMAS JEFFERSON) and participated in the unsuccessful negotia-

tions with the Spanish government to sell Florida.

In 1808 Monroe made his first tentative effort to secure the nomination for president. The unsuccessful effort temporarily alienated him from James Madison, the man who was nominated. The two quickly reconciled, however, and in 1811, before the end of Monroe's third term as governor of Virginia, Madison appointed him secretary of state. Monroe employed his superb administrative and organizational skills so successfully in Madison's cabinet that he remained in office until 1817. He played a vital role during the War of 1812 (see JAMES MADISON), serving, after the dismissal of John Armstrong, as the secretary of war in 1814 and 1815.

In 1816 Monroe won the Democratic-Republican party's nomination for president and the general election. During Monroe's first term in office rival political parties disappeared. Monroe was so popular and the nation appeared so prosperous and content that in 1817 a Boston newspaper coined the phrase "era of good feelings" to describe the mood that had settled upon the country. The panic of 1819 and the depression that followed, however, soon turned those feelings from good to bad.

Although Monroe won a landslide reelection in 1820 (he lost only one vote in the electoral college), he had to confront large issues. Monroe's two administrations spanned the national expansion of the U.S. population into the Midwest and a dramatic period of growth in the national economy. They also heralded the divisive role that slavery was going to play in the territories, although the matter was temporarily resolved in 1820 by the Missouri Compromise (see HENRY CLAY). At this time, the United States also asserted its role as protector of the newly independent nations of Latin America with the pronouncement of the Monroe Doctrine.

The Monroe Doctrine was prompted by a dispute with Russia over the boundary of Alaska and by an invitation from Great Britain to issue a joint declaration concerning Latin

America. During the Napoleonic Wars, Spain's Latin American colonies had declared their independence. Now, there was a growing threat that European powers would again attempt to colonize the region. Great Britain favored keeping the former colonies independent for commercial development and trade purposes. The United States also supported Latin American independence. However, Secretary of State JOHN QUINCY ADAMS successfully persuaded President Monroe to reject the British joint declaration offer. Instead, he inserted into Monroe's message to Congress on December 2, 1823, a succinct statement: "The American continents, by the free and independent condition which they have assumed and maintain, are henceforth not to be considered as subjects for future colonization by any European powers." In effect, the United States had announced a clear foreign policy position separate from Great Britain. Although dismissed by European nations at the time, the Monroe Doctrine became the foundation of U.S. foreign policy in the Americas. Eventually, the Monroe Doctrine achieved meaning as a result of the actions of later presidents who referred to it for the rationale of U.S. actions in the region.

Foreign policy proved to be the area of greatest success for Monroe. During his administration, the Florida question was resolved through a treaty with Spain in 1819 (see ANDREW JACKSON). In addition, the boundary line with Canada was settled along the 49th parallel and the Great Lakes were demilitarized.

It was also during the Monroe administration that an experiment was tried by the American Colonization Society to resolve the slavery issue in the United States. The idea, which Monroe endorsed, was to send the descendants of slaves in America to Africa. A region in equatorial Africa was colonized by the United States and named Liberia. The idea was that freed American slaves would voluntarily return to live in Africa. Eventually, the sponsors of the idea dreamed, there would be no more slave problem or racial problem in the United States. The fact that, as Americans, blacks had no more connection to Africa than European-descended Americans had to their ancestral homes was overlooked.

Four candidates sought the Democratic-Republican party's nomination for president in 1824. Although Andrew Jackson won the most popular votes, no candidate secured enough electoral votes in the general election to become president, and the outcome of the contest was thrown into the House of Representatives. John Quincy Adams managed to become Monroe's successor when Henry Clay supported him against Andrew Jackson. However, the so-called Era of Good Feelings, which had begun to wither under the strain of sectional interests during Monroe's second term, had definitely come to an end. Jackson's followers labeled the Adams–Clay deal a corrupt bargain, formed a highly successful opposition camp to Adams's policies, and began the campaign that culminated four years later in the election of Andrew Jackson as president.

Monroe retired to his Virginia estate in 1825. Four years later, he served as presiding officer of the Virginia Constitutional Convention.

BIBLIOGRAPHY

Ammon, Harry, *James Monroe: Quest for National Identity*, 1971; Brown, Stuart G. (ed.), *Autobiography of James Monroe*, 1959; Cresson, W. P., *James Monroe*, 1946; Hamilton, S. M. (ed.), *Writings of James Monroe*, 1898–1903; Wilmerding, Lucius, Jr., *James Monroe: Public Claimant*, 1960.

Morgenthau, Henry, Jr.

(May 11, 1891–February 6, 1967)
Secretary of the Treasury

As President FRANKLIN D. ROOSEVELT's secretary of the treasury from 1934 to 1945, Henry Morgenthau worked to stabilize the value of the dollar during the Great Depression and oversaw the raising of the capital necessary to win World War II.

Born in New York City, Morgenthau studied architecture at Cornell University. After completing his studies, he purchased a farm in New York and published the *American Agriculturalist* magazine. He was appointed New York commissioner of conservation by his friend and neighbor, Franklin Delano Roosevelt, who became governor of New York in 1928.

Soon after Roosevelt assumed the presidency in 1933, he appointed Morgenthau chairman of the Federal Farm Board and governor of the Farm Credit Administration. In these positions Morgenthau administered the distribution of government loans designed to ease the debt burden of farmers.

In 1934 Roosevelt appointed Morgenthau secretary of the treasury. Morgenthau remained in office until shortly after President Roosevelt's death, a period that encompassed the economic turmoil of the Great Depression and World War II. A financially conservative man, Morgenthau at first opposed the Keynesian economists (see FRANKLIN DELANO ROOSEVELT and HARRY S TRUMAN) in the New Deal, who advocated deficit spending, but later accepted the necessity of unbalanced budgets. During World War II he directed the war bonds drives that helped to raise the capital necessary for defeating Germany and Japan.

In his book, *Germany Is Our Problem* (1945), Morgenthau outlined a plan to ensure that Germany would never again threaten world peace. His proposal to convert Germany from an industrial to an agricultural nation was briefly considered and then dismissed as impractical. He played an important role before his retirement, however, in obtaining U.S. membership in the International Monetary Fund and the World Bank.

BIBLIOGRAPHY

Blum, John M., *From the Morgenthau Diaries, 1951–1967*, condensed and revised as *Roosevelt and Morgenthau*, 1970; Everest, Allen, *Morgenthau, the New Deal, and Silver*, 1950; Hammond, Paul, "Directives for the Occupation of Germany," in Harold Steen (ed.), *American Civil-Military Decisions*, 1963; Morgenthau, Henry, Jr., *Germany Is Our Problem*, 1945; Schlesinger, Arthur, Jr., "Morgenthau Diaries," *Collier's*, September 27–November 1, 1917.

Morrow, Dwight Whitney

(January 11, 1873–October 5, 1931)
Diplomat, Senator

Dwight Whitney Morrow was born in Huntington, West Virginia. After graduating from Amherst College in 1895 and Columbia Law School in 1899, Morrow established residence in Englewood, New Jersey. He became an expert in banking and finance law while working in New York City for the Wall Street firm headed by former Speaker of the House THOMAS B. REED (Reed, Simpson, Thacher and Barnum) and became a full partner in 1905. In 1914 he joined the banking house of J. P. Morgan and Company.

When the United States entered World War I, Morrow acted as an adviser to the Allied Maritime Transport Council and served as chief civilian aide to General John J. Pershing.

In 1927 President CALVIN COOLIDGE appointed Morrow ambassador to Mexico. Relations between the United States and Mexico had been strained ever since the Mexican Revolution of 1910 had turned into a violent civil war. American forces had seized Veracruz in 1914, and General Pershing had led the army into Mexico in 1916 in a futile effort to catch the rebel leader Pancho Villa.

Morrow's service in Mexico was remarkably successful. He carefully diffused the tense situation between the two nations by negotiating a procedure for developing a payment plan that Mexico felt was reasonable for expropri-ated American property. Instead of bellicose threats and arrogant disdain for Mexican culture, Morrow established close, harmonious relations with Mexico's leaders.

The success of the good feelings he developed among Mexicans came to mark a new spirit in U.S. relations with Latin America. This spirit stood for cooperation and compromise rather than coercion through economic pressure and/or military invasion.

In 1930 President HERBERT HOOVER named Morrow a delegate to the London Naval Conference. Later that year, Morrow won election to the U.S. Senate from New Jersey but died after only a few months in office.

BIBLIOGRAPHY

Nicolson, Harold, *Dwight Morrow,* 1935.

Morse, Wayne Lyman

(October 20, 1900–July 22, 1974)
Senator

Library of Congress

Born in Madison, Wisconsin, Wayne Morse graduated from the University of Wisconsin in 1923, earned a master's degree there in 1924, and received law degrees from the University of Minnesota in 1928 and Columbia University in 1932.

From 1924 to 1929 he taught law at the University of Wisconsin and at the University of Minnesota. He became an associate professor at the University of Oregon Law School in 1930, and served as dean and professor there from 1931 to 1944. While at the law school, Morse became a leading authority on labor arbitration.

After serving on numerous World War II boards and committees, Morse was elected to the Senate in 1944 as a Republican. He was reelected in 1950 as an independent and, after joining the Democratic party in 1954, successfully ran for reelection in 1956 as a Democrat. After an unsuccessful bid for the Democratic presidential nomination in 1960, Morse became increasingly alarmed by the American military involvement in South Vietnam.

Morse was never afraid to take an unpopular stand. In 1947 he supported labor legislation and opposed the then popular Taft-Hartley Act (see HARRY S TRUMAN) because he believed that it unfairly restricted the power of the unions. He also supported federal aid to education programs and measures benefiting blacks and farmers. A well-read and articulate opponent of the war in Vietnam (see LYNDON BAINES JOHNSON and RICHARD MILHOUS NIXON), Morse was one of two senators to vote against the Tonkin Gulf Resolution in 1964, which President Lyndon Johnson used to justify a massive military buildup in South Vietnam. Morse also voted against all appropriations bills for the war. His controversial criticisms of the Tonkin Gulf Resolution and American military intervention in Vietnam made him politically vulnerable and contributed to his defeat in a 1968 bid for reelection.

BIBLIOGRAPHY

Smith, Arthur, *Tiger in the Senate: Wayne Morse*, 1962.

Morton, Levi Parsons

(May 16, 1824–May 16, 1920)
Vice President, Diplomat, Representative

L evi P. Morton was a Wall Street banker with only six years of experience in politics when he was nominated for vice president by the Republican party in 1888. The son of a Vermont minister, Morton, unable to afford college, began his business career as a storekeeper in Hanover, New Hampshire. Quickly mastering the wholesale and importing business, he moved to Boston and then New York, where, in 1855, he became the head of a wholesale firm. His company failed in 1861 when Southern debts became worthless; but Morton paid his creditors in full and then opened a Wall Street banking firm in 1863.

Extremely successful in banking, Morton was soon a well-known figure in the world of international finance. His frequent contacts with political figures prompted him to enter politics as a Republican candidate for Congress from New York in 1876. Although defeated then, he served in the House of Representatives from 1879 to 1881. He resigned from the House in 1881 to accept an appointment as minister to France after he had declined the Republican nomination for vice president and the post of secretary of the navy in the JAMES A. GARFIELD administration.

After losing two bids for the Senate in 1885 and 1887, Morton accepted the vice presidential nomination in 1888. Elected with BENJAMIN HARRISON, Morton earned a reputation for scrupulous fairness in his role of presiding over the Senate. In 1895, as an advocate of civil service reform, he was elected governor of New York. As governor, he kept his campaign pledge to resist all efforts of the party bosses to use the awarding of government offices for political purposes. After completing his term in 1897, he returned to banking and, at age seventy-five, founded the Morton Trust Company.

BIBLIOGRAPHY

McElroy, R. M., *Levi Parsons Morton: Banker, Diplomat and Statesman*, 1930.

Moynihan, Daniel Patrick

(March 16, 1927–)
Diplomat, Senator

During the course of over three decades in public service, Daniel Patrick Moynihan served as an adviser to four presidents and as a senator from New York.

Born in Tulsa, Oklahoma, Moynihan grew up in New York City under humble circumstances. He joined the navy in 1944, and received a B.A. from Tufts University in 1948 and an M.A. from the Fletcher School of Law and Diplomacy in 1949. A Fulbright Fellowship enabled him to study at the London School of Economics and Political Science in 1950 and 1951.

From 1955 to 1958 Moynihan worked in a variety of staff positions in the administration of Governor W. Averell Harriman of New York. In 1960 Moynihan joined the JOHN F. KENNEDY campaign for president as an urban affairs research specialist. He became special assistant to Secretary of Labor ARTHUR GOLDBERG in 1961 and assistant secretary of labor in 1963. During the two years he spent in this position, Moynihan helped draft antipoverty program legislation. In 1965 he wrote *The Negro Family: The Case for National Action*, a controversial report that attributed a good deal of urban black poverty to the instability of black family life.

In addition to working in the government, Moynihan continued to pursue an academic career. He was awarded a Ph.D. from Tufts University in 1961 and coauthored (with Nathan Glazer) *Beyond the Melting Pot* (1963), an important work of urban sociology. From 1965 to 1969 Moynihan taught at the John F. Kennedy School of Government at Harvard University and wrote prolifically about urban poverty and social welfare.

Although a Democrat, Moynihan joined the administration of Republican president RICHARD NIXON in 1969 as the director of the Urban Affairs Council. He designed Nixon's family assistance plan, a dramatic proposal that would have eliminated much of the nation's complex and inefficient welfare system in favor of a simple guaranteed annual income for any family falling below the poverty line. The proposal won in the House but was defeated in the Senate. Moynihan then resigned in 1971 and returned to Harvard.

In 1973 President Nixon appointed Moynihan as ambassador to India. As soon as he returned from India in early 1975, President GERALD FORD appointed him as ambassador to the United Nations, where he served for eight months.

After achieving an upset victory in the New York Democratic primary in 1976, Moynihan was elected to the Senate. Although initially labeled a neoconservative, Moynihan gradually assumed a more traditional liberal Democratic perspective. He continued to fight for major welfare reform, sought to protect the interests of the disadvantaged and elderly, and came to believe in the need to implement strategic arms reductions and improved relations with the Soviet Union.

BIBLIOGRAPHY

Moynihan, Daniel P., *Beyond the Melting Pot: The Negroes, Puerto Ricans, Jews, Indians, and Irish of New York City,* 1963, *Maximum Feasible Misunderstanding; Community Action in the War on Poverty,* 1969, *Toward a National Urban Policy,* 1970, *The Politics of a Guaranteed Income: The Nixon Administration and the Family Assistance Plan,* 1973, *Coping: On the Practice of Government,* 1974, *A Dangerous Place,* 1978, *Loyalties,* 1984, and *Family and Nation,* 1986.

Muhlenberg, Frederick Augustus Conrad

(January 1, 1750–June 4, 1801)
Speaker of the House, Representative

Frederick Augustus Conrad Muhlenberg was a well-known Lutheran pastor before entering politics and becoming the first Speaker of the House of Representatives.

Muhlenberg was born in Trappe, Pennsylvania, into a prominent family. He was educated at the University of Halle in Germany. Upon his return to Philadelphia in 1770, he was ordained a Lutheran minister. In 1773, after serving as pastor in various churches in Pennsylvania, Muhlenberg was chosen pastor of Christ (Lutheran) Church in New York City. A supporter of the American Revolution, Muhlenberg left New York City when it was occupied by British forces under General William Howe in 1776 and resumed his ministerial duties in rural Pennsylvania.

In 1779 Muhlenberg was elected as a delegate to the Continental Congress. He never returned to the ministry. He served in the Continental Congress until 1780. From 1780 to 1783 he was elected to the Pennsylvania state legislature, where he was chosen speaker.

Muhlenberg presided over the state constitutional ratification convention and was elected as a moderate Federalist to the U.S. House of Representatives. In 1789 he was elected the first Speaker of the House of Representatives. After being briefly displaced in the Second Congress by Jonathan Trumbull, he was reelected Speaker in the Third Congress and every one thereafter until 1797.

In 1796, despite the unpopularity in Pennsylvania of the treaty JOHN JAY had negotiated with Great Britain concerning American maritime trade rights (see JOHN JAY), Muhlenberg cast the deciding vote in the House to appropriate funds enabling its ratification. This act hurt him politically, and in his second effort to win the Pennsylvania governor's office in 1796 (the first was in 1793), he was overwhelmingly defeated.

Muhlenberg, who had always managed to work harmoniously with THOMAS JEFFERSON's supporters, left the Federalist party in 1799 and became a Democratic-Republican. In 1800, shortly before his death, he was appointed by the governor to be the receiver general of the Pennsylvania Land Office.

BIBLIOGRAPHY

Wallace, Paul A. W., *The Muhlenbergs of Pennsylvania,* 1950.

Murphy, Frank

(April 13, 1893–July 19, 1949)
Attorney General, Associate Justice of the Supreme Court

Throughout his varied public service career as a liberal Democratic mayor, colonial administrator, governor, attorney general, and judge, Frank Murphy fought to protect civil liberties and to increase government responsibility for social welfare.

Murphy was born in Harbor Beach, Michigan, to Irish American parents. After earning his law degree from the University of Michigan in 1914, Murphy practiced law in Detroit. He was an army officer during World War I, and took advantage of an army educational program after the war to study law briefly at Lincoln's Inn in London and at Trinity College, Dublin.

Upon his return to Detroit in August 1919, Murphy obtained an appointment as assistant U.S. attorney for eastern Michigan. In 1924 he won election as a judge of the recorder's court and remained on the bench until he was elected mayor of Detroit in 1930.

During his successful campaign for mayor, Murphy had stressed the need for the city government to help the depression-era unemployed and became well known for his relief efforts. He led the crusade of the nation's mayors for federal help that resulted in the enactment of the Emergency Relief and Construction Act by Congress in July 1932.

In return for his strong campaign support, President FRANKLIN D. ROOSEVELT appointed Murphy governor general of the Philippines in 1932 and U.S. high commissioner in 1935. Murphy returned to Michigan in 1936 at Roosevelt's request to run for governor. Elected that year with the aid of the Roosevelt reelection landslide victory, Murphy assumed the office of governor in January 1937, at the height of the United Automobile Workers (UAW) sit-down strike at General Motors (GM) plants in Flint. Although he dispatched troops to Flint, Murphy refused, even after GM had obtained a court order, to use troops to remove the striking workers. Instead, he persuaded GM to recognize the UAW and, in so doing, contributed greatly to the success of the labor movement in what many observers regarded, at the time, as the decade's pivotal, capital–labor struggle. At first Murphy was widely praised for his mediation efforts. However, as workers throughout the auto and other industries, inspired by the success of the Flint unionists, staged their own strikes, Murphy was criticized for not having enforced the law and for his excessively prolabor sympathies. Michigan voters ousted him from office in 1938.

President Roosevelt named Murphy as attorney general in 1939 and as associate justice of the Supreme Court in 1940. Although Murphy was frequently in dissent while on the Court because of his beliefs that individual liberty was as necessary in wartime as in peacetime, and that criminals should have the same procedural rights in state courts as in federal courts, many of his minority positions eventually became the view of the majority of the Court. For example, one of his most famous dissents was in the case of *Korematsu* v. *United States* (1944), in which he attacked as racist the wartime evacuation and internment of Japanese Americans.

BIBLIOGRAPHY

Fine, Sidney, *Frank Murphy,* 1984; Howard, J. Woodford, Jr., *Mr. Justice Murphy: A Political Biography,* 1968; Hunt, Richard D., *High Ministry of Government: Frank Murphy,* 1965.

Muskie, Edmund Sixtus

(March 28, 1914–   )
Secretary of State, Senator

Edmund Muskie was born in Rumford, Maine. He graduated from Bates College in Lewiston, Maine, in 1936. After completing his studies at Cornell Law School in 1939, he established a law practice in Waterville, Maine. During World War II Muskie served as a naval officer. He returned to Maine after the war, helped invigorate the Democratic party there, and won election to the state legislature, where he served from 1947 until 1951. In 1954 he was elected governor as a Democrat in predominately Republican Maine. Four years later, he won election to the U.S. Senate.

Muskie established a record in the Senate as a moderate liberal and became a leader in legislation to curtail air and water pollution. He was nominated as HUBERT HUMPHREY's vice president by the fractured Democratic party in 1968 and helped run a strong campaign, but the Humphrey–Muskie ticket was unable to defeat the Republican combination of RICHARD NIXON and SPIRO AGNEW.

Encouraged by the close outcome of the 1968 presidential race, Muskie decided to try for the Democratic party's nomination for president in 1972. However, the unfair tactics and false accusations employed by Nixon's aides dedicated to ensuring Nixon's reelection caused Muskie to lose control of his emotions during the New Hampshire primary and eventually abandon his quest for the nomination.

After losing his bid for the presidency, Muskie resumed his Senate career. As chairman of the Senate Budget Committee, he vainly sought to curtail government spending during President GERALD FORD's administration. In 1980, after the secretary of state (see CYRUS VANCE) resigned over a policy dispute with President JIMMY CARTER, Carter chose Muskie to replace him. Muskie served in the position for only a brief period, however, because Carter was not reelected in 1980.

Muskie returned to Maine in January 1981 and resumed the practice of law.

BIBLIOGRAPHY

Muskie, Edmund S., *Journeys*, 1972; Nevin, David, *Muskie of Maine*, 1972.

Nelson, Donald Marr

(November 17, 1888–September 29, 1959)
Diplomat, Government Agency Director

As chairman of the War Production Board during World War II, Donald Nelson played a vital role in facilitating the conversion of the American civilian economy into the "arsenal of democracy."

Nelson was born in Hannibal, Missouri, and graduated from the University of Missouri in 1911 with a bachelor's degree in chemical engineering. He had intended to pursue his doctorate, but a temporary job as a chemist at Sears, Roebuck and Company became his permanent career. Between 1912 and 1939 he worked his way up the administrative ladder of the company from the testing laboratory to the office of executive vice president.

In 1940 President FRANKLIN D. ROOSEVELT asked Nelson to provide government economic boards with assistance in converting industry to defense and war purposes. Released from Sears, Nelson became acting director of procurement in the Treasury Department and chairman of the National Defense Advisory Commission.

In January 1942 Roosevelt created the War Production Board (WPB) and appointed Nelson as its head. The WPB was meant to be a "superagency" that would oversee the conversion of the economy from a civilian into a massive war production machine. Though the WPB successfully allocated vital raw materials and facilitated, for a time, harmonious management and labor relations, it never achieved the degree of power and efficiency it sought. The authority delegated to it was not sufficient, and Nelson was not hard-nosed enough in bureaucratic infighting. One such fight with army leaders over the best way to implement reconversion back to a civilian economy once the war was over led to Nelson's departure from the WPB in August 1944. He was then sent as Roosevelt's personal representative (with cabinet rank) to accompany Major General Patrick J. Hurley on a special mission to the Soviet Union and China during 1944 and 1945. He retired from government service in May 1945.

BIBLIOGRAPHY

Nelson, Donald Marr, *Arsenal of Democracy*, 1946.

Nixon, Richard Milhous

(January 9, 1913–)
President, Vice President, Senator, Representative

After finally achieving his dream of becoming president in 1968, Richard Nixon became the first U.S. chief executive to resign from office. It was a dramatic ending to a long and controversial political career marked by early unscrupulous election campaign tactics and later foreign policy accomplishments.

Nixon was born in Yorba Linda, California, and grew up in Whittier. He graduated from the small Quaker-run Whittier College in 1934 and, thanks to a scholarship and part-time work, managed to complete his law studies at Duke University in 1937. After serving as a town counsel and corporate tax lawyer, Nixon moved to Washington, D.C., in January 1942 to work in the Office of Price Administration. That August he joined the navy and served in the Pacific as a lieutenant.

National Archives

After the war Nixon entered California politics. In his campaign for the U.S. House of Representatives, Nixon branded his Democratic opponent, Jerry Voorhis, as a tool of organized labor because he had accepted campaign donations from the Congress of Industrial Organizations' Political Action Committee. Nixon also claimed that the committee was communist-dominated. The slander was unfounded, but voters responded to it and gave Nixon a solid victory.

In Congress, Nixon won a national reputation for his aggressive behavior as a member of the House Un-American Activities Committee (HUAC). In a famous trial, he supported the claims of Whittaker Chambers that Alger Hiss, a respected diplomat and president of the Carnegie Endowment for International Peace, had been a member of the Communist party before World War II and had spied for the Soviet Union. Hiss was eventually convicted of perjury. Capitalizing on his newfound notoriety, Nixon decided in 1950 to run for the U.S. Senate against Democratic representative Helen Gahagen Douglas. Once again, Nixon, relying on unsubstantiated evidence and innuendo, won the election by labeling his opponent a communist.

Nixon's youth, anticommunist reputation, and California residence made him an ideal running mate for DWIGHT D. EISENHOWER in 1952. During the campaign Nixon was almost forced off the Republican ticket because of the discovery that a special campaign fund had been set up by wealthy supporters to help defer his Senate campaign costs. It was alleged that Nixon used some of the funds in an inappropriate personal manner. Nixon went on national television with his family. The group included a dog called Checkers—a gift Nixon said he would not return. His talk (thereafter referred to as the Checkers speech), an effective, tearful denial of wrongdoing, stymied efforts to force his resignation. Because of Eisenhower's illnesses and distaste for internal party politics, Nixon assumed the task of pacifying various Republican party groups and took many overseas goodwill trips during his eight years as vice president. It was on one such trip to Moscow that he seized upon the opportunity to debate Soviet leader Nikita Khrushchev about the benefits of capitalism over communism. This exchange, known as the kitchen debate because it took place in the kitchen appliance display at the American National Exhibition in Moscow, brought Nixon enormous popularity in the United States.

In 1960 Nixon easily won the Republican nomination for president, but he was defeated in the general election by Democrat JOHN F. KENNEDY in a very close race. Many political analysts attributed his narrow loss to the mistake of agreeing to debate Kennedy on live television. The haggard and stony-faced Nixon, although a brilliant debater, was no match for the youthful and photogenic Kennedy. A majority of the television audience felt that Kennedy had won, but radio listeners felt that Nixon had.

Two years later, Nixon ran for governor of California and, after losing badly to the Democratic incumbent, held a news conference in which he attacked the press for its alleged anti-Nixon bias. He concluded with the sarcastic comment, "You won't have Nixon to kick around anymore, because, gentlemen, this is my last press conference." Nixon moved to New York City and became a partner of a large Wall Street law firm. In 1964, when other Republicans refused to endorse conservative BARRY GOLDWATER, Nixon campaigned on his behalf. This, plus frequent appearances for Republican candidates across the nation, enabled Nixon to make a remarkable political comeback in 1968. This time, running against Democrat HUBERT HUMPHREY and third-party candidate GEORGE WALLACE, he won.

Nixon posed as a candidate of the "silent majority," of the average Americans whose interests had been ignored by a liberal Democratic party preoccupied with the problems of American blacks and the media-grabbing antics of the nation's privileged, university youth. Nixon campaigned against more welfare for blacks, against cultural permissiveness and political radicalism, and for law and order and respect for authority and tradition. His election, in retrospect, was a watershed in American political history because it signaled the breakup and decline of the liberal coalition that had dominated American politics since the New Deal.

Nixon assumed the presidency in 1969 at a difficult time in American history. High inflation, domestic civil rights protests and the war in Vietnam (see LYNDON BAINES JOHNSON) had split the nation along age, class, and racial lines. During his first term Nixon gradually withdrew American forces from South Vietnam. Under his "Vietnamization plan," the South Vietnamese army was trained to take over the fighting and to use American air power to force North Vietnam to relinquish its quest for total victory. In 1970 American bombing of communist bases in Cambodia and Laos succeeded in disrupting enemy supply lines but unleased a fury of domestic political protest.

Undaunted, Nixon continued to alternate between increased bombing and a willingness to negotiate as American ground combat forces were withdrawn. Finally, in January 1973, after massive American B-52 bombing attacks, North Vietnam agreed to a negotiated peace. But this "peace with honor" turned out to be little more than an opportunity for the United States to pull out of a war it could not win. South Vietnam fell under the domination of the North in 1975. In addition, the bombing had dramatically enlarged the area of conflict in Indochina, undermining sources of stability in Cambodia and giving an opening for the Khmer Rouge and their policies of mass murder.

Nixon's other foreign policy achievements were less controversial. Pursuing a policy of peaceful coexistence called détente (see HENRY ALFRED KISSINGER), he improved relations with the Soviet Union. He visited Moscow in 1972, and Soviet party leader Leonid Brezhnev came to the United States in 1973. Their talks resulted in a large grain sale to the Soviet Union by the United States and the beginning of talks on limiting strategic nuclear weapons. Nixon also visited the People's Republic of China in 1972, thereby opening communications with that country and substantially reducing tensions in the world. During the 1973 Yom Kippur War, the Nixon administration, along with the Soviet Union, successfully pressured Israel, Egypt, and Syria to cease hostilities. With peace restored, Nixon made a friendly visit to Israel and four Arab nations in 1974.

In domestic politics, Nixon's efforts to curtail the federal government's role in civil rights advocacy and social welfare provision met with mixed results. He dismantled many liberal programs of the 1960s, slowed down the progress of school integration, and ap-

pointed four conservative justices to the Supreme Court. Yet the Democratic Congress blocked his legislation to prohibit forced busing, stymied numerous attempts to cut social programs, and refused to confirm two of his Supreme Court nominees. Nixon, moreover, sometimes initiated policies more liberal than conservative, as in his imposition of wage and price controls in 1971 and his Family Assistance Plan proposal (1970), a bold welfare program that would have guaranteed each American family a minimum annual income.

Partially out of a desire to stop leaks of classified Vietnam War–related information to the press and out of a desire to ensure his own reelection in 1972, Nixon authorized the establishment of a team of agents (nicknamed the Plumbers) to tap telephones illegally and burglarize the offices of opponents. When they were caught in the Democratic party's national campaign office in the Watergate building in Washington, D.C., in June 1972 and arrested, Nixon authorized the payment of large sums of campaign contribution money to maintain their silence and promised them clemency after the election. (He had previously authorized the infiltration of the student New Left and antiwar movements to spy on them and to provoke their members to ever more extreme actions.) In the fall, Nixon was elected by an overwhelming majority against his Democratic rival, GEORGE MCGOVERN.

Shortly after Nixon began his second term, his vice president, SPIRO AGNEW, was forced to resign for income tax evasion (see SPIRO AGNEW). Then the cover-up Nixon had authorized of the activities of the clandestine Plumbers operation began to unravel. Over the course of the next two years Nixon and the nation experienced his gradual political destruction. A nationally televised Senate investigation piled up evidence of his guilt in obstructing justice and in abusing the powers and privileges of his office for personal and political gain. Finally, in August 1974, Nixon was forced by a Supreme Court decision to turn over tapes he had made of conversations in his office detailing his efforts to prevent the discovery of his involvement in the cover-up of the Watergate break-in. Faced with certain impeachment by Congress, Nixon resigned.

One month later, President Gerald Ford granted Nixon a full pardon from any federal prosecution. Nixon accepted the pardon but never admitted that he had ever done anything illegal. In retirement he continued to travel and write about foreign policy issues.

Nixon's penchant for secrecy and illegality had the long-term effect of not only diminishing his achievements, but also diminishing the stature of the presidency.

BIBLIOGRAPHY

Ambrose, Stephen E., *Nixon: The Education of a Politician, 1913–1962,* 1987; Bernstein, Carl, and Bob Woodward, *The Final Days,* 1976; Evans, R., Jr., and R. Novak, *Nixon and the White House: Frustration of Power,* 1971; Nixon, Richard M., *RN: The Memoirs of Richard Nixon,* 1978, *The Real War,* 1980, and *No More Vietnams,* 1985; Parmet, Herbert S., *Richard Nixon and His America,* 1990; Thornton, Richard C., *The Nixon–Kissinger Years: Reshaping America's Foreign Policy,* 1989; White, Theodore H., *The Making of the President,* 1960.

Norris, George William

(July 11, 1861–September 2, 1944)
Senator, Representative

In 1910 Norris, in the fourth of his five consecutive terms as a U.S. representative from Nebraska, was successful in his crusade to strip Speaker of the House JOSEPH G. CANNON of his dictatorial power. Two years later, Norris began the first of his five consecutive terms in the Senate. Officially a Republican, during his four decades in Congress, Norris strove to be "independent of all parties."

Born in Sandusky County, Ohio, Norris attended Baldwin University and the Northern Indiana Normal School. He studied law at Valparaiso University and was admitted to the bar in 1883. He moved to Furnas County, Nebraska, where from 1895 to 1902 he was judge of the district court. After serving in the House of Representatives from 1903 to 1913, he moved on to the Senate.

Norris was a Progressive (see THEODORE ROOSEVELT) whose roots were in the Midwest Populist (see JAMES BAIRD WEAVER) traditions that stressed curbing the power of the "Interests," increasing the political power of the "People," and using the federal government for purposes of economic regulation and social welfare. Consistent with these beliefs, Norris supported Roosevelt on the Progressive party ticket in 1912. Unlike Roosevelt, however, he opposed American entry into World War I on the grounds that it would benefit the elite classes rather than the masses of ordinary Americans. For similar reasons, he opposed American participation in the League of Nations (see WOODROW WILSON).

For years Norris envisioned a federal program to turn the vast energy of the powerful, flood-prone Tennessee River into a great source of hydroelectric power for the whole region—the government taking on the role of economic development and energy generation (and in the process taking it away from private industry)—but his efforts were frustrated by Presidents CALVIN COOLIDGE and HERBERT HOOVER. In recognition of his role as principal author of the legislation during FRANKLIN D. ROOSEVELT's first term that finally created the Tennessee Valley Authority (TVA) in 1933, the Norris Dam carries his name. The TVA was soon hailed as a model liberal success in government planning.

Because of his support for many of Roosevelt's New Deal policies and active campaigning on behalf of Roosevelt in his first two presidential election campaigns, Norris was expelled from the Republican party in 1936. He won reelection anyway as an independent.

Concerned with administrative reform, in 1932 Norris authored the Twentieth Amendment to the Constitution, which abolished the "lame duck" session of Congress and changed the date of the presidential inauguration from March to January. He also wrote the Nebraska constitutional amendment that in 1934 established a unicameral legislature for that state.

With the outbreak of World War II, Norris reluctantly supported the revision of American neutrality laws so that lend-lease military assistance could be provided to Great Britain (see FRANKLIN DELANO ROOSEVELT). In 1942, at age eighty-one, Norris failed to win reelection to the Senate in a three-way race and retired from politics.

BIBLIOGRAPHY

Lief, Alfred, *Democracy's Norris,* 1939; Lowitt, Richard, *George W. Norris: The Persistence of a Progressive, 1913–1933,* 1971; Norris, George W., *Fighting Liberal,* 1945; Zucker, Norman L., *George W. Norris,* 1966.

Nye, Gerald Prentice

(December 19, 1892–July 17, 1971)
Senator

Fervently Progressive, thoroughly provincial, and intensely emotional in his public speeches, Senator Gerald Nye of North Dakota was a leading proponent of American isolationism during the 1930s.

Nye was born in Hortonville, Wisconsin. After graduating from high school he worked on and owned newspapers in Wisconsin, Iowa, and North Dakota. In 1924 Nye supported the presidential bid of Progressive candidate ROBERT M. LA FOLLETTE. In 1925 he was appointed to fill a vacant seat in the U.S. Senate from North Dakota, and a year later was elected to the first of three consecutive terms as a Progressive Republican member of North Dakota's Nonpartisan League, an agrarian movement founded to fight domination of the state's economy by eastern financial "special interests."

Nye quickly established a reputation in the Senate as a strong advocate of farm relief at home and avoidance of American involvement in events abroad. In 1927 he chaired the Senate committee that investigated the Teapot Dome scandal (see WARREN GAMALIEL HARDING), and he led the fight to prevent the United States from joining the World Court. At first a supporter of FRANKLIN D. ROOSEVELT's New Deal, Nye broke with the president first over his foreign policy, then over his domestic legislative efforts.

In 1934 Nye introduced a resolution in the Senate calling for an investigation of the weapons industry. He became the chairman of the Senate committee charged with conducting the highly publicized probe (1934–1937) that revealed the mammoth size and influence of the arms industry in business, financial, and political affairs. He became nationally well known through a series of speeches he delivered blaming the weapons industry—"the merchants of death"—for the "unnecessary" entry of America into World War I.

During the late 1930s Nye played a key role in shaping and enacting a series of neutrality acts (see WILLIAM EDGAR BORAH) designed to prevent American involvement in European conflicts. In 1940 he won a seat on the Senate Foreign Relations Committee and fought a vain effort to prevent passage of the Lend-Lease Act (see Franklin Delano Roosevelt). After the Japanese attack on Pearl Harbor (see Roosevelt), Nye supported the prosecution of the war. After losing his bid to win a fourth term in the Senate in 1944, Nye became

a management consultant in Washington, D.C., from 1946 until his retirement in 1960.

BIBLIOGRAPHY

Cole, Wayne S., *Senator Gerald P. Nye and American Foreign Relations*, 1962.

O'Connor, Sandra Day

(March 26, 1930–)
Associate Justice of the Supreme Court

U.S. Supreme Court

The first woman appointed to the U.S. Supreme Court, Justice O'Connor has, in her judicial decisions, remained true to her conservative political and legal beliefs.

Born in El Paso, Texas, O'Connor spent her early childhood on the family's 155,000-acre ranch in southeastern Arizona. A brilliant student, she graduated from high school at age sixteen and completed the normal seven-year undergraduate and law school programs at Stanford University in five years. At Stanford she met John Jay O'Connor and married him after her graduation in 1952.

O'Connor worked as a civilian lawyer for the U.S. Army's Quartermaster Corps in Germany from 1954 to 1957. Upon her return to the United States in 1957, she settled in Phoenix, Arizona. In Phoenix she established her own law firm and became assistant attorney general for the state of Arizona in 1965. She

served as a Republican in the Arizona Senate from 1969 to 1974 and became, in 1972, the senate's majority leader, the first woman in any state to hold that office. O'Connor earned a reputation as a tough debater and strict party leader. Once, when a committee member angrily yelled at her: "If you were a man, I'd punch you right in the mouth," she calmly replied, "If you were a man, you could."

In 1974 O'Connor was elected judge of the superior court of Phoenix, a position she held until 1979, when Democratic governor Bruce Babbitt named her to the state court of appeals. In July 1981 President Ronald Reagan fulfilled a campaign pledge to place the first woman on the Supreme Court by nominating Sandra Day O'Connor as an associate justice. He had told his aides to find a woman who was both a political and a judicial conservative. In her Senate confirmation hearings, O'Connor said she believed that judges should interpret the laws as narrowly as possible (that is, strict constructionism; see THOMAS JEFFERSON and MELVILLE WESTON FULLER) and not try to become legislators by broadening statutes to include their own political views.

During her first eight years as an associate justice, O'Connor took conservative positions. She identified herself as a meticulous legal thinker devoted to precedent and judicial process. Her most controversial position to date has dealt with abortion rights. In 1983 she strongly dissented from the Court majority's reaffirmation of the right of women to legal abortions, and in 1988 she sided with the majority in a decision that allowed states to impose legal restrictions narrowing the right of women to have abortions. Her actions angered feminists and caused Judy Goldsmith, president of the National Organization for Women, to comment: "Having a woman on the Court gave us the possibility of a representative female perspective. It did not guarantee it."

In another decision, though, she incurred the wrath of fellow associate justice ANTONIN SCALIA for not being conservative enough by voting to allow teenage girls the alternative of obtaining permission from a judge to have an abortion instead of notifying parents. She has emerged as a moderate antiabortionist and as an individual striving to balance her interpretations of the Constitution with a high regard for Supreme Court precedent and traditions, including those set during the EARL WARREN years.

BIBLIOGRAPHY

"Going Against the Grain," *Time*, June 27, 1983; Hackett, George, "All Eyes on Justice O'Connor," *Newsweek*, May 1, 1989; McLoughlin, Merrill, "Sandra Day O'Connor: Woman in the Middle," *Ladies Home Journal*, November 1989; Magnuson, Ed, "The Brethren's First Sister," *Time*, July 2, 1981; "Sizing Up Ms Justice," *Newsweek*, July 18, 1983; Williams, Marjorie C., and Al Kamen, "America's Most Influential Women," *Readers' Digest*, December 1989.

Olney, Richard

(September 15, 1835–April 8, 1917)
Secretary of State, Attorney General

In his brief terms as attorney general and then as secretary of state, Richard Olney managed to establish long-term policy legacies.

Born in Oxford, Massachusetts, Olney graduated from Brown University in 1856 and Harvard Law School two years later. Admitted to the Massachusetts bar in 1859, Olney began practicing law in Boston. In 1873 he was elected to the Massachusetts legislature as a Democrat. However, after serving only one term, despite several attempts, he was never able to win reelection in the increasingly Republican party–dominated state.

In 1893 President GROVER CLEVELAND chose Olney to be his attorney general. Olney was the first government official to employ an injunction to stop a strike. In 1894 the injunction he obtained against the Pullman strikers resulted in the imprisonment of EUGENE DEBS, president of the American Railway Union, for contempt of court. He also persuaded President Cleveland to send troops to crush worker resistance on the pretext of protecting the mail, even though John Peter Altgeld, the Democratic governor of Illinois, said federal troops were not needed to maintain law and order. The U.S. Supreme Court later upheld

Olney's novel use of the injunction and established his action as a precedent for "government by injunction."

Although he had acted swiftly and harshly to crush the Pullman strike, Olney was not philosophically opposed to labor organizations. Aware of the need of workers to have an avenue to redress their grievances with management, he supported the movement that culminated in the Arbitration Act of 1898.

In 1895 Olney was appointed secretary of state and became directly involved in negotiations with Great Britain over a boundary dispute it was having with Venezuela. The United States had the right to intervene, declared Olney, because "it is practically sovereign on this continent." This viewpoint of the American right to participate in all foreign affairs in the Western Hemisphere became known as the Olney Corollary to the Monroe Doctrine (see JAMES MONROE). The boundary dispute was eventually settled through international arbitration as a result of the U.S. intervention.

Olney returned to private law practice at the end of the Cleveland administration in 1897 and, although he was briefly mentioned as a possible presidential candidate in 1904, declined to try for the nomination. He also turned down opportunities to be the ambassador to Great Britain and governor of the Federal Reserve Board.

BIBLIOGRAPHY

James, Henry, *Richard Olney*, 1923.

O'Neill, Thomas Philip, Jr.

(December 9, 1912–   )
Speaker of the House, Representative

In a political career that spanned half a century of state and national legislative service, Thomas "Tip" O'Neill, Jr., was careful to follow a political maxim for which he was often quoted: "All politics is local."

O'Neill, who was born in Cambridge, Massachusetts, was nicknamed Tip after a professional baseball player, James O'Neill, famous for hitting foul balls off the tip of his bat. After graduating from Boston College in 1936, he won election to the Massachusetts House of Representatives as a Democrat and strong supporter of FRANKLIN D. ROOSEVELT's New Deal.

In 1949 O'Neill was elected speaker of the Massachusetts House. He served in this office until he was elected to the U.S. House of Representatives in 1952. By 1966, he had solidified his political base so well that the Republican party no longer even bothered to nominate a candidate to run against him.

While serving in the U.S. House of Representatives as a staunch liberal Democrat until 1986, O'Neill continued his strong support for New Deal social programs along with voting for civil rights legislation, antipoverty programs, Medicare, national health care, environmental protection, reductions in the defense budget, and busing to achieve school integration.

At first O'Neill had strongly supported the war in Vietnam (see LYNDON BAINES JOHNSON and RICHARD MILHOUS NIXON), but after the 1968 Tet offensive, he became a vocal critic of administration policy and an advocate of the need for the United States to withdraw. This won him great favor with the student element of his constituency, but, as he later said, his real strength derived from his strong support among blue-collar workers, and "I had a helluva time" trying "to sell them."

In 1971 he was elected assistant majority leader and two years later, majority leader. He served in this post during the congressional investigation of the Watergate scandal (see RICHARD MILHOUS NIXON), correctly predicting that President Nixon would resign before it would be necessary to have an impeachment trial.

In 1977 O'Neill was elected Speaker of the House and became known for his skill at finding grounds for compromise. He held this post until he retired from politics in 1986. After RONALD REAGAN won the presidency in 1980 and the Republicans gained control of the Senate, O'Neill became the highest-ranking elected official of the Democratic party. As Speaker at the height of Reagan's popularity, O'Neill found it extremely difficult to obtain enough votes to prevent enactment of crucial parts of the Reagan agenda, such as tax cuts, social welfare cuts, and increases in defense spending.

BIBLIOGRAPHY

O'Neill, Thomas P., *Shades of Gray*, 1987, and *Man of the House: The Life and Political Memoirs of Speaker Tip O'Neill*, with William Novak, 1987.

Orr, James Lawrence

(May 12, 1822–May 5, 1873)
Diplomat, Speaker of the House, Representative

James Lawrence Orr was born in Pendleton District (now Anderson County), South Carolina. After studying law at the University of Virginia, he was admitted to the bar in 1842. Two years later, he was elected to the state legislature. In 1848 he won election to the first of five successive terms in the U.S. House of Representatives, serving as Speaker from 1857 until 1859.

At first a supporter of fellow Democrat STEPHEN A. DOUGLAS and the need to preserve the Union, Orr changed his position and became a champion of secession when ABRAHAM LINCOLN was elected president in 1860.

After a brief military role in organizing a Confederate regiment (Orr's Regiment of Rifles), he was elected in December 1861 to the Confederate senate and remained there throughout the Civil War. A frequent critic of JEFFERSON DAVIS, Orr accepted the fact that the South was destined to lose the war before most of his colleagues and advised seeking a negotiated settlement in 1864.

An advocate of accommodation, Orr was elected governor of South Carolina in 1865 as a supporter of President ANDREW JOHNSON's Reconstruction plans. However, once again shifting his position to match political reality, he quickly became a Radical Republican with the collapse of Johnson's popularity. While this ensured his position in the short run, it cost him the support of his white constituents. In 1868 Orr was elected to a two-year term on the circuit bench.

At the Republican national convention in 1872, Orr supported President ULYSSES S. GRANT's anti–Ku Klux Klan policy (see ULYSSES SIMPSON GRANT). Later that year he was appointed minister to Russia. Orr died of pneumonia in St. Petersburg just a few months after his arrival.

BIBLIOGRAPHY

Cyclopedia of Eminent and Representative Men of the Carolinas, 1892; Perry, B. F., *Reminiscence of Public Men*, 1893; Simkins, F. B., and R. H. Woody, *South Carolina During Reconstruction*, 1932.

Otis, James

(February 5, 1725–May 23, 1783)
Revolutionary Leader

From 1761 to 1769 James Otis was the political leader of Massachusetts and the chief publicist of the American cause. His pamphlets explaining the patriot perspective on the relationship between the American colonies and England laid the broad theoretical groundwork for American independence.

Otis was born in West Barnstable, Massachusetts. After graduating from Harvard in 1743, he studied law and was admitted to the bar in 1748. Two years later, he established a law practice in Boston and quickly rose to prominence. By 1760, he was king's advocate general of the vice admiralty court at Boston. He resigned his position in 1761 rather than abide by the British policy of issuing writs of assistance that authorized searches for smuggled goods without specifying either the location or the items. During Otis's argument in court on behalf of Boston merchants against the legality of the writs, JOHN ADAMS later observed: "American independence was then and there born."

Otis was elected to the Massachusetts General Court (colonial legislature) in 1761. That same year his father was also reelected speaker of the Massachusetts House, and the father–son team soon managed to unite opponents of the Crown into a powerful opposition block. Otis's activities in the colonial legislature, as a member of the "Sons of Liberty," as head of the Massachusetts Committee of Correspondence, and as author of several widely distributed pamphlets defending the reasoning behind protests of British colonial policy enabled him to become the recognized leader of the patriot cause in Massachusetts from 1761 to 1769.

Otis hoped to find a nonviolent solution to the growing tension with England. He initially advocated colonial representation in Parliament, not independence, which he said shortly after serving as a delegate to the Stamp Act Congress in New York in 1765, "none but rebels, fools, or madmen, will contend for. . . . Were these colonies left to themselves, tomorrow, America would be a meer shambles of blood and confusion." However, in 1768 he helped SAM ADAMS draft the Massachusetts circular letter in opposition to the greater duties imposed by the Townshend Act.

His activities helped to unite all the colonies, although he remained opposed to direct action against the British. When he was described in 1869 by the commissioners of customs to England as a traitor, he was infuriated. Otis published an open letter in which he called the commissioners liars. A confrontation with one of the commissioners in a Boston tavern led to blows, and Otis suffered a severe head wound from which he never fully recovered. He became subject to spells of irrational behavior and had to be placed in the care of his brother. His political career was effectively ended.

BIBLIOGRAPHY

Mullett, C. F. (ed.), "Some Political Writings of James Otis," *University of Missouri Studies*, vol. 4, nos. 3, 4, 1929; Tudor, William, *Life of James Otis*, 1823.

Paine, Thomas

(January 29, 1737–June 8, 1809)
Revolutionary Leader

Perhaps no other writer than Thomas Paine did more to inspire Americans to obtain their independence from Great Britain and to endeavor to spread the principles of the American Revolution to Europe.

Paine was born in Thetford, England. After working in a variety of jobs with only debt to show for his efforts, Paine decided to move to Philadelphia. Aided by a letter of introduction from BENJAMIN FRANKLIN, Paine managed to earn a living as the editor of the *Pennsylvania Magazine* and as a journalist after his arrival in Philadelphia in November 1774.

Paine followed closely the events that led up to the American Revolution. At first he believed the colonies should avoid armed rebellion, but once actual fighting had begun he became convinced that only complete independence would work. In January 1776, he published his forty-seven-page pamphlet *Common Sense,* explaining his reasoning in bold, direct language. Paine advocated a declaration of independence to secure European aid and to unite the colonies. The new, unspoiled, democratic America had to break its ties with England in order to evolve in its own unique way. Once independence had been achieved, America could establish a central democratic republican form of government that could serve as a model and beacon to the rest of the world. *Common Sense* was phenomenally successful and had a tremendous impact on American public opinion.

Library of Congress

After the publication of the Declaration of Independence, Paine briefly served in the Continental Army, but his mission was to write, not fight. During the war he published a series of widely read pamphlets that bolstered American revolutionary morale. For example, in December 1776, after the dismal performance of the American forces in the New York campaign, Paine's first *American Crisis* pamphlet began with the famous line, "These are the times that try men's souls."

Undoubtedly in appreciation for his writing efforts and need to earn a living, he was appointed by the Continental Congress as secretary of the Foreign Affairs Committee in April 1777. He fulfilled his duties properly for two years, but in 1779 he was forced to resign after indiscreetly mentioning in a newspaper article information about secret French aid known to him only because of his official position.

Once the Revolution was won, Paine, who earned no profits from his pamphlets, was awarded a confiscated Loyalist farm in New Rochelle by New York and £500 by Pennsylvania. He lived in relative comfort on his farm until traveling to Europe in 1787 and becoming involved in the French Revolution.

While living in London, Paine wrote *The Rights of Man* (1791–1792). These pamphlets defended the actions of the French government, attacked England's hostility to the French Revolution and support of a monarchy, and argued that all people had natural civil rights. The British government issued a warrant for his arrest and Paine fled to France, where he was initially hailed as a hero. He soon became embroiled in the political turmoil there and ended up imprisoned from December 1793 until American intervention secured his release in November 1794.

Financially destitute and in weakened health, Paine returned to America in 1802, where he spent the last seven years of his life on his farm in New Rochelle.

BIBLIOGRAPHY

Aldridge, A. Owen, *Man of Reason: The Life of Thomas Paine*, 1959, and *Thomas Paine's American Ideology*, 1984; Foner, Eric, *Tom Paine and Revolutionary America*, 1977; Hawke, David F., *Paine*, 1947; Powell, David, *Tom Paine: The Greatest Exile*, 1985; Williamson, Audrey, *Thomas Paine*, 1973.

Palmer, Alexander Mitchell

(May 4, 1872–May 11, 1936)
Attorney General, Representative

The mass arrests of accused radicals and the deportation of aliens accused of being disloyal during the "Red Scare" of the post–World War I years were known as the Palmer Raids, ordered by Attorney General A. Mitchell Palmer.

Alexander Mitchell Palmer was born into a prominent Quaker family in Moosehead, Pennsylvania. He graduated from Swarthmore College in 1891. After studying law and being admitted to the bar in 1893, Palmer established a practice in Stroudsburg and became one of Pennsylvania's most successful attorneys.

Active in the state Democratic party, Palmer quickly assumed a leadership role. In 1908 he won the first of three consecutive terms to the U.S. House of Representatives.

At the Democratic national convention in 1912, Palmer was the floor leader of the bloc of delegates committed to securing the presidential nomination for WOODROW WILSON. For his loyalty, President Wilson offered Palmer the position of secretary of war. Palmer declined the nomination because of his pacifist Quaker faith.

In 1914 Palmer, at Wilson's request, gave up his seat in the House of Representatives and made an unsuccessful bid to win election to the Senate. After the United States entered World War I, Palmer accepted the post of alien property custodian. The position involved the resale of $600 million in seized enemy property to American citizens. Critics charged that he sold seized property for below-market value to friends for personal profit, but a congressional investigation in 1921 cleared him of all accusations.

In 1919 President Wilson appointed Mitchell U.S. attorney general. During his two years in office, Palmer attempted, with little success due to his limited powers and resources, to prevent labor strikes and to prosecute illegal industry price fixing. His most controversial action concerned his vigorous prosecution of men and women who were suspected of disloyalty to the United States because of their radical political beliefs. Although his authorization of raids, arrests, and deportations of such well-known radical political aliens as Emma Goldman were deplored by defenders of civil liberties, they brought him popular acclaim. In 1920, at the Democratic national convention, he almost won the party's presidential nomination. In historical perspective, his zeal appears excessive, though it must be understood as part of a wave of antiradical and anti-immigrant hysteria that swept through the nation in the aftermath of World War I.

At the conclusion of the Wilson administration in March 1921, Palmer returned to his private law practice.

BIBLIOGRAPHY

Coben, Stanley, *A. Mitchell Palmer: Politician*, 1963; Murray, Robert K., *Red Scare: A Study in National Hysteria, 1919–1920*, 1955.

Parker, Alton Brooks

(May 14, 1852–May 10, 1926)
Candidate for President

B orn and educated in Cortland, New York, Parker graduated from Albany Law School in 1873. He established a successful law practice in Kingston and became an important figure in the New York Democratic party. Elected in 1877 as an Ulster County surrogate, he remained in that position until he managed David B. Hill's successful 1885 campaign for governor. From 1885 to 1889 Parker was a justice of the New York Supreme Court, and until 1892 served on the bench of the New York Court of Appeals. In 1897 he was elected chief justice of that court.

Parker's judicial record was generally liberal, especially in labor cases. The combination of his liberal opinions on the bench with his reputation for honesty, record of party loyalty, and conservative personal philosophy made Parker an appealing potential presidential candidate to Democratic party leaders. They hoped he would be able to win over conservative Republican voters unhappy with THEODORE ROOSEVELT's reforms without losing the support of the liberal wing of the Democratic party. Fearing that he might discredit himself as a judge, Parker did nothing to promote his own candidacy in 1904. He broke with the free-silver wing of the Democratic party by stating to the Democratic convention that he considered the gold standard to be "firmly and irrevocably established." This act might have cost him the nomination had he run in the previous two elections when the silver Democrats merged platforms with the Populists (see WILLIAM JENNINGS BRYAN and JAMES BAIRD WEAVER). However, by 1904 the free-silver issue had lost its urgency, and Parker was nominated on the first ballot.

The immense popularity of Roosevelt, combined with the conflict within the Democratic party over the silver versus gold standard issue, led to Parker's overwhelming defeat in the 1904 election. Parker returned to New York City and resumed his private law practice. He was elected president of the American Bar Association from 1906 to 1908 and remained active in Democratic party politics until his death.

BIBLIOGRAPHY

Grady, J. R., *The Lives and Public Services of Parker and Davis*, 1904; *New York Times*, May 11, 1926; O'Brien, M. J., "Memoir," *New York County Lawyers' Association Year Book*, 1926.

Paterson, William

(December 24, 1745–September 9, 1806)
Associate Justice of the Supreme Court, Senator, Revolutionary Leader

Patriot, legislator, and Supreme Court justice, Paterson is remembered as the defender of the interests of small states at the Constitutional Convention and author of the New Jersey Plan.

Born in county Antrim, Ireland, Paterson arrived with his parents in Delaware in 1747 and grew up in Princeton, New Jersey. He graduated from the College of New Jersey (now Princeton University) in 1763 and earned a master's degree three years later. Admitted to the bar in 1769, Paterson established a law practice in New Jersey, eventually settling near New Brunswick.

After serving in several colonial government and legislative positions, Paterson was chosen as the new state's first attorney general in 1776. He retained this post, also serving in the Continental Congress, until 1783.

As the leader of his state's delegation to the Constitutional Convention in 1787, Paterson championed the rights of small states to be equally represented in the new federal government alongside the large states. He advocated adoption of what became known as the New Jersey Plan. The plan called for a federal government consisting of three branches—legislative, judicial, and executive. The legislative branch was to be a unicameral (single-house) body in which each state had equal representation regardless of size or population. Paterson's plan gave way to a compromise between the large and small states that brought about the establishment of a bicameral (two-house) federal legislature consisting of the Senate (membership provided by two members from each state) and the House of Representatives (membership based proportionally on the population of each state).

Elected one of New Jersey's first senators in 1789, Paterson resigned from the Senate to become governor in 1790. Three years later, President GEORGE WASHINGTON appointed Paterson to the Supreme Court. During his term as an associate justice of the Supreme Court from 1793 to 1806, Paterson supported decisions that established the Constitution as the supreme law of the land. By deciding in favor of the supremacy of the federal government over state governments, Paterson also contributed to the acceptance of the Supreme Court as the final arbiter of constitutional questions.

BIBLIOGRAPHY

Shriner, C. A., *William Paterson*, 1940; Wood, Gertrude S., *William Paterson of New Jersey, 1745–1806*, Ph.D. thesis, Columbia University, 1933.

Pennington, William

(May 4, 1796–February 16, 1862)
Speaker of the House, Representative

William Pennington was born in Newark, New Jersey, into a prominent family. He graduated from the College of New Jersey (now Princeton University) in 1813 and completed his legal studies in 1817.

For the next nine years, while his father was a district judge, Pennington was clerk of the district and circuit courts.

In 1828 he was elected to the New Jersey legislature and, in 1837, running as a member of the Whig party, chosen governor and chancellor of the state. His one controversial decision while governor concerned the manner in which he resolved the disputed congressional election results of 1838. The Democrats claimed to have won five out of the six congressional district election races, but the county clerks certified that all six seats had been won by Whig candidates. Amidst charges of corruption, Pennington claimed that he did not have the authority as governor to challenge the results and certified the Whig candidates as the legal winners. The battle was continued in the U.S. House of Representatives. The Whig and Democratic parties were so evenly balanced in the House that whichever group was seated would determine the voting majority. Finally, three months after Congress had assembled, it decided to overturn Pennington's decision and seated the Democratic candidates.

Pennington failed to win reelection as governor in 1843 but remained active in politics. He never accomplished his dream of being appointed an ambassador in Europe or of becoming state chancellor again, but in 1858 he was elected to Congress. Eight weeks after the Congress assembled, Pennington was chosen as a compromise candidate to be its new Speaker. His term as Speaker is recalled chiefly for his frequent errors concerning the proper administration of House etiquette and procedural rules.

BIBLIOGRAPHY

Nixon, J. T., *The Circumstances Attending the Election of William Pennington . . . as Speaker*, New Jersey Historical Society Proc., vol. 2, 1872; Elmer, L. Q. C., *The Constitution and Government of . . . New Jersey*, New Jersey Historical Society Collections, vol. 7, 1872.

Pepper, Claude Denson

(September 8, 1900–April 1, 1989)
Senator, Representative

Claude Denson Pepper, liberal congressional champion and folk hero to older Americans, was born near Dudleyville, Alabama. After graduating from the University of Alabama at Tuscaloosa in 1921 and Harvard Law School in 1924, Pepper practiced law in Perry, Florida. In 1929 Pepper won election to the Florida state legislature as a Democrat and sponsored his first "senior citizen" legislation—a bill exempting persons over sixty-five from having to obtain licenses to fish. He lost a reelection fight in 1931 because he voted against a legislative resolution censuring Lou Henry Hoover, the wife of President HERBERT HOOVER, for inviting a black man to a White House function. His willingness to affirm his liberal politics even if it meant losing votes and elections became a hallmark of his career.

Pepper moved to Tallahassee, Florida, in 1931 and held a number of state offices while establishing a successful law practice there. He lost his first effort to win election to the U.S. Senate in 1934 by a narrow margin, but was elected to complete the remainder of a term in the Senate two years later. A strong supporter of New Deal legislation and President FRANKLIN D. ROOSEVELT's anti-isolationist foreign policy, Pepper won reelection to two full six-year terms in 1938 and 1944.

Although Pepper generally supported President HARRY S TRUMAN's legislative goals, he became increasingly convinced that the administration was wrong in its conclusion that the Soviet Union posed an expansionist military threat. He also opposed the U.S. buildup of a nuclear arsenal. Instead, Pepper favored providing economic aid to the Soviet Union and a policy of patience rather than confrontation. As result of an unusually distorted picture of his record in Congress, he was not renominated for a third term in 1950. During the campaign, Pepper's opponent accused him of being soft on communism and used racist and smear tactics to discredit Pepper.

After his reelection defeat, Pepper returned to his law practice in Tallahassee. He remained active in politics and began his second political career in Washington, D.C., when he won election to the House of Representatives in 1962. In Congress Pepper supported LYNDON JOHNSON's Great Society programs and strongly endorsed Medicaid and Medicare. At first he supported the U.S. involvement in Vietnam (see LYNDON BAINES JOHNSON and RICHARD MILHOUS NIXON), but by 1968 he had become convinced that the United States should withdraw.

From 1977 until 1983 Pepper was chairman of the House Select Committee on Aging. In this post he vigorously condemned "ageism" as just as wrong as racism and sexism. Long convinced that mandatory retirement was "an extravagant waste of people," he sponsored a bill in 1978 that halted mandatory retirement for most federal employees and raised the retirement age to seventy for workers in industry.

Pepper gained his greatest influence after 1983 when he became chairman of the House Rules Committee. He was a driving force in Congress that year to implement legislation designed to guarantee the financial solvency of the Social Security system and to prevent cuts in benefits.

BIBLIOGRAPHY

New York Times Magazine, November 28, 1981; Pepper, Claude D., and Hays Gorey, *Eyewitness to a Century,* 1987, *Political Profiles: The Nixon/Ford Years,* 1979, and *Politics in America,* 1982; *Washington Post Magazine,* June 27, 1971.

Perkins, Frances

(April 10, 1882–May 14, 1965)
Secretary of Labor

Frances Perkins was the first woman in the country's history to serve as a member of the cabinet.

Born in Boston, Massachusetts, Perkins graduated from Mount Holyoke College in 1902 and earned a master's degree from Columbia University in 1910. A dedicated teacher and social worker committed to using the legislative process to obtain health and working condition improvements for the poor, Perkins became executive secretary of the New York Consumers' League in 1910. In 1911 Perkins was a witness to the Triangle Shirtwaist Company fire in which 146 workers, most of them women, lost their lives. The disaster, the result of hazardous conditions and the lack of fire escapes, made an indelible impression on Perkins, who thenceforth spent her life fighting such conditions.

While lobbying successfully for the fifty-four-hour workweek bill in 1912, she became a close friend of the leader of the New York State Assembly, ALFRED E. SMITH. When Smith became governor in 1918, he asked Perkins to become the first woman to serve on the state Industrial Commission. During her tenure, she reinvigorated the factory inspection and workmen's compensation divisions. Appointed to the Industrial Board in 1923, as a member (1923–1926) and then as chair (1926–1929), she worked to advance labor legislation. After FRANKLIN D. ROOSEVELT was elected governor of

New York in 1928, Perkins, appointed industrial commissioner, became one of his most important advisers. She gained national prominence during the early years of the Great Depression for her criticisms of the optimistic statistical employment reports issued by HERBERT HOOVER's administration.

When Roosevelt was elected president in 1932, he appointed Perkins secretary of labor. Perkins vigorously cleaned out the corrupt Bureau of Immigration; strengthened the department's statistical, conciliation, and job placement services; and created the Department of Labor Standards to provide guidance for state labor departments. She was not only the first woman to serve in the cabinet, she was also one of the most important (as well as the longest-serving) ever to hold the office. She presided over and encouraged labor's rise to power and played an important role in securing such crucial New Deal reforms as the Social Security Act (1935) and the Fair Labor Standards Act (1938).

Perkins's advice helped to restrain Roosevelt from ordering federal intervention to end the 1934 general strike in San Francisco. This, combined with rumors linking her to Harry Bridges, the radical leader of the longshoremen's union, caused certain groups to brand her a socialist. When she postponed de-

National Archives

portation hearings for Bridges in 1938 on technical grounds, the House Un-American Activities Committee launched a campaign to impeach her. Although the impeachment effort failed, Perkins decided to resign. Roosevelt, however, never lost faith in her and prevailed upon her to remain at her post.

During World War II Perkins concentrated on protecting labor standards and defending the validity of her department's cost-of-living index against charges that it discriminated against labor. After serving in the transitional period for President HARRY TRUMAN, Perkins resigned on July 1, 1945. In addition to serving on the U.S. Civil Service Commission from 1946 to 1953 and publishing a memoir, *The Roosevelt I Knew* (1946), Perkins lectured at universities across the country before settling at Cornell University in 1955. She died at the age of eighty-three, after a series of strokes.

BIBLIOGRAPHY

Martin, George Whitney, *Madam Secretary, Frances Perkins,* 1976; Mohr, Lillian Holman, *Frances Perkins, that Woman in FDR's Cabinet!* 1979; Severn, William, *Frances Perkins: A Member of the Cabinet,* 1976.

Pickering, Timothy

(July 17, 1745–January 29, 1829)
Secretary of State, Secretary of War, Senator, Representative, Postmaster General

Federalist and early follower of GEORGE WASHINGTON, Timothy Pickering held many offices in the young U.S. government.

Born in Salem, Massachusetts, Pickering graduated from Harvard College in 1763. Admitted to the bar five years later, he quickly discovered that politics and not the practice of law was his true vocation.

At the start of the American Revolution, Pickering was commissioned a colonel in the Massachusetts militia. His knowledge of military tactics and distinguished performance during the winter campaign of 1776–1777 led to his appointment by General Washington as adjutant general in 1777. He served in this post until he became a member of the Board of War and Ordnance the following January. From 1780 until the end of the war in 1783, he was quartermaster general.

In 1787 Pickering established permanent residence in the Wyoming valley of Luzerne County in Pennsylvania. He represented Luzerne County in the convention that ratified the U.S. Constitution in 1787 and the Pennsylvania constitutional convention in 1789 and 1790. After helping to negotiate several treaties with Indian tribes for the new federal government, Pickering was appointed postmaster general. He served in that post from 1791 until he became secretary of war in January 1795. Eight months later, upon the resignation of EDMUND RANDOLPH, Pickering assumed the office of secretary of state.

When he became president in 1797, JOHN ADAMS made the mistake of keeping Pickering, a secret ally of Adams's rival ALEXANDER HAMILTON, as secretary of state. Although unaware of Pickering's spying for Hamilton, Adams finally dismissed him in 1800 when he discovered that Pickering had attempted to sabotage his efforts to avoid going to war with France.

After his dismissal, Pickering briefly returned to Pennsylvania and then moved back to Massachusetts. Although he failed to win election to the U.S. House of Representatives in 1802, he was chosen a year later to serve a term in the Senate. Defeated for reelection to the Senate in 1811, he served as a member of the Executive Council of Massachusetts for one year and then won election to the first of two more terms in the House of Representatives. He served in the House from 1813 to 1817.

A staunch Federalist, Pickering opposed the purchase of Louisiana (see THOMAS JEFFERSON) and the War of 1812 (see JAMES MADISON). Embittered at the growing power of the Democratic-Republicans and the decline of the Federalist party in the national legislature, Pickering supported the short-lived movement for the secession of New England, New York, and New Jersey from the Union.

BIBLIOGRAPHY

Pickering, Octavius, and C. W. Upham, *The Life of Timothy Pickering,* 4 vols., 1867–1883; Prentiss, Harvey Putnam, *Timothy Pickering As the Leader of New England Federalism, 1800–1815,* 1934.

Pierce, Franklin

(November 23, 1804–October 8, 1869)
President, Senator, Representative

Chosen as a candidate from the North who could please the South, Franklin Pierce, as fourteenth president, tried to find the way to compromise during the fateful years of the 1850s but succeeded only in splitting the country further apart.

Born in Hillsboro, New Hampshire, Pierce graduated from Bowdoin College in 1824 and was admitted to the New Hampshire bar three years later. Encouraged by his father, who was governor, he immediately entered politics. In 1829 he was elected to the first of four terms in the New Hampshire legislature, where, from 1831 to 1832, he served as speaker.

In 1832 he was elected as a Democrat to the U.S. House of Representatives, served two terms, and then moved on to serve one term in the Senate from 1837 to 1842. A loyal Democrat while in Congress, Pierce respected the right of states to determine the slavery issue but opposed federal funding of internal improvements (see JOHN CALDWELL CALHOUN). Pierce did not believe that the Constitution authorized such expenditures by the central government. He left Washington to live in Concord, New Hampshire, in 1842 to earn enough money to support his growing family.

President JAMES K. POLK appointed Pierce district attorney in 1845 and in 1846 invited him to become his attorney general, but Pierce declined the offer as well as an appointment to the Senate and instead enlisted in the army during the Mexican War (see JAMES KNOX POLK).

Library of Congress

In 1847, as a brigadier general, he joined General WINFIELD SCOTT in Mexico; because of an accident and illness, however, he did not participate in any battles.

Pierce returned to New Hampshire in 1850, where he resumed his former role as leader of the Democratic party. When the Democratic convention became deadlocked in 1852 between the supporters of JAMES BUCHANAN, STEPHEN A. DOUGLAS, WILLIAM L. MARCY, and LEWIS CASS, Pierce was eventually chosen as a compromise candidate acceptable to Southern and New England voters who could support the party platform of abiding by the Compromise of 1850 (see HENRY CLAY). In the general election Pierce, running against Whig Winfield Scott and Free-Soiler JOHN P. HALE, carried every state but four.

"Harmony" was the key word in Franklin Pierce's inaugural address on March 4, 1853. The compromise measures of 1850, he said, were "strictly constitutional and to be unhesitatingly carried into effect." Convinced that expansion was the way to prevent the country from dividing over slavery, he embarked on an aggressive campaign to acquire new territory. Agents were dispatched to buy Alaska, Cuba, the northern part of Mexico, and a naval base in Santo Domingo and to secure the annexation of Hawaii.

Pierce's expansionist dreams were frustrated by the hostility of Northern congressmen who, protecting the interests of their constituents, feared the growth of business competition in the West and the disinterest of

European powers. JAMES GADSDEN, the minister to Mexico, did manage to secure a small strip of territory in northern Mexico, settling a boundary dispute arising from the Treaty of Guadalupe Hidalgo that ended the Mexican War and pleasing parties interested in building a southern route for a transcontinental railroad (see GADSDEN). But other efforts met no success. Frustrated by their inability to convince Spain to sell Cuba, the American ministers to Spain, England, and France met at Ostend, Belgium, to agree on a united approach in dealing with Spain. They decided to notify Washington that Cuba was too vital to U.S. slave interests to lose. It should, they said, be seized if Spain continued to refuse to sell it. Although Pierce quickly distanced himself from his ministers once their feelings were published in what became known as the Ostend Manifesto, the damage was done. He was branded in the North as a proslavery, warlike expansionist.

Pierce's administration was overshadowed by the controversy that resulted from his support of the Kansas-Nebraska Act in 1854. In order to secure Senate approval of his appointments and passage of treaties with Canada and Mexico, Pierce agreed to support the repeal of the Missouri Compromise of 1820 (see HENRY CLAY). Popular sovereignty—the vote of the people who lived there—would determine whether slavery would be allowed in the Kansas and Nebraska territories.

The results of the Kansas-Nebraska Act were disastrous for both the nation and the Democratic party. The Democrats lost control of Congress in the 1854 elections, and the slavery issue was reopened in the territories.

Determined to administer popular sovereignty as fairly as possible, Pierce appointed a Southerner governor of Nebraska and a Northerner governor of Kansas. He divided the other offices equally between the pro- and antislavery factions. Trouble developed almost immediately between Northern and Southern settlers in Kansas, however, as pro- and antislavery supporters raced to move into the state in sufficient numbers to determine the majority. Soon, bands of armed men were killing each other over slavery, and "Bleeding Kansas" threatened to degenerate into anarchy. Finally, in February 1856, Pierce ordered federal troops into the area and succeeded in restoring order, but it was too late. Passions over slavery had been further inflamed, and North and South were more irreconcilable than before. Pierce, too, suffered consequences. He was unable to secure renomination. The Democratic party chose James Buchanan instead.

After retiring from the presidency, Pierce took an extended tour of Europe and then returned to Concord, New Hampshire. At first he supported ABRAHAM LINCOLN's efforts to preserve the Union, but he later became a bitter critic because of Lincoln's emergency suspensions of personal and property constitutional rights. His attacks on Lincoln made Pierce very unpopular in New England, and he died in social and political obscurity.

BIBLIOGRAPHY

Nichols, Roy Franklin, *Franklin Pierce*, 1931.

Pinchback, Pinckney Benton Stewart

(May 10, 1837–December 21, 1921)
Senator, Representative (elected but did not serve)

Pinckney B. S. Pinchback was born in Macon, Georgia, the son of a white Mississippi planter and a former slave. Because his father had emancipated his mother, Pinchback was born free. To avoid enslavement after his father's death in 1848, Pinchback moved with his mother to Ohio. He attended high school in Cincinnati and then obtained work on riverboats as a cabin boy and steward.

In 1862 Pinchback reached New Orleans, where he raised two companies of black soldiers, known as the Corps d'Afrique, but was denied a captain's commission because of his race.

After the Civil War Pinchback decided to remain in Louisiana to take advantage of the opportunities Reconstruction offered for blacks to enter politics. In 1868, as a Republican, he won election to the state senate. In the senate he was elected president pro tempore and briefly served as lieutenant governor on the death of the incumbent in 1871. From December 9, 1872, to January 13, 1873, he was acting governor while the elected official underwent impeachment proceedings.

Pinchback's race negated his two efforts to win election to national office. Although he won the 1872 race for congressman-at-large, he never actually held office because his Democratic opponent successfully challenged the election results. In 1873 he was elected by the state legislature to the U.S. Senate, but once again the election results were challenged. The members of the Senate refused to allow Pinchback to take his seat while the election challenge remained unresolved. Pinchback finally accepted the futility of his quest and surrendered his claim to serve in the Senate in 1876 in return for payment of the salary that he would have earned up until that time.

Aware of the hopelessness of remaining in the Republican party in Louisiana after the end of Reconstruction, Pinchback joined the Democratic party in 1877. He held his last public office—surveyor of customs in New Orleans—in 1882.

In 1887, at age fifty, Pinchback earned his law degree from Straight University (now Dillard University) in New Orleans and passed the bar, but he never practiced law in Louisiana. Instead, in 1890, he settled in Washington, D.C.

BIBLIOGRAPHY

Lonn, Ella, *Reconstruction in Louisiana*, 1918; Simmons, W. J., *Men of Mark*, 1887.

Pinchot, Gifford

(August 11, 1865–October 4, 1946)
Government Agency Director

As a conservationist and Progressive political leader, Gifford Pinchot pioneered the establishment of the federal government's role in regulating the use of natural resources.

Pinchot was born in Simsbury, Connecticut. After graduating from Yale University in 1889, he studied the scientific management of forests in Europe. Upon his return to the United States, Pinchot became a well-known advocate of the need for public regulation of private industry's use of national forest lands in order to encourage conservation. In 1898 Pinchot was appointed by President WILLIAM MCKINLEY to head the Division of Forestry in the Department of Agriculture (renamed the U.S. Forest Service in 1905).

Because President THEODORE ROOSEVELT shared his passion for conservation and shrewd courting of private interest groups concerned with the need to protect national forests from overexploitation, Pinchot commanded considerable political power. During his twelve years in office, Pinchot successfully implemented a single federal government vision of national forest management: "to make the forest produce the largest amount of whatever crop or service will be most useful, and to keep on producing it for generation after generation of men and trees."

In 1910 President WILLIAM HOWARD TAFT dismissed Pinchot for publicly criticizing his decision to support Secretary of the Interior RICHARD BALLINGER's leasing of public land in Alaska to private coal-mining interests. Conservationists concluded that Taft was reneging on the commitment to preserving the nation's public lands for future generations and encouraged Theodore Roosevelt to challenge Taft for the Republican nomination for president in 1912. When the Republicans nominated Taft, Pinchot worked for Roosevelt to become the candidate of the Progressive party (see THEODORE ROOSEVELT).

After failing to win election to the U.S. Senate from Pennsylvania in 1914, Pinchot served as Pennsylvania's commissioner of forestry from 1920 to 1922, and, as a Republican, won election to two terms (1923–1927 and 1931–1935) as governor of Pennsylvania.

Pinchot remained active in politics and the conservation movement for the rest of his life. He still had enough influence in the 1930s, much to the consternation of Secretary of the Interior HAROLD L. ICKES, to block the reorganization of the Department of the Interior and the U.S. Forest Service into a new Department of Conservation and Public Works. Ickes by the 1930s had become more of a "preservationist" than a conservationist, which meant he wanted to set aside lands for parks, monuments, and wilderness preserves and to prevent businesses from using any resources on that land for industrial or commercial use. Conservationists thought in terms of making the most efficient use of natural resources, preservationists in terms of excluding natural resources from any kind of use except that of personal enjoyment (see HAROLD LE CLAIRE ICKES).

In addition to his public service work, Pinchot also served as a visiting lecturer at the Yale University School of Forestry from 1903 to 1936.

BIBLIOGRAPHY

Fausold, Martin L., *Gifford Pinchot*, 1961; Hays, Samuel P., *Conservation and the Gospel of Efficiency: The Progressive Conservation Movement, 1890–1920*, 1972; McGeary, M. Nelson, *Gifford Pinchot*, 1960; Pinchot, Gifford, *Breaking New Ground*, 1947; Pinkett, Harold T., *Gifford Pinchot: Private and Public Forester*, 1970.

Pinckney, Charles Cotesworth

(February 25, 1746–August 16, 1825)
Diplomat, Candidate for President

Charles Cotesworth Pinckney, brother of Thomas Pinckney, was born in Charles Town (Charleston), South Carolina, and educated in England. He had graduated from Oxford University and been admitted to the English bar before returning to South Carolina in 1769. In South Carolina Pinckney immediately established a successful law practice and became active in local politics. He was elected to the provincial assembly in 1769, the provincial congress in 1775, the South Carolina House of Representatives in 1778, and the state senate in 1779. During the American Revolution he fought in numerous battles, rising in rank from captain to brigadier general. In 1782 he was again elected to the South Carolina House of Representatives.

A prominent delegate to the Constitutional Convention in 1787, Pinckney later declined President George Washington's offers to appoint him commander of the army, a Supreme Court justice, or secretary of war; but he accepted the post of minister to France in 1796. His diplomatic mission frustrated by the refusal of the revolutionary French government to receive him, Pinckney decided to return to the United States. A year later he returned to Paris as one of the agents in the mission that culminated in the notorious XYZ Affair (see John Adams).

Nominated as the Federalist candidate for vice president in 1800, Pinckney received only sixty-four electoral votes to finish well behind Thomas Jefferson. (Alexander Hamilton had tried to prevent Adams's reelection by having Federalist electoral college members cast their ballots for Pinckney as president.) In 1804 his party chose him to oppose Jefferson's virtually certain reelection; Pinckney lost by a landslide, 162 electoral votes to 14. Federalist Pinckney was nevertheless nominated for president again in 1808, and defeated again, this time by James Madison.

Despite his three electoral defeats, Pinckney remained active in various public affairs until his death in Charleston in 1825.

BIBLIOGRAPHY

Zahniser, Marvin R., *Charles Cotesworth Pinckney*, 1967.

Pinckney, Thomas

(October 23, 1750–November 2, 1828)
Diplomat, Representative

Thomas Pinckney, brother of Charles Cotesworth Pinckney, was born in Charles Town (Charleston), South Carolina, but grew up in England, where he attended Oxford University, the Middle Temple, and then, in Caen, France, the royal military academy. He returned to Charleston in 1774 and established a law practice. A patriot, Pinckney trained recruits during the American Revolution. He fought in Florida as well as South Carolina before being wounded and captured by the British at the Battle of Camden in 1780.

After the war Pinckney was elected governor of South Carolina from 1787 to 1789. From 1792 to 1796 he served as U.S. minister to Great Britain. Although unable to resolve the difficult issue of American neutral shipping rights, as a special envoy to Spain from 1794 to 1795, Pinckney negotiated the favorable Treaty of San Lorenzo. Pinckney's treaty, as it was also called, established commercial relations between Spain and the United States, granted the United States free navigation of the Mississippi River through Spanish territory, and fixed the boundaries of Louisiana and Florida.

After losing a bid to be elected vice president as the Federalist candidate in 1796, Pinckney was elected to the House of Representatives. While serving in Congress from 1797 to 1801, Pinckney supported Federalist policies.

As a major general in the War of 1812 (see JAMES MADISON), Pinckney fought at the Battle of Horseshoe Bend. He spent the last years of his life conducting and writing about successful crop rotation and animal breeding experiments he performed on his plantation near Charleston.

BIBLIOGRAPHY

Bemis, S. F., *Pinckney's Treaty,* 1926.

Polk, James Knox

(November 2, 1795–June 15, 1849)
President, Speaker of the House, Representative

James K. Polk was one of the most effective chief executives in American history. In his single term in office he accomplished all of his major objectives. During his administration more than a million square miles of new territory were added to the United States. But this also revived the slavery controversy in a major and divisive way that polarized the country and led to a civil war a dozen years later—a consequence, in part, of the "achievements" of Polk's administration.

Born in Mecklenburg County, North Carolina, the frequently sick and frail Polk was strong-willed enough to survive a gallstone operation without the benefit of anesthesia at age sixteen. Deeply religious, his teacher noted that "his moral conduct was . . . exemplary . . . he never missed a recitation nor omitted the punctilious performance of any duty."

Library of Congress

After graduating from the University of North Carolina in 1818, he moved to Tennessee and was admitted to the bar. A successful attorney, he developed a close personal friendship with ANDREW JACKSON. In 1824, after serving two terms in the Tennessee legislature, he was elected to the U.S. House of Representatives as a Jacksonian Democrat.

Physically slender and of medium height, the somber, secretive, thin-lipped Polk quickly earned a reputation as an industrious Democrat. Polk said he worked so hard that "he had but little opportunity to read newspapers." He described himself as "the hardest-working man in this country." He expected, and obtained, no less industrious behavior from his subordinates. As a member of the House Ways and Means Committee in 1832, he supported Jackson's opposition to the rechartering of the Bank of the United States (see NICHOLAS BID-

DLE). In 1835 he became Speaker of the House. His close identification with Jackson made him an easy target for Southern radicals angry over the president's stands on tariff legislation and nullification (see JOHN CALDWELL CALHOUN). Although challenged to duel on several occasions during heated House debates, Polk refused to be provoked.

In 1839, at the request of the Tennessee Democratic party, Polk left Washington to run a successful campaign for governor. He was not reelected in 1841, however, and was again defeated in 1843. Although MARTIN VAN BUREN appeared to be the logical choice for the Democratic nomination in 1844, the convention chose "dark horse" Polk after Andrew Jackson persuaded party leaders that Polk's strong support for the annexation of Texas and Oregon would enable him to defeat HENRY CLAY.

During the campaign Clay avoided answering how he would handle the question of the admission of Texas. If Texas were admitted to the Union as a slave state, the delicate balance in the Senate between slave and free states would be disrupted. There were already many more (148 to 82) representatives in the House from free than slave states.

Polk did not equivocate. Following the advice of Jackson, he made the acquisition of "all of Oregon, and all of Texas" the cornerstone of his campaign. Polk won the close race with 170 electoral votes to Clay's 105.

The virtually unknown Polk was to become the only "strong" president between Jackson and ABRAHAM LINCOLN. Shortly after his inauguration in 1845, Polk told Secretary of the Navy George Bancroft that he had four things he wanted to accomplish as president: "one, a reduction of the tariff; another, the independent treasury; a third, the settlement of the Oregon boundary question; and, lastly, the acquisition of California." He achieved all of his objectives during his four years in office.

First, disregarding his campaign pledge, Polk informed Great Britain of his willingness to settle the Oregon boundary dispute at the 49th parallel. (The Oregon territory had been jointly occupied by the two countries as a result of their inability to resolve their separate claims to the area.) The British countered by insisting on the Columbia River for the boundary line. Polk refused to budge. War seemed likely. At the same time, without waiting to settle the issue with England, Polk ordered General ZACHARY TAYLOR to take American troops into the disputed Rio Grande region of Texas. War had already begun between Mexico and the United States when Polk received news of Great Britain's acceptance of the 49th parallel. Able to focus all its power in one region, the United States soon overwhelmed Mexico.

Under the terms of the Treaty of Guadalupe Hidalgo of 1848, Mexico recognized the Rio Grande as the southern border of Texas and surrendered control of New Mexico and California to the United States in return for $15 million. Polk had already secured passage in 1846 of the Independent Treasury Act, which provided the secretary of the treasury with legal guidelines, and the Walker tariff, which greatly reduced tariff duties.

In his last annual message to Congress in 1848, Polk announced that gold had been discovered in California, attacked Clay's American System (see HENRY CLAY), and advised that the issue of slavery should not be allowed to hinder the settlement and development of the newly acquired territory. Exhausted and prematurely aged due to his overwork and poor health, Polk decided not to run for reelection in 1848. He died only a few months after retiring from office.

BIBLIOGRAPHY

McCormac, Eugene I., *James K. Polk*, 1922; Quaife, Milo M. (ed.), *Diary of James K. Polk*, 1910; Sellers, Charles G., Jr., *James K. Polk*, 1957; Weaver, Herbert, and Paul H. Bergeron (eds.), *Correspondence of James K. Polk, 1817–1832*, 1969.

Pomeroy, Theodore Medad

(December 31, 1824–March 23, 1905)
Speaker of the House, Representative

Theodore M. Pomeroy was born in Cayuga, New York. He graduated from Hamilton College in Clinton, New York, in 1842, was admitted to the bar in 1846, and established a law practice in Auburn, New York. From 1851 to 1856 he served as district attorney of Cayuga County, and in 1857 he was elected to the state legislature.

In 1860 Pomeroy won election to the U.S. House of Representatives as a Republican. He was reelected in 1862, 1864, and 1866 but declined to run in 1868, after being elected Speaker of the House. Thus, he served as Speaker for only one day, March 3, 1869.

After leaving Congress, Pomeroy became first vice president of the American Express Company and after 1870 embarked on a banking career in Auburn, New York. In 1875 and 1876 he was mayor of Auburn and from 1878 to 1879 served in the state senate.

BIBLIOGRAPHY

Kennon, Donald R., *The Speakers of the U.S. House of Representatives: A Bibliography, 1789–1984*, 1985.

Powell, Adam Clayton, Jr.

(November 29, 1908–April 4, 1972)
Representative

During his eleven successive terms in the House of Representatives the controversial Baptist minister Adam Clayton Powell, Jr., was a prominent civil rights spokesman and symbol for black Americans.

Powell was born in New Haven, Connecticut, but grew up in Harlem, New York. After earning a bachelor's degree from Colgate University in 1930 and a master's two years later from Columbia University, Powell became a minister. He eventually succeeded his father as the leader of the 13,000-member Harlem Abyssinian Baptist Church, where he continued to preach until 1971.

As a young minister during the Great Depression, Powell organized and led a series of successful civil rights protests that obtained jobs and public housing for blacks. In 1941 he became the first black ever elected to the city council. Four years later, he won the first of eleven consecutive terms as a Democrat in the U.S. House of Representatives. The outspoken young congressman refused to abide by racist prohibitions against his freedom of movement in Washington, D.C. He did not hesitate to challenge racist remarks by fellow legislators, sought to end discrimination in the military services, and tried to deny federal funds to any project where racial discrimination was practiced.

In addition to his civil rights efforts, Powell also became known for his high absentee record and extraordinary accomplishments as chairman of the House Committee on Education and Labor from 1960 to 1967. He explained the apparent contradiction of his success by claiming that cutting political deals did not require being in frequent attendance; it just meant knowing who to call, what to offer, what to ask for, and when to be present to vote. He played an important part in the drafting and enactment of the 1961 Minimum Wage Bill, the Manpower Development and Training Act, the Anti-Poverty Bill, the Juvenile Delinquency

Act, the Vocational Education Act, and the National Defense Educational Act.

Powell was often criticized for his extravagant social life, but he successfully claimed to his loyal black constituents that he wasn't doing anything white members of Congress did not do; he just wasn't bothering to hide his behavior. However, his political career began to unravel after he was successfully sued for slander and cited for criminal contempt of court (for ignoring the civil suit). The full House membership voted in 1967 to exclude him from any further service in Congress. Powell won a special election called to fill his vacant House position, and was seated in January 1969. He was, however, fined $25,000 for his alleged misuse of payroll and travel funds, and he lost his seniority.

Though the Supreme Court ruled in 1969 that Powell's expulsion from the House had been unconstitutional, Powell's political career ended in 1970 when he failed to win the Democratic nomination for reelection. He died in Miami shortly after retiring.

BIBLIOGRAPHY

Powell, Adam Clayton, Jr., *Adam by Adam*, 1971.

Quayle, James Danforth

(February 4, 1947–   )
Vice President, Senator, Representative

At the age of thirty-three Dan Quayle became the youngest candidate ever elected to the U.S. Senate in Indiana. Eight years later, he became vice president of the United States.

James Danforth Quayle was born into a prominent family in Indianapolis, Indiana. He graduated from DePauw University in 1969. From 1969 until 1974 Quayle held a series of state government positions and attended Indiana University Law School.

As soon as he graduated from law school and passed the bar in 1974, Quayle joined the family's publishing business as an associate publisher and general manager of the *Huntington Herald-Press*. He entered national politics in 1976 by winning a surprising upset election victory as a conservative Republican against an incumbent Democrat. Two years later, he was reelected to Congress by the widest margin in the district's history.

Although his accomplishments as a representative were negligible, Quayle decided to run for the Senate in 1980. With a campaign strategy that portrayed the Democratic incumbent, three-term senator Birch Bayh, as a liberal Democrat in favor of abortion and spending taxpayer money on social programs, Quayle scored another impressive upset election victory. Six years later, Quayle won reelection by the widest margin (61 percent) ever achieved in a statewide race in Indiana history. While in the Senate, Quayle generally supported the policies of President RONALD REAGAN.

In 1988 Republican presidential nominee GEORGE BUSH selected Quayle to be his vice presidential running mate. In explaining his choice, Bush cited Quayle's conservative views and voting record in Congress, his youthful good looks, and his Midwest background. Although considerable controversy followed Bush's selection of Quayle on the grounds that he was intellectually unqualified and lacked the experience necessary for taking over the presidency if that should prove necessary, the Bush–Quayle ticket went on to defeat soundly the Democrats MICHAEL DUKAKIS and Lloyd Bentsen.

BIBLIOGRAPHY

Fenno, Richard F., Jr., *The Making of a Senator: Dan Quayle*, 1989.

Rainey, Henry Thomas

(August 20, 1860–August 19, 1934)
Speaker of the House, Representative

As Speaker of the House of Representatives during President FRANKLIN D. ROOSEVELT's first year in office, Henry Rainey helped to secure the speedy passage of New Deal legislation.

Rainey was born on a farm near Carrollton, Illinois. He earned his bachelor's degree from Amherst College in 1883 and a master's in 1886. He also completed a law degree in 1885 from the Union College of Law, Chicago, and thereupon established a law practice in Carrollton.

In the presidential campaign of 1896 (see WILLIAM JENNINGS BRYAN), Rainey donated his considerable public speaking talent to the Democratic party by delivering speeches around the nation. Six years later, he was elected to the U.S. House of Representatives from Illinois. Thereafter, with the exception of the years 1921 to 1923, Rainey was reelected every two years until his death.

A member of the Progressive wing of the Democratic party (see WOODROW WILSON),

Rainey advocated tariff reduction and free silver. During his years in Congress he helped to secure passage of the Underwood Tariff (1913), which lowered duties, and played an important part in the drafting and passage of World War I revenue bills.

From 1931 to 1933 Rainey was the Democratic party's floor leader in Congress, and from 1933 to 1934, Speaker of the House. As Speaker, he pushed through passage of President Roosevelt's New Deal legislation in record time with only minor changes.

BIBLIOGRAPHY

Amherst Graduate Quarterly, May 1933; *History of Green County, Illinois,* 1872, pp. 494–495; *Memorial Services,* House Document No. 236, 1974, Congress, I Session; Morrison, H. A., *Honorable Henry Thomas Rainey . . . Record of Services,* 1934; *New York Times,* August 10, 20, 21, 26, 1934.

Randall, Samuel Jackson

(October 10, 1828–April 13, 1890)
Speaker of the House, Representative

Born in Philadelphia, Samuel Jackson Randall attended the University Academy in that city. He founded his own iron and coal company before serving a term in the Pennsylvania state senate in 1858, then winning the first of thirteen consecutive terms in the U.S. House of Representatives in 1862. Randall was a member of the Democratic party, which opposed high tariffs. However, as

a representative from a protectionist area of the country, he staunchly defended the need for high tariffs and consistently voted in their favor.

From 1875 to 1888 Randall controlled the Democratic party in Pennsylvania. A powerful figure in the House, he served as Speaker from 1876 to 1881. As Speaker, he presided over the sessions that led to the compromise that resolved the disputed election between SAM-UEL J. TILDEN and RUTHERFORD B. HAYES for the presidency in 1876.

Because of his refusal to support President GROVER CLEVELAND's efforts to reduce the tariff in 1887, Cleveland denied Randall any further patronage appointments. Cleveland's action, combined with the debilitating effects of ter-minal cancer, led to Randall's loss of political power in Pennsylvania and isolation in Washington.

BIBLIOGRAPHY

Fuller, H. B., *The Speakers of the House*, 1909.

Randolph, Edmund

(August 10, 1753–September 12, 1813)
Secretary of State, Attorney General

Born into a distinguished Virginia family, Edmund Randolph studied at William and Mary College and in his father's law office before beginning a remarkably successful national political career.

An aide-de-camp to GEORGE WASHINGTON during the Revolution, he became attorney general of his state at the age of twenty-three. He was elected to the Continental Congress three years later and in 1786 was chosen to be governor of Virginia.

As a delegate to the Constitutional Convention, Randolph presented the Virginia Plan—the core of the Constitution's plan for a national government. However, because he opposed a one-man executive branch and feared the power given the central government by the completed document, he refused to sign the Constitution. Nevertheless, in the crucial Virginia ratification convention, he supported adoption of the Constitution as the only practical course of action.

Library of Congress

President Washington appointed Randolph to be attorney general and, after THOMAS JEFFERSON resigned in 1794, to be the new secretary of state. Randolph was opposed to Jay's Treaty with the British in 1795 (see JOHN JAY), and documents came to light implying Randolph had improperly supplied information to the French. When questioned by Washington as to whether he had obtained bribes from a French diplomat, Randolph was humiliated and resigned. He was later completely vindicated. He returned to his private law practice and in 1807 led the successful defense of AARON BURR at the former vice president's trial for treason.

BIBLIOGRAPHY

Conway, Moncure D., *Omitted Chapters of History: Life and Papers of Edmund Randolph*, 1888.

Randolph, John

(June 2, 1773–May 24, 1833)
Diplomat, Senator, Representative

John Randolph spent twenty-six years in the House of Representatives fighting all legislation by the national government that he felt threatened state sovereignty.

Born in Prince George County, Virginia, Randolph briefly attended the College of New Jersey (now Princeton University), Columbia, and William and Mary before becoming a lawyer. In 1799, after attracting considerable public attention in a spirited debate with PATRICK HENRY, Randolph was elected to the U.S. House of Representatives. He served in the House, except for brief periods, until 1829.

A sharp-tongued, brilliant debater, Randolph was elected chairman of the Ways and Means Committee and quickly became floor leader of the Republicans. At first a strong supporter of THOMAS JEFFERSON, Randolph, a strict constructionist (see MELVILLE WESTON FULLER), left the Republican party when Jefferson supported the acquisition of Florida. Jefferson's increasing conviction for the need of the president to be able to interpret the Constitution broadly caused Randolph to become a virulent critic. The result was the loss of his committee chairmanship. Infuriated, Randolph led the opposition in the House to Jefferson's embargo policy, the declaration of war in 1812 (see JAMES MADISON), the establishment of a national bank (see ALEXANDER HAMILTON), protective tariffs, and western expansion.

The owner of a large plantation and hundreds of slaves, Randolph earned tremendous popularity in the South with his furious denunciations of any intervention by the federal government concerning the institution of slavery. He maintained that the Constitution gave the federal government no powers to limit the expansion of slavery. It was on this basis that Randolph opposed the Missouri Compromise in 1820 and became an enemy of its chief architect, HENRY CLAY.

Concerning the tariff of 1824, Randolph said, "I do not stop to argue the constitutionality of this bill; I consider the Constitution a dead letter. . . . A fig for the Constitution . . . there is no magic in this word 'union.'" Even more ominously, later that year he promised to use "every . . . means short of actual insurrection" to block the passage of an internal improvements act (see JOHN CALDWELL CALHOUN). To him, "Asking one of the States to surrender part of her sovereignty is like asking a lady to surrender part of her chastity."

Randolph's sarcastic wit, flamboyant attire, and meanspirited, emotional attacks on opponents made him feared by everyone in Congress. Critics began to wonder if he was mentally ill because he often appeared in the House booted, spurred, carrying a whip, and brandishing his pistol. After Clay helped JOHN QUINCY ADAMS secure the presidential election in 1824 and then became secretary of state, Randolph's attacks on their "corrupt bargain" were so venomous that he and Clay engaged in a bloodless duel in 1826.

From 1825 until 1827 Randolph served in the U.S. Senate, and in 1830 he briefly served as President ANDREW JACKSON's minister to Russia. Although he was forced to return to the United States in 1831 because of ill health, he immediately began delivering speeches attacking Jackson's position that a state could not refuse to obey a federal law (nullification—see JOHN CALDWELL CALHOUN). He died in Philadelphia in 1833.

BIBLIOGRAPHY

Adams, Henry, *John Randolph*, 1882; Bruce, William C., *John Randolph of Roanoke*, 1922; Garland, H. A., *Life of John Randolph*, 1856; Kirk, Russell, *John Randolph of Roanoke*, 1964.

Rankin, Jeannette

(June 11, 1880–May 18, 1973)
Representative

Jeannette Rankin was the first woman ever elected to the U.S. House of Representatives and the only member of Congress to vote against U.S. entry in both World War I and World War II.

Rankin was born near Missoula, Montana. After graduating from the University of Montana in 1902, she did social work and became a leader in the woman suffrage movement. (Montana was one of the few states at that time in which women could vote.)

In 1916, as a Republican, she won Montana's at-large seat in the House of Representatives. Three days after beginning her term in the House in 1917, she voted against the declaration of war on Germany. She was not re-elected in 1918.

Rankin won another term in Congress in 1940. Consistent with her indomitable pacifism, she was the only member of Congress to vote against the declaration of war on Japan after the Pearl Harbor attack (see FRANKLIN DELANO ROOSEVELT). Following an unsuccessful effort to win election to the Senate in 1943, she spent the rest of her life fighting for women's rights.

In her eighties she led a brigade of 5,000 anti–Vietnam War (see LYNDON BAINES JOHNSON and RICHARD MILHOUS NIXON) protesters in Washington, D.C. She refused, however, to do the same a few years later for abortion and equal pay: "Certainly I believe in the right of abortion and in an end to discrimination on the basis of sex," she explained. "But I cannot march with you on such superficial issues."

BIBLIOGRAPHY

Josephson, Hannah Geffen, *Jeannette Rankin, First Lady in Congress: A Biography*, 1974; McFadden, Robert D., "Ex-Rep. Jeannette Rankin Dies; First Woman in Congress, 92," *New York Times*, May 20, 1973.

Rayburn, Samuel Taliaferro

(January 6, 1882–November 16, 1961)
Speaker of the House, Representative

Sam Rayburn served in the House of Representatives for almost fifty years, longer than anyone else in American history. He held the office of Speaker for seventeen years, twice as long as the previous record holder, HENRY CLAY.

Rayburn was born near Kingston (in Roane County), Tennessee, and grew up in Fannin County, Texas. After graduating from the Mayo Normal College (now East Texas State University), he taught school for three years.

He won election as a Democrat to the Texas legislature in 1906, studied law at the University of Texas, and was admitted to the bar in 1908. Rayburn served in the state legislature until 1913, the last two years as speaker. In 1912 he was elected to the first of his record-breaking twenty-five consecutive terms in the U.S. House of Representatives. In Congress, before the 1930s, Rayburn was a fairly typical Southern Progressive Democrat. He favored free trade, aid to farmers, states' rights, and

Prohibition; was relatively indifferent to urban problems and organized labor; and distrusted big business.

During the 1930s Rayburn became a staunch supporter of FRANKLIN D. ROOSEVELT's New Deal, and helped to draft and enact legislation to regulate public utilities and the bond and stock markets. He was also a major proponent of rural electrification.

Rayburn was elected majority leader in 1937 and, three years later, Speaker of the House. He was Speaker in every Democratic-controlled Congress for the rest of his life (1940–1946, 1950–1952, 1956–1961) and became one of the most powerful men in Washington. Rayburn's most often-quoted advice to new members of Congress—"If you want to get along, go along"—reflected his own distaste for ideological politics and personal conflict. His skills at persuasion and constructive compromise enabled him to become a master at behind-the-scenes discussion to obtain the votes he needed. Only on rare occasions, such as the Selective Service extension controversy in 1941 and the Rules Committee fight of 1961, did he attempt to use force to persuade reluctant legislators. In the former case, Rayburn managed to overcome strong isolationist sentiment to secure the passage of legislation to extend the military service terms of draftees four months before the Japanese attack at Pearl Harbor (see FRANKLIN DELANO ROOSEVELT).

Rayburn was a quiet opponent of civil rights legislation for most of his career. Finally, in 1957 and 1960 he lent his active support to a bill designed to ensure voting rights for blacks. Throughout the 1950s Rayburn worked closely with Senate Democratic leader LYNDON JOHNSON, his one-time protégé. Together they guided legislation through the Democratic-controlled Congress. Rayburn's hopes that Johnson would be nominated for president in 1960 were crushed by the dashing JOHN F. KENNEDY. Although Rayburn advised against it, Johnson agreed to be Kennedy's running mate. The Kennedy–Johnson Democratic ticket was successful in 1960. A loyal Democrat, Rayburn worked to secure backing of the Kennedy administration's liberal legislative agenda. He died shortly after winning the battle to add liberal members to the House Rules Committee. Political commentators described it as the fiercest internal struggle in the House in fifty years. Even with Rayburn's considerable skill and prestige squarely on the line, the victory vote was a narrow 217 to 212.

BIBLIOGRAPHY

Caro, Robert, *The Years of Lyndon Johnson: The Path to Power,* 1982; Dorough, C. Dwight, *Mr. Sam,* 1962; Dulaney, H. G., and Edward H. Phillips (eds.), *Speak, Mr. Speaker,* 1978; Mooney, Booth, *Roosevelt and Rayburn: A Political Partnership,* 1971; Steinberg, Alfred, *Sam Rayburn: A Biography,* 1975.

Reagan, Ronald Wilson

(February 6, 1911–   )
President

Ronald Reagan's presidency may well be regarded as one of the twentieth century's most important, both for undermining the liberal tradition that had dominated American politics since FRANKLIN DELANO ROOSEVELT and for preparing the way for the end of the cold war. Reagan began his political career as a Roosevelt Democrat and grew up to hate high taxes, big government, and communism. As a leader of the conservative wing of the Republican party, he emphasized the desirability of economic freedom and incentives and of removing the federal government from the regulation of industry and commerce.

Reagan was born in Tampico, Illinois. After graduating from Eureka College in 1932, he began working as a sports announcer for a small radio station in Davenport, Iowa, and in 1933 for a Des Moines station.

Reagan, who had done some acting in college, was recruited by a Hollywood talent scout for the Warner Brothers studio while covering baseball spring training on radio in California. Over the course of a film career that lasted until 1964, he made more than fifty movies and became, he later observed, "the Errol Flynn of the B's (low-budget movies)."

National Archives

During World War II Reagan served for three years in the U.S. Army making training films. After his discharge with the rank of captain, he returned to his film career. In 1947 he was elected to the first of five consecutive one-year terms as president of the Screen Actors Guild. It was a difficult period to lead the union due to the investigations by the House Un-American Activities Committee into the alleged infiltration of the Hollywood movie industry by communists. Reagan cooperated with the blacklisting of suspected communist sympathizers in the industry. He was convinced they were trying to subvert well-meaning liberals in the film business, but he also viewed the committee and its chairman, J. Parnell Thomas, as "a pretty venal bunch."

Reagan revered the efforts of President Franklin D. Roosevelt to alleviate the suffering of people like his unemployed shoe salesman father during the Great Depression. However,

he began to change his liberal Democratic allegiance during the late 1940s and early 1950s in the face of the massive increase in the size of the federal government. During this period he occasionally acted in and served as the host of the television program "General Electric Theater."

In 1962 Reagan became a Republican. After he taped an effective speech for use in television ads—"A Time for Choosing"—in support of BARRY GOLDWATER's unsuccessful 1964 campaign for president, many wealthy Republican conservatives became convinced that he was the best candidate available for representing their views. A number of them agreed to finance a bid by him to run for governor of California. In 1966 Reagan won the Republican nomination for governor and then the general election on a campaign platform that promised to crack down on college campus radicals, eliminate welfare fraud, and reduce taxes. He was reelected four years later by a wide margin.

Through pragmatic compromise and a masterful ability to marshal public opinion, Reagan managed to fulfill many of his campaign pledges while governor. The dramatic growth in welfare payments was halted; and by freezing state government hiring and reducing social spending, budget surpluses were obtained that were used to reduce local property taxes.

Reagan decided not to run for reelection in 1974 as governor in order to concentrate on securing the Republican party nomination for president in 1976. Although he came within sixty convention votes of winning the nomination in 1976, convincing a majority of Republican delegates to abandon the popular incumbent GERALD FORD proved too difficult. After Ford was defeated by Democrat JIMMY CARTER, Reagan began campaigning for the 1980 Republican nomination.

At first, Reagan adopted a conservative front-runner campaign strategy. However, after he lost the Iowa caucus race to GEORGE BUSH, he adopted a vigorous approach that quickly overwhelmed Bush and eliminated the perception that at age sixty-eight Reagan might be too old to be president. President Carter, burdened by soaring inflation, high unemployment, and an unresolved hostage situation of Americans in Iran, attempted to portray Reagan as a trigger-happy extremist who would involve the nation in war. Democrats also attacked Reagan's support for antiabortion legislation, advocacy of the use of federal funds for parochial schools, and support for a constitutional amendment to reestablish prayer in public schools.

Reagan disarmed Carter's charge that he was an unstable extremist by projecting a warm and friendly image during several television debates. Reagan managed to keep the campaign focused on domestic economic and foreign policy issues. At the end of his final televised debate with Carter, Reagan succinctly summed up the race in many voters' minds: "Ask yourself, are you better off now than you were four years ago?"

During the campaign Reagan promised that, if elected, he would lower taxes, increase defense spending, and reduce the budget deficit. He said that an economic theory known as supply-side economics (quickly nicknamed Reaganomics) would make these apparently contradictory goals possible. The idea was that reduced taxes would spur investment, which would increase productivity and jobs. More people working and increased business revenue would produce greater tax revenues. Social programs could be cut because fewer people would need them.

Two months after assuming office, an assassination attempt by a deranged gunman was barely averted. The president was shot in the chest but survived, thanks to swift medical care. He recovered while Congress debated his tax and budget proposals, and made a dramatic return to address a joint session of Congress in support of his goals. Budget cuts totaling $39 million were followed by the enactment of a 25 percent tax cut for individuals spread over three years and faster write-offs of capital investments for business.

Reaganomics achieved mixed results from 1981 to 1989. The nation experienced a recession in 1982 that was induced by the tight money supply policy of the Federal Reserve. The Federal Reserve's goal was to smother inflation with high interest rates. Unemployment dropped from double-digit levels in 1982 to 7 percent by 1987, and inflation declined from 13.5 percent in 1980 to 5 percent by 1982. From 1983 to 1990 the nation enjoyed one of the longest stretches of uninterrupted economic growth in its history. On the other hand, Reagan's balanced budget never materialized. Instead, by 1988 the national debt had soared past $3 trillion. To fund the debt the Federal Reserve was forced to keep interest rates high in order to attract foreign capital. In effect, the budget deficits of the Reagan spending and tax-cutting approach had resulted in a new tax many Americans had to pay through high interest rates, the profits from which flowed to relatively small groups of lenders at home and abroad. Although growth was slowed, the federal government was not, as promised, reduced in size. The results of deregulation have been ambiguous at best: if it stimulated vigorous economic growth, it also encouraged certain economic practices that seriously weakened important sectors of the U.S. financial system. These problems did very little to dampen enthusiasm for Reagan, who continued to be hailed for his opposition to government spending and for his reinvigoration of the capitalist economy. He further satisfied his supporters by placing two conservative justices on the Supreme Court, SANDRA DAY O'CONNOR and ANTONIN SCALIA.

In the area of foreign policy, Reagan adopted a hostile attitude toward the Soviet

Union, which he described as the "Evil Empire." He proposed the Strategic Defense Initiative (dubbed Star Wars by the press) to provide the United States with a protective shield from nuclear attack as part of the largest peacetime military buildup in U.S. history. In October 1983 he ordered the invasion and occupation of Grenada, allegedly to prevent a communist takeover of that nation. Just two days earlier, 241 U.S. Marines had been killed by a terrorist bombing attack in Lebanon. The tragedy led Reagan to order the swift withdrawal of American forces from the country. Reagan also authorized U.S. funding of anticommunist guerrillas (Contras) in Nicaragua.

By the election campaign of 1984, most Americans felt better off economically—inflation and unemployment were down and the economy was expanding. Further, their fears about becoming involved in a war were diminished. As a result, Reagan was reelected by the largest number of electoral votes in history.

Reagan's greatest pride as president was to have started down the road toward nuclear disarmament through one-on-one diplomacy with Soviet leader Mikhail Gorbachev. His foreign policy will ultimately be judged by his role in bringing about the end of the cold war. Reagan's supporters claim that his vast defense expenditures and determination to battle communist aggression everywhere brought the Soviet Union to its knees. His critics contend that the capitulation of the Soviet Union was due to long-brewing problems inside the Soviet Union and not to American pressure.

The Nicaragua and Lebanon hostage situation led to the most serious crisis of the Reagan administration. In 1987 it was discovered that, contrary to his pledge never to deal with terrorists, Reagan had, at the very least, not attempted to stop subordinates from arranging a complicated arms-for-hostages swap by circumventing congressional restrictions and selling weapons to Iran in exchange for the release of hostages. The profits of these sales were then used to obtain equipment for the Contras.

Reagan denied all knowledge of the existence of the arms-for-hostages deal when challenged by the press and a special congressional prosecutor; but such a statement, while it relieved him from guilt of any wrongdoing in the Iran–Contra scandal, was an admission that he did not know what his subordinates were doing. The man whose vision of America was so popular seemed to be out of touch with so many things, small and large.

Despite the scandal, Reagan managed to recover his prestige and popularity before he left office. He retired to his home in California in 1989 after seeing his former vice president, George Bush, sworn into office as his successor. Reaganomics will ultimately be judged on whether the nation experiences economic decline or a more prosperous future.

BIBLIOGRAPHY

Dallek, Robert, *Ronald Reagan: The Politics of Symbolism*, 1984; Deaver, Michael K., *Behind the Scenes*, 1988; Edwards, Anne, *Early Reagan*, 1987; Reagan, Ronald, *An American Life: The Autobiography*, 1990; Speakes, Larry, *Speaking Out: The Reagan Presidency from Inside the White House*, 1988; Wills, Garry, *Reagan's America: Innocents at Home*, 1987.

Reed, Thomas Brackett

(October 18, 1839–December 7, 1902)
Speaker of the House, Representative

Thomas Brackett "Czar" Reed is remembered for his firm control of the flow of legislation through the House of Representatives during his two terms as Speaker in the 1890s.

Reed was born in Portland, Maine. After graduating from Bowdoin College in 1860, he moved to California and taught school while studying law. Although admitted to the California bar in 1863, Reed decided to return to Maine. His pursuit of a law career was briefly interrupted by an eighteen-month stint in the U.S. Navy in 1864 and 1865, but upon his discharge from the service he established a law practice in Portland and became active in Republican politics. Elected to the state assembly in 1867, he served two years there before winning a seat in the state senate in 1869. From 1870 to 1873 he served as attorney general of Maine.

Reed began his national political career in 1876 when he won his first of eleven consecutive terms in the U.S. House of Representatives. By 1882 he had become the leader of the Republicans in the House and had developed a reputation as a brilliant parliamentarian with a gift for delivering memorable quips at just the right moment in debate to deflate the ego of his opponent. He supported the gold standard, a strong navy, and high protective tariffs.

When the Republicans gained control of the House in the elections of 1888, Reed was elected Speaker. While serving in that office from 1889 to 1891 and from 1895 to 1899, he pushed through the so-called Reed Rules, which greatly increased the power of the Speaker. One of his changes ended the practice of the Speaker to count only members who answered present during roll calls. This tradi-

tion had enabled members to observe activity in the House without having their views recorded. It also often prohibited a vote being taken on a bill when a quorum was not present. Since the lack of a quorum meant that no legislation could be passed, not voting present was an effective way for congressmen to halt House business and to oppose a bill without ever having to publicly declare a position. Speaker Reed introduced the practice of counting all those members of Congress who were recognized in the chamber whether representatives answered when their names were called or not. This change greatly increased the flow of legislation through the House and forced representatives to publicly announce their positions much more frequently. The result was a dramatic enhancement of the chances of securing the passage of popular Republican legislation. Reed also arbitrarily used his Speaker's power not to recognize representatives who wished to speak. This enabled him to control the flow of debate in the House.

Reed was considered the most likely candidate to win the Republican party nomination for president in 1896, but his refusal to declare publicly his unequivocal support for the gold standard (see WILLIAM JENNINGS BRYAN) before the convention undermined his credibility. His refusal to actively recruit delegates, the way MARK HANNA did for WILLIAM MCKINLEY prior to the convention, destroyed his chances.

At first Reed supported the administration of fellow Republican William McKinley, but a breach developed between the two in 1898 when Reed refused to support the U.S. war with Spain (see WILLIAM MCKINLEY, JR.). Reed was so opposed to the U.S. annexation of Hawaii and the acquisition of overseas colonial possessions that he resigned from Congress in 1899. He spent the last few years of his life practicing law in New York City.

BIBLIOGRAPHY

McCall, Samuel W., *The Life of Thomas Brackett Reed*, 1914; Robinson, William Alexander, *Thomas B. Reed*, 1930.

Rehnquist, William Hubbs

(October 1, 1924–   )
Chief Justice of the Supreme Court, Associate Justice of the Supreme Court

First as an associate justice from 1972 to 1986 and then as chief justice of the Supreme Court, William Rehnquist has encouraged the movement of the Court away from a broadly interpretative judicial philosophy favored by liberals toward the strict constructionist position (see THOMAS JEFFERSON and MELVILLE WESTON FULLER) preferred by conservatives.

Rehnquist was born in Milwaukee, Wisconsin. He enrolled at Stanford University in 1942, but his education was interrupted for three years (1943–1946) while he served in the Army Air Force during World War II. After graduating from Stanford University in 1948, he earned a master's degree in political science at Harvard University in 1949 and a law degree from Stanford in 1952.

He joined Supreme Court Associate Justice Robert H. Jackson's staff as a clerk in January 1952. He moved to Arizona in 1953 and practiced law in Phoenix for the next three years. During this period he became active in the conservative wing of the Arizona Republican party. In 1958, while serving as a special Arizona state prosecutor, he helped to bring charges against several officials accused of state highway fraud. When fellow Arizona political ally Richard G. Kleindienst was appointed deputy attorney general in 1969, he named Rehnquist to the post of assistant attorney general in charge of the Office of Legal Counsel.

The Office of Legal Counsel interprets the Constitution and government statutes for the president and the attorney general and gives legal advice to all departments of the government. Unlike predecessors in this position, Rehnquist assumed a highly visible profile. He frequently appeared at legislative committee meetings to defend the constitutionality of controversial actions by President RICHARD M. NIXON that included expanding the Vietnam War (see LYNDON BAINES JOHNSON and RICHARD MILHOUS NIXON) into Cambodia, refusing to disclose government documents to members of the press, and arresting hundreds of antiwar protesters in Washington, D.C.

Convinced that the liberal Supreme Court under EARL WARREN's leadership had gone too far in its interpretation of the Constitution to protect the rights of the accused, Rehnquist argued for supporting "no knock" police entry, pretrial detention, wiretapping, and electronic surveillance. He was hailed by conservatives for these views and championed as the "brains of the Justice Department"; but his advocacy of such tough law-and-order positions earned him the animosity of liberals, who unsuccessfully attempted to block his confirmation to the Supreme Court after President Nixon nominated him in October 1971.

As an associate justice, Rehnquist remained true to his judicial philosophic beliefs: He usually adopted the most conservative perspective in his judicial opinions. In 1986 President RONALD REAGAN chose Rehnquist to succeed Chief Justice WARREN BURGER. As chief justice, Rehnquist has voted with the majority on several controversial cases. Some of his decisions include giving states the right to impose tighter restrictions on abortion, limiting the rights of death row inmates in state prisons to last-minute appeals, and reconsidering 1866 civil rights laws that gave minorities the right to sue private parties for racial discrimination. His opinions have been less conservative in cases involving rent-controlled housing and free speech.

BIBLIOGRAPHY

Boles, Donald E., *Mr. Justice Rehnquist, Judicial Activist: The Early Years*, 1987; Davis, Sue, *Justice Rehnquist and the Constitution*, 1989.

Revels, Hiram Rhoades

(September 1822–January 16, 1901)
Senator

Hiram Rhoades Revels was the first black American to serve as a U.S. senator. Revels was born in Fayetteville, North Carolina. After training for the seminary at Ohio and Knox College in Illinois, Revels was ordained a minister of the African Methodist church in 1845. He preached throughout the Midwest and eventually settled in Baltimore, Maryland, where he became the pastor of a church and principal of a school for blacks.

Library of Congress

During the Civil War Revels helped to raise and organize black Union regiments in Maryland and Missouri. He enlisted in 1864 and served as a chaplain in a Mississippi regiment before briefly occupying the post of provost marshal of Vicksburg, Mississippi.

After the war Revels settled in Natchez, Mississippi, and embarked upon a political career as a Republican. First as an alderman in 1868, then as a state senator, he managed to balance his religious and political duties. In January 1870 he was elected to the U.S. Senate seat once occupied by JEFFERSON DAVIS. In a conciliatory gesture toward whites, Revels recommended the full restoration of civil and political rights to all ex-Confederates.

After leaving the Senate in 1871, Revels became the president of Alcorn University, a Mississippi college for blacks. In 1873 he was secretary of state ad interim of Mississippi, and in 1874 he was dismissed as president of Alcorn University by the Republican governor. According to his critics, Revels had alienated blacks and deferred too much to Democrats. The next year, Revels joined the Democratic opposition and helped to defeat the reelection of the Republican carpetbag government. He was reappointed president of Alcorn University by the new Democratic governor in 1876 and later that year became the editor of the *Southwestern Christian Advocate*.

BIBLIOGRAPHY

Garner, J. W., *Reconstruction in Mississippi*, 1901.

Roberts, Owen Josephus

(May 2, 1875–May 17, 1955)
Associate Justice of the Supreme Court

During the late 1930s, Associate Justice Owen Roberts provided the swing vote that shifted the majority opinion of the Supreme Court from opposition to New Deal legislation to support for it.

Roberts was born in Philadelphia. He earned his B.A. degree (1895) and law degree (1898) at the University of Pennsylvania. While teaching law at the University of Pennsylvania from 1898 to 1918, he also practiced law in Philadelphia and, from 1901 to 1904, served as assistant district attorney of Philadelphia County.

During World War I Roberts acted as special deputy attorney general in Pennsylvania charged with prosecuting cases arising under the Espionage Act. In 1924 President CALVIN COOLIDGE appointed Roberts and Senator Atlee Pomerene special prosecuting attorneys to investigate the Teapot Dome scandal (see WARREN GAMALIEL HARDING). Their efforts exposed as fraudulent several leases at Teapot Dome, Wyoming, and Elk Hills, California, naval oil reserves, and led to the conviction of former secretary of the interior ALBERT B. FALL.

President HERBERT HOOVER appointed Roberts to the Supreme Court in 1930. Although a lifelong Republican, Roberts quickly established a reputation for unpredictability and inconsistency as a justice. From 1933 to 1936 he voted with the conservative members of the Court, thereby helping to constitute the majority that declared the National Industrial Recovery Act and the first Agricultural Adjustment Act (see FRANKLIN DELANO ROOSEVELT) unconstitutional. Roberts was evidently intimidated by the overwhelming reelection of President Franklin D. Roosevelt in 1936 and the president's scheme the following year to "pack" the Court with additional justices in order to secure the liberal majority Roosevelt

desperately needed. Roberts supported the Social Security Act as a proper exercise of the federal government's taxing and spending power, and in 1938 he agreed that the second Agricultural Adjustment Act was a legal regulation of interstate commerce.

In 1941 President Roosevelt appointed Roberts to head a commission investigating the Japanese attack on Pearl Harbor (see FRANKLIN DELANO ROOSEVELT). The commission's controversial report cited dereliction of duty on the part of the top military officers at Pearl Harbor as the cause of the catastrophe.

Although Roberts was erratic even in his support for protecting civil rights, it was in this area that he wrote his most eloquent opinion. In *Korematsu* v. *United States* (1944), he disagreed with the majority and opposed the detention and relocation of Japanese Americans during World War II.

Following the retirement of Chief Justice CHARLES EVANS HUGHES, Roberts became disturbed by what he deemed to be the Court's lack of attention to precedent when deciding cases. He grew increasingly isolated and disgruntled. Estranged from his colleagues and labeled by the press as the "man of many minds" whose "switch in time" had "saved nine," Roberts decided to retire in 1945 to pursue a variety of civic, educational, and philanthropic activities. From 1948 to 1951 he served as the dean of the University of Pennsylvania Law School.

BIBLIOGRAPHY

Leonard, Charles A., *Search for a Judicial Philosophy: Mr. Justice Roberts and the Constitutional Revolution of 1937,* 1971.

Rockefeller, Nelson Aldrich

(July 8, 1908–January 26, 1979)
Vice President

Despite an enviable record of public service that included four terms as governor of New York and two years as vice president, and the Rockefeller family fortune (the combined total of which exceeds that of the wealth of many nations), Nelson Rockefeller never achieved what he most desired—the Republican nomination for president.

Nelson Aldrich Rockefeller was born in Bar Harbor, Maine, on the birthday of the then richest man in the world, his grandfather, John D. Rockefeller, who had built Standard Oil into one of the world's greatest corporations. He was named after his maternal grandfather, NELSON ALDRICH, a powerful U.S. senator and unabashed champion of big business in government.

After graduating from Dartmouth College in 1930, Rockefeller invested in a Standard Oil subsidiary in Venezuela. Although it was a relatively small investment by Rockefeller standards, he quickly became so knowledgeable about Latin American problems that in 1940 President FRANKLIN D. ROOSEVELT appointed him coordinator of inter-American affairs. Four years later, he became assistant secretary of state for American republic affairs but was dismissed in 1945 by President HARRY TRUMAN.

In 1952 DWIGHT D. EISENHOWER appointed Rockefeller to serve on a presidential advisory committee on government organization that recommended, among other reforms, the creation of the Department of Health, Education, and Welfare. Rockefeller was appointed the first under secretary of the new department. A year later, he became special assistant to the president for foreign affairs, but he grew so frustrated by his inability to influence Eisenhower that he resigned in December 1955 and returned to New York to run for elective office. He confided to a friend that he had learned a lesson from his years in Washington: appointive office would never satisfy him because "you can't have a real voice in your party until you've proved you know how to get the votes."

In 1958 he won the first of four consecutive terms as governor of New York. Ambitious and driven to make a large-enough impact in New York to win the presidency, Rockefeller assumed the responsibility for raising taxes to fund a wide array of new state services in education, transportation, health, welfare, housing, and environmental protection. At this time Rockefeller represented the epitome of the Eastern Republican Establishment, which had come to support a great many of the domestic changes created by the New Deal and in foreign policy was decidedly internationalist in outlook. Rockefeller tried, after losing the 1960 Republican presidential nomination to RICHARD NIXON, to develop a more conservative image. After his landslide reelection victory in 1962, he was the leading contender for the 1964 Republican nomination. He might have won the nomination then except for his unfavorably perceived decision to divorce his wife of over thirty years to marry a woman eighteen years younger and a shift in control within the Republican party away from the liberal Eastern Establishment to the more conservative, anticommunist, and unilateralist elites of the Southwest and West. Conservative senator BARRY GOLDWATER of Arizona was nominated instead. Rockefeller halfheartedly made one last try to win the presidential nomination in 1968, but he entered the race too late to overcome Richard Nixon's lead.

In December 1973 Rockefeller resigned from the governorship. He planned to concentrate his energy on developing the Commission on Critical Choices for America, which he had organized. However, following the forced resignation of President Nixon due to the Watergate scandal (see RICHARD MILHOUS NIXON),

Vice President GERALD FORD became president and nominated Rockefeller to be his vice president. After undergoing close public scrutiny by Congress into his vast private wealth, Rockefeller became vice president on December 19, 1974.

In spite of the fact that President Ford designated him to lead several important committees, the vice presidency was a disappointment to Rockefeller. He was unable to win the support of conservative Republicans and was perceived as such a liability to Ford's election chances in 1976 that he withdrew from consideration to be Ford's running mate. He returned to New York after leaving Washington in 1976 and concentrated on developing his art collection until his death.

BIBLIOGRAPHY

Persico, Joseph E., *The Imperial Rockefeller: A Biography of Nelson A. Rockefeller,* 1982; Underwood, James E., and William J. Daniels, *Governor Rockefeller in New York: The Apex of Pragmatic Liberalism in the U.S.,* 1984.

Rogers, William Pierce

(June 23, 1913–)
Secretary of State, Attorney General

William Rogers was chosen to be secretary of state by long-time friend President-elect RICHARD NIXON in 1969 because of his skill as a negotiator rather than for his experience in foreign affairs.

Rogers was born in Norfolk, New York. He graduated from Colgate University in 1934 and received his law degree from Cornell in 1937. After a short stint with a Wall Street law firm, he joined the staff of the crime-busting Republican district attorney THOMAS E. DEWEY.

During World War II he served as a naval officer in the Pacific. In March 1948 Rogers became chief counsel of the Special Committee to Investigate the National Defense Program. His primary accomplishment was uncovering "five-percenters," government officials who received kickbacks for obtaining federal contracts for clients.

Rogers left government service in 1950 to join the Washington, D.C., office of a New York law firm. In 1952 he played an important role in securing the Republican nomination for DWIGHT D. EISENHOWER by convincing the convention's credentials committee to seat the Eisenhower rather than the ROBERT A. TAFT delegates from four disputed Southern states. When vice presidential nominee Nixon was almost forced off the ticket because of the discovery of a fund that California business executives had raised to help him financially during the campaign, it was Rogers who convinced him to go on television and make his dramatic "Checkers" speech (see RICHARD MILHOUS NIXON).

In 1952 President Eisenhower appointed Rogers deputy attorney general, a position in which he counseled Vice President Nixon during the president's illnesses and trips abroad.

From October 1957 until the end of the Eisenhower administration in January 1961, Rogers served as attorney general. He made the enforcement of the 1957 Civil Rights Act one of his department's highest priorities and worked to secure the voting rights of blacks and school integration.

In 1961 Rogers returned to his New York law practice. He was a delegate to the United

Nations General Assembly in 1965, and in 1967 to the fourteen-nation ad hoc committee on Southwest Africa.

Upon his appointment of Rogers as secretary of state, President Nixon explained that he needed a man of Rogers's caliber to handle the delicate negotiations that he was sure would end the Vietnam War (see LYNDON BAINES JOHNSON and RICHARD MILHOUS NIXON). Actually, most foreign policy matters were handled by the president and his special White House assistant on foreign affairs, Dr. HENRY A. KISSINGER, who succeeded Rogers as secretary of state in 1973.

BIBLIOGRAPHY

Newsweek, March 3, 1969; *New York Times Magazine*, July 27, 1969.

Roosevelt, Anna Eleanor

(October 11, 1884–November 7, 1962)
Diplomat

Eleanor Roosevelt was the first wife of a president to use her unique position to fight for the rights of minorities, women, and the destitute. In 1939, when the Daughters of the American Revolution refused to let Marian Anderson, a black singer, perform in Washington's Constitution Hall, Eleanor Roosevelt resigned from the organization. Then she helped arrange for Anderson to give a triumphant outdoor concert on federal property at the Lincoln Memorial.

Niece of THEODORE ROOSEVELT, Anna Eleanor Roosevelt was born in New York City. Although her wealthy background assured her social position and her attendance at the best private schools provided her with ample training, she had a difficult childhood with an unsympathetic mother and an alcoholic father. Her parents died when she was very young, leaving her to be raised by a strict grandmother. The young Eleanor considered herself unattractive and never acquired an arrogant upper-class demeanor. Shy instead of coy, clumsy instead of poised, she was just as surprised as everyone else when her dashing, handsome, distant cousin FRANKLIN D. ROOSEVELT proposed marriage. At the time, eschewing the life of privilege and ease, Eleanor was doing volunteer social work among New York City's poor.

For fourteen years after their marriage, until 1919, Eleanor dutifully suffered domination by Franklin's mother, Sara, bore six children, and fulfilled the traditional social obligations of a wealthy politician's wife. The discovery at the end of World War I that her husband loved another woman prompted Eleanor Roosevelt to establish an identity of her own. Instead of devoting an afternoon a week to aid the less fortunate, she made it a full-time career. She also became active in women's affairs and the Democratic party. When Franklin Roosevelt was stricken later that year with polio, she helped him to continue his political career by taking over some of his tasks. Franklin returned to active political life in 1928 and won election as governor of New York, and Eleanor resumed her own growing public life.

After her husband's election as president in 1932, Eleanor refused to live only in Franklin's shadow. She worked in the slums, visited workers in mines and factories, held press conferences, and wrote a newspaper column. Strongly committed to civil equality for black Americans, she was often the only person close to the White House who was willing to speak up on the issue. When her sometimes controversial statements and behavior on behalf of the less fortunate worried his aides, President

Roosevelt smiled and replied, "I can always say, I can't do a thing with my wife." Although despised by some for her outspokenness, Eleanor was admired and loved by many more for her tireless efforts to encourage social reform for blacks, women, youth, and the poor.

Her frequent trips across the country enabled her to learn the mood of the public. She became a major domestic policy adviser in Roosevelt's administration. As one New Deal aide recalled, "No one who ever saw Eleanor Roosevelt sit down facing her husband, and holding his eye firmly, say to him, 'Franklin, I think you should . . .' ever forgot the experience." She served briefly as codirector of the Office of Civilian Defense in 1941 and played a major role in Roosevelt's selection of FRANCES PERKINS as secretary of labor, the first woman to hold a cabinet-level position.

During World War II Eleanor Roosevelt visited troops in the United States, England, the Caribbean, and the South Pacific. After Franklin's death in 1945, she continued her public life, writing her newspaper column, serving as a delegate until 1952 to the United Nations (where she was instrumental in drafting the Declaration of Human Rights), and working with emotionally disturbed children. She supported reform Democrats in New York and worked for ADLAI STEVENSON (III) in his campaigns for president in 1952 and 1956. President JOHN F. KENNEDY reappointed her to the United Nations in 1961, the year before she died.

BIBLIOGRAPHY

Hansen, William P., and John Haney (eds.), *Eleanor Roosevelt*, 1987; Hareven, Tamara, *Eleanor Roosevelt: An American Conscience*, 1968; Lash, Joseph P., *Eleanor and Franklin*, 1971, and *Eleanor: The Years Alone*, 1972; Roosevelt, Eleanor, *This Is My Story*, 1937, *This I Remember*, 1949, and *On My Own*, 1958.

Roosevelt, Franklin Delano

(January 30, 1882–April 12, 1945)
President

The only president ever to serve more than two terms, Franklin Delano Roosevelt was elected to office in 1932 and was reelected three more times before he died near the end of World War II. During the twelve years of his presidency Roosevelt aroused both intense loyalty and opposition. His critics and supporters agree, however, that more than any other president, Roosevelt was the architect of the American welfare state and established government responsibility for individual social welfare. Roosevelt's impact upon the United States through his social and economic legislation was huge and lasting.

No other president in the twentieth century has enjoyed the adulation of the masses to the degree conferred on FDR. He was the first president to use mass communication (the radio) to its full advantage. Through his speeches and famous "fireside chats," FDR sounded like a kind uncle or grandfather to millions of Americans who had never heard a president speak before. Hundreds of thousands sent him letters detailing their plight, asking for his assistance, and thanking him for his help.

Franklin D. Roosevelt spent his early years at the family estate in Hyde Park, New York, and attended the exclusive Groton School before going on to Harvard University and Columbia University Law School. In 1905 he married ANNA ELEANOR ROOSEVELT, his distant cousin and the niece of THEODORE ROOSEVELT. He ran for the New York Senate in 1910. Although a Democrat in an overwhelmingly Republican district, Roosevelt won an impressive victory. He quickly made a name for himself by challenging the Tammany Hall (see WILLIAM MARCY TWEED) political machine's control over the Democratic party. In 1913 he was chosen by Josephus Daniels, President WOODROW WILSON's new secretary of the navy, to be assistant secretary of the navy, the same post Theodore Roosevelt had once held. In 1920 Roosevelt ran as the vice presidential candidate with JAMES COX. Although the Democratic party lost the election, Roosevelt used the opportunity to establish a national reputation.

Library of Congress

His political future seemed assured when, in 1921, he was stricken with polio (infantile paralysis) and almost completely paralyzed.

For two years he struggled to teach himself how to cope with the disease and the loss of the use of his legs. Many people thought his paralysis would be an insurmountable obstacle to a political career, but instead of giving up, with the help of his wife Roosevelt developed a bold, active personal style that more than compensated for his inability to stand without assistance. Prior to his illness Roosevelt had appeared to many of his contemporaries as a spoiled rich man dabbling in politics. Little of his liberalism or political seriousness was apparent before his bout with polio. Once, when asked how he could be so patient with a political opponent, he said, "If you had spent two years in bed trying to wiggle your big toe, after that anything else would seem easy."

In 1928, with the encouragement of AL SMITH, the outgoing governor, Roosevelt managed to win the race for governor of New York. With the onset of the Great Depression, Roosevelt became known for his willingness to use the state government to relieve wide-spread misery and established a reputation as a compassionate, reform-oriented chief executive. He was reelected in 1930.

In many respects Roosevelt seemed the ideal candidate to recapture the White House for the Democrats in 1932. Still, it wasn't until after JOHN NANCE GARNER withdrew from the race at the Democratic convention and instructed his Texas and California delegates to vote for Roosevelt that Roosevelt was able to win the nomination on the fourth ballot. Then he captured the attention of the nation by flying to Chicago to become the first candidate to directly address a convention immediately after nomination. He said, "You have nominated me and I know it, and I am here to thank you for the honor. Let it . . . be symbolic that in so doing I broke traditions. Let it be from now on the task of our Party to break foolish traditions. . . . I pledge you, I pledge myself, to a new deal for the American people."

During the campaign Roosevelt promised to balance the federal budget and to provide direct aid to the needy. Although vague on exactly how he would accomplish this, he exuded tremendous confidence that he could do what was necessary to end the depression: "The country needs, and, unless I mistake its temper, the country demands bold, persistent experimentation. It is common sense to take a method and try it. If it fails, admit it frankly and try another. But above all, try something."

Roosevelt carried all but six states and defeated HERBERT HOOVER by over 7 million votes: 22,821,857 to 15,761,841. Roosevelt also stymied the efforts of the Socialist and Communist parties to capitalize on the economic turmoil gripping the nation. Socialist candidate NORMAN THOMAS obtained less than a million votes, and the Communist party's representative, William Foster, managed to win only 100,000 votes.

Roosevelt, confident of victory, had begun preparing for the presidency months before his campaign and election. Besides a core of loyal political assistants, he had enlisted the aid of a number of college professors, REXFORD TUGWELL, Adolph Berle, Jr., and Raymond Moley—nicknamed the brain trust—to assist him so that once in office he could move swiftly to deal with the national crisis.

In his inaugural address Roosevelt announced that he would call Congress into an immediate special session to obtain the legislation necessary to deal with the banking crisis and the collapse of the economy. He told the nation that if Congress hesitated, he would ask it "for broad executive power to wage a war against the emergency, as great as the power that would be given to me if we were in fact invaded by a foreign foe. This great Nation will endure as it has endured, will revive and prosper. So, first of all, let me assert my firm belief that the only thing we have to fear is fear itself. . . ."

The special session of Congress Roosevelt called convened on March 9, 1933, and adjourned on June 16. During that Hundred Days more important legislation was passed than at any other comparable period in U.S. history. The three aims of the New Deal were recovery, relief, and reform. The first New Deal legislation concentrated on recovery and relief. To accomplish these goals, Roosevelt had to overcome deep-seated American prejudices against a strong federal government.

Two days after assuming office, Roosevelt issued a proclamation closing all of the nation's banks. The special session of Congress passed an emergency banking bill just three days later that gave the president broad powers over the nation's banks, currency, and foreign exchange. Roosevelt went on radio to talk informally to the public about what he had authorized the Federal Reserve Board and Treasury Department to do and to promise: "I

can assure you that it is safer to keep your money in a reopened bank than under the mattress." The combination of decisive action and personal persuasion worked. Public confidence in reopened banks was restored.

Roosevelt also took the nation off the gold standard and devalued the currency by 40 percent to make American goods more competitive abroad, raise prices of goods at home, and reduce individual debt. As one would anticipate, those in debt applauded, but creditors, such as those holding bonds and long-term mortgages, were enraged.

The most popular New Deal measures were those that tried to relieve the suffering of the approximately 25 percent of the labor force who were unemployed. Roosevelt knew local and state agencies had run out of funds, so he created the Federal Emergency Relief Administration, headed by HARRY HOPKINS, to give money to local relief agencies. The Civil Works Administration (1933), the Civilian Conservation Corps (1933), the Public Works Administration (1933), and later the Works Progress Administration (1935) were also created to provide temporary relief jobs. Among the other innovative programs were the Agricultural Adjustment Administration (AAA, 1933), which attempted to buoy farm prices by limiting production; the Home Owners' Loan Corporation (1933), which worked to protect people from mortgage foreclosures; the National Recovery Administration (NRA, 1933), which was designed to regulate business competition; the National Labor Relations Board (1935), which was established to guarantee the right of labor to organize; the Social Security Act, which set up an old-age pension system; and the Tennessee Valley Authority (TVA) project, which brought low-cost power and jobs to millions of people in the Tennessee River valley area.

Although these efforts failed to end the Great Depression, they did provide a sense of the government's commitment to alleviating the suffering and led to Roosevelt's landslide reelection in 1936. They also marked the first extensive use of government's fiscal powers—

what would later be termed Keynesian (after English economist John Maynard Keynes) policies—to stimulate mass purchasing and thereby promote economic recovery (see HARRY S TRUMAN). Then in 1937, after the Supreme Court angered Roosevelt by declaring (in 1935) the NRA and AAA unconstitutional, he made a costly political blunder by launching a plan to increase the size of the Court by six more judges, to fifteen, so that he could appoint enough new justices to overcome the existing five-member conservative majority. Public reverence for the Court and Roosevelt's miscalculation that he could orchestrate the election defeat of congressional opponents in 1938 resulted in his first major congressional setback. This "court-packing" plan, combined with the 1937 recession and his apparent unwillingness to curb a wave of sit-down strikes, sharply limited his political power. The Republicans and conservative Democrats won enough seats in the 1938 congressional elections to halt further substantial New Deal legislation, though Roosevelt did put through the Executive Reorganization Act in 1939, which enlarged and strengthened the executive branch of the government. World War II, not innovative New Deal legislation, returned the nation to prosperity.

By the time he won reelection in 1936, it was clear to Roosevelt that ominous dictatorial regimes in Japan, Germany, and Italy were going to solve their economic problems through military expansion. Roosevelt hoped to keep the United States out of war, but as World War II began in 1939, he worked to bring about the repeal of the Neutrality Act of 1935 (see WILLIAM EDGAR BORAH) so that he could provide aid to Great Britain. In 1940 he decided to run for an unprecedented third term. Promising to keep Americans out of any foreign wars, Roosevelt easily defeated his Republican rival, WENDELL WILLKIE, 449 electoral votes to 82.

After his reelection Roosevelt obtained congressional approval to provide lend-lease aid to Great Britain and, in 1941, to the Soviet Union. The Lend-Lease Act, passed mainly to allow the British more credit to buy war supplies, provided for the sale, transfer, exchange, or lease of arms or equipment to any country whose defense was vital to the United States. (Total lend-lease aid by the end of the war would amount to nearly $50 billion.) American ships and planes also began convoying supply ships far out into the North Atlantic and reporting German submarine locations to the British navy. In the Far East the United States attempted in 1941 to halt Japan's military expansion by announcing a potentially crippling embargo of vital war materiel and oil to Japan. Instead of backing down, Japan launched a surprise attack on December 7, 1941, designed to wipe out the U.S. Pacific fleet stationed at Pearl Harbor in Hawaii. In asking Congress for a declaration of war against Japan, the president declared December 7 as "a date which will live in infamy." Germany and Italy then declared war, and the United States found itself fighting adversaries in both Asia and Europe.

During the war congressional conservatives managed to dismantle some of the New Deal's innovative programs and forced Roosevelt to orchestrate economic mobilization in a manner that gave considerable authority and profit opportunities to corporate elites. Although severely criticized for various aspects of his direction of the war effort, Roosevelt behaved in his characteristically pragmatic fashion. His goal was to win the war with as few American casualties as possible. To do this he needed to keep the wartime alliance of Great Britain, the Soviet Union, and the United States together until after Germany and Japan were defeated, and he did. At the same time, war-induced prosperity in combination with a widespread belief among Americans that they were fighting "the Good War" sustained national unity and enough of Roosevelt's popularity to gain him reelection to a fourth term in 1944.

Roosevelt did not live to see the end of World War II. At the Allied summit at Yalta in 1945 he had been unable to secure a Poland free of Soviet domination, but he did manage to obtain a Soviet promise to join the war against Japan and to participate in the United Nations. Critics attack his refusal to challenge Soviet domination of Eastern Europe, but supporters point out that it was merely an acceptance of political reality—Soviet troops occupied the region. Ordered by his doctors to rest after his return from Yalta, Roosevelt traveled to his favorite retreat at Warm Springs, Georgia, where he suffered a massive cerebral hemorrhage and died.

Perspectives on FDR over the years have varied widely. In the 1930s his Republican opponents saw him as a virtual socialist. Liberal historians of the 1940s and 1950s lionized him for leading a popular crusade to restore prosperity and justice in America. The radical historians of the 1960s viewed him as a servant of capital, seeking mainly to restore capitalism to health and not truly interested in helping the downtrodden. Still others have stressed the pragmatic, nonideological nature of his approach—his willingness to try policies that promised to work and that seemed feasible. None of these interpretations, however, has sought to deny the centrality of FDR and his New Deal in the shaping of modern America.

BIBLIOGRAPHY

Burns, James M., *Roosevelt: The Lion and the Fox*, 1956, and *Roosevelt: The Soldier of Freedom*, 1970; Davis, Kenneth S., *FDR*, 3 vols., 1979–1986; Fraser, Steve, and Gary Gerstle (eds.), *The Rise and Fall of the New Deal Order, 1930–1980*, 1989; Freidel, Frank, *Franklin D. Roosevelt*, 4 vols., 1953–1973; Leuchtenberg, William, *FDR and the New Deal, 1932–1940*, 1963; Schlesinger, Arthur M., Jr., *The Age of Roosevelt*, 3 vols., 1957–1960; Ward, Geoffrey C., *Before the Trumpet: Young Franklin Roosevelt, 1882–1905*, 1985, and *A First-Class Temperament: The Emergence of Franklin Roosevelt*, 1989.

Roosevelt, Theodore

(October 27, 1858–January 6, 1919)
President, Vice President

Although largely opposed by the political establishment, Theodore Roosevelt fought to give the common citizen "a square deal." Many of his ideas for reform, considered radical in their day, have become accepted by both political parties. An avowed nationalist with imperialist leanings, he also transformed the United States into a major international and military power. He brought both the presidency and the nation into the twentieth century.

Theodore Roosevelt was born into a prosperous family in New York City. His early education came from private tutors. Because he suffered from asthma and poor eyesight, he tried to build himself up physically through exercise and sport and practiced hard at horseback riding, boxing, and shooting. He also developed an early interest in nature and in military affairs. Later he attended Harvard University and was elected to Phi Beta Kappa. While at Harvard, he began writing *The Naval War of 1812*, which was published two years after he graduated in 1880. In 1881, at the age of twenty-three, he was elected to the New York State legislature, where he served three one-year terms and supported the Progressive reform wing of the Republican party.

Following the tragic death of his young wife, Roosevelt spent two years in the Dakota Territory, ranching and writing history. In 1886 he ran unsuccessfully for mayor of New York City. He did not return to public office until President BENJAMIN HARRISON appointed him to the Civil Service Commission in 1889. Opposed to the spoils system, Roosevelt worked hard to revise civil service examinations and search out fraud. In 1895 he became president of the police commission of New York City. His reforms brought opposition from both Democrats and Republicans in the city government.

President WILLIAM MC-KINLEY appointed Roosevelt assistant secretary of the navy in 1897. Roosevelt used this post to ready the navy for war with Spain; he wanted to end Spanish rule of Cuba and the Philippines, and expand American influence in the Caribbean and the Pacific. When the Spanish-American War (see WILLIAM MC-KINLEY, JR.) broke out in 1898, Roosevelt joined the 1st Regiment of U.S. Cavalry Volunteers, the "Rough Riders," as a colonel. He led the now famous charge up San Juan Hill near Santiago, returned to the United States a national hero, and was elected governor of New York in November 1898.

Library of Congress

An active and popular governor, Roosevelt supported civil service reform, social reform, and the labor movement. He also passed a tax on corporate franchises, outlawed racial discrimination in the public schools, and urged the conservation of New York's natural resources. Although a moderate reformer, his stand on many issues made him unpopular with business leaders and the Republican party bosses in the state. To remove him from state politics, the bosses nominated him as President McKinley's running mate in 1900, a post considered largely ceremonial. The McKinley-Roosevelt ticket won easily.

When McKinley was assassinated in September 1901, the forty-two-year-old Roosevelt became the youngest person ever to be president. Although he promised to continue McKinley's policies, including retaining a number of his cabinet members, Roosevelt made it

clear that he would be his own president. He would certainly be one of the most vigorous and well-liked presidents. He considered himself a man of all the people, and while he embraced the new reform movement that was sweeping the country (one that would become known as "Progressivism") and constantly preached morality and social change, he was not a radical in economics or in politics.

In 1902 Roosevelt ordered the Justice Department to bring suit against the Northern Securities Company under the provisions of the Sherman Anti-Trust Act (see BENJAMIN HARRISON). The suit was successful, and the railroad monopoly, owned by some of the country's wealthiest businessmen, was dissolved. This action earned Roosevelt a reputation as a "trust buster"; however, he believed that, in general, trusts should be regulated rather than dissolved.

During his first term, Roosevelt intervened in the prolonged national coal strike to force a settlement, a move considered a victory for labor; he created the Bureau of Corporations to investigate the practices of any interstate corporation; and he supported the conservation of American forests, lakes, rivers, and coal reserves.

In foreign policy, he confronted problems that involved the United States in world diplomacy. Since the United States had acquired an overseas empire, Roosevelt set out to protect it by strengthening the navy and the army. By his bullying methods of obtaining the land in Panama to build a canal and of threatening the rest of the world from interfering in Latin American and Western Hemisphere affairs—the Roosevelt Corollary to the Monroe Doctrine (see JAMES MONROE)—Roosevelt put the other nations on notice that the United States was becoming a world power. (See also HENRY WHITE and JOHN MILTON HAY.)

Roosevelt was reelected by a landslide in 1904. During his second term, he continued to press for reforms at home—his so-called Square Deal—though Congress would eventually defy his stand against the abuses of the rich and powerful business community. He approved the Hepburn Act giving the Interstate Commerce Commission the power to regulate railroad rates and services, the Pure Food and Drug Act, and the Meat Inspection Act. He began construction of the Panama Canal and mediated the end of the Russo-Japanese War, for which he won the Nobel Peace Prize in 1906. He worked for the development of natural resources and assigned millions of acres of land to national parks and reserves. He was responsible for the "gentlemen's agreement" curbing Japanese immigration to the United States and sent an American fleet around in the world to give meaning to his expression "Speak softly and carry a big stick."

Roosevelt supported the candidacy of his secretary of war, WILLIAM HOWARD TAFT, in 1908. By 1912, however, he felt Taft had been won over by reactionary elements. When Taft won the Republican nomination, Roosevelt ran against him on the Progressive, or Bull Moose, party ticket. This caused the votes to be split, and Democrat WOODROW WILSON won the election. Though this defeat ended Roosevelt's career in national politics, many of the Progressive ideas he had championed lived on in the Wilson administration (see WOODROW WILSON).

Historians have not been able to reach consensus on a simple definition of Progressivism. The Progressive movement, however, had been gaining momentum since about 1900. It favored many of the reforms backed by the earlier agrarian Populists (see JAMES BAIRD WEAVER) and struck out at the domination of the "Interests"—big business and the wealthy few. Many Progressives were middle-class and college-educated people who wanted to fight corruption and help the disadvantaged poor, as well as better their own condition. Often centered in large cities, they wrote exposés of poor working conditions in industry and of corruption in government, brought new ideas to education, and fostered reform in all areas of city life and administration. Progressivism also drew on the support of groups, such as workers and consumers, who either were interested in such specific issues as worker's compensation and child labor or felt a more general commitment to tame the power of the "Interests." (See ROBERT MARION LA FOLLETTE and HENRY AGARD WALLACE for discussion of later Progressive movements.)

Roosevelt backed CHARLES EVANS HUGHES for the presidency in 1916 and was an ardent supporter of the military effort in World War I. Although he opposed Wilson's Fourteen Points, he was, with reservations, in favor of the League of Nations (see WOODROW WILSON). In 1919 he died of malaria, contracted a few years earlier on an expedition to Brazil.

BIBLIOGRAPHY

Andrews, Wayne (ed.), *Autobiography of Theodore Roosevelt*, 2d ed., 1958; Beale, Howard K., *Theodore Roosevelt and the Rise of America to World Power*, 1956; Blum, John M., *Republican Roosevelt*, 1954; Burton, David H., *Theodore Roosevelt: Confident Imperialist*, 1969; Chessman, G. Wallace, *Governor Theodore Roosevelt*, 1965, and *Theodore Roosevelt and Politics of Power*, 1969; Harbaugh, William H., *Power and Responsibility: Life and Times of Theodore Roosevelt*, 1961; Lodge, Henry Cabot, and Theodore Roosevelt, *Selections from Correspondence*, 2 vols., 1925; Lorant, Stefan, *Life and Times of Theodore Roosevelt*, 1959; Morison, Elting E., et al. (eds.), *Letters of Theodore Roosevelt*, 8 vols., 1951–1954, and *Works of Theodore Roosevelt*, 24 vols., 1923–1926; Mowry, George E., *Theodore Roosevelt and the Progressive Movement*, 1946; Pringle, H. F., *Theodore Roosevelt*, 1958; Roosevelt, Nicholas, *Theodore Roosevelt*, 1967; Wagenknecht, Edward C., *Seven Worlds of Theodore Roosevelt*, 1958.

Root, Elihu

(February 15, 1845–February 7, 1937)
Secretary of State, Secretary of War, Diplomat, Senator

Elihu Root served in the cabinets of two presidents, won the Nobel Peace Prize, and completed a term in the U.S. Senate in addition to developing a successful domestic and international law practice.

Root was born in Clinton, New York. After graduating from Hamilton College in Clinton in 1864, he obtained his law degree from New York University Law School in 1867 and became a successful corporate attorney. Root became directly involved in politics for the first time when he agreed to serve as U.S. district attorney for the southern district of New York from 1883 to 1885. In 1894 he managed the state constitutional convention of New York and the following year became that body's president.

When THEODORE ROOSEVELT began his political career by unsuccessfully campaigning for mayor of New York City, Root was at his side serving as confidant and adviser. His close relationship to Roosevelt was a major factor in President WILLIAM MCKINLEY's decision to choose Root as the secretary of war in 1899. At first, Root was reluctant to accept the appointment. He told the emissary of the news: "Thank the President for me, but say that it is quite absurd. I know nothing about war. . . . " It was not until it was explained to him that it would be his responsibility to establish and direct the governments of the newly acquired colonies of the Philippines and Puerto Rico that Root changed his mind. This was a task he felt superbly trained to administer.

Although Root stressed the guarantee of individual liberties in Puerto Rico and the Philippines, he placed the protection of U.S. interests first and accepted responsibility for the army's brutal crushing of the Philippine independence effort. As secretary of war, Root also oversaw the reorganization of the army, created the Army War College, and established the policy of regularly rotating officers from staff to line positions. Root, an exhausted man, resigned from office in 1903, but only two years later, after the death of JOHN HAY, President Theodore Roosevelt appointed him secretary of state.

As secretary of state from 1905 to 1909, Root worked to improve relations with Latin America and Japan. During a tour of Latin America in 1906, he succeeded in easing tensions that had risen over U.S. actions in Panama. In 1908 he managed to convince Japan to confirm the U.S. Open Door policy (see WILLIAM MCKINLEY, JR.) in China with the Root-Takahira Agreement.

In 1909 Root accepted an appointment to the U.S. Senate. He had never run for office because he feared the political capital his opponent might make of the fact that he had been WILLIAM "BOSS" TWEED's defense attorney in Tweed's 1873 trial for corruption of urban politics. Tweed, leader of the Tammany Hall political machine (see WILLIAM MARCY TWEED), was eventually convicted of establishing political corruption in New York on an unprecedented scale.

The next year, in addition to fulfilling his Senate duties, Root served as chief U.S. consul of the International Court of Justice at The Hague, Holland, in the North Atlantic fisheries arbitration case. The Permanent Court of Arbitration settled the dispute between the United States and Great Britain over Canadian and U.S. territorial fishing rights in the North Atlantic. In recognition of his work as secretary of state and at The Hague in favor of the use of diplomacy and arbitration to settle international disputes, Root was awarded the 1912 Nobel Peace Prize.

Also in 1912, as chairman of the Republican national convention, Root ended his long personal friendship with Theodore Roosevelt because he felt obligated as a matter of principle to support WILLIAM HOWARD TAFT's reelection. Roosevelt never fully forgave Root.

A strong proponent of the need to help the Allies defeat Germany in World War I, Root was critical of WOODROW WILSON's policy of neutrality but did not criticize him until after retiring from the Senate in 1915. After the war Root, with reservations designed to assure critics of American sovereignty, advocated U.S. membership in the League of Nations (see WOODROW WILSON). In 1920 he helped to create the League's Permanent Court of International Justice. As president of the Carnegie Endowment for International Peace from 1910 to 1925, he worked for the free international exchange of scientific knowledge.

In 1921 Root accepted his last diplomatic appointment. President WARREN G. HARDING selected him to be one of the four U.S. delegates to the International Conference on the Limitation of Armaments in Washington, D.C. (commonly known as the Washington Conference).

BIBLIOGRAPHY

Bacon, Robert, and James B. Scott (eds.), *Addresses of Elihu Root,* 1925; Jessup, P. C., *Elihu Root,* 2 vols., 1938; Leopold, Richard W., *Elihu Root and the Conservative Tradition,* 1954.

Rostow, Walt Whitman

(October 7, 1916–)
Presidential Adviser

Walt Rostow was an important economic theorist before being appointed by President JOHN F. KENNEDY to chair the Policy and Planning Council of the State Department. In this position and as a special assistant to President LYNDON JOHNSON from 1966 to 1969, Rostow was one of the strongest advocates of the massive U.S. military intervention in Vietnam (see LYNDON BAINES JOHNSON and RICHARD MILHOUS NIXON). He also played a major role in the 1965 decision to begin bombing North Vietnam.

Rostow was born in New York City. After earning his B.A. from Yale in 1936, he became a Rhodes scholar and studied at Balliol College, Oxford University from 1936 to 1938. He earned his Ph.D. in economics from Yale in 1940. Oxford University awarded him a master's degree in 1946, and Cambridge University granted him another master's degree in 1949.

Rostow taught economics at Columbia University in 1940 and 1941, then entered the State Department. From 1942 until the end of World War II in 1945, he worked with the Office of Strategic Services. After the war he held a number of State Department positions in Europe, specializing in foreign aid development problems. He also taught at Oxford and Cambridge. He returned to the United States in 1950 and from then until 1960 was a professor of economic history at Massachusetts Institute of Technology.

In 1957 Senator John F. Kennedy recruited Rostow as an economic foreign policy adviser. During Kennedy's successful bid to win the presidency in 1960, Rostow originated the campaign's popular "New Frontier" slogan. In November 1961 he was appointed counselor of the State Department and chairman of its Policy and Planning Council by President Kennedy. In this capacity and as a special assistant to Lyndon B. Johnson from 1966 to 1969, the staunchly anticommunist Rostow exerted a major influence on U.S. foreign policy.

After leaving government service in 1969, Rostow became a professor of economics and history at the University of Texas.

BIBLIOGRAPHY

Rostow, Walt W., *The Stages of Economic Growth*, 1960 (reprint 1971), *The United States in the World Arena*, 1960, *Politics and the Stages of Growth*, 1971, and *The Diffusion of Power*, 1972.

Rush, Benjamin

(January 4, 1746–April 19, 1813)
Revolutionary Leader

Benjamin Rush was a medical as well as a political reformer. In addition to serving in the Continental Congress and signing the Declaration of Independence, Rush was surgeon general of the American Continental Army, professor of medical theory and practice at the University of Pennsylvania, and leader of efforts to improve penitentiary and mental hospital conditions.

Rush was born in Byberry (now a part of Philadelphia), Pennsylvania. He graduated from the College of New Jersey (now Princeton University) in 1760 and earned his medical degree from the University of Edinburgh in 1768. Upon his return to America in 1769, Rush established a medical practice and became a professor of chemistry, the first in the thirteen colonies, at the College of Philadelphia. He also assumed an increasingly active role in revolutionary political protest activities. In June 1776 he was elected to

Library of Congress

the Provincial Congress, and one month later, he was chosen to represent Pennsylvania in the Continental Congress. He arrived in Philadelphia just in time to be one of the signers of the Declaration of Independence.

From April 1777 until January 1778 Rush served as surgeon general of the Continental Army. The dismal health conditions he encountered in the army led him to demand that Dr. Shippen, the physician director general, be dismissed; instead, General GEORGE WASHINGTON established a committee to study Rush's charges. The investigating committee refused to support Rush's allegations. Washington sided with the committee, and Rush resigned in protest. His military career came to an end, but the affair did result in Rush's writing a pioneering article on improving sanitary conditions in the military: *Directions for Preserving the Health of Soldiers* (1778).

After his brief military experience, Rush returned to Philadelphia and became a highly respected medical professor and social reform advocate. The causes he championed included abolishing slavery; improving public education, especially for women; regulating the consumption of alcoholic beverages; establishing a modern penitentiary system; and treating insanity as a mental illness capable of improvement through scientific treatment. In 1783 he helped found Dickinson College and three years later established the first free dispensary in the United States.

Rush was a strong advocate in the mid-1780s of the need to create a more powerful central government. His efforts led to his election as a delegate to Pennsylvania's ratifying convention. At the convention, he and jurist James Wilson orchestrated the effort that culminated in the ratification of the federal Constitution. Two years later, he and Wilson worked together again to secure a new state constitution for Pennsylvania. Its adoption in 1789 ended Rush's political career. Thenceforth, he concentrated on his medical research and teaching.

In 1792, with the absorption of the College of Philadelphia into the University of Pennsylvania, Rush became that university's professor of theory and practice. His reliance upon the bleeding and purging of patients, particularly in the yellow fever epidemic of 1793, aroused considerable medical controversy. (He worked heroically and noted the coincidence of mosquitoes to the disease, but hurt rather than helped most of his patients by draining them of too much of their blood.) Although his advocacy of bleeding was largely discredited by critics who correlated the death rate of his patients to the amounts of blood he withdrew, Rush never admitted his error. Nevertheless, he became an exceptionally popular teacher at the University of Pennsylvania and made notable contributions to treating psychic disorders. His *Medical Inquiries and Observations upon the Diseases of the Mind* (1812) was the first detailed American study of mental illness and possible treatments.

In 1797, in recognition for his efforts on behalf of securing the ratification of the Constitution, President JOHN ADAMS appointed Rush treasurer of the U.S. Mint at Philadelphia. He held this post until his death.

BIBLIOGRAPHY

Corner, G. W. (ed.), *The Autobiography of Benjamin Rush*, 1948; Ginger, Carl, *Revolutionary Doctor: Benjamin Rush*, 1966; Goodman, Nathan G., *Benjamin Rush, Physician and Citizen, 1746–1813*, 1934; Hawke, David F., *Benjamin Rush: Revolutionary Gadfly*, 1971; Runes, D. O., *The Selected Writings of Benjamin Rush*, 1947; Schutz, John A., and Douglas Adair (eds.), *Dialogues, John Adams and Benjamin Rush, 1805–1813*, 1960.

Rusk, Dean

(February 9, 1909–   )
Secretary of State, Diplomat

Dean Rusk, the quiet, loyal secretary of state in the administrations of JOHN F. KENNEDY and LYNDON B. JOHNSON, had a simple approach to fulfilling the duties of his office. He summed it up in his comment that he agreed with President HARRY S TRUMAN's dictum that "the president makes foreign policy."

Born David Dean Rusk in Cherokee County, Georgia, to poor tenant farmer parents, Rusk graduated from Davidson College in Davidson, North Carolina, in 1931 and, as a Rhodes scholar, earned his master's degree three years later from Oxford University. He then taught government and became dean of faculty at Mills College in Oakland, California. After serving in Southeast Asia in World War II as deputy chief of staff for the China-Burma-India theater, Rusk returned to Washington, D.C., where he worked in both the war and state departments. Assistant secretary of state during the Korean War, he was closely involved in the decision to commit American forces there in 1950 and in the peace negotiations with Japan the following year. In 1951 he was chosen president of the Rockefeller Foundation, a position he held from 1952 until President-elect Kennedy chose him to be secretary of state in 1960.

Rusk assumed a low profile under the dynamic young President Kennedy, who viewed foreign policy as his own specialty. Although Kennedy never had cause to complain about Rusk's imperturbable behavior during the Cuban Missile Crisis and several other critical times, such as the war in Laos, the botched U.S.–supported Bay of Pigs invasion of Cuba, the East German construction of the Berlin Wall, and the U.S. buildup in South Vietnam, he often commented that "[Rusk] never gives me anything to chew on. . . . You never know what he is thinking."

After Kennedy's assassination in 1963 President Johnson, who felt quite differently toward Rusk than Kennedy, asked Rusk to remain in office as his secretary of state until 1969. Johnson, much less adroit in foreign affairs than Kennedy, appreciated Rusk's unflagging support for his policy of pursuing military victory in South Vietnam (see LYNDON BAINES JOHNSON and RICHARD MILHOUS NIXON) until peace talks began in 1968. Johnson described Rusk as "Number One in the Cabinet and . . . Number One with me."

Upon leaving government service, Rusk, described by the historian Arthur Schlesinger, Jr., as a man of "exceptional intelligence, lucidity and control with a talent for concise and dispassionate exposition [who is] irrevocably conventional," taught international law at the University of Georgia.

BIBLIOGRAPHY

Cohen, Warren, *Dean Rusk*, 1980; Schoenbaum, Thomas J., *Waging Peace and War: Dean Rusk in the Truman, Kennedy, and Johnson Years*, 1988.

Rutledge, John

(September 1739–July 18, 1800)
Associate Justice of the Supreme Court, Revolutionary Leader

South Carolina planter-aristocrat John Rutledge was a leader in the American Revolution; yet after independence was won, he strongly opposed a democratically elected national government. He argued instead for the election of the president by Congress and for the selection of representatives by the state legislatures.

Rutledge was born in Charleston, South Carolina. After admission to the English bar in 1760, he returned to Charleston and was elected to the colonial legislature. He was a delegate to the Stamp Act Congress in 1765 and to the First and Second Continental Congresses. Rutledge was chairman of the committee that wrote South Carolina's constitution in 1776, and was elected president of the General Assembly in 1776 and then governor of South Carolina in 1779. He served in Congress from 1782 to 1783, and in 1787 was a delegate to the federal Constitutional Convention. A fierce patriot, Rutledge performed courageously during the American Revolution to free South Carolina from British rule. Nevertheless, at the Constitutional Convention he argued that wealth should be used as the basis for determining political representation and opposed any restrictions on the institution of slavery.

In 1789 Rutledge was named senior associate justice of the U.S. Supreme Court by GEORGE WASHINGTON. He resigned in 1791 to become chief justice of the South Carolina Supreme Court. In 1795 he asked President Washington to appoint him Chief Justice of the Supreme Court. Washington acceded to Rutledge's request; but because of Rutledge's fierce denunciation of Jay's Treaty (see JOHN JAY), the Senate refused to confirm him, even though he had already presided over the August term of the Court.

BIBLIOGRAPHY

Barry, Richard, *Mr. Rutledge of South Carolina*, 1942.

St. John, John Pierce

(February 25, 1833–August 31, 1916)
Candidate for President

John Pierce St. John was born in Brookville, Indiana. After being admitted to the bar at Charleston, Illinois, in 1861, he served as a Union officer in the Civil War. In 1869 he established a law practice in Olathe, Kansas. Four years later, St. John was elected to the Kansas senate as a Republican. In the senate he quickly established a reputation as a supporter of the Prohibition movement. He was elected governor of Kansas in 1878 on a strong antiliquor platform. As governor of Kansas for two terms from 1879 to 1883, St. John successfully supported a Prohibition amendment to the state constitution. After his effort to win election to a third term in 1882 failed, he devoted his considerable speaking abilities to promoting the cause of Prohibition.

In 1884 he was the National Prohibition party's candidate for president. Because most of his votes were secured in the key state of New York and came at the expense of the Republican presidential candidate, JAMES G. BLAINE, St. John was blamed by Republicans for securing the election of Democrat GROVER CLEVELAND.

In addition to his Prohibition work, St. John supported the free-silver movement (see WILLIAM JENNINGS BRYAN) and championed woman suffrage.

BIBLIOGRAPHY

Alexander, Orline St. John, *The St. John General*, 1907; Cutler, W. G. (ed.), *History of the State of Kansas*, 1883; Frederickson, Edna Tutt, *John P. St. John, the Father of Constitutional Prohibition*, Ph.D. dissertation, University of Kansas, 1931; *Who's Who in America*, 1914–1915.

Scalia, Antonin

(March 11, 1936–)
Associate Justice of the Supreme Court

Antonin Scalia, the first Italian American ever to serve on the Supreme Court, has played an important role in moving the Court to the political right.

Scalia was born in Trenton, New Jersey, and grew up in Queens, New York. He graduated from Georgetown University in 1957 and received a law degree from Harvard University in 1960. Scalia practiced law in Cleveland, Ohio, until 1967, when he left private practice to accept a teaching post at the University of Virginia Law School.

From 1971 to 1977 Scalia served under Presidents RICHARD NIXON and GERALD FORD in various legal positions. For the next five years he taught at the University of Chicago Law School, where he earned the admiration of President RONALD REAGAN for his articles arguing that the Supreme Court should interpret the Constitution from a strict constructionist (see THOMAS JEFFERSON and MELVILLE WESTON FULLER) point of view. He also earned a national reputation as a strong advocate of federal and state deregulation of the marketplace.

In 1982 he was appointed to the U.S. Court of Appeals for the District of Columbia, and in 1986, was named by President Reagan as an associate justice of the Supreme Court.

In his decisions during his first four years on the Supreme Court, Justice Scalia opposed racially based affirmative action programs, denied that the Constitution guaranteed a woman the right to have an abortion, advocated a more narrow interpretation of the free speech protections covered under the First Amendment, and defended the power of the executive branch over that of Congress.

BIBLIOGRAPHY

Chicago Tribune, August 3, 1986; *Christian Science Monitor*, June 19, 1986; *New Republic*, June 10, 1985; *New York Times*, June 19, 1986.

Schurz, Carl

(March 2, 1829–May 14, 1906)
Secretary of the Interior, Diplomat, Senator

Carl Schurz was a radical political reform advocate during the revolutions of 1848 in Europe before settling in the United States and becoming a successful political leader and journalist. Schurz was born in Liblar, near Cologne, Prussia, and studied at the University of Bonn. He was forced to flee from Bonn in 1849 because of his revolutionary activities. Several years later, he immigrated to America. He settled in Wisconsin in 1855 and quickly became a well-known abolitionist leader in the large German immigrant community there.

Schurz's gift for public speaking and ability to campaign in both English and German led to his nomination by the Republican party for lieutenant governor in 1857. After losing the general election, he studied law and was admitted to the Wisconsin bar.

First as a delegate to the 1860 Republican national convention, then as a vigorous campaign worker, Schurz supported ABRAHAM LINCOLN for president. In turn, President Lincoln appointed Schurz minister to Spain in 1861, but Schurz resigned from office in April 1862 in order to join the Union army. He was commissioned a brigadier general of volunteers and quickly rose to the rank of major general.

In 1868 Schurz was elected to the U.S. Senate by the Missouri state legislature. During his single term in the Senate (1869–1875), Schurz opposed many of the programs of ULYSSES GRANT. Disgusted by the rampant "spoils system" management of the government during President Grant's first term, Schurz helped to organize the new reform Liberal Republican party in 1872 and backed the presidential candidacy of HORACE GREELEY.

In 1876, to the dismay of his Liberal Republican party friends, Schurz supported the election of RUTHERFORD B. HAYES for president. President Hayes rewarded Schurz by naming him secretary of the interior. While secretary of the interior, Schurz implemented the practice of competitive examinations for civil service positions, improved the treatment of Indians, worked to conserve natural resources, and began the development of national parks.

Schurz completed his term as secretary of the interior in 1881, then became editor of the *New York Evening Post*. After resigning from the *Post* in 1884 over a policy dispute, Schurz spent the rest of his life practicing law and writing articles on contemporary affairs.

BIBLIOGRAPHY

Bancroft, Frederic (ed.), *Speeches, Correspondence and Political Papers of Carl Schurz,* 6 vols., 1913; Easum, Chester V., *Americanization of Carl Schurz,* 1929; Fuess, Claude M., *Carl Schurz, Reformer,* 1932; Schurz, Carl, *Reminiscences,* 3 vols., 1907–1908.

Scott, Winfield

(June 13, 1786–May 29, 1866)
Candidate for President

Known as Old Fuss and Feathers for his meticulous dress and behavior, Winfield Scott, the founder of America's professional army, was born near Petersburg, Virginia. He briefly attended William and Mary College and studied law before joining the army in 1808. He was tried and suspended from active duty in 1809 for a year for questioning the competence of his commanding officer. Scott used the year to read everything he could about military tactics and returned to his command in 1811.

Scott was so frustrated by the incompetence he found in the army that he would have resigned in disgust if he had not been so eager to participate in the War of 1812 (see JAMES MADISON). As soon as the fighting began, he traveled to New York and gallantly tried to whip recalcitrant American militia troops into combat-ready soldiers. Wounded and briefly captured in the fighting around the Great Lakes, Scott made such an impression in battle that he was promoted, though only twenty-eight, to brigadier general in 1814. He used the authority provided by his new rank to train, and then command in several battles, the American army's best fighting force. Severely wounded at the Battle of Lundy's Lane on July 25, 1814, Scott became a national hero.

After the war Scott used the free time provided by peace to study abroad and write about military tactics. He also indulged his passions for fine food and elegant uniforms and on three occasions served presidents with distinction. When South Carolina threatened to secede over the tariff controversy in 1832, President ANDREW JACKSON sent Scott to Charleston as a show of force. Scott proved to be diplomatic with the enraged Carolinians, and he played a crucial role in resolving the crisis. After being ordered by President Jackson in 1835 to pacify the Creek and Seminole Indians in Florida without sufficient supplies

and men, Scott was questioned by a board of inquiry for his failure and then exonerated of any wrongdoing. Ordered by President MARTIN VAN BUREN to engage British troops along the Maine-Canada border in the late 1830s, Scott won international recognition for his successful diplomatic handling of the emergency, which averted a war and led to a final settlement of the long-term boundary dispute in the Webster-Ashburton Treaty of 1842.

As general in chief of the army at the outbreak of the war with Mexico (see JAMES KNOX POLK), Scott devised a plan for winning the war, but Democratic president JAMES K. POLK did not want to allow the possibility of any more glory accruing to a potential political rival. Finally, once it became clear that a quick victory was not going to be attained and under pressure from Secretary of War WILLIAM L. MARCY and others, Polk relented and allowed Scott to implement his plan for a bold thrust directly at the heart of Mexico. The plan called for an amphibious assault on Veracruz and a march inland along the same route Cortés had used to attack the Aztecs in Mexico City. After overcoming tremendous logistical problems and defeating numerically superior Mexican armies in his path, Scott managed to occupy Mexico City on September 14, 1847. As soon as Mexico had been defeated, the Polk administration embarked on a campaign to discredit Scott's remarkable accomplishments in central Mexico. He was relieved of command and summoned to Washington to appear before a court of inquiry. He was cleared of all charges. A bill to promote him from general in chief of the army to lieutenant general was submitted, but because of Democratic political opposition it was not passed until 1855.

Although his name was mentioned several times as a possible Whig party candidate for president, it was not until 1852, when the party was disintegrating over the slavery issue, that he received the nomination. The Whigs hoped his military glory could carry him to the White House over the sectionalism tearing the party and nation apart. Although this strategy had worked earlier with the selection of ZACHARY TAYLOR, this time the Whig party miscalculated. Scott, brilliant as a general, was a poor campaigner. He was soundly defeated by Democrat FRANKLIN PIERCE.

After his election defeat, Scott remained as head of the army. When the Civil War began, he developed sound plans for the Union, including the blockade of Southern ports that was eventually taken up as part of the strategy. Conflict with General GEORGE MCCLELLAN, however, forced President ABRAHAM LINCOLN to allow him to retire in the fall of 1861.

BIBLIOGRAPHY

Elliot, Charles W., *Winfield Scott: The Soldier and the Man,* 1937; Scott, Winfield, *Memoirs of Lieutenant General Scott,* 1864; Smith, D. H. Arthur, *Old Fuss and Feathers: The Life of Winfield Scott,* 1937.

Sedgwick, Theodore

(May 9, 1746–January 24, 1813)
Speaker of the House, Senator, Representative

Theodore Sedgwick was born in West Hartford, Connecticut. He began his studies at Yale in 1761 but was expelled before graduation for misbehavior. After being admitted to the bar in 1766, he established a practice at Sheffield, Massachusetts. (In 1772, his B.A. degree was awarded by Yale and dated as if he had graduated with his class in 1765.)

Sedgwick's military participation in the American Revolution consisted of serving as General John Thomas's aid during the ill-fated invasion of Canada. From 1780 to 1788 he practiced law and served in the Massachusetts legislature, the last year as speaker of the house. From 1785 to 1788 Sedgwick was also a delegate to the Continental Congress and played a leading role in suppressing Shays's Rebellion in Massachusetts. In this 1786 incident, state troops were sent to put down an uprising, led by Daniel Shays, of destitute farmers who were unable to pay their taxes and were defying the state government.

After working to secure the adoption of the new federal Constitution, Sedgwick was elected to the U.S. House of Representatives. He served in the House until he was elected to the Senate in 1796. During his three years in the Senate, he was president pro tempore for several weeks in 1798. He returned to the House in 1799 as a Federalist supporter of JOHN ADAMS for one more two-year term and was elected Speaker. Although he served on numerous committees while in Congress, his most important accomplishment in the House occurred during the controversy that surrounded the ratification of Jay's Treaty (see JOHN JAY). Sedgwick played a major role in establishing the precedent that the Constitution did not grant the House the right to participate in treaty making.

In 1802 Sedgwick was appointed to the Massachusetts Supreme Court. He was still serving in this position at the time of his death.

BIBLIOGRAPHY

Welch, Richard E., Jr., *Theodore Sedgwick, Federalist: A Political Portrait*, 1965.

Seward, William Henry

(May 16, 1801–October 10, 1872)
Secretary of State, Senator

William Henry Seward's independent spirit influenced the course of American politics for almost half a century, from the election of JOHN QUINCY ADAMS through the administration of ANDREW JOHNSON.

Born in Florida, New York, Seward graduated from Union College in 1820 and was admitted to the New York bar in 1822. After establishing his practice in Auburn, New York, Seward entered politics as a strong supporter of "John Quincy Adams . . . and better government" in a state dominated by followers of THOMAS JEFFERSON.

Library of Congress

As a member of the New York Anti-Mason party, Seward was elected to the state senate in 1830. Defeated for reelection in 1833, he was nominated by the new Whig party for governor in 1834 but failed to win election. Running again in 1838, he was elected governor twice before an economic depression enabled the Democrats to regain control of the state legislature as well as the governor's office. While governor, he became strongly identified with the growing antislavery movement when he refused to surrender three black sailors for extradition to Virginia as runaway slaves.

A firmly committed antislavery advocate by 1848, Seward discovered that the public mood in New York had altered enough to enable his election to the U.S. Senate on an antislavery platform. When the old Whig party merged with the new Republicans in 1855, he became one of the most outspoken representatives of the antislavery North. As a U.S. senator from 1849 to 1861, Seward saw the slavery issue as "an irrepressible conflict" between North and South. He believed the issue of extending slavery into the territories was not negotiable because slavery was prohibited by "a higher law than the Constitution." He opposed the Compromise of 1850 (see HENRY CLAY and MILLARD FILLMORE), the Kansas-Nebraska Act (see FRANKLIN PIERCE), the Lecompton Constitution (see JAMES BUCHANAN and ROBERT JOHN WALKER), and the Dred Scott decision (see ROGER BROOKE TANEY).

Seward sought the Republican presidential nomination in 1860 and was deeply disappointed when the party chose ABRAHAM LINCOLN as its candidate instead. Nevertheless, he campaigned vigorously for Lincoln, and after Lincoln's election he accepted an appointment as secretary of state in 1861.

Seward undoubtedly felt superior to Lincoln. Shortly after assuming office, he wrote Lincoln a memo that made it clear he expected the president to treat him as the real leader of the administration. He told Lincoln to divert attention from American disunion by precipitating a war with Spain and France. If Lincoln didn't know how to perform this feat, Seward said he would handle the problem himself. Lincoln replied by reminding Seward that whatever had to be done by executive authority, as the president he would do it himself.

The relationship between Seward and Lincoln remained difficult; but there is no doubt that Seward's performance as secretary of state, first under Lincoln, then under Andrew Johnson, was exemplary. Well aware of the need for public support, he conducted all diplomatic correspondence with a keen appreciation for how it might influence public opinion. He skillfully averted European intervention in the Civil War (mainly through the efforts of CHARLES FRANCIS ADAMS, U.S. minister to Great Britain) and later secured France's promise of withdrawal from Mexico.

An expansionist at heart, he had opposed the purchase of Cuba in the 1850s because it conflicted with his antislavery views. After the Civil War the farsighted Seward negotiated the purchase of Alaska in 1867, an act that at the time was promptly dubbed "Seward's folly." Seward also anticipated the U.S. acquisition of Hawaii.

The night Lincoln was assassinated, Seward, who had been hurt earlier in a carriage accident and confined to his bed with much of his body in a cast, was also attacked by a knife-wielding coconspirator. (Seward's cast actually helped saved his life by deflecting some of the assailant's stabs long enough for Seward's cries to summon help.) After his recovery, instead of retiring, Seward drew on hidden reserves of energy and assumed a central role in the administration of Andrew Johnson.

Favoring a moderate Reconstruction policy, Seward staunchly supported President Johnson's conciliatory policy toward the South. He even traveled around the North with Johnson in 1866 and spoke on the president's behalf, at great cost to his own popularity, in order to demonstrate his support for Johnson's very poorly received policy speeches.

During the impeachment proceedings against Johnson, Seward remained loyal to the president. All efforts to entice him into the Radical camp were met with an emphatic "I will see you damned first." Retiring from public service in 1869, even though he was partially crippled, Seward traveled around the world. He returned to his Auburn, New York, home in 1871, where paralysis gradually overcame his once hardy constitution. He died on October 10, 1872.

BIBLIOGRAPHY

Baker, G. E. (ed.), *Works of William H. Seward*, 5 vols., 1853–1854; Bancroft, Frederic, *Life of W. H. Seward*, 1900; Seward, F. W. (ed.), *Autobiography of William H. Seward, 1801–1834*, 2 vols., 1877–1891; Van Deusen, Glyndon G., *William Henry Seward*, 1967.

Seymour, Horatio

(May 31, 1810–February 12, 1886)
Candidate for President

Born in Pompey Hill, New York, Seymour was educated at Geneva Academy (now Hobart College) and at a military school in Middletown, Connecticut. He also studied law at Utica, New York, and was admitted to the bar in 1832.

Seymour entered politics by serving as military secretary to New York governor WILLIAM L. MARCY for six years. He was elected state assemblyman in 1841, and became mayor of Utica the next year. In 1844 he reentered the assembly and, after pushing through important canal legislation, was elected speaker in 1845. Following the split in the New York Democratic party over the slavery issue in 1848, Seymour played an important role as arbitrator between the opposing groups.

Nominated six times for governor, he won the office twice, first in 1852 and again ten years later. Although opposed to ABRAHAM LINCOLN's election and the Emancipation Proclamation, he nevertheless supported restoration of the Union and urged loyalty to the president. As governor, he worked diligently to maintain the state's quota in Union forces and moved swiftly to quell antidraft riots in 1863. However, to the end of his life, he insisted that the extra-constitutional powers assumed by Lincoln's administration were the most dangerous issues to arise from the Civil War.

Aware of the difficulty in running against the popular war hero General ULYSSES S. GRANT, Seymour was not eager to be nominated for president by the Democrats in 1868. "I could not accept the nomination if tendered," he said at the Democratic convention that year. But when he was chosen on the twenty-second ballot as a compromise candidate between Eastern and Western Democrats, "the Great Decliner," as his enemies dubbed him, accepted. Seymour always felt that this was the greatest political blunder of his life. He campaigned vigorously but lost by over 300,000 votes.

After his defeat, Seymour continued to play an important role in the Democratic party, notably in his efforts to help SAMUEL TILDEN reform Tammany Hall (see WILLIAM MARCY TWEED) and end corrupt machine politics in New York City.

BIBLIOGRAPHY

Stewart, Mitchell, *Horatio Seymour*, 1938.

Sherman, James Schoolcraft

(October 24, 1855–October 30, 1912)
Vice President, Representative

Born in Utica, New York, in 1855, James Sherman earned his undergraduate and law degrees from Hamilton College in Clinton, New York. After being admitted to the state bar in 1879, he became a successful banker and businessman. In 1884 he was elected mayor of Utica as a Republican, and three years later he won a seat in the U.S. House of Representatives. He served as a member of Congress almost without interruption from 1887 until his election as WILLIAM H. TAFT's vice president in 1909.

Apparently uninterested in having his name associated with major legislation, Sherman concentrated his energy while in Congress upon perfecting parliamentary procedures. He wrote most of the measures proposed by the House Rules Committee between 1887 and 1909. His firm and fair manner when he presided over the House earned him the trust and respect of his colleagues; but when Speaker THOMAS BRACKETT REED retired, Sherman was unable to win enough votes to succeed him.

In 1906 Sherman was named chairman of the Republican congressional campaign committees; and in 1908, after THEODORE ROOSEVELT had selected Taft as his successor, Republican congressional leaders agreed upon Sherman for the vice presidency to balance the ticket. As vice president, he presided over the Senate with the same fairness and low profile he had perfected in his congressional career.

Sherman never complained about the lack of opportunity the vice presidency offered to establish his own political identity. When Taft, caught in the middle of a New York political battle between Sherman and Roosevelt, sided first with Sherman, then with Roosevelt, and finally blamed the fight on Sherman, the vice president dutifully kept quiet.

Taft had more than one reason to regret the renomination of Sherman as his running mate in 1912, the first vice president to be so honored since JOHN C. CALHOUN. Sherman died before the election, thus weakening an already losing cause.

BIBLIOGRAPHY

Biographical Directory of the American Congress, 1928; *New York Herald,* October 31, 1912; Sherman, James Schoolcraft, *Memorial Address Delivered at a Joint Session of the Senate and the House,* 1913; *Who's Who in America,* 1910–1911.

Sherman, John

(May 10, 1823–October 22, 1900)
Secretary of State, Secretary of the Treasury, Senator, Representative

In a political career that spanned almost half a century, John Sherman achieved virtually every political goal he desired and was awarded almost every honor the American political system can provide, except the presidency.

Born in Lancaster, Ohio, Sherman began the study of law at age fourteen. He was admitted to the bar in 1844 and established a practice in Mansfield, Ohio, before moving to Cleveland in 1853. Active in politics as a member of the Whig party and strongly opposed to slavery, Sherman helped to organize the new Republican party in Ohio after passage of the Kansas-Nebraska Act (see FRANKLIN PIERCE). In 1854 he was elected to the first of three successive terms in the House of Representatives. As chairman of the Ways and Means Committee, Sherman quickly rose to prominence in the House and played an important role in securing the enactment of the Morrill tariff of 1861, a protectionist tariff that sharply raised duties. In 1861 Sherman moved on to the Senate, where, with the exception of the four years he served as secretary of the treasury from 1877 to 1881, he would remain until 1897.

As chairman of the Senate Finance Committee, Sherman played a crucial role in formulating government financial policy during

Reconstruction. Although he had supported the use of paper money (greenbacks) during the Civil War, he deplored the inflationary effects of relying on anything but gold as the foundation of the nation's monetary system. In 1875 Sherman oversaw the enactment of the Specie Resumption Act, and while secretary of the treasury, he directed its successful implementation in 1879. Once again, the dollar, including the remaining greenbacks in circulation, was redeemable in gold.

Although unsuccessful in securing the Republican nomination for president in 1880, 1884, and 1888, Sherman gave his name to two important pieces of legislation passed in 1890: the Sherman Anti-Trust Act, which made it a crime for business firms to combine to prevent competition; and the Sherman Silver Purchase Act, which dramatically increased the amount of silver purchased by the federal government.

Library of Congress

The silver was to be used to back the printing of paper money, called treasury notes. The goal was to foster debt relief for farmers through inflation.

President WILLIAM MCKINLEY appointed Sherman secretary of state in 1897 in order to secure a seat in the Senate for his political adviser, MARCUS A. HANNA. The combination of Sherman's advanced age, failing memory, and opposition to the acquisition of overseas colonies as a result of the Spanish-American War led McKinley to request that Sherman resign from the cabinet in 1898.

BIBLIOGRAPHY

Burton, Theodore E., *John Sherman*, 1906; Sherman, John, *Recollections of Forty Years in the House, Senate, and Cabinet*, 2 vols., 1895; Thorndike, R. S. (ed.), *The Sherman Letters*, 1894.

Sherman, Roger

(April 19, 1721–July 23, 1793)
Senator, Representative

During a lifetime of dedicated public service, Roger Sherman earned the distinction of being the only American to help draft and sign the Continental Association of 1774, the Declaration of Independence, the Articles of Confederation, and the Constitution—the four historic documents of the American revolutionary period.

Born in Newton, Massachusetts, into humble circumstances, Sherman was largely self-taught. He earned a living as a cobbler before moving to New Milford, Connecticut, in 1743 to become a surveyor (from 1745 to 1758) and general store owner with his brother. In 1754 he was admitted to the Connecticut bar and one year later was elected to the colonial legislature. In 1761 he moved to New Haven, where he purchased a second store and then another in Wallingford. While building up his personal fortune, Sherman continued to serve in public office. With the exceptions of 1756 to 1757 and 1761 to 1764, he served until 1785 in the state legislature. Other offices he held included justice of the peace (1765 to 1766) and judge in the state superior court (1766 to 1788).

Although he supported the right of the colonists to protest British rule, Sherman at first opposed violent confrontation. During the Revolution, as a member of both the Connecticut legislature and the Continental Congress (from 1774 to 1781, and from 1783 to 1784), Sherman fought for adequate taxation to support the war effort and sound money. From 1784 to 1793 he served as mayor of New Haven.

At the Constitutional Convention in 1787 Sherman was one of the most outspoken advocates of a strong central government. He presented what became known as the Connecticut Compromise (see OLIVER ELLSWORTH) to resolve the issue of fair representation for large and small states in the new national legislature. The Connecticut plan called for establishing two houses of Congress—the House of Representatives, in which the composition would be determined by population, and the Senate, in which each state would have equal representation regardless of size or population. After helping to secure ratification of the Constitution in Connecticut, Sherman served two years in the House of Representatives (from 1789 to 1791) and two years in the U.S. Senate (from 1791 to 1793). He died in office.

BIBLIOGRAPHY

Boardman, Roger S., *Roger Sherman, Signer and Statesman*, 1938; Boutell, L. H., *Roger Sherman*, 1896.

Shultz, George Pratt

(December 13, 1920–   )
Secretary of State; Secretary of Labor; Secretary of the Treasury

George Shultz held three cabinet-level posts. A trained economist and specialist in labor relations, Shultz put his strong skills as a negotiator to use in service to five presidents.

Shultz was born in New York City. He graduated from Princeton University in 1942 and served in the Marines in the Pacific as an artillery officer. After obtaining his doctorate in industrial economics from the Massachusetts Institute of Technology (MIT) in 1949, he taught at MIT until 1955 and coauthored (with Charles Myers) a standard text in labor relations, *Dynamics of a Labor Market*.

In 1957 he became a professor at the Graduate School of Business at the University of Chicago and, five years later, the dean of the Graduate School of Business, a position he held until 1969. During this period he also developed an impressive record as an arbitrator of labor–management disputes and served as an economic and labor consultant in the administrations of DWIGHT EISENHOWER, JOHN KENNEDY, and LYNDON JOHNSON. Although a conservative Republican, he was well regarded both by business leaders, who liked his distaste for involving government officials in labor disputes, and by union officials, who appreciated his faith in collective bargaining.

In 1969 Republican president RICHARD NIXON chose Shultz to be secretary of labor. Shultz managed to maintain good relations with labor while in this position, even though he opposed raising the minimum wage and supported paying construction workers hired to meet racial minority quotas lower than union wages.

In June 1970 Nixon appointed Shultz to head the newly created Office of Management and Budget. In this post Shultz publicly supported, while privately disagreeing with, controversial Nixon economic policies that included a ninety-day wage and price freeze in 1971. In May 1972 he became secretary of the treasury, but his continuing disagreements with Nixon prompted his resignation in March 1974.

U.S. Department of State

From 1974 until he was appointed secretary of state by President RONALD REAGAN in 1982, Shultz was an executive of the Bechtel Corporation and president of the Bechtel Group, Inc., a huge engineering and construction firm based in San Francisco. While secretary of state from 1982 until 1989, Shultz followed a pragmatic, incremental approach to dealing with foreign affairs. He was never a member of Reagan's inner circle of advisers and threatened to resign several times when left out of important decisions (most notably the dispatching of American troops to Grenada in 1983; see RONALD WILSON REAGAN). Ironically, this isolation worked to his personal advantage, since it validated his claim in congressional testimony regarding the Iran-Contra scandal (see REAGAN and WILLIAM JOSEPH CASEY) that he had recommended during cabinet discussions not to proceed with exchanging weapons for American hostages held by pro-Iranian forces in Lebanon.

Shultz had his greatest diplomatic successes toward the end of the Reagan administration. In 1988 he helped to negotiate arms agreements with the Soviet Union, along with an agreement for the withdrawal of all Soviet forces from an eight-year occupation of Afghanistan (see JAMES EARL CARTER, JR.).

When asked how he had managed to emerge from both the Watergate (see RICHARD MILHOUS NIXON) and the Iran-Contra scandals with an enhanced image for honesty while so many around him lost credibility, Shultz replied: "The way to maintain your integrity is to act with integrity. I think it's very simple."

In 1989 Shultz retired to the Stanford University campus in Palo Alto, California, to serve as a part-time professor in the Graduate School of Business and to write his memoirs.

BIBLIOGRAPHY

Current Biography, 1988; Dam, Kenneth W., and George P. Shultz, *Economic Policy Beyond the Headlines,* 1977; Rees, Albert, and George P. Shultz, *Workers and Wages in the Urban Labor Market,* 1970; Shultz, George P., *Risk, Uncertainty, and Foreign Economic Policy,* 1981; Shultz, George P., and Arnold R. Weber, *Strategies for the Displaced Worker,* 1966; Shultz, George P., and Thomas L. Whisler (eds.), *Management Organization and the Computer,* 1960.

Simpson, Jerry

(March 31, 1842–October 23, 1905)
Representative

Kansas Populist party crusader Jerry Simpson was born in Westmoreland County, New Brunswick, Canada. Largely self-educated, he obtained a job as a cook on a Great Lakes boat at age fourteen and discovered a career. He rose through the ranks over the next decade to become a captain. In 1879 he traded the life on the lakes for a farm and sawmill near Holton, Kansas. He sold this property in 1884 and purchased a cattle ranch near Medicine Lodge, Kansas. Simpson lost his herd during a harsh winter, and he was forced by debts to become the town marshal.

While marshal, Simpson became involved in local politics. Originally a Republican, he switched his allegiance to the Union Labor party and made two unsuccessful efforts to win election to the state legislature in 1886 and 1888 before joining the new Populist (People's) party (see James Baird Weaver). Simpson's lack of success in his agricultural endeavors was mirrored across the West. He was a perfect representative of the fate of his neighbors and an ideal choice for the Populist party candidate for Congress in 1890.

While successfully campaigning for Congress, Simpson accused his well-dressed banker opponent of wearing silk stockings. A reporter sarcastically commented that Simpson was so crude he did not know enough to wear socks. Simpson shrewdly turned the hostile comment into a boast and nicknamed himself Sockless Jerry. It was the name by which he was known for the rest of his political career.

Simpson was reelected to Congress in 1892 but lost in 1894 due to a split in the Populist party. After the Populists united forces with the Democratic party in 1896 (see William Jennings Bryan), he was returned to Congress. He failed to win reelection to Congress in 1898 for a second time and, after proving unable to secure the endorsement of the Populist party convention for the Senate, retired from politics.

During his three terms in Congress, Simpson supported a graduated income tax; government ownership of railroad, telegraph, and telephone companies; paper money; shorter working hours for industrial laborers; and free silver coinage.

BIBLIOGRAPHY

Bicha, Karel D., "Jerry Simpson, Populist," *Journal of American History*, 1967; Diggs, A. L., *The Story of Jerry Simpson*, 1908.

Slidell, John

([unknown] 1793–July 29, 1871)
Diplomat, Senator, Representative

Diplomat, Louisiana Democratic party leader, and power behind the presidency for most of James Buchanan's administration, Slidell is chiefly remembered for his role in the *Trent* affair (see Charles Francis Adams and John Slidell) during the Civil War.

Slidell was born in New York City in 1793. He graduated from Columbia College in 1810 and went into the mercantile business. The embargo policy of the United States during the War of 1812 (see JAMES MADISON) forced his firm into bankruptcy, and Slidell moved to New Orleans in 1819. His commercial legal skills were in demand in New Orleans, and Slidell quickly established a successful law practice.

After losing his first bid to win a seat in Congress in 1828 as a Jacksonian Democrat, Slidell served as federal district attorney of New Orleans from 1829 to 1833. Two tries to win election to the Senate in 1834 and 1836 failed, but he won election to Congress in 1842 and served one term from 1843 to 1845. In Congress Slidell supported slavery and lower tariffs, except, as in the case of sugar, when tariffs protected a vital Louisiana commodity.

In 1844 Slidell helped JAMES K. POLK win Louisiana and therefore the presidency. President Polk appointed Slidell commissioner to Mexico shortly after taking office in 1845. Slidell's mission was to negotiate a settlement of the dispute over the southern border of the Republic of Texas (see JAMES KNOX POLK) and the purchase of New Mexico and California. Fearful of the political consequences of even meeting with Slidell to discuss such unpopular issues (Mexico did not recognize the independence of Texas), the Mexican government refused to accept his appointment. The failure of Slidell's mission paved the way for the U.S. decision to acquire the desired Mexican territory through military conquest (see JAMES KNOX POLK).

Slidell lost another race for the Senate in 1848, but he was successful on his fourth try in 1853. While a senator from 1853 until 1861, Slidell supported the Southern goals of repealing the Missouri Compromise (see HENRY CLAY) and acquiring Cuba to expand the number of slave states. A political opponent of STEPHEN A. DOUGLAS, Slidell was an early supporter of James Buchanan for president. In 1856, after having previously backed Buchanan as the Democratic party's nominee in 1848 and 1852, Slidell managed Buchanan's successful campaign for the presidency. Until the election of ABRAHAM LINCOLN in 1860 prompted the move toward secession, Slidell was Buchanan's closest adviser. His access to federal patronage also enabled him to control the Louisiana Democratic party at this time.

In 1861 JEFFERSON DAVIS appointed Slidell the Confederacy's minister to France. He and fellow Confederate diplomat JAMES M. MASON, the minister to England, were removed by the Union Navy from the British mail packet *Trent* on the high seas and held at Fort Warren in Boston. The incident almost precipitated a break in diplomatic relations between the United States and the British and French governments, but President Lincoln defused the crisis by allowing the agents to proceed to their destinations.

While Confederate minister to France, Slidell was never able to persuade the French government to recognize the independence of the Confederacy or to provide it with significant aid because Napoleon III refused to act without the support of England.

Slidell remained in Paris after the collapse of the Confederacy and died in July 1871.

BIBLIOGRAPHY

Sears, Louis M., *John Slidell*, 1925; Willson, Beckles, *Slidell in Paris*, 1932.

Smith, Alfred Emanuel

(December 30, 1873–October 4, 1944)
Candidate for President

After establishing a reputation as a reform governor in New York, Alfred E. Smith became the first Roman Catholic ever nominated for president by a major American political party.

Reared in poverty on New York City's Lower East Side, Smith had to leave school in his teens and go to work as a newsboy and a fish market employee. He entered politics in 1894 as a campaign worker for an opponent of the Tammany Hall (see WILLIAM MARCY TWEED) political machine's candidate for mayor. Smith's candidate did not win, but another reform candidate did. Smith was rewarded for his anti–Tammany Hall campaign efforts with a patronage position as a legal documents process server.

Smith's views toward Tammany Hall gradually mellowed, and in 1903 he was elected to the state assembly with the support of the organization. Ten years later, he was chosen speaker. In 1911 Smith was appointed to a special commission to investigate working conditions in factories. Reform legislation he recommended that eventually became law included sanitary, health, and fire laws; minimum wage and working hour regulations for women and children; and improved workmen's compensation laws.

At the state constitutional convention in 1915, Smith's work on behalf of budget reform and home rule for New York City won the admiration of many senior politicians in the state as well as of political reporters. "He has," said

Library of Congress

FRANKLIN D. ROOSEVELT, "a marvelous faculty for cutting the Gordian knots of argument . . . with the sharp sword of common sense."

In the fall of 1915 the popular Smith was elected sheriff of New York City and, in 1917, president of New York City's board of aldermen. One year later, with the support of both Tammany Hall and reform elements in the Democratic party, Smith was elected to the first of four terms as governor. Due to a Republican landslide in 1920, Smith was not re-elected, but he was returned to office in 1922, 1924, and 1926.

As governor, Smith earned a reputation as an honest and progressive administrator with a flair for appealing to New York's working class. He refused to give up his Lower East Side pronunciation of words, such as "raddio" for radio, and seemed to be always wearing a brown derby hat and smoking a cigar. His greatest accomplishment in office was securing the passage of a constitutional amendment that enabled him to reorganize the cumbersome machinery of the state government into a modern, efficient bureaucracy. This feat, plus the social welfare legislation he supported for women, children, the insane, and factory workers, made him immensely popular.

A logical choice to be a Democratic party candidate for president, Smith made his first unsuccessful run for the nomination in 1924. It was during this campaign that supporter Franklin Roosevelt described him with a name that stuck, the "Happy Warrior," in honor of his enthusiasm.

Unable to win the nomination then because of his support for the repeal of Prohibition and prejudice against his Catholic faith, Smith made another—this time successful—try in 1928 but lost the general election to HERBERT HOOVER. Many pundits agreed with H. L. Mencken that the reason Smith lost was because "those who fear the Pope outnumber those who are tired of the Anti-Saloon League," but it is unlikely that any Democratic candidate would have been able to win the presidency when the nation had experienced almost a decade of peace and prosperity under Republican leadership.

Smith was a man of many parts: He was a reformer, a machine politician, a devout Roman Catholic, a technocrat, and a cigar-chomping man of the people. As such, he appealed to many people and had a powerful state and national impact on American politics. Although Smith lost by a wide margin in 1928, he did very well in large urban centers in the North and Midwest. This pattern reflected the dramatically rising voter-participation rates of immigrants and their children. The coalescing of these voters into a coherent ideological and electoral block was a critical component of Roosevelt's liberal New Deal coalition. The election of 1928, in other words, showed the New Deal coalition in the making. Also, an unusually large number of New Deal administrators came out of New York (FRANCES

PERKINS is a prominent example) and had first gained their experience as Smith appointees. New York under Smith had become a laboratory for social welfare reform, and many of the successful policies and implementors went on to national prominence during the New Deal.

After 1928 Smith never ran for public office again. Instead, he became president of the Empire State Building Corporation, the company that built and managed the Empire State Building. His political opinions became increasingly conservative during the Great Depression, and he emerged as one of Roosevelt's most ardent critics. Smith labeled Roosevelt's oratorical appeals to the common citizen demagogic and considered the New Deal's programs to be experiments in socialism that, instead of ending the depression, would only increase the power of the federal government's mushrooming bureaucracy. In 1936 and 1940 Smith supported Roosevelt's Republican opponents and only renewed his friendship with Roosevelt during World War II.

BIBLIOGRAPHY

Freidel, Frank (ed.), *Governor Alfred E. Smith: The Politician as Reformer*, 1981; Handlin, Oscar, *Al Smith and His America*, 1987; Josephson, Matthew, and Hannah Josephson, *Al Smith: Hero for the Cities*, 1969; O'Connor, Richard, *The First Hurrah*, 1970; Smith, Alfred E., *Up to Now*, 1929.

Smith, Margaret Madeline Chase

(December 14, 1897–   )
Senator, Representative

Margaret Chase Smith is the only woman ever elected to four successive terms in the U.S. Senate.

Margaret Chase was born in Skowhegan, Maine. Unable to afford to attend college, she worked as a teacher and in a number of different business office management positions before marrying Clyde Harold Smith in 1930. When he was elected to the U.S. House of Representatives in 1936, Smith became her husband's secretary and, after his death in 1940, his successor in Congress. She was reelected in 1942, 1944, and 1946.

During her eight years in the House, Smith supported New Deal social legislation, worked to improve the status of women in the armed forces, and opposed making the House Un-American Activities Committee a permanent body.

In 1947 Smith won the first of four successive terms in the Senate. As a senator, she continued the same independent voting pattern she had established in the House. Smith frequently supported liberal Democratic domestic programs, and advocated a strong military and firm anticommunist foreign policy. In 1950, in a "declaration of conscience" that was formulated and signed by Smith and six other Republicans, she attacked fellow Republican JOSEPH MCCARTHY's anticommunist guilt-by-association and intimidation tactics. She said, "I don't want to see the Republican party ride to political victory on the four horsemen of calumny—fear, ignorance, bigotry, and smear."

Although frequently mentioned as a Republican vice presidential possibility, the offer was never extended. Smith retired from politics after losing her bid to win reelection to a fifth Senate term in 1972.

BIBLIOGRAPHY

Clymer, Eleanor, and Lillian Erlich, *Modern American Career Women*, 1959; *Ladies Home Journal*, January 1961; *National Business Woman*, October 1960; *Time*, September 5, 1960.

Smith, Robert

(November 3, 1757–November 26, 1842)
Secretary of State, Secretary of the Navy

Robert Smith was born in Lancaster, Pennsylvania. After graduating from the College of New Jersey (now Princeton University) in 1781, he studied law and was admitted to the bar in Baltimore, Maryland. Smith quickly established a successful practice in Baltimore that specialized in admiralty cases. From 1793 to 1798 he was a member of the state legislature, and was appointed by President THOMAS JEFFERSON as secretary of the navy in 1801.

As secretary of the navy, Smith worked diligently to enforce the Embargo Act of 1807, even though he felt that the effort to influence the actions of France and England through restrictions on American trade was counterproductive and doomed to failure.

President JAMES MADISON appointed Smith secretary of state in 1809. Smith became increasingly convinced of the futility of forcing trade restrictions upon American commerce to change British behavior during the Napoleonic Wars, and debates at cabinet meetings between Smith and Madison over the continuation of the trade restriction approach grew increasingly strident. Smith realized that Napoleon was taking advantage of the situation to manipulate the United States into a confrontation with England. Madison, wanting to believe that France was acting in good faith in response to the pressure of reduced trade with the United States, refused to believe Smith's warning. Instead, the president accepted Napoleon's statement that he would cease all French interference with American maritime trade and ordered the resumption of American shipping to France while ordering a halt in February 1811 to all trade with Great Britain and its colonies (see JAMES MADISON).

Relations between Smith and Madison's principal ally in the cabinet, Secretary of the Treasury ALBERT GALLATIN, though never good, deteriorated to such a degree that Gallatin submitted his resignation to Madison in March 1811. An enraged Madison declined to accept Gallatin's resignation and, in a private meeting with Smith, vented his frustrations over Smith's discordant behavior, alleged inefficiency, and breach of trust. Smith resigned as secretary of state, returned to Baltimore, and published a scathing indictment of the president's treatment of him that effectively ended Smith's political career.

BIBLIOGRAPHY

Bemis, Samuel F., *American Secretaries of State and Their Diplomacy*, 1929.

Stanton, Edwin McMasters

(December 19, 1814–December 24, 1869)
Secretary of War, Attorney General

Over the course of a single decade, Edwin M. Stanton served in the cabinets of JAMES BUCHANAN, ABRAHAM LINCOLN, and ANDREW JOHNSON. As secretary of war, he played a crucial role in ensuring the success of President Lincoln's goal of reunifying the nation through military victory.

Born in Steubenville, Ohio, Stanton attended Kenyon College in Gambier, Ohio, from 1831 to 1834. Unable to earn enough money to complete his studies, Stanton studied law in his guardian's office until being admitted to the bar in 1836. His quick mind, attention to detail, and industriousness enabled him to establish a reputation as an expert in complex criminal, patent, and land title litigations. Stanton began his increasingly prosperous law practice in Ohio, moved to Pittsburgh, Pennsylvania, in 1847, and nine years later settled in Washington, D.C.

Prior to 1860 Stanton had held only two minor political offices: prosecuting attorney of Harrison County, Ohio, from 1837 to 1839, and reporter of Ohio Supreme Court decisions from 1842 to 1845. Acting as U.S. counsel in 1858, Stanton's masterful handling of fraudulent California land claims won him an appointment as President Buchanan's attorney general in 1860. At cabinet meetings Stanton advised Buchanan to take a much firmer stand against secession than the president was willing to risk in the waning months of his term (see JAMES BUCHANAN). Nevertheless, Stanton was a supportive lieutenant. Buchanan wrote of him in 1862: "He was always on my side and flattered me ad nauseam."

A staunch Unionist, Stanton supported JOHN C. BRECKINRIDGE for president in 1860 in the hope that his election would prevent the country from splitting apart over slavery. Lincoln, who had had the opportunity to observe Stanton's qualities while working on a patent case in 1856, chose Stanton to be his new secretary of war in 1862, replacing SIMON CAMERON. Lincoln needed a patriotic, able, and energetic administrator to manage the bloated and inefficient War Department. Both men were suspicious of each other's motives at the start, but respect and trust gradually evolved. In the course of vigorously pursuing the daunting task of managing the War Department during the Civil War, Stanton's honesty and vigorous administration won the president's admiration.

Short-tempered with subordinates who could not perform as diligently and efficiently as he, Stanton set high standards for performance and honesty. He systematized troop organization and disbursement procedures, investigated corrupt contractors, and virtually eliminated patronage appointments to obtain critically essential military efficiency. There is no doubt that his ability to master massive amounts of detail and to make quick decisions was a decisive factor in ensuring civilian control of the immense military force recruited during the war while at the same time improving its combat effectiveness.

What supporters saw as decisive and bold behavior often led critics to attack Stanton for arrogance and brutality. ULYSSES S. GRANT, who saw the dark side of the secretary of war when Stanton publicly, and unnecessarily harshly, rebuked William T. Sherman for exceeding his authority in granting surrender terms to Confederate General Joseph E. Johnston, said Stanton "cared nothing for the feeling of others" and seemed to find it more pleasurable "to disappoint than to gratify."

After Lincoln's assassination, President Andrew Johnson made the mistake of retaining Stanton in office even though it became increasingly clear that Stanton supported the Radical Republicans' Reconstruction program and not Johnson's conciliatory approach. Finally, in August 1867, after months of squabbling, Johnson suspended Stanton from office in spite of Stanton's supporters in Congress who had passed the Tenure of Office Act, which forbade the president from dismissing a cabinet officer without the consent of the Senate. Encouraged by Radical congressional leaders eager to force a political confrontation with a president they despised, Stanton refused to vacate his post until after the effort to remove Johnson from office by impeachment had failed (see ANDREW JOHNSON).

In 1867 Stanton explained his decision to remain in office on the grounds that, as a cabinet department head, he was not "bound to accord with the President on all grave questions of policy or administration"; but after the impeachment trial of Johnson, Stanton admitted that "he had never doubted the constitutional right of the President to remove members of his Cabinet without question from any quarter whatever."

President Grant nominated Stanton as an associate justice of the Supreme Court in 1869, but the fifty-five-year-old Stanton died before he could take his seat.

BIBLIOGRAPHY

Gorham, George C., *Life and Public Services of Edwin M. Stanton*, 2 vols., 1899; Thomas, Benjamin P., and H. M. Hyman, *Stanton*, 1962.

Stettinius, Edward Riley, Jr.

(October 22, 1900–October 31, 1949)
Secretary of State, Diplomat

Industrialist and diplomat Edward R. Stettinius, Jr., was secretary of state during the last years of World War II and the first U.S. ambassador to the United Nations.

Born in Chicago, Illinois, Stettinius attended, but did not graduate from, the University of Virginia. A successful financier and businessman, Stettinius left his position as a vice president at General Motors in 1934 to join U.S. Steel. One year after becoming chairman of the board at U.S. Steel in 1938, he accepted an appointment to the War Resources Board. He resigned from private industry in 1940 to devote all his attention to government service.

After a year on the Council of National Defense, in which he successfully encouraged the development of synthetic rubber, and two years as administrator of the lend-lease program (see FRANKLIN DELANO ROOSEVELT), he became under secretary of state in 1943. Appointed secretary of state in 1944, Stettinius became one of President Franklin D. Roosevelt's most trusted advisers at the important Yalta Conference in 1945. There, Roosevelt, Winston Churchill, and Joseph Stalin agreed on the terms of the Soviet Union's entry into the war against Japan and on the plans for the United Nations; the three also attempted (with considerably less success) to define the territorial boundaries and political characters of postwar Poland and Germany.

Stettinius helped found the United Nations (UN) as leader of the U.S. delegation to the UN charter conference at San Francisco in April 1945. In June he resigned his position as secretary of state to become the first U.S. delegate to the United Nations. He left that post in 1946 to become rector of the University of Virginia.

BIBLIOGRAPHY

Walker, Richard, L., *Edward R. Stettinius, Jr., 1944–1945,* 1965.

Stevens, Thaddeus

(April 4, 1792–August 11, 1868)
Representative

Thaddeus Stevens led the Radical Republicans in Congress during the Reconstruction period and was the primary instigator in the impeachment of President ANDREW JOHNSON.

Born in Danville, Vermont, Stevens grew up in poverty after his father abandoned the family. Although a sickly child, Stevens refused to allow his financial and physical handicaps to quell his ambition. He gained admission to Dartmouth College and after graduating in 1814 moved to Pennsylvania. He was admitted to the bar in that state in 1816 and established a law practice in Gettysburg.

Stevens invested his earnings in local real estate and the relatively unprofitable char-

Library of Congress

coal-iron industry. He began his political career in 1833 in the state legislature, where he served until 1841 as a member of the Federalist party, taking stands against slavery and freemasonry. He quickly established a reputation as an aggressive, fiercely uncompromising leader in Pennsylvania affairs. In addition to protecting banking interests, Stevens supported extending the free public school system of Philadelphia throughout the state in 1834. When public reaction set in against increased taxes in 1835, he helped to prevent the repeal of the free school law "as an act for branding and marking the poor."

During this period Stevens, a determined abolitionist, defended fugitive slaves free of charge. He once reportedly paid $300 to secure the release of a hotel servant who was about to be sold away from his family.

After eight years in the state legislature, Stevens was elected to the House of Representatives as a Whig in 1848 and served until 1853. Opposed to the Compromise of 1850 (see HENRY CLAY and MILLARD FILLMORE), he was especially virulent and caustic in his denunciation of the Fugitive Slave Law, taunting Southerners for devoting their lives "to selecting and grooming the most lusty sires and the most fruitful wenches to supply the slave barracoons." After leaving the House in 1853 in disgust over the moderation of his colleagues on the slave issue, Stevens joined the new Republican party in 1856. Reelected to the House in 1858 as a Republican, Stevens used his sarcastic wit, knowledge of parliamentary procedure, and eloquence to become the leader of the Radical Republicans. First as the chairman of the Ways and Means Committee, then as the head of the Appropriations Committee, Stevens commanded tremendous authority in the House until his death in 1868.

Stevens's passion earned him the admiration of many of his colleagues. However, his stubbornness, harsh language, and vindictive nature, while making him a formidable adversary, prevented him from achieving greatness. As chairman of the House Ways and Means Committee during the Civil War, Stevens urged President ABRAHAM LINCOLN to deal harshly with the "rebels" of the South ("Oh, for six months of stern old [ANDREW] JACKSON!" was one of his frequent admonitions). He called for the emancipation of all slaves and the confiscation of planter estates in the South to be divided into small farms for the freed slaves.

During the Civil War, Stevens helped to secure the passage of increased protective tariffs, encouraged the construction of railroads through government subsidies, backed the issuing of paper (greenback) money, and fought to allow blacks to enlist in the Union army.

After Andrew Johnson became president, Stevens served on the Joint Committee on Reconstruction, where he openly battled against the conciliatory policies of the president (see ANDREW JOHNSON). He succeeded in imposing military reconstruction on the South, which he viewed as a "conquered province" with which Congress could do as it pleased. However, more moderate Republicans, like LYMAN TRUMBULL and William Pitt Fessenden, played a more important role in crucial facets of Reconstruction than radicals like Stevens and CHARLES SUMNER.

It was Stevens who introduced the resolution in the House calling for the impeachment of President Johnson. However, his failing health prevented him from taking part in the trial itself. Deeply depressed by the president's acquittal, Stevens died shortly thereafter.

BIBLIOGRAPHY

Brodie, Fawn M., *Thaddeus Stevens*, 1959; Current, Richard, *Old Thad Stevens*, 1942.

Stevenson, Adlai Ewing

(October 23, 1835–June 14, 1914)
Vice President, Representative

Born in Christian County, Kentucky, Adlai Ewing Stevenson became a successful lawyer in Illinois. He was almost forty when he won a seat as a Democrat in the House of Representatives in 1874. During two nonconsecutive terms in Congress in the 1870s, Stevenson represented the low-tariff, pro-silver money views of Midwestern farmers and laborers.

As first assistant postmaster general during President GROVER CLEVELAND's first (1885–1889) term, Stevenson carried out the unpleasant task of removing over 40,000 Republican postmasters in order to provide jobs for Democratic party workers.

A strong supporter of Cleveland, who favored "hard money" or the gold standard, Stevenson was placed on the ticket in 1892 to please "soft money" or silver standard supporters. Stevenson presided over the Senate with tact and diplomacy, loyally supporting the administration in spite of his opposite economic views.

Stevenson ran for vice president on the unsuccessful 1900 Democratic ticket headed by WILLIAM JENNINGS BRYAN, and in 1908 he lost a close race for governor of Illinois before retiring from public life. His grandson, ADLAI E. STEVENSON (III), was twice an unsuccessful presidential candidate in the 1950s.

BIBLIOGRAPHY

Stevenson, Adlai Ewing, *Memoirs*, 1909.

Stevenson, Adlai Ewing

(February 5, 1900–July 14, 1965)
Diplomat, Candidate for President

Adlai Stevenson was the Democratic party's presidential nominee in the elections of 1952 and 1956. His principal significance lay, according to political historian Theodore H. White, in placing the "virus of morality in the bloodstream of both parties." Condemning the use of "soft soap, slogans, gimmicks, bandwagons, and all the other infernal machines of modern politics" as "contempt for people's intelligence, common sense, and dignity," Stevenson introduced wit, masterful command of the language, and moral tone in contemporary American presidential campaigning.

Stevenson, grandson of ADLAI EWING STEVENSON, who was GROVER CLEVELAND's vice president, ran twice for the presidency as a Democrat against a man he knew he could not beat, popular World War II military hero DWIGHT D. EISENHOWER.

Born in Los Angeles and raised in Bloomington, Illinois, Stevenson grew up in a house frequented by famous politicians and intellectuals. His father was active in Illinois politics and saw to it that Stevenson's intellectual development was enhanced by frequent trips throughout America and to Europe. Stevenson graduated from Princeton University in

1922 and then attended Harvard Law School for two years before returning to Cincinnati to work briefly as a newspaper reporter. He completed his law studies at Northwestern University in 1926 and immediately began a law career in Chicago, but he never enjoyed making money and winning cases as much as performing public service.

Stevenson's government career began in 1933 when he went to Washington, D.C., to work in the New Deal Agricultural Adjustment Administration. In 1934 he became chief attorney of the newly created Federal Alcohol Control Administration, a position he left the following year to return to Chicago and resume his law practice. He maintained his interest in politics by becoming active in the Chicago Council on Foreign Relations and was elected its president in 1935.

During the next few years, Stevenson developed a reputation as a superb speaker on foreign affairs. In June 1940, in the face of tremendous antiwar sentiment throughout the country, he agreed to chair the controversial Committee to Defend America by Aiding the Allies. In 1941 he became principal attorney for Secretary of the Navy WILLIAM FRANKLIN (FRANK) KNOX. This position required him to serve as Secretary Knox's speech writer and representative on various interagency committees. In late 1943 and early 1944, he headed a mission to Italy to determine what relief role the Foreign Economic Administration should play there. The next year he transferred to the State Department and participated in the preparatory conferences for the founding of the United Nations (UN). He served as a UN delegate in 1946 and 1947.

United Nations

In 1948 Stevenson was elected governor of Illinois. During his four-year administration, he drew able people into the state government and improved the police force, highway and educational systems, and welfare programs. He vetoed an anticommunist measure because he regarded it as "more dangerous to ourselves than to our foes" and sent in the National Guard to Cicero in 1951 to defend blacks from white rioters.

Although Stevenson preferred to serve a second term as governor, he accepted a draft by the Democratic party to be the candidate for president in 1952. Stevenson's carefully crafted, well-reasoned speeches were no match for Dwight D. Eisenhower's popularity. Too many people perceived him as an "egghead," as soft on communism, and as too progressive on civil rights. He won only nine states, losing 442 electoral votes to 89; but his campaign was not a failure for the nation. Stevenson's enthusiasm and affection for campaigning attracted many young people into politics. He especially appealed to young liberals. His second try for the presidency in 1956 resulted in an even more lopsided defeat. He won only 73 electoral votes. In 1960 he reluctantly agreed to try a third time for the nomination, but the Democratic convention selected the dynamic JOHN F. KENNEDY instead.

Stevenson wanted to be secretary of state in the Kennedy administration, but President Kennedy appointed him ambassador to the United Nations, the post Stevenson wanted least. Ironically, it was while serving at the UN and appearing in nationally televised sessions that millions of Americans first grew to appreciate Stevenson's intellectual abilities and forthrightness. During the Cuban Missile Crisis in 1962 (see JOHN F. KENNEDY), when Soviet Ambassador Valerian Zorin hedged on answering Stevenson's questions regarding the presence of Russian missiles in Cuba, Stevenson indignantly cried, "I am prepared to wait until hell freezes over!"

Though Stevenson agilely defended American policies, he never had the opportunity he hoped for to help shape the foreign policies of the Kennedy or LYNDON JOHNSON administrations. The result was that he was placed in the awkward position of having to argue at the UN for actions he did not agree with, such as the invasion of Cuba in 1961 and the invasion of the Dominican Republic in 1965. Stevenson remained silent when his advice was misrepresented, as when President Kennedy told reporters Stewart Alsop and Charles L. Bartlett that "Adlai had wanted a Munich" and had recommended capitulating to the Soviets during the missile crisis. Actually, Stevenson had

suggested trying to negotiate for the removal of all Soviet military bases in Cuba before ordering air strikes. (President Kennedy ordered an embargo and did negotiate. Air strikes were not employed.)

In 1965, just when Stevenson had decided it was time to retire so that he could "sit in the shade with a glass of wine . . . and watch the people dance," he was stricken by a fatal heart attack in London.

BIBLIOGRAPHY

Cochran, Bert, *Adlai Stevenson: Patrician Among Politicians,* 1969; Martin, John B., *Adlai Stevenson and the World,* 1977; Ross, Lillian, *Adlai Stevenson,* 1966; Stevenson, Adlai, *Major Campaign Speeches of Adlai Stevenson,* 1952, and *Putting First Things First: A Democratic View,* 1960; Walton, Richard J., *The Remnants of Power: The Tragic Last Years of Adlai Stevenson,* 1968.

Stevenson, Andrew

(January 21, 1784–January 25, 1857)
Diplomat, Speaker of the House, Representative

Andrew Stevenson was born in Culpeper County, Virginia. After graduating from the College of William and Mary, he studied law, was admitted to the bar, and established a practice in Richmond.

Stevenson was elected to the Virginia House of Delegates in 1809 and served, with the exception of 1817, until 1821. After two unsuccessful campaigns for Congress in 1814 and 1816, he was finally elected to the U.S. House of Representatives in 1821. A Jacksonian Democrat (see ANDREW JACKSON), Stevenson was elected Speaker of the House in 1827 with the help of MARTIN VAN BUREN and re-

tained his post until his resignation from Congress in 1834.

During the nullification controversy (see JOHN CALDWELL CALHOUN), Stevenson supported the supremacy of the national government and played an important role in ensuring that Virginia did not follow South Carolina's separatist stance. He supported Van Buren for vice president in 1832 and for president in 1836.

In 1834 Stevenson was nominated to be minister to Great Britain by President Andrew Jackson, but partisan politics prevented his confirmation by the Senate until 1836. He served in London until 1841 without incident except for one embarrassing mistake: he advised British investors that the campaign to destroy the Bank of the United States (see NICHOLAS BIDDLE and ROGER BROOKE TANEY) would fail. Although he remained active politically upon his return to the United States, his influence waned, and hopes of obtaining an appointment in the JAMES K. POLK administration never materialized.

BIBLIOGRAPHY

Adams, John Q., *The Memoirs of John Quincy Adams*, vols. 6–12, 1875–1877; Ambler, C. H., *Sectionalism in Virginia*, 1910; Bassett, C. H., *The Life of Andrew Jackson*, 1967; Bowers, C. B., *The Party Battles of the Jackson Period*, 1922; McMaster, J. B., *A History of the People of the U.S.*, vol. 6, 1906.

Stimson, Henry Lewis

(September 21, 1867–October 20, 1950)
Secretary of State, Secretary of War, Diplomat

During the exhausting around-the-clock workdays of World War II, Secretary of War Stimson was described by another cabinet-level colleague and confidant of President FRANKLIN D. ROOSEVELT as a "heroic figure of sincerity and strength." In the course of his long career in public service, Stimson served in the cabinets of two Republican and two Democratic presidents.

Henry Lewis Stimson was born in New York City. He graduated from Yale University in 1888 and, after completing his legal studies at Harvard Law School in 1890, became an attorney in fellow Republican ELIHU ROOT's New York law firm. In 1906 President THEODORE ROOSEVELT appointed Stimson to his first governmental office, U.S. attorney for the Southern District of New York. Stimson left this post in 1909 to run for public office.

In 1910 he won the Republican nomination for governor of New York but lost in the general election. The following year President WILLIAM HOWARD TAFT appointed Stimson secretary of war. Stimson served as secretary of war until 1913, when he returned to private law practice. During World War I he joined the army and served as a colonel in the artillery in France. He then returned to New York City to practice law.

In 1927 President CALVIN COOLIDGE sent Stimson to arbitrate an election and reestablish a constitutional government in Nicaragua, then occupied by U.S. troops. From 1900 on, the United States had frequently intervened in Latin America to protect American investments, to cripple radical movements, and to defend countries against real or imagined European aggressors. Stimson's adroit handling of that difficult assignment led Coolidge to appoint him governor of the Philippines. Two years later, President HERBERT HOOVER chose Stimson to be secretary of state.

As secretary of state, Stimson headed the American delegations to the London Naval Conference in 1930 and the Geneva Disarmament Conference in 1932. At these conferences agreements to adhere to restrictions on the development and deployment of military weapons were negotiated. The Japanese invasion of Manchuria in 1931 led to his announcement of what became known as the Stimson Doctrine, under which the United States refused to recognize the annexation of territory through aggression. He returned to private law practice in 1933 but continued to speak out on foreign policy issues.

Stimson's advocacy of aid to Great Britain at the outbreak of World War II and President

Franklin D. Roosevelt's desire to form a bipartisan cabinet led Roosevelt to appoint Stimson, identified as a conservative corporate lawyer, as secretary of war in 1940. Roosevelt's appointment of Stimson also reflected the ebbing of New Deal liberal energies and of Roosevelt's decision to exchange his "Dr. New Deal" hat for a "Dr. Win-the-War" one. When questioned how he, a Republican, could support the policies of the Democratic Roosevelt administration, Stimson replied: "I have abandoned everything except a consideration of the defense of the country."

As secretary of war, Stimson energetically oversaw the creation of the mammoth American military-industrial complex. "If you are going to try to go to war, or to prepare for war, in a capitalist country," he once explained, "you have got to let business make money out of the process or business won't work." Under Stimson's leadership, with Roosevelt's support, the government offered enormous inducements to American industry to retool for the war effort and thereby reinvigorated American capitalism after more than a decade of depression. Many of Stimson's appointments were "dollar-a-year-men," corporation executives who were paid only one dollar a year but were allowed to remain on their corporation payrolls while in government service. This further strengthened government–business ties.

In 1945, as the chief presidential adviser on atomic policy, Stimson recommended the dropping of atomic bombs on Japanese cities. He later defended his controversial recommendation as necessary to avoid the sacrificing of American soldiers in a costly invasion. After his retirement at the end of World War II in September 1945, President HARRY TRUMAN awarded Stimson the Distinguished Service Medal.

BIBLIOGRAPHY

Current, Richard N., *Secretary Stimson, A Study in Statecraft*, 1954; Ferrell, Robert H., *Kellogg and Stimson*, 1961; Morison, Elting E., *Turmoil and Tradition: Henry L. Stimson*, 1960; Rappaport, Armin, *Henry L. Stimson and Japan: 1931–1933*, 1963; Stimson, Henry L., *On Active Service in Peace and War*, 1948.

Stockton, Richard

(October 1, 1730–February 28, 1781)
Revolutionary Leader

Patriot and signer of the Declaration of Independence Richard Stockton was born near Princeton, New Jersey, into a prominent family. He graduated from the College of New Jersey (now Princeton University) in 1748, was admitted to the bar in 1754, and practiced law in New Jersey.

After he returned from a trip to England and Scotland in 1767 in his role as trustee of the College of New Jersey, Stockton, who had previously avoided public service, began to play a prominent role in New Jersey politics. In 1768 he was appointed to the state legislature, and six years later to the supreme court of New Jersey.

Politically a moderate, Stockton at first advocated reconciliation with England; but in 1774, after the closing of the Port of Boston, he wrote and sent to Lord Dartmouth "An Expedient for the Settlement of the American Disputes," in which he argued for the necessity of establishing a plan of self-government for the American colonies as independent states free of parliamentary rule. Unless such a plan was implemented, he warned, war would be unavoidable. Stockton's document was utilized in formulating the petition of the Continental Congress to the king in July 1775. The lack of success in appealing to the British Crown led Stockton, after he became a member of the Continental Congress in 1776, to advocate a declaration of independence.

While he was in Congress, Stockton was nominated for governor of New Jersey. He and William Livingston received the same number of votes in the state legislature, so it was decided to make Livingston governor and Stockton chief justice of the supreme court. Stockton declined the honor in order to continue his work in Congress.

During the summer of 1776 Stockton served on a number of important congressional committees. In the fall of that year he was appointed to inspect the condition of the soldiers in the northern army. Caught by surprise in the British invasion of New Jersey, Stockton was captured while attempting to ensure the safety of his family. Imprisoned in New York during the bitter cold of winter with insufficient clothing and shelter, his health rapidly deteriorated. Congress eventually managed to secure his release through a prisoner exchange, but it was too late: Stockton never regained his strength and remained an invalid until his death a few years later.

BIBLIOGRAPHY

Stockton, T. C., *The Stockton Family of New Jersey*, 1911.

Stone, Harlan Fiske

(October 11, 1872–April 22, 1946)
Attorney General, Chief Justice of the Supreme Court, Associate Justice of the Supreme Court

Harlan Fiske Stone's philosophy about the law and the role of the Supreme Court in American society led him to concur with the thrust of the dissents of OLIVER WENDELL HOLMES and LOUIS BRANDEIS, and to play a vital role in paving the way for the revolutionary decisions of the Court under EARL WARREN.

Stone was born in Chesterfield, New Hampshire. He graduated from Amherst College in 1894 and, after completing his legal studies at Columbia University in 1898 and being admitted to the bar, practiced law in New York City while teaching at Columbia. By 1910 he had become the dean of the Columbia School of Law. During his fourteen years as dean of the law school he continued to teach and earned a reputation as a superb law instructor.

During World War I Stone served on the national board created by President WOODROW WILSON to determine the legitimacy of the claims of conscientious objectors.

Stone left Columbia in February 1923 to devote himself to his private legal practice. In April 1924 President CALVIN COOLIDGE appointed Stone attorney general. Stone's assignment was to restore the image of the department that was tarnished by the Teapot Dome scandal (see WARREN GAMALIEL HARDING). In less than a year in office, he appointed J. EDGAR HOOVER as the new director of the Federal Bureau of Investigation (FBI) and reorganized the FBI along the lines of Scotland Yard. He also initiated an antitrust suit against the Aluminum Corporation of America. In March 1925 President Coolidge nominated

Stone as an associate justice of the Supreme Court.

Despite his conservative political connections, Stone came to share the liberal views of Brandeis and Holmes that the law is "a human institution for human needs." It is not, he argued, "an end, but a means to an end—the adequate control and protection of those interests, social and economic, which are the special concern of government and hence of law." The achievement of this goal is best "attained through reasonable accommodation of law to changing economic and social needs." For this reason, in 1936 he sided with the liberal minority in opposing the conservative majority's ruling that the Agricultural Adjustment Act was unconstitutional.

In *United States* v. *Carolene Products Company* two years later, Stone, in one of the most famous footnotes in the Court's history, provided the ideological foundation for a whole new era of judicial activism by the Warren Court in the 1950s and 1960s. In this footnote, Stone defined three basic areas in which the Court should employ special judicial scrutiny: legislative encroachment on First Amendment freedoms; government action impeding or corrupting the political process; and official conduct adversely affecting the rights of racial, religious, or national minorities.

In June 1941 Democratic president FRANKLIN D. ROOSEVELT appointed Stone chief justice. During his five years as chief justice, Stone came to rue the sweeping scope of his *Carolene* footnote because of the way it was beginning to be interpreted by liberal judicial activists. Both liberals and conservatives, he feared, were much too inclined to enforce their personal convictions without regard to the need to carefully weigh competing values "within the bounds of reasonableness."

BIBLIOGRAPHY

Konefsky, S. J., *Chief Justice Stone and the Supreme Court,* 1945; Mason, Alpheus Thomas, *Harlan Fiske Stone: Pillar of the Law,* 1956; Stone, Harlan Fiske, *Public Control of Business,* 1940.

Story, Joseph

(September 18, 1779–September 10, 1845)
Associate Justice of the Supreme Court, Representative

Joseph Story was a dominant figure in the U.S. Supreme Court's early history. In 1816 he wrote the Supreme Court majority opinion that established the Court's right to judicial review of state court decisions. In addition, the opinions he wrote on admiralty cases during the War of 1812 (see JAMES MADISON) became models of international law.

Born in Marblehead, Massachusetts, Story graduated from Harvard University in 1798. Three years later, he opened his own law practice in Salem. A Jeffersonian Republican, Story was elected to the Massachusetts legislature in 1805 and served until 1807, when he left to complete the remainder of a term in the U.S. House of Representatives. In 1811 he returned to the Massachusetts legislature and was elected speaker of the state house.

Appointed to the Supreme Court by James Madison in 1811, Story was a distinguished member of the Court and seemed the logical successor to Federalist chief justice JOHN MARSHALL in 1835. However, ANDREW JACKSON was president, and he was not about to select a man who had once supported JOHN QUINCY ADAMS. Jackson chose ROGER B. TANEY instead.

Story's concise and logical writings were notable for the range of subjects they covered.

In 1832 he began his *Commentaries on the Constitution of the United States,* which appeared in three volumes the next year. The year before he had published *Bailments,* and in 1836 he completed *Equity Jurisprudence.* A strong supporter of the broad interpretation of the meaning of the Constitution, Story argued in 1837 that Congress had exclusive right to regulate state and foreign commerce. His hatred of slavery was reflected in his decision in *United States* v. *The Schooner Amistad* (1841), in which he freed a cargo of mutinous slaves so that they could be returned to Africa. In 1842 he wrote the rules of equity practice for the Court.

Although he remained on the Supreme Court until his death in 1845, Story, who had accepted a chair at Harvard Law School in 1829, was also a teacher. Thus, through his teaching, as well as through his writings, Story played a major role in the establishment of American equity jurisprudence.

BIBLIOGRAPHY

Dunne, Gerald T., *Justice Joseph Story and the Rise of the Supreme Court,* 1971; Schwartz, Mortimer D., and John C. Hogan (eds.), *Joseph Story: Eminent Jurist,* 1959.

Sumner, Charles

(January 6, 1811–March 11, 1874)
Senator

Senator Charles Sumner, an abolitionist leader before the Civil War and a powerful foe of conciliation toward states that had seceded after the war, considered his field to be "in morals, not politics."

Born in Boston, Sumner attended Harvard College and graduated from Harvard Law School in 1833. Admitted to the Massachusetts bar in 1834, Sumner traveled to Europe in 1837 to study judicial institutions. Upon his return in 1840, he became passionately committed to abolishing slavery.

Sumner's dedication to preventing the expansion of slavery into the territories led him

Library of Congress

to begin his career in politics. After joining an unsuccessful effort to have the Whig party in Massachusetts take a strong antislavery stand, Sumner joined the Free Soil party and backed MARTIN VAN BUREN's presidential bid in 1848. When a coalition of Free Soilers and Democrats won control of the Massachusetts legislature in 1851, Sumner was elected to the first of four Senate terms despite strong conservative opposition in Boston.

In the Senate the brilliant, vain, and uncompromising Sumner proposed repealing the Fugitive Slave Act of 1850 (see MILLARD FILLMORE) on the grounds that slavery, which was sectional, should not be recognized by the federal government like freedom, which was national. But it was against the Kansas-Nebraska Act (see FRANKLIN PIERCE) that Sumner directed his full rage in 1854. Calling it a "swindle" and a "rape," he labeled STEPHEN A. DOUGLAS a "noisome, squat, and nameless animal." Although his efforts did not succeed in defeating the bill, they helped arouse public opinion in the North and encouraged the creation of the Republican party.

In May 1856 Sumner delivered a fierce denunciation against those he held responsible for "The Crime Against Kansas." In his speech, he attacked Senator ANDREW P. BUTLER of South Carolina as a Don Quixote paying his vows to "the harlot, Slavery." Two days later, Sumner was beaten unconscious with a heavy cane at his Senate desk by Representative PRESTON BROOKS, a nephew of Butler. Sumner was so badly injured in the attack that he did not resume his career in the Senate for three years. But once back he quickly demonstrated that he had not changed by delivering a speech, "The Barbarism of Slavery," against the institution of slavery and all those who supported it.

At first pleased that the secession of the South had rid the nation of slavery, Sumner became a strong supporter of the Union once the Civil War began. During the war he became chairman of the Senate Committee on Foreign Relations. His personal acquaintance with European leaders and customs helped him explain the Union cause abroad. In 1861 Sumner helped to avert an international crisis by urging President ABRAHAM LINCOLN to free two Confederate diplomats who were removed by Americans from a British ship, the *Trent,* on its way to England. (After the war, Sumner unsuccessfully pushed for England to pay a huge amount in wartime damages be-

cause of its alleged support of the Confederacy [see HAMILTON FISH].) He also fought for the abolishment of slavery in the District of Columbia and the creation of the Freedmen's Bureau to help blacks make the difficult transition from slavery to freedom.

Sumner believed that Southern society needed to be completely reorganized to ensure equal rights for blacks. The federal government could force Radical Reconstruction ideas upon the South because the states that had seceded had committed political suicide and were no longer protected by the Constitution. Although often frustrated by what he viewed as President Lincoln's tardy efforts to help blacks, Sumner grew to respect Lincoln's integrity and long-range intentions. He did not respect President ANDREW JOHNSON's policies and became a leader of the movement to have him removed from office through the impeachment process.

After Johnson's impeachment trial and acquittal, Sumner's obsession with "absolute human equality" seemed unrealistic to new members of Congress. This, plus his hostility to the new administration of ULYSSES S. GRANT, enabled his opponents to remove Sumner as chairman of the Senate Foreign Relations Committee in 1871. Increasingly incapacitated by a debilitating heart condition, Sumner died after a long period of illness in 1874 from a heart attack in Cambridge, Massachusetts.

BIBLIOGRAPHY

Donald, David H., *Charles Sumner,* 2 vols., 1960–1970; Pierce, Edward L., *Memoir and Letters of Charles Sumner,* 4 vols., 1877–1893; Sumner, Charles, *Works,* 15 vols., 1870–1883.

Taft, Robert Alphonso

(September 8, 1889–July 31, 1953)
Senator

Robert Taft was called Mr. Republican, a title that not only reflected his national prominence as a powerful leader in the Senate, but also characterized the values of the middle America he represented and held dear—honesty, thrift, hard work, and common sense.

Grandson of Alphonso Taft, the attorney general under President ULYSSES S. GRANT, and son of WILLIAM HOWARD TAFT, the twenty-seventh president, Robert A. Taft started his career as a lawyer. After studying at Yale and Harvard, he established a law practice in Cincinnati, Ohio, in 1913.

Unable to enlist in World War I because of poor eyesight, Taft served as assistant consul for the U.S. Food Administration and after the war helped HERBERT HOOVER handle American relief activities in Europe. These experiences reinforced his basic convictions about the inefficiency of federal regulatory agencies and the selfishness of European nations.

From 1919 until 1939 Taft was a successful attorney and an active Republican in Cincinnati. He was elected in 1921 to the Ohio state legislature, chosen majority leader in 1925 and speaker in 1926, and served in the state senate from 1931 to 1932. In 1938 he entered the U.S. Senate. From 1946 to 1952 he dominated the powerful Republican policy committee and in 1953 served as the majority leader. His best-known piece of legislation was the Taft-Hartley Act of 1947, designed to check what Taft considered to be the excess power of unions.

Although Taft was a conservative Republican, his Senate career was not without its inconsistencies. As a laissez-faire economist, he was vehemently opposed to the national recovery and relief programs of the New Deal (see FRANKLIN DELANO ROOSEVELT); yet he supported federal aid for housing and education. He believed in equal opportunity and a balanced budget and fought legislation that in his view got in the way of individual liberty or frustrated the growth of businesses. In foreign affairs, he opposed lend-lease (see ROOSEVELT), selective service, and American entry into World War II. After the war he opposed the commitment of large numbers of American ground troops in Europe, U.S. membership in the North Atlantic Treaty Organization (NATO), and U.S. policies in Asia. These positions earned him an isolationist label from Republican critics who had come to regard international intervention as necessary. Taft considered himself a pragmatist who appreciated that the United States did not have the economic or political capability necessary for resolving problems all around the world. Finally, Taft savagely attacked American foreign aid programs and other aspects of the Truman Doctrine (see HARRY S TRUMAN), which extended aid for the containment of communism abroad, while he did not attack the communist witch-hunting of fellow Republican senator JOSEPH MCCARTHY.

Although he was called Mr. Republican in the Senate and was greatly respected as a man of honor and impeccable honesty, Taft's habit of expressing his views in bold, blunt terms prevented him from winning his party's presidential nomination in 1940, 1948, and 1952. Taft also lost popularity because of his lingering isolationism and anti–New Deal animus at a time when many Republicans were embracing American involvement in Europe and Asia and accepting the basic tenets of New Deal reform. Taft spent the last year of his life as the Senate floor leader for President DWIGHT D. EISENHOWER's programs.

BIBLIOGRAPHY

Kirk, Russell, and James McClellan, *The Political Principles of Robert A. Taft,* 1967; Patterson, James T., *Mr. Republican,* 1972; Taft, Robert A., *Foreign Policy for Americans,* 1951; White, William S., *The Taft Story,* 1954.

Taft, William Howard

(September 15, 1857–March 8, 1930)
President, Secretary of War, Chief Justice of the Supreme Court

Twenty-seventh president of the United States and distinguished jurist, William Howard Taft was the most outstanding member of a notable political family. He graduated from Yale in 1878 and earned his law degree at Cincinnati Law School while helping in his father's unsuccessful campaign for governor of Ohio. Following the campaign, President CHESTER A. ARTHUR named the younger Taft district collector of internal revenue in 1882. Opposed to the appointment of new people in his department for purely political reasons, Taft resigned from the office the next year but remained active in local Republican politics. In 1887, at age thirty, he was named to fill a vacancy on the state superior court and then won election for a full term the next year.

In 1890 President BENJAMIN HARRISON appointed Taft solicitor general, the federal government's attorney before the Supreme Court. The following year he was appointed a federal superior court judge. "I love judges," he said, "and I love courts. They are my ideals that typify on earth what we shall meet in the hereafter in heaven under a just God." As a federal judge, Taft strengthened the Sherman Anti-Trust Act (see BENJAMIN HARRISON) by becoming the first federal judge to state that laborers had a right to strike. President WILLIAM MCKINLEY knew that Taft coveted a seat on the Supreme Court and promised to appoint him if he would become the governor of the newly annexed Philippine islands. Taft

Library of Congress

agreed and arrived there in 1901, planning to leave as soon as possible. Instead, he ended up loving the job of administering reforms there so much he declined two nomination offers to the Supreme Court by President THEODORE ROOSEVELT.

Roosevelt, a close friend since Taft's days as solicitor general, finally managed to get him to return to Washington by appointing him secretary of war. In Washington, Taft quickly became Roosevelt's most trusted confidant and adviser. Although Roosevelt secured the nomination of Taft to be his political successor at the Republican convention in 1908, Taft had reluctantly accepted the honor because he could not be appointed chief justice. On a platform of preserving Roosevelt's programs, Taft beat his Democratic rival, WILLIAM JENNINGS BRYAN, by over a million votes.

Having to serve after the immensely popular Teddy Roosevelt was perhaps Taft's greatest handicap. He knew that the standard to which he was going to be compared was too high for him to match. He wrote to Roosevelt shortly after taking office, "I fear that a large part of the public will feel as if I had fallen away from your ideals. . . . I have not the facility for educating the public as you had through talks with correspondents. . . ."

During his four years in office, Taft managed to obtain a slight lowering of tariff rates with the Payne-Aldrich Tariff. He vigorously enforced the Sherman Anti-Trust Act and backed legislation that gave the Interstate Commerce Commission jurisdiction over the communications industry and increased railroad rate-setting powers. In the area of government reform, Taft instituted efficiency measures in the federal government; sponsored the Publicity Act, which opened the lists of campaign contributions in races for the House of Representatives; brought 9,000 assistant postmasters into the civil service; advocated the Sixteenth Amendment, which authorized a federal income tax; and supported the Seventeenth Amendment, which provided for the direct popular election of U.S. senators.

His problems with the Progressives in his own party began when he developed a close working relationship with their enemy, the conservative and dictatorial Speaker of the House JOSEPH CANNON. He angered conservationists because he believed the manner in which Roosevelt had conserved huge tracts of land from development in the West—by placing them in the public domain under the guise of water-power or irrigation sites—had been illegal.

In the foreign policy arena, his secretary of state, PHILANDER C. KNOX, is best remembered for creating "dollar diplomacy" as a policy to further American business interests abroad. Knox's efforts to secure a reciprocity treaty with Canada were stymied by Canadian fears of annexation, and opposition in the Senate doomed U.S. agreement to settling international disputes through arbitration at The Hague.

Tired of the burdens of the presidency, Taft only agreed to run for a second term in 1912 to prevent the election of his former friend and now rival for the nomination, Theodore Roosevelt. Taft was sure that if elected again, Roosevelt would undermine constitutional government. The split in the Republican party that resulted when Taft won the nomination and Roosevelt decided to run on the Progressive or Bull Moose ticket (see THEODORE ROOSEVELT) assured the victory of Democrat WOODROW WILSON.

Miserable during his last year as president, Taft had added considerable weight to his already portly figure. He happily returned to private life in 1913 at age fifty-five. During World War I President Wilson named him cochairman of the National War Labor Board and then, in 1921, to the position he had always wanted more than any other, chief justice of the Supreme Court. As chief justice, Taft won congressional support for reforms in the federal judiciary that allowed the Court to have more discretion in selecting which cases it would hear. He wrote the majority opinion in *Myers* v. *United States* (1926), a decision that asserted the president's right to remove executive appointees without the advice and consent of the Senate; he was part of a majority that denied Congress the right to use taxes as a weapon to restrict practices it disapproved of; and he helped to limit the powers of individual states in the regulation of commerce and to enlarge federal powers in the same sphere.

The nine years he spent as chief justice were the happiest of his political career. "The truth is," he said, "that in my present life I don't remember that I ever was president." He died from a heart ailment a month after retiring from the Supreme Court.

BIBLIOGRAPHY

Mason, Alpheus T., *William Howard Taft: Chief Justice,* 1983; Pringle, Henry F., *The Life and Times of William Howard Taft,* 2 vols., 1939.

Tallmadge, James

(January 28, 1778–September 29, 1853)
Representative

James Tallmadge was born in Stanford, New York. He graduated from Rhode Island College (now Brown University) in 1798 and established a successful law practice in Poughkeepsie, New York.

After serving as Governor GEORGE CLINTON's private secretary in 1813, he briefly served as a brigadier general of the New York militia during the War of 1812 (see JAMES MADISON). In 1816 Tallmadge was elected to the U.S. House of Representatives as a Democrat. His most notable accomplishment during his two-year term in the House concerned an amendment he introduced in 1819 to the bill authorizing the admission of Missouri as a state.

At the time of Missouri's request for statehood, there was an even balance of eleven free and eleven slave states. The de facto political agreement between slave and free states in the Union was that the balance would be retained. The problem was that there was no free state ready to join the Union in 1819.

Tallmadge's amendment called for the gradual abolishment of slavery in Missouri by prohibiting the importation of any new slaves into the area after it became a state and granting freedom to all blacks born there in the future. His amendment, which was approved by the House but defeated in the Senate, touched off more than a year of fierce and divisive national debate. The issue was temporarily resolved in 1820 by the Missouri Compromise (see HENRY CLAY).

By the terms of the compromise, Missouri was admitted as a slave state and Maine (formerly a part of Massachusetts) as a free state. To avoid having to confront the issue in the future, an imaginary line was drawn through all the lands acquired by the Louisiana Purchase (see THOMAS JEFFERSON) excluding slavery "forever" north of 36°30' (the southern boundary of Missouri), except for the state of Missouri itself.

Tallmadge declined to be renominated for a second term and returned to his law practice. In 1821 and again in 1846 he was a delegate to state constitutional conventions. He was elected to the New York legislature in 1824 and served as lieutenant governor from 1825 to 1827.

BIBLIOGRAPHY

Andrews, G. B., *A Sermon Occasioned by the Death of the Honorable James Tallmadge*, 1853; *New York Daily Times*, October 1, 1853; *Poughkeepsie Eagle*, October 8, 1853.

Taney, Roger Brooke

(March 17, 1777–October 12, 1864)
Attorney General, Secretary of the Treasury, Chief Justice of the Supreme Court

On the basis of Chief Justice Roger Brooke Taney's ruling in the *Dred Scott* case of 1857, Senator CHARLES SUMNER predicted that Taney's name would be "hooted down the page of history." A later chief justice, CHARLES EVANS HUGHES, acknowledged that Taney's ruling was in error but said that he was "a great chief justice." He remains one of the most controversial figures in American history.

Taney was born on his family's ancestral plantation in Calvert County, Maryland. He graduated from Dickinson College in 1795 and went on to study law in Annapolis. He started a private law practice and became prominent in Maryland politics, serving from 1816 to 1821 in the state senate. In 1827 he was named Maryland attorney general.

Although originally a Federalist, Taney supported Democrat ANDREW JACKSON in his unsuccessful bid for the presidency in 1824. Taney also supported Jackson in 1828 and, after Jackson's victory, became a leading figure in the Democratic party. In 1831 Jackson appointed him U.S. attorney general.

Taney took a leading role in the so-called Bank War. When Congress passed a rechartering bill for the Second Bank of the United States (see NICHOLAS BIDDLE) four years ahead of time in 1832, Jackson vetoed it with a strong message written by Taney. The national bank became an issue in the 1832 election, as Jackson had intended, and he took his reelection as a sign that the public agreed with his position. Jackson wanted to continue to press the issue of the bank and had Taney, whom he had named secretary of the treasury, begin removing government deposits from the bank, a process that eventually led to its demise. The Senate, however, refused to confirm Taney's appointment and also refused him confirmation as associate justice to the Supreme Court in 1835. When JOHN MARSHALL died in 1835, Jackson nominated Taney as chief justice, and this time the Senate, under new leadership, confirmed the appointment, which Taney held until his death in 1864.

Taney was a less fierce nationalist than Marshall, and his Court would tend to back

Library of Congress

Jackson's ideas of "democratizing" the country's economic and political life by broadening the scope of powers given to the people through their state and other local authorities. In *Charles River Bridge* v. *Warren Bridge* (1837), for example, Taney supported the idea that contracts between a state and a business corporation should be interpreted to favor the state, for "the happiness and prosperity of the community." Thus a company that had a prior long-term contract for a toll bridge over the Charles River between Boston and Cambridge—and hence a monopoly on bridge traffic—could not prevent a second company from receiving another state contract to construct a competitive toll-free bridge.

In *Cooley* v. *Board of Port Wardens* (1852), going beyond Marshall's opinion that Congress had the exclusive power to regulate interstate commerce, Taney's ruling allowed the states to regulate interstate commerce in matters of local concern where there was no previous federal statute. It furthermore limited federal rulings in interstate commerce to matters of national concern.

In the great majority of cases until 1856, Taney avoided political involvement; he believed that the Supreme Court was mandated to interpret the Constitution, not to rewrite the law. Until the *Dred Scott* case, he was a proponent of the idea of judicial restraint.

The *Dred Scott* case (formally *Scott* v. *Sandford,* 1855), however, brought politics and the issue of slavery directly to the court. Personally, Taney was opposed to slavery and hoped that the institution would gradually pass away. He believed that the Constitution recognized slavery, however, and in his majority decision in the case ruled that no black could qualify as a citizen and could not sue in federal courts. Furthermore, he ruled that slaves were property and that Congress possessed no power to pass a law that would deprive people of their property in the territories. The ruling did not question the right of a state to prohibit slavery, but the idea that the federal government had no right to act on the question was extraordinary. White extremists in the South were delighted, and abolitionists in the North were horrified. This hugely controversial decision voided the Missouri Compromise of 1820 (see HENRY CLAY), polarized already hardened views on slavery both in the North and the South, and brought the country closer to civil war.

Taney served his final years as chief justice under the cloud of the *Dred Scott* decision. He took a strong stand for civil liberty in wartime, however, in *ex parte Merryman* (1861), holding that President ABRAHAM LINCOLN could not suspend the writ of habeas corpus, thus defending the rights of the individual against arbitrary martial law.

BIBLIOGRAPHY

Harris, Robert J., "Chief Justice Taney," *Vanderbilt Law Review*, 10, 1957; Lewis, Walker, *Without Fear or Favor: Chief Justice Roger Brooke Taney*, 1965; Swisher, Carl B., *Roger B. Taney*, 1935.

Taylor, John W.

(December 19(?), 1753–August 21, 1824)
Senator

The political philosopher John Taylor was one of the first American politicians to articulate the doctrine of states' rights. Taylor was born on the family estate in Carolina County, Virginia. He attended the College of William and Mary but left before graduating to study law. He was admitted to the Virginia bar in 1774.

During the revolutionary war, Taylor served in the Virginia militia and the Continental Army and, from 1779 to 1781, in the Virginia House of Delegates. He was reelected to the Virginia legislature and served from 1783 to 1785 and from 1796 to 1800. In 1798 Taylor introduced the Virginia Resolutions, written by JAMES MADISON in opposition to the Alien and Sedition Acts (see JOHN ADAMS and THOMAS JEFFERSON), in the Virginia House of Delegates. The resolutions formed a basis for the doctrine of states' rights.

From 1792 to 1794, in 1803, and from 1822 until his death, Taylor served in the U.S. Senate. Taylor, a loyal Jeffersonian Republican, attacked ALEXANDER HAMILTON's Federalist programs, declaring in *An Enquiry into the Principles and Tendencies of Certain Public Measures* (1794) that Hamilton's financial development program was unconstitutional and biased in favor of business interests over small farmers. When President THOMAS JEFFERSON was criticized in 1804 for exceeding his constitutional authority in the purchase of Louisiana (1803), Taylor came to his defense and published *A Defence of the Measures of the Administration of Thomas Jefferson*.

Taylor's greatest work of political philosophy, *An Inquiry into the Principles and Policy of the Government of the United States*, was published in 1814. In it Taylor declared that only a nation composed of small farmers could preserve democracy. The best way to prevent the central government, which he was convinced was dominated by "the business class," from gradually increasing its power at the expense of individual liberty was for the states to vigorously protect their constitutional rights against federal government encroachment.

BIBLIOGRAPHY

Beard, C. A., *The Economic Origins of Jeffersonian Democracy,* 1915; Mudge, E. T., *The Social Philosophy of John Taylor of Caroline,* 1939.

Taylor, Zachary

(November 24, 1784–July 9, 1850)
President

Library of Congress

Although he served less than sixteen months as president, popular career soldier and national hero Zachary "Old Rough and Ready" Taylor played an important part in the events that led up to the Compromise of 1850 (see HENRY CLAY and MILLARD FILLMORE).

Born in Orange County, Virginia, Taylor grew up on a farm near Louisville, Kentucky, a member of a large, distinguished Virginia family. In 1808 he joined the army and was commissioned a first lieutenant of infantry. Four years later as a captain, Taylor so ably defended Fort Harrison in Indiana that he was promoted as the first brevet major in the U.S. Army. In 1814, after again performing with distinction at the Battle of Credit Island in Illinois, Taylor was promoted to full major.

Promoted to colonel in 1832, he fought that year in the Black Hawk War against the Sac and the Fox Indians and earned his nickname "Old Rough and Ready" fighting the Seminole Indians in Florida from 1837 to 1840. The name was bestowed by his men after his courageous, determined, and improvised tactical skill resulted in a rare victory against the Seminole at the Battle of Okeechobee. "He looked like a man born to command," a fellow officer had written in 1832. Yet, in traditional military terms, his appearance and behavior were odd. A short man with a large head, Taylor's usual attire, whether in battle or not, consisted of baggy pants, a plain coat bearing no insignia, and a farmer's wide-brimmed straw hat. He reviewed his troops or observed a battle's progress seated sideways on his horse with one leg crossed over the saddle.

The Mexican War (see JAMES KNOX POLK and WINFIELD SCOTT) enabled Taylor to win his greatest glory. In 1846 President Polk ordered Taylor to lead a small American army of 2,300 men to the Rio Grande. Texas, which had just been annexed, claimed the Rio Grande as its southern border. Mexico claimed that the border was actually much farther north at the Nueces River. Fighting broke out between the two armies near Matamoros in April 1846. In the next two days, although confronting a Mexican force twice as large as his own, Taylor won two victories at the battles of Palo Alto and Resaca de la Palma. He was immediately embraced as a national hero and mentioned as a possible candidate for president. The apolitical Taylor, who had never voted, replied that the idea of running for president "seems . . . too visionary to require a serious answer."

During the summer of 1846 Taylor was promoted to major general and led his volunteer army of 6,000 men in the fierce battle for Monterrey. Fearful that Taylor would become a rival candidate for president, Polk then decided to transfer most of Taylor's regular army troops to General Winfield Scott's invasion of Mexico. Infuriated, Taylor led 5,000 of his men deeper into Mexico instead of withdrawing into a defensive position. General Santa Anna's decision to attack at Buena Vista with four times as many men on February 22, 1847, provided Taylor with his most spectacular victory. The Mexicans lost twice as many men as the Americans and retreated the next day. Buena Vista, more than any other event in his career, made Taylor president.

After being nominated by the Whig party in 1848, Taylor shrewdly promised that if elected, he "would not be the mere president of a party . . . [but] endeavor to act independent of party domination and should feel bound to administer the Government untrammeled by party schemes." With the Democratic party divided over the slavery issue and the appearance of the Free Soil party (see LEWIS CASS and MARTIN VAN BUREN), Taylor was elected.

President Taylor assumed office at a time of national crisis. The central issue of his ad-ministration concerned whether slavery was going to be allowed into the new territory acquired from the Mexican War. Southerners wanted the Mason-Dixon line extended to California. Northerners wanted slavery contained. Armed conflict had broken out between antislavery settlers and proslavery Texans over land claimed by both sides in the New Mexico territory.

After assuming the presidency, Taylor, a slaveholder himself, made it clear that he did not support the extension of slavery into the newly acquired territory. He met Southern threats of secession with the promise that if any state tried to leave the Union, he would personally lead the U.S. Army against it. With the nation on the verge of civil war, the great compromisers Senators Henry Clay and STEPHEN A. DOUGLAS attempted to put together a series of bills—which became known as the Compromise of 1850—that could settle the issue by giving both sides some of what each wanted. California would be admitted as a free state; the people in the territories would have the right through the ballot box to determine whether their state would be free or not; a strict fugitive slave law requiring Northerners to send all runaway slaves back to their owners would be implemented; and the slave trade would be abolished in Washington, D.C.

Taylor wanted to end national debate on slavery permanently; he was sure this could be accomplished by halting the extension of slavery and guaranteeing the right of existing slave states to maintain the institution. He did not agree with Clay and Douglas's compromise approach and promised to stymie their efforts through the use of his veto power. California would have to be admitted alone as a free state, and the South would have to accept that fact. With the president hostile to compromise, Congress became deadlocked, and armed rebellion seemed inevitable. Then Taylor attended the Fourth of July festivities at the unfinished Washington Monument. Exhausted from the heat, he drank large amounts of milk that had spoiled. Within hours he was gravely ill with gastroenteritis. He died five days later. His tragic death enabled his successor, MILLARD FILLMORE, to secure the passage of the Compromise of 1850.

BIBLIOGRAPHY

Dyer, Brainerd, *Zachary Taylor*, 1946; Hamilton, Holman, *Zachary Taylor*, 1941–1951; Samson, W. H. (ed.), *Letters from the Battlefields of the Mexican War*, 1908.

Thomas, Norman Mattoon

(November 20, 1884–December 16, 1968)
Candidate for President

The leader of the Socialist party from the 1920s to the 1960s, Norman Thomas was an important critic of American society and politics, a role he maintained even as his party declined into political insignificance.

Thomas was born in Marion, Ohio. After graduating from Princeton University in 1905, he served as a social worker at the Spring Street Presbyterian Church and Settlement House in New York City.

In 1911 Thomas graduated from the Union Theological Seminary and became pastor of the East Harlem Presbyterian Church and chairman of the American Parish, a federation of Presbyterian churches and social welfare agencies located in poor immigrant neighborhoods in New York City. His encounter with poverty, in combination with his opposition to World War I, prompted him to resign from the pastorate in 1918 and join the Socialist party.

In 1924 Thomas ran for governor of New York at the head of the Progressive party (see THEODORE ROOSEVELT) and Socialist party tickets. He lost, but in the process he discovered that running for office provided a valuable opportunity to gain public attention for his causes. In subsequent years he ran as the Socialist candidate for alderman, mayor of New York City, state senator, governor, and, from 1928 to 1948, six times for president.

The hardship of the depression rekindled American voter interest in the Socialist party, which under Thomas's leadership advocated public works, unemployment insurance, minimum wage laws, a shorter work week, and abolition of child labor. In the presidential election of 1932, Thomas gained his highest popular vote, 884,781 (2 percent of the total vote). However, the success of the New Deal and internal factionalism undermined the Socialist party's influence.

Thomas's early attraction to the Soviet Union's communist experiment soured after he made a trip there in 1937, and he was completely disillusioned about Soviet communism after the signing of the Nazi–Soviet nonaggression pact in 1939. He became one of communism's most vociferous critics. During the late 1930s Thomas strongly supported efforts to keep America out of World War II. He believed that a war to end fascism abroad would result in the embracing of fascist values and the suppression of civil liberties at home. After the Japanese attack on Pearl Harbor (see FRANKLIN DELANO ROOSEVELT), he supported the U.S. war effort as unavoidable, but he opposed the internment of Japanese Americans on the West Coast, the mass saturation bombing of cities, the use of nuclear weapons, and the U.S. wartime alliance with the Soviet Union.

Thomas's opposition to war further isolated the Socialist party. Then the advent of the cold war made the discussion of any socialist alternative—even one specifically opposed to communism—impossible. Thomas received only 95,908 popular votes in 1948 and from that point refused to run for president or to hold any elected offices within the Socialist party. He advocated turning the party into an educational and research body. Nevertheless, he remained the unofficial spokesman of the Socialist party for the rest of his life. Although Thomas supported the U.S. defense of South Korea as part of the United Nations' effort (see HARRY S TRUMAN), he opposed American military involvement in Vietnam (see LYNDON BAINES JOHNSON and RICHARD MILHOUS NIXON).

BIBLIOGRAPHY

Fleischman, Harry, *Norman Thomas: A Biography, 1884–1968,* 1969; Seidler, Murray B., *Norman Thomas: Respectable Rebel,* 1967; Thomas, Norman, *As I See It,* 1932, *A Socialist's Faith,* 1951, *Great Dissenters,* 1961, and *Socialism Re-examined,* 1963.

Thurmond, James Strom

(December 5, 1902–   )
Candidate for President, Senator

Described by the liberal magazine *New Republic* as "a determined defender of lost causes," the conservative Strom Thurmond was a pivotal figure in the movement of white southerners out of the Democratic party during his over forty years in national politics.

Born in Edgefield, South Carolina, Thurmond graduated from Clemson College in 1923, taught high school from 1923 to 1929, and served as a public school superintendent from 1929 to 1933. He was admitted to the bar in 1930 and became a city and county attorney from 1933 to 1938 before moving on to the state senate and a position as a circuit court judge.

When the United States entered World War II, Thurmond volunteered for duty and became a much-decorated officer in the 82d Airborne Division. Upon his return from active duty in 1946, Thurmond, a Democrat, was elected governor of South Carolina. He served in that office from 1947 to 1951. In 1948 Thurmond ran as a States' Rights, or Dixiecrat, candidate for president against fellow Democratic party candidate HARRY S TRUMAN. Thurmond was outraged by the inclusion of a civil rights plank in the 1948 Democratic party platform and by Truman's support for federal civil rights legislation that, if passed, would endorse the black struggle for equality and threaten the southern states' commitment to segregation. Thurmond's campaign, dedicated to opposing any program of "social equality by Federal fiat," managed to win over a million votes and the thirty-nine electoral votes of four southern states. From 1951 to 1955 he established a successful law practice in Aiken, South Carolina.

Thurmond began his U.S. Senate career in 1954 by winning the only successful write-in campaign for the Senate in history. In 1957 he set a filibuster record in a vain attempt to prevent the passage of civil rights legislation. Besides his opposition to federal civil rights enactments, Thurmond claimed that the government did not properly appreciate the degree of the "communist threat" and needed to pursue a much more vigorous military defense posture.

In 1964 Thurmond abandoned the Democratic party, became a Republican, and managed to secure South Carolina's support for BARRY GOLDWATER in his unsuccessful 1964 race against Democratic president LYNDON B. JOHNSON. Thurmond's help at the Republican convention in 1968 also ensured RICHARD NIXON's nomination. Although most southerners did not follow Thurmond into the Republican party, they did vote, in increasing numbers, for Republican presidents. This voting pattern shift played a crucial role in the rise and political success of the so-called New Right.

BIBLIOGRAPHY

Lachicotte, Alberta, *Rebel Senator: Strom Thurmond of South Carolina*, 1966; Thurmond, Strom, *The Faith We Have Not Kept*, 1968.

Tilden, Samuel Jones

(February 9, 1814–August 4, 1886)
Candidate for President

As the Democratic party's nominee in 1876, Samuel J. Tilden lost to RUTHERFORD B. HAYES in the most controversial election in U.S. history. He had risen to prominence in the Democratic party as one of the country's most successful champions of government reform.

Tilden was born in New Lebanon, New York. After an intermittent education due to illness, he briefly attended Yale and then graduated from New York University. He was admitted to the bar in 1841 and soon became a highly successful corporation lawyer. His specialty was managing the complexities of reorganizing and refinancing railroads. Growing wealthy from his legal fees, he considerably augmented his fortune through shrewd investments in railroads, iron mines, and real estate.

An ardent Jacksonian Democrat in the 1830s, Tilden worked to elect President JAMES K. POLK in 1844. He became a leader of the Barnburners, a Democratic faction in New York committed to free-soil (antislavery) principles. Although a delegate to the Free-Soil national convention in 1848 (see MARTIN VAN BUREN), he did not join the new Republican party in the early 1850s but instead chose to stay in the Democratic party.

Remaining on the periphery of politics during the Civil War, he opposed ABRAHAM LINCOLN's election, encouraged opposition to the power of the federal government, and supported ANDREW JOHNSON's conciliatory Reconstruction policy toward the South against the plan of the Radical Republicans.

As chairman of the state Democratic committee from 1866 to 1874, Tilden won national recognition by ousting New York City's infamous Tweed Ring (see WILLIAM MARCY TWEED) of corrupt politicians and reforming the state governmental and judicial bodies.

Renowned as a reformer, Tilden was elected governor of New York in 1874. While governor he reformed the state's economic structure and smashed the fraudulent Canal Ring that was growing rich on funds allocated for canal improvements. Defeated by Hayes in the bitterly disputed presidential election of 1876 (see RUTHERFORD BIRCHARD HAYES), Tilden declined to run in 1880 and 1884. He died in 1886, leaving over $3 million to help found the New York Public Library.

BIBLIOGRAPHY

Bigelow, John, *The Life of Samuel J. Tilden*, 1895; Flick, Alexander C., and Gustav S. Lobrano, *Samuel Jones Tilden: A Study in Political Sagacity*, 1939; Kelley, Robert L., "Samuel J. Tilden," *Historian*, 26, 1963.

Tillman, Benjamin Ryan

(August 11, 1847–July 3, 1918)
Senator

The fury of his anger over the unfair lot of the small farmer and the venom of his barbs at those he held responsible enabled "Pitchfork Ben" Tillman to dominate South Carolina politics for over twenty years.

Benjamin Ryan Tillman was born in Edgefield County, South Carolina. Largely self-educated, he earned a living as a small (400 acres) "upcountry" farmer in South Carolina after the Civil War.

Tillman rose to political prominence during the hard economic times in Reconstruction-era South Carolina. He shrewdly capitalized on what small farmers and poor whites perceived to be the self-interested rule of the Tidewater lawyer and merchant "Bourbon aristocracy." Convinced, as he explained, that he was the only man with "the brains, the nerve and the ability to organize the common people against the aristocracy," Tillman founded the Farmers' Association in 1886. This power base, combined with a unique, earthy, public speaking ability, enabled him to quickly win control of the Democratic party. For the next two decades, first as governor (1890–1894) and then as a senator (1895–1918), Tillman dominated South Carolina politics.

In 1892, after he had attacked the state legislature as "dead, rotten driftwood" on "the tide which swept from the mountains to the seaboard" because it would not support his goals, his supporters were overwhelmingly elected. As governor, Tillman supported agricultural education, taxation reform, state government regulation of railroads, and the creation of a state monopoly on the sale of liquor. He used his control of the state consti-tutional convention, which he convened in 1895, to establish property and education voting requirements that made it possible to legally prevent blacks from voting.

In 1894 Tillman chose his successor for governor and won the first of four consecutive terms in the U.S. Senate. In the Senate, Tillman supported free silver (the use of silver as well as gold to back U.S. currency; see WILLIAM JENNINGS BRYAN) and became a strong ally of the Populists (see JAMES BAIRD WEAVER). His attacks on fellow Democratic president GROVER CLEVELAND's support for the gold standard—"Send me to Washington, and I'll stick my pitchfork into his [Cleveland's] old ribs!"—expressed the frustration of debt-burdened small farmers and earned him his nickname of Pitchfork Ben.

Tillman viciously attacked Cleveland at the Democratic convention in 1896 and actively supported the candidacy of young free silver candidate William Jennings Bryan. Although his grip on South Carolina politics gradually diminished after the election of a "Bourbon aristocrat" to the governor's office in 1902, and he was seriously incapacitated by strokes in 1908 and 1910, Tillman was still reelected to a final term in the Senate in 1912.

BIBLIOGRAPHY

Cooper, William J., Jr., *The Conservative Regime: South Carolina, 1877–1890*, 1968; Simkins, Francis B., *Pitchfork Ben Tillman: South Carolinian*, 1944.

Tompkins, Daniel D.

(June 21, 1774–June 11, 1825)
Vice President, Representative

The popular young governor of New York Daniel D. Tompkins seemed the ideal choice to be JAMES MONROE's running mate in 1816. The Monroe ticket won, but it was a hollow victory for Tompkins. While governor of New York during the War of 1812 (see JAMES MADISON), he had secured badly needed loans on personal credit for both the New York and federal governments. Because he had failed to keep accurate records of his financial transactions, after the war both governments claimed that he owed them money. Tompkins, of course, pressed his own claims. New York settled the matter by declaring that Tompkins owed the state nothing and vice versa, and the federal government withheld Tompkins's annual vice presidential salary of $5,000.

Tompkins ran unsuccessfully for a fifth term as governor of New York in 1820, the same year in which he was reelected vice president. Depressed by his long campaign for reimbursement of salary, he began to drink heavily and left Washington more than two years before the end of his second term. Vin-dicated the year before his death when Congress paid him $95,000, Tompkins died in 1825, unsatisfied. He claimed that with interest, the government actually owed him $660,000.

It was a tragic end to a remarkably successful political life begun fifty years earlier in Scarsdale, New York. Tompkins had graduated from Columbia College in 1795 and been admitted to the bar two years later. Popularly known as the farmer's boy, he had been elected to Congress in 1804. He resigned to serve on the New York Supreme Court before being elected governor of New York as a Republican in 1807, 1810, 1813, and 1816. As governor, he worked for improvements in educational facilities, a reformed penal code, and the abolition of slavery.

BIBLIOGRAPHY

Hastings, Hugh (ed.), *Public Papers;* Irwin, Ray Watkins, *Daniel D. Tompkins,* 1968.

Truman, Harry S

(May 8, 1884–December 26, 1972)
President, Vice President, Senator

Give 'em hell" Harry Truman, the man who had left the White House in 1953 labeled a failure, lived to see historians and political commentators agree that he had actually been one of the nation's greatest presidents.

Truman grew up on a farm near Independence, Missouri. As a young man, he developed a passion for reading history books. He could not afford to attend college and worked at a series of clerical and farm jobs until his National Guard unit was mobilized in 1917. During World War I he served as an artillery officer in France, rising to the rank of captain.

After failing in a clothing store venture in Kansas City in 1922, an army friend, the nephew of political boss Tom Pendergast, persuaded Truman to run for district judge. He was elected but failed to win reelection in 1924. With Tom Pendergast's help, Truman won the race for chief judge of Jackson County in 1926. In 1934 Pendergast, looking for a "man of unimpeachable character and integrity" to restore the image of his political machine, helped Truman win election to the U.S. Senate. Truman was never subservient to Pendergast and voted for President FRANKLIN D. ROOSEVELT'S New Deal legislation, which Pendergast opposed. However, Truman was still viewed with suspicion by the Roosevelt administration.

When Pendergast was arrested and imprisoned for income tax evasion in 1939, Truman, financially unable to launch an expensive reelection campaign, considered retiring from the Senate. But his pride was hurt, once it became clear that Roosevelt preferred to support Truman's opponent, and he decided to wage an unconventional reelection campaign. With no money to buy advertising, Truman traveled around the state talking to people wherever he found them. The strategy worked, and he won a narrow reelection victory in 1940.

During the campaign Truman had decided that the rapidly growing defense program the United States was developing was riddled with waste and inefficiency. Upon his return to the Senate he succeeded in establishing and chairing the Special Committee to Investigate the National Defense Program. Throughout the massive spending of World War II Truman and his committee made headlines by exposing corporations that padded military expense costs. By 1944, when President Roosevelt chose him to be his fourth-term running mate, Truman was a respected figure in the Senate. Changing political winds had convinced Roosevelt that he needed a vice presidential running mate in the 1944 election with a far less liberal reputation than HENRY WALLACE, and Truman seemed safe.

Library of Congress

Truman assumed the office of president after the unexpected death of Roosevelt on April 12, 1945. He became president during an extraordinarily difficult period with very little preparation. Roosevelt had not included him in cabinet or important policy meetings. During his first two years in office, Truman had to confront the immensely difficult tasks of rebuilding the nations ravaged by World War II and containing the powerful appeal of communism. He had to negotiate the future of the U.S. and Soviet presence in Europe and the Middle East with Joseph Stalin, decide whether to use the atomic bomb to end the war with Japan, confront Soviet domination of Eastern Europe, cope with massive labor unrest and postwar inflation in the United States, and deal with a hostile, newly elected Republican Congress.

Truman was unable to persuade Congress to agree to wage and price controls after World War II ended, and, as he had predicted, prices soared. Organized labor responded by seeking wage increases. By the end of 1946 millions of workers were on strike. Truman attempted to use the influence of the White House to help negotiate settlements in the railroad and coal-mining industries. When his efforts failed, he threatened to use the army to run the trains, pressuring the strikers back to work after only a few days, and obtained an injunction to prevent the coal miners from striking.

Truman refused, however, to be labeled antiunion and vetoed the antilabor Case bill in 1946. When the Republicans won control of Congress in the 1946 elections, they passed the Taft-Hartley Act, designed to curtail the power of organized labor, over Truman's veto.

Truman was in an awkward political position in 1947. He was viewed as antilabor by unions and antibusiness by executives because of his support of wage and price controls. He was also unpopular in the South because he favored civil rights legislation and in the Northeast because of his unsophisticated demeanor. In addition, deteriorating conditions in the war-ravaged world seemed to be undoing all that Americans thought World War II had won. Western Europe was impoverished, Eastern Europe had fallen under the Soviet Union's domination, the communists were winning the civil war in China, and the conflict between the Jews and Arabs in Palestine was outstripping the British ability to control it. Truman wrote, "Charlie Ross [Charles G. Ross, Truman's press secretary] said I'd shown that I'd rather be right than President, and I told him I'd rather be anything than President."

Truman refused to accept the negative judgment of his critics. Stymied on the domestic front, he moved boldly in the international arena to contain communism. The Truman Doctrine of 1947, precipitated by a civil war in Greece between communists and noncommunists, declared the determination of the United States to use its military might to contain communism and fight communist insurgencies in every corner of the world. Among the many programs Truman initiated through bipartisan foreign policy support in Congress were the Marshall Plan (see GEORGE CATLETT MARSHALL) and the North Atlantic Treaty Organization (NATO). American forces also protected the defeated Nationalist Chinese forces on the island of Formosa (Taiwan).

Unable to secure civil rights legislation in Congress, Truman used his office to publicize the issue and, through executive action, to order the integration of the armed forces. (It was only in the Korean War, however, that integration of the armed forces was achieved.) His actions caused a revolt in his own party. The Southern wing refused to endorse his re-election in 1948 and ran its own candidate, Governor J. STROM THURMOND of South Carolina, for president as a states' rights "Dixiecrat."

With his own party split and the Republicans united behind a confident moderate candidate, THOMAS E. DEWEY, governor of New York, Truman's election defeat in 1948 seemed certain to everyone but Truman. Running against what he labeled the "do-nothing" Republican Congress, Truman ran a vigorous campaign. He traveled across the nation and spoke to people from the back of his presidential campaign train. The result was a narrow election victory and a stunning political upset. He defeated Dewey 303 electoral votes to 189. Thurmond received 39 electoral votes.

Truman's second term was dominated by a period of mass hysteria over communist spies and infiltrators in America and by the Korean War. Truman did not support the questionable "witch hunt" activities of the House Un-American Activities Committee, or of Senator JOSEPH MCCARTHY of Wisconsin, but he was unable to prevent their excesses. He vetoed the McCarran Internal Security Act of 1950, which required all communists to register with the Justice Department; provided for the deportation of any alien who had ever been a communist; and prohibited the employment of communists or their supporters in positions relating to national defense. Congress passed it anyway.

When North Korean forces invaded South Korea in 1950, Truman, without obtaining a declaration of war from Congress, ordered American forces to the area before the United Nations voted to halt the aggression. General Douglas MacArthur was placed in overall command of UN forces and succeeded in driving the North Koreans out of South Korea. Truman then authorized him to pursue North Korean forces up to the Yalu River border with China. MacArthur was sure Chinese troops would not intervene and that Korea would be liberated by Christmas. Instead, half a million Chinese troops entered North Korea, and UN troops were put on the defensive. MacArthur demanded the right to launch air strikes at enemy supply bases in China.

Truman refused, fearful of provoking Soviet intervention and a third world war. MacArthur publicly criticized Truman's decision in 1951 and was ordered by Truman not to discuss the subject with reporters. When Republican minority leader Joseph Martin made public a letter from MacArthur in which he again criticized Truman in public, an infuriated Truman accepted the political consequences of his extremely unpopular action and relieved MacArthur of command.

Truman was booed at the opening game of the 1951 baseball season in Washington. Having a favorable job rating of only 25 percent in the polls, and plagued by charges of corruption in government due to the actions of friends he had trusted, Truman decided not to run for reelection in 1952. He subsequently was snubbed by the newly elected DWIGHT D. EISENHOWER during his inauguration ceremony and judged a failure as president by contemporaries. The day Truman left Washington to return to his home in Independence, Missouri, he wrote to his daughter: "There is an epitaph in Boot Hill cemetery in Arizona which reads, 'Here lies Jack Williams. He done his damnedest! What more can a person do?' Well, that's all I could do. I did my damnedest, and that's all there was to it!"

Truman spent the last two decades of his life writing his memoirs, establishing the Truman Library, and traveling. He continued to offer his "plain talk" solutions to important issues until his death.

Truman's reputation began to improve during the eight years of the boring and allegedly ineffectual Eisenhower administration. By 1960 and the return of the Democrats to the White House, his reputation was intact. However, Truman has been subjected to a second round of criticism since then, largely over his handling of communism abroad and at home. Some scholars think that his limited understanding of international relations and his blunt, untutored style of diplomacy hurt U.S. relations with the Soviet Union and hastened the outbreak of the cold war. Also, the Truman Doctrine is seen by some scholars as a misun-

derstanding and misapplication of GEORGE KENNAN's strategy of containment and the cause of many costly and ill-considered American interventions overseas, culminating in the Vietnam War (see LYNDON BAINES JOHNSON and RICHARD MILHOUS NIXON). Finally, historians of the anticommunist hysteria at home locate its roots not in the actions of Senator Joseph McCarthy but in those of Truman, with his containment doctrine and his demand that all government employees sign loyalty oaths.

Historians continue to be impressed, however, with Truman's success in consolidating the gains of the New Deal (protecting labor's right to organize; guaranteeing welfare for the poor, the aged, and the disabled) and his efforts to extend the principles of the New Deal with his own proposal—the Fair Deal—for liberal reforms. Moreover, his combination of vast military expenditures abroad and significant outlays for social welfare at home ("guns and butter") became the Keynesian [after English economist John Maynard Keynes] formula—government expenditures to stimulate consumer purchasing power (see FRANKLIN DELANO ROOSEVELT)—on which a generation of Democratic politicians and presidents (JOHN F. KENNEDY and Lyndon B. Johnson) staked their political success.

BIBLIOGRAPHY

Cochran, Bert, *Harry Truman and the Crisis Presidency,* 1973; Donovan, Robert J., *Tumultuous Years: The Presidency of Harry S Truman,* 1949–1953, 1984; Gaddis, John Lewis, *The United States and the Origins of the Cold War,* 1972, and *Strategies of Containment,* 1982; Hamby, Alonzo L., *Beyond the New Deal: Harry S Truman and American Liberalism,* 1973; Jenkins, Roy, *Truman,* 1986; Miller, Merle, *Plain Speaking: An Oral Biography of Harry S Truman,* 1974; Paterson, Thomas G., *The Origins of the Cold War and Strategies of Containment,* (2d ed.), 1974; Rogin, Michael, *The Intellectuals and McCarthy: The Radical Spectre,* 1967; Truman, Harry S, *Memoirs,* 2 vols., 1955, 1956; Truman, Margaret, *Harry S Truman,* 1973.

Trumbull, Jonathan

(March 26, 1740–August 7, 1809)
Speaker of the House, Senator, Representative

Jonathan Trumbull was born in Lebanon, Connecticut, into a prominent family. He graduated from Harvard College in 1759. Three years later, he was awarded a master's degree. In 1774, 1775, 1779, 1780, and 1788, Trumbull represented Lebanon in the state legislature. He was speaker of the house in the latter year.

Trumbull occupied several important non-combat roles in the American Revolution. From July 1775 until he resigned to look after the accounts of his brother, General Joseph Trumbull, Trumbull acted as paymaster of the patriot troops. In 1778 he was the unanimous choice of Congress to be the comptroller of the treasury, but he held this post for only six months before resigning. Two years later, he accepted an appointment as General GEORGE WASHINGTON's secretary. He served on Washington's staff until the end of the war in 1783.

When the first national elections were held under the new Constitution, Trumbull was elected to the House of Representatives. He served in the House from 1789 to 1795, the last two years as Speaker. In 1794 he was elected to the U.S. Senate but resigned two years later to become the deputy governor of Connecticut. When the governor died in 1797, Trumbull succeeded him. He was reelected annually every year for the rest of his life.

Trumbull was a staunch Federalist and adamant opponent of THOMAS JEFFERSON's Democratic-Republican policies. While governor, Trumbull did everything he could to undermine the enforcement of the Embargo Act of 1807. In 1809 he even refused to authorize the use of the state militia by the secretary of war to enforce the embargo on the grounds that it was an unconstitutional infringement of states' rights. To bolster the legitimacy of his position before the special session of the state legislature called to deal with the crisis, Trumbull shrewdly justified his action by quoting from Democratic-Republican JAMES MADISON's Virginia Resolutions (see THOMAS JEFFERSON).

BIBLIOGRAPHY

Trumbull, Jonathan, *Jonathan Trumbull, Governor of Connecticut, 1764–1784,* 1919; Weaver, Glenn, *Jonathan Trumbull: Connecticut's Merchant,* 1913.

Trumbull, Lyman

(October 12, 1813–June 25, 1896)
Senator

Lyman Trumbull's political career reflects the turmoil of the Civil War era in American political history. He began as a Democrat, joined the Republican party, emerged from his three terms in the U.S. Senate as a member of the Liberal Republican party, and finally returned to the Democratic party in 1876.

Trumbull was born in Colchester, Connecticut. He taught school in Georgia from 1833 until he was admitted to the bar in 1836. He then moved to Belleville, Illinois, in 1837, established a legal practice, and embarked upon a remarkably successful and broad political career in state government. He was elected to the state legislature as a Democrat in 1840, served as Illinois secretary of state from 1841 to 1843, and as a justice of the state supreme court from 1848 until elected to the U.S. House of Representatives in 1854.

Trumbull never actually became a U.S. representative. Before the House convened, he was elected as a compromise candidate to the U.S. Senate, where he eventually served three terms (1855–1873).

Trumbull joined the newly created Republican party in 1855 and led the opposition to his fellow Illinois senator STEPHEN A. DOUGLAS's popular sovereignty solution in favor of congressional jurisdiction for deciding whether Kansas would be admitted as a slave or free state. During the Civil War, Trumbull was a firm supporter of ABRAHAM LINCOLN's policies. Although he often agreed with and supported Radical Republican Reconstruction legislation (Trumbull introduced the Civil Rights Bill, helped to override a presidential veto, and helped draft the Thirteenth Amendment), he refused to support Republican efforts to re-

move President ANDREW JOHNSON from office. Trumbull was one of only a few Republicans to vote against Johnson's impeachment.

In 1872 he was one of the founders of the Liberal Republican party. He campaigned vigorously for the doomed presidential candidacy of HORACE GREELEY, then returned to the practice of law in Chicago. He rejoined the Democratic party in 1876 and served as one of SAMUEL J. TILDEN's advisers in the disputed presidential election of that year (see RUTHERFORD BIRCHARD HAYES). Four years later, he was the unsuccessful Democratic candidate for governor of Illinois.

BIBLIOGRAPHY

Ross, E. D., *The Liberal Republican Movement*, 1919; White, Horace, *Life of Lyman Trumbull*, 1913.

Tugwell, Rexford Guy

(July 10, 1891–July 21, 1979)
Presidential Adviser

Born in Sinclairville, New York, Rexford Tugwell earned his Ph.D. from the University of Pennsylvania in 1922, where he attended the Wharton School of Finance and Commerce.

Tugwell became a professor of economics at Columbia University. His articles in favor of government regulation and, when necessary, management of the economy caught the attention of FRANKLIN D. ROOSEVELT during his two terms as governor of New York.

National Archives

During Roosevelt's 1932 presidential campaign, Tugwell became a member of Roosevelt's inner circle of advisers known as the brain trust. After his election Roosevelt appointed Tugwell assistant secretary and then under secretary of agriculture before making him head of the Rural Resettlement Administration. Tugwell was associated with the planning impulse in New Deal policy, an impulse that shaped critical policy of the First New Deal, especially the National Recovery Act and the Agricultural Adjustment Act. When this impulse lost influence in New Deal circles, as it did around

1936, Tugwell's close association with Roosevelt came to an end. Critics accused Tugwell of being a socialist and radical, but many of the innovative programs he helped initiate and implement helped farmers through the hardships of the depression.

From 1941 to 1946 Tugwell served as governor of Puerto Rico. In 1946 he accepted an appointment at the University of Chicago and taught there until 1957, when he moved to Santa Barbara, California, to become a senior staff member at the Center for the Study of Democratic Institutions.

BIBLIOGRAPHY

Current Biography, 1963; *New York Times*, July 24, 1979; Tugwell, Rexford G., *The Light of Other Days*, 1963, and *The Stricken Land*, 1946.

Tweed, William Marcy

(April 3, 1823–April 12, 1878)
Representative

As the head of Tammany Hall, the Democratic party organization in New York City, William Marcy Tweed became infamous for his greed and arrogant abuse of political power.

Tweed was born in New York City. After leaving public school at age eleven, he joined his father as a chair maker and was an apprentice saddler before attending a bookkeeping school for several months. At age seventeen he became the bookkeeper of a small brushmaking firm his father partly owned. By nineteen, he was a member of the firm.

In 1848 Tweed organized a new volunteer fire engine company in New York City, at that time a sure way to enter politics. He lost his first bid to win election for assistant alderman in 1850, but one year later he succeeded as a candidate of the Democratic party in a predominately Whig district. Two years later, he was elected to Congress, but Tweed served only one two-year term because he preferred to exercise more influence at the local government level. While serving in Congress, Tweed held onto his position as alderman. His term as a representative ended in 1855 and within a year he was elected the chairman of the New York City Board of Supervisors and a school commissioner.

A master of political strategy, Tweed used his new positions to increase his political power by accepting bribes and placing allies in key positions to distribute patronage jobs. He soon dominated the New York Democratic party. In 1857 he was elected to the governing board of New York City's powerful Democratic political machine, Tammany Hall. Eleven years later, he was chosen to head the organization.

Tweed used his power in New York City and the state legislature in Albany, as well as in the governor's office after 1868, to institute graft at taxpayers' expense on an unprecedented scale. Although he had no training as an attorney, he opened a law office through which huge fees were paid by businesses to obtain city and state contracts, a printing company through which all state documents had to be submitted regardless of the cost and, in his largest scheme, a marble company that billed the state government exorbitant rates for the stone required to build a new county courthouse.

Because of the false billing submitted for the courthouse, the original cost of the building skyrocketed from an estimated $500,000 to $12 million. The level of overall greed and corruption evident in the construction of the courthouse led to an investigation of Tweed's methods of robbing the public treasury by *Harper's Weekly* and the *New York Times*. Aided by articles in these publications after 1870, and especially the cartoons drawn by Thomas Nast in *Harper's Weekly*, public indignation was aroused. Tweed only confirmed the accusations made by Nast when he made the mistake of offering the cartoonist $500,000 to stop producing drawings about him.

As a result of the efforts of a Democratic reform committee led by SAMUEL J. TILDEN, later governor of New York, Tweed was convicted of forgery and grand larceny in 1871 and sentenced to twelve years in jail. He was released in 1875 after the sentence was reduced on appeal, but he was immediately rearrested and returned to jail to await trial for civil damages. Unable to pay the $3 million bail, Tweed decided to escape and fled first to Cuba and then Spain. He was recaptured in Spain after Spanish officials identified him from Nast's cartoons. Tweed was arrested and returned to jail, where he unsuccessfully attempted to secure leniency by cooperating in the arrests and trials of former conspirators and by detailing his own corrupt activities.

Tweed's health had begun to deteriorate rapidly after 1875, and he died in jail before ever standing trial for the civil damages.

BIBLIOGRAPHY

Callow, Alexander B., Jr., *Tweed Ring*, 1968; Cynch, D. T., *Tweed*, 1927; Mandelbaum, Seymour, *Boss Tweed's New York*, 1965.

Tyler, John

(March 29, 1790–January 18, 1862)
President, Vice President, Senator, Representative

John Tyler was the first vice president to become president following the death of the incumbent. He served only for the remainder of WILLIAM HENRY HARRISON's term because of a fierce battle with political rivals in Congress from within his own party. The crowning achievement of his administration was the annexation of Texas.

Tyler was born on his family's plantation in Charles City County, Virginia. In 1811, four years after he graduated from the College of William and Mary, Tyler began to practice law and was immediately elected to the Virginia House of Delegates. After serving several terms in the Virginia legislature, he was elected to the U.S. House of Representatives in 1816, the governorship of Virginia in 1825, and the U.S. Senate in 1827.

Tyler believed that the federal government derived its power from the states. Therefore, it was improper for the federal government to contemplate the use of force to make the states acquiesce to national laws, as President ANDREW JACKSON had threatened to do during the nullification crisis (see JOHN CALDWELL CALHOUN). Throughout his political career, Tyler consistently defended the institution of slavery and the interests of his Virginia slave-owning-class background. He opposed the Missouri Compromise in 1820 (see HENRY CLAY) while in the House on the grounds that the Constitution did not authorize Congress to legislate any matters pertaining to slavery. In 1834 he warned: "The Southern states are in constant apprehension lest the national government should be converted into a mere majority machine."

In 1836, rather than support a directive by the Virginia legislature to vote to expunge from Senate records the 1833 censure of

Andrew Jackson that he had supported, Tyler resigned from office, thereby enhancing his reputation as an implacable opponent of Jackson and increasing his appeal to Whig party members.

For the presidential race of 1836, the Whig party adopted a strategy of running regional candidates for president and vice president in the hope of drawing enough votes to prevent MARTIN VAN BUREN from receiving a majority and thereby forcing the election into the House of Representatives. Tyler was nominated for vice president by two of the three sections and came in second in the third. The Whig strategy failed and Van Buren won enough electoral votes to assume the office of president.

In 1839, at the Whig national convention, Tyler was nominated for the vice presidency to balance the ticket after William Henry Harrison was nominated as president. The Harrison–Tyler ticket—with the campaign slogan "Tippecanoe and Tyler too"—was successful, but Harrison died after only a month in office. On April 6, 1841, Tyler became president.

President Harrison had called Congress into special session to facilitate the enactment of HENRY CLAY's "American system" legislation (see CLAY), the main plank of the Whig party's platform. Tyler could not bring himself to support Clay's program because of his apprehension over its intrusion upon the rights of the states. Enraged, Clay, who planned to run for president himself in 1844, organized congressional support to force Tyler from office. After Tyler vetoed two bills authorizing a new Bank of the United States (see NICHOLAS BIDDLE and ROGER BROOKE

Library of Congress

TANEY), Clay engineered the resignation of the entire cabinet. Only Secretary of State DANIEL WEBSTER remained in office in order to conclude the delicate negotiations over the Maine boundary that resulted in the Webster–Ashburton Treaty (1842).

Despite accusations by Whig party leaders that he was acting in the same dictatorial fashion as the despised Andrew Jackson, Tyler refused to resign from office. Two days after the cabinet resignations, he nominated new secretaries. The day after his new choices were confirmed by the Senate, the Whig members of Congress expunged Tyler from the party on the grounds that he was seeking to create a new, distinct political base. A year later, in 1842, the Whig-dominated House of Representatives even passed a resolution claiming that Tyler was courting impeachment for vetoing a protective tariff bill.

Tyler persevered, and succeeded in forcing Congress to pass a much less protective tariff. Although his political situation improved somewhat after the Whigs lost control of the House in the 1842 elections, he remained a man without a political party base and continued to be able to exercise domestic political influence negatively only through the use of his veto power. By the end of his term in office, he had vetoed more bills than any other president, and he became the first president ever to have one of his vetoes overridden by Congress.

In addition to his success in negotiating the Webster-Ashburton Treaty, Tyler also extended the Monroe Doctrine (see JAMES MONROE) to include the Hawaiian islands (1842), negotiated a new trade treaty with China

(1844), and brought about the annexation of Texas by joint resolution in the final days of his term of office.

Tyler considered running as an independent for president in 1844. With the nomination of JAMES K. POLK by the Democratic party (Polk supported the annexation of Texas), Tyler instead decided to retire from politics. He returned to his plantation in Virginia and only reentered the national political scene in 1861 as the leader of an unsuccessful effort to find a compromise capable of averting the outbreak of fighting between the North and South. After Virginia seceded, he briefly served in the provisional Confederate Congress. In November 1861, shortly before his death, he was elected to the Confederate House of Representatives.

BIBLIOGRAPHY

Morgan, Robert J., *A Whig Embattled: The Presidency under John Tyler,* 1954 (reprint 1974); Tyler, Lyon G., *The Letters and Times of the Tylers,* 3 vols., 1884–1886 (reprint 1970).

Underwood, Oscar Wilder

(May 6, 1862–January 25, 1929)
Senator, Representative

Oscar W. Underwood led the fight in the Senate to secure approval of President WOODROW WILSON's foreign policy objectives and was a major contender for the Democratic party's presidential nomination in 1912 and 1924.

Underwood was born in Louisville, Kentucky. After graduating from the University of Virginia in 1884, he was admitted to the bar and established a law practice in Birmingham, Alabama.

Underwood was elected to the U.S. House of Representatives in 1894. While serving as floor leader (1911–1915), he introduced the Underwood Tariff Act of 1913, which dramatically reduced tariff rates and removed many articles from tariff protection. (The Underwood Tariff passed but was never put into effect because of the outbreak of World War I.) He also played a vital role in securing passage of the Federal Reserve Act.

Elected to the first of two terms in the Senate in 1914, Underwood quickly assumed a leadership role in securing approval of President Wilson's foreign policy objectives. Although he felt Wilson should have shown more willingness to compromise with his Senate critics, Underwood led the doomed battle to secure ratification of the Treaty of Versailles and U.S. participation in the League of Nations (see WOODROW WILSON). He was Democratic party floor leader in the Senate from 1921 to 1923, and once again in 1924 a major contender for the Democratic party nomination for president. Underwood might have won his party's endorsement except for his well-known opposition to the national prohibition of alcohol and his decision to publicly attack the resurgence of the Ku Klux Klan (see *Ulysses Simpson Grant*).

In 1928, a year after he retired from the Senate, Underwood served as a delegate to the Pan American Conference held in Havana, Cuba.

BIBLIOGRAPHY

Underwood, Oscar W., *Drifting Sands of Politics,* 2d edition, 1931.

Upshur, Abel Parker

(June 17, 1791–February 28, 1844)
Secretary of State, Secretary of the Navy

Abel Parker Upshur was born in Northampton County, Virginia. He attended the College of New Jersey (now Princeton) but was expelled for participating in a student demonstration. He briefly moved on to Yale University, but soon abandoned his studies there without graduating to pursue the study of law in Richmond, where he established a successful practice. From 1812 to 1813 and from 1825 to 1827, Upshur served in the Virginia House of Delegates. As a delegate to the Virginia constitutional convention in 1829 and 1830, he opposed efforts to make the state government more democratic on the grounds that majority rule was dangerous to property rights and social institutions.

From 1826 to 1841, Upshur served as a justice on Virginia's supreme court. A strong supporter of the institution of slavery, a devout proponent of the superiority of states' rights over those of the federal government, and a firm believer that banks ought to be able to function without government regulation, Upshur gradually became one of the principal spokesmen for the Southern perspective of the limited power for the national government.

In 1841 President JOHN TYLER chose Upshur to be secretary of the navy and in 1843, after DANIEL WEBSTER resigned, to be his secretary of state. While secretary of state, Upshur began negotiations that resulted in the annexation of Texas in 1845, an event he did not live long enough to see. The accidental explosion of a cannon aboard the warship *Princeton* killed him and a number of other top officials in the Tyler administration.

BIBLIOGRAPHY

Hall, Claude H., *Abel Parker Upshur: Conservative Virginian*, 1963.

Vallandigham, Clement Laird

(July 29, 1820–June 17, 1871)
Representative

Clement Laird Vallandigham was the most prominent political leader of the Peace Democrats, or so-called Copperheads, during the Civil War.

Vallandigham was born in New Lisbon (now Lisbon), Ohio, and attended Jefferson College (now Washington and Jefferson), in Canonsburg, Pennsylvania. After reading law, he was admitted to the bar in 1842 and established a practice in Dayton, Ohio. He was elected to the Ohio legislature in 1845 and 1846, and became the editor of the local Democratic newspaper, the *Dayton Empire*.

Although personally opposed to slavery, Vallandigham believed that adherence to the Constitution left the issue of emancipation up to the individual state and not the federal government. After two unsuccessful efforts as the Democratic candidate for the U.S. House of Representatives in 1852 and 1854, he won a contested race on his third try in 1856, was seated in May 1858, and was reelected by narrow margins in November 1858 and in 1860.

In the House, Vallandigham supported compromise efforts to avoid the Civil War. Although he disagreed with STEPHEN A. DOUGLAS's popular sovereignty solution to the issue of extending slavery into the territories, he supported Douglas for president in 1860 on the grounds that he was the most viable candidate to defeat ABRAHAM LINCOLN. When fighting broke out between Union and Confederate forces, Vallandigham opposed all efforts to increase the size of the Union army and vigorously attacked Republican party leaders as the perpetrators of the violence. He campaigned for reelection in 1862 on the slogan he hoped the national Democratic party would adopt: "To maintain the Constitution as it is, and to restore the Union as it was." Although he attracted large crowds of supporters and became known as the leader of the Peace Democrats (Copperheads), he was soundly defeated.

Increasingly outspoken as the war continued, Vallandigham became the leader of the antiwar group known as the Sons of Liberty and urged young men to refuse to serve in the Union army. In a political speech delivered in Ohio in May 1863, he declared that the real reason for the Civil War was not to save the Union, but to free blacks and enslave whites. The speech infuriated General Ambrose E. Burnside, the Union military commander of Ohio. He had Vallandigham arrested and tried by a military court on grounds of treason for "declaring sympathies for the enemy." Vallandigham was sentenced to imprisonment for the remainder of the war. The arrest and trial of a political opponent was a political embarrassment to Lincoln. In order to avoid making Vallandigham into a martyr, Lincoln commuted his sentence and exiled him to the Confederacy.

Vallandigham escaped from the Confederacy to Bermuda and then to Ontario, Canada, where he remained until he decided to risk returning in order to participate in the election of 1864. Lincoln chose to ignore Vallandigham's return. The Democratic party platform in 1864 contained the demand for the immediate cessation of hostilities and the pursuit of a negotiated settlement of the war largely as a result of Vallandigham's efforts. The Union victories of 1864 doomed the Democrats' chances for winning the presidency and destroyed Vallandigham's national influence.

He remained active in Democratic party politics for the rest of his life but was never elected to public office again.

BIBLIOGRAPHY

Gray, Wood, *The Hidden Civil War: The Story of the Copperheads,* 1942; Klement, Frank, *Limits of Dissent: Vallandigham and the Civil War,* 1970; Milton, G. F., *Abraham Lincoln and the Fifth Column,* 1942; Porter, G. H., *Ohio Politics during the Civil War Period,* 1911; Randall, J. G., *Constitutional Problems under Lincoln,* 1926; Vallandigham, James L., *Clement Laird Vallandigham,* 1872.

Van Buren, Martin

(December 5, 1782–July 24, 1862)
President, Vice President, Secretary of State, Senator

As President ANDREW JACKSON's campaign manager, political confidant, secretary of state, vice president, and finally, handpicked successor, Martin Van Buren played a major role in national politics. According to the historian Arthur Schlesinger, Jr., "Van Buren's understanding of the new functions of public opinion, as well as of Congress, furnished the practical mechanisms [that] transformed Jackson's extraordinary popularity into the instruments of power. . . . Without them, the gains of Jacksonian democracy would have been impossible."

Library of Congress

Born in Kinderhook, New York, Van Buren was the son of a truck farmer and tavern keeper. His formal education was limited to the local elementary school and the private Kinderhook Academy. At age fourteen he began his legal education by working in a local law office. In 1803, at age twenty-one, Little Van—he was only 5 feet, 6 inches tall—passed the bar and established his own successful practice in Kinderhook.

By 1808 Van Buren was surrogate of Columbia County. In 1812 he was elected to the state senate on an anti–U.S. Bank platform. In the state senate, he supported the War of 1812 (see JAMES MADISON), the construction of the Erie Canal, the revision of the New York constitution, and proposed legislation to eliminate imprisonment for debt.

Van Buren assumed command of the wing of the New York Republican party (called the Bucktails) that opposed the rule of DEWITT

CLINTON. By 1816 he had accumulated enough anti-Clinton followers to win appointment as state attorney general, but he was forced out of office three years later when Clinton was elected governor. Van Buren rebounded from this setback by launching a successful campaign for the U.S. Senate the following year. When he set out for Washington, D.C., in 1821 to begin his national political career, Van Buren left behind a well-organized political machine based on patronage known as the Albany Regency.

In the Senate Van Buren earned the title "Red Fox of Kinderhook" because of his shrewd political judgment and care to avoid taking a stand on controversial issues. A firm supporter of front-runner WILLIAM CRAWFORD for president in 1824, Van Buren was dismayed when Crawford was forced out of the race by a paralyzing stroke and JOHN QUINCY ADAMS was elected. Returned for another term to the Senate in 1827, Van Buren became an avid supporter of Andrew Jackson. To ensure the success of the Jackson ticket in New York, Van Buren gave up his seat in the Senate and ran for governor. Although elected governor, he quickly resigned after only two and a half months in office in order to become President Jackson's secretary of state.

Van Buren established an intimate relationship with Jackson that was based upon mutual trust and appreciation for each other's political talents. He was the most powerful man in Jackson's inner circle of advisers known as the

Kitchen Cabinet. It was Van Buren who welded the disparate groups of anti-Adams forces into the cohesive Democratic party that overwhelmingly reelected Jackson in 1832.

While secretary of state, Van Buren reached a settlement with England on West Indian trade, negotiated American access to the Black Sea with Turkey, and persuaded the French to pay American damage claims from the Napoleonic Wars. However, his greatest accomplishment was not in foreign policy but at home in managing to replace JOHN C. CALHOUN as Jackson's successor.

In 1830 Jackson and Calhoun clashed over the issue of nullification (see JOHN CALDWELL CALHOUN). Van Buren seized the opportunity to remind an angry Jackson that Calhoun had also lied about the fact that he had opposed Jackson once before—when Jackson had invaded Florida in 1818. Van Buren also capitalized upon the dilemma posed by the Peggy Eaton affair for Jackson (see JOHN CALDWELL CALHOUN).

Jackson appointed Van Buren minister to Great Britain in 1831 while Congress was in recess. When Congress reconvened, the Senate refused to confirm his appointment by one vote—cast by vengeful Vice President John C. Calhoun. Calhoun's action prevented Van Buren's appointment, but it backfired by encouraging Jackson to choose Van Buren to be his vice presidential running mate in 1832.

Four years later, running as Jackson's designated successor against a fragmented field of several opposition candidates, Van Buren easily defeated his rivals, garnering 170 electoral votes to his nearest rival WILLIAM HENRY HARRISON's 73. In his inaugural address, Van Buren promised to adhere to Jackson's policies; but a severe economic depression, known as the Panic of 1837, which lasted throughout his administration, quickly undermined his popularity. Firmly committed to avoiding increasing federal government power, Van Buren's approach to coping with the hard economic times consisted of supporting the gold standard, removing federal deposits from all private banks (the federal

government had lost more than $10 million due to the failure of state banks), and establishing an independent treasury (Independent Treasury Act, 1836).

As the depression worsened, Van Buren was attacked as incompetent and heartless. Against great opposition, he managed to secure legislation that established a so-called independent treasury, or subtreasury system. Government funds would be placed in an independent treasury in Washington and in subtreasuries in certain other cities for exclusive use by the government through its agents. Thus no bank could use government money for speculative purposes. He also instituted the ten-hour workday for all laborers on federal projects, an act that did nothing to endear him to the average voter in the face of continued hardship. More positively received were the talks initiated with Canada to avoid war over the Maine boundary. These resulted in the Webster-Ashburton Treaty of 1842.

In many ways the campaign of 1840 was a replay of the campaign Van Buren had helped Jackson win in 1828 against John Quincy Adams. Despite his modest beginnings, Van Buren was successfully portrayed by the Whigs as an effete, insensitive aristocrat as opposed to "Log Cabin and Hard Cider" military hero William Henry Harrison. Van Buren won only 60 electoral votes versus Harrison's 234.

Van Buren returned to Kinderhook, New York, where he moved into a completely remodeled Italo-Gothic mansion named Lindenwald that he furnished with antiques. He planned to run for president again in 1844 and might have secured the Democratic nomination if he had not lost the support of Jackson and many other Democrats because of his refusal to support the annexation of Texas. Van Buren was against the admission of another slave state and feared a war with Mexico. The Democrats chose expansionist JAMES K. POLK instead.

In 1848 the wing of the New York Democratic party that opposed the extension of slavery into the newly won territory from Mexico, known as the Barnburners, nominated a reluctant Van Buren. A month later, a coalition of other disgruntled Democrats and Whigs met in Buffalo, New York, formed the Free Soil party, which was pledged to a platform against slavery, and also nominated Van Buren. The party's slogan was "Free soil, free speech, free labor, and free men." The Democrats nominated LEWIS CASS and the Whigs, Mexican War hero ZACHARY TAYLOR. Taylor went on to win the election.

After the 1848 election Van Buren spent several years traveling in Europe, where he collected antiques to furnish Lindenwald. Back in Kinderhook in 1855, Van Buren lived in relative obscurity until his death.

BIBLIOGRAPHY

Curtis, James C., *The Fox at Bay: Martin Van Buren and the Presidency, 1837–1841*, 1970; Niven, John, *Martin Van Buren: The Romantic Age of American Politics*, 1983; Wilson, Majoe L., *The Presidency of Martin Van Buren*, 1984.

Vance, Cyrus Roberts

(March 27, 1917–)
Secretary of State, Secretary of the Army

Cyrus Roberts Vance was born in Clarksburg, West Virginia. He graduated from Yale in 1939 and, after earning his law degree from there in 1942, joined the navy. He served in the Pacific during World War II, and in 1947 began to practice law in New York City.

A Democrat, Vance obtained a number of important posts over the course of his long government career. From 1957 until 1960, he was a special counsel for Senate investigating committees, and then, briefly, general counsel for the Department of Defense. In 1962 he became secretary of the army. From 1964 until 1967, during the height of the American military buildup in South Vietnam, he was deputy secretary of defense.

Vance supported American involvement in Vietnam (see LYNDON BAINES JOHNSON and RICHARD MILHOUS NIXON) until 1968. Then the military situation in South Vietnam and the domestic turmoil the war was causing in America convinced him to advise President Lyndon Johnson to stop the aerial bombing of North Vietnam and to initiate efforts to obtain a negotiated settlement of the war. During the last year of the Johnson administration, Vance served as a negotiator at the Paris peace talks with North Vietnam. He also participated in the diplomatic efforts that led to the end of the war between Greece and Turkey over Cyprus.

Vance returned to the private practice of law from 1969 until President JIMMY CARTER appointed him secretary of state in 1976. As secretary of state from 1977 until 1980, Vance championed the need for détente with the Soviet Union (see RICHARD MILHOUS NIXON and HENRY ALFRED KISSINGER). He also led efforts to obtain nuclear arms reductions, to improve relations with China, and to ease tensions in the Middle East by promoting negotiations between Israel and its hostile Arab neighbors.

Deeply concerned over the collapse of American relations with Iran after the overthrow of Shah Mohammad Reza Pahlavi and the seizure of American embassy personnel by militant Islamic fundamentalists in November 1979, Vance counseled patience and nonviolence. Without informing Vance, President Carter authorized a military mission to rescue the hostages (see JAMES EARL CARTER, JR.). Military helicopters crashed in an Iranian desert and the mission failed. Vance felt compelled to resign, the first American secretary of state to do so since WILLIAM JENNINGS BRYAN in 1915.

President Carter accepted his resignation on April 28, 1980. Since then, Vance has been an active consultant on foreign policy and arms control issues. In 1985 he was named vice chairman of the Council on Foreign Relations.

BIBLIOGRAPHY

McLellan, David S., *Cyrus Vance*, 1985; Vance, Cyrus R., *Hard Choices: Four Critical Years in Managing America's Foreign Policy*, 1983.

Vandenberg, Arthur Hendrick

(March 22, 1884–April 18, 1951)
Senator

During two decades in the U.S. Senate, Arthur H. Vandenberg evolved from a devout isolationist to a firm and important legislative supporter of America's need to participate in the United Nations and the North Atlantic Treaty Organization (NATO; see HARRY S TRUMAN).

Born in Grand Rapids, Michigan, Vandenberg attended the University of Michigan Law School but did not graduate due to poor health. Instead of becoming a lawyer, Vandenberg became the editor of the *Grand Rapids Herald*. From 1906 until his appointment to fill a vacant Senate seat in 1928, his newspaper position made him a powerful and influential force in Michigan politics. He was elected to a full term in the Senate in 1934 and reelected in 1940 and 1946.

At first, as chairman of the Senate Committee on Foreign Relations, Vandenberg was a staunch isolationist. He opposed lend-lease but altered his views after the Japanese attack on Pearl Harbor (see FRANKLIN DELANO ROOSEVELT), a day, he said later, that "ended isolation for any realist." His conversion to internationalism was gradual, however, and his support of Presidents Franklin D. Roosevelt's and HARRY TRUMAN's foreign policies was not unqualified. Secretary of State DEAN ACHESON noted a certain ritual of statesmanship in Vandenberg's position on such projects as the United Nations Relief and Rehabilitation Administration: first "opposition and then gesta-

tion, and finally a demand for political concessions before giving his full weighty stamp of approval."

In 1945 Vandenberg served as a delegate to the United Nations Conference in San Francisco. The following year he attended the Paris conference of foreign ministers as an adviser, and in 1947 he was a delegate to the Pan American Conference in Rio de Janeiro.

As a leader of Truman's efforts to develop a bipartisan foreign policy, Vandenberg played an important role in converting the isolationist Midwest wing of the Republican party to internationalism and to the support of the Democratic party's foreign policy initiatives. A great fear of communism spurred on the conversion. Vandenberg supported the Marshall Plan (see GEORGE CATLETT MARSHALL and HARRY S TRUMAN) and introduced the resolution stating "America's determination . . . to exercise the right of individual or collective self-defense," the basis for U.S. participation in NATO.

Vandenberg was president pro tempore of the Senate from 1947 to 1949 and died in office.

BIBLIOGRAPHY

Vandenberg, A. H., Jr., and J. H. Morris (eds.), *Private Papers of A. H. Vandenberg*, 1952.

Vardaman, James Kimble

(July 26, 1861–June 25, 1930)
Senator

James K. Vardaman was an outspoken isolationist whose efforts to thwart American involvement in World War I proved extremely nettlesome to President WOODROW WILSON's foreign policy goals.

Vardaman was born near Edna, Texas, and grew up in Mississippi. He read law at Carrollton and was admitted to the bar in 1882. In addition to his law practice, Vardaman edited a number of local newspapers and served in the Mississippi House of Representatives from 1890 to 1896 (speaker, 1894). During the Spanish-American War (see WILLIAM MCKINLEY, JR.), he was an army officer in Santiago, Cuba.

In 1904 Vardaman won election to the governorship by appealing to the disaffected poor white voter. He let his black hair grow to his shoulders, put on a white suit, hooked a dozen white oxen up to a huge eight-wheeled lumber wagon, and toured the state delivering passionate, populist speeches tailored to addressing the needs of poor white farmers. The "White Chief," as he was soon called, also warned that allowing blacks to obtain an education was a mistake because it threatened the proper dominance of the white man. The combination of spectacle, racism, and populism (see JAMES BAIRD WEAVER) brought him victory.

In 1912 Vardaman won election to the Senate, where he opposed President Woodrow Wilson's foreign policy initiatives on the grounds that any U.S. involvement in World War I would require an unjustifiable loss of life. Wilson was so angered by Vardaman's opposition to the war effort in 1918 (he was one of only six senators to vote against the declaration of war against Germany) that he made a direct appeal to the voters of Mississippi to oust Vardaman from office. The patriotic fervor that swept the nation after the United States entered the war proved to be too much even for the once immensely popular Vardaman, and he failed to win renomination then and in one later attempt.

BIBLIOGRAPHY

Holmes, William F., *The White Chief: James Kimble Vardaman*, 1970.

Varnum, Joseph Bradley

(January 29, 1750 or 1751–September 11, 1821)
Speaker of the House, Senator, Representative

A staunch Jeffersonian Republican, Joseph Bradley Varnum was the only New Englander in Congress to support the War of 1812 (see JAMES MADISON).

Born in Dracut, Massachusetts, Varnum received little formal education before marrying and raising a family of twelve on his small farm in Massachusetts. A captain of the militia during the American Revolution, Varnum participated in the battle of Lexington, the campaign against British forces under General John Burgoyne in 1777, and the fighting in Rhode Island the following year.

After serving in the state legislature from 1780 until 1795, Varnum became a moderate anti-Federalist. Elected a delegate to the state ratifying convention in 1788, he supported the adoption of the federal Constitution with reservations and the promise of the addition of a Bill of Rights. In 1794 he defeated the Federalist candidate by a narrow margin to win election to the House of Representatives.

In Congress Varnum benefited from the increasing popularity of THOMAS JEFFERSON and the Democratic-Republican party. Varnum supported the new party's political agenda and was chosen Speaker in 1807. Although his support for Jefferson's extremely unpopular Embargo Act of 1807, which prohibited all foreign trade to and from American ports, hurt him politically at home, Varnum still managed to win reelection every two years until 1810.

In 1810 the Massachusetts legislature chose Varnum as a compromise candidate for the U.S. Senate. During his one term from 1811 to 1817, Varnum served as president pro tempore of the Senate and as the acting vice president. Varnum also was the only New Englander to strongly support the need to go to war against the British in 1812. His position was unfavorable in Massachusetts, and he was attacked by a mob in Boston and soundly rejected by the voters in an 1813 run for governor. Despite the unpopularity of his position, Varnum never altered his views about the desirability of expanding the United States through military conquest.

Unable to win a second term in the Senate, Varnum returned to Massachusetts and was promptly elected to the Massachusetts legislature. His last public service was as a delegate to the state constitutional convention in 1820.

BIBLIOGRAPHY

Gardiner, A. B., and J. M. Varnum, biographical sketch, *Magazine of American History*, September 1887; Varnum, J. M., *The Varnums of Dracut in Massachusetts*, 1907.

Vinson, Frederick Moore

(January 22, 1890–September 8, 1953)
Secretary of the Treasury, Chief Justice of the Supreme Court, Representative

Frederick M. Vinson is recalled more for his service in the U.S. House of Representatives and accomplishments as an official in the executive branch than for his work as a chief justice of the Supreme Court.

Vinson was born in Louisa, Kentucky, and earned both his B.A. (1909) and law degrees (1911) from Centre College in Danville. After being admitted to the bar in 1911, he established a practice in Louisa and embarked upon a career in politics. In 1922 he won election to the U.S. House of Representatives, where he served three consecutive terms (1923 to 1929) before failing to win reelection in 1928—the year he managed the unsuccessful presidential campaign of AL SMITH. He was reelected in 1930, then to three more consecutive terms (1931 to 1938).

While serving as a member of the House Ways and Means Committee from 1931 to 1938 (and chairman of the taxation subcommittee after 1936), Vinson became an expert on tax and fiscal affairs. The combination of Vinson's fiscal expertise, superb political skills, and position on the powerful Ways and Means Committee enabled him to become a leader of his party in the House and to play a vital role in the enactment of President FRANKLIN D. ROOSEVELT's revenue bills and other New Deal legislation.

In 1938 President Roosevelt appointed Vinson a justice of the U.S. Court of Appeals for the District of Columbia. Five years later, he was named chief justice of the three-member Emergency Court of Appeals, which handled cases arising under the Emergency Price

Control Act. In May 1943 Vinson resigned from the court of appeals to assume directorship of the Office of Economic Stabilization. He was appointed federal loan administrator in March 1945 and director of the Office of War Mobilization and Reconversion in April of that year. After a brief three-month stint in that position, President HARRY S TRUMAN appointed Vinson secretary of the treasury. His primary task was to adapt the economy to the postwar world. Perhaps his most important accomplishments involved his role in establishing the International Bank for Reconstruction and Development and the International Monetary Fund.

In June 1946 Truman nominated Vinson as chief justice of the Supreme Court. The brilliance and political skill Vinson had displayed in his legislative and government careers did not translate into a leadership position on the Supreme Court. He lacked the breadth of legal intellect necessary to be an outstanding justice. His view of the Court's institutional role, shaped by his years in the House, was to avoid using the Court's constitutional power to set social policy. Thus, his most important opinions, upholding the right of the federal government to restrict the civil liberties of communists and to seize essential industries

(and suspend organized labor's rights) in times of national emergencies, defended actions taken by the Congress and President Truman. Civil rights proved a more vexing problem for him. While his rulings in *Sweatt* v. *Painter* (1950) and *McLaurin* v. *Oklahoma State Regents* (1950) invalidated the "separate but equal" test as applied to professional and graduate schools of state universities, he remained reluctant to challenge the very legitimacy of the segregation system that had dominated southern life since the 1890s. He died just as the Court was getting ready to decide the critical *Brown* v. *Board of Education of Topeka, Kansas* (see EARL WARREN). The supporters of integration thought that his absence from the Court improved their chances of winning a landmark decision against segregation.

BIBLIOGRAPHY

Bolner, James, "Fred M. Vinson: 1890–1938, the Years of Relative Obscurity," *Register of the Kentucky Historical Society*, 1965; Frank, John, "Fred Vinson and the Chief Justiceship," *University of Chicago Law Review*, 1954; Pritchett, C. H., *Civil Liberties and the Vinson Court*, 1954.

Volcker, Paul Adolph

(September 5, 1927–   )
Chairman of the Federal Reserve Board

Under Chairman Paul Volcker's direction, the Federal Reserve, by curbing the growth of the money supply and establishing high interest rates, helped end a period of unprecedented inflation in the United States in the late 1970s and early 1980s.

Volcker was born in Cape May, New Jersey. He graduated from Princeton in 1949 and earned a master's degree from the Harvard Graduate School of Public Administration in

1951. From 1953 until 1969 Volcker worked for the U.S. Treasury, the Federal Reserve Bank in New York City, and the Chase Manhattan Bank of New York.

In 1969 President RICHARD NIXON appointed Volcker under secretary for monetary affairs, with special responsibility for international money matters. While in this position in the early 1970s, Volcker helped to establish a floating international monetary system to replace the rigidly regulated system that had been in existence since the Bretton Woods Agreement of 1944.

From 1975 until 1979 Volcker was president of the Federal Reserve Bank of New York. In 1979 President JIMMY CARTER appointed Volcker chairman of the Federal Reserve Board, an independent federal agency that directs the U.S. banking system and manages the nation's money supply. Volcker saw the country through one of its most difficult economic eras since the Great Depression—a period of soaring inflation that he helped to tame by restricting the money supply and by forcing interest rates up to record double-digit levels. Although his policies contributed to a tough recession in 1982, they appeared to have stimulated the long period of economic growth that ensued.

After completing two terms (President RONALD REAGAN reappointed him in 1983) as chairman of the Federal Reserve in August 1988, Volcker returned to New York and split his time between a partnership in a Wall Street investment banking firm and a part-time professorship of international economic policy at Princeton University.

BIBLIOGRAPHY

Neikirk, William R., *Volcker, Portrait of the Money Man*, 1987; *New York Times*, August 18, 1971; Sterngold, James, "Volcker, the Deal-Making Professor," *New York Times*, March 3, 1988.

Wade, Benjamin Franklin

(October 27, 1800–March 2, 1878)
Senator

Benjamin Franklin Wade is recalled chiefly for his lifelong opposition to slavery and desire as a senator to ensure a Reconstruction of the Union that would secure rights and power for freed slaves and Unionists.

Wade was born near Springfield, Massachusetts. In 1821 he moved with his parents to Andover, Ohio. Largely self-educated, he tried several occupations before deciding to study law. He was admitted to the Ohio bar in 1827, settled in Jefferson, and developed a successful law practice.

In 1837, after serving a term (1835–1837) as Ashtabula County prosecuting attorney, Wade was elected as a member of the Whig party to the state senate. An opponent of slavery, his opposition to a tough new fugitive slave law led to his reelection defeat in 1839. A third try in 1841 was successful. During his second term in the state senate he worked to undermine the effectiveness of the fugitive slave law. In 1847 he was appointed justice of the third judicial district. Although committed to opposing slavery, while on the bench he avoided antislavery activities.

In 1851 the Whig-dominated state legislature elected Wade to the U.S. Senate. He won reelection in 1857 and 1863 as a Republican. In the Senate, Wade established a reputation as a fiercely dedicated, uncompromising abolitionist. He opposed the fugitive slave laws (see MILLARD FILLMORE) and, with his colleague Senator SALMON P. CHASE, fought the Kansas-Nebraska Act (see FRANKLIN PIERCE) in 1854. As a member of the Committee of Thirteen during the movement toward secession by the South in the winter of 1860–1861, Wade opposed the Crittenden plan for holding the Union together (see JOHN JORDAN CRITTENDEN). The time, he believed, for seeking a political compromise had passed.

During the Civil War Wade played a leading role in orchestrating the activities of the

Radical Republicans in Congress. In 1861 he founded and became chairman of the Committee on the Conduct of the War, which sought to pump more vigor and determination into the Union war effort. Dissatisfied with the lack of protection ABRAHAM LINCOLN's Reconstruction plan provided Unionists and freed slaves in the South, Wade cosponsored the Wade–Davis bill (see ANDREW JOHNSON).

The Wade–Davis bill required each Southern state to make a list of all its white male residents. A state government could not be recognized until a majority of the people on its voting list had taken an oath to support the Constitution. Then a state had to hold an election to choose delegates to write a new state constitution. No one could vote in that delegate election or serve as a delegate until he had promised to support the Constitution and sworn that he had never held office under the Confederacy or fought in the Confederate army.

Lincoln decided not to sign the Wade–Davis bill into law in July 1864. In an effort to avoid a confrontation with the Radical Republicans over Reconstruction policy, Lincoln announced that Southern states had a choice:

they could follow the Wade–Davis plan, or they could implement his plan.

President Andrew Johnson's decision to adhere to Lincoln's plans after Lincoln's assassination prompted Wade to lead the successful Radical Republican effort in Congress to seize control of Reconstruction policy. In 1867 Wade was chosen president pro tempore of the Senate. At that time, this position meant that he would become president if Johnson were removed from office. This fact, plus Wade's enthusiasm for impeaching Johnson and securing his conviction in the Senate, actually helped President Johnson. The thought of the domineering, vitriolic Wade in the office of the president concerned many Republicans.

After failing to win reelection to the Senate and losing a bid for the Republican nomination for vice president in 1868, Wade retired from politics. He returned to Ohio and resumed his law practice.

BIBLIOGRAPHY

Riddle, Albert G., *Life of Benjamin F. Wade,* 1886;
Trefousse, Hans L., *Benjamin Franklin Wade,* 1963.

Wagner, Robert Ferdinand

(June 8, 1877–May 4, 1953)
Senator

Robert F. Wagner guided so many key New Deal bills through the U.S. Senate that he was dubbed the "legislative pilot of the New Deal." His most significant accomplishment involved the drafting and enactment of the National Labor Relations Act (the Wagner Act).

Wagner was born in Nastätten, Germany. He moved with his family to New York when he was eight years old. He earned a B.A. from the College of the City of New York in 1898 and a law degree at New York Law School two

years later. He became involved in the Tammany Hall political machine (see WILLIAM MARCY TWEED) in 1898 while developing a prosperous law practice.

From 1904 to 1918, first as a state assemblyman and then as a state senator, Wagner shrewdly balanced Tammany Hall loyalty requirements with efforts to initiate social reform legislation. In the state senate, Wagner became known for his investigations of factory working conditions. Along with AL SMITH, he cosponsored over sixty bills to reform working conditions and establish a minimum wage. With the support of the Tammany Hall organization, fifty-six of the bills eventually became law.

In 1918 Wagner won election to a fourteen-year term on the district court in New York. During his seven years as a state supreme court justice, he worked to protect the rights of labor. In 1922 he issued the first injunction in America requiring an employer to abide by an agreement made with workers. Wagner resigned from the bench in 1926 to run for the first of four consecutive U.S. Senate terms.

Library of Congress

Even before the Great Depression began, Wagner argued for the need to have the federal government relieve urban unemployment. In 1932, when the depression was at its worst, Wagner managed to convince Republican president HERBERT HOOVER to support congressional passage of the Relief and Construction Act, the first legislation that gave the federal government the responsibility for preserving a desirable level of national employment.

After the election of Democratic president FRANKLIN D. ROOSEVELT, Wagner helped draft and obtain Senate approval for several important New Deal bills that committed the federal government to aid the national economy. Among the most important of these was the National Industrial Recovery Act in 1933, designed to prevent unfair competitive practices and to improve labor standards, and his own National Labor Relations Act in 1935 (the Wagner Act), which created the National Labor Relations Board to aid unions by prohib-

iting employers from engaging in unfair labor practices. Wagner also sponsored the bills that authorized the Civilian Conservation Corps, the Railroad Retirement Act, the farm-mortgage refinancing plan, federal low-cost subsidized housing, federal health programs, and the Social Security Act.

Wagner did not always agree with the goals of the Roosevelt administration. He fought Roosevelt's Supreme Court–packing plan in 1937 and disapproved of his proposal to reorganize the executive branch in 1938. He never won Roosevelt's support for a new federal antilynching law, which would protect blacks in the South from being hanged by groups of white vigilantes, or a full employment bill.

While chairman of the Senate banking committee during World War II, Wagner continued to press for additional social legislation with little success. His last major legislative accomplishment was the Public Housing Act of 1949, enacted shortly before his resignation from the Senate that year because of ill health. He had also become a strong proponent of the need for the United States to support the creation of the Jewish state of Israel in the Middle East. His son, Robert F. Wagner, Jr., was mayor of New York City from 1954 to 1965.

BIBLIOGRAPHY

Huthmacher, Joseph, J., *Senator Robert F. Wagner and the Rise of Urban Liberalism,* 1968.

Waite, Morrison Remick

(November 29, 1816–March 23, 1888)
Chief Justice of the Supreme Court

As chief justice of the United States Supreme Court for fourteen years, Waite proved to be a far-seeing magistrate who made important contributions to constitutional law, most notably in the preservation of legislative as opposed to judicial power.

Born into a distinguished legal family in Lyme, Connecticut, Waite graduated from Yale College in 1837, moved to Maumee, Ohio, the next year, and was admitted to that state's bar in 1839. He was elected to a single term in the Ohio legislature in 1849. In 1850 he moved to Toledo and established a successful practice specializing in corporate finance and real estate matters for railroad clients.

Always active politically behind the scenes during the 1850s, Waite made a second unsuccessful try for Congress in 1862. He was a staunch defender of the Union cause in Ohio during the Civil War, and his record of serving only one term in the Ohio legislature is not an accurate reflection of his political influence. He performed such an important part in securing Ohio's loyalty to the Union that he was offered an appointment as a reward to the Ohio Supreme Court, which he declined so that he could serve as an unofficial adviser to the governor.

In 1871 Waite served as one of the American counselors in the arbitration of Civil War claims against England. His capable performance in Geneva was undoubtedly a significant factor in President ULYSSES S. GRANT's selection of him for chief justice after the first two nominees, George H. Williams and Caleb Cushing, were not approved by the Senate.

In *Munn* v. *Illinois* (1877), Waite held that when private property becomes "clothed with a public interest," it should be publicly regulated. In *Pensacola Telegraph Co.* v. *Western Union Telegraph Co.* (1878), he contributed to the expansion of congressional power over interstate commerce. These cases established a lasting precedent in matters concerning public utilities. Waite felt that "until Congress acts" (and it did not until the Interstate Commerce Act of 1887), such laws were essential to a given state's welfare. In *Stone* v. *Farmers' Loan and Trust Company* (1886), however, he insisted on reasonable state laws and cautioned that "this power . . . of regulation is itself [not] without limit." No state, he warned, could take over private property without due process of law.

Waite was firmly committed to protecting legislative power from encroachment by the judiciary. His most important decision in the area of civil rights—*Reynolds* v. *United States* (1879)—concerned upholding the power of the United States to make bigamy a crime in spite of Mormon claims of protection on the grounds of religious freedom.

BIBLIOGRAPHY

Magrath, C. Peter, *Morrison R. Waite*, 1963; Trimble, Bruce B., *Chief Justice Waite*, 1970.

Walker, Robert John

(July 19, 1801–November 11, 1869)
Secretary of the Treasury, Senator

Two passions, politics and financial speculation, dominated Robert J. Walker's life. Critics claimed that Walker often confused the two. Supporters noted that if he did, the nation benefited.

Walker was born in Northumberland, Pennsylvania. He graduated at the top of his class from the University of Pennsylvania in 1819 and was admitted to the bar in Pittsburgh in 1821. Although he had become a leader of the Democratic party in Pennsylvania within a few years, the need to earn more money led Walker to join his brother in Natchez, Mississippi, in 1826. The two established a lucrative law practice in Natchez, and within a decade Walker had enough money to run for national political office.

In 1835, aided by a letter (which may have been forged) from President ANDREW JACKSON encouraging voters to support his candidacy, Walker was elected as a Jacksonian Democrat to the first of his two successive terms in the Senate.

While in the Senate, Walker supported low tariffs; the passage of the Independent Treasury Act of 1836, which provided for the deposit of government funds in subtreasuries rather than in banks (see MARTIN VAN BUREN); protection for the institution of slavery; and the expansion of the United States through the annexation of Texas (see JAMES KNOX POLK). He also played an important role in the passage of the Preemption Act of 1841. This act permitted settlers on unsurveyed public lands to locate a claim of 160 acres and after six months of residence purchase it from the government for as little as $1.25 an acre.

In return for Walker's shrewd handling of his compromise "dark horse" selection by the Democratic convention in 1844, President James K. Polk named Walker secretary of the treasury in 1845. A close adviser to the president, Walker helped resolve the conflict with England over the ownership of the Oregon Territory (see JAMES KNOX POLK). He also oversaw the implementation of lower tariff rates (the Walker Tariff of 1846 carried his name). A diligent and efficient administrator, Walker managed to secure a badly needed loan in Europe to help finance the war with Mexico (see JAMES KNOX POLK), established what became the model for warehousing imported goods to the United States for inspection, and sponsored the bill that created the Department of the Interior.

After leaving office in 1849, Walker capitalized on his political contacts by becoming a lobbyist and land speculator. In 1851 and 1852 he acted as an agent in London for selling Illinois Central Railroad securities, then accepted appointment as governor of the volatile Kansas Territory in March 1857. Walker's hopes that this office would lead to a Senate seat were dashed when his actions in Kansas were interpreted by Southerners as a betrayal.

As territorial governor, Walker authorized a state constitutional convention to meet in Lecompton, Kansas, in 1857. This convention was to determine, based upon majority (popular sovereignty) rule, whether the Kansas Territory should seek to be admitted to the Union as a slave or free state. Walker wanted a fair representation of the territory's slave and antislave population to participate. However, because local election districts had been gerrymandered (see ELBRIDGE GERRY) in favor of proslavery candidates and the election returns were in the control of local proslavery officials, antislavery advocates refused to participate. The proslavery forces produced what became known as the Lecompton Constitution (see JAMES BUCHANAN). The issue of rejecting or accepting the document's proslavery position, not whether to accept or to reject the whole document, was then submitted to a popular referendum. Once again, antislavery advocates refused to participate. After the election, slavery forces ignored the fact that less than a majority of the state's citizens had voted, declared the Lecompton Constitution ratified, and sent it to President James Buchanan to submit to Congress. Two months later, in January 1858, when the newly elected Kansas legislature submitted the Lecompton Constitution as a whole to the people, the majority of Kansas voters rejected it. Nevertheless, and despite Walker's appeal for the president to ignore the Lecompton Constitution as a fraud, President Buchanan decided to submit it to Congress. Faced with a lack of support in Kansas and in the White House, Walker resigned as territorial governor.

During the Civil War, Walker returned to England and was successful in selling bonds to finance the North's war effort. Long convinced of the need for the United States to acquire more territory (he had supported the annexation of the Yucatan and Cuba while secretary of the treasury), Walker helped in the successful effort to purchase Alaska and at the time of his death hoped that the United States would acquire Nova Scotia.

BIBLIOGRAPHY

Dodd, William Edward, *Robert J. Walker, Imperialist,* 1914; Shenton, James P., *Robert John Walker: A Politician from Jackson to Lincoln,* 1961.

Wallace, George Corley

(August 25, 1919–   )
Candidate for President

First as a segregationist governor who defiantly claimed that state sovereignty gave him the right to exclude black students from state public schools, then as a third-party candidate for president, George Corley Wallace articulated a discontent with Democratic party liberalism that made him a hero to millions of American voters in the 1960s.

Wallace was born in Clio, Alabama. In 1936, while a junior in high school, Wallace won the state Golden Gloves bantamweight boxing championship and boxed professionally to help support himself while he studied at the University of Alabama Law School from 1937 until he graduated in

AP/Wide World Photos

1942. During World War II Wallace served in the air force in the Pacific.

In 1947 Wallace was elected as a Democrat to the first of two terms in the state legislature. At the Democratic national convention in 1948, Wallace led the fight against the insertion of a strong civil rights plank in the party platform. However, he refused to join other southern delegates who walked out of the convention when the statement was endorsed by the convention.

Wallace served as a state circuit court judge from 1953 to 1959. He achieved statewide notoriety in this post because of his defiance of a federal court order to produce voting records in 1956. The U.S. Civil Rights Commission wanted the records in order to investigate charges of discrimination against black voters. He lost his first bid for governor in 1958 but was elected in 1962 by promising to lead the fight against integration of schools and other public facilities in Alabama. "Segregation now, segregation tomorrow, and segregation forever!" became his popular, defiant cry.

The pressure to end segregation—in schools, colleges, hotels, restaurants, employment, and all American life—was intense when he assumed the governor's office. In April 1963 Martin Luther King, Jr., and the Southern Christian Leadership Conference began a drive employing nonviolent tactics to end segregation in Birmingham, Alabama. The brutal reaction of the Birmingham police force—the unleashing of police dogs and of high-powered hoses on demonstrators—was seen on national television.

Governor Wallace supported the actions of the Birmingham police and two months later stood in the path of two black students to prevent them from enrolling at the University of Alabama. The issue, he said, raised a fundamental constitutional question concerning the usurpation of state authority by the federal government. However, four hours later, after President JOHN F. KENNEDY dispatched federalized units of the Alabama National Guard to the university, Wallace backed down and allowed black students to register.

Ineligible by state law to succeed himself, Wallace had his wife, Lurleen, run for governor in 1966, with the understanding that he would continue to set the policies for the state. Lurleen died in office in 1968, the same year Wallace ran for president at the head of the American Independent party's national ticket.

Racial turmoil and the Vietnam War (see LYNDON BAINES JOHNSON and RICHARD MILHOUS NIXON) dominated the 1968 presidential campaign. During the year both Martin Luther King, Jr., and Democratic senator ROBERT F. KENNEDY were assassinated, and numerous ra-

cial riots erupted in American cities. Wallace reiterated his opposition to federal enforcement of public school integration, attacked the liberal Supreme Court under EARL WARREN for coddling criminals, advocated halting government efforts to prevent racial discrimination in the sale or rental of all housing, and promised to win in Vietnam. "I think," he said, "we've got to pour it on there."

Wallace did not think he could win the general election as a third-party candidate. His goal was to appeal to enough discontented voters to keep either of the major parties from winning so that the election would be thrown into the House of Representatives. In the House his supporters could use their votes for trading purposes to achieve Wallace's goals.

Wallace won 10 million popular votes (13 percent of the total) and the electoral votes of five southern states. He attracted the support not only of southern whites, but also of significant numbers of northern white ethnics who felt betrayed by the Democratic party's willingness to accommodate the demands of blacks and university youth. Republican candidate Richard Nixon won by only 43.4 percent of the total vote. This was the lowest winning majority since the three-way presidential race in 1912, but Nixon secured enough electoral votes to be declared the winner. Still, the power of Wallace's appeal was not lost on Nixon, and he increasingly tailored his rhetoric to attract Wallace supporters into the Republican party.

In 1969 the Alabama state constitutional bar against gubernatorial succession was repealed, and the following year Wallace was elected governor. During his second term in office, Wallace was much more moderate on racial issues and won considerable black support. On May 15, 1972, while campaigning in Laurel, Maryland, for Democratic primary votes in a new effort to win the Democratic party nomination for president, Wallace was shot by a disturbed spectator. Wallace survived, but he was forced to abandon his campaign. His wounds left him permanently paralyzed from the waist down.

Two years later, Wallace was elected to a third term as governor. He made one last, unsuccessful try for the Democratic party presidential nomination in 1976. Before his retirement from politics in 1987 due to complications from his gunshot wounds, he completed a fourth term as governor (1982–1986).

BIBLIOGRAPHY

Frady, Marshall, *Wallace*, 1968.

Wallace, Henry Agard

(October 7, 1888–November 18, 1965)
Vice President, Secretary of Agriculture, Secretary of Commerce, Candidate for President

During his two decades in national politics, Henry Agard Wallace served as President FRANKLIN D. ROOSEVELT's secretary of agriculture and vice president and President HARRY S TRUMAN's secretary of commerce. He also ran as the Progressive party's candidate for president in 1948, changed political parties twice, and underwent a drastic public reversal of his early positive attitudes toward the Soviet Union.

Born in Adair County, Iowa, Wallace graduated from Iowa State College with a degree in agriculture in 1910. A Republican, Wallace joined the family business and became an associate editor of the influential farm magazine *Wallaces' Farmer*. When his father retired in 1924, Wallace became editor and merged the magazine with the *Iowa Homestead* four years later. In addition to his magazine responsibilities, Wallace developed a successful new strain of corn and founded a company to market it.

Wallace firmly believed in the goals of Progressivism (see THEODORE ROOSEVELT), which, until the 1920s, had carried significant influence in the Republican party. Frustrated by the collapse of the Republicans' Progressive wing (see ROBERT MARION LA FOLLETTE) and by the party's increasingly conservative farm policies, Wallace supported the Democrat ALFRED E. SMITH for president in 1928 and played an important role in ensuring Iowa's support for Franklin D. Roosevelt in 1932. In 1933 President Roosevelt appointed Wallace secretary of agriculture. In this position Wallace supervised the Agricultural Adjustment Administration's controversial efforts to regulate farm prices by limiting production and destroying surplus crops and livestock.

By the late 1930s Wallace had come to be seen as a leader of the left wing of the Democratic party, a sizable group whose political plans for the United States closely resembled those of social democrats in Europe. During World War II Wallace extended this vision and became identified with a worldwide struggle for democracy that would usher in the "People's Century." This was in stark contrast to the "American Century" vision of Henry Luce, the founder of *Time* magazine, who pictured a world rebuilt under American tutelage.

When President Roosevelt chose Wallace as his running mate in 1940, many Democratic party leaders protested. "Just because the Republicans have nominated an apostate Democrat [see WENDELL LEWIS WILLKIE]," said one, "let us not for God's sake nominate an apostate Republican." During his term as vice president from 1941 to 1945, Wallace made several goodwill tours of Latin America and Asia and briefly chaired the Board of Economic Warfare.

Wallace's open support of the Soviet Union and his continued insistence on extending the New Deal at home stirred controversy about his views and brought him increasing opposition, both within the Democratic party and among the American people at large. Roosevelt's advisers convinced the president, whom they were afraid would not live through a fourth term, to drop Wallace from the ticket in 1944 in favor of the more conservative Harry S Truman.

Instead of vice president, Roosevelt appointed Wallace as his new secretary of commerce. Wallace was confirmed by the Senate on March 1, 1945, just a month before Roosevelt's death. Truman asked Wallace to remain in office, but after Wallace criticized Truman's "get tough" policy toward the Soviet Union in a speech in September 1946, Truman asked for Wallace's resignation.

Wallace became editor of the *New Republic* magazine, and in 1948 accepted the presidential nomination of the newly formed and communist-influenced Progressive party. Running on a platform that attacked the Marshall Plan (see GEORGE CATLETT MARSHALL and HARRY S TRUMAN), advocated disarmament, and called for peaceful relations with the Soviet Union, Wallace garnered more than a million popular votes but failed to carry a single state. Two years later, Wallace resigned from the Progressive party after it condemned his support of the U.S. intervention in Korea. In 1952 Wallace wrote an article that appeared in the magazine *This Week* entitled "Why I Was Wrong," in which he confessed that he had been wrong about trusting the Soviet Union. In a complete reversal, his once positive feelings toward the Soviet Union were now replaced by deep enmity.

During the 1950s Wallace retired from national politics to his farm in New York and concentrated his energies on developing new strains of crops and running his Hi-Bred Corn Company.

BIBLIOGRAPHY

Macdonald, Dwight, *Henry Wallace,* 1948; Markowitz, Norman D., *The Rise and Fall of the People's Century,* 1973; Schapsmeier, Edward L., and Frederick H. Schapsmeier, *Henry A. Wallace of Iowa, 1910–1965,* 2 vols., 1968–1970; Wallace, Henry A., *America Must Choose,* 1934, and *Sixty Million Jobs,* 1945.

Warren, Earl

(March 19, 1891–July 9, 1974)
Chief Justice of the Supreme Court

One of the great modern chief justices, Earl Warren's name became synonymous with the fight for civil rights and the preservation of individual freedoms. Born in Los Angeles, Warren graduated from the University of California at Berkeley in 1912, and earned his law degree from the University of California in 1914. Warren's early career was marked by law practice, service in the army in World War I, and various prosecutorial positions, which led to his appointment as California's attorney general in 1939.

Warren was elected governor of California with unprecedented bipartisan support in 1942, 1946, and 1950. As a Republican governor with Democratic support, Warren increased old age and unemployment benefits; overhauled the state penal system; inaugurated a public works program of new schools, highways, hospitals, and parks to meet the needs of the state's expanding population; and reduced taxes. He proposed a statewide compulsory health insurance program and fought a loyalty oath requirement for the state university's faculty. These progressive measures were offset by three other positions. He favored a loyalty pledge for all state employees, signed a bill outlawing the Communist party in California, and supported the internment of West Coast Japanese Americans during World War II. This last action Warren deeply regretted in later life.

Library of Congress

In 1948 Warren ran for vice president on the Republican ticket with THOMAS E. DEWEY and suffered the only defeat of his political career. After an unsuccessful bid for the presidential nomination in 1952, Warren backed DWIGHT D. EISENHOWER. After his election, Eisenhower named Warren chief justice of the Supreme Court.

During Warren's tenure from 1953 to 1969, the Court faced a variety of critical issues, but the most important decisions involved civil rights questions. As Warren explained, "The very atmosphere in which we live is charged with the subject." Despite his early reputation as a "hard" prosecutor, Warren consistently backed the broad interpretation of the constitutional protections of the individual. His opinions, based on a sense of fairness as much as legal precedent, brought him both praise and criticism.

Warren's first major opinion, delivered on May 17, 1954, for a unanimous court, involved the desegregation of schools. *Brown* v. *Board of Education of Topeka, Kansas* overturned the sixty-year-old "separate but equal" doctrine that had allowed segregated schools. The Warren Court held that separate educational facilities were inherently unequal, and that racially segregated schools deprived children of equal educational opportunities. Desegregation, the Court decreed, should be implemented "with all deliberate speed." This ruling was later extended to transportation, recreation, and other activities. *Brown* v. *Board of Education* is generally agreed to have given impetus to the civil rights movement. It also triggered massive resistance in the South, forcing President Eisenhower to send in federal troops to enforce the Court's decrees.

Warren delivered many other decisions for the Court that cut across a wide spectrum to safeguard individual liberties and made him the most controversial judge of his time. First as a dissenter, then as the voice of the majority in *Reid* v. *Covert* (1957) and *Kinsella* v. *United States, et al.* (1960), Warren argued that the trial of civilians by the military was always unconstitutional. *Engle* v. *Vitale* (1962) found prayers in public schools unconstitutional. *Gideon* v. *Wainwright* (1963) ruled that felony defendants were entitled to a lawyer despite their inability to pay. *Escobedo* v. *Illinois* (1964) held that a defendant must be allowed access to a lawyer before being questioned by police. *Miranda* v. *Arizona* (1966) confirmed the obligation of authorities to inform a criminal suspect of his or her rights.

As chief justice, Warren supported broadening the interpretation of the Fourteenth Amendment to apply to state governments the restrictions placed on the federal government in the Bill of Rights. In *Baker* v. *Carr* (1962), he ordered state legislatures to apportion representation so that each citizen's role would carry equal weight. In *Reynolds* v. *Sims* (1964), Warren, speaking for the Court, argued that state election districts that were not apportioned on a "one man, one vote" population basis were unconstitutional because they denied citizens equal protection under the law.

After President JOHN F. KENNEDY's assassination, Warren reluctantly agreed to accept President LYNDON B. JOHNSON's request that he head the official investigation into the matter. The conclusion of the Warren Commission that Lee Harvey Oswald acted alone has never been disproven, but it continues to remain a source of controversy.

BIBLIOGRAPHY

Cox, Archibald, *Warren Court: Constitutional Decision as an Instrument of Reform*, 1968; Katcher, Leo, *Earl Warren: A Political Biography*, 1967; Kluger, Richard, *Simple Justice: The History of Brown v. Board of Education and Black America's Struggle For Equality*, 1976; Pollack, Jack Harrison, *Earl Warren: The Judge Who Changed America*, 1979; Schwartz, Bernard, *Super Chief; Earl Warren and His Supreme Court, A Judicial Biography*, 1983; Warren, Earl, *The Memoirs of Earl Warren*, 1977; White, G. Edward, *Earl Warren: A Public Life*, 1982.

Washburne, Elihu Benjamin

(September 23, 1816–October 22, 1887)
Secretary of State, Diplomat, Representative

Elihu Benjamin Washburne was born on a small farm in Livermore, Maine. After briefly attending Harvard Law School in 1839, he established a law practice in Galena, Illinois. The profits from successful investments in western lands enabled Washburne to enter politics as a Whig candidate for Congress in 1848. Although he failed to win election then, four years later he won a seat in the House of Representatives that he retained for the next sixteen years (1853 to 1869).

In Congress Washburne earned a reputation for honesty. As chairman of the committee on appropriations, he became known as a devout protector of the taxpayer from special interest group raids upon the Treasury and from corruption in the distribution of western lands. He was nicknamed the watchdog of the treasury.

During the Civil War Washburne was a loyal supporter of ABRAHAM LINCOLN and ULYSSES S. GRANT. As a Radical Republican during Reconstruction, he was one of President ANDREW JOHNSON's sharpest critics.

In recognition of his support, President Grant appointed Washburne secretary of state in 1869. Washburne assumed the office but resigned only five days later in order to become the minister to France. Grant had evidently appointed him secretary of state solely to enhance his diplomatic prestige in Europe.

During the siege of Paris in the Franco-Prussian War and the subsequent chaos of the Paris Commune, Washburne was the only foreign diplomat to remain in the city. Upon his return to the United States, he launched an unsuccessful attempt to secure the Republican nomination for president in 1880. When Grant decided to try for a third term, Washburne loyally offered his support. Grant lost the nomination and blamed his defeat on Washburne's candidacy. The two men never spoke to each other again.

BIBLIOGRAPHY

Hunt, Gaillard, *Israel, Elihu, and Cadwallader Washburne*, 1925.

Washington, Bushrod

(June 5, 1762–November 26, 1829)
Associate Justice of the Supreme Court

Bushrod Washington was born in Westmoreland County, Virginia, into a distinguished family. (GEORGE WASHINGTON was his uncle.) He graduated from William and Mary College in 1778 and served in the American Revolution from 1780 to 1782 before being admitted to the bar and establishing a practice, first in Alexandria, and then Richmond in 1790. Active in local politics, he was a member of the Virginia House of Delegates and served in 1788 in the Virginia convention that adopted the Constitution.

In 1798 he was appointed associate justice of the Supreme Court by President JOHN ADAMS. At the time, the appointment did not seem important, since it was believed that the Supreme Court would play a very small part in national affairs compared to the executive and legislative branches. Instead, during the course of his thirty-one years on the Supreme Court, Washington participated, as a strong supporter of Chief Justice JOHN MARSHALL'S views, in the cases that established the foundation for the Supreme Court's vital role in American political life. He also rendered a number of important decisions concerning admiralty and commercial law.

Bushrod Washington was executor of George Washington's estate and helped John Marshall in writing his biography of George Washington. After the death of Martha Washington, Bushrod established his residence at Mount Vernon.

BIBLIOGRAPHY

Binney, Horace, *Bushrod Washington*, 1852; Carson, H. L., *History of the Supreme Court in the U.S.*, 2 vols., 1902; Warren, Charles, *The Supreme Court in the U.S.*, 1926.

Washington, George

(February 22, 1732–December 14, 1799)
President, Revolutionary Leader

George Washington played an indispensable role in the founding of the United States. The American Revolution might well have been lost without Washington's leadership and the young nation torn apart without his unifying presence.

Library of Congress

Washington was born on the family plantation in Westmoreland County, Virginia. He received little formal education except from tutors. A great deal of the knowledge and self-confidence he acquired came from his older half-brother, Lawrence, who was educated in England and served as a surrogate father after the death of their father in 1743.

Even as a youth, the tall and hardy Washington was possessed of exceptional dignity and self-confidence. Lawrence's marriage into the powerful Fairfax family enabled Washington to enter the world of the wealthy Virginia planter class. In 1747 he accompanied George Fairfax on a land-surveying mission in the Shenandoah Valley. Fascinated by the frontier, Washington became a strong supporter (and land speculator) of the Ohio Company's efforts to foster the development of the West.

With the death of his half-brother in 1752, Washington moved into Mount Vernon, a large estate, and thanks to the efforts of Colonel William Fairfax was appointed at the age of twenty-one a major in the Virginia militia.

Washington's first military action occurred on the frontier. During a campaign to dislodge French and Indian troops in the Ohio Valley, Washington's men were forced to surrender, and he had to sign a statement acknowledging that he had "assassinated" the leader of a small French force his men had ambushed. Disillusioned by his first military experience and bitter over a British ruling that colonial officers could not rise above the rank of captain, Washington resigned his commission in 1754. The following year, as General Edward Braddock's civilian adviser, Washington returned to the scene of his disgrace. Braddock refused to heed his advice about the necessity of learning to fight like the Indians in the wilderness, and Braddock's troops were decimated by a French and Indian ambush. Washington won widespread praise for taking control of the situation after Braddock was mortally wounded and organizing a successful retreat. A grateful Virginia legislature appointed him colonel and commander in chief of the state militia. For the next several years Washington endured the frustrating burden of trying to defend settlers from hit-and-run Indian raids with too few men and supplies. Finally, in 1758, after a combined British and American force succeeded in driving the French from the Ohio Valley, Washington was able to retire from military service.

After his return to civilian life at Mount Vernon, Washington married a rich widow, Martha Custis, in 1759. Two years later, he inherited Mount Vernon, and during his thirties lived the life of a wealthy planter. He successfully speculated in land and served in the Virginia House of Burgesses from 1759 to

1774. Washington was also a patriot. He opposed the Stamp Act in 1765 (see JOHN ADAMS and SAMUEL ADAMS), and when other Virginians urged caution after the Boston Tea Party, he declared that the cause of Massachusetts was the cause of all America. From 1774 to 1775 he served as a delegate to the Continental Congress. When war came, the forty-three-year-old Washington was unanimously chosen to lead the American forces.

Washington felt that he lacked sufficient military experience to take charge of the war effort, but he also knew that there was no other qualified leader available. The combination of his inexperience in leading large numbers of troops in battle, the inexperience of the militias, poor supplies, lack of naval support, and the sectional hostilities between the North (especially New England) and the South almost lost the war by the winter of 1776. But Washington gradually acquired a masterful sense of military skill through his errors. His ability to learn under duress and refusal to accept defeat kept an American army in the field.

On Christmas eve in 1776, he launched a successful surprise attack at Trenton, New Jersey, that reversed a long series of defeats, then succeeded again with another surprise attack at Princeton on January 2, 1777. These two raids enabled Washington to preserve the American forces. Even after the dismal winter of 1777–1778 at Valley Forge, Washington refused to consider the idea of defeat. Within a year the defeat of the British army at Saratoga, New York, led to French support, and gradually Washington was able to train and equip a credible army. Then, at the Battle of Yorktown in 1781 with French troop and naval support, Washington was able to entrap the main British force in the colonies under the command of Lord Cornwallis.

Washington could not have forced Cornwallis to surrender without French help, but the victory at Yorktown and the credit for winning what turned out to be the decisive battle of the war belonged to Washington.

One final incident of the war demonstrated Washington's commitment to republican government. In 1782 a large number of army officers held a meeting to contemplate action to obtain years of back pay they were owed by Congress. Washington heard that a march on Congress might occur and made it clear that he did not condone such an action. His example of sacrifice (he requested compensation only for his expenses) silenced further discussion of the matter by the officers, and his appeal to Congress led to its decision to pay the men the full five years of compensation they were owed.

At the end of the war in 1783, Washington was the most famous man in America. He returned to Mount Vernon, but was soon convinced that the Articles of Confederation did not provide a central government strong enough to ensure the success of the republic he had fought so hard to create. After participating in a series of preliminary meetings, Washington agreed to preside over what became the Constitutional Convention in Philadelphia in 1787. The impact of Washington's support for ratification of the new Constitution is incalculable, but it was undoubtedly tremendous. The fear of creating a new king was negated by the general knowledge that Washington would assume the office of president.

After the new government was organized, Washington was unanimously chosen to be president. He was reelected to a second term in 1792. It was, as historian Clinton Rossiter observed, "no easy task to be the first occupant of a mistrusted office under a dubious Constitution."

Washington assumed the office of president on April 30, 1789, acutely aware that everything he did established a precedent (for example, that the president has the power to select and nominate executive officers and the power to remove them). He hoped to prevent the rise of divisive partisanship and sectionalism by appointing the most talented people available to his cabinet. He chose THOMAS JEFFERSON to be secretary of state, ALEXANDER HAMILTON secretary of the treasury, HENRY KNOX secretary of war, EDMUND RANDOLPH attorney general, and Samuel Osgood postmaster general. The group was representative of the various regions and political perspectives of the new nation. To clearly demonstrate that he was the president of all the people in all the states, Washington traveled the length of the country and received the warm applause of a grateful public.

Washington's administrative style was to listen to the arguments of both sides about an issue, investigate the facts, make up his mind, then stick tenaciously to his decision. He was sure that the people would eventually come to see the wisdom of the course of action that he had chosen. This method of leadership was perfectly suited to implementing the brilliant economic legislative proposals developed by Alexander Hamilton. Before Washington left office in 1796, the nation had a sound currency, adequate tax revenue to meet government expenses, an internationally respected credit rating, an adequate network of sound banks, and the start of a tax system designed to aid the development of manufacturing and maritime commerce. So much accomplished in such a short period aroused considerable controversy. There was even a short-lived Whiskey Rebellion (see ALEXANDER HAMILTON) in 1794 by farmers in western Pennsylvania opposed to paying an excise tax. Washington led an army against the farmers who were terrorizing the tax collectors, but the farmers chose not to join battle.

The first goal of Washington's foreign policy was to keep the United States at peace. (See JOHN JAY.) Washington knew that the young republic had to concentrate on establishing its economy and government and could not afford to become embroiled in European conflicts. His second objective was to obtain British and Spanish concessions that would facilitate the settlement of the Ohio Valley. His last major goal was to obtain commercial trade markets for the United States in order to stimulate the economy and to bring in tariff revenue to support the government.

The support Washington gave for Hamilton's nationalist financial measures and his decision not to support Jefferson's belief that the United States was treaty-bound to aid France in its war with Great Britain in 1793 proved to be too much for Jefferson. He resigned at the end of the first of Washington's two terms in office and founded the Democratic-Republican party to oppose the Federalist perspective personified by Hamilton.

Although tension continued between settlers and Indians in the West, organized armed resistance by the Indians was crushed by General Anthony Wayne in 1794. Two years later, the British finally evacuated the forts they had continued to hold within American territory. In 1795 Spain agreed to allow U.S. farmers the right to navigate the entire length of the Mississippi River and three years of tax-free access to the port of New Orleans to ship their produce. The southern boundary of the United States with Florida was also agreed upon.

With the new government provided by the Constitution firmly established, Washington decided not to seek reelection in 1796, thereby establishing the tradition of two terms for the presidency upheld until FRANKLIN D. ROOSEVELT was elected to a third term in 1940. (Presidents are now restricted to two terms by the Twenty-second Amendment.) Disheartened by the rise of the two-party system, he retired to Mount Vernon. His famous Farewell Address admonished the country to avoid foreign entanglements.

Washington answered the call to duty one more time in 1798 when he agreed to assume command of an army to be raised in the event of war with France. Fortunately, he prevailed upon President John Adams to ignore the war fever in the nation—at the cost of sacrificing Adams's reelection chances—to successfully pursue a peaceful compromise solution. His last public statements defended the Alien and Sedition Acts (see JOHN ADAMS and THOMAS JEFFERSON) and denied the states' rights concept advocated in the Kentucky and Virginia Resolutions (see THOMAS JEFFERSON).

"Washington's life," noted political analyst Garry Wills, "verged on legend, even as he lived it, because . . . he came close enough for others to accept him as a literal fulfillment of the age's aspirations." Historians agree that his achievements qualify him for a place among the great leaders of world history.

BIBLIOGRAPHY

Alden, John R., *George Washington: A Biography*, 1984; Fitzgerald, John C., *George Washington Himself*, 1933 (reprint 1975); Flexner, James T., *George Washington: A Biography*, 4 vols., 1965–1972, and *Washington: The Indispensable Man*, 1974 (reprint 1979); Ford, Paul L., completed by John A. Carrol and Mary Ashworth, *The True George Washington*, 7 vols., 1948–1957; Higginbotham, Don, *George Washington and the American Military Tradition*, 1985; Irving, Washington, *Life of George Washington*, 5 vols., 1883 (reprint 1983); Jackson, Donald, and Dorothy Twohig (eds.), *The Diaries of George Washington*, 6 vols., 1976–1979; Morgan, Edmund S., *The Genius of George Washington*, 1980; Nettels, Curtis P., *George Washington and American Independence*, 1951 (reprint 1977); Wills, Garry, *Cincinnatus: George Washington and the Enlightenment*, 1984.

Watson, Thomas Edward

(September 5, 1856–September 26, 1922)
Candidate for President, Senator, Representative

Populist party (see JAMES BAIRD WEAVER) candidate and writer Tom Watson was a leader in the crusade for political reform at the turn of the century.

Watson was born in Columbia County, Georgia. He attended Mercer University for two years, then studied law and was admitted to the bar in 1875. As a criminal lawyer in Thomson, Georgia, he quickly established a thriving practice.

At age twenty-three, he embarked upon a political career as an agrarian reformer. His fierce denunciations of Northern industrialist "special interests" won him a statewide reputation and in 1882, a two-year term in the Georgia House of Representatives.

Watson became convinced that the only way for the South to throw off the yoke of Northern domination was to form an alliance with the agrarian West. In 1890 he ran for Congress as a Democrat on the Farmers' Alliance platform. After winning election, he abandoned the Democratic party and declared that he was a Populist. In Congress he supported the Farmers' Alliance platform, supported organized labor, and sought the free delivery of rural mail. He also edited and published the *People's Party Paper* (1891) and the *The People's Party Campaign Book* (1892).

In 1896 Watson was nominated to be the Populist candidate for vice president. Watson's dedication to the Populist cause led him to swallow his pride and to agree to appear on the same ticket as Democrat WILLIAM JENNINGS BRYAN. It was a humiliating national campaign experience for Watson. The effort to fuse the Democrats and Populists did not succeed, and Republican WILLIAM MCKINLEY won the presidency.

Watson retired from politics in 1896 to write popular history and biography, returning, however, in 1904 to run as the Populist party candidate for president. He won only 117,183 votes but attracted considerable attention. He made a final, nominal effort for the presidency in 1908.

Dismay over his lack of political success caused Watson to grow embittered. His Populist reform zeal was twisted into hatred for

Catholics, blacks, Jews, and socialists. He even championed the Ku Klux Klan (see ULYSSES SIMPSON GRANT).

Watson's opposition to U.S. entry into World War I and the draft led to his political resurrection. After narrowly losing a race for Congress in 1918, he was overwhelmingly elected to the Senate in 1920 on a platform calling for the restoration of civil liberties and opposition to U.S. participation in the League of Nations (see WOODROW WILSON). During his two years in the Senate, Watson fought Wood-

row Wilson's foreign policy goals and voted against U.S. participation in the league. He died in office.

BIBLIOGRAPHY

Brewton, W. W., *The Life of Thomas E. Watson,* 1926; Watson, Thomas E., *Life and Speeches of Thomas E. Watson,* 1908; Woodward, C. Vann, *Tom Watson: Agrarian Rebel,* 1955.

Weaver, James Baird

(June 12, 1833–February 6, 1912)
Candidate for President, Representative

Born in Dayton, Ohio, James Baird Weaver grew up on the Michigan and Iowa frontiers. He entered Cincinnati Law School in 1855, graduated a year later, and practiced law in Iowa until he enlisted in the Union army in 1861. By the time he left the service in 1865, he had been promoted to brevet brigadier general.

Weaver returned to Iowa after the Civil War and, as a member of the Republican party, was elected district attorney of the second Iowa judicial district in 1866. The following year he accepted an appointment as a federal assessor of internal revenue. He remained in this position until 1873. In 1874 he made an unsuccessful bid to win the Republican party nomination for Congress. When a try for the nomination for governor also failed the next year, Weaver, who had found himself in disagreement with the Republican party's support for the gold standard, decided to join the Greenback party. The Greenback party supported the use of silver as well as gold to back government-issued paper money. The goal was to increase the money supply in order to reduce the debt burden of farmers. As a candidate of the Greenback party, Weaver

won election to Congress in 1878. In 1880 he polled more than 300,000 popular votes as the party's nominee for president, but he failed to win any electoral votes. Weaver's first attempt to return to Congress in 1882 was unsuccessful; but in 1884, with the support of the Democratic and Greenback–Labor parties, he was elected to two consecutive terms in Congress, where he served from 1885 to 1889.

In July 1892 a group composed primarily of western and southern farmers, convinced of the need for radical economic and political reform, met in Omaha, Nebraska, and established the Populist (People's) party. The party platform called for the free coinage of silver; an increase in the money supply to $50 per person; an income tax upon the wealthy; government ownership of railroad, telegraph, and telephone companies; a shorter working day for industrial laborers; and the direct election of senators. After helping to found the Populist party, Weaver, although he knew he had virtually no chance of winning the White House, accepted its nomination for president in 1892. He managed to win over a million popular votes and twenty-two electoral votes.

A strong advocate of uniting all reform and "soft money" elements into one party, Weaver played a major part in uniting the Democratic and Populist parties before retiring from national politics. In 1896 he encouraged the Populist party endorsement of WILLIAM JENNINGS BRYAN for president after Bryan had won the Democratic party nomination.

BIBLIOGRAPHY

Haynes, F. E., *James Baird Weaver*, 1919.

Weaver, Robert Clifton

(December 29, 1907–   )
Secretary of Housing and Urban Development

Robert C. Weaver was the first black American ever appointed to the cabinet. Weaver was born in Washington, D.C. He earned a bachelor's degree in economics in 1929 and a master's two years later at Harvard. After spending a year as a professor of economics at the Agricultural and Technical College of North Carolina in Greensboro, Weaver returned to Harvard and earned a Ph.D. in economics in 1934.

In 1933 Weaver began a long career in the federal government. He held a number of different staff positions in the New Deal government of Democratic president FRANKLIN D. ROOSEVELT, serving as an expert on manpower, housing, and urban and black affairs. He founded the so-called black cabinet, a group of knowledgeable New Deal government officials who worked behind the scenes to integrate the federal government and to ensure that black Americans obtained a share in the New Deal–sponsored relief projects, subsidized housing, and federally funded jobs.

After World War II Weaver briefly served with the United Nations Relief and Rehabilitation Administration mission in the Soviet Union, and held a wide variety of teaching and private foundation positions. Two books he published at this time—*Negro Labor, a National Problem* (1946) and *The Negro Ghetto* (1948)—reinforced his reputation as a leading national expert on black economic and racial housing pattern issues.

From 1955 to 1961 Weaver held various New York state and city housing posts and was appointed by President JOHN F. KENNEDY to the federal Housing and Home Finance Agency in 1961. He also published two more books: *The Urban Complex* (1964) and *Dilemmas of Urban America* (1965).

President LYNDON B. JOHNSON appointed Weaver as the secretary of Housing and Urban Development (HUD) in 1966. While at HUD, Weaver attempted to encourage housing integration. He viewed the de facto segregation patterns of whites in the suburbs and blacks in the inner cities as the root cause of segregated schools and many other racial problems in America.

Upon leaving federal government service in January 1969, Weaver became president of Baruch College (1969–1970), professor of urban affairs at Hunter College (1970–1978), and director of urban programs for Hunter College's Brookdale Center on Aging.

BIBLIOGRAPHY

Current Biography, 1961; *New York Times*, December 31, 1960; *Who's Who Among Black Americans*, 1990–1991.

Webster, Daniel

(January 18, 1782–October 24, 1852)
Secretary of State, Senator, Representative

As orator, champion of the Union, and constitutional lawyer, Daniel Webster was one of the great statesmen of his day. Like his contemporary HENRY CLAY, he aspired to the presidency. Because of his identification with Northern sectional interests, however, he was unable to attain that office.

Born in Salisbury, New Hampshire, Webster graduated from Dartmouth College in 1801 and was admitted to the bar in 1805. By 1808 he had established a reputation in New Hampshire for legal expertise and considerable political skill. A Federalist, he denounced THOMAS JEFFERSON'S policies and the War of 1812 (see JAMES MADISON). After explaining his political views in a popular speech called "The Rockingham Memorial Address," he was elected to the U.S. House of Representatives in 1812 as a Whig. Webster served there until his decision to move to Boston in 1816, where he subsequently pursued a highly successful legal practice that involved several precedent-setting appearances before the U.S. Supreme Court. His arguments in *Dartmouth College* v. *Woodward* (1819), *McCulloch* v. *Maryland* (1819), and *Gibbons* v. *Ogden* (1824) were supported by Chief Justice JOHN MARSHALL and earned Webster the title Expounder of the Constitution.

After a brief period in the Massachusetts House of Representatives in 1822, Webster was asked to represent Boston in the U.S.

Library of Congress

House of Representatives as a member of the Federalist party. Although distrustful of JOHN QUINCY ADAMS, Webster supported the president's national development programs. In 1827 he was elected to the Senate and became a leader of the legislators who were against ANDREW JACKSON. Reelected to the Senate as a Whig in 1833, Webster, along with Henry Clay and JOHN C. CALHOUN, was destined to play a crucial role in national politics during the next two decades.

As the elected representative of an industrial state, Webster argued in 1828 for higher protective tariffs. He attacked Calhoun's theory of nullification in a famous debate in 1830 with South Carolina senator ROBERT HAYNE on the grounds that the Union had been established by the people through their state governments. Therefore, once the federal government had been established, it could not be dissolved by the states. "Liberty and Union, now and forever, one and inseparable!" Webster declared.

Webster was one of three regional Whig candidates for president in 1836. The Whigs hoped that together the three might draw enough votes to deny Democrat MARTIN VAN BUREN a majority. If the strategy worked, the election would be thrown into the House, where a Whig could have a better chance of being elected. Van Buren won 170 electoral votes to 124 for the Whig candidates combined.

In recognition of his help in securing WILLIAM H. HARRISON's election in 1840, Webster was appointed secretary of state. During the nation's first succession crisis—upon the death of President Harrison—it was Webster who defined how the transition should be handled by Vice President JOHN TYLER; and it was Webster, alone among the members of the Harrison cabinet, who stood by Tyler when Henry Clay, trying to isolate Tyler from the Whig party in order to secure the presidency for himself, engineered a mass cabinet resignation on September 11, 1841. "Where am I to go, Mr. President?" asked Webster that day in a remarkable display of political courage, since he knew that if he did not quit, his party would make him suffer for it. "You must decide for yourself," said Tyler. "If you leave it to me, Mr. President, I will stay where I am," replied Webster. The Tyler presidency survived.

Among Webster's successes as secretary of state was the Webster-Ashburton Treaty (see MARTIN VAN BUREN), which set the northeastern boundary of Maine and committed the United States to participate in efforts to end the slave trade. When Webster resigned from the cabinet in 1843 because of his opposition to the annexation of Texas (see JAMES KNOX POLK), Tyler accepted his departure with regret.

Webster returned to the Senate in 1845 and opposed the extension of slavery into the territories. He hoped to be nominated by the Whig party for president in 1848, but his nationalist vision and his position on slavery prevented his selection. The convention chose the Mexican War hero ZACHARY TAYLOR instead.

With the Union in danger of a civil war over slavery, Webster, against considerable public hostility in the North, backed Clay's compromise efforts. In the course of debate, he spoke in favor of compromise, "not as a Massachusetts man, nor as a Northern man, but as an American." Abolitionists never forgave his statement that slavery was an evil, but not so great an evil as disunion.

When MILLARD FILLMORE became president after Taylor's death in 1850, Webster was again appointed secretary of state. Denied the Whig nomination for president in 1852 in favor of another military hero, WINFIELD SCOTT, Webster angrily predicted his party's demise. He died shortly before the general election.

BIBLIOGRAPHY

Baxter, Maurice G., *Daniel Webster and the Supreme Court,* 1966; Brown, Norman D., *Daniel Webster and the Politics of Availability,* 1969; Current, Richard N., *Daniel Webster,* 1955; Curtis, George T., *Life of Daniel Webster,* 1870; Fuess, Claude M., *Daniel Webster,* 2 vols., 1930; Van Tyne, C. H. (ed.), *Letters of Daniel Webster,* 1902.

Weinberger, Caspar

(August 18, 1917–)
Secretary of Defense, Secretary of Health, Education, and Welfare

Prior to becoming RONALD REAGAN's secretary of defense and orchestrating an unprecedented peacetime buildup of American military forces, Caspar Weinberger had earned a reputation as a budget slasher at both the state and federal government levels.

Weinberger was born in San Francisco. He graduated from Harvard in 1938 and earned his law degree from Harvard Law School in 1941.

During World War II he served as a captain on General Douglas MacArthur's intelligence staff. After the war he practiced law in California and, in 1952, was elected as a Republican to the California state legislature. He was reelected in 1954 and 1956.

From 1962 to 1964 Weinberger was chairman of the California Republican Central Committee. During the late 1960s he held various California state posts, including that of cost-cutting finance director in 1968 in Governor Ronald Reagan's administration.

His Washington career began in 1969, when President RICHARD NIXON appointed him to the Federal Trade Commission. Weinberger quickly moved to the Office of Management and Budget, where, as deputy director (1970–1972) and director (1972–1973), he gained experience in dealing with Pentagon budgets. In November 1972 President Nixon appointed Weinberger, now well known as the man placed in charge of a department when budget cuts are imminent, secretary of health, education, and welfare.

Weinberger left public service in 1975 and returned to San Francisco, where he managed engineering and construction firms until President-elect Reagan appointed him secretary of defense in 1980 and charged him with restoring the American military and nuclear arsenal to a position of clear superiority over the Russians. The extent of American weakness before 1980 and the effectiveness of the post-1980 buildup are hotly debated issues, but the collapse of communism in 1989 allowed Reagan and Weinberger supporters to claim that this vast buildup helped bring the Soviet Union and its allies to their knees. Weinberger resigned from office in November 1987 in order to care for his ill wife.

BIBLIOGRAPHY

Austen, Ian, "The Flawed Legacy of 'Cap the Knife,'" *McLean's*, November 16, 1987; Griffiths, Dave, "Weinberger's Legacy: A Stronger Nation and a Management Mess," *Business Week*, November 16, 1987; *New York Times*, November 29, 1972; *Washington Post*, May 17, 1972; Weinberger, Caspar, *Fighting for Peace: Seven Critical Years in the Pentagon*, 1990; *Who's Who in America*, 1981.

Wheeler, Burton Kendall

(February 27, 1882–January 7, 1975)
Senator

Senator Burton K. Wheeler was one of the most prominent leaders of the isolationist movement in the years immediately preceding the entry of the United States into World War II.

Wheeler was born in Hudson, Massachusetts. He graduated from the University of Michigan in 1905 with a degree in law, was admitted to the bar the following year, and practiced law in Butte, Montana, until 1911, when he was elected to the Montana House of Representatives.

From 1913 to 1918 he served as U.S. district attorney for Montana and developed a controversial reputation as a radical because he refused to prosecute pacifists. In 1922 he was elected to the U.S. Senate as a Democrat, despite his opponents' efforts to smear his reputation. In 1924 Wheeler ran as ROBERT M. LA FOLLETTE's vice presidential running mate on the Progressive party ticket. After their ticket's defeat, Wheeler returned to the Democratic party and supported the candidacy of ALFRED E. SMITH for president in 1928 and FRANKLIN D. ROOSEVELT in 1932.

After Roosevelt became president in 1933, Wheeler generally supported New Deal legislation. In 1937, however, he was one of the first senators to oppose Roosevelt's proposed Court-packing Judiciary Reorganization Bill.

Roosevelt and Wheeler mended their political alliance, but their reconciliation was short-lived due to Wheeler's opposition to the administration's campaign for military preparedness. Wheeler even made a brief bid to win the Democratic party's presidential nomination in 1940 as a Peace candidate. Although this effort failed, he was elected to his fourth, and last, term in the Senate.

BIBLIOGRAPHY

Wheeler, Burton K., *Yankee from the West*, 1962.

Wheeler, William Almon

(June 30, 1819–June 4, 1887)
Vice President, Representative

William Almon Wheeler was unknown outside his home state of New York when he was nominated to be the vice presidential running mate of RUTHERFORD B. HAYES in 1876 in order to secure a sectional balance on the Republican party ticket.

Born in Malone, New York, Wheeler was financially unable to attend the University of Vermont for more than two years. Nevertheless, in 1845, after returning to Malone and studying on his own with a tutor, he was admitted to the New York state bar. Wheeler's law practice was so successful that after six years he retired to manage a local bank and serve as the trustee for the mortgage holders of the Northern Railway.

Always active in politics, at first as a Whig and then as a Republican, Wheeler served as a district attorney from 1846 to 1849, and later in the New York state legislature as both an assemblyman and a senator. From 1861 to 1863 and from 1869 to 1877 he served in the U.S. House of Representatives. Wheeler's main contribution in Congress was the successful arbitration of a highly controversial 1874 election dispute in the state of Louisiana.

Wheeler's refusal to benefit from the "Salary Grab" Act of 1873 (Congress raised its own pay by 50 percent) enhanced his reputation as a congressman of exceptional honesty. That plus his New York origins made him an attractive, if little known, vice presidential candidate to the Republicans in 1876 (see RUTHERFORD BIRCHARD HAYES). His lack of public stature was evident in a letter Hayes wrote to his wife in January 1876: "I am ashamed to say, Who is a Wheeler?" During his term of office as vice president, however, Wheeler became a close friend of President Hayes. Wheeler retired to his home in Malone, New York, in 1881 and, declining further public service, died there six years later.

BIBLIOGRAPHY

Wheeler, A. B., *The Genealogy and Encyclopedic History of the Wheeler Family in America*, 1914.

White, Edward Douglass

(November 3, 1845–May 19, 1921)
Chief Justice of the Supreme Court, Associate Justice of the Supreme Court, Senator

Library of Congress

Born in Lafourche Parish, Louisiana, White attended the Jesuit College in New Orleans and Georgetown College (now Georgetown University) in Washington, D.C., before briefly serving in the Confederate army. He was admitted to the bar in 1868 and established a successful law practice.

In 1874 he was elected to the Louisiana senate and in 1879 and 1880 served as a judge on the state supreme court. Elected to the U.S. Senate in 1890, he served there until he was appointed associate justice of the Supreme Court by President GROVER CLEVELAND in 1894. President WILLIAM H. TAFT selected White to be chief justice in 1910.

White—the first Southerner to head the Supreme Court since ROGER TANEY was appointed in 1836—was generally a conservative on the bench. In his twenty-seven years on the Supreme Court, he left a puzzling, often self-contradictory record. His legal writings were once described as "models of what judicial opinions ought not to be."

In *Lochner* v. *New York* (1905), for example, he dissented when the Court upheld the invalidation of a ten-hour day for bakers; but he also dissented in *Bunting* v. *Oregon* (1917), when the Court upheld a similar law and overruled *Lochner.* Then, in 1916, he wrote the decision upholding the constitutionality of the Adamson Act, which established an eight-hour day for railroad workers.

His most notable contribution to legal jurisprudence occurred in 1911 when he wrote the controversial "rule of reason" decision in the antitrust case against the Standard Oil Company. In this decision, which dissolved the Standard Oil complex, the court abandoned a literal interpretation of the language of the Sherman Anti-Trust Act (see BENJAMIN HARRISON) and held that only unreasonable combinations were considered illegal. The ruling would play an important role in the history of the government's efforts to regulate the economy.

BIBLIOGRAPHY

Hagemann, Gerard, *Man on the Bench,* 1962;
Klinkhamer, Marie Carolyn, *Edward Douglass White,* 1945.

White, Henry

(March 29, 1850–July 15, 1927)
Diplomat

Over the course of a long and distinguished career of foreign service, Henry White earned the title of America's first professional diplomat.

White was born into a prominent family in Baltimore, Maryland, and educated by tutors. From 1865 until he returned to the United States to marry in 1879, White lived with his family in France, Germany, Italy, and England.

In 1883 President CHESTER A. ARTHUR appointed White secretary of the American legation in Vienna and the following year, first secretary of the American legation in London. He remained in London until President GROVER CLEVELAND replaced him with a Democratic appointee in 1893. Four years later, Republican president WILLIAM MCKINLEY reappointed White first secretary in London.

After succeeding McKinley in 1901, President THEODORE ROOSEVELT credited White with being an important ingredient in the development of the exceptionally close diplomatic relations between the United States and Great Britain that began to emerge at the time of the Spanish-American War (see WILLIAM MCKINLEY, JR.). White's unique ability to interpret the subtle nuances of English and American culture proved to be of great help in the Hay-Pauncefote Treaty negotiations (1901), which permitted the United States to build the Panama Canal, the settlement of the Alaskan boundary dispute (1903), and resolution of the Venezuelan controversy in 1897.

President Roosevelt appointed White ambassador to Italy in 1905 and ambassador to France in 1907.

President WILLIAM HOWARD TAFT replaced White as ambassador to France in 1909; but the following year when Taft asked him, White agreed to head the American delegation to the fourth Pan American Conference in Buenos Aires. In 1911 White settled in Washington, D.C. Until Democratic president WOODROW WILSON asked White to serve on the bipartisan peace commission in 1918, White was virtually retired.

BIBLIOGRAPHY

Mowat, R. B., *Americans in England,* 1935; Nevins, Allan, *Henry White: Thirty Years of American Diplomacy,* 1930.

White, Hugh Lawson

(October 30, 1773–April 10, 1840)
Candidate for President, Senator

Born in Iredell County, North Carolina, White moved to what is now the eastern part of Tennessee in 1787. After fighting in the Creek and Cherokee wars, he became secretary to Governor William Blount in 1793. Upon completing his law studies in Lancaster, Pennsylvania, in 1796, he returned to Tennessee and established a law practice in Knoxville.

White held a number of state government positions before beginning the first of his several terms in the U.S. Senate in 1825. A Democrat, White at first supported President ANDREW JACKSON's policies, but a rift between the two men began in 1831 when White made known his opposition to Jackson's choice of MARTIN VAN BUREN as his political successor. Jackson, infuriated that he could not persuade White to support Van Buren, threatened to ruin him if he dared to openly challenge Van Buren's nomination for president. Instead of being intimidated, White delivered a speech in 1835 in which he declared his support for limiting presidential patronage and allowed the legislatures of Alabama and Tennessee to nominate him for president. After Van Buren won the Democratic party's presidential nomination in 1836, White ran as an independent candidate for president. He won the electoral votes of Tennessee and Georgia, but he was not able to prevent Van Buren's election.

In 1840, rather than obey directions from the Tennessee legislature to vote for Van Buren's independent treasury bill (see MARTIN VAN BUREN), White resigned from the Senate.

BIBLIOGRAPHY

Abernathy, T. P., *From Frontier to Plantation in Tennessee*, 1932.

White, John

(February 14, 1802–September 22, 1845)
Speaker of the House, Representative

John White was born near Cumberland Gap (now Middleboro), Kentucky, into a prominent family. After attending Greenville College, he studied law and was admitted to the Kentucky bar in 1823. He settled in Richmond, established a successful law practice, and became an admirer and friend of HENRY CLAY.

Two years after winning election to the state legislature in 1832, he was elected as a Whig to the first of five consecutive terms in the U.S. House of Representatives. While in Congress, he supported Whig party positions, opposing President ANDREW JACKSON's fight against rechartering the Bank of the United States (see NICHOLAS BIDDLE and ROGER BROOKE TANEY) and President MARTIN VAN BUREN's subtreasury plan (see VAN BUREN). Although he eventually changed his position, at first he opposed the annexation of Texas (see JAMES KNOX POLK) as a slave state.

In 1841 White was elected Speaker of the House. He served in this position until January 1843, then completed one more term in the House before retiring from politics to resume his private law practice in Richmond. In February 1845 White accepted appointment as judge of the Nineteenth Judicial District of Kentucky. For unknown reasons, he committed suicide just a few months later.

BIBLIOGRAPHY

Smith, William Henry, *Speakers of the House of Representatives of the United States*, 1928.

Williams, Roger

(January 16, 1603–March 15, 1683)
Colonial Leader

The religious intellectual Roger Williams established the colony of Rhode Island and left a legacy of respect for the principle of religious freedom in America.

Williams was born in London, England. A protégé of Sir Edward Coke, he attended Charterhouse. After graduating from Pembroke College, Cambridge, England, in 1627, he became an Anglican chaplain. In 1629 he participated in the Puritan conference at Sempringham called to decide whether the Puritans should immigrate to New England. Williams arrived in the Massachusetts Bay Colony in February 1631. Although offered the chance to preach in Salem, he decided that the Puritans were not "separated" enough in their beliefs from the Church of England and settled instead in Plymouth. After only a year in Plymouth, however, he decided that conditions were no better there and accepted a second offer in 1633 to preach in Salem.

In Salem, Williams immediately caused a furor by arguing that the Puritans' Massachusetts Bay royal charter was invalid because the king could not give away land that belonged to the Indians without their consent. He compounded his unpopularity by writing a letter to King Charles I accusing him of being an ally of the Devil. Reprimanded by the Massachusetts General Court, Williams apologized for his actions. He was back before the court in 1635 for his belief that no government had the right to punish people for violating the first four commandments nor could it administer an oath to a nonbeliever. When he refused to back down from these positions, he was banished from Massachusetts.

In April 1636 the unrepentant Williams decided to found a new colony, Providence, Rhode Island, upon land he secured from the Narragansett Indians. He attracted settlers to his colony by generously distributing land to anyone willing to accept his belief that "no

man should be molested for his conscience." Williams's good relations with the Narragansetts even helped the Puritans who had exiled him when he agreed to negotiate an end to the Pequot War in 1637. During the hostilities, the colonists nearly wiped out the Pequot tribe, who had fought back against the continuing takeover of the lands by Europeans.

In 1639 Williams briefly joined the Baptist church. He quickly left the Baptists, and for the rest of his life he considered himself a "Seeker"—someone who accepted no creed but believed in the fundamental truth of Christianity. To protect his new colony from being crushed by the hostile Puritans or usurped by another colonizer, Williams returned to England in 1642 to secure a royal charter. On the journey he wrote *A Key into the Language of America* (1643), which illustrated his appreciation for American Indian cultures. In England he also published *Mr. Cotton's Letter Lately Printed, Examined, and Answered* (1644), in which he rebutted the Puritan clergyman John Cotton's claim that those who encouraged groups of settlers to separate from the New England Puritan colonies threatened the ability of the Puritans to establish a reform church. Williams argued that no government had the right to persecute a man for his religious beliefs.

Williams secured his charter and returned to Providence in March 1644, committed to establishing a democratic government. He was forced to return once again to England in 1651 to defend the validity of his charter against another claimant. He succeeded, and upon his return to Providence was elected to the first of three terms as president of the colony.

Although Williams had saved the colony from court intrigue, he was unable to prevent the catastrophic Indian uprising known as King Philip's War in 1675. For three years the

Wampanoags, under the leadership of a chief known as King Philip, terrorized some New England towns in retaliation for the taking of their lands. Eventually the Wampanoags, and what power they still wielded, were destroyed. The situation was so desperate that even Williams, now over seventy-two years old, shouldered a musket and participated as a militia captain in military maneuvers during the war. The devastation of the conflict wiped out Williams's personal fortune and ended his vision of peaceful coexistence between the European and Native American cultures.

In his last years, Williams defended the right of Quakers to practice their religion unimpeded in Rhode Island. This did not, however, prevent him from publishing *George Fox Digg'd Out of His Burrowes* in 1676 to illustrate the error of Quaker theology. Williams hoped that the religious fanaticism of the Quakers might reinvigorate interest in Puritan theology. The increasingly secular preoccupations of the inhabitants of New England troubled his deeply religious soul.

BIBLIOGRAPHY

Garrett, John, *Roger Williams: Witness Beyond Christendom, 1603–1683*, 1970; Gilpin, W. Clark, *The Millenarian Piety of Roger Williams*, 1979; Miller, Perry, *Roger Williams: His Contribution to the American Tradition*, 1953 (reprint 1962); Morgan, Edmund S., *Roger Williams: The Church and the State*, 1967; Winslow, Ola Elizabeth, *Master Roger Williams, a Biography*, 1957.

Willkie, Wendell Lewis

(February 18, 1892–October 8, 1944)
Candidate for President

In a meteoric rise to national political prominence, Wendell Willkie, a corporation president and a member of the Democratic party until 1939, was nominated by the Republican party for president in 1940.

Born in Elwood, Indiana, Willkie earned both his bachelor's (1913) and law degrees (1916) from Indiana University. After serving in France during World War I, he returned to Akron, Ohio, and began working as a corporate lawyer. Within a few years he had earned a reputation as a superb courtroom attorney and expert counsel for protecting the interests of utilities companies.

Active in the Ohio Democratic party, Willkie quickly became well known for his hostility to a revival in the 1920s of the Ku Klux Klan (see ULYSSES SIMPSON GRANT) and his belief in the need for the United States to join the League of Nations (see WOODROW WILSON). In 1929 Willkie joined a New York law firm that represented Commonwealth and Southern Corporation, a

Library of Congress

utility holding company with divisions in eleven states. In 1933 he became president of the company. Many of Commonwealth's subsidiaries were in areas destined to become part of the New Deal's Tennessee Valley Authority (see FRANKLIN DELANO ROOSEVELT). The skillful battle Willkie led in the courts and media with the government to avert the TVA project proved unsuccessful, but his points concerning private versus public control of utilities brought him national attention.

Disheartened by what he perceived to be the unsound economic principles of some of the New Deal's agencies, Willkie decided to quit the Democratic party and join the Republican party in 1939. Through speeches and magazine articles attacking the New Deal, Willkie earned a reputation as one of FRANKLIN D. ROOSEVELT's most articulate critics. By 1940 he had become the unofficial leader of business opposition to the New Deal.

Even though Willkie had never held public office and did not decide to try for the Republican party's presidential nomination in 1940 until a few months before the convention, his articles had won him the backing of the business community. His personal warmth and charisma gave birth to a grass-roots swelling of support that culminated at the Republican convention with a sixth ballot victory to shouts of "We want Willkie!" The enthusiasm of Willkie's followers and the willingness of business leaders to contribute to his campaign convinced Republican party leaders that Willkie was the best candidate available to defeat Roosevelt.

Ironically, after winning the nomination, Willkie floundered on how best to campaign against Roosevelt, a man who represented many of the same ideals he believed in. However, as soon as he began concentrating on the flaws in Roosevelt's policies for economic recovery, he found his theme and managed to succeed in waging a surprisingly vigorous and dynamic campaign against the popular Roosevelt.

Willkie's supporters attempted to capitalize on Roosevelt's decision to seek an unprecedented third term with the slogan "Out stealing third," but the Democrats countered by pointing to Roosevelt's track record as a leader and replied, "Better a third-termer than a third-rater!" Willkie's dynamic campaign efforts garnered him more popular votes than any Republican prior to that time, but the combination of Roosevelt's popularity and the uneasiness among voters about changing leaders at the start of World War II led to his loss to Roosevelt by over 5 million popular votes and an electoral vote of 449 to 82.

After the election, Willkie supported the administration's aid to the Allies and served as the president's personal envoy on a world trip in 1942, about which he wrote a best-selling book, *One World*, published in 1943. The book explained the rise of nationalism among European colonies in Africa and Asia and the need of the West to prepare for a new world based on these nations becoming independent. In addition to his diplomatic efforts, Willkie fought at home for protecting the civil rights of minorities and the civil liberties of everyone.

Instead of currying favor among conservatives of the Republican party, Willkie infuriated them. In a highly publicized U.S. Supreme Court case, Willkie represented a naturalized citizen whom the federal government wanted to deport because he was an admitted communist. Through his speeches, articles, and personal contacts, Willkie attacked isolationist sentiment and argued for the need of the Republican party to support American participation in an international organization dedicated to ensuring world peace.

Aware that he had lost the support of Republican party leaders, Willkie tried to win the 1944 presidential nomination by taking his case directly to rank-and-file party members. He was convinced that once the people heard his message he would garner their support. Instead, he came in last in a four-way race in

the Wisconsin primary. After this dismal showing, he gave up all hope of winning the Republican nomination and withdrew from the campaign.

In the general election he refused to support President Roosevelt or his own party's nominee, THOMAS E. DEWEY, before a series of heart attacks led to his death in October in New York City.

BIBLIOGRAPHY

Barnard, Ellsworth, *Wendell Willkie*, 1966; Barnes, Joseph, *Willkie*, 1952; Dillon, Mary E., *Wendell L. Willkie*, 1952; Johnson, Donald B., *Republican Party and Willkie*, 1960; Moscow, Warren, *Roosevelt and Willkie*, 1968.

Wilmot, David

(January 20, 1814–March 16, 1868)
Senator, Representative

Representative David Wilmot became widely known as the author of the Wilmot Proviso, an amendment he tried to have attached to the bill funding the peace negotiations with Mexico. The proviso would have prohibited slavery in any of the territory acquired as a result of the Mexican War (see JAMES KNOX POLK). It passed in the House several times but never became law because of Southern opposition in the Senate. The controversy surrounding Wilmot's proposal demonstrated the growth of the sectional hostility that would culminate in the Civil War.

Wilmot was born in Bethany, Pennsylvania. After being admitted to the state bar in 1834, he established a practice with GALUSHA A. GROW in Towanda, Pennsylvania. Wilmot was a Democratic member of the U.S. House of Representatives from 1845 to 1851. In 1848 he supported the Free-Soil candidacy of MARTIN VAN BUREN for president against Democrat LEWIS CASS. After passage of the Kansas-Nebraska Act (see FRANKLIN PIERCE), Wilmot played an important role in the creation of the Republican party.

Wilmot ran unsuccessfully for governor of Pennsylvania in 1857. He was appointed in 1861 to complete the remainder of a term in the Senate and was a loyal supporter of ABRAHAM LINCOLN. At the end of his brief Senate career in 1863, Wilmot was appointed judge of the U.S. Court of Claims, a position he retained until his death.

BIBLIOGRAPHY

Going, Charles B., *David Wilmot, Free-Soiler*, 1924.

Wilson, Charles Erwin

(July 18, 1890–September 26, 1961)
Secretary of Defense

Charles E. Wilson was secretary of defense during President DWIGHT D. EISENHOWER's first term, a period of the cold war characterized by intense scrutiny of American military preparedness and strength.

Wilson was born in Minerva, Ohio. He graduated from Carnegie Institute of Technology (now Carnegie-Mellon University) in 1909 with a degree in electrical engineering. The following year he began his career as an engineer with the Westinghouse Electric and Manufacturing Company in Pittsburgh, and in 1926 became president and general manager of the Delco Remy Corporation, a subsidiary of General Motors (GM).

From 1929 to 1939 he was vice president of GM, in charge of labor relations and production planning. In 1937 he presided over the negotiations that resulted in GM's historic recognition of the United Automobile Workers union. The other major American car manufacturers quickly followed GM's example.

Wilson became president of General Motors in 1941 and orchestrated the immense wartime production of GM for the government. After World War II he made GM a pioneer in labor relations by offering workers unprecedented income security, in the form of cost-of-living adjustments and annual pay increases tied to productivity improvements. In return, Wilson demanded and largely won labor peace.

Wilson was named secretary of defense by President-elect Eisenhower in 1952. His controversial tenure began at his Senate confirmation hearings. When asked if he could make a decision that was good for the United States but bad for General Motors, he replied: "Yes, sir, I could. I cannot conceive of one because for years I thought what was good for our country was good for General Motors, and vice versa."

With the Korean War concluded, Wilson's primary task was the politically unrewarding one of cutting the size of the defense establishment to peacetime proportions. He also supported cutting funds for conventional forces and relying upon nuclear weapons in order to obtain "More Bang for a Buck."

After he had resigned in 1957, critics charged that his poor leadership had led to a "missile gap" between the United States and the Soviet Union that left the United States vulnerable to attack. (The "missile gap" was later proven to be nonexistent, but Democratic presidential candidate JOHN F. KENNEDY used it to political advantage in 1960.)

BIBLIOGRAPHY

Drucker, Peter, *Adventures of a Bystander,* 1979; Sloan, Alfred P., *My Years with General Motors,* 1964.

Wilson, Henry

(February 16, 1812–November 22, 1875)
Vice President, Senator

Henry Wilson, born Jeremiah Jones Colbath, rose from poverty as an indentured farmer and cobbler to become the eighteenth vice president of the United States. After changing his name to Wilson on his twenty-first birthday, he settled in Natick, Massachusetts, and became a successful shoe manufacturer.

In 1840 he was elected as a Whig to the Massachusetts state legislature, where he served until 1852. Leaving the Whig party in 1848 because of its evasiveness on the slavery issue, he helped to organize the Free-Soil party (see MARTIN VAN BUREN) and became editor of its newspaper, the *Boston Republican.* In 1854 he briefly joined the American, or Know-Nothing, party (see MILLARD FILLMORE) in the mistaken notion that it would unite the political forces in the nation against slavery. Appalled at the intolerance of many of the party's supporters and the refusal of the party leaders to take a stand on the slavery issue, he cut off further involvement in 1855. That same year the Massachusetts legislature elected him to the U.S. Senate as a Republican, where he remained until 1872.

Wilson quickly became one of the Senate's most energetic abolitionists. His first speech condemned the institution of slavery and called for the repeal of the fugitive slave law

(see FILLMORE). After playing an active role in helping to organize the new Republican party, Wilson vigorously campaigned for ABRAHAM LINCOLN's election in 1860.

As chairman of the Senate's military affairs committee during the Civil War, Wilson worked tirelessly to secure the passage of the legislation necessary to raise, organize, train, and provision the huge Union military machine. After the war he joined the Radicals in opposing ANDREW JOHNSON's conciliatory Reconstruction program, in favor of their own much more forceful legislation that sought to obtain full civil and political rights for blacks in the South. After long tours through the South, however, he gradually adopted a more sympathetic and tolerant attitude toward the South.

In 1872 Wilson was elected vice president on the ticket with ULYSSES S. GRANT, but he died in 1875 before his term of office was completed.

BIBLIOGRAPHY

McKay, Ernest, *Henry Wilson, Practical Radical: A Portrait of a Politician,* 1971; Nason, Elias, and Thomas Russell, *The Life and Public Services of Henry Wilson,* 1881.

Wilson, Woodrow

(December 28, 1856–February 3, 1924)
President

Woodrow Wilson had already been brilliantly successful, as a distinguished professor of political science and as the innovative president of Princeton University, before he began his remarkable political career as governor of New Jersey and president of the United States.

Born in Staunton, Virginia, Wilson grew up in Augusta, Georgia, and Columbia, South Carolina. In 1873 Wilson entered Davidson

College, but he was forced to drop out due to illness. Two years later, he entered Princeton University and graduated in 1879. Wilson briefly attended the University of Virginia Law School, but once again illness intervened. He completed his law studies at home and was admitted to the Georgia bar in 1882.

Dissatisfied and unsuccessful as an attorney, in 1883 Wilson decided to become a college professor like his father and enrolled in a doctoral program at Johns Hopkins University. He received his Ph.D. in political science in 1886 and, after the publication of his thesis, *Congressional Government,* in 1887, achieved scholarly recognition.

Wilson taught at Bryn Mawr College from 1885 to 1888, and Wesleyan University from 1888 to 1890. While at Wesleyan, he wrote *The State.* In 1890 Wilson accepted a teaching position at Princeton University.

During his twelve years as a professor at Princeton, Wilson published nine scholarly books, including his largest work, *History of the American People,* and several dozen journal articles. The remarkable reputation he had acquired in academia was rewarded in 1902 when he was named president of the university.

As president from 1902 to 1910, Wilson succeeded in reorganizing Princeton's course of studies and departmental structure, and introduced the preceptoral system of education. He failed to achieve his goal of eliminating Princeton's anti-intellectual, class-based eating clubs in 1908. He also lost a much more important and bitterly fought campaign to control the location and management of the newly created Graduate College. These de-

Library of Congress

feats played an important role in providing him with sufficient incentive to plunge into the race for governor of New Jersey in 1910. Colonel George Harvey, editor of *Harper's Weekly,* had first proposed the idea of Wilson's running for governor—and eventually for president—to Wilson in 1906. With Harvey's guidance, Wilson had shortly thereafter begun to use speaking engagements to identify himself carefully with the need for progressive political reforms, lower tariffs, and control of the trusts.

When Wilson was offered the Democratic nomination for governor in 1910, the party bosses assumed they were selecting a figurehead. Wilson surprised them by becoming an exceptionally vigorous and independent administrator. Before the Democratic convention in 1912, Wilson had managed to push through the New Jersey legislature a comprehensive Progressive agenda instituting direct primaries and election reform, new state regulations of public utilities, workmen's compensation, municipal reform, and reorganization of the school system. Although Wilson campaigned across the nation and entered several primaries, by the time the Democratic convention met in 1912, his chances of securing the nomination seemed bleak against Speaker of the House CHAMP CLARK. Then the convention deadlocked, and on the forty-sixth ballot Wilson was chosen.

Two weeks later, at the Republican convention, former president THEODORE ROOSEVELT refused to accept defeat in his bid to win another term in the White House when President HOWARD TAFT was renominated. Roosevelt instead decided to seek the presidency as the candidate of the Progressive, or Bull Moose, party. During the national campaign Wilson promised prosperity and reform based on a "New Freedom" that consisted of reducing tariffs, breaking up the trusts, and creating a sound national banking and credit system. The split of the Republican vote enabled Wilson to win with 6,296,547 votes to Roosevelt's 4,118,571 and Taft's 3,486,720. Socialist candidate EUGENE V. DEBS won almost a million votes.

Shortly after assuming office, Wilson called Congress into special session to emphasize the importance of obtaining new tariff legislation. Six months later, after a difficult battle in the Senate, Wilson finally obtained his goal. The Underwood Act increased the number of duty-free products, reduced tariff rates from 40 percent to 26 percent, and, as a rider to the bill made possible by the passage of the Sixteenth Amendment, imposed the first income tax.

While the effort to secure passage of the tariff was raging, Wilson was also working to secure the passage of legislation to reform the banking system. In an address to a joint session of Congress in June 1913, he said, "It is absolutely imperative that we should give the businessmen of this country a banking and currency system. . . . We must not leave them without the [necessary] tools of action. . . ."

On December 23, 1913, after another hard-fought campaign in the Senate had been won, Wilson was able to sign the Federal Reserve Act into law. The act created a national banking system composed of twelve regional banks, coordinated and regulated by a Federal Reserve Board appointed by the president. The system was also authorized to issue a new national currency, Federal Reserve notes.

Wilson obtained the last piece of his three-pronged New Freedom program in 1914 when he signed a bill establishing the Federal Trade Commission. The body was designed to prevent unfair business competition.

The remarkable success of the first Wilson administration on the domestic front was not matched in the foreign policy arena. Frustrated efforts to control events in the Mexican Revolution led first to the brief occupation of Veracruz in 1914 and then, in 1916–1917, to the futile expedition of American forces under General John J. Pershing into Mexico to catch the revolutionary leader Pancho Villa. Equally unsuccessful efforts to control events in Haiti and the Dominican Republic led to their occupation by the U.S. Marines in 1915 and 1916.

After the outbreak of war in Europe in 1914, Wilson gradually became increasingly preoccupied with foreign policy issues. Initially, the position of the administration was to adopt a policy of strict neutrality. This became increasingly difficult in the face of German submarine attacks on merchant shipping. When the British passenger ship *Lusitania* was torpedoed in May 1915 and more than 100 Americans died, Wilson warned Germany that such acts would provoke U.S. retaliation. After American public opinion was again aroused when a second passenger liner, the *Arabic,* was sunk in August, the German government did finally promise Wilson that it would no longer authorize attacks on passenger ships. When Wilson protested the torpedoing of a merchant ship, the *Sussex,* in March 1916, the German government's promise was expanded to a pledge to obey international law in regard to attacks on merchant vessels on the high seas.

Renominated in 1916, Wilson won reelection by a narrow margin with the campaign slogan "He Kept Us Out of War."

Wilson's hopes of mediating an end to the war were dashed early in 1917 when Germany issued a proclamation declaring its intent to pursue a policy of unrestricted submarine attacks. After the loss of more American lives with the sinking of several merchant ships, Wilson asked Congress for a declaration of war on April 2, 1917. "The world," he said, "must be made safe for democracy."

Perhaps Wilson's most successful accomplishments during the war consisted of the appointment of General Pershing to lead the American Expeditionary Force in Europe and insisting that American troops fight as units independent of British and French control. Other accomplishments included obtaining passage of a new military draft law from a reluctant Congress, empowering BERNARD M. BARUCH to oversee economic mobilization as head of the War Industries Board, and taking control of the railroads. When Germany was forced to capitulate in 1918, it was Wilson who negotiated the surrender terms and then obtained Allied approval based on his famous Fourteen Points. Eight pertained to territorial adjustments; others called for open treaty negotiations, freedom of the seas, removal of economic barriers and equality of trade, reduction of armaments, and impartial adjustment of colonial claims. The most important points to Wilson were his call for the creation of the League of Nations and the concept of self-determination. In the fight to make the league a reality, Wilson would sacrifice his health and many of his other points.

Determined to be remembered as the man who established the framework for permanent peace, Wilson decided to lead the American delegation to the peace conference in Paris in 1919. His tumultuous greeting in Europe and description as the "apostle of peace" confirmed Wilson's resolve to see to it that the league was an integral component of any proposed peace treaty.

Considering the desire for revenge of the war-weary Allies, the intricate maze of complex political and economic issues, and the hidden agendas of the other principal negotiators representing Great Britain, France, and Italy, Wilson accomplished a great deal in Paris. Although Germany was forced to relinquish its colonies, virtually eliminate its armed forces, and accept a huge war reparations burden, Wilson prevented its dismemberment. He also played an important role in the creation of a new Poland and, most important of all, achieved his most cherished goal: the creation of the League of Nations.

Wilson mistakenly assumed that once he won European endorsement for the treaty and support for the establishment of the league, the U.S. Senate would approve his actions. Even after he toured the nation in a dramatic appeal for popular support that so exhausted

him he suffered a debilitating stroke, he could not secure the treaty's ratification in the Senate. Opposition was based on the isolationist fear that participating in the League of Nations would compromise American sovereignty in conducting foreign affairs and embroil America in future European conflicts.

Unable to lead the debate for public support due to the paralysis caused by his stroke in October 1919, Wilson nevertheless refused to compromise. He refused to discuss any plans to secure Senate votes by changing the language of the treaty to eliminate the commitment of America to collective security and participation in the league. The result was a stalemate that lasted until Wilson's view was reputed with the Republican landslide victory in the 1920 elections.

Wilson was awarded the 1919 Nobel Peace Prize for his efforts to establish the league. He retired from the White House a sick and crippled man in 1921, and lived the life of a recluse in Washington until his death several years later.

He left a remarkable political legacy. More than any other president of this century, Wilson defined the meaning of modern liberalism and made the Democratic party its advocate. Labeled Progressivism at the time, this ideology called upon the government to take an active role in economic affairs, to control and regulate the economically powerful (banks, railroads, corporations—the "Interests") and to protect the economically disadvantaged (the "People"). The Federal Reserve System, the Federal Trade Commission, the income tax amendment, support for laws supporting unions, workmen's compensation, and limitations on child labor need to be seen in this light.

Wilson became president at a time when the country was struggling to come to terms with the vast inequalities of wealth and power that the new industrial system had generated, and his legislative agenda both responded to these popular concerns and further emboldened the advocates of far-reaching change. Thus, the American Socialist party reached the zenith of its power in the years of Wilson's presidency, the labor movement organized millions of workers, and women won the right to vote.

These developments have led many historians to view Wilson as a great champion of the American people. More recently, scholars have emphasized the conservative aspects of Wilson's presidency: the use of government power to stabilize and protect capitalist interests (Federal Reserve); Wilson's willingness during World War I to suspend fundamental civil liberties, to throw political dissenters like EUGENE DEBS into jail, to tolerate Attorney General A. MITCHELL PALMER's raids and deportation of alien radicals. But none of this revisionism reduces Wilson's significance as the president who presided over and guided America's emergence as a modern nation and world power. He, along with Theodore Roosevelt, established the presidency as the most important branch of the federal government after forty years of weak chief executives.

BIBLIOGRAPHY

Brooks, Emile J., *An Historical and Political Assessment of Woodrow Wilson as President of the United States*, 2 vols., 1986; Cooper, John Milton, *The Warrior and the Priest*, 1983; Ferrell, Robert H., *Woodrow Wilson and World War I: 1917–1921*, 1986; Lathan, Earl (ed.), *The Philosophy and Policies of Woodrow Wilson*, 1975; Link, Arthur S., *Woodrow Wilson and the Progressive Era, 1910–1917*, 1954, *Higher Realism of Woodrow Wilson and Other Essays*, 1971, and *Woodrow Wilson: Revolution, War, and Peace*, 1979; Mulder, John M., *Woodrow Wilson: The Years of Preparation*, 1978.

Winthrop, John

(January 12, 1588–March 26, 1649)
Colonial Leader

John Winthrop was one of the most powerful political leaders in Massachusetts Bay during the colony's critical formative years.

Winthrop was born into a prominent family in Edwardstone, England. He was admitted to Trinity College, Cambridge, in 1602, but left before graduating to marry at age seventeen. While attending Trinity, Winthrop had a religious conversion experience and became a member of the Puritan Church.

In 1613 Winthrop was admitted to Gray's Inn and became a prosperous London attorney. In 1626 he was appointed one of the limited number of attorneys for the court of wards and liveries, and he frequently drafted petitions to be submitted to Parliament. However, due to the tumult of the economic, political, and religious changes taking place in England at that time, his legal business began to decline around 1629. This fact, plus his deepening commitment to Puritanism, convinced him to join the migration of Puritans to New England as a member of the Massachusetts Bay Company.

To protect themselves from the interference of the Crown in their quest to establish a religious haven, the Puritans broke with tradition and took their charter and governing body (General Court) with them. In effect, the charter became the constitution of the Massachusetts Bay Colony and the General Court a representative legislature.

In October 1629 Winthrop was chosen to be the colony's first governor. Six months later, along with about 600 other settlers, Winthrop set sail for New England. While crossing the Atlantic, he wrote in his journal what he thought the colony ought to aspire to be—"A Modell of Christian Charity"—and how this Puritan goal could be accomplished. He had no faith in democracy and believed instead in government by religious aristocracy. He felt it essential that representatives should govern for life.

Within a few months of his arrival in Massachusetts in June 1630, dozens of permanent communities were established and Winthrop had founded the city of Boston. Thousands of additional settlers, many of whom were not Puritans, poured in during the next few years to make Massachusetts a phenomenal colonial settlement success story. The large number of settlers and the fact that they had established their own government gave Winthrop a unique position as compared to the situation in other American colonies. However, his behavior was restricted by the need to balance the growing pressure for representative democracy in the colony with the demand by the Puritan elders for enforcing stern adherence to the settlement's religious vision.

Winthrop appreciated that religion and politics were inextricably intertwined in the Massachusetts Bay Colony, but he had trouble reconciling the conflict that arose between the pressure for democracy and the vision of religious purity. He practiced great discretion while governor during his first four years in office. Nevertheless, when the freemen of the colony won the right to elect government officials and members of the General Court in 1634, Winthrop, who was identified as a leader in the effort to prevent this development, was not reelected. Two years later, Winthrop's management of the colony from 1630 to 1634 was reviewed by the Puritan elders, and he was rebuked for being too tolerant.

The impact of these two events encouraged Winthrop to adopt a more consistent conservative stance. He resolved to be more severe in demanding adherence to the colony's religious vision. In 1637, while serving as deputy governor, he successfully advocated the banishment of Anne Hutchinson and all her followers from Massachusetts Bay Colony for deviating from the tenets of Puritanism. (She challenged the right of the Puritan elders to rule the colony by claiming that people could obtain divine guidance directly from God.) When Hutchinson asked for the reason for her banishment, Winthrop replied: "Say no more; the Court knows wherefore and is satisfied."

On a personal, short-term political level, Winthrop's support for enforcing adherence to conservative religious goals in Massachusetts Bay Colony was successful. From 1637 until his death in 1649, with the exception of a few years when he served as a member of the Executive Council, Winthrop was annually reelected governor. He served a total of twelve terms as governor and played a vital role in shaping the theocratic policy of the colony.

In addition to his Massachusetts government work, Winthrop, who had been an early advocate of the need to establish a confederation of the New England colonies for military defense purposes, helped frame a confederation agreement and served as first president of the New England Confederation in 1645. His journal, *The History of New England from 1630 to 1649*, is an important source of early colonial American history.

BIBLIOGRAPHY

Forbes, Allyn B. (ed.), *Winthrop Papers, 1498–1649*, 5 vols., 1929–1947; Hosmer, James K. (ed.), *Winthrop's Journal: History of New England, 1630–1649*, 2 vols., 1908; Morgan, Edmund S., *The Puritan Dilemma: The Story of John Winthrop*, 1958.

Winthrop, Robert Charles

(May 12, 1809–November 16, 1894)
Speaker of the House, Senator, Representative

Born in Boston, Massachusetts, Robert Charles Winthrop graduated from Harvard College in 1828. He studied law under Daniel Webster and was admitted to the bar in 1831. In 1840 Winthrop was elected to the U.S. House of Representatives and became Speaker in 1847. Although personally opposed to slavery, Winthrop followed a moderate path on the issue of allowing its expansion into the territories in the futile hope of avoiding civil war through compromise. He was not elected to a second term as Speaker in 1849 because of the opposition of Free-Soilers (see Martin Van Buren).

In 1850 Winthrop was appointed to complete Secretary of State Daniel Webster's unexpired term in the U.S. Senate. After offering only mild opposition to the fugitive slave bill (see Millard Fillmore) in the hope of easing sectional tensions, Winthrop was defeated for a full term in 1851 by the abolitionist Charles Sumner.

Winthrop never sought political office again after 1851. He devoted the rest of his life to literature and education. A popular orator, he delivered his "Oration on the Hundredth Anniversary of the Surrender of Lord Cornwallis" to both houses of Congress in 1881 and spoke in 1885 at the dedication of the Washington Monument.

──────

BIBLIOGRAPHY

Winthrop, Robert C., *Memoir of Robert C. Winthrop*, 1897.

Wirt, William

(November 8, 1772–February 18, 1834)
Attorney General, Candidate for President

A highly effective attorney general, William Wirt represented the United States in some of the most famous early Supreme Court cases.

Born in Bladensburg, Maryland, Wirt obtained little formal schooling before moving to Virginia in 1792 and gaining admission to the bar. He practiced law in Culpeper County until 1799 and then moved to Richmond, where he was almost im-

Library of Congress

mediately elected to his first of three terms as clerk of the House of Delegates. In 1807 he served as the assistant prosecuting attorney in the treason trial of Aaron Burr. His eloquence and expertise combined with the sensationalism of the trial earned him national fame.

In 1817 President James Monroe chose Wirt to be attorney general of the United States. Wirt remained in office until the end of John Quincy Adams's administration in 1829. As attorney general, he represented the United States before the Supreme Court in such landmark cases as *McCulloch* v. *Maryland* (1819), *Gibbons* v. *Ogden* (1824), and *Dartmouth College* v. *Woodward* (1819) (see JOHN MARSHALL). In addition to his legal duties, Wirt displayed considerable administrative expertise. He reorganized the government's legal department for greater efficiency and introduced the practice of having his opinions published as precedents for the future. When ANDREW JACKSON became president, Wirt moved to Baltimore and resumed his private law practice.

In 1832 Wirt reluctantly accepted the nomination for president of the Anti-Mason party at a time when public sentiment against Freemasonry was strong. A supporter of HENRY CLAY, he hoped that his candidacy might be able to unite all those opposed to Andrew Jackson's reelection (Jackson was a Mason) in a manner Henry Clay, whom the Anti-Masons refused to endorse, could not. However, when the Whigs decided to nominate Clay over Wirt anyway, Wirt unsuccessfully endeavored to help Clay win by only halfheartedly campaigning.

In addition to his legal and political careers, Wirt achieved considerable success as a writer. In 1803 his popular *The Letters of a British Spy* was published. This work was followed the next year by *The Rainbow*, in 1810 by *The Old Bachelor*, and in 1817 by *Sketches of the Life and Character of Patrick Henry.*

BIBLIOGRAPHY

Kennedy, John Pendleton, *Memoirs of the Life of William Wirt, Attorney General of the United States,* 2 vols., 1949.

Wright, James Claude, Jr.

(December 22, 1922–)
Speaker of the House, Representative

Born in Fort Worth, Texas, Jim Wright studied at Weatherford (Texas) College and the University of Texas. During World War II he served in the South Pacific in the U.S. Air Force. After the war, Wright returned to Fort Worth and became a partner in a national trade extension and advertising firm. In 1946, as a liberal Democrat, he was elected to the Texas legislature. After failing to win reelection in 1948, Wright adopted a much more conservative political platform.

In 1954 Wright was elected to the U.S. House of Representatives. He won reelection every two years thereafter for the next thirty-three years. In 1987 he became Speaker of the House and immediately established a reputation for vigorous, though brusque, leadership.

During Wright's brief two-year tenure as Speaker, the House passed legislation to provide aid for the homeless, funds to clean up the nation's waters, and catastrophic illness insurance for the elderly (later rescinded). Wright also led efforts to find a negotiated settlement to the confrontation between the United States and the Sandinista government of Nicaragua.

Although he never admitted violating any House rules, Wright was forced to resign as Speaker in 1989 because of alleged ethical violations in which he was accused of using his political office to secure financial gain for himself and his family.

BIBLIOGRAPHY

Barry, John M., *The Ambition and the Power: Jim Wright and the Will of the House,* 1989.

Yancey, William Lowndes

(August 10, 1814–July 27, 1863)
Representative

William Lowndes Yancey did more perhaps than any other single Southern political leader to encourage the secession movement.

Yancey was born in Warren County, Georgia. He attended Williams College from 1830 to 1833 but did not graduate. After reading law in Greenville, South Carolina, he moved to Alabama in 1837, established a successful law practice, and began publishing a newspaper.

From 1841 to 1844 Yancey served in the state legislature, then won election to the U.S. House of Representatives. During his term in the House (1844–1846), his fiercely sectionalist and proslavery sentiments (he even demanded the resumption of the slave trade) branded him a Southern extremist. Embittered and disillusioned by the hostile reception of his beliefs in Washington, Yancey resigned from Congress in 1846 and moved to Montgomery, Alabama. He planned to avoid any further involvement in politics, but the attempt of the Wilmot Proviso (see JOHN CALDWELL CALHOUN) to exclude slavery from the newly acquired territories could not be ignored. At the Democratic national convention in 1848, he introduced a series of resolutions, known as the Alabama Platform, which demanded that Congress protect slavery in the territories. The Democratic convention rejected Yancey's demands, but the state legislatures of Alabama and Georgia, along with several state conventions in other Southern states, adopted them on their own. Within a few years, Yancey's Alabama Platform had become the political creed of the South.

During the 1850s Yancey publicly expressed hope that secession could be avoided, but he had begun to conclude that secession was inevitable. After 1858 he was adamant that if the Republicans won the presidency in 1860, secession would be necessary.

At the national Democratic party convention in 1860, Yancey repeated his demand for the party to endorse his Alabama Platform. When the convention refused, Yancey and his followers stormed out of the convention. The Northern Democrats nominated STEPHEN A. DOUGLAS for president. The Southern Democrats chose JOHN C. BRECKINRIDGE. After Republican candidate ABRAHAM LINCOLN won the presidency, Yancey wrote the Alabama ordinance of secession and played a leading role in the creation of the Confederacy.

Yancey was elected to the Confederate Senate, where he served until his death in 1863.

BIBLIOGRAPHY

Du Bose, John Witherspoon, *The Life and Times of William Lowndes Yancey*, 1892 (reprint, 1942); Venable, Austin L., *The Role of William L. Yancey in the Secession Movement*, 1945.

Young, Andrew Jackson, Jr.

(March 12, 1932–)
Diplomat, Representative

First as a civil rights activist, then as a congressman, diplomat, and mayor, Andrew Young has devoted his life to improving the quality of life for blacks and poor people both in the United States and around the world.

Young was born in New Orleans, attended segregated black public schools, and earned a bachelor's degree from Howard University in Washington, D.C., in 1951. In 1955 he was awarded a B.D. from Hartford (Connecticut) Theological Seminary and ordained a minister in the United Church of Christ.

United Nations

For two years he was a pastor for several small Alabama and Georgia churches. Despite numerous threats, he also led a black voter registration drive in Georgia. In 1957 he accepted a position with the National Council of Churches. He spent the next four years working with inner-city black youth and once again leading a voter registration drive, this time in New York City.

In 1961 Young joined the Southern Christian Leadership Conference (SCLC), the civil rights organization led by Martin Luther King, Jr. He became King's trusted associate and in 1964, SCLC's executive director. After King's assassination in 1968, he became SCLC's executive vice president. Frustrated by the lack of change the SCLC and other civil rights organizations had accomplished from working outside of the political system, Young decided to try another approach and to run for national office himself.

In 1972, two years after an unsuccessful first try, Young became the first black from Georgia to win a seat in the U.S. House of Representatives since the Reconstruction era. He was reelected to Congress in 1974 and 1976.

A close friend of JIMMY CARTER, Young helped Carter win the black vote in the South during his races for governor of Georgia and for president. In January 1977 President Carter appointed Young ambassador to the United Nations.

Young's dedication to helping the world's poor aroused considerable controversy during his term at the United Nations. He frequently argued the need for the industrialized nations to help the third world nations, and made no effort to hide his lack of support for continuing to determine U.S. relations with foreign countries on the basis of whether they were pro- or anticommunist. He also had serious misgivings about the American pro-Israeli stance in the Middle East, especially the U.S. policy of not meeting with representatives of the Palestine Liberation Organization (PLO). Unable to persuade President Carter to authorize his meeting with the PLO, Young decided to act on his own. When the fact that he had held clandestine meetings in New York City with members of the PLO was disclosed in the press, Young was forced to resign.

In 1981 Young was elected mayor of Atlanta and reelected in 1985. Five years later, in July 1990, he was elected one of the two finalists in the Democratic primary contest for governor of Georgia but failed to secure the nomination.

BIBLIOGRAPHY

Ebony, February 1973; *New York Times Magazine,* February 6, 1977; *Saturday Review,* October 16, 1976; *Who's Who Among Black Americans,* 1990–1991.

American Political Leaders: A Timeline

All names in the timeline appear with first-name initial only (e.g., G. Washington).

The first column includes all the presidents, in boldface, followed by dates indicating when they served. Also included in the first column are unsuccessful candidates for that presidential term; their names appear in italics.

Every other American political leader mentioned in the book is found under the column marked for the office held, within the appropriate presidential administration. Leaders who served in the same position during more than one administration are listed only under the first one. For example, Associate Justice J. Story, who served under six presidents, is listed with President Madison because his service began in 1811. Some leaders, such as A. Burr or H. Clay, who held more than one office, will appear under more than one column. Dates following names of leaders indicate the years served in that office and appear in abbreviated form (e.g., under Chief Justice, J. Jay 89–95). The full dates here are, of course, 1789–1795, and readers should not find the lack of centuries confusing if they will refer back to the dates of the presidential administration given in the first column.

Positions of leaders who appear in the columns labeled Cabinet and Other are abbreviated to save space. The abbreviations used are the following:

Asst. A.G.	Assistant Attorney General
Asst. War	Assistant Secretary of War
A.G.	Attorney General
Ch. Cook Co.	Chairman of the Cook County [Chicago] Democratic Central Committee
Ch. Fed. Res.	Chairman of the Federal Reserve Board
Dir. CIA	Director of the Central Intelligence Agency
Dir. FBI	Director of the Federal Bureau of Investigation
Gov. Agc. Dir.	Government Agency Director
Post. Gen.	Postmaster General
Pres. Adv.	Presidential Adviser
Pres. CSA	President of the Confederate States of America
Pres. Sec. Bk.	President of the Second Bank of the United States
Agr.	Secretary of Agriculture
Army	Secretary of the Army
Comm.	Secretary of Commerce
Def.	Secretary of Defense
Ed.	Secretary of Education
HEW	Secretary of Health, Education, and Welfare
HUD	Secretary of Housing and Urban Development
Int.	Secretary of the Interior
Lab.	Secretary of Labor
Navy	Secretary of the Navy
Trans.	Secretary of Transportation
Treas.	Secretary of the Treasury
War	Secretary of War

The last column lists some major events and legislation in American history. These milestones help place the leaders in their time.

Leaders who served before formation of the government under the Constitution are not listed on the timeline. They are:

COLONIAL LEADERS: W. Bradford, T. Hutchinson, R. Williams, J. Winthrop

REVOLUTIONARY LEADERS: S. Adams, J. Dickinson, B. Franklin, J. Hancock, P. Henry, G. Mason, J. Otis, T. Paine, B. Rush, R. Stockton

PRESIDENT	VICE PRESIDENT	SECRETARY OF STATE	CABINET	DIPLOMAT	CHIEF JUSTICE
G. Washington 1789–1793 *J. Adams*	J. Adams 89–93	T. Jefferson 90–93	E. Randolph A.G. 89–94 H. Knox War 89–94 A. Hamilton Treas. 89–95 T. Pickering Post. Gen. 91–95	T. Jefferson 85–89 T. Pinckney 92–96	J. Jay 89–95
G. Washington 1793–1797 *J. Adams* *G. Clinton*	J. Adams 93–97	E. Randolph 94–95 T. Pickering 95–97	T. Pickering War 95	J. Jay 94–95 J. Monroe 94–96 J. Q. Adams 94–01 C. Pinckney 96–97 R. King 96–03	J. Rutledge 95 O. Ellsworth 96–00
J. Adams 1797–1801 *T. Jefferson* *C. Pinckney* *A. Burr*	T. Jefferson 97–01	T. Pickering 97–00 J. Marshall 00–01		E. Gerry 97–98 J. Marshall 97–98	
T. Jefferson 1801–1805 *A. Burr* *J. Adams* *C. Pinckney* *J. Jay*	A. Burr 01–05	J. Madison 01–09	R. Smith Navy 01–09 A. Gallatin Treas. 01–14	R. Livingston 01–04 J. Monroe 03–07 N. Biddle 04–07	J. Marshall 01–35
T. Jefferson 1805–1809 *C. Pinckney*	G. Clinton 05–09		J. Breckinridge A.G. 05–06		
J. Madison 1809–1813 *G. Pinckney* *G. Clinton*	G. Clinton 09–12	R. Smith 09–11 J. Monroe 11–17		J. Q. Adams 09–14	
J. Madison 1813–1817 *D. Clinton*	E. Gerry 13–14		J. Monroe War 14–15 W. Crawford War 15–16 W. Crawford Treas. 16–25	W. Crawford 13–15 A. Gallatin 16–23	
J. Monroe 1817–1821 *R. King*	D. Tompkins 17–21	J. Q. Adams 17–25	J. Calhoun War 17–25 W. Wirt A.G. 17–29 L. Cheves Pres. Sec. Bk. 19–22	J. Forsyth 19–23	
J. Monroe 1821–1825 *J. Q. Adams*	D. Tompkins 21–25		N. Biddle Pres. Sec. Bk. 23–29		

ASSOCIATE JUSTICE	SPEAKER OF THE HOUSE	SENATOR	REPRESENTATIVE	OTHER	EVENT
J. Rutledge 89–91	F. Muhlenberg 89–91 J. Trumbull 91–93	W. Paterson 89–90 R. Lee 89–92 O. Ellsworth 89–96 R. King 89–96 J. Monroe 90–94 R. Sherman 91–93 A. Burr 91–97 J. Taylor 92–94	R. Sherman 89–91 E. Gerry 89–93 J. Trumbull 89–95 T. Sedgwick 89–96 J. Madison 89–97 F. Muhlenberg 89–97 J. Dayton 91–99 N. Macon 91–15		First Inaugural 1789 Bill of Rights 1791
W. Paterson 93–06 S. Chase 96–11	F. Muhlenberg 93–97	A. Gallatin 93–94 J. Trumbull 95–96 R. Stockton 96–97 T. Sedgwick 96–99	A. Gallatin 95–01 E. Livingston 95–01 J. Varnum 95–11 A. Jackson 96–97		Second Inaugural 1793 Whiskey Rebellion 1794 Jay's Treaty 1794
B. Washington 98–29	J. Dayton 97–99 T. Sedgwick 99–01	A. Jackson 97–98 J. Dayton 99–05	T. Pinckney 97–01 J. Marshall 99–00 J. Randolph 99–13		XYZ Affair 1797–98 Alien and Sedition Acts 1798
	N. Macon 01–07	D. Clinton 02–03 J. Taylor 03 J. Q. Adams 03–08 T. Pickering 03–11	J. Story 03–09 D. Tompkins 04		Presidential Election Decided in House of Representatives 1801 Louisiana Purchase 1803
	J. Varnum 07–11	H. Clay 06–07 W. Crawford 07–13	J. Story 07–09 R. Johnson 07–19		Embargo Act 1807
J. Story 11–45	H. Clay 11–14	H. Clay 10–11 J. Varnum 11–17	L. Cheves 11–15 W. King 11–16 J. Calhoun 11–17		Battle of Tippecanoe 1811 War of 1812 1812–15
	L. Cheves 14–15 H. Clay 15–20	R. King 13–25 N. Macon 15–28	R. Stockton 13–15 T. Pickering 13–17 D. Webster 13–17 J. Forsyth 13–18 J. Randolph 15–17 H. Clay 15–21 P. Barbour 15–25 W. Harrison 16–19		Hartford Convention 1815 Second Bank of the United States 1816
		J. Crittenden 17–19 J. Forsyth 18–19 R. Johnson 19–29 W. King 19–44	J. Tallmadge 17–19 J. Tyler 17–21 L. McLane 17–27 J. Randolph 19–25		Era of Good Feelings 1817 Missouri Compromise 1820
	P. Barbour 21–23 H. Clay 23–25	M. Van Buren 21–28 T. Benton 21–51 J. Forsyth 22–24 A. Jackson 23–25 R. Hayne 23–32	J. Buchanan 21–31 A. Stevenson 21–34 W. Mangum 23–26 J. Forsyth 23–27 S. Houston 23–27 D. Webster 23–27 E. Livingston 23–29		Monroe Doctrine 1823 Henry Clay's "American System" 1824

President	Vice President	Secretary of State	Cabinet	Diplomat	Chief Justice
J. Q. Adams 1825–1829 *W. Crawford* *H. Clay* *A. Jackson*	J. Calhoun 25–29	H. Clay 25–29		R. King 25–26 A. Gallatin 26–27 W. Harrison 28–29	
A. Jackson 1829–1833 *J. Q. Adams*	J. Calhoun 29–32	M. Van Buren 29–31 E. Livingston 31–33	R. Taney A.G. 31–33 L. McLane Treas. 31–33 L. Cass War 31–36	L. McLane 29–31 J. Randolph 30 J. Buchanan 31–33	
A. Jackson 1833–1837 *H. Clay* *W. Wirt*	M. Van Buren 33–37	L. McLane 33–34 J. Forsyth 34–41	R. Taney Treas. 33–34 A. Kendall Post. Gen. 35–40 B. Butler War 36–37	E. Livingston 33–35 A. Stevenson 36–41 L. Cass 36–42	R. Taney 36–64
M. Van Buren 1837–1841 *W. Harrison* *H. L. White* *D. Webster* *W. Mangum*	R. Johnson 37–41	J. Forsyth 37		G. Dallas 37–39	
W. Harrison 1841 *M. Van Buren* *J. Birney* **J. Tyler** 1841–1845	J. Tyler 41	D. Webster 41–43 A. Upshur 43–44 J. Calhoun 44–45	J. Crittendon A.G. 41 A. Upshur Navy 41 J. Bell War 41	E. Everett 41–45 W. King 44–46	
J. Polk 1845–1849 *H. Clay* *J. Birney*	G. Dallas 45–49	J. Buchanan 45–49	R. Walker Treas. 45–49 W. Marcy War 45–49	J. Slidell 45 L. McLane 45–46	

Associate Justice	Speaker of the House	Senator	Representative	Other	Event
	J. Taylor 25–27 A. Stevenson 27–34	J. Randolph 25–27 W. Harrison 25–28 H. L. White 25–40 L. McLane 27–29 J. Tyler 27–36 D. Webster 27–41	E. Everett 25–35 J. Polk 25–39 J. Randolph 27–29 P. Barbour 27–30 J. Bell 27–41		T. Jefferson and J. Adams Die July 4, 1826 Tariff of Abominations 1828
		E. Livingston 29–31 J. Forsyth 29–34 J. Clayton 29–36 W. Marcy 31–32 G. Dallas 31–33 W. Mangum 31–35 H. Clay 31–42 J. Calhoun 32–43	R. Johnson 29–37 J. Q. Adams 31–48	F. Blair Pres. Adv. 30–45	Webster-Hayne Debate 1830 Nullification Controversy 1832
P. Barbour 36–41	J. Bell 34–35 J. Polk 35–39	J. Buchanan 34–45 J. Crittendon 35–41 R. Walker 36–45	M. Fillmore 33–35 F. Pierce 33–37 J. White 33–43 J. Hammond 35–36 L. Boyd 35–37 J. Jones 35–45		Rise of Whig Party 1834 End of Second Bank of the United States 1836
	R. Hunter 39–41	F. Pierce 37–42	J. Mason 37–39 M. Fillmore 37–43 R. Hunter 37–43 J. Giddings 39–42 L. Boyd 39–55		Independent Treasury Act 1840
	J. White 41–43 J. Jones 43–45	W. Mangum 41–53 J. Crittenden 42–48 D. Atchison 43–55	H. Fish 43–45 J. Hale 43–45 J. Slidell 43–45 S. Douglas 43–47 H. Hamlin 43–47 R. Winthrop 43–50 H. Cobb 43–51 A. Johnson 43–53 J. Giddings 43–59 W. Yancey 44–46		Webster-Ashburton Treaty 1842
	J. W. Davis 45–47 R. Winthrop 47–49	L. Cass 45–48 S. Cameron 45–49 J. Clayton 45–49 J. Calhoun 45–50 D. Webster 45–50 A. Butler 46–57 S. Houston 46–59 J. Davis 47–51 J. Hale 47–53 J. Bell 47–59 S. Douglas 47–61 R. Hunter 47–61 J. Mason 47–61 W. King 48–53 H. Hamlin 48–57	J. Davis 45–46 R. Hunter 45–47 D. Wilmot 45–51 A. Lincoln 47–49 H. Greeley 48–49		Annexation of Texas 1845 Mexican War 1846–48 Wilmot Proviso 1846–47 Gold Discovered in California 1848

President	Vice President	Secretary of State	Cabinet	Diplomat	Chief Justice
Z. Taylor 1849–1850 *L. Cass* *M. Van Buren* **M. Fillmore** 1850–1853	M. Fillmore 49–50	J. Clayton 49–50 D. Webster 50–52 E. Everett 52	J. Crittenden A.G. 50–53		
F. Pierce 1853–1857 *W. Scott* *J. Hale*	W. King 53	W. Marcy 53–57	J. Davis War 53–57	J. Gadsden 53–54 J. Buchanan 53–56 G. Dallas 56–61	
J. Buchanan 1857–1861 *J. Frémont* *M. Fillmore*	J. Breckinridge 57–61	L. Cass 57–60 J. Black 60–61	J. Black A.G. 57–60 H. Cobb Treas. 57–60 E. Stanton A.G. 60–61		
A. Lincoln 1861–1865 *S. Douglas* *J. Breckinridge* *J. Bell*	H. Hamlin 61–65	W. Seward 61–69	S. Cameron War 61–62 S. P. Chase Treas. 61–64 E. Stanton War 62–68	C. Schurz 61–62 J. Slidell 61–62 C. Adams 61–68 S. Cameron 62 W. Evarts 63–64	S. P. Chase 64–73
A. Lincoln 1865 *G. McClellan* **A. Johnson** 1865–1869	A. Johnson 65		W. Evarts A.G. 68–69	J. Hale 65–69	
U. Grant 1869–1873 *H. Seymour*	S. Colfax 69–73	E. Washburne 69 H. Fish 69–77	W. Belknap War 69–76	E. Washburne 69–77 J. Orr 72	
U. Grant 1873–1877 *H. Greeley*	H. Wilson 73–75		B. Bristow Treas. 74–76	J. Foster 73–85	M. Waite 74–88

Associate Justice	Speaker of the House	Senator	Representative	Other	Event
	H. Cobb 49–51 L. Boyd 51–55	H. Clay 49–52 S. P. Chase 49–55 L. Cass 49–57 W. Seward 49–61 J. Fréacmont 50–51 R. Winthrop 50–51 H. Fish 51–57 B. Wade 51–69 C. Sumner 51–74	T. Stevens 49–53 J. Orr 49–59 J. Breckinridge 51–55 T. Hendricks 51–55 G. Grow 51–63		Compromise of 1850
	N. Banks 56–57	E. Everett 53–54 J. Clayton 53–56 J. Benjamin 53–61 J. Slidell 53–61 J. Crittenden 55–61 J. Hale 55–65 H. Wilson 55–72 L. Trumbull 55–73	T. Benton 53–55 W. Tweed 53–55 N. Banks 53–57 P. Brooks 53–57 E. Washburne 53–69 H. Cobb 55–57 J. Sherman 55–61 S. Colfax 55–69		Gadsden Purchase 1853 Kansas-Nebraska Act 1854
	J. Orr 57–59 W. Pennington 59–61	J. Hammond 57–60 S. Cameron 57–61 J. Davis 57–61 H. Hamlin 57–61 A. Johnson 57–62 S. P. Chase 60–61	C. Adams 58–61 C. Vallandigham 58–63 R. Conkling 59–63 T. Stevens 59–68		Dred Scott Decision 1857 Lecompton Constitution 1857 Lincoln-Douglas Debates 1858
D. Davis 62–77	G. Grow 61–63 S. Colfax 63–69	J. Breckinridge 61 D. Wilmot 61–63 J. Sherman 61–77 T. Hendricks 63–69	W. Wheeler 61–63 T. Pomeroy 61–69 I. Donnelly 63–69 J. Blaine 63–76 J. Garfield 63–81 S. Randall 63–90	J. Davis Pres. CSA 61–65	Civil War 1861–65 Emancipation Proclamation 1863
		F. Frelinghuysen 66–69 S. Cameron 67–77 R. Conkling 67–81	R. Conkling 65–67 R. Hayes 65–67 N. Banks 65–73 M. Kerr 65–73 B. Butler 67–75		Abraham Lincoln Assassinated 1865 A. Johnson Impeached 1868
	T. Pomeroy 69 J. Blaine 69–75	C. Schurz 69–75 H. Hamlin 69–81 T. Bayard 69–85 H. Revels 70–71 F. Frelinghuysen 71–77	G. Hoar 69–77 W. Wheeler 69–77		Créacdit Mobilier Scandal 1872
	M. Kerr 75–76 S. Randall 76–81	P. Pinchback 73 (elected but did not serve) A. Johnson 75 J. Blaine 76–81	P. Pinchback 72 (elected but did not serve) J. Cannon 73–91 R. Bland 73–95 A. Stevenson 75–77 N. Banks 75–79 B. Bruce 75–81 W. McKinley 76–91		Resumption of Specie Payments 1875 Disputed Election of 1876

President	Vice President	Secretary of State	Cabinet	Diplomat	Chief Justice
R. Hayes 1877–1881 *S. Tilden*	W. Wheeler 77–81	W. Evarts 77–81	J. Sherman Treas. 77–81 C. Schurz Int. 77–84		
J. Garfield 1881 *W. Hancock* *J. Weaver* **C. Arthur** 1881–1885	C. Arthur 81	J. Blaine 81 F. Frelinghuysen 81–85	W. Gresham Post. Gen. 83–84 W. Gresham Treas. 84	H. Hamlin 81–82 L. Morton 81–85 H. White 83–09	
G. Cleveland 1885–1889 *J. Blaine* *J. St. John* *B. Butler*	T. Hendricks 85	T. Bayard 85–89			M. Fuller 88–10
B. Harrison 1889–1893 *G. Cleveland*	L. Morton 89–93	J. Blaine 89–92 J. Foster 92–93		R. Lansing 92–14	
G. Cleveland 1893–1897 *B. Harrison* *J. Weaver*	A. E. Stevenson 93–97	W. Gresham 93–95 R. Olney 95–97	R. Olney A.G. 93–95 J. Carlisle Treas. 93–97	T. Bayard 93–97	
W. McKinley 1897–1901 *W. Bryan*	G. Hobart 97–99	J. Sherman 97–98 W. Day 98 J. Hay 98–05	J. Long Navy 97–02 E. Root War 99–04	J. Hay 97–98 G. Hoar 98 W. Day 98–99	
W. McKinley 1901 *W. Bryan* *E. Debs* **T. Roosevelt** 1901–1905	T. Roosevelt 01		P. Knox A.G. 01–04 W. Taft War 04–08		
T. Roosevelt 1905–1909 *A. Parker* *E. Debs* *T. Watson*	C. Fairbanks 05–09	E. Root 05–09			
W. Taft 1909–1913 *W. Bryan* *E. Debs* *E. Chafin*	J. S. Sherman 09–12	R. Bacon 09 P. Knox 09–13	R. Ballinger Int. 09–11 H. Stimson War 11–13	R. Bacon 09–12 H. White 10–11	E. White 10–21

Associate Justice	Speaker of the House	Senator	Representative	Other	Event
J. Harlan 77–11		D. Davis 77–83 G. Hoar 77–04 W. Hampton 79–91	B. Butler 77–79 J. Keifer 77–85 J. Carlisle 77–90 T. Reed 77–99 N. Aldrich 79–81 L. Morton 79–81 A. Stevenson 79–81 J. Weaver 79–81		
	J. Keifer 81–83 J. Carlisle 83–89	B. Harrison 81–87 J. Sherman 81–97 N. Aldrich 81–11	J. Long 83–89 C. Crisp 83–96 D. Henderson 83–03		J. Garfield Assassinated 1881 Pendleton Act 1883
		W. Evarts 85–91	J. Weaver 85–89 R. La Follette 85–91 J. S. Sherman 87–91		Interstate Commerce Act 1887
	T. Reed 89–91 C. Crisp 91–95	J. Carlisle 90–93 E. White 91–94	T. Watson 91–93 W. Bryan 91–95 J. Simpson 91–95		Sherman Anti-Trust Act 1890 Rise of Populist Party 1892
E. White 94–10	T. Reed 95–99	B. Tillman 95–18	J. Clark 93–95 C. Curtis 93–07 J. S. Sherman 93–09 J. Cannon 93–13 F. Gillett 93–25 G. Grow 94–03 O. Underwood 95–15		
	D. Henderson 99–02	M. Hanna 97–04 C. Fairbanks 97–05 A. Beveridge 99–11 W. Dillingham 00–23	R. Bland 97–99 J. Simpson 97–99 J. Clark 97–21	G. Pinchot Gov. Agc. Dir. 98–10	Spanish-American War 1898 Open Door Policy 1899
O. Holmes 02–32 W. Day 03–22	J. Cannon 03–11	P. Knox 04–09	N. Longworth 03–13 G. Norris 03–13 H. Rainey 03–21 J. Garner 03–33		W. McKinley Assassinated 1901 Work Begins, Panama Canal 1904
		R. La Follette 06–25 C. Curtis 07–13 W. Borah 07–40	E. Denby 05–11 J. Keifer 05–11 C. Hull 07–21 J. Cox 08–12		Hepburn Act, Pure Food and Drug Act, and Meat Inspection Act 1906
C. Hughes 10–16	J. Clark 11–19	E. Root 09–15 A. Fall 12–21	J. Cox 09–13 A. Palmer 09–14 J. Byrns 09–36 V. Berger 11–13 J. W. Davis 11–13 J. Byrnes 11–25		Ballinger-Pinchot Controversy 1910

President	Vice President	Secretary of State	Cabinet	Diplomat	Chief Justice
W. Wilson 1913–1917 *T. Roosevelt* *W. Taft* *E. Debs* *E. Chafin*	T. R. Marshall 13–17	W. Bryan 13–15 R. Lansing 15–20	W. McAdoo Treas. 13–19 N. Baker War 16–21	E. House 14–17 H. Hoover 14–19 A. Dulles 16–18	
W. Wilson 1917–1921 *C. Hughes*	T. R. Marshall 17–21	B. Colby 20	A. Palmer A.G. 19–21	H. White 18–19 J. W. Davis 18–21	
W. Harding 1921–1923 *E. Debs* *J. Cox*	C. Coolidge 21–23	C. Hughes 21–25	W. Hays Post. Gen. 21–22 H. Daugherty A.G. 21–24 E. Denby Navy 21–24 A. Fall Int. 21–25 H. Hoover Comm. 21–28 A. Mellon Treas. 21–32	E. Root 21–22	W. Taft 21–30
C. Coolidge 1923–1925			H. Stone A.G. 24–25	F. Kellogg 23–25	
C. Coolidge 1925–1929 *J. W. Davis* *R. La Follette*	C. Dawes 25–29	F. Kellogg 25–29		H. Stimson 27–29 D. Morrow 27–30	
H. Hoover 1929–1933 *A. Smith* *N. Thomas*	C. Curtis 29–33	H. Stimson 29–33		C. Dawes 29–32 A. Mellon 32–33	C. Hughes 30–41
F. Roosevelt 1933–1937 *H. Hoover* *N. Thomas*	J. Garner 33–37	C. Hull 33–44	J. Farley Post. Gen. 33–40 H. Wallace Agr. 33–40 F. Perkins Lab. 33–45 H. Ickes Int. 33–46 H. Morgenthau, Jr. Treas. 34–45		

Associate Justice	Speaker of the House	Senator	Representative	Other	Event
L. Brandeis 16–39		J. Vardaman 13–19 G. Norris 13–43 W. Harding 15–21 O. Underwood 15–27 C. Curtis 15–29	A. Barkley 13–27 J. Rayburn 13–61 M. London 15–19 J. Cannon 15–23 N. Longworth 15–31	B. Baruch Pres. Adv. 16	Federal Reserve Act 1913 Federal Trade Commission Act 1914 Sinking of the *Lusitania* 1915
	F. Gillett 19–25	P. Knox 17–21 F. Kellogg 17–23 H. Johnson 17–45	J. Rankin 17–19 F. La Guardia 17–21 W. Bankhead 17–40 V. Berger 19–21 (elected but did not serve)	G. Creel Gov. Agc. Dir. 17–19 B. Baruch Gov. Agc. Dir. 18–19	U.S. in World War I 1917–18 Treaty of Versailles 1919
		T. Watson 21–22	M. London 21–23		Washington Armament Conference 1921
		B. Wheeler 23–47	V. Berger 23–29 F. Vinson 23–29 C. Hull 23–31 F. La Guardia 23–33 H. Rainey 23–34	J. Hoover Dir. FBI 24–72	Teapot Dome Scandal 1921
H. Stone 25–41	N. Longworth 25–31	F. Gillett 25–31 H. L. White 25–40 G. Nye 25–45 H. Black 27–37 A. Barkley 27–49 R. Wagner 27–49 A. Vandenberg 28–51	J. Martin 25–67 O. De Priest 28–35		
O. Roberts 30–45 B. Cardozo 32–38	J. Garner 31–33	D. Morrow 31 C. Hull 31–33 H. Long 31–35 J. Byrnes 31–41	J. McCormack 29–71 F. Vinson 31–38 M. Dies, Jr. 31–45		Stock Market Crash 1929
	H. Rainey 33–34 J. Byrns 35–36 W. Bankhead 36–40	W. McAdoo 33–39 H. Truman 35–45 C. Pepper 36–51	W. Lemke 33–41 E. Dirksen 33–48 F. Maverick 35–39	R. Tugwell Pres. Adv. 33–36 J. Kennedy Gov. Agc. Dir. 34–35 L. Henderson Gov. Agc. Dir. 34–35	New Deal 1933 Social Security Act 1936

PRESIDENT	VICE PRESIDENT	SECRETARY OF STATE	CABINET	DIPLOMAT	CHIEF JUSTICE
F. Roosevelt 1937–1941 *H. L. White* *A. Landon* *W. Lemke* *E. Browder* *N. Thomas*	J. Garner 37–41		H. Hopkins Comm. 38–40 F. Murphy A.G. 39–40 H. Stimson War 40–45 W. Knox Navy 40–44	J. Kennedy 37–40	
F. Roosevelt 1941–1945 *W. Willkie* *N. Thomas*	H. Wallace 41–45	E. Stettinius 44–45	J. Forrestal Navy 44–47	H. Hopkins 41 A. Dulles 42–45 D. Nelson 44–45	H. Stone 41–46
F. Roosevelt 1945 *T. Dewey* *N. Thomas* **H. Truman** 1945–1949	H. Truman 45	J. Byrnes 45–47 G. Marshall 47–49	H. Wallace Comm. 45–46 F. Vinson Treas. 45–46 J. Forrestal Def. 47–49	E. Stettinius 45–46 E. Roosevelt 45–52 A. E. Stevenson 46–47 J. Dulles 46–48	F. Vinson 46–53
H. Truman 1949–1953 *T. Dewey* *J. Thurmond* *H. Wallace* *N. Thomas*	A. Barkley 49–53	D. Acheson 49–53	G. Marshall Def. 50–51	J. McCloy 49–52 J. Dulles 51 D. Rusk 51 C. Bowles 51–53 G. Kennan 52–53	
D. Eisenhower 1953–1957 *A. E. Stevenson*	R. Nixon 53–57	J. Dulles 53–59	M. Durkin Lab. 53 O. Hobby HEW 53–55 C. Wilson Def. 53–57 E. Benson Agr. 53–60	W. Donovan 53–54 C. Luce 53–57 H. Lodge, Jr. 53–60	E. Warren 53–69
D. Eisenhower 1957–1961 *A. E. Stevenson*	R. Nixon 57–61	C. Herter 59–61	W. Rogers A.G. 57–61		

ASSOCIATE JUSTICE	SPEAKER OF THE HOUSE	SENATOR	REPRESENTATIVE	OTHER	EVENT
H. Black 37–71 F. Frankfurter 39–62 W. Douglas 39–75 F. Murphy 40–49	S. Rayburn 40–46	H. Lodge, Jr. 37–44 C. Pepper 37–51 R. Taft 39–53	L. Johnson 37–49 E. Kefauver 39–49 M. Smith 40–48	T. Arnold Asst. A.G. 39–43 W. Knudsen Gov. Agc. Dir. 40–45	International Relations Deteriorate 1937–38 World War II Begins in Europe 1939
J. Byrnes 41–42			J. Rankin 41–43 H. Jackson 41–53 J. Fulbright 43–45 C. Luce 43–47 W. Lemke 43–50 C. Herter 43–53	L. Henderson Gov. Agc. Dir. 41–43 D. Lilienthal Gov. Agc. Dir. 41–45 J. McCloy Asst. War 41–45 D. Nelson Gov. Agc. Dir. 42–44 W. Donovan Gov. Agc. Dir. 42–45 C. Bowles Gov. Agc. Dir. 43–46	Lend-Lease Act 1941 Japan Bombs Pearl Harbor, U.S. Enters WWII 1941
	J. Martin 47–49	W. Morse 45–69 J. Fulbright 45–75 H. Lodge, Jr. 47–53 J. McCarthy 47–54	Sh. Adams 45–47 A. Powell, Jr. 45–67 S. Ervin 46–47 R. Nixon 47–51 J. F. Kennedy 47–53 C. Albert 47–77	D. Lilienthal Gov. Agc. Dir. 46–50 B. Baruch Gov. Agc. Dir. 46–47	Germany Surrenders 1945 Atomic Bomb Attack on Japan 1945 Japan Surrenders 1945 Beginning of Cold War 1946 Marshall Plan, 1946 Truman Doctrine 1947 Taft-Hartley Act 1947
	S. Rayburn 50–52	J. Dulles 49 L. Johnson 49–61 E. Kefauver 49–63 H. Humphrey 49–65 M. Smith 49–73 J. Dulles 51 R. Nixon 51–53 E. Dirksen 51–69	E. McCarthy 49–59 G. Ford 49–73		NATO (North Atlantic Treaty Organization) 1949 Korean War 1950–53 McCarthy Era 1950–54
	J. Martin 53–55 S. Rayburn 56–61	J. F. Kennedy 53–57 B. Goldwater 53–60 H. Jackson 53–83 S. Ervin 54–74 A. Barkley 55–56 J. Thurmond 55–	M. Dies 53–59 T. O'Neill 53–86 J. Wright 55–89	A. Dulles Dir. CIA 53–61 R. Daley Ch. Cook. Co. 53–76 Sh. Adams Pres. Adv. 53–58	*Brown* v. *Board of Education of Topeka* 1954 Suez Crisis 1956
		J. F. Kennedy 59–61 E. McCarthy 59–71 E. Muskie 59–81	G. McGovern 57–61 C. Bowles, 59–61	Z. Brzezinski Pres. Adv. 60–66	Civil Rights Act 1957 Cuban Revolution 1959

President	Vice President	Secretary of State	Cabinet	Diplomat	Chief Justice
J. F. Kennedy 1961–1963 *R. Nixon*	L. Johnson 61–63	D. Rusk 61–69	A. Goldberg Lab. 61–62 R. Kennedy A.G. 61–64 R. McNamara Def. 61–68 C. Vance Army 62–64	E. Roosevelt 61–62 A. Stevenson 61–65	
L. Johnson 1963–1965				C. Bowles 63–68 H. Lodge, Jr. 63–77	
L. Johnson 1965–1969 *B. Goldwater*	H. Humphrey 65–69		R. Weaver HUD 66–69 J. Mitchell A.G. 67–72 C. Clifford Def. 68–69	P. Harris 65–67 A. Goldberg 65–68	
R. Nixon 1969–1973 *H. Humphrey* *G. Wallace*	S. Agnew 69–73	W. Rogers 69–73	G. Shultz Lab. 69–70 J. Mitchell A.G. 69–72 G. Shultz Treas. 72–74	G. Bush 72–74	W. Burger 69–86
R. Nixon 1973–1974 *G. McGovern*	S. Agnew 73 G. Ford 73–74	H. Kissinger 73–77	C. Weinberger HEW 73–75	D. Moynihan 73–75	
G. Ford 1974–1977	N. Rockefeller 74–77				
J. Carter 1977–1981 *G. Ford* *E. McCarthy*	W. Mondale 77–81	C. Vance 77–80 E. Muskie 80	P. Harris HUD 77–79 P. Harris HEW 79–81	A. Young 77–79 A. Goldberg 77–78	
R. Reagan 1981–1985 *J. Carter* *J. Anderson*	G. Bush 81–85	A. Haig 81–82 G. Shultz 82	C. Weinberger Def. 81–87 G. Shultz Treas. 81–89 E. Dole Trans. 83–87	J. Kirkpatrick 81–85	
R. Reagan 1985–1989 *W. Mondale*	G. Bush 85–89		J. Baker Treas. 85–88 W. Bennett Ed. 85–89		W. Rehnquist 86–
G. Bush 1989– *M. Dukakis*	D. Quayle 89–	J. Baker 89–	E. Dole Lab. 89–90 J. Kemp HUD 89–		

Associate Justice	Speaker of the House	Senator	Representative	Other	Event
A. Goldberg 62–65	J. McCormack 62–71	E. Kennedy 62–	R. Dole 61–69 J. Anderson 61–81	M. Bundy Pres. Adv. 61–66 W. Rostow Pres. Adv. 61–69	Bay of Pigs Invasion 1961 Cuban Missile Crisis 1962
		G. McGovern 63–81	C. Pepper 63–89		J. F. Kennedy Assassinated 1963 Civil Rights Act 1964 Escalation of War in Vietnam 1964
T. Marshall 67–		R. Kennedy 65–68 W. Mondale 65–75 E. Brooke 67–79	T. Foley 65– G. Bush 67–71 A Powell, Jr. 67–71		Great Society Legislation 1965–68
W. Rehnquist 72–86	C. Albert 71–77	B. Goldwater 69–87 R. Dole 69– H. Humphrey 71–78	S. Chisholm 69–83 B. Abzug 71–77 J. Kemp 71–89	J. Ehrlichman Pres. Adv. 69–73 A. Haig Pres. Adv. 69–72 H. Haldeman Pres. Adv. 69–73	Watergate Break-in 1972
		J. Helms 73–	B. Jordan 73–77 A. Young 73–77	A. Haig Pres. Adv. 73–74	Roe v. Wade 1973 U.S.–N. Vietnam Ceasefire 1973
				G. Bush Dir. CIA 75–76	Nixon Resigns 1974 Détente Begins 1974 U.S. Bicentennial 1976
	T. O'Neill 77–86	D. Moynihan 77– N. Kassebaum 78–	D. Quayle 77–81 G. Ferraro 79–83	Z. Brzezinski Pres. Adv. 77–81 P. Volcker Ch. Fed. Res. 79–88	Carter Energy Program 1977 Camp David Accords 1978 Iranian Hostage Crisis 1979
S. O'Connor 81–		D. Quayle 81–89		W. Casey Dir. CIA 81–87 J. Baker Pres. Adv. 81–85	Tax Cut Legislation 1981 U.S. Invades Grenada 1983
A. Scalia 86–	J. Wright 87–89				Gramm-Rudman Act 1985 Iran-Contra Scandal 1986
	T. Foley 89–				U.S. Invades Panama 1989 Persian Gulf War Begins 1991